Demonic Divine

Front cover illustration:
Shri Devi, Magzor Gyalmo
Queen who Has the Power to Turn Back Armies
Central Tibet, mid-18th century
Mineral pigments on cloth
Collection of Shelley and Donald Rubin (Cat. no. 31, detail)

Back cover illustration:
Mahakala Vyagra Vahana, Tiger-rider
Tibet, late 18th–early 19th century
Mineral pigments on cloth
Rubin Museum of Art (Cat. no. 17, detail)

Demonic Divine: Himalayan Art and Beyond

By Rob Linrothe and Jeff Watt

Essays by Rob Linrothe and Marylin Rhie

Foreword by Matthieu Ricard

Contributions from Carly Busta

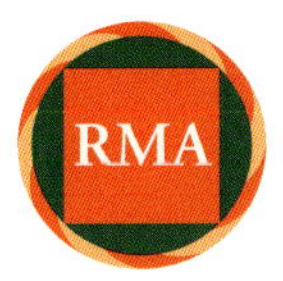

Rubin Museum of Art, New York
Serindia Publications, Chicago

This catalog is published in conjunction with the exhibition *Demonic Divine: Himalayan Art and Beyond,* held at the Rubin Museum of Art, New York, from 2 October 2004 to 9 January 2005, and *Wrathful Deities in Buddhist Art: An installation to celebrate the opening of the Rubin Museum of Art,* held at the Asia Society, New York from 23 March to 22 August 2004.

Published by the Rubin Museum of Art, New York, and Serindia Publications, Chicago

Library of Congress Cataloging-in-Publication Data

Demonic Divine: Himalayan art and beyond / by Rob Linrothe and Jeff Watt; with a foreword by Matthieu Ricard.
p. cm.
Item is published in conjunction with the exhibition "Demonic Divine: Himalayan art and beyond" held at the Rubin Museum of Art, New York, October 2, 2004–January 9, 2005.
Includes index.
ISBN 1-932476-08-3 (pbk.)
ISBN 1-932476-15-6 (Hardcover)
1. Art, Buddhist—Himalayan Mountains Region—Exhibitions. 2. Art, Tibetan—Himalayan Mountains Region—Exhibitions. 3. Gods, Buddhist—Himalayan Mountains Region—Exhibitions.
I. Linrothe, Robert N., 1951– II. Watt, Jeff.
N8193.H56D46 2004
704.9'48943'095496—dc22
2004002992

Exhibition Curator: Rob Linrothe
Exhibition Advisor: Jeff Watt
Exhibition Coordinator: Lisa Arcomano
Project Assistants: Hannah Stephenson, Carly Busta
Catalog Production: Carly Busta

Designer: Heads Inc.
Design Advisor: Milton Glaser, Inc.
Separations by: Snoeck-Ducaju & Zoon
Printed and bound in Belgium by Snoeck-Ducaju & Zoon

Contents

The Demonic Divine

PREFACE BY DONALD RUBIN

If you are new to Himalayan art, you may be horrified by many of the paintings and sculptures in this book. Some of the images seem to come directly from Dante's *Inferno*: scenes of death and destruction, decapitation, monstrous beings with garlands of severed heads gorging on human hearts, in short, a human hell more terrifying than any horror movie.

But we are all familiar with this. We see unspeakable horrors every day in the media—not just as entertainment, but also as real events: murders, crime scenes, even holocausts. The images of September 11th will forever haunt us. Memories of the World War II death camps and "ethnic cleansing" in Bosnia and Rwanda are still fresh in our minds. Hideous cruelty is sadly common to the human condition.

Yet, curiously, each severed head and each mangled corpse in these Himalayan works of art is a metaphor for the opposite: the destruction of hatred, revenge, anger, egotism, ignorance and greed—evils Christianity once called deadly sins.

Just as Dante journeyed through hell and purgatory before reaching paradise, followers of the sacred traditions of the Himalayas find the path to enlightenment through transforming the dark side of the mind and gaining inner freedom from destructive emotions. These violent paintings are meant to aid us in our journey to understand the nature of the heart, and beyond that to the hard work of change. As such, they are metaphors for compassion—a compassion neither passive nor gentle—but an affirmative, active, and courageous force.

While most religions try to show us the path to enlightenment by way of concern for others and a system of ethics, followers of these Himalayan traditions, in addition, find it in conquering our limitations by going to war with our personal demons, which are none other than jealousy, hatred, greed, and other mental toxins. The goal is to transform the root of human destructiveness, the negative in us nourished by unhealthy egos grown from our ignorance. Divine demons in the art show us the hellish fury that must be summoned from within to crush, sever, boil, and burn that ignorance. They are visualizations of our own inner battle, and exhortations to victory.

In essence, these "wrathful deities" are the policemen of the soul. They are protectors of all beings and sacred teachings—preventing people from harming themselves and others and fighting for our safety against the insidious cancers of self-deception and egotism.

Acknowledgments

ROB LINROTHE

The image of the "demonic divine" may be recognized in a number of religious and artistic traditions, both visual and literary. Representations of the demonic divine feature the liminal, reason violating, category conflating "grotesque" (i.e., *grottoesque*), in the original sense of the term. Thus the elegant monstrosities of Raphael's Loggia, and their Roman inspirations, similarly merge improbable parts to create fanciful hybrids. These latter images, John Ruskin's "sportive grotesques," still invite visual pleasure in whimsy, fantastic imagination or clever intellectual matches. In some images, the humorous grotesque is prominent, while in other traditions, it was the *horreur sacrée* that was induced. In still others, there was room for both.

Himalayan artists developed this mode of art to such a degree that the two almost become synonymous. This followed from the evolving religious values and concerns, which developed nuanced categories of demonic divine. The rich holdings of the Rubin Museum of Art and the Shelley and Donald Rubin collection has made it possible to explore some of the variations of the theme in Himalayan art. The generosity of many museums and collectors in the northeastern United States has also allowed us to touch on the demonic divine in other cultures, for it can be found in a number of other art traditions. The aim is not to claim universality, however, either in our coverage in the exhibition or in the theme itself. Nor do we intend to suggest that a dancing skeleton couple in contemporary Mexico somehow "means" the same as one in a nineteenth-century

Tibetan painting, or that the visual similarities between an Etruscan gorgon mask and the face of Mahakala share a historical root. Nevertheless, it is surprising how often artists in completely disparate cultural traditions have drawn on similar imagery of death, decay, sinister violence, and hybridity to convey the unsettling demonic divine.

Our primary debt of gratitude, after the one owed the invariably unknown artists, must go to the collectors, institutional and private, who have made their works available. From the beginning, Shelley and Donald Rubin have encouraged the concept and supported the implementation, and I hope they are pleased with the result. At the American Museum of Natural History, Charles Spencer, Division Chair and Curator, Meso-American Archaeology; Enid Schildkrout, Curator, African Ethnology; Kristen Mable, Registrar for Archives and Loans/Anthropology; Naomi Goodman, Collections Assistant, African Ethnology; and Christina Elson, Researcher, Meso-American Archaelogy, have been generous with time and expertise. At the Asia Society Museum, Amy V. McEwen, Collections Manager and Museum Registrar; Helen Abbott, Assistant Director; and Colin MacKenzie, Associate Director and Curator at the time were similarly helpful. Noel Valentin, Registrar, and Fatima Bercht, Chief Curator, of El Museo del Barrio were enthusiastic about the idea almost from its inception. At the Brooklyn Museum of Art, Amy Poster, Curator of Asian Art; Edna Russmann, Curator, Department of Egyptian, Classical and Ancient Middle Eastern Art; the late James Romano, Curator of Egyptian art, Jennifer Lesslie, Assistant Registrar for Domestic Loans; and Marc Mayer, Deputy Director of Art, all helped guide us and our loan requests through the proper channels. At the Metropolitan Museum of Art, Sean Hemingway, Associate Curator, Department of Greek and Roman art, took time and care to help us locate the right object for the exhibition and arranged for approvals and photographs; we also thank his colleagues in the same department, Michael Baran and Carlos A. Pićon, as well as Frances Redding Wallace, Associate Registrar, Loans; and Minora Collins, Registrar. At the University of Pennsylvania Museum of Archaeology and Anthropology, we thank Lynn C. Makowsky, Keeper, Mediterranean Section; Jeremy A. Sabloff, The Williams Director; and Juana Dahlan, Assistant Registrar, Loans.

Four private collectors have been singularly generous in making available their fine works of art, Himalayan, Indian and Chinese. A long-time supporter of the Rubin Museum of Art, Navin Kumar, has been unstinting in his loans, which bolster the show in critical ways. So too, Michael and Beata McCormick, genuine enthusiasts, have encouraged us to use those works in their collection of Himalayan art which we felt best enhanced the exhibition. Michael Cohn, of Michael Cohn Antiquities, and Lillian Schloss have graciously lent fine sculptures from India and China, respectively.

Many scholars and colleagues have extended critical help to us. First and foremost, E. Gene Smith, of the Tibetan Buddhist Resource Center, has an impressive generosity matched only by the wealth of his experience and knowledge, and his undimmed enthusiasm for Tibetan history and its sources. We have benefited enormously from all of it. To Tudeng Nima (Alak Zenkar Rinpoche) and Ngawang Topgyal we are similarly grateful. Christian Luczanits and Arthur Leeper have also given excellent advice, counsel, and inspiration. Alan and Denise Farancz have tolerated with good humor our frequent interruptions of their work with questions needing their professional expertise.

The catalog is greatly enhanced by Marylin Rhie, whose essay on Mahakala is a major contribution to the study of Himalayan art. As always, she has been a pleasure to work with. Matthieu Ricard's foreword adds just the right insider's perspective to our attempt to limn from the outside a key component of religious practice. His writing as well as his person always lifts the spirit.

Within the Rubin Museum of Art, our Collections Manager and Exhibitions Coordinator, Lisa Arcomano, has been untiring in her labors. She and her staff, including Hannah Stephenson and Dudu Etzion, have eased the gestation and labor pains of this project tremendously, very tangibly. Our former colleague, Ben Brinkley, helped in numerous ways to negotiate the pitfalls of terminology and definitions. Bob Baylis, a Trustee of the RMA, helped to make some key introductions. Moke Mokotoff, who has been involved with the Rubin Museum of Art since well before it was even conceived, also gave critical support at various moments along the way. And Marilena Christodoulou, the RMA Director of Finance and Development, always calmly dispensed excellent advice and organized the means to desired ends.

The production of the catalog naturally required the work of many talented people. The look of the book is due to So Takahashi, whose style of understated elegance and accessibility we appreciated. Milton Glaser and Katja Maas of Milton Glaser, Inc., also helped in the design, particularly of the essays. Gary Hawkey of IOColor in Seattle, gave us very useful advice, and Michael Sakkalli and Stijn Blontrock of Snoeck-Ducjau & Zoon in Belgium have overseen the printing production. Martina D'Alton resolutely steered us toward clarity and concision, and Elizabeth Johnson and Ilaria Fusina sifted through the text carefully, eliminating many inconsistencies and errors. And the indefatigable Shane Suvikapakornkul of Serindia, our co-publisher and friend, saw the project through to the end.

Above all, I wish to personally thank my collaborators on this exhibition and catalog, Jeff Watt and Carly Busta. Carly Busta wrote five of the catalog entries (13, 19–20, 27, 29–30), and Jeff contributed research to most of the Himalayan art entries, as well as writing the introduction on Bön wrathful deities and the entry for catalog number 59. Working with the two of them on this project helped me rediscover the truth of what a minor character, an academic, points out in Vikram Seth's mammoth novel, *A Suitable Boy* (New York: HarperCollins, 1993): "Writing is yitself discovery. Yexplication is yexploration" (spelling as in the original, p. 1273). I have learned a great deal while completing this project, not all of it about the dark, wild, and demonic imagery of the Himalayas, but most of it from them.

New York
April 2004

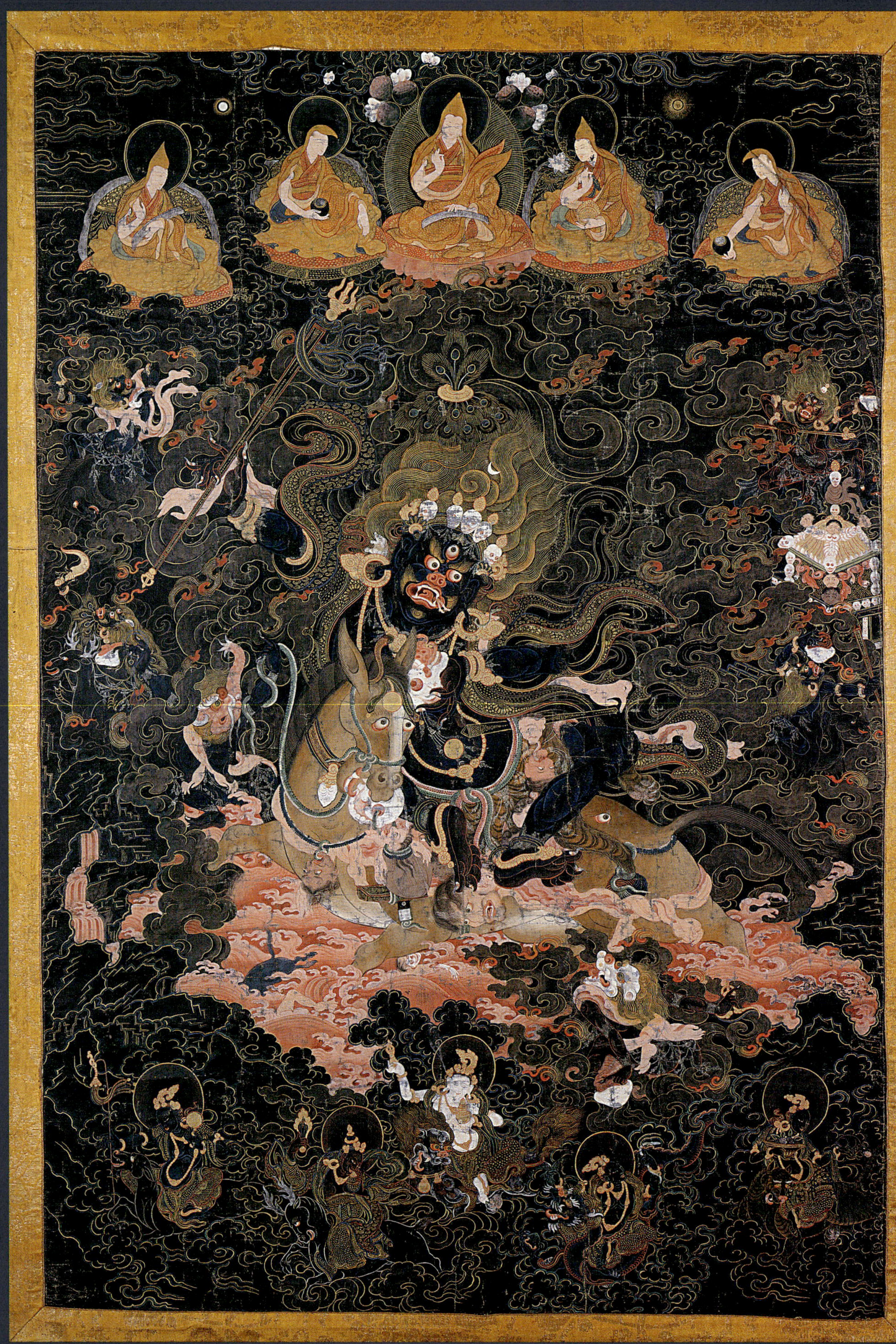

Cat. no. 31

Foreword

MATTHIEU RICARD

What is it about sacred art that makes it sacred? It is not just that it draws its images and ideas from one or another of the world's religions. Truly sacred art awakens in the mind a direct experience deeper than our ordinary selves and the material world.

According to Buddhism, the mind's fundamental nature is a state of peace and lucid clarity, which lies beyond the reach of our thought processes, concepts, and ordinary feelings. This ultimate nature of the mind is the Buddha-nature, a primordially perfect state, which is also sometimes termed primordial wisdom, pure awareness, or enlightenment. From this primordial wisdom, as if from a brilliant sun, rays of compassion shine forth. Love and compassion, when they are true and unconditional, are not something that the ordinary mind fabricates. They arise as the spontaneous radiance of wisdom.

The sun may at times be hidden from us behind the clouds, but that makes no difference to the sun itself. Its own brilliance can never be obscured. Likewise, primordial wisdom and compassion are always present within every sentient being, even when hidden by clouds of hatred, obsession, pride, jealousy, and, first and foremost, ignorance.

In Buddhist terms, ignorance is not just a lack of knowledge or information. It is, rather, a persistent blindness to the true nature of mind and phenomena. It is ignorance that divides things into self and other, near and far, good and bad, and that sees things as having a true, substantial existence. Primordial wisdom, on the other hand, sees that the ultimate nature of everything is emptiness, *shunyata.* The view of emptiness is the understanding that phenomena are devoid of intrinsic, autonomous, and permanent existence.

Although it might at first seem a nihilistic view of the world, this is far from being the case. Emptiness does not imply nothingness. Rather, it refers to the infinite potential for phenomena to appear in a vast network of interdependent processes—which would be impossible if everything consisted of inert, immutable, self-contained entities.

Wrathful appearance

In such a context, how can we understand the so-called wrathful deities, the focus of so many contemplative practices in Tibetan Buddhism? In essence, their awesome appearance expresses the invincible power of compassion.

Imagine a mother whose child was about to be run over by a car. She would not hesitate, or gently say, "Please move away from the road." She would immediately grab the child and pull him forcibly to safety. Her act is violent in appearance only. In truth she has saved her child's life.

In such situations, sheer compassion dictates decisive action. But we should not mistake this for a cheap excuse to use violence whenever it suits our self-centered designs. Wrathfulness here is a way of depicting the formidable energy of a compassion that cannot bear the suffering of beings. There is no trace of hatred or anger in it.

This becomes clear when we examine some examples of the symbolism associated with wrathful deities. Their hair bristles upward in a blazing mane out of overwhelming compassion for the intense suffering of beings caught up in delusion. If they have only one head, it symbolizes the absolute truth, while if they have three heads, these represent the three dimensions of Buddhahood (*trikaya*), as well as the transformation of the three main mental poisons—desire, anger, and ignorance.

Their two arms represent the union of wisdom (the realization of emptiness) and skillful means (compassion); while if they have six arms, these are to remind us of the six transcendent perfections (*paramitas*): generosity, discipline, patience, diligence, concentration, and wisdom. Their two legs represent absolute space (*dharmadhatu*) and awareness (*vidya*), inseparable; if four, they symbolize the four boundless qualities—love, compassion, joy, and impartiality. The fifty-eight dry skulls that some wrathful deities wear symbolize the death of the fifty-eight kinds of deluded thought. Their razor-sharp wings symbolize penetrating wisdom. Their three eyes symbolize perfect knowledge of the past, present, and future.

These deities are not seen as having material, tangible bodies of flesh, blood, and bone, but bodies of light, vivid and translucent like a rainbow, and totally immaterial, like the reflection of the moon in water. They are not just lifeless images, but full of wisdom and love and the power to help beings.

Many meditational deities have both peaceful and wrathful forms. The process of transition from peaceful to wrathful is called "peacefulness transfigured into wrathfulness" (*shi ba khro bo gnas gyur*). Once again, this shows how wrathfulness is simply a way in which the peaceful nature of primordial wisdom becomes manifest, a very dynamic way required to free beings from particular kinds of suffering. Such a change of gear is needed to break through the shell of dualistic clinging to reality, to clean up the mess made by ignorance, sweep away the mind's obscurations, purify toxic thoughts, and dissolve destructive emotions. But deep within, the heart is still at peace.

The wisdom-wrath of these deities therefore symbolizes the subjugation of hatred and the other mental poisons that create suffering for both ourselves and others. It is said that the demon Rudra, who embodied all the negativity of the human mind, was subjugated by the wisdom deities Hayagriva and Vajrapani. As a sign of victory, Hayagriva and Vajrapani clad themselves in the accoutrements of the vanquished demon and assumed his physical appearance, showing that wisdom always lies deep within ignorance, love behind the hideous face of hatred, and compassionate strength behind blind violence.

For someone who aspires to reach enlightenment, all forms should be perceived as the manifestation of primordial purity, all sounds as the echo of emptiness and all thoughts as the play of wisdom. One no longer needs to distinguish between beautiful and ugly, harmonious and discordant. Beauty has become omnipresent and one is fulfilled and serene all the time. As it is said, "In a continent of gold, you cannot find ordinary stones."

Ordinary beauty is certainly a source of joy, but spiritual beauty has a unique value, because it inspires in us the conviction that enlightenment both exists and can be attained. It is this beauty that sacred art seeks to express, be it Buddhist, Christian, Hindu, or Islamic, and whether its mode of expression is music, dance, painting, or simple contemplation. Sacred art is not just a representation of symbols and ideas. It is a direct experience of inner peace, free from attachment to the illusory solidity of the ego and the phenomenal world.

Shechen Monastery, Nepal
July 2003

Reader's Notes

The Rubin Museum of Art is abbreviated to "RMA." Accession numbers for RMA holdings are preceded by C (formerly in the Shelley and Donald Rubin Cultural Trust) and F (formerly in the Shelley and Donald Rubin Foundation).

In captions, we use the following conventions:
HA followed by a number (HA 6510). This indicates the item number on the Himalayan Art Website, www.himalayanart.org. In the text of essays or entries, we refer to it as "Himalayan Art Website item," followed by the number.

References to TBRC are to the Tibetan Buddhist Resource Center website, www.tbrc.org. Item numbers are prefaced by "W" or "P," referring to the titles of written works (W) or to people (P).

Toh. refers to the Tohoku University catalogue of the Derge Kanjur and Tanjur, *A catalogue of the Tohoku University collection of Tibetan works on Buddhism*, published by the Seminary of Indology, Tokyo University 1953, Sendai Japan.

In the essays and catalog entries, illustrations of objects in the exhibition are referred to by their catalog number (cat. no.). Illustrations in the two essays are referred to by figure number (fig.). Figure numbers referring to illustrations in Linrothe's essay are preceded by a "1." ("fig. 1.1"), in Rhie's essay by a "2." ("fig. 2.1").

The main deities on eight paintings (cat. nos. 16–18, 31–32, 46, 50–51) have each been numbered on a black-and-white chart provided at the end of the catalog section, with the notes and overflow text. A key to the chart immediately follows the latter. References to the deities referred to in the charts and the keys are preceded by the catalog number ("cat. key 46.21," for example).

Transcription systems

The issue of transcription is always a vexing one, rarely more so than with Tibetan writing. Nothing is likelier to set off heated debate among scholars and educators. Scholars want a system that will allow them to reconstruct the Tibetan spelling of the original, including the "silent" letters (silent, that is, in some regions of Tibet) and those combinations which fundamentally alter the pronunciation (variously in different regions of Tibet). The general reader, however, wishes to have something approximating a pronounceable word, which, to choose random examples, *rta-mgrin* or *spyan-ras-gzigs*, are not. There is no solution that will satisfy everyone's legitimate concerns, and since we hope this catalog will be of use to the educated and interested public and to some scholars as well, we have compromised. We have chosen to spell the preceding examples "Tamdrin" and "Chenrezig" in the text, and provide in the notes an equivalent version of important names or terms in the modified Wylie transcription. Inscriptions are gerenally given in Wylie, again in the notes. The system used in the text is one we call "RMA Standard," developed by Jeff Watt and Ben Brinkley. The index only references the RMA Standard version. An explanation of this transcription system, with examples, is found in a document titled "Romanization Key: A Note on the Romanization of Sanskrit and Tibetan Language," at www.himalayanart.org/books/romanization.pdf. It also covers the treatment of Sanskrit terms, without diacritical marks and rendering both palatal and retroflex sibilants as "sh." We apologize for inconsistencies and ask the indulgence of our readers if we haven't fulfilled the hopes of F. W. Thomas for a strictly rigorous approach to transcribing Tibetan. In 1925 he tartly penned the following expectation:

> It is to be hoped that in the future writers on Tibet will show respect for an old literary language by presenting Tibetan words in the form of an exact transliteration according to an accepted system, regardless of pronunciation, which readers unacquainted with the language will in any case distort—in obedience, it would seem, to a perverse instinct misguiding all alike, whether *docti* or *indocti*, in the presence of unknown vocables. [In Foreword to A. H. Francke, *Antiquities of Indian Tibet*, vol. 2, *The Chronicles of Ladakh and Minor Chronicles* (Calcutta: Superintendent Government Printing, 1926), pp. v–vi.]

Chinese words are given in Pinyin except with names of living authors, whose choice of romanizing their names is respected.

Essays

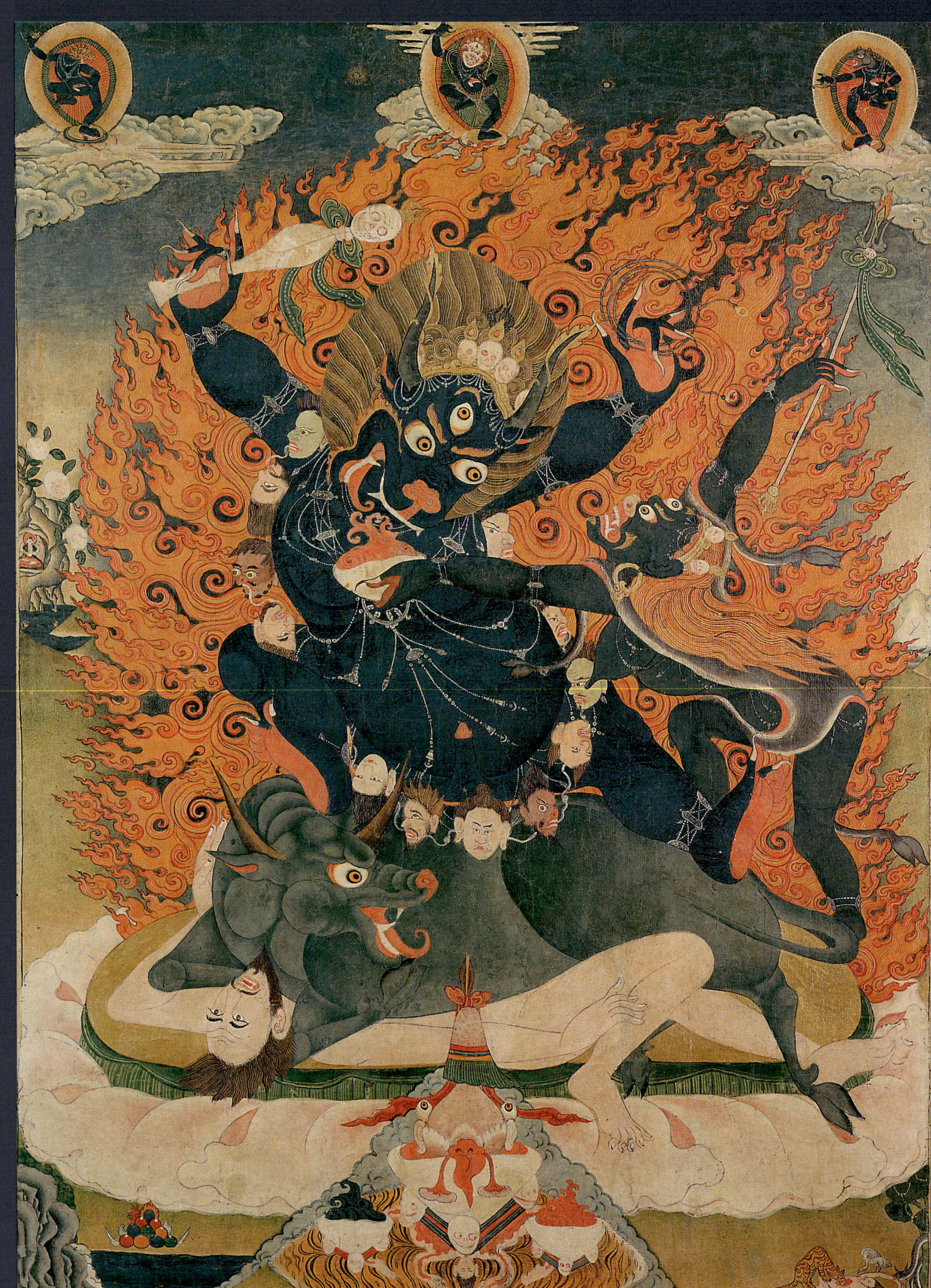

Protection, Benefaction, and Transformation

WRATHFUL DEITIES IN HIMALAYAN ART

ROB LINROTHE

Facing page: Fig. 1.1.
Yama Dharmaraja
Tibet, 19th c.
Mineral pigments on cloth; 33¼ x 23¾ in. (84.45 x 60.33 cm).
F1997.31.7 (HA 404).

O mighty destroyer of selfishness-demons[,]
With body of wisdom unchained from all bonds,
Yamantaka come brandish your skull-headed bludgeon
Of egoless wisdom, of voidness and bliss.
Without any misgiving now wield your fierce weapon
And wrathfully swing it three times round your head.

With all of your fierceness come smash this foul enemy!
Burst ego-concepts with your wisdom's great might!
With your boundless compassion protect us from suffering
The miseries caused by our self-centred actions;
Destroy our self-cherishing once and for all![1]

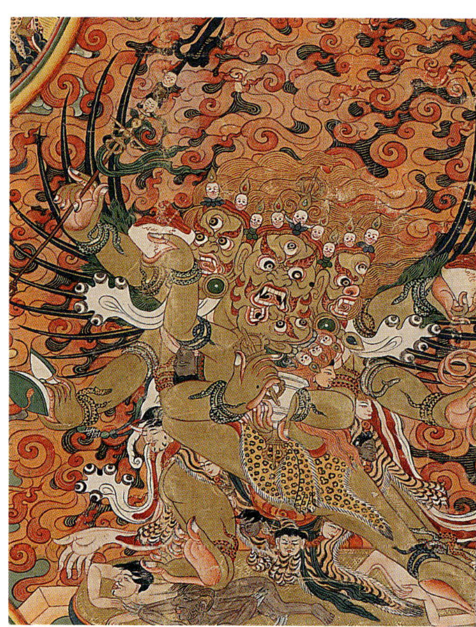

Fig. 1.2.
Six-armed Buddha Heruka with consort Krodhishvari (detail of Chemchog Heruka *tangka*)
Tibet, 19th c.
Mineral pigments on cloth; overall size 33 x 14 3/4 in. (83.82 x 37.47 cm).
F1998.3.9 (HA 613).

1

One of the most conceptually sophisticated, visually dynamic, and varied aspects of Himalayan art is its treatment of wrathful deities. This is the subject of the inaugural feature exhibition of the Rubin Museum of Art (RMA). The prominence of wrathful deities in Himalayan art, both Buddhist and Bön (Tibet's indigenous religion), is accurately reflected in the RMA collection, where it forms one of the collection's deepest strengths.

Taken together, these works convey the expressive power and graphic innovation of generations of Himalayan artists. Although Himalayan artists brought this genre to a zenith, it was not their invention alone. Much before them, the *Kashyapaparivarta*, one of the earliest Mahayana Buddhist texts from India, refers to a painting of a wrathful Dangerous Protector (*yaksha*) that is so terrifying, when its painter looked at it, he fainted away in fright![2] Some of the paintings and sculptures in the exhibition rival this legendary painting in intensity, though hopefully they will not literally sweep anyone off their feet, or cause a loss of consciousness in the galleries.

*

> Fearful am I to fear itself, with my necklace made of a string of heads, and dancing furiously on a solardisk. Black am I and terrible, a crossed vajra on my head, my body smeared with ashes, and my mouths sending forth the sound HUM. But my inner nature is tranquil, and holding Nairatmya in loving embrace, I am possessed of tranquil bliss.[3]

At the heart of the concept of the "demonic divine" is an intriguing paradox. It is embodied in the actual works of art, as well as in the texts which, in many cases, inspired them. This paradox is that compassion can take a terrifying form. As one learned Tibetan explained it, "Although certain meditational deities are wrathful [i.e. Wrathful Buddhas], their wrath is but a manifestation of compassion."[4] Put differently, what appears as our worst nightmare actually embodies our deepest potential. The spine-shivering violence in the descriptions and images is gruesome, direct, and palpable. Yet the menace is directed at those who would force human aspiration to its knees. Ultimately, the images model for us adamant attitudes for rooting out personal faults and flaws. Though they grasp dangerous weapons, snarl furiously, and make threatening gestures, wrathful deities are neither malignant nor harmful to humans. Though their features are exaggeratedly grotesque, they have our profoundest interests and welfare at heart.

> The wrath of the Vidyarajas [wrathful "kings of wisdom"], their weapons and the blazing flames of their aureoles are directed against the darkness of *avidya* [ignorance] which prevents men from gaining emancipation. They are therefore really beneficent.[5]

The crucial phenomenon underlying

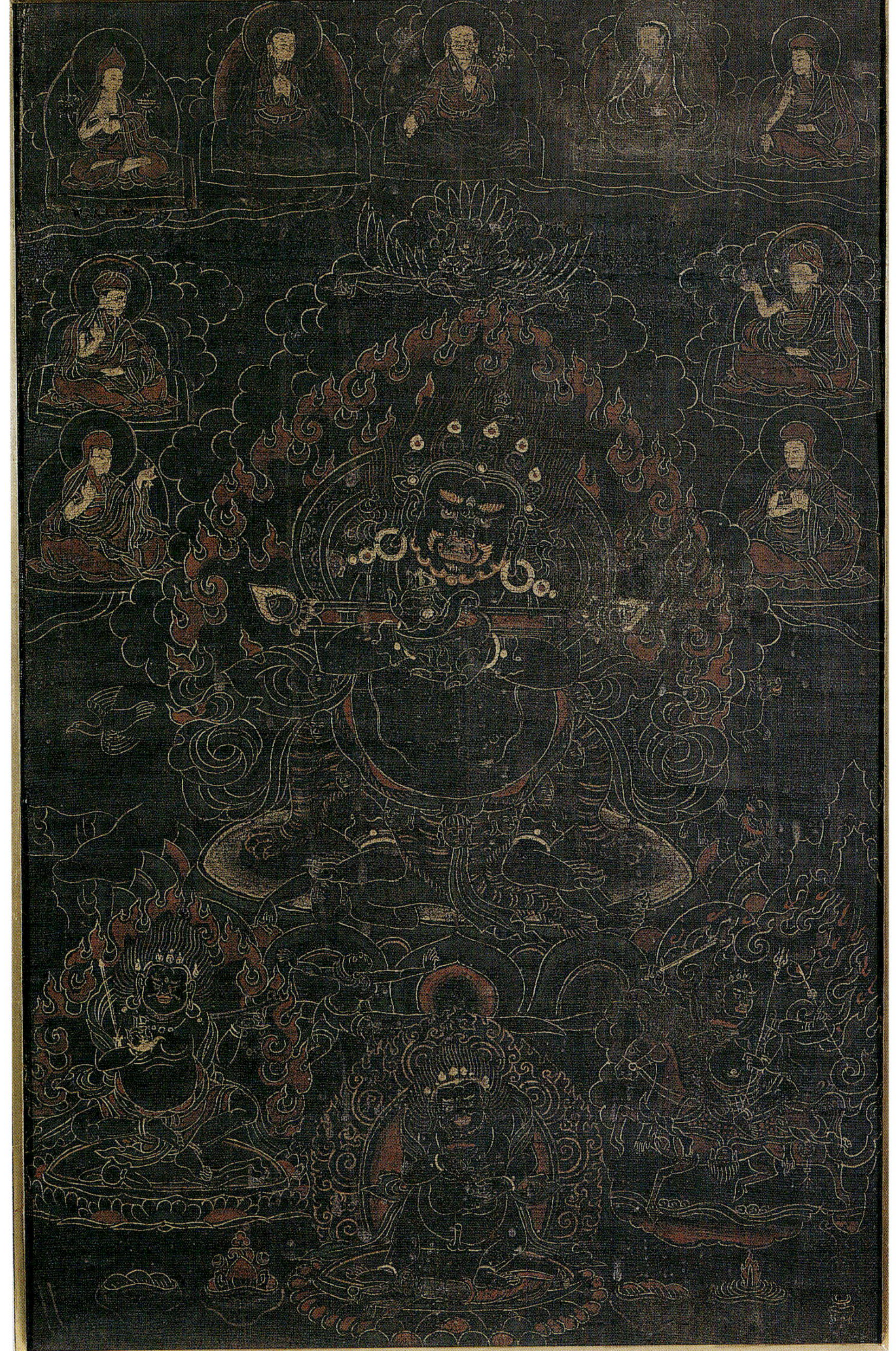

Fig. 1.3.
Mahakala Panjarnata
Tibet, 18th c.
Mineral pigments on cloth; 18½ x 12 in. (46.99 x 30.48 cm).
F1996.28.1 (HA 502).

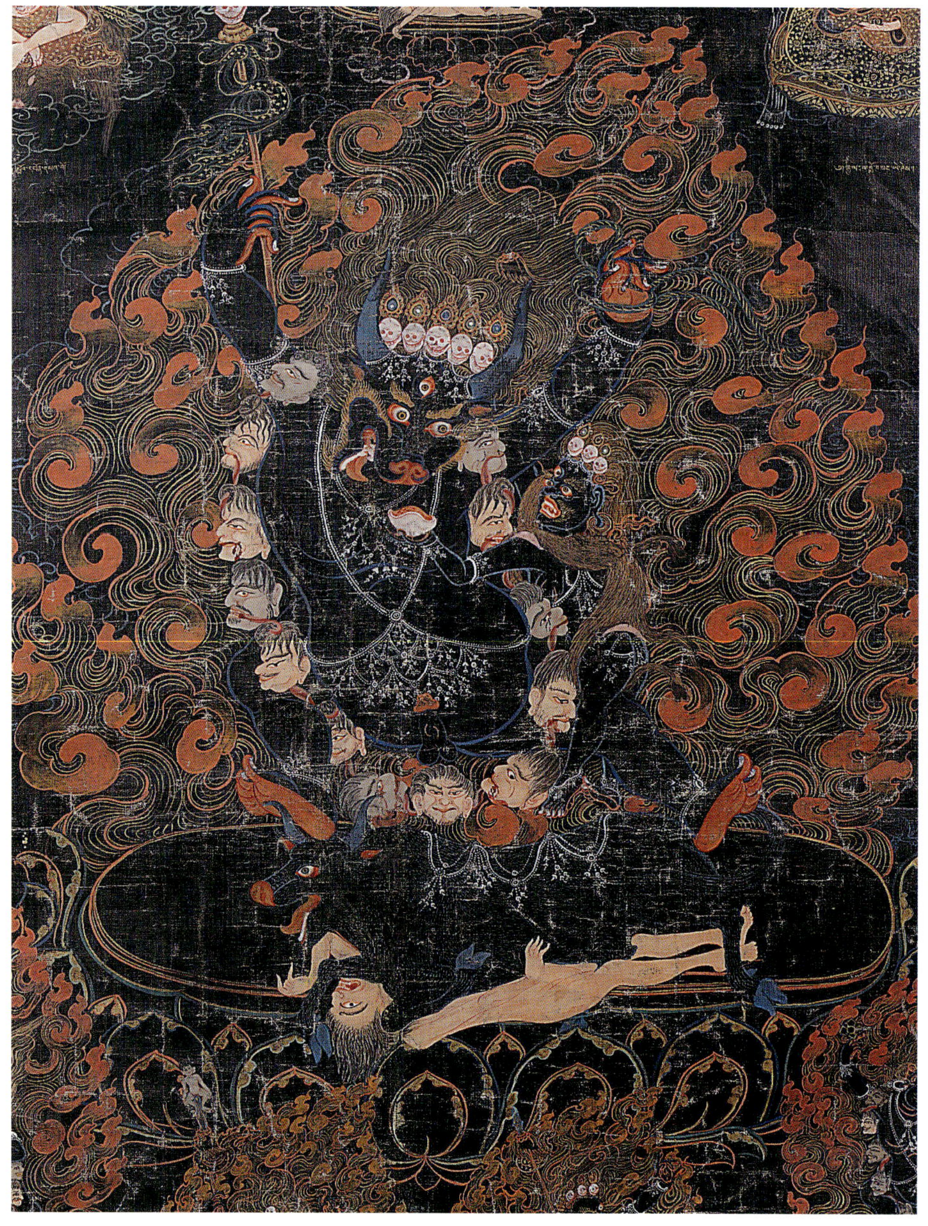

Fig. 1.4.
Yama with garland of heads (detail of Yama Dharmaraja *tangka*)
Tibet, 18th c.
Mineral pigments on cloth; overall size 31 x 22 in. (78.74 x 55.88 cm).
Collection of Shelley and Donald Rubin (HA 809).

their appearance is this: wrathful deities adopt the forms of what they are engaged in destroying. In the process they exaggerate the hyperbole of defiance, power, and intimidation displayed by the obstacles. These enemies are the inner and outer enemies experienced in mundane human existence, and it is as if, in their defeat, they surrender their very essence, as embodied in their appearance. Thus, the destroyer of death is even more terrifying in appearance than his victim—death. He "terrifies the terrifiers."[6] But these are adopted forms, contingent poses imposed from outside for the purposes of the transformation of benighted sentient beings. This power of "miraculous transformation" (Sanskrit: *vikurvanabala*), to "transform . . . at will, subjecting the forms of the world—all lacking substantiality—to manipulation," derives from the ultimate realization of reality.[7] The horrifying forms do not emerge from within these wrathful deities as expressing the inner essence. Just the opposite. The forms instead symbolize the performance of a task the early Mahayana philosopher, Nagarjuna, prescribes for every Buddhist:

> If you become angry
> Merely owing to an injury,
> Then why not be angry with anger,
> Which destroys your goal of liberation?[8]

As embodiments, or personifications, of the destruction of obstacles, the appearances of wrathful deities give us confidence in their abilities to master that which is malignant in human life: illness, misfortune, ingrained destructive patterns of behavior, the capacities to lust, hate, and envy, and the ability to act out of selfishness and ignorance, faculties with which we are all endowed. Liturgies recited in meditation not only list some of these obstacles, but also instruct the deities on what to do with the obstacles:

> Out of compassion and your commitments prescribed by the Victorious Buddhas, free me quickly from enemies and interferers—with all hateful enemies, harmful interferers, demons and interruption-makers, seize them, bind them, tie them up! Summon them, drag them and make them your slaves! . . . Dismember them, trample them, make them bewildered! Subdue them, destroy them, demolish them

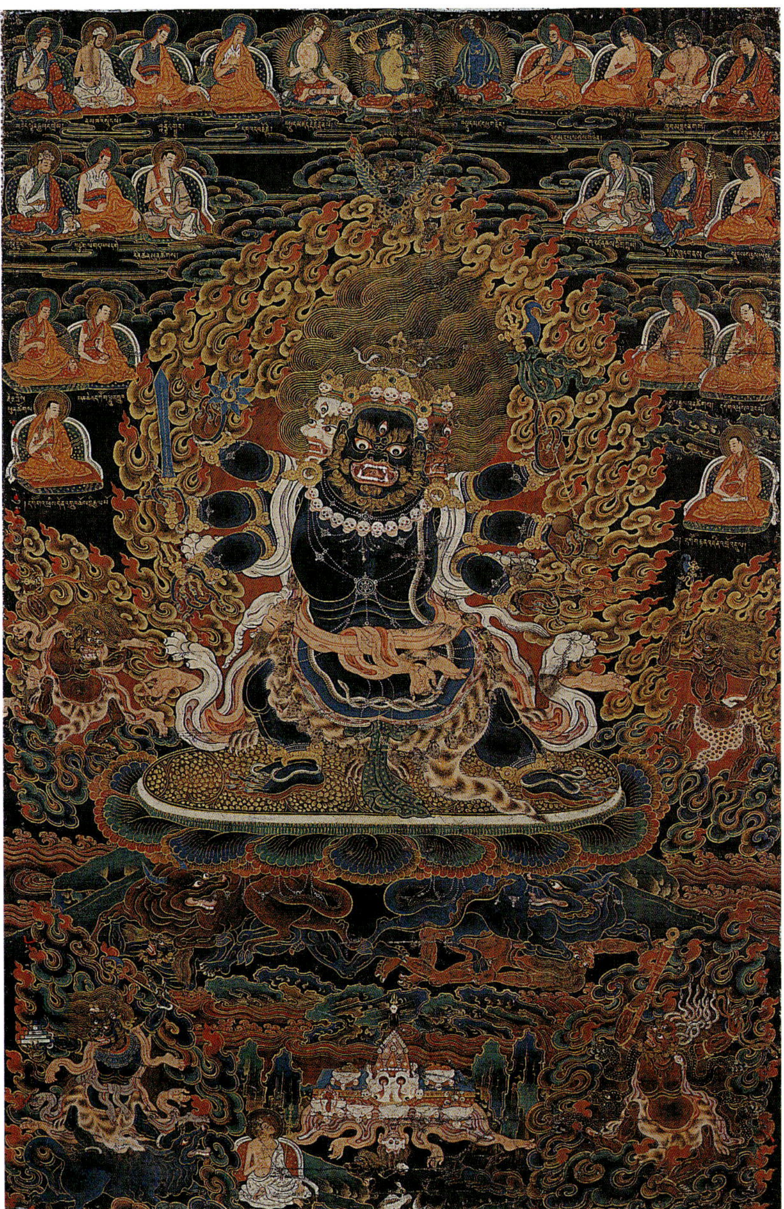

Fig. 1.5.
Krishna Yamari (detail)
Tibet, 18th c.
Mineral pigments on cloth; overall size 20¾ x 13¼ in. (52.7 x 33.65 cm).
F1998.16.3 (HA 661).

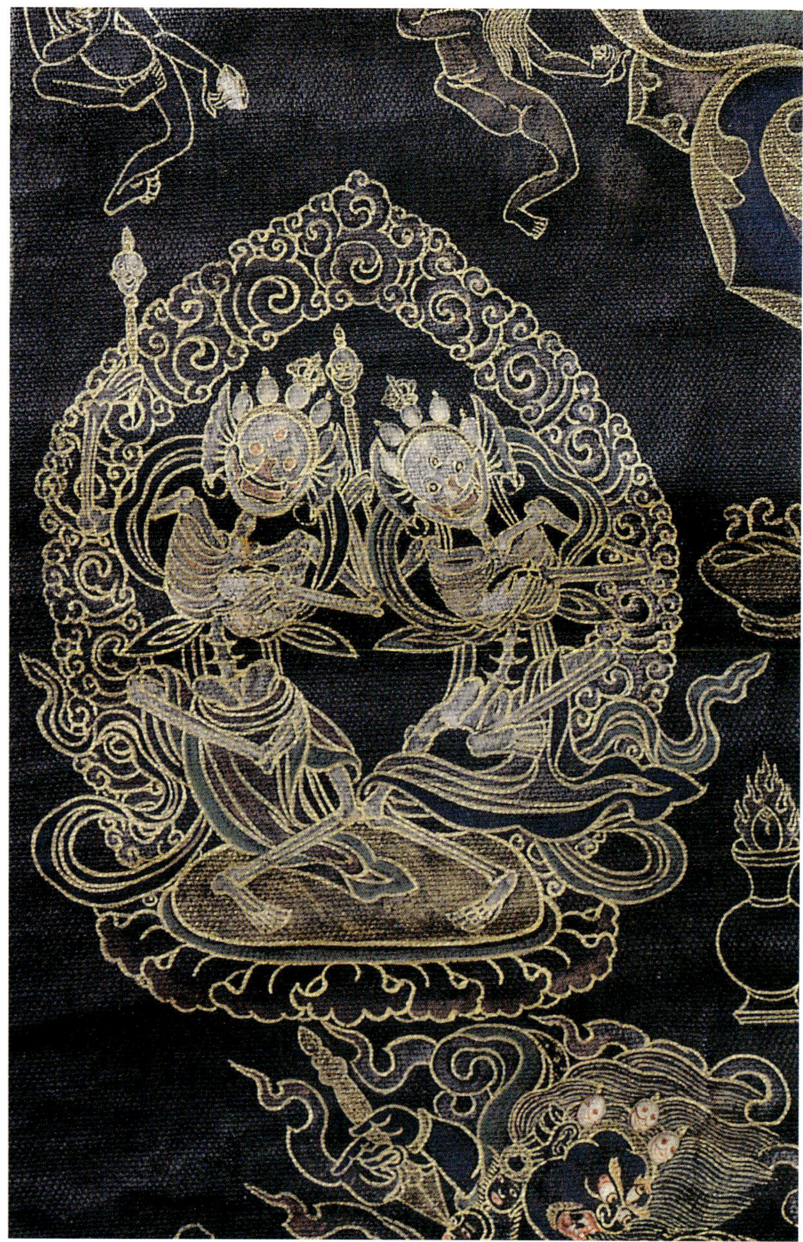

Fig. 1.6.
Chitipati (detail of Mahakala Panjarnata *tangka*)
Tibet, 18th c.
Mineral pigments on cloth; overall size 31 x 23¼ in. (78.74 x 59.05 cm).
Collection of Shelley and Donald Rubin (HA 730).

fully so that not even an atom of them might remain.[9]

The *Manjushrimulakalpa*, an early Indian Esoteric Buddhist text compiled by the eighth century, sums up the tasks of a certain group of minor wrathful deities as "destroyers of death, destruction, epidemics, ruin and tamers of all beings without exception; bestowers upon the faithful; discharged for the practitioners of rituals of malediction, increase, and pacification."[10]

So, wrathful deities are not malevolent, despite their appearance. Indeed, thinking them so actually does one harm, at least according to the pervasive system of between-birth experience embodied in the *Bardotodol*, known popularly in the West as the *Tibetan Book of the Dead*. According to this text, the disembodied consciousness of the recently deceased will encounter wrathful forms, and if she is repelled by the frightful appearance, this leads to rebirth in less fortunate circumstances. If, by contrast, she recognizes them as compassionate forms of the Buddha, she will be led to enlightenment. A lengthy description of "the great, glorious Buddha Heruka" indicates that he has three faces, six arms, and four legs, carrying a wheel, axe, and sword in his proper right hands, and a bell, plow, and skull bowl in the left, that he is fierce and flashing with menace, and that he is embraced by his consort Buddha Krodhishvari (the Female Lord of Wrath; fig. 1.2). The following instructions are given to prepare her for the encounter:

> Thus they rise manifestly before you, having emerged from within your own brain! Do not fear them! Do not be terrified! Do not hate them! Recognize them as an image of your own awareness. He is your own Archetype Deity, so do not panic! In fact, they are really Lord Vairochana [Buddha] Father and Mother, so do not be afraid! The very moment you recognize them, you will be liberated![11]

Even earlier, Nagarjuna wrote this verse:

> If water be set on fire,
> How is it to be extinguished?
> If fear comes from the protector,
> Who will protect from fear?[12]

In sum, the terrifying appearance reflects the power to destroy the obstacles that block a fulfilling, compassionate, and wise life, which in turn will ultimately lead to enlightenment. The more terrifying the appearance, the more powerful the obstacles that can be decimated. The mandate given to Himalayan artists was to express this very conundrum, benevolent wrath, and they responded to the task with great imagination and verve. Without neglecting the religious requirements of a specified number of heads, hands, and attributes, Himalayan artists found many ways to profitably exaggerate and illuminate the theme. One response was the adaptation and development of "black-ground" (*nag-tang*) painting as particularly effective and appropriate to the demonic-divine (fig. 1.3).[13] These paintings are among the most expressive of the *horreur sacrée.* Artists also developed awesome haloes of flames, through which the deities stare with bulging eyes. Some of the wrathful figures are garlanded with strung-together decapitated human heads which loll naturalistically, their tongues protruding (fig. 1.4). Crowned with skulls, the mouth of the deity is often agape, with sharp white fangs surrounding a long snakelike tongue, which emerges as if the deity is simultaneously laughing and roaring, "as if he gulps down the entire multitude of interrupting worldly demons."[14] "A 'mist of illnesses' comes forth from the mouth and a terrific storm is supposed to be blowing from the nostrils of the flat nose."[15]

Another text gives a useful description:

> All ten of the terrible ones have yellowish-red hair flaming up; their brows and eyelashes flare intensely orange [fig. 1.5]. Each face has three eyes and four sharp fangs, which grind horribly. Their fierce loud laughs HA HA reverberate, and their faces are wrinkled with intensity of expressions. They have big bellies. Their hair is bound by blue Ananta snakes, red Takshaka snakes serve as earrings [other snakes serve as necklaces, bracelets, sashes, belts and

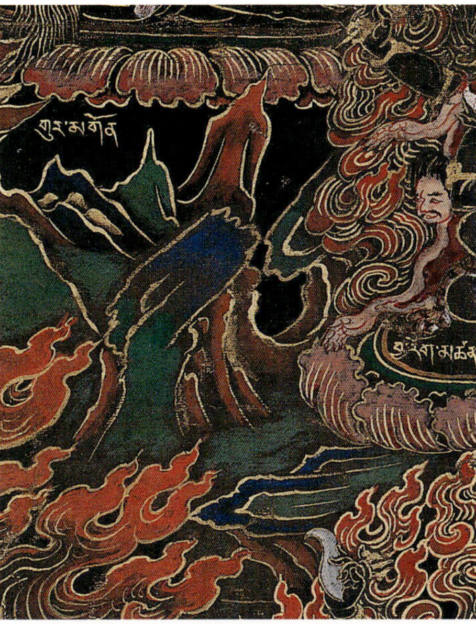

Fig. 1.7.
Mountains
(detail of cat. no. 16).

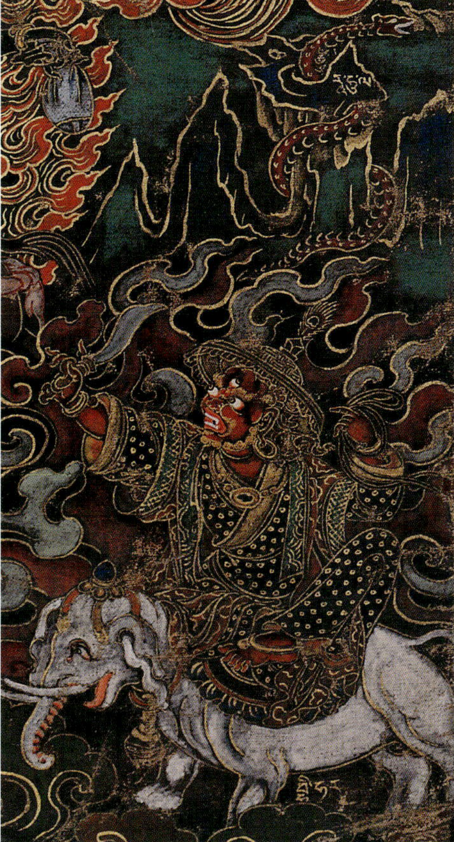

Fig. 1.8.
Mountains with dragon
(detail of cat. no. 16).

> anklets]. Intense wisdom-fire blazes from their bodies; they stand in the center ready to punish all evil beings.[16]

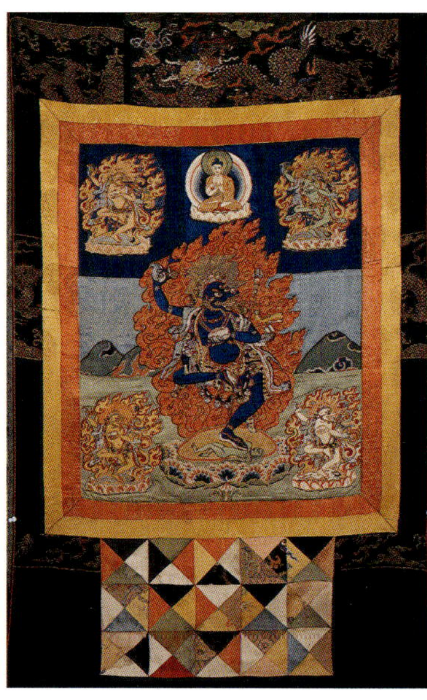

Fig. 1.9.
Simhamukha
Tibet, 18th c.
Applique of Chinese silk, with embroidery; 52 x 33½ in. (132 x 85.09 cm).
C2003.42.1 (HA 65258).

Such descriptions have a graphic quality that may have been informed by paintings and sculptures, even as the texts would have inspired artists in turn. In some cases the grotesqueries border on the humorous in their sheer exuberance and extremity. The male and female pair of dancing skeletons, the Chitipati, illustrates this well (fig. 1.6).

The setting in these paintings was also calibrated to the theme of the central wrathful figures. When not inhabiting charnel (cremation) grounds, craggy mountains in haunted colors make the earth itself seem eerie (fig. 1.7). As a contemporary Tibetan artist describes it,

> The atmosphere in the painting [of wrathful deities] should be fiery and smouldering and at times, depending on various aspects, contain dragons and birds of prey circling about the sky [fig. 1.8].[17]

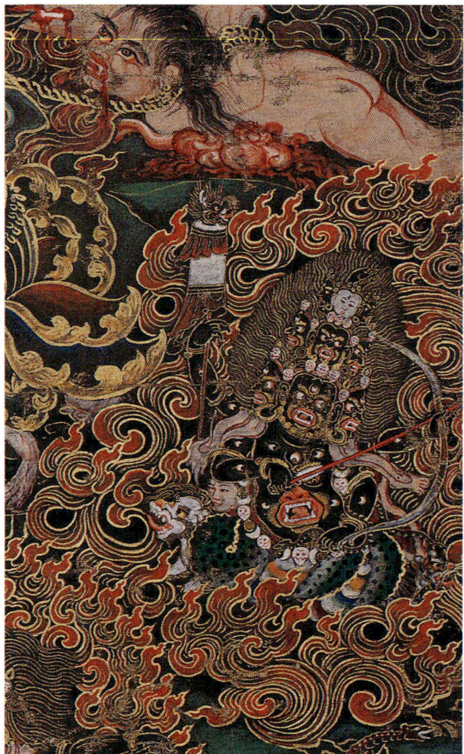

Fig. 1.10.
Rahula
(detail of cat. no. 16).

The artists seem to relish the opportunity to give rein to their visual imagination, and the artworks are vivid records of the artists' creativity, sparked by the religious ideas that came down to them and the desire to surpass past artists in clothing the ideas in forms.

2

The artists employed a number of visual strategies in order to enhance the power of the wrathfulness in their images. One is a kind of "fantastic naturalism." Others are a related hybridity, agitated line, dramatic color, exaggeration, and graphic depictions of sexuality and violence. Many-armed, multiheaded deities, with skin colors that range across the spectrum, should be unbelievable. Yet the artists are able to craft the disparate parts together with surprising conviction. The proportions and the joins are designed so that it seems that if such a being were to exist, it would look like this! It all the more a triumph when the hybridity of creature-parts come into play, when a lion's head is placed on a woman's body (fig. 1.9), a buffalo head is grafted to a big-bellied blue body (cat. no. 50), a blue wolf's head to a red humanoid body (cat. no. 7), the torso of a big-bellied human male turns into a coiled snake (fig. 1.10), or a bird's beaked head is placed atop a human torso (fig. 1.11).

Drama is enhanced with "psychedelic" color contrasts—especially the deep reds glimmering out of a black background, or a black figure silhouetted by an orange backdrop of flames (cat. no. 37). The flames, clouds, and scarves trail in a specified direction, as if whipped by the dynamic momentum of the main figures. The stances and poses are often exaggerated—the hips are flung far out of line with the central axis, or the legs are outstretched and the toes curled upward (fig. 1.5, cat. no. 33). The "archer's pose" (*alidhasana*), in which one leg is extended straight out, and the other is bent sharply at the knee, is probably the most common across all classes of wrathful deities. A kind of dancing pose (*ardhaparyanka*) is also adopted, placing the weight of the body on one slightly bent leg and raising the other flexed at the knee (figs. 1.9, 1.12). Both of these poses, along with rarer ones unique to particular deities (figs. 1.3, 1.13, cat. no. 40), are energetic and dynamic. In this sense they are visual expressions of the activity of the deity, but from the aesthetic point of view, the poses shatter any expectation for a static icon.

Body proportions are generally of two types, dwarfish and big-bellied (fig. 1.13), or tall and slender (cat. no. 37).[18] This distinction again cuts across all classes of wrathful deities, though there is a tendency for more worldly deities to be "weightier" while more of the highest "meditation" deities, what we are calling Wrathful Buddhas, are athletic or warriorlike. (The three broad classes of wrathful deities are discussed below.)

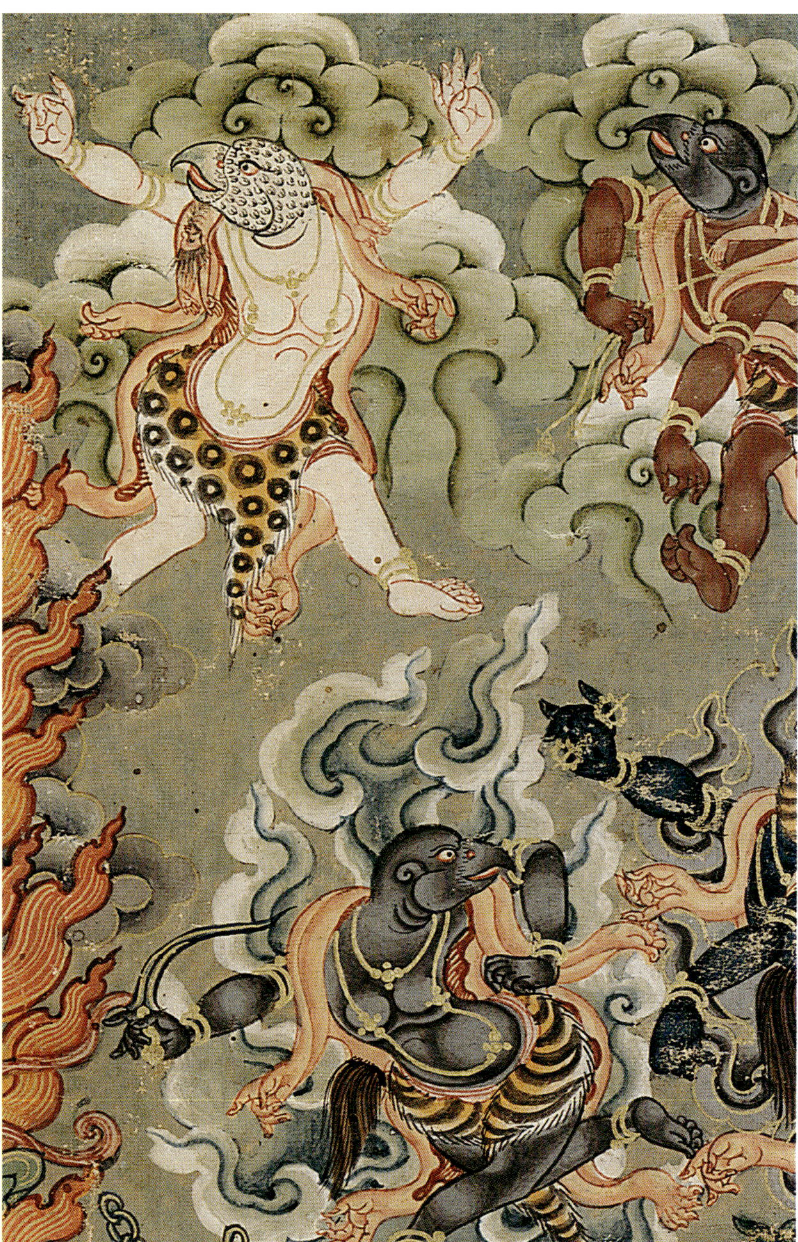

Fig. 1.11.
Animal-headed deities (detail of Chemchog Heruka *tangka)*
Nyingma lineage
Tibet 19th c.
Mineral pigments on cloth; overall size 29 x 21 in. (73.66 x 53.34 cm).
Collection of Shelley and Donald Rubin (HA 702).

Artists exaggerate the eyes of wrathful deities, underscoring the faces' furious countenances. In sculptures, the eyes bulge out of their sockets, and red pigment is painted

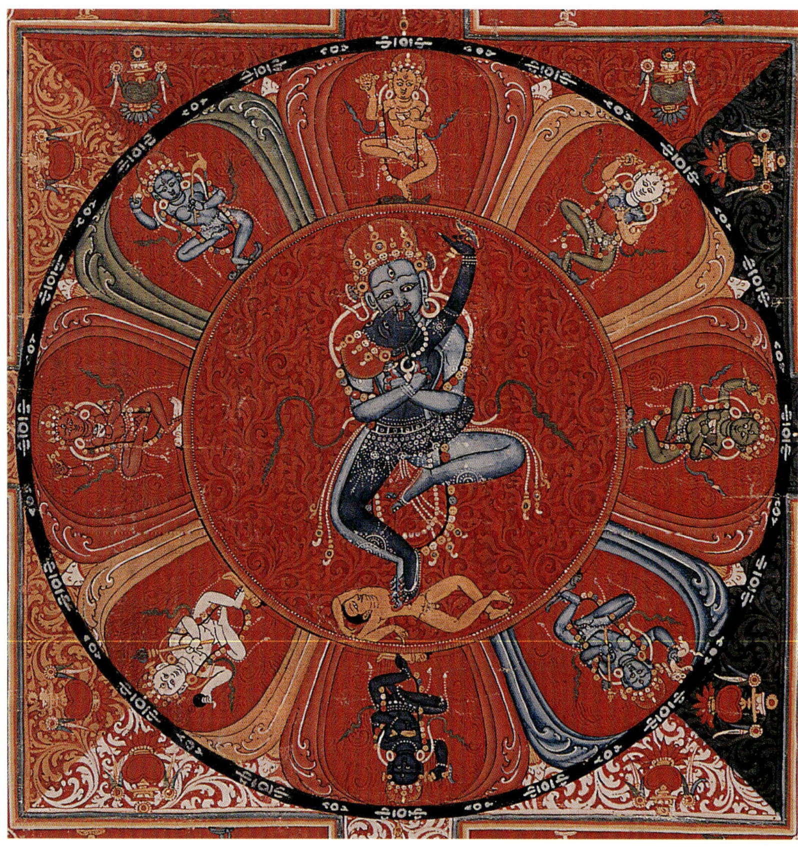

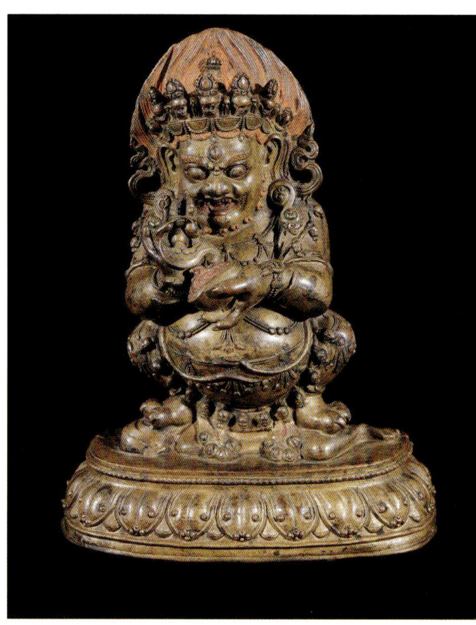

Top: Fig. 1.12.
Two-armed Hevajra embracing Nairatmya with eight goddesses (detail of Hevajra Mandala *tangka*)
Tibet, 16th c.
Mineral pigments on cloth; overall size 20½ x 16¾ in. (52.07 x 42.54 cm).
C2002.24.7 (HA 65123).

Right: Fig. 1.13.
Mahakala Panjarnata
Tibet, 18th c.
Metalwork; H. 11 in. (27.94 cm).
C2001.7.1 (HA 65018).

around the rims as if to suggest the eyes are bloodshot (cat. no. 17). *Tangka* painters create mesmerizing eyes by contrasting the red rims with relatively small pupils swimming in orbs of white (fig. 1.14). Flaming eyebrows often enhance the effect—even on a vertically oriented "third eye" (fig. 1.15). Many of these figures appear to look directly out at the viewer, but a surprising number look ever-so slightly askance (fig. 1.16), to the side or above (fig. 1.17). As far as I know, only one deity, Ekajati, squeezes her normal pair of eyes completely shut, but she has a fortuitous third eye that she keeps open (fig. 1.18). The more typical, wide eyes convey both the all-seeing nature of the deities, and their incensed reaction to the obstacles they observe.

Gaping mouths emitting ferocious laughs are the norm. Fangs are prominent, and sometimes pointed tongues. Scarves trail, curl, and whip, echoing the movements of the flames which invariably frame the wrathful deities. Scarves and flames are devices that work to suggest the extension of the deity's power radiating outward. Hair echoes the movement of the flames and scarves, frequently waving upward and diagonally away (fig. 1.19), though sometimes spiking up or rounding off. Adding to the terrifying appearance are ubiquitous snakes as ornaments around ankles, wrists, and hair.

The deities, male and female alike, are naked, or nearly so. Although adorned with ribbons and jewels, their genitals are not obscured. Vajrabhairava and forms of Yama Dharmaraja (cat. nos. 46, 34) are shown graphically ithyphallic, and the breasts of the female deities are invariably emphasized, either as full and round or withered and drooping with elongated nipples (fig. 1.20, cat. nos. 1, 7, 58). The results are images that have a huge impact on the viewer, with effects calculated to underscore the central paradox of wrathful compassion. For, the uglier and scarier they are, the more powerful the obstacles that can be overcome.

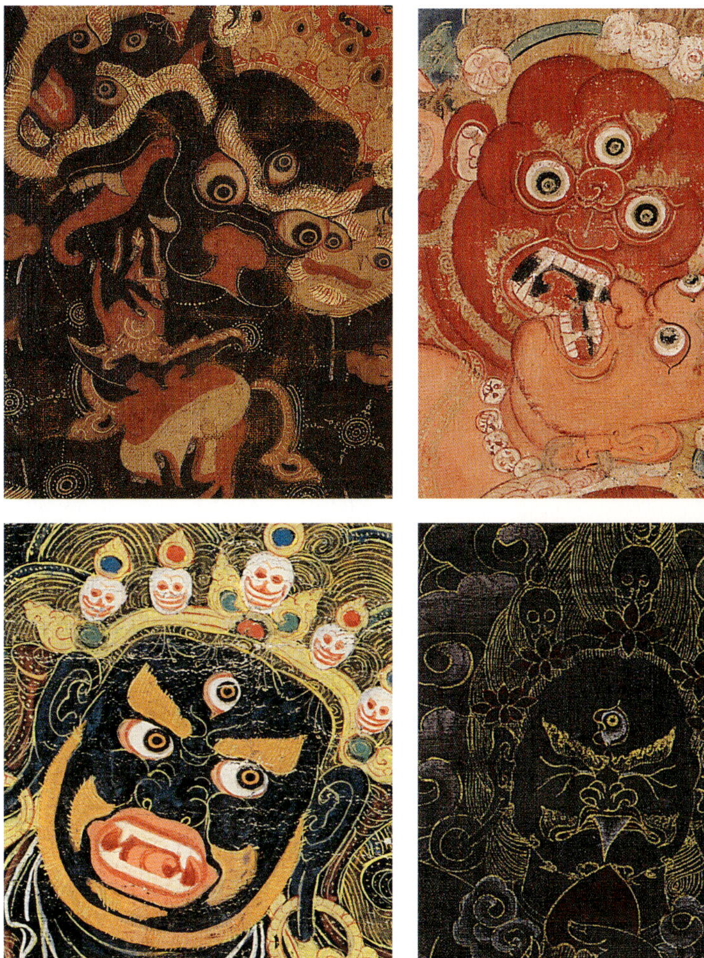

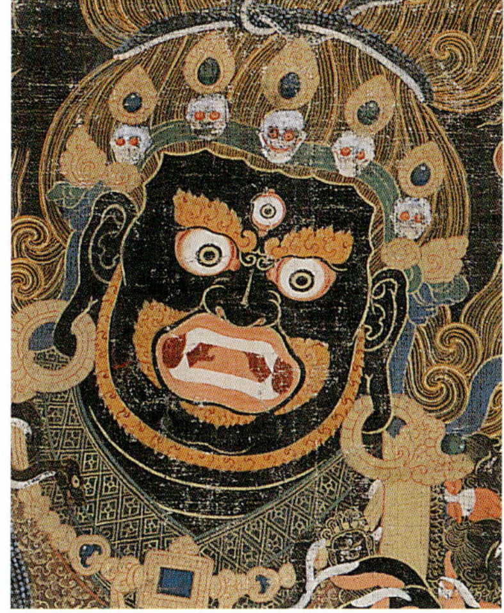

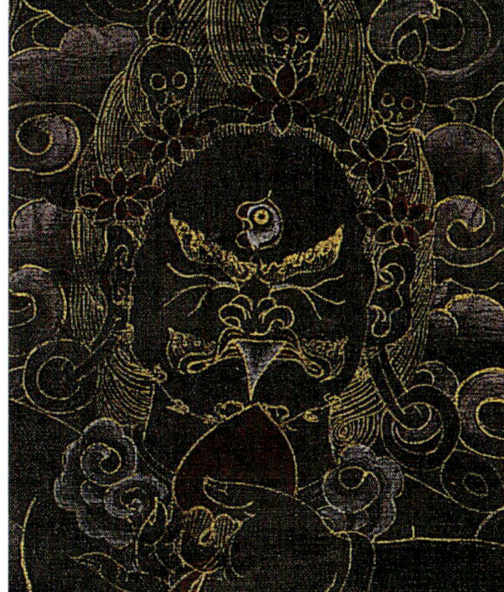

Top Row, Left to Right:
Fig. 1.14.
Head of Vajrabhairava (detail of Vajrabhairava *tangka*)
Tibet, 18th c.
Mineral pigments on cloth; overall size 24 1/2 x 16 in. (62.23 x 40.64 cm).
Collection of Shelley and Donald Rubin (HA 198).

Fig. 1.15.
Heads of central figures (detail of Rakta Yamari *tangka*)
Tibet, 18th c.
Mineral pigments on cloth; overall size, 17 x 15 1/2 in. (43.18 x 39.37 cm).
Collection of Shelley and Donald Rubin (HA 1036).

Fig. 1.16.
Head of Mahakala (detail of Mahakala Danda *tangka*)
Tibet, 17th c.
Mineral pigments on cloth; overall size 40 1/2 x 27 1/4 in. (102.87 x 69.215 cm)
Collection of Shelley and Donald Rubin (HA 22).

Bottom Row, Left to Right:
Fig. 1.17.
Head of Mahakala (detail of Mahakala Maning *tangka*)
Tibet, 18th c.
Mineral pigments on cloth; overall size 27 1/2 x 21 1/2 in. (69.85 x 54.61 cm).
Collection of Shelley and Donald Rubin (HA 878).

Fig. 1.18.
Head of Ekajati (detail of Ekajati *tangka*)
Tibet, 19th c.
Mineral pigments on cloth; overall size 23 1/2 x 17 1/2 in. (59.69 x 44.45 cm).
Collection of Shelley and Donald Rubin (HA 263).

Perhaps the effect of activating fear in the beholder are even intended to stimulate a moral reaction. "Horror and distress at the world may be most valuable to Buddhist ethics in their ability to generate compassion."[19]

Another very striking aspect, palpable in most images of wrathful deities, is the savage subject matter. Almost all of the deities carry weapons. Knives, swords, clubs, and fetters are particularly prominent, but so are "trophies" of conquest such as the brain-filled skull bowls, the flayed skins of animals and humans, human hearts held up in triumph, drums made of two brain-pans stuck together, and creatures of all varieties being trampled and crushed underfoot (fig. 1.20). At the bottom of many such paintings, a set of offerings symbolizing the presentation of the senses and consciousness depicts bloodshot eyes attached to stemlike optic nerves, a tongue, heart, ears, nose, and skin, "represented as having been torn or ripped from the body, and assembled as a 'flower offering'"(fig. 1.21).[20] The graphic violence of such images mirrors the drastic statements made in texts and commentaries, such as this verse credited to Dharmarakshita:

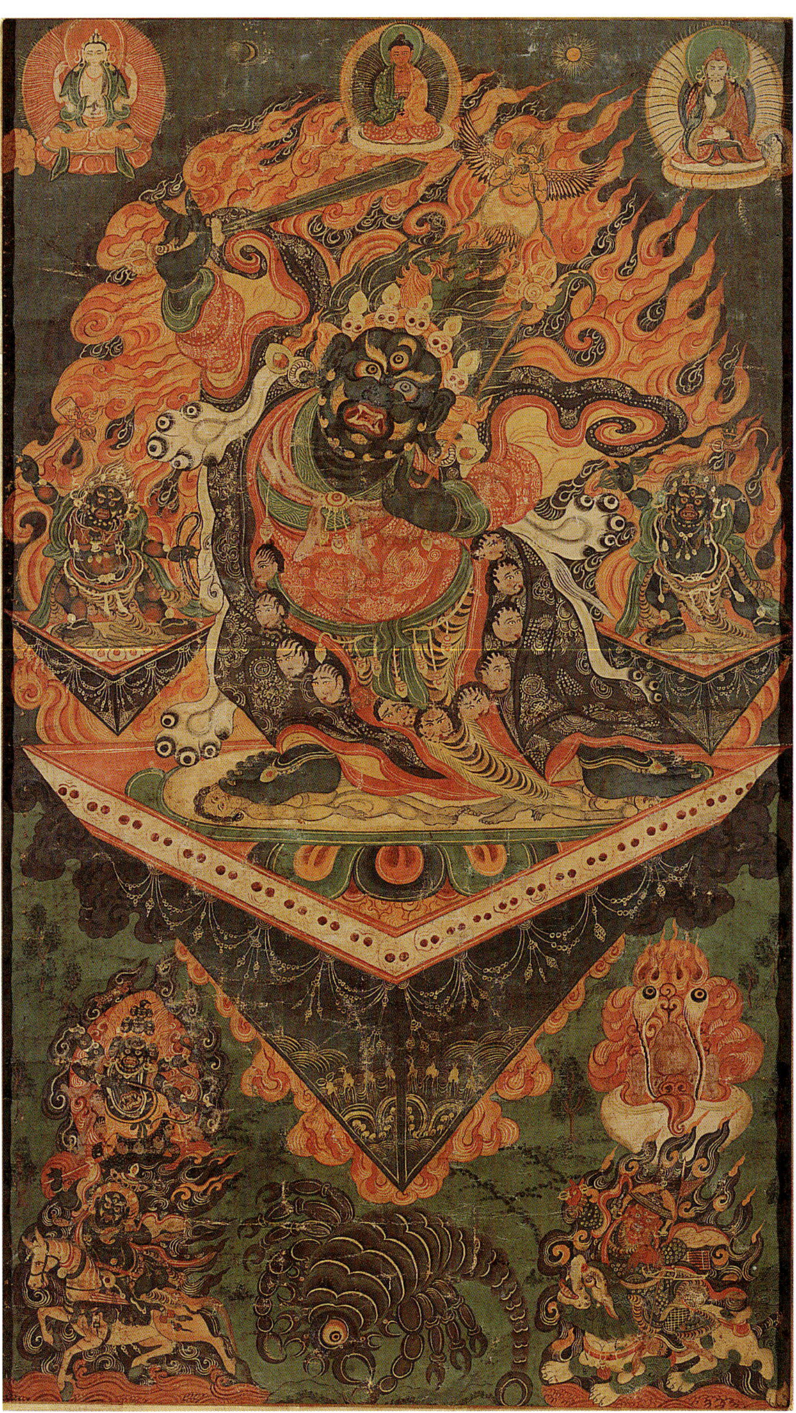

Batter him, batter him, rip out the heart
Of our grasping for ego, our love for ourselves!
. . . .
Tear out the heart of this self-centered butcher
Who slaughters our chance to gain final release! [21]

In the paintings depicting Dorje Legpa and Maning Mahakala featured in the exhibition (cat. nos. 2, 16), they literally hold hearts in their proper left hands, just as this verse commands. Recently, more attention has been paid to the violence in Esoteric Buddhist literature, which can be understood literally or metaphorically.[22] Ronald Davidson has argued that it must be seen against the backdrop of the social reality of India when these religious teachings emerged, beginning in the seventh century.[23] At that time, the empires that had kept the peace over large areas of India and promoted monastic Buddhism were collapsing and being replaced by an ongoing series of aggressive, small, conquest armies, headed by unscrupulous warriors. In reaction, committed Buddhists sought ways both to create an ideology of justifiable violence that would attract these leaders and to give themselves the tools to defend Buddhism against Hindu absolutists. Certainly, the increasingly violent metaphors for inner conquest appearing in Esoteric Buddhist art between the seventh and thirteenth centuries have been clearly charted.[24]

Be that as it may, north of India, in Tibet and the other Himalayan regions, this form of Buddhism ultimately found a very fertile, hospitable ground. Buddhism faced new and different obstacles in the process of being transplanted to this region. The enforced "conversion" of pre-Buddhist, native Himalayan deities, especially those belonging to the category of Dangerous Protectors (see below) is evidence of the difficulties and accommodations made in splicing Esoteric Buddhism to Tibetan religious practice.[25] Many of the chthonic, animistic deities of Tibet and the surrounding regions survived somewhat uneasily as oath-bound protectors, sometimes preserving their earlier practical, protective functions intact. Yet there is no question that, over time, the metaphors, conventions, and imagery embedded in Indian Esoteric Buddhist texts and art were wholeheartedly embraced and then radically developed by religious practitioners and artists in the Himalayas. The images of wrathful deities are distinctive, and at least for contemporary Westerners, have come to be characteristic of, or identified with, Himalayan cultures.

Still, the idea of the demonic divine is not peculiar to Esoteric Buddhism or to Himalayan cultures. Many different cultures have drawn on similar thematic concepts or have used parallel visual languages of distortion, wrath, and hybridity. These parallels, which are neither absolute nor universal, are the subject of a section of *Demonic Divine: Himalayan Art and Beyond* (cat. nos. 9, 13, 19–20, 23–24, 27, 29–30, 41, 48–49, 62–63). By juxtaposing objects and comparative images in various media representing Himalayan and non-Himalayan cultures, it will become clear that although retaining their distinctiveness, Himalayan cultures are by no means unique in developing the theme to the extent they do.

3

The exhibition *Demonic Divine: Himalayan Art and Beyond* is organized thematically into three groupings of functionally related wrathful deities. In the Himalayan traditions, the three groups are not defined as neatly as this, but this set of three draws on categories that do exist in the traditions. The divisions, therefore, are a mixture of etic and emic ways of looking at wrathful deities.

The first group, the wrathful **Dangerous Protectors** (fig. 1.22), for example, help ensure health, wealth, and happiness by delivering the faithful from "outer" enemies, visible and invisible. They protect particular

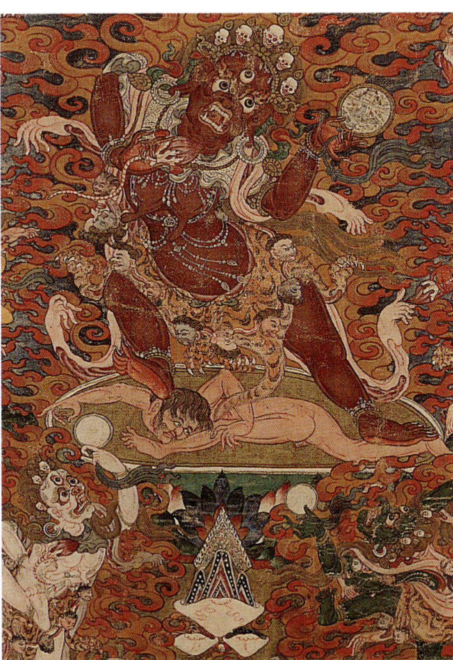

Facing page: Fig. 1.19.
Hayagriva
Tibet, 19th c.
Mineral pigments on cloth; 26 x 14 3/4 in. (66.04 x 37.46 cm).
Collection of Shelley and Donald Rubin (HA 4).

Fig. 1.20.
Drogdze Wangmo (detail of Drogdze Wangmo *tangka)*
Tibet, 19th c.
Mineral pigments on cloth; 17 1/4 x 14 3/4 (43.81 x 29.21 cm).
F1996.7.1 (HA 421).

locales from invasion and pestilence, or cure poisonous snake-bites and illnesses. They control the environmental forces and elements in which they are embedded, along with the fates and fortunes of humans. Some of these dangerous gods originated very early as indigenous nature gods in Tibet and were "converted" to Buddhism after the seventh century. Others, particularly the wealth gods, were brought from India where they originated in sedimentary layers of ancient culture as pre-Buddhist gods. In the hierarchy of the three categories we propose here, the Dangerous Protectors are the lowest group, a fractious and dangerous lot, monitored by higher deities to ensure they preserve their vows to protect and benefit the faithful. Many of them ride horses, lions, goats, or other animals (fig. 1.23). They tend to wear armor, reinforcing their martial nature (fig. 1.22, cat. nos. 3, 4). They are guardian warriors who are oath-bound protectors.

Among the wrathful Dangerous Protectors, the incorporation into Buddhism of gods of circumscribed territories or

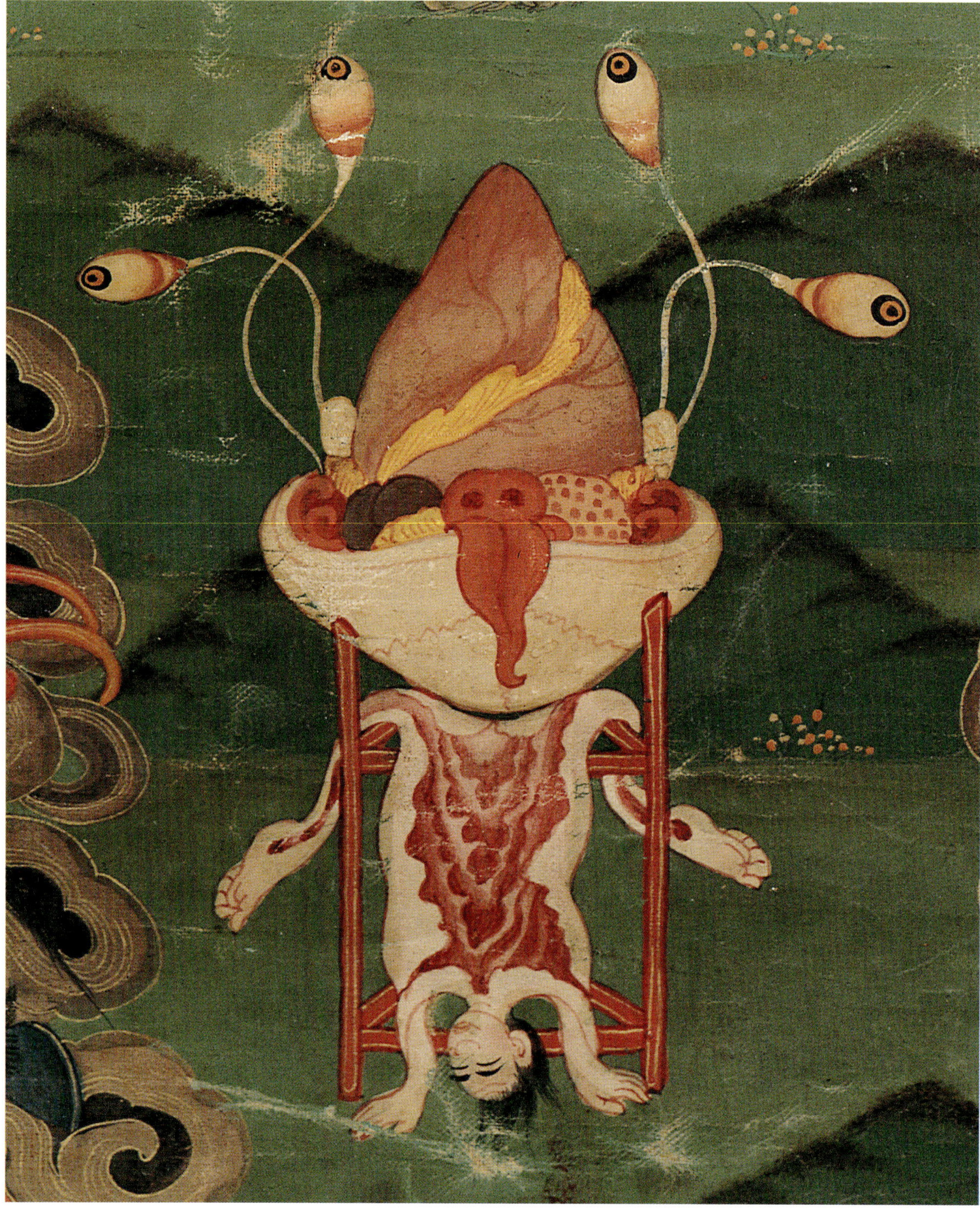

locales, such as mountain gods, is a complex process, one that continues to be an issue today.[26] A large number of these deities are said to have been tamed by Padmasambhava in the eighth century, but

> Tibetan Buddhist ritual specialists continue that process of subjugation, incorporating complex [ritual] practices to the protectors into their repertoires, while laypeople, with this-worldly pragmatic concerns, make regular daily offerings as well as special emergency offerings to some of these beings as circumstances require.[27]

Dorje Legpa is an example of an indigenous Tibetan spirit subjugated by Padmasambhava, who bound him by oath into a protector of *terma* (revealed treasure) texts (fig. 1.23, cat. no. 2). Pehar is another oath-bound protector converted by Padmasambhava (cat. no. 6). Since the seventeenth century, he has been promoted by the Gelugpa as the protector of the Tibetan state, while Shangpa Karpo (fig. 1.25) is accepted as a worldly protector of Tibet.[28]

In some regions, worship of the mountains gods is limited to lay people, even though the deities are seen as converts to Buddhism, and the protection of religion is one of their functions. However, territory gods are dangerously ambivalent. As the scholar Pascale Dollfus writes,

> How the gods act depends on people's behavior towards them. They are regularly worshiped—individually or collectively—by the nomads to ensure their benevolence and their help so that prosperity increases and disease spares the cattle.[29]

One example of a territory god is Draglha Gonpo (The Protector, God of the Rock; cat. no. 3). He is especially associated with a region of eastern Tibet known as Serta. Another is Machen Pomra (fig. 1.26), represented here by one of the minor gems of the Rubin collections, a fourteenth-century painting in which the protector wears a robe imitating Sassanian roundel brocade, a memory of early Tibetan court culture. Although he originated as a mountain deity, and retains his appearance as a kingly warrior, in the later Tibetan Buddhist system he became a more generalized protector of religious teachings.[30]

The Dangerous Protectors are given at least nominal duties to protect religion within their domains, but the primary responsibilities are more mundane: to

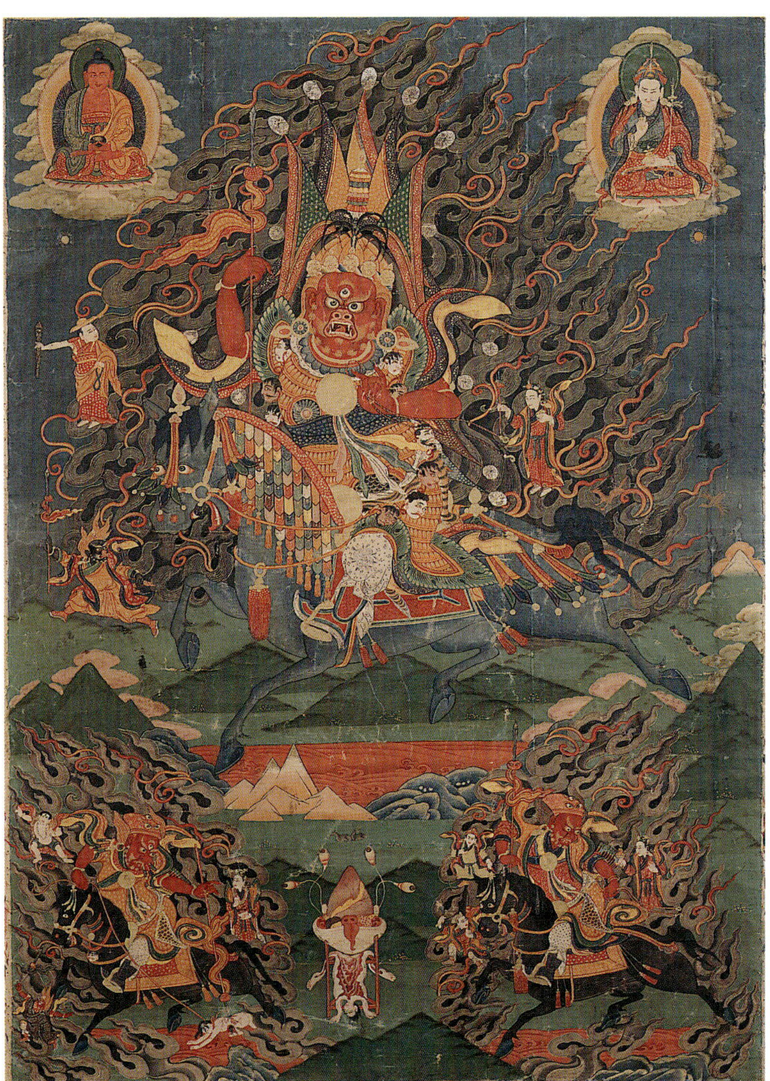

Facing page Fig. 1.21.
Sense offerings
(detail of fig. 1.22).

Fig. 1.22.
Red Vaishravana
Tibet, 19th c.
Mineral pigments on cloth; 26¼ x 19 in. (66.67 x 48.26 cm).
F1997.7.3 (HA 103).

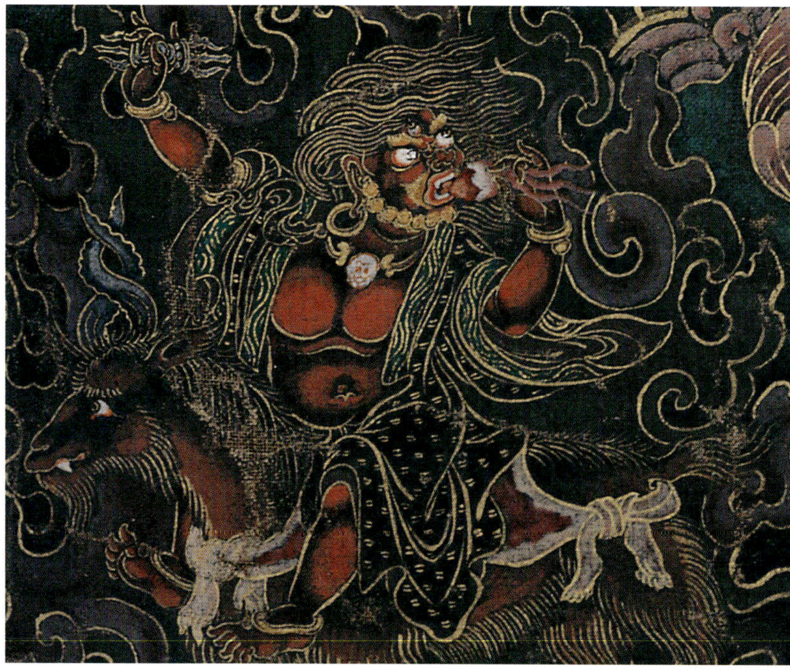

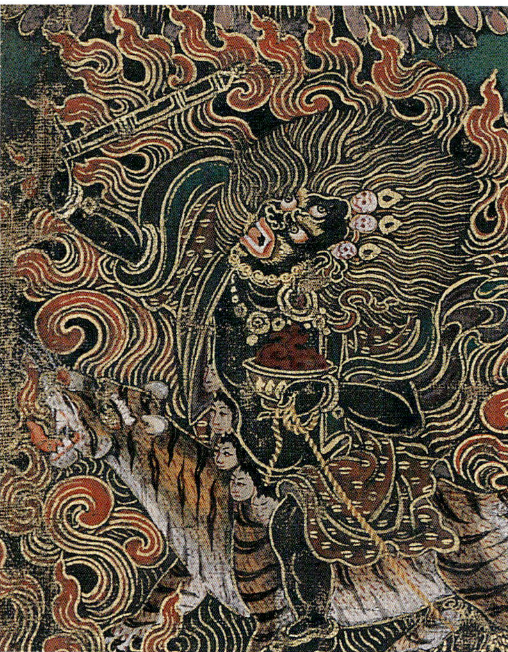

Top: Fig. 1.23.
Dorje Legpa
(detail of cat. no. 16).

Right: Fig. 1.24.
Vyaghra Vahana (detail of cat. no. 16).

ensure the birth of sons, to protect humans and livestock against diseases and epidemics, to avert accidents and bad omens, and to destroy or contain obstacle-creating demons. For this reason, they are designated "worldly." In the predominantly Gelugpa system that René de Nebesky-Wojkowitz studied and published, they were known as *jigtenpai sungma* or *jigten gyi chokyang* (wordly). [31]

The second of our heuristic groupings is the wrathful **Enlightened Protectors**, sometimes also known as the "Supramundane Protectors" or "those who have passed beyond the six spheres of existence" (*jigten ledepai sungma*; fig. 1.27).[32] No longer merely gods—the Enlightened Protectors are usually the primary protectors of particular teachings, of miraculously discovered "treasure texts," of lineages, rituals, or meditation practices. These teachings tend to require initiations in order to be revealed and are psychically dangerous to practice. Therefore, initiations call for special protectors to ensure the safety and mental stability of the initiate at a time of vulnerability. For example, Yama Dharmaraja was one of the protectors of Tsongkapa (1357–1419), and simultaneously of the Gelugpa lineage and the Varjabhairava practices (cat. nos. 33–36). Panjarnata Mahakala (figs. 1.3, 1.27, cat. nos. 18, 21, 22) is the main protector of the Sakya tradition, while Shadbhuja Mahakala (cat. no. 28) is the special protector of the Shangpa Kagyu and Gelugpa lineages. Magzor Gyalmo (cat. nos. 31–32) is a wrathful form of the peaceful goddess Sarasvati originating in India. In Tibet, she has come to be revered as the special protector of the Dalai Lamas and the Namgyal College of the Potala Palace, as well as being invoked for divination rituals.[33]

Compared to the wrathful Dangerous Protectors, a larger proportion of the wrathful Enlightened Protectors derive from Indian Buddhism, and more Himalayan images survive from earlier periods. They are considered realized, or enlightened beings, in contrast to the Dangerous Protectors.

A popular Tibetan rule of thumb, still current today, distinguishes the appearance of Dangerous Protectors and Enlightened Protectors quite simply: those who wear boots are Dangerous Protectors, and those who do not are Enlightened Protectors.It is certainly the case that most of the Enlightened Protectors—and all the Wrathful Buddhas—are barefoot. However, there are exceptions among the Enlightened Protectors. For instance, the Maning, Vyaghra Vahana, Legden, and Danda forms of Mahakala, who are generally an Enlightened Protectors, wear boots (cat. nos. 15–17, 25). Enlightened Protectors are also much more likely to wear an Indian-style *dhoti* (wraparound skirt).

The distinction between what we are calling "Dangerous" and "Enlightened" Protectors refers more to the status of the protectors, than to the goal that is sought. That is, these categories do not map neatly onto this-world (Sanskrit: *laukika*) benefits, such as health, longevity, and wealth, or pleasures (*bhoga*) and attainments of a spiritual nature (Sanskrit: *lokottara*) such as liberation (*moksha*). Both classes of protectors can provide this-world benefits, which are recognized as conveying the necessary means to pursue spiritual goals. At the same time, it must be the case that Dangerous Deities cannot directly help the cause of enlightenment or spiritual attainments, else they would, as it were, help themselves. Enlightened Protectors may provide material and spiritual benefits, but Dangerous Protectors are available for the former, and only indirectly for the latter.

An important subset of Enlightened Protectors are those who are focused on bestowing or protecting wealth. Jambhala, with his gem-spitting mongoose, is one member of this set.[34] White six-armed Mahakala is also a wealth-bestowing deity, and a painting in the Rubin collections (Himalayan Art Website item 853) seems to visually express this fecundity with its ornamental scrollwork and floral volutes which produce gems and fruit in equal profusion.[35] He stands on two white Ganapati, derived from Ganesha, the Hindu god of plenty, who grin at each other as gems roll out of their mouths onto a plate below, framed by a grisly sense offering. Perhaps the most deliciously macabre images depicting Enlightened Protectors are those of the Chitipati pair of skeletons (figs. 1.6, 1.27, lower left, cat. nos. 10–12). Although especially associated with Chakrasamvara and Vajravarahi meditation, on their own they protect from thieves. An inscription on a

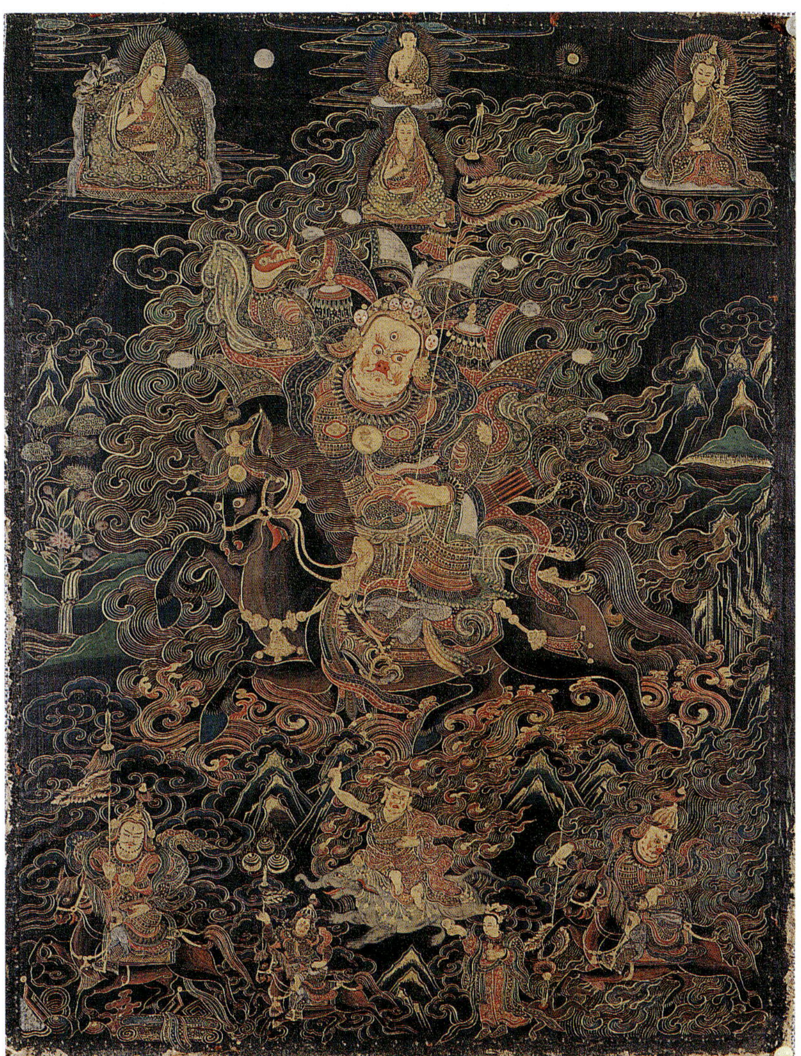

Fig. 1.25.
Shangpa Karpo
Tibet, 19th c.
Mineral pigments on cloth; 19¼ x 14¼ in. (48.89 x 36.83 cm).
Collection of Shelley and Donald Rubin (HA 853).

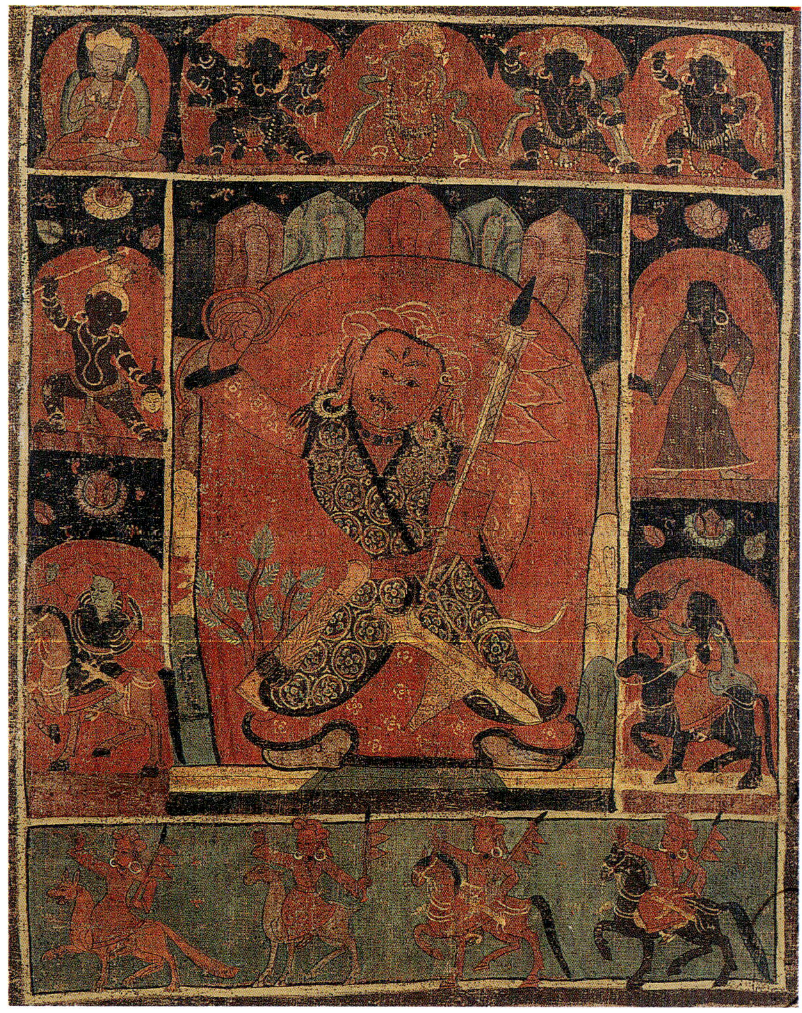

Fig. 1.26.
Machen Pomra
Tibet, 14th c.
Mineral pigments on cloth; 15½ x 12 in. (39.37 x 30.48 cm).
Collection of Shelley and Donald Rubin (HA 938).

work in the Rubin collections has an elaborate curse on anyone who steals from the owner.[36]

The third category, the **Wrathful Buddhas**, is the most important of the three in terms of religious practice (fig. 1.28). In fact they help constitute the set of paramount deities in the pantheons of Esoteric Buddhism, Bön, and Hinduism. Within Himalayan Buddhism, even if they do not look like the traditional robe-clad figure of a monk, Wrathful Buddhas are understood to be totally enlightened Buddhas. Large cycles of teachings, including the ritual texts, commentaries, and liturgies to support them, are dedicated to these deities. Historically, they emerged after the eighth century in India; none of them (with the exception of the forms of Padmasambhava) is a Himalayan creation.[37] Wrathful Buddhas take terrifying forms in order to subdue the most tenacious, deeply rooted, and powerful inner and outer demons who are often given the name Rudra, one of the designations associated with Shiva in Hinduism. Leaving aside the historical connections and mutual appropriations among Shaivite Tantric Hindus and Esoteric Buddhists in India, Esoteric Buddhists used Shiva, who is perceived as the Supreme Lord, as a symbol of paramount egoism and pride. Because Shiva-Rudra has so many paranormal powers, the collective wisdom of the Buddhas is forged together to produce the ferocious forms of Wrathful Buddhas, the only ones who can defeat Rudra in his various aspects.[38]

The Wrathful Buddhas are understood as, in a sense, images of the enlightened mind itself, as expressing the nature of your own mind.[39] They are what are known as "tutelary deities," sometimes called "archetype deities," with a personal connection to aspirants. That is to say, a deity in this group is one "on whom one's practice may be centered."[40] In Esoteric Buddhist practice, one visualizes one of these deities as emanating in front of you. You offer him/her praise and veneration, but then visualize yourself as becoming identical to the deity, followed in due course by a dissolution of the union. In the process, initiated practitioners "cultivate a sense of divine pride, the strong feeling . . . that you are the *actual* fully enlightened emanation body of a buddha. . . . [Y]ou should feel from the depths of your being that you *are* Heruka [a class of Wrathful Buddhas] that you and he are an inseparable unity."[41] Jamgön Kongtrul (1813–99) instructs simply:

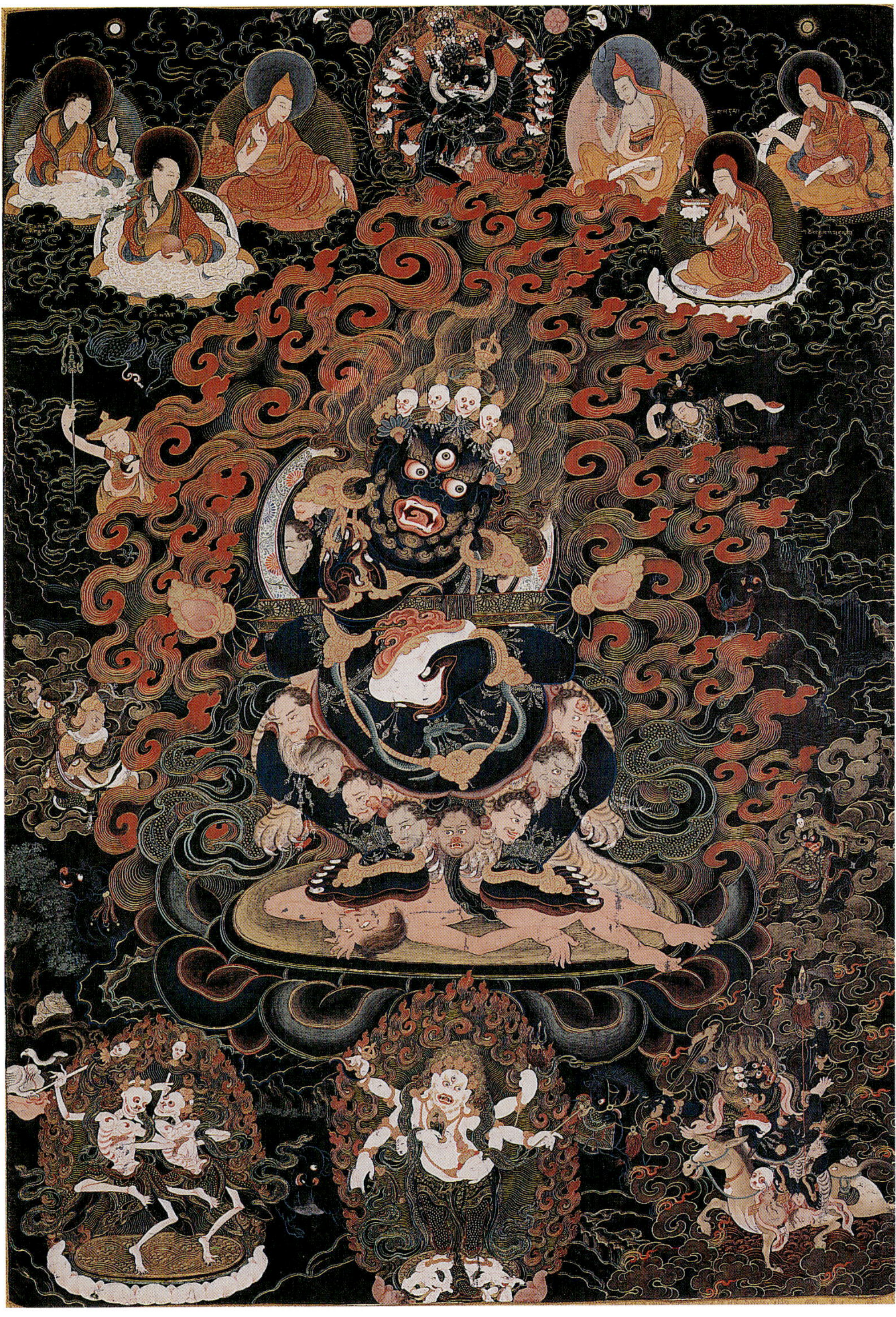

Fig. 1.27.
Mahakala
Tibet, 18th c.
Mineral pigments
on cloth; 33³/4 x 23 in.
(85.72 x 58.42 cm).
C2001.1.4 (HA 65004).

Fig. 1.28.
White Chakrasamvara with consort
Tibet, 18th c.
Mineral pigments on cloth; 38½ x 26½ in. (97.79 x 67.31 cm).
Collection of Shelley and Donald Rubin (HA 432).

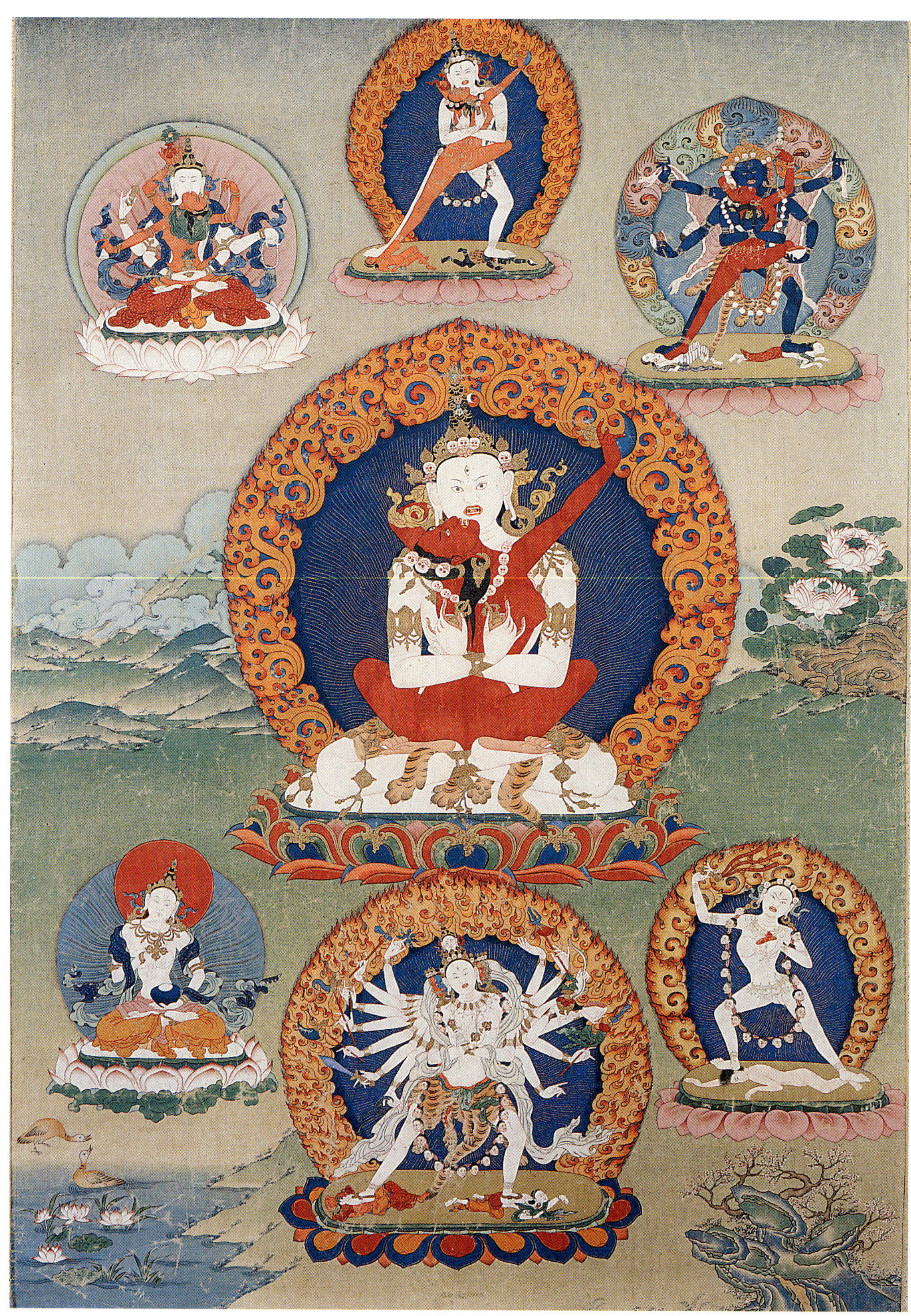

> Meditate that you instantly become a heruka such as Chakrasamvara, masculine and feminine in union, with all the adornments [fig. 1.28].[42]

And Tsongkhapa writes:

> In a split second I myself become the blue-black Fury Vajra [Guhyasamaja], with three faces, black, white, and red; six arms holding vajra, wheel, and lotus in the right, and bell, jewel, and swords in the left; embraced by Touch Vajra similar to myself [fig. 1.29].[43]

In summing up the three classes of wrathful deities, they can be related to their functions, as long as it is understood that the highest deities function at all three levels, and the middle group functions at the first and second levels. With that caveat, one can say that the wrathful Dangerous Protectors are involved with the protection of the body and the endowment of material life. The wrathful Enlightened Protectors concentrate on dispensing blessings and psychic protection against madness and other personal dangers. The Wrathful Buddhas provide both the means and the end of spiritual transformation and total enlightenment. The three classes do not correlate with gender differences. There are male and female examples of all three types, from the oath-bound animal-headed protectresses (cat. no. 7) to the wrathful forms of Shri Devi (cat. nos. 31, 32) and the wisdom-bestowing, knife-wielding Vajravarahi (cat. nos. 57, 58).

One final point about the three categories of Dangerous Protectors, Enlightened Protectors, and Wrathful Buddhas: they may all appear in the same composition. It is not at all unusual for paintings that feature Enlightened Protectors to depict Wrathful Buddhas above, even Dangerous Protectors as well. For instance, in catalog number 17, featuring the Vyaghra Vahana form of Mahakala, the Wrathful Buddha Vajrapani appears just to the left of top center, while below the central figure, in the lower right is the snake-bodied Dangerous Protector Rahula. By the same token, in catalog number 50, the Wrathful Buddha Vajrabhairava and his consort dominate the composition. Starting in the upper left and right corners are various forms of Mahakala (cat. key 50.9–13, 50.22), Chitipati (cat. key 50.14), Shri Devi (cat. key 50.15–16), all Enlightened Protectors. In the lower right corner is Tsiu Marpo (associated with Samye monastery), accompanied by other Dangerous Protectors, including Damchen

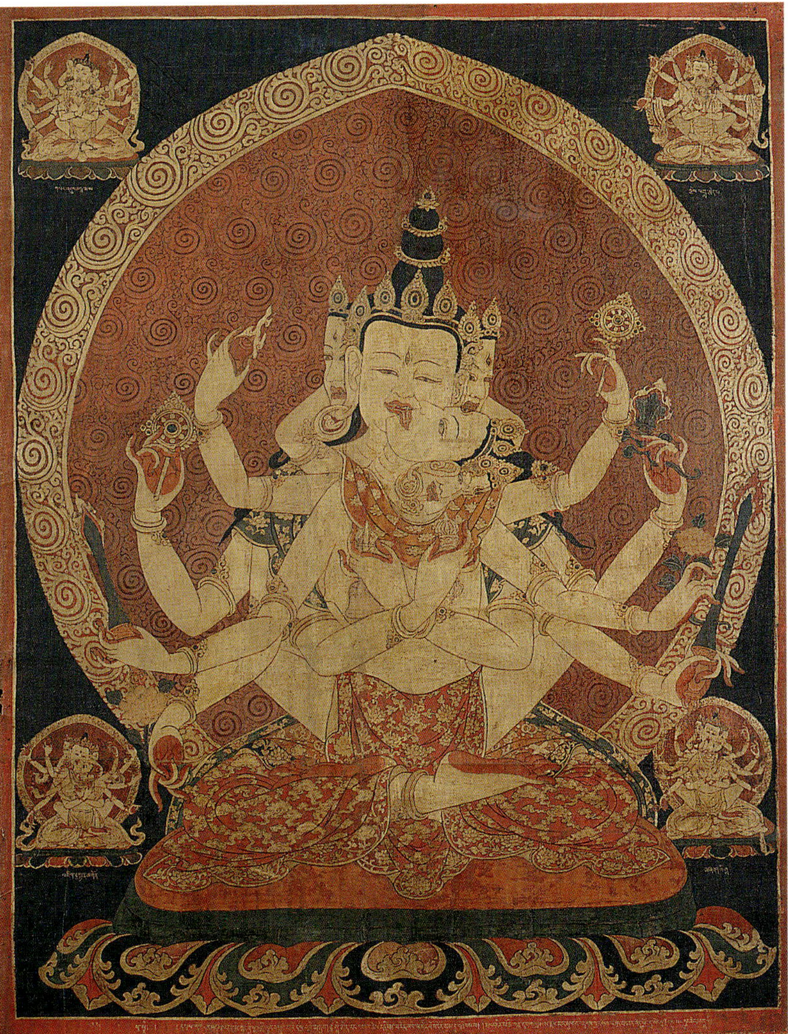

Fig. 1.29.
Akshobhyavajra Guhyasamaja
Central Tibet, 16th c.
Mineral pigments on cloth; 29¾ x 22¾ in. (75.56 x 57.78 cm).
F1997.31.13 (HA 487).

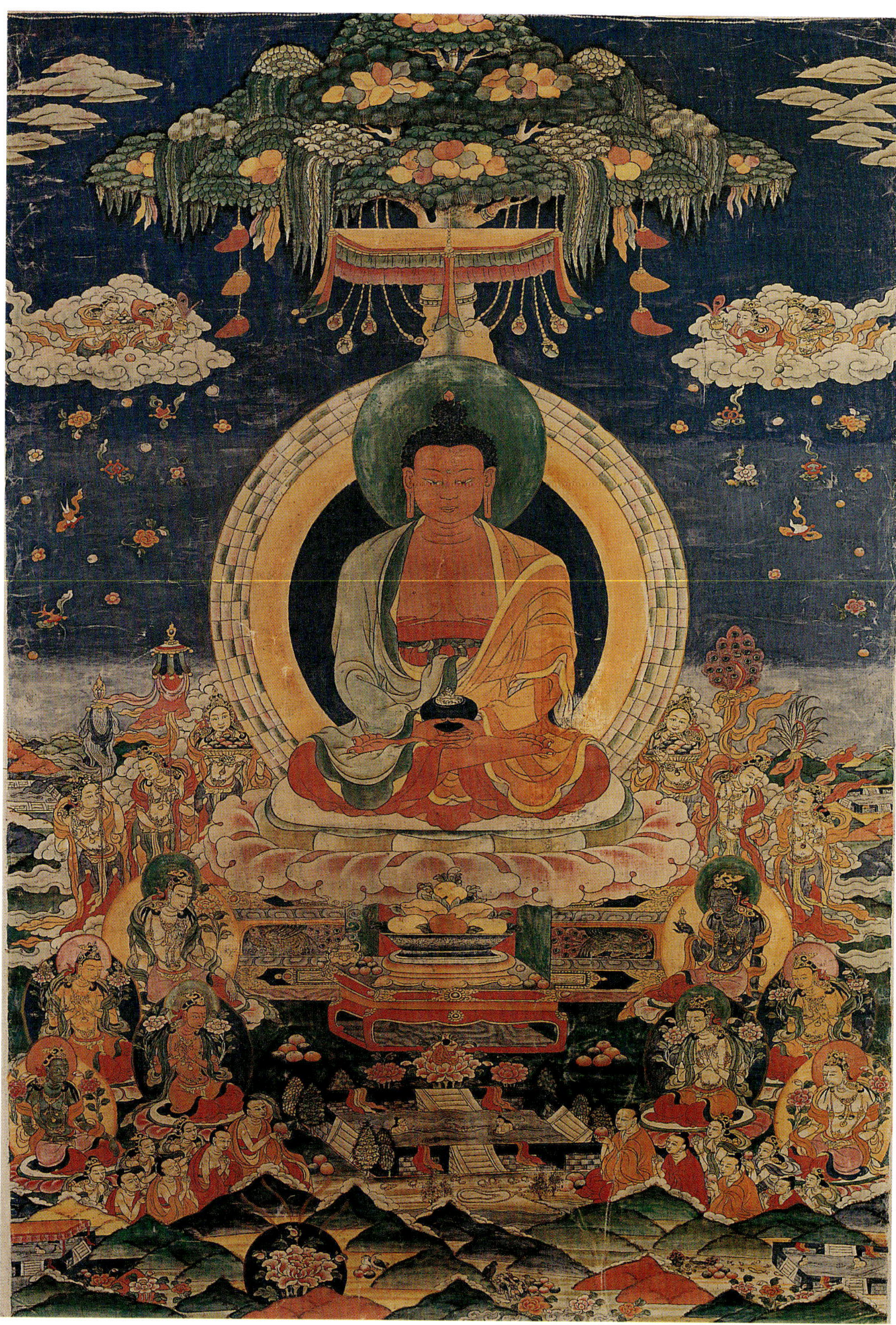

Fig. 1.30.
Amitabha Buddha
Central Tibet, 19th c.
Mineral pigments on cloth; 39 1/2 x 25 1/2 in. (97.79 x 64.77 cm).
F1997.6.3 (HA 85).

Garwai Nagpo (cat. key 50.23) and Dorje Yudronma (cat. key 50.24). The relative placement of these three types within a single composition, correlated to their relative size and centrality, clearly indicates the respective hierarchical importance of the Wrathful Buddhas, the Enlightened Protectors, and the Dangerous Protectors.

4

The concept underlying the images of an angry Buddha or a menacing divinity poses a challenge to outsiders, especially those from Western traditions. The shock of seeing figures whose only familiar referents in Judaeo-Christian-Islamic art are demons led many Westerners to assume that Buddhists in the Himalayan regions were devil-worshipers. This reaction can be sensed even in the descriptions of travelers who were more than superficially familiar with the Himalayan people, art, and religions. For instance, L. Austine Waddell, who published more than one book about the region in the late nineteenth and early twentieth centuries, based on extensive firsthand experience, has this to say about the Gonkang (see appendix to this essay), a shrine dedicated to wrathful protectors in Tibet:

> One of the rooms was the Devils' Chamber of Horrors (Gon-k'ang), a sort of satanic Aladdin's cave in the dark, designed to awe and impress the superstitious pilgrims. Here are collected the hideous colossal images of all the demons which infest the world and prey upon the poor Tibetans. They have the forms of men, but the heads of ogres and monstrous beasts, the hideous creations of a nightmare, and all are eating human bodies and surrounded by a variety of weapons.[44]

Later, a kind of psycho-anthropological interpretation was applied to these images, by which they were understood as expressing unconscious urges submerged within Himalayan society:

> Kept secret under the earth the mGon khang [hall of protective deities in Tibetan monasteries] was both that domain of the unconscious teeming with the untrammeled appetites and impulses of life, and Tibet's subconscious stored with the memories of ancient heathen times and of both old and recent wars.[45]

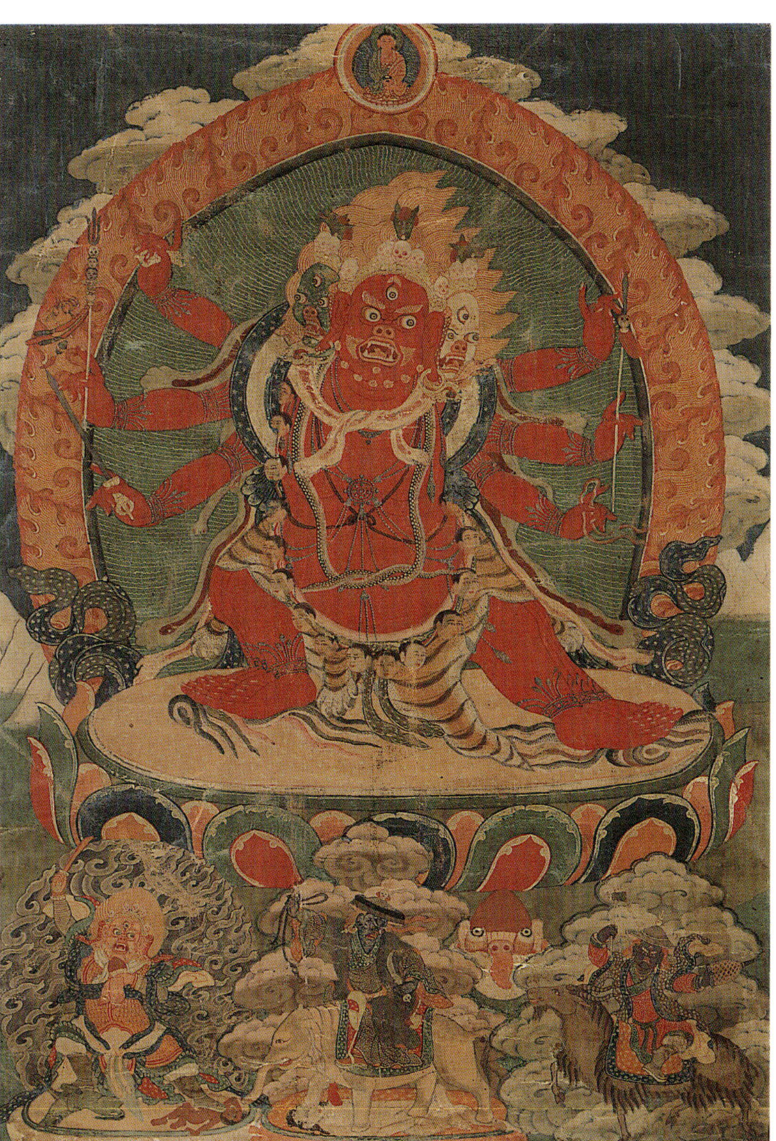

Fig. 1.31.
Hayagriva
Central Tibet, 19th c.
Mineral pigments on cloth; 20 x 14 in. (50.8 x 35.5 cm).
Collection of Shelley and Donald Rubin (HA 65).

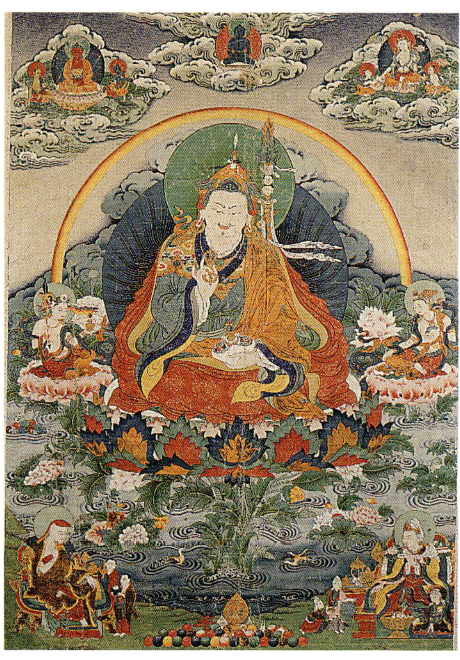

Fig. 1.32.
Padmasambhava
Tibet, 19th c.
Mineral pigments on cloth; 27½ x 19 in. (69.85 x 48.57 cm). F1997.12.1 (HA 188).

Facing page: Fig. 1.33.
Padmasambhava as Guru Dragpo
Tibet, 19th c.
Mineral pigments on cloth; 25¼ x 19½ in. (64.13 x 49.53 cm). Collection of Shelley and Donald Rubin (HA 9).

Recently, the same deities have been ambitiously interpreted in a much more positive light. The Wrathful Buddha Vajrabhairava (see fig. 1.14, cat. nos. 46, 47, 50)—here referred to as an "archetype deity"—has been described as:

> Exterminator of death, as a self-adopted archetypal embodiment. He is created in imaginative samadhi [meditative state of unity] in order to navigate the deep, deep spaces of dying and death, in order to accelerate the development of one's compassionate side, the evolutionary element most essential to becoming enlightened. Vajrabhairava embodies full enlightenment adamant in confrontation with the most profound demons of the individual and collective unconscious.[46]

It is fascinating to track the evolution of Westerners' reactions to the same images. There may be a grain of truth in all three of the ones represented here, along with others. Still, they probably shed more light on the interpreters than on the Himalayan cultures that stimulated them. The purpose of this exhibition is not to "correct" such attitudes, nor to put forward an "authentic" understanding, but to celebrate the audacious creativity and originality of Himalayan artistry.

5

As already established, this exhibition concentrates on images of figures that are angry or threatening in aspect. Within Himalayan religion and art, the three categories of Dangerous Protectors, Enlightened Protectors, and Wrathful Buddhas are actually much broader than the present selection of artworks seems to imply. For, in fact, there are Dangerous Protectors and Enlightened Protectors who are peaceful in aspect. Moreover, Wrathful Buddhas form a substantial subset of a larger grouping of tutelary deities, or *yidam*, many of whom are as beneficent in appareance as they are in function. In other words, belonging to these three functional categories ultimately is not based on visual character but on activity. The wrathful forms, however, dominate these three groupings, even if some peaceful deities also eliminate obstacles with equal facility. Furthermore, the wrathful deities probably embody the process most perfectly, in function and in appearance. They can more readily be perceived to be actively involved in the processes of protection against enemies, benefaction of worldly and spiritual wealth, purification, and transformation. By contrast, the peaceful forms embody the beneficent result, not the terrifying methods.

Wrathful and peaceful forms can be understood in a different way as well. Certain deities have more than one form—indeed, sometimes a multitude of forms. Some forms of the same deity are peaceful, some "semiwrathful," and others "terrific." The peaceful form may emphasize the compassionate activity of a particular deity, while the wrathful form underscores the wisdom or transformative power of the deity. "So in

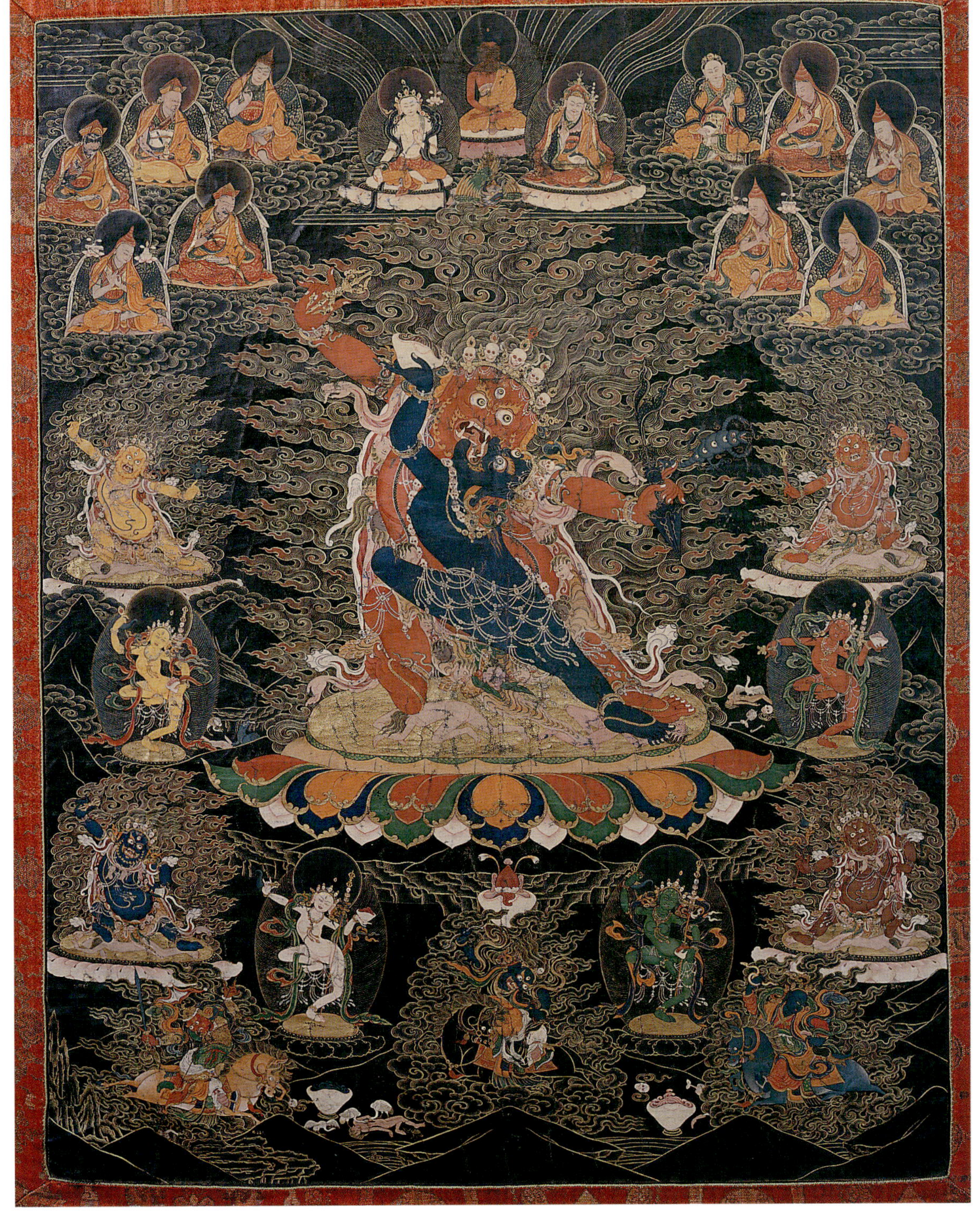

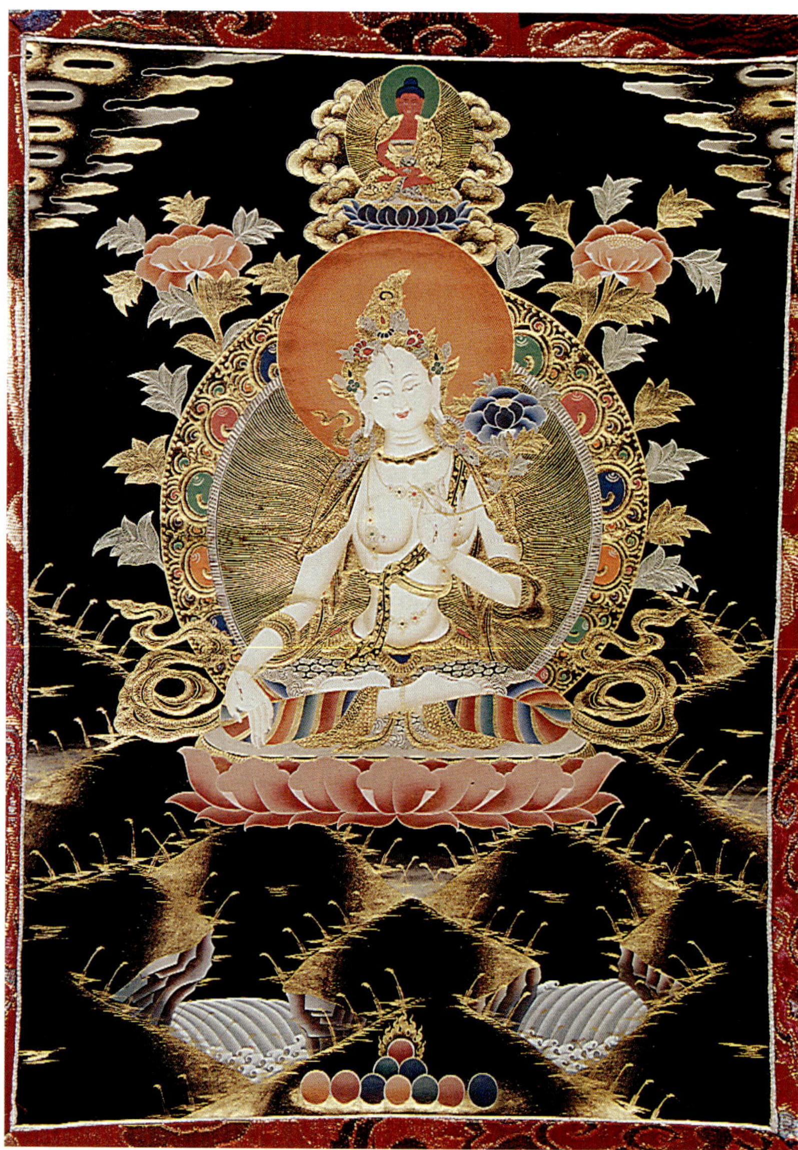

Fig. 1.34.
Tshering Dorje (artist).
White Tara
Northern India, 2001
Pigments on cloth;
17 x 13 in. (43.18 x 33.02 cm).
Private Collection.

the tantras it is said that the Buddhas' form manifestations are indeterminate and cannot be precisely defined, since they appear in accordance with the perspectives and dispositions of the beings needing to be tamed."[47] Which form is manifested depends on the task at hand. Neither form is necessarily "truer" than the other. The appearances of pacific and wrathful are most emphatically not binaries signifying "good" and "evil."

In one section of the exhibition, a pair of images was selected to illustrate this point. Wrathful and pacific forms of Vajrapani are juxtaposed (cat. nos. 65, 66). Other examples can be suggested as well. Hayagriva, for instance, is considered in some lineages to be the manifestation of the wrathful activity of Amitabha Buddha (figs. 1.30, 1.31). Padmasambhava has eight major emanations, and several of them are wrathful.

One of the two founders of the Rubin Museum of Art, Donald Rubin, is particularly fond of the concept of "equivalence of form." He finds it an apt expression of the duality he experiences in the human psyche, filled as it is with positive and negative impulses, or constructive and destructive forces. One of the features he admires in Himalayan art is its psychologically sophisticated recognition of the richness and variety of human experience, the willingness of the artists to confront not just the pious platitudes of superficial morality, but the darker sides as well.

6

Responding to their own intuitive attraction for the distinctive achievements of Himalayan art, RMA founders Donald and Shelley Rubin have succeeded over the years in assembling an impressively large array of black-ground *tangkas* (*nag-tang*).[48] With more than eighty examples to draw from, black-ground *tangkas* are clearly one of the strengths of the Rubin collections. They constitute a natural sub-topic within the *Demonic Divine: Himalayan Art and Beyond* exhibition.[49]

Since the seventeenth century, the themes of *nag-tang* paintings are nearly always wrathful deities of one or more of the three categories defined above. Admittedly, there is a contemporary movement of Tibetan painters in the exile community working for Western clients, or for Tibetan clients exposed to Western tastes, who use

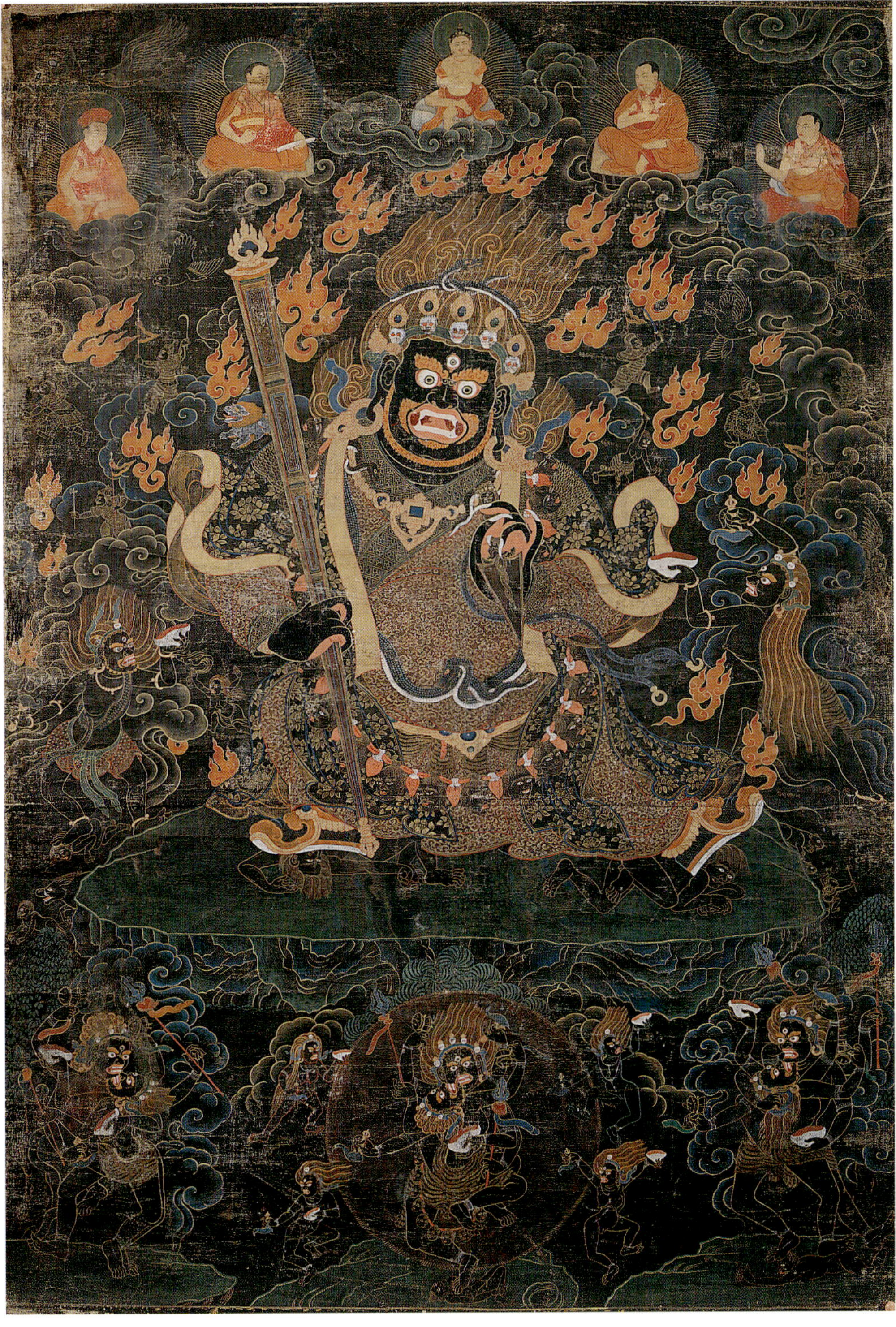

Fig. 1.35.
Mahakala Danda
Tibet, 17th c.
Mineral pigments
on cloth; 40 1/2 x 27 1/4 in.
(102.87 x 69.21 cm).
Collection of Shelley and
Donald Rubin (HA 22).

Fig. 1.36.
Bodhisattva of the Sun (detail of a hanging banner)
From Cave 17
Dunhuang (China), 9th c.
Mineral pigments on silk; overall length 83 in. (213 cm), painted area 35¼ x 10 in. (89.6 x 25.4 cm).
Collection of the British Museum 1919.1-1.0121.

Facing page: Fig. 1.37.
Shri Devi as Palden Lhamo
Bhutan, 19th c.
Mineral pigments on cloth; 18 x 14 in. (45.72 x 35.56 cm).
F1998.1.2 (HA 602).

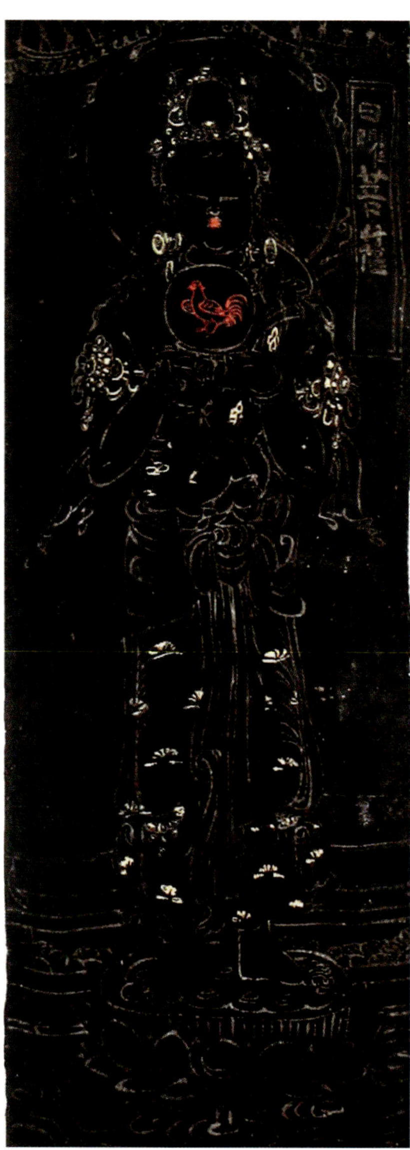

this style for peaceful themes, including Shakyamuni Buddha and Tara. Tshering Dorjay, a painter and sculptor born of parents from Sakya in 1959, can be considered a representative of this type of exile artist. He studied painting in Mussoorie with Amdo Jamyang, and now works in Darjeeling, Katmandu, and Leh. His painting of 2001, a White Tara of distinctly peaceful demeanor, is set against a dark background (fig. 1.34). This use of *nag-tang* is exceptional, however. Generally, most contemporary artists working for monastic clientele use the black-ground painting type in the traditional wrathful manner. They have their own versions of the origins of *nag-tang*:

> The supposed genesis of the Black Thanka is quite interesting. It is said the ashes of a holy lama were applied to a canvas and later a deity was drawn upon it in gold.[50]

Traditional black-ground paintings are characterized by linear outlining in silver and gold against a dark background, which is usually black, though sometimes blue, and a minimal or at least restrained use of other colors. The range of color and modeling is quite wide. Compare the limited use of gold and red in figure 1.3 with the much more varied colors of figure 1.35. There is a general tendency to add more colors over time—keeping the exposed skin of the central figure unpainted—but that criterion alone cannot be used to date images. Most scholars agree that black-ground *tangkas* were not widespread until the seventeenth century. Of the eighty examples in the Rubin collections, none are known to be earlier than that date. The "earliest dated manifestation of the 'black thanka' genre of painting" is the "Gold Manuscript" in the Fournier Collection of the Musée Guimet in Paris created between 1674 and 1681 by the Fifth Dalai Lama.[51] A few *nag-tang* paintings have been attributed over the years to the fifteenth and sixteenth centuries, but rather tentatively.[52] Recently, the date of the earliest known black-ground painting has been pushed back considerably by Aldo Mignucci, who has dated two paintings in a private collection to the early and late fourteenth century.[53] Following that, a painting in the John and Berthe Ford collection, now at The Walters Art Museum, Baltimore, has been given a fifteenth-century attribution.[54]

There are some intriguing earlier prece-

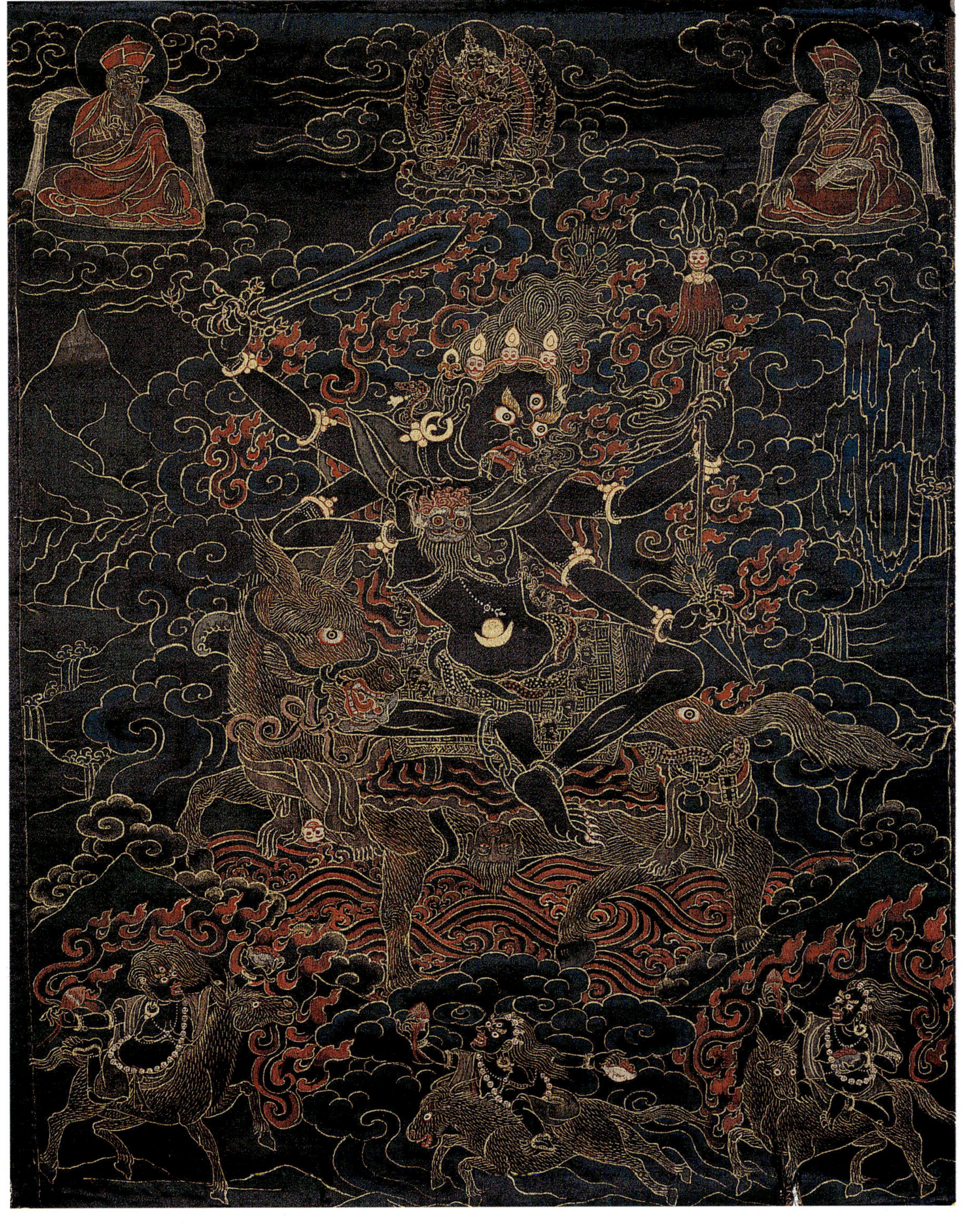

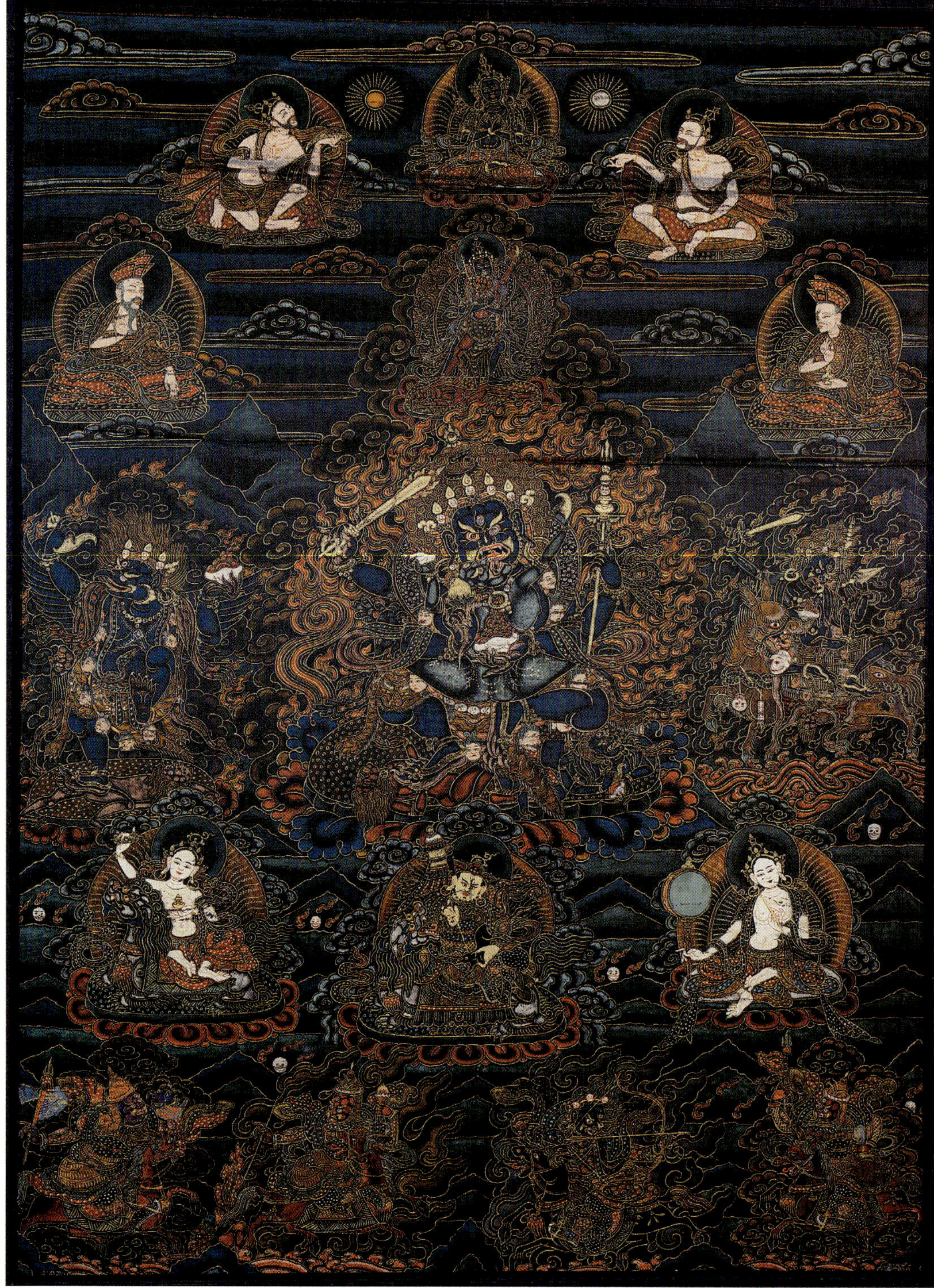

Fig. 1.38.
Mahakala Chaturbuja
Tibet, 19th c.
Mineral pigments
on cloth; 26 x18½ in.
(66.04 x 46.99 cm).
Collection of Shelley
and Donald Rubin
(HA 113).

dents for these paintings. The earliest are Tang dynasty (618–906) illuminated frontispieces of Chinese Buddhist manuscripts which use gold and silver pigments to draw Buddhist themes on paper stained a deep purple.[55] This technique continued to be used at the Chinese courts of the Song, Yuan, Ming, and Qing periods.[56] Just as it spread to Korea and Japan, such lavish editions of Buddhist texts were probably don ated to Tibetans who visited the court, and these texts could have contributed to the development or pervasiveness of the black-ground convention. Indeed, there is evidence that in the royal Tibetan period (ca. seventh to ninth century), "royal commands were written in gold on blue paper or silk."[57] A similar palette of silver paint on very dark blue is used on some paintings on silk found at Dunhuang, which the Tibetans ruled for more than half a century spanning the eighth and ninth centuries (fig. 1.36).[58] Outlines of deities and other patterns were painted in yellow and white, substitutes for gold and silver. Besides the two outline colors, only red was added.

Other possible sources for later black-ground *tangkas*, more proximate in time, are illuminated manuscripts from Nepal dating to the eleventh and twelfth centuries.[59] Gold and silver letters are written on a black ground, and at either ends are illuminations, though the depictions of the deities framing the text are not necessarily against black. Tibetans made their own versions of such texts, and a page in the exhibition depicts Vajrapani and Vaishravana, datable to the late thirteenth century (cat. no. 54). The yellow pigment used on both figures is mica-flecked and was used intentionally to give it a sparkle. These are not considered black-ground paintings, however, primarily because the figures are not outlined with gold or silver ink. Bodies are modeled and color is applied. In addition, the repertoire of subject is not limited to wrathful deities. They are, nevertheless, not remote from a black-ground aesthetic.

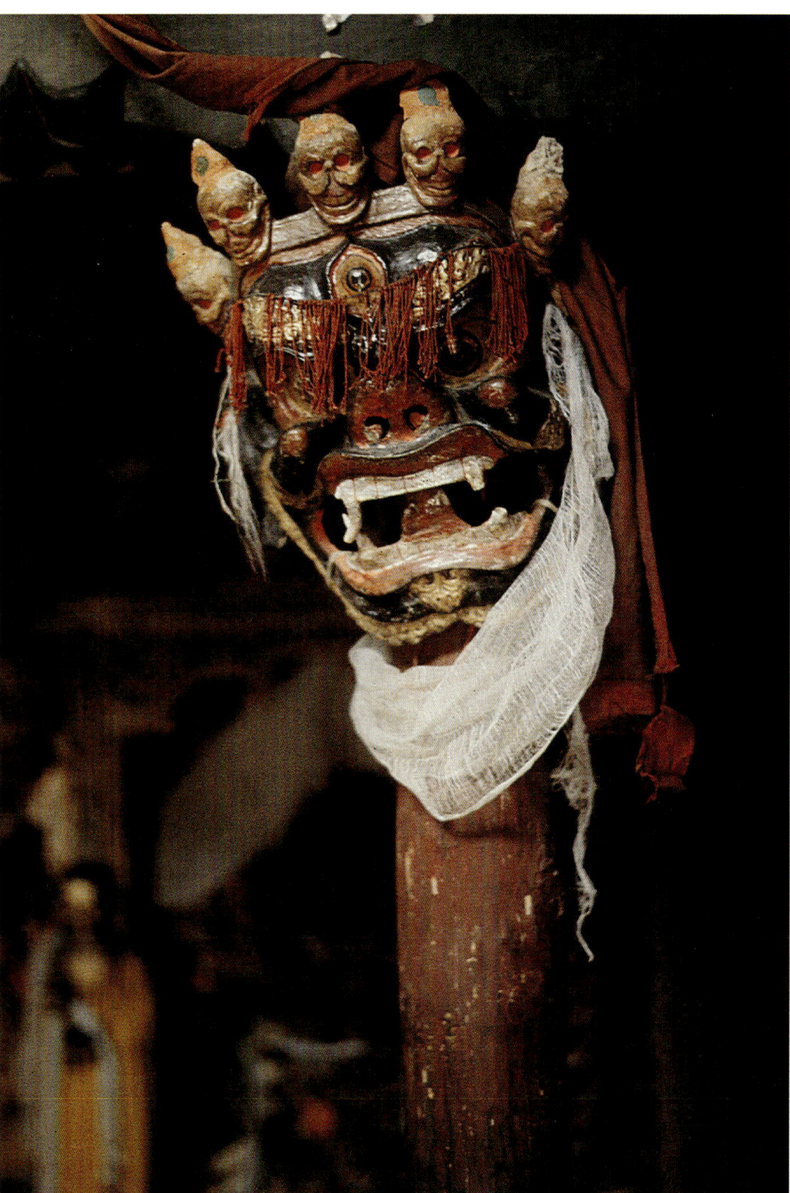

Fig. 1.39.
Cham-dance mask hanging on a pillar in the Gonkang in Bardan monastery Zangskar (India).

An intermediate stage between texts written on black with gold and silver pigments and seventeenth-century black-ground *tangkas* may be found in some early murals and paintings. For instance, in the murals at the Sumtsek temple at Alchi, Ladakh, in western Tibet (now part of India), painted in the late twelfth or early thirteenth century,

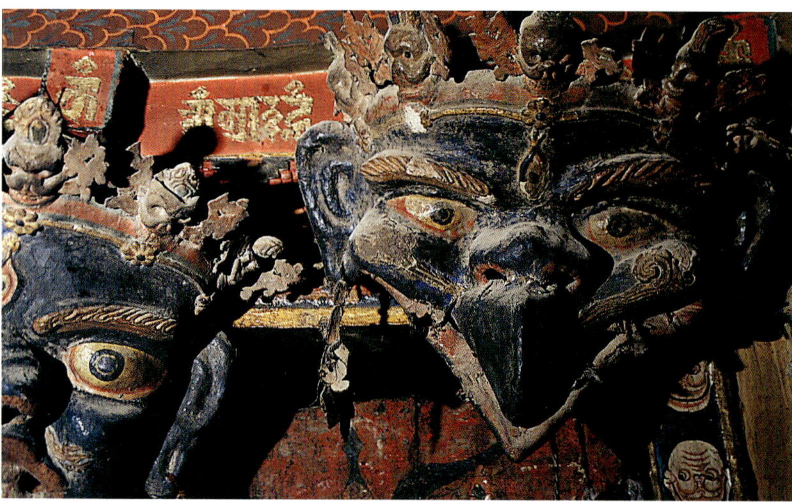

Fig. 1.40.
Cham-dance masks hanging on the entrance to the Gonkang in Korzok monastery
Tsomoriri,
Zangskar (India).

Facing page: Fig. 1.41.
Hevajra in a mural in the assembly hall of Hemis monastery
Ladakh (India), ca. 19th c.

artists used a similar dark blue for both the background on which Mahakala, Magzor Gyalmo, and Remati are posed, and for the dark blue-black skin of Mahakala.[60] Gold is also plentifully applied, with similar effect. But at Alchi, and at several other western Tibetan sites including the caves at Dungkar,[61] the same dark blue is also used as the backdrop for mandalas and many other themes at the site and was not exclusively reserved for wrathful deities the way it was in later times. Another difference is that the later artists tend to restrict the use of opaque colors, either by choosing only a few colors and relying on line, or else applying color only to certain parts of the picture, such as the skin of the deities or the flames surrounding them. At Alchi, by contrast, full use of color appears.

There is a small group of yet earlier paintings, including some of the earliest surviving central Tibetan works on cloth, which likewise feature wrathful deities with a bright red nimbus of flames against a dark blue, or nearly black, background. They are generally dated to the twelfth century.[62] Two of them are included in the catalog (cat. nos. 37, 53). They have such strong connections with Indian painting of the eleventh and twelfth centuries—unfortunately known almost exclusively through manuscript illumination—that at least for the Rubin Achala (cat. no. 37), an Indian origin cannot be completely ruled out. Nonetheless, they are not true black-ground paintings in the technical sense, consisting only of gold-painted outlines against a dark background with a minimal or localized use of color. On the other hand, in the paintings that I have been able to examine thoroughly in person—including the two in the exhibition—what is similar to classical *nag-tang* is that the bodies of the main figures are left "in reserve," as it were, with the dark color of the background coming through as the skin of the deity.

Despite the technical barrier to including them as *nag-tang*, it is not an insurmountable stretch from the black or midnight-blue ground widely used in painting between the eleventh and fourteenth centuries for wrathful deities, mandalas, and other themes in central and western Tibet, to the later black-ground *tangkas*. If, Mignucci has tried to demonstrate, black-ground paintings as we now know them had begun by the fourteenth century, then we have a continuous tradition of *nag-tang* drawing on a multitude of prior sources: Indian, Nepalese, and Chinese.[63] Early black-ground painting, which was not originally exclusively wrathful in theme, was recognized by Tibetan artists for its potential to enhance the power of wrathful deity painting. They continued to develop it, to draw out the fullest and richest dramatic effects.

One significant later development in black-ground painting was made by Bhutanese artists, for which two Rubin collections paintings will serve as examples (figs. 1.37, 1.38). Their innovations, both subtle and distinctive, have to do with modeling with dark colors, a particular shade of blue, certain tendencies toward patterning, and a slight, but palpable, luminescent effect. In terms of modeling, although the dark blue color employed is not graded, it is added in alternating bands with the dark blue background, especially noticeable in

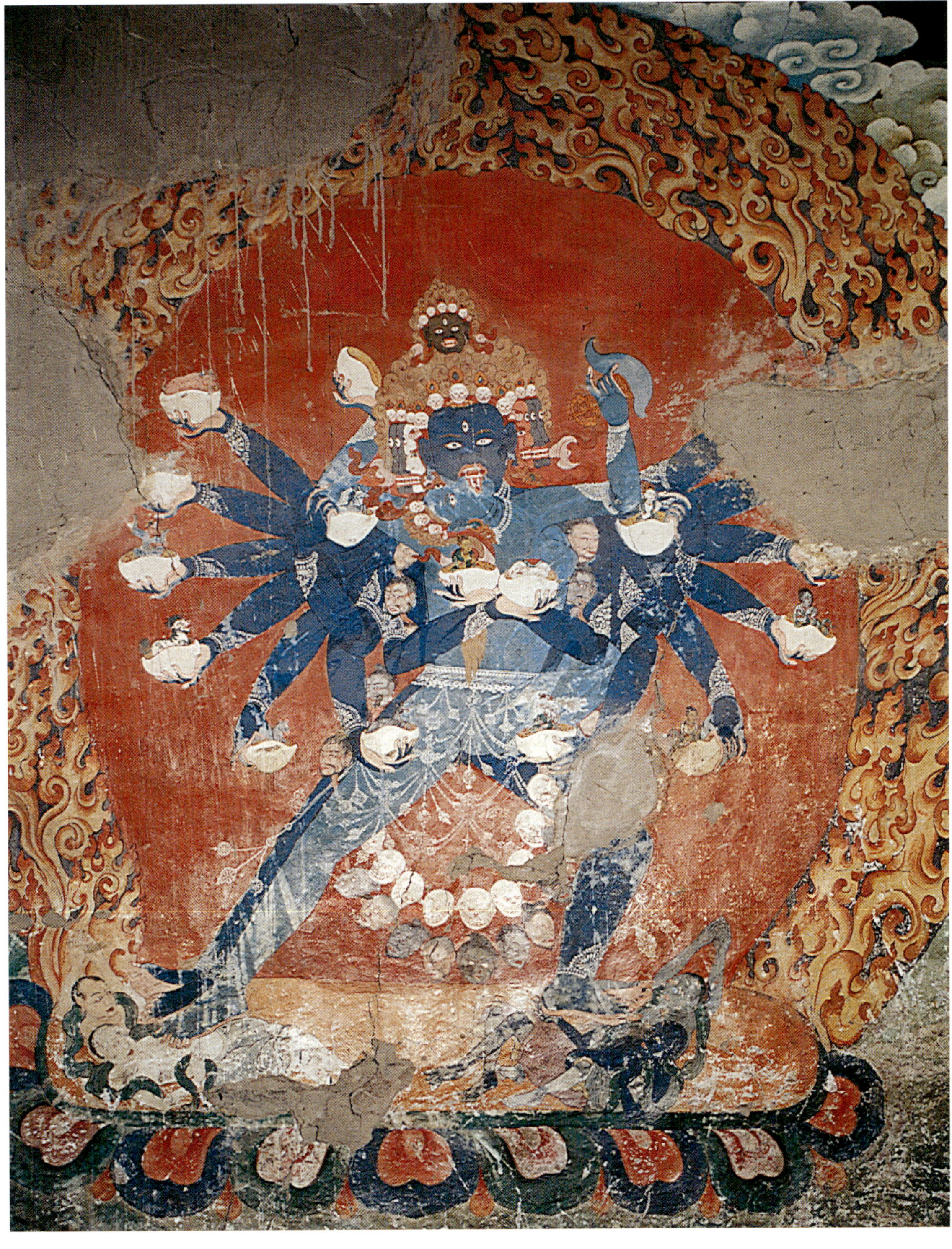

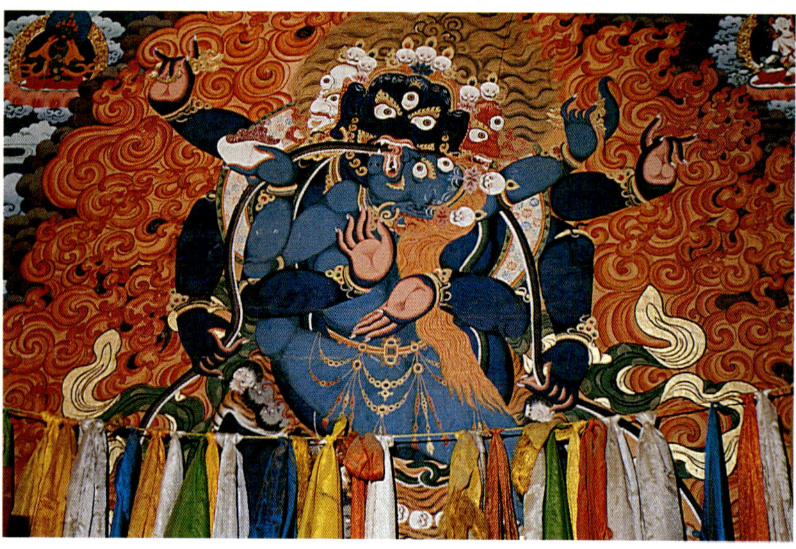

Fig. 1.42.
Mahachakra Vajrapani in a mural in the assembly hall of Sengge Shong Mango monastery
Amdo Rebgong
Qinghai (China), ca. 19th c.

the sky and the clouds. The same shade of dark blue—possibly indigo—appears on both Rubin examples, though the larger painting (fig. 1.38) uses a regular rotation between the dark indigo and a slightly lighter shade. In this and in other details, the Bhutanese artists seem to delight in a patterning effect, quite evident, for instance in the pools of blood below Shri Devi at the center of figure 1.37 and in the center left of figure 1.38. The luminescent effect seems to derive from the use of dark colors to model an already black figure, resulting in the illusion of glowing colors. Landscape in Bhutanese painting is often minimized, pushed to the very bottom or sides of the composition. Rarely does a coherent sense of continuous space unite all the figures, as can be found in contemporary painting of other styles. This may enhance the sense of the deities looming out of void, a prized quality in the *nag-tang*.

7

In Himalayan religious contexts, paintings and sculptures of wrathful deities are found in a variety of situations, including private altars and shrines in the homes of lay people as well as the rooms of monks and initiated practitioners. One also finds wrathful deities among the images carved on small rocks and stacked with etched prayers on so-called *mani*-walls. On cliffs where outlines of Buddhist deities are carved in low relief, wrathful deities are frequently included. But the most concentrated locus of wrathful-deity *tangka* and sculpture is the local monastery. Within the halls of each monastery, there are typically three sites where wrathful deities are particularly likely to be placed. The first is the Gonkang, the room devoted to the deities who protect the monastery, the lineage, and the teachings in which the monastery traditionally specializes. Not only are the wrathful deities in the majority there, but in fact it is rather unusual to find peaceful forms in the Gonkang.

Giuseppe Tucci, probably the greatest scholar of Tibetan art in the twentieth century, who grounded his scholarship in fieldwork and linguistic studies, has written a description of the Gonkang that is unsurpassed in detail and sweep. It is phenomenologically astute, dramatically narrating the feelings of the outsider who is allowed to venture into the Gonkang. It also accurately summarizes the types of objects, inhabitants, and activities one is likely to encounter there. Tucci's masterful account is included in the appendix to this essay, reproducing a small section of his magnum opus, *Tibetan Painted Scrolls*. Only on one score would I attempt to supplement his discussion. It is common, at least in western Tibet, to find those masks that have been retired from the *cham*-ritual dance performances to be hung on the entrance to or the walls of the Gonkang. They actually add to the eerie and disorienting experience Tucci recounts so vividly (figs. 1.39, 1.40).

Another locale where wrathful deities inevitably find their place in Himalayan monasteries—Buddhist (of all lineages) or Bön—is in the main assembly hall. Although sculptures and murals of Wrathful Buddhas are placed on the main altar—

while *tangkas* depicting them are hung in front or above the altar—they and the Enlightened Protectors are frequently found on the back (entrance) wall or along the side walls toward the back. For example, on the back wall of the main assembly hall at Hemis, in Ladakh, is a damaged but still beautiful Hevajra mural (fig. 1.41). On the distant, opposite side of Tibet, in Amdo Rebgong, a mural of Mahachakra Vajrapani from the nineteenth century is one of three murals to survive the Cultural Revolution (1966–76) in the Sengge Shong Mango assembly hall. It is placed on a side wall close to the entrance, behind a low curtain of *katak*-scarves (fig. 1.42). The practice of having the wrathful deities near the entrance wall in shrines that do not particularly feature wrathful deities on the rest of the walls is not just a modern tendency. Over the doorways of the three stories at the late twelfth-century Sumtsek, at Alchi, one finds Mahakala, Yamantaka, and Achala.[64] The same tendency is attested by the fifteenth-century Qutan Dian temple of the Drotsang Dorjee Chang monastery, also in northern Amdo. There, on the side walls immediately adjacent to the entrance wall, appear different forms of Mahakala, including Panjarnata (fig. 1.43). In that location, he acts as a protector.

The third place within a monastery where multiple representations of the demonic divine are frequently to be found in Himalayan monasteries is on the outer walls of various halls, within the porch. One encounters here mainly the Dangerous Protectors, the localized deities who are afforded an ambiguous recognition at best. Their status is rarely high enough to earn them the sanction of monastic authorities steeped in Buddhist theology. So the Dangerous Protectors are rarely brought into the halls themselves, though they can be promoted to the Gonkang. Yet their importance in the lives of devotees and tonsured monks and nuns ensures that they find a place somewhere in the complex, and

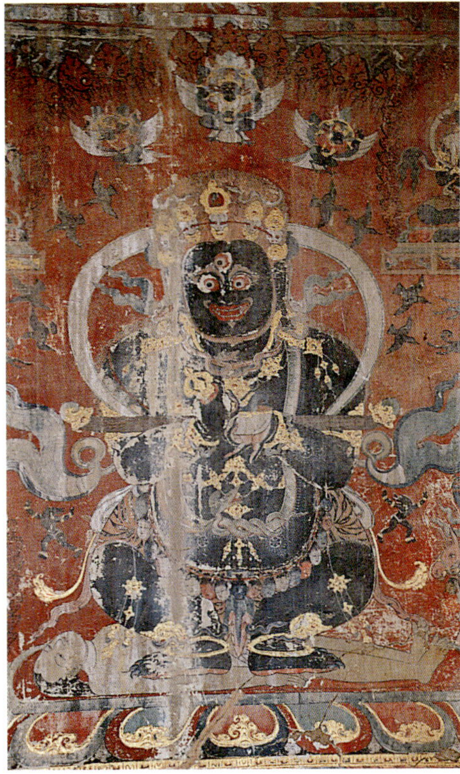

Fig. 1.43.
Mahakala Panjarnata in a mural in the Shakyamuni hall in Drotsang Dorjee Chang temple
Northern Amdo
Qinghai (China), early 15th c.

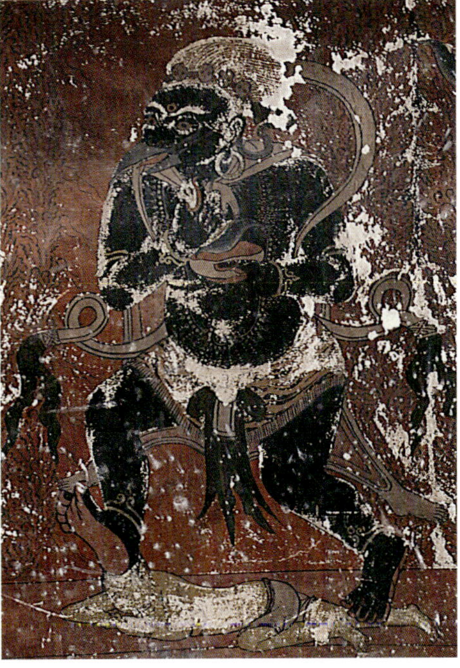

Fig. 1.44.
Raven-headed deity in a mural in the Mahakala hall in Drotsang Dorjee Chang temple
Northern Amdo
Qinghai (China), early 15th c.

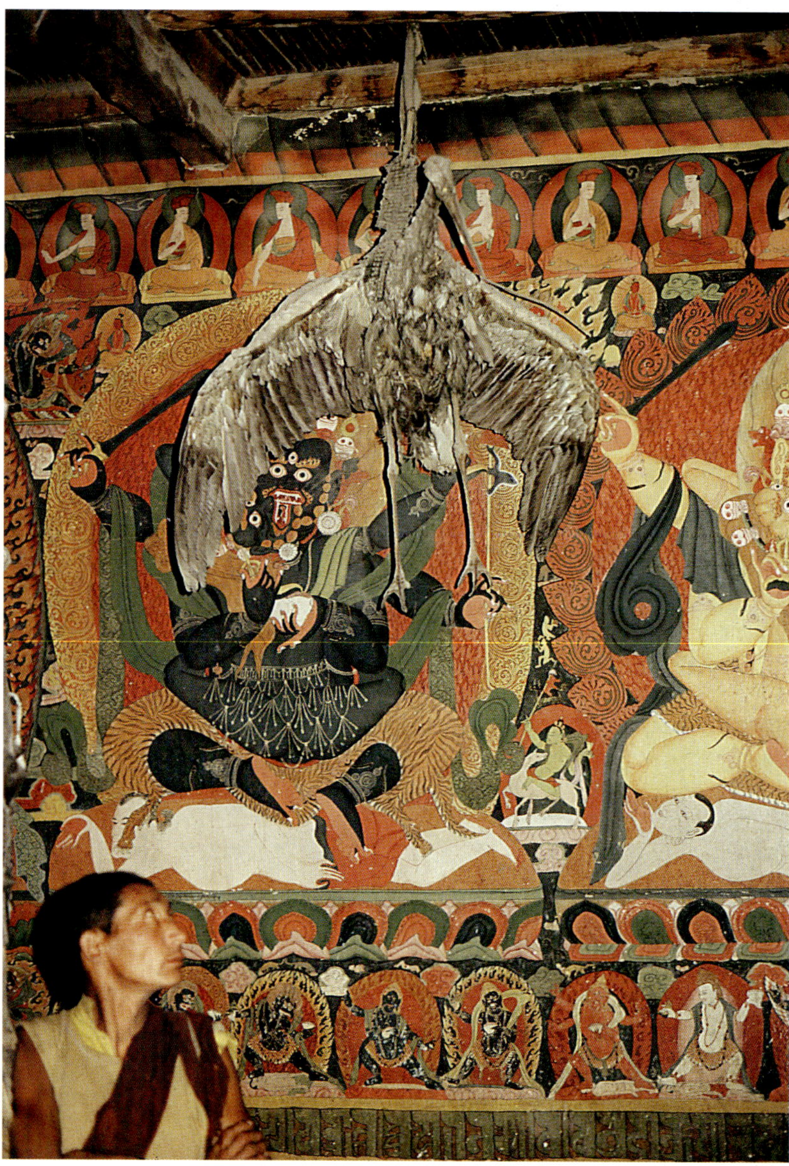

Fig. 1.45.
A stuffed crane displayed in the Gonkang of Phyang monastery
Ladakh (India).

it is often in the liminal zone of the entrance porch, where neither Enlightened Protectors, nor Wrathful Buddhas would be displayed. The Dangerous Protectors lead the way into the main hall, flanking the entrance. Just inside, one will see representations of Enlightened Protectors on the back wall. Moving forward toward the altar, the Wrathful Buddhas, alongside their own more peaceful forms, take paramount positions.

The formal qualities that we recognize as wrathful bring together quite different groups of deities, who function in a variety of ways, and are found in distinctive locales. Himalayan cultures have developed the potential of the demonic divine in subtle and nuanced ways, calibrating them to different inner needs and locating them in appropriate settings. Himalayan artists have been at the forefront of this development. Their achievements in visually fusing the awe-inspiring with the terrifying are worth enjoying, celebrating, and respecting, in all their forms.

APPENDIX: TUCCI ON GONKANG

The following is an excerpt from Giuseppe Tucci, *Tibetan Painted Scrolls*, translated by Virginia Vacca, volume 1, *Classification of the Tankas*, (Rome: la Libreria Dello Stato, 1949), section 5, pp. 320–23. The illustrations and figure numbers have been added.

We shall also dwell at length on the tankas of the mGon k'an, because, although they too obey certain fixed schemes, they often attain the highest artistic expression Tibetan art is capable of. They are called tankas of the mGon k'an because they are almost always arranged in the mGon k'an and represent the deities venerated there. mGon k'an, literally, means "the mGon po's house"; the mGon po is the "Lord", i.e. the *Yi dam*, the protecting deity of the sect or convent; in fact each sect has its patron, its terrible defender, the terrific and warlike aspect of the merciful deity who protects the devotees from the dangers of evil powers. The Sa skya pa [for instance] have Gur mgon and P'ur pa, the dGe lugs pa have Ye ses mgon po.

The *Yi dam* rules and guides a host of lesser beings, *srun ak'or or bstan srun* [fig. 1.44], nearly all aboriginal deities, which Buddhism later accepted, transforming them into the terrible keepers of the Law; many of them are local demons who, after the triumph of Buddhism, were taken on as custodians of the temple built on the place they used to garrison, of its treasures and of its fortunes. *Yi dam* or mGon po, surrounded by the pageant of their terrible followers thus reside and receive their cult in the mGon k'an, mysterious shrines into which it is very difficult to be admitted. The doors giving access to them are low and narrow. On the doors are painted monstrous faces. The visitor, even before entering, feels hesitating and lost in a half-light which the feeble light of a lantern seems to make gigantic, plumbing its doubtful depths. The monks too are restless and anxious. The locks creak, keys are turned, the doors open. One has the

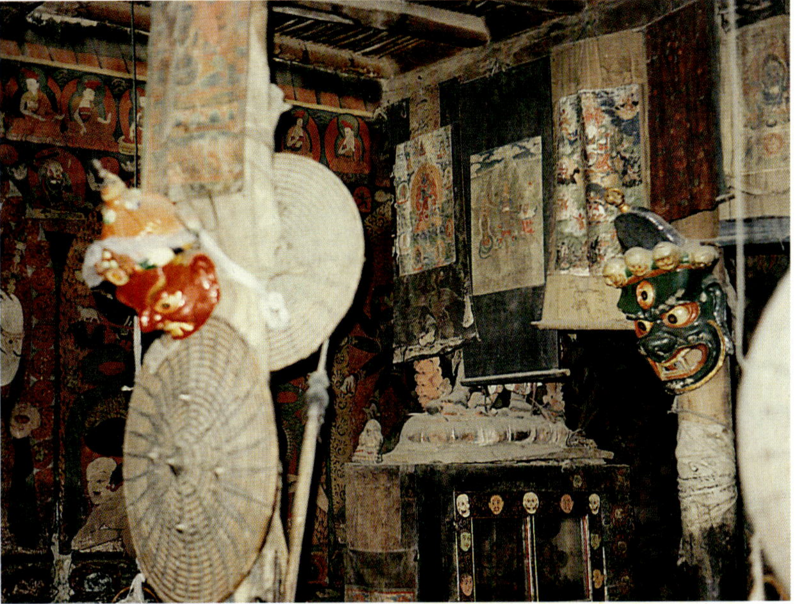

Fig. 1.46.
Spears and shields tied to a pillar in the Gonkang of Phyang monastery Ladakh (India).

impression of plunging headlong into bottomless night, into solidified darkness. Then the lamp, prevailing little by little over the gloom, sculpts and carves against the black background forms and aspects which do not belong to this world. You would think you were looking out over primordial chaos, where the vital urge finds expression in uncertain and contradictory waverings or becomes incorporated into indistinct shapes, immediately abandoned as by a sudden repentance, but so suddenly that the two images overlap, melt one into the other and monsters are born out of them, figures which are neither beast nor man, but are nevertheless one and the other, without yet reaching a definite aspect of their own: the beast has a human expression, the man grins and twists like a brute.

An elementary, chaotic, contradictory world, like the images formed in a feverish delirium. There is no cruelty or malice in their eyes, but the fury of monsters, exploding with the violence of a storm; you expect them not to speak but to howl like the wind, not to move with a wild animal's agility but to hurl themselves about with a

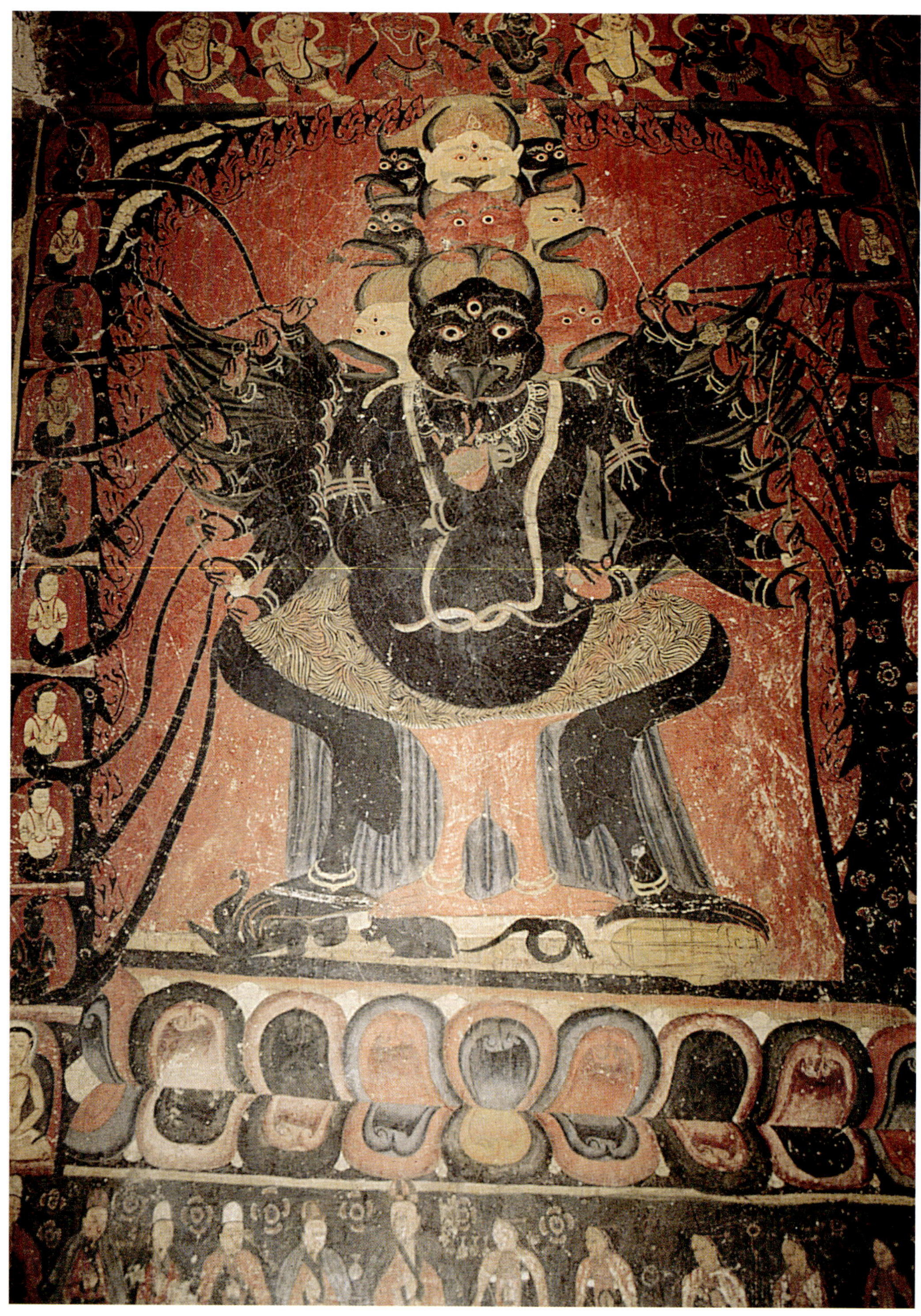

Fig. 1.47.
Eighteen armed nine-headed *naga*-controlling Garuda in a mural on the back wall of Guru Lakahang
Near Phyang
Ladakh (India), ca. late 14th c.

hurricane's uncontrollable vehemence. The shrine proper is reached little by little, plodding and groping in the dark. All around, stuffed animals hang from the ceiling: dogs, yaks, horses, wolves; stiff, filled with straw, covered with the dust of centuries; their hair falls off and drops down every time a breath of air blows through the place [fig. 1.45].

They are the *spyan gzigs*, the god's messengers. All round, war trophies [fig. 1.46] and remains of enemies and brigands, killed through the favor of the same deities who protect the temple. And as the temple is a projection of the universe, indeed cosmos in its essential paradigm, they also defend all men from all sorts of perils and evils.

Meanwhile in that cave, which seems to sink into the abysses of the earth, deep thuds echo with a constant rhythm and are repeated by mysterious hollows. One advances in the anxious anticipation of being confronted at any moment by something mysterious; one is led on by a resigned and awed curiosity; it is no longer possible to turn back. Little by little the thuds become nearer, until the *sancta sanctorum* is reached, where a priest, squatting in the ritual pose, recites litanies and invocations in a monotonous voice, beating rhythmically on a large drum with a crooked drumstick. The dark and empty rooms multiply its echo. These priests pass their lives in the mGon k'an, voluntary comrades of the deities incumbing on all sides with their monstrous figures; they are buried in darkness, as though plunged into primordial chaos to live the drama of creation over again in that silence. When one enters, they do not move nor look up; they remain with closed eyes, murmuring secret formulas, almost a lullaby soothing and putting to sleep forces hidden within the images; as if, were the crooning interrupted for an instant, they might wake up and break loose in all their fury. The place itself captivates by its mystery, its shadows, its silences; the faith, the pious awe of religious souls who have passed through the place or lived there for centuries, seem to create a sacred atmosphere, in which the manifestation of the god's divine spirit is felt to be imminent. As if to show materially that these mGon k'an sink back into the origin of all things, they are often underground.

*

The tankas of the mGon k'an correspond marvelously to the atmosphere of the place meant to receive them: their pervading colours are red and black; in the most ancient, of the Guge school, the dark blue or black figures on monstrous deities emerge from the dark red background [fig. 1.47]; in the most recent ones these roles are reversed: on the black background the figures stand out surrounded by vivid gleams of flame. In some of them . . . we must almost guess at the presence of the goddess from the vivid red of her eyes, mouth and hands and from the flames surrounding her; she suddenly springs out of the awful darkness of cosmic night, all aflame [cat. no. 22].

At other times, terrific deities and gruesome offering of human skulls, eyes and entrails are traced out in thin goldenlines. But in both cases the effect is equally obtained: the contrast of strong colours, black backgrounds, fiery images emerging from them in sudden epiphanies, represent in an extremely striking manner the atmosphere of *tremendum* pervading all the mGon k'an.

Notes

1. Dharmarakshita, *The Wheel of Sharp Weapons: A Mahayana Training of the Mind*, 2nd revised edition, trans. Geshe Ngawang Dhargyey, Sharpa Tulku, Khamlung Tulku, Alexander Berzin, and Jonathan Landaw (Dharamsala: Library of Tibetan Works and Archives, 1994), p. 22. Dharmarakshita's "Wheel of Sharp Weapons" was brought to Tibet and translated by his disciple Atisha (982–1054) and Dromton. This text is accepted as authentic by the Gelugpa lineage, but its authorship is considered suspect by others, according to a personal communication from Jeff Watt, Director of the Himalayan Art Website and Curator, Rubin Museum of Art. However, even if these suspicions are well-founded, it would be a Tibetan composition of pre-15th-century date, and still relevant for my purposes of suggesting the Tibetan understanding of wrathful deities.
2. "Just as a painter, paralysed with fear, Kashyapa, falls headlong and goes off into a faint because of the frightening features of a *yaksa* drawn by himself, so all the unenlightened worldlings stray through *samsara* because of forms, sounds, smells, tastes and [objects of] touch created by themselves, not knowing what those things really are." Bhikkhu Pasadika, "The Kasyapaparivarta ['Od-srung-gi le'u]-Prolegomena," *Tibet Journal* 5, no. 4 (1980): 51.
3. David Snellgrove, *The Hevajra Tantra: A Critical Study*, 2 vols. (London: Oxford University Press, 1959), II.v.8–11, p.110.
4. Geshe Ngawang Dhargyey, in Dharmarakshita, *Wheel of Sharp Weapons*, p. 56.
5. Dietrich Seckel, "Buddhist Art," *Encyclopaedia of Buddhism*, ed. G. P. Malalasekera (Sri Lanka, 1973), p. 485.
6. Sharpa Tulku and Michael Perrott, *A Manual of Ritual Fire Offerings* (Dharamsala: Library of Tibetan Works and Archives, 1987), p. 59.
7. Glenn Wallis, *Mediating the Power of Buddhas: Ritual in the Mañjusrimulakalpa* (Albany: SUNY, 2002), pp. 34, 163.
8. Nagarjuna, *Nitishaastraprajnadanda* in Tarthang Tulku et al., *Elegant Sayings* (Berkeley: Dharma Publishing, 1977), p. 48.
9. Kyabje Phabongkha Dechen Nyingpo, *Meditation on Vajrabhairava*, 2nd ed., comp. and trans. Sharpa Tulku and Richard Guard (Dharamsala: Library of Tibetan Works and Archives, 2000), pp. 71–72.
10. Wallis, *Mediating the Power of Buddhas*, p. 122.
11. Robert A. F. Thurman, *The Tibetan Book of the Dead* (New York: Bantam Books, 1994), pp. 152–53.
12. Tarthang Tulku, *Elegant Sayings*, p. 20.
13. Black-ground *tangkas* in the exhibition include catalog nos. 1, 2, 6, 16, 17, 31, 33, 37, 50, 53.
14. Martin J. Boord, *A Bolt of Lightning From the Blue: The vast commentary on Vajrakila that clearly defines the essential points* (Berlin: Edition Khordong, 2002), p. 8.
15. Réne de Nebesky-Wjkowitz, *Oracles and Demons of Tibet: The Cult and Iconography of the Tibetan Protective Deities* (The Netherlands: Mouton and Co., 1956), p. 6.
16. Robert A. F. Thurman, *Essential Tibetan Buddhism* (Edison: Castle Books, 1997), p. 226, from a visualization and recitation manual arranged by Tsongkhapa.
17. Pemal Namdol Thaye, *Tibetan Thanka Painting: Portrayal of Mysticism* (Grafton, Australia: G. C. Shannon, 2000), p. 39.
18. For more on these distinctions, as well as other traits of the higher classes of wrathful deities, see Rob Linrothe, "Delivering Threats, Threatening Deliverance: Forms and Functions in Indo-Tibetan Esoteric Buddhist Wrathful Deities," Part One, *Oriental Art* 46, no. 2 (2000): 24–35; Part Two, *Oriental Art* 46, no. 3 (2000): 92–105.
19. Maria Heim, "The esthetics of Excess," *Journal of the American Academy of Religion* 71, no. 3 (2003): 549.
20. Robert Beer, *The Encyclopedia of Tibetan Symbols and Motifs* (Boston: Shambhala, 1999), p. 325.
21. Dharmarakshita, *Wheel of Sharp Weapons*, p. 12. See also page 56, where the "self-centered butcher" is glossed as Yama, the god of death.
22. For example, an American Academy of Religion panel at the national conference in November 2000, was devoted to the topic of "Buddhism and Violence." For abstracts of the talks, refer to www.aarweb.org /annualmeet/2000/pbook/abstract.asp?Abs' A22.
23. Ronald M. Davidson, *Indian Esoteric Buddhism: A social history of the Tantric movement* (New York: Columbia University Press, 2002).
24. Rob Linrothe, *Ruthless Compassion: Wrathful Deities in Early Indo-Tibetan Esoteric Buddhist Art* (London: Serindia, 1999).
25. For the early phases of this process, and the way it was understood and mythologized in later Tibet, see Matthew Kapstein, *The Tibetan Assimilation of Buddhism: Conversion, Contestation, and Memory* (Oxford/New York: Oxford University Press, 2000).
26. Hildegard Diemberger, "The Horseman in Red on Sacred Mountains of La stod lho (Southern Tibet)," in *Tibetan Mountain Deities, Their Cults and Representations*, ed. Anne-Marie Blondeau (Vienna: Österreichische Akademie der Wissenschaften, 1998), p. 46.
27. Elisabeth A. Stutchbury, "Raja Gephan—The Mountain Protector of Lahul," in *Tibetan Mountain Deities*, p. 161.
28. Information on Dorje Legpa, Pehar and Shangpa Karpo derived from the entries by Jeff Watt on the Himalayan Art Website.
29. Pascale Dollfus, "Mountain Deities Among the Nomadic Community of Kharnak," in *Ladakh: Culture, History, and Development between Himalaya and Karakoram*, ed. Martijn van Beek, Kristoffer Brix Bertelsen, and Poul Pedersen (New Delhi: Sterling Publishers, 1999), p. 98.
30. Information on Draglha Gonpo and Machen Pomra taken from the entries by Jeff Watt on the Himalayan Art Website. Katia Buffetrille has discussed the relationship between mountain deities and warrior-kings, who are assimilated to the mountain divinity. Both bear similar responsibilities and thus are given similar appearances. Katia Buffetrille, "One Day the Mountains Will Go Away: Preliminary remarks on the flying mountains of Tibet," pp. 77–89 in *Reflections of the Mountain: Essays on the History and Social Meaning of the Mountain Cult in Tibet and the Himalayai*, ed. Anne-Marie Blondeau and Ernst Steinkellner (Vienna: Österreichischen Akademie der Wissenschaften, 1996).
31. Gyurme Dorje, "A rare series of Tibetan banners," in Nigel Allen, ed., *Pearls of the Orient: Asian Treasures from the Wellcome Library* (London: Serindia, 2003), p.161. Nebesky-Wjkowitz, *Oracles and Demons of Tibet*, pp. 3–5.
32. Martin Willson and Martin Brauen, *Deities of Tibetan Buddhism: The Zürich Paintings of the Icons Worthwhile to See* (Bris sku mthon ba don ldan) (Boston: Wisdom Publications,

2000), p. 489; Nebesky-Wjkowitz, *Oracles and Demons of Tibet*, pp. 3–5.

33. Most of these examples have been taken from the entries by Jeff Watt on the Himalayan Art Website.
34. Himalayan Art Website items 65174, 65026.
35. Himalayan Art Website item 351.
36. Himalayan Art Website item 1065.
37. Such statements are made from a secular, historical, nonreligious perspective and are not meant to bedisrespectful. Himalayan Buddhists naturally do not accept that the emanations of Padmasambhava are Himalayan "creations," nor for that matter that the other deities were "created" in India. See Linrothe, *Ruthless Compassion*.
38. The root narratives of such Wrathful Buddhas as Trailokyavijaya and Vajrakila both feature similar stories of subduing forms of Shiva. Just as Yamantaka and Vajrabhairava take on aspects of the form of Yama, the Hindu God of Death, so too Hevajra and Chakrasamvara can be shown to take on aspects of the forms of Shiva.
39. "The clear form of the deity is the luminous appearance of your own mind." Jamgön Kongtrul Lodrö Thaye, *Creation and Completion: Essential Points of Tantric Meditation*, intro., trans. and annot. Sarah Harding (Boston: Wisdom Publications, 1996), p. 41.
40. Willson and Brauen, *Deities of Tibetan Buddhism*, p. 511. In Sanskrit, they are *ishtadevata*, in Tibetan, *yidam*.
41. Lama Thubten Yeshe, *Introduction to Tantra: A Vision of Totality* (Boston: Wisdom Publications, 1987), p. 137.
42. Jamgön Kongtrul Lodrö Thaye, *Creation and Completion*, p. 40. See also Venerable Gyatrul Rinpoche, *Generating the Deity*, trans. Sangye Khandro (Ithaca, N.Y.: Snow Lion Publications, 1992).
43. Thurman, *Essential Tibetan Buddhism*, p. 216.
44. L. Austine Waddell, *Lhasa and its Mysteries, with a record of the British Tibetan Expedition of 1903–1904* (New York: Dover, 1988), pp. 228–29.
45. Fokke Sierksma, *Tibet's Terrifying Deities: Sex and Aggression in Religious Acculturation* (The Hague: Mouton, 1966), p. 166.
46. Robert A. F. Thurman, "The Evolutionary Art of Buddhist Tibet," in Marylin M. Rhie, and Robert A. F. Thurman, *Worlds of Transformation: Tibetan Art of Wisdom and Compassion* (New York: Tibet House and the Shelley and Donald Rubin Foundation, 1999), p. 37.
47. Khenpo Namdrol, *The Practice of Vajrakilaya* (Ithaca, N.Y.: Snow Lion Publications, 1999), pp. 38–39.
48. Now dispersed into the RMA and Rubin personal collections.
49. Black-ground *tangkas* in the exhibition include catalog nos. 1, 2, 6, 16, 17, 31, 33, 37, 50, 53.
50. Thaye, *Tibetan Thanka Painting*, p. 27.
51. Heather Stoddard, "The Style and Artistic Context" in Samten Karmay, *Secret Visions of the Fifth Dalai Lama* (London: Serindia, 1988), p. 12. Also, Nathalie Bazin et al., *Rituels tibétains: Visions secrètes du Ve Dalaï Lama* (Paris: Musée national des Arts asiatiques-Guimet, 2002), no. 35.
52. For example, Pratapaditya Pal, *Art of the Himalayas: Treasures from Nepal and Tibet* (New York: Hudson Hills Press, 1991), cat. no. 92.
53. Aldo Mignucci, "Tibetan Black *Thang-kas*: New Evidence on the Origins of a Painting Tradition," *Annali di Ca' Foscari* 39, no. 3 (Serie Orientale, 2000): 1–10; idem, "Tibetan Black Thangkas: Origins and Early Development of a Painting Tradition," symposium talk, April 5, 2003, Art Institute of Chicago, in conjunction with the opening of the exhibition *Himalayas: An Aesthetic Adventure*. See also Pratapaditya Pal et al., *Himalayas: An Aesthetic Adventure* (Chicago: Art Institute of Chicago, 2003), pp. 201–12, and Bazin et al., *Rituels tibétains*, no. 41.
54. Pratapaditya Pal, *Desire and Devotion: Art from India, Nepal, and Tibet in the John and Berthe Ford Collection* (Baltimore: The Walters Art Museum, 2001), cat. no. 145.
55. Although the earliest extant ones are Japanese copies of the eighth century, Meech-Pekarik has "no doubt that the gorgeous technique . . . was imported from China." Pratapaditya Pal and Julia Meech-Pekarik, *Buddhist Book Illuminations* (London: Ravi Kumar Publications, 1988), p. 237.
56. See, for instance, the 14th-century manuscript in the Schoyen collection, MS2457/1; www.nb.no/baser/schoyen/5/5.17/ms24571.jpg; consulted August 2003.
57. Cristina Anna Scherrer-Schaub, "Towards a Methodology for the Study of Old Tibetan Manuscripts: Dunhang and Tabo," *Tabo Studies II: Manuscripts, Texts, Inscriptions, and the Arts*, ed. C. A. Scherrer-Schaub and E. Steinkellner (Rome: Istituto Italiano per l'Africa e l'Oriente, 1999), p. 7.
58. Roderick Whitfield and Anne Farrer, *Caves of the Thousand Buddhas: Chinese Art from the Silk Route* (New York: George Braziller, 1990), cat. nos. 45, 47, pp. 66–70.
59. Heather Stoddard, "The Style and Artistic Context" in Samten Karmay, *Secret Visions of the Fifth Dalai Lama* (London: Serindia, 1988), p. 11; Mignucci, "Tibetan Black *Thang-kas*: New Evidence," p. 2.
60. Roger Goepper and Jaro Poncar, *Alchi: Ladakh's Hidden Buddhist Sanctuary, the Sumtsek* (London: Serindia, 1996), p. 30.
61. Thomas J. Pritzker, "A Preliminary Report on Early Cave Paintings of Western Tibet," *Orientations* 27, no. 6 (1996): 206–27. Helmut Neumann, "The Wheel of Life in the Twelfth Century Western Tibetan Cave Temple of Pedongpo," in *Buddhist Art and Tibetan Patronage, Ninth to Fourteenth Centuries*, ed. Deborah Klumburg-Salter and Eva Allinger (Leiden: Brill, 2002), pp. 75–84.
62. Three are in the Rubin collections; see Himalayan Art Website items 594, 65088, 65128. Another is in the Essen collection, now in the Museum der Kulturen, Basel, Switzerland; Gerd-Wolfgang Essen and Tsering Tashi Thingo, *Die Götter des Himalayan: Buddhistische Kunst Tibets, Die Sammlung Gerd-Wolfgang Essen*, vol. 1 (Munich: Prestel-Verlag, 1989), no. I-99. A related image in a Swiss private collection has three such wrathful deities against a black background in a register below a green Tara; Pal, *Himalayas: An Aesthetic Adventure*, cat. no. 116. See also the Chakrasamvara mandala in Steven M. Kossak and Jane Casey Singer, *Sacred Visions: Early Paintings from Central Tibet* (New York: The Metropolitan Museum of Art, 1998), cat. no. 2. One could include in this group several others from the same exhibition, but the amount of restoration precludes confidence.
63. Mignucci, "Tibetan Black *Thang-kas*: New Evidence," pp. 1–10.
64. Goepper and Poncar, *Alchi*, pp. 30–31, 150–52, 211–13.

Mahakala

MARYLIN M. RHIE

SOME *TANGKAS* AND SCULPTURES FROM THE RUBIN MUSEUM OF ART

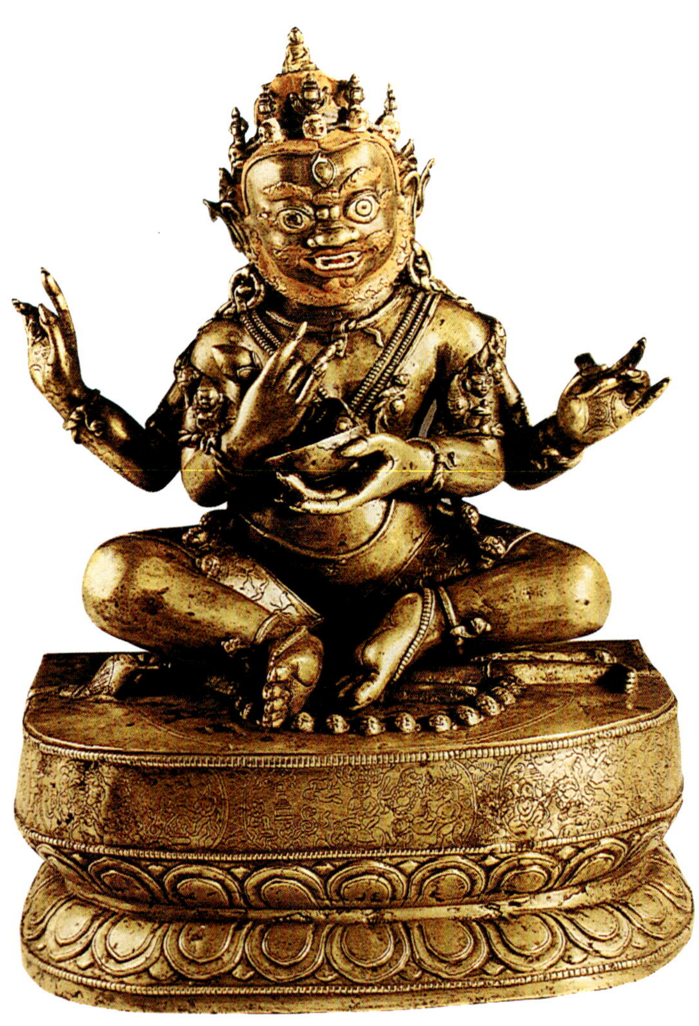

Fig. 2.1.
Four-armed Mahakala
Central Tibet, 12th c.
Gilt copper; H. 17 in.
(43 cm).
Tibet Museum, Lhasa.

The wrathful deity Mahakala is both a protector (*dharmapala*) and an archetype (*yidam*) in Tibetan Buddhist practice.[1] The long and fruitful history of Mahakala in Tibetan art reflects these two forms. Using primarily paintings (*tangkas*)[2] and sculptures from the Rubin collections now housed in the new Rubin Museum of Art, this essay seeks to lay out the main directions of Mahakala's depiction in Tibetan art. Most attention is given to "seeing" the images, like "reading" the object as a text. In this way we can understand to a degree some of the numerous forms and appearances of Mahakala—how the artistic schools express and depict him over time and in different regions of Tibet—and we can note the popularity of certain forms with certain Tibetan Buddhist orders and their practice. Mahakala is a major icon, however, and by no means is this essay exhaustive. Its emphasis is on an initial chronological and comparative presentation with some attention given to regional focus and sectarian issues, all of which hold the prospect for deeper analysis and study concerning one of the most important icons of Tibet.

The origins and sources for Mahakala are to be found in India, though there has been the suggestion of some foreign influences and the Indian origins are obscure and not certain.[3] It may be that at least some forms could be traced to Nagarjuna.[4] Possibly there has been some relation to or assimilation of certain aspects of the Hindu god Shiva.[5] It appears that Mahakala may have become more popular in Nepal than in India, though this is still hard to judge. More investigation in the future may clarify the early developments. His introduction into Tibet is, however, more definite, especially with regard to certain forms. For example, the Panjarnata Mahakala (Lord of the Pavilion) was introduced by Rinchen Zangpo (958–1055) and the six-armed (Shadbhuja) form of Mahakala, both the blue/fierce and the white/wealth aspects, traces a clear lineage back to the Indian Mahasiddha Shavaripa. The great Indian sage Atisha who came to Tibet in 1042 and died there in 1054, introduced several forms of Mahakala that became important for the Kadampa order.[6]

In general, Mahakala is usually shown as blue or black, though he appears in red, yellow, green, and white forms as well, but more rarely. He can be two-armed, four-armed, or six-armed, as a rule.[7] Each of these forms has some distinctly different qualities and aspects, and each is usually accompanied by a different assortment of attendants in his entourage. His most characteristic and pervasive symbolic attributes are the skull bowl (*kapala*) filled with blood and curved knife chopper (*kartri*). In the multiarmed forms he holds other implements, such as the sword, trident, wand or scepter (*khatvanga*) often topped with a trident and three heads, lance, small hand drum (*damaru*), fresh heart, lasso, and wooden gong (*gandi*). Various texts describe his customary appearance as fearsome and terrible, inspiring awe. He has flaring yellow-orange hair, wears a crown of five human skulls, and scowls fearfully with gaping mouth revealing gnashing fangs and curled tongue. He has three angry, wide open, red-rimmed eyes. Around his corpulent torso, with its seat of energy in his large belly, is a garland of fifty severed heads denoting the severed ego-centered passions. A large green snake encircles his body; he wears a tiger skin as loin cloth; and numerous snakes come from his hair and adorn his body as ornaments, as do other jewels or little bells. He tramples on (or is sometimes said to be rising up from sitting on) the corpse of defeated ego or the elephant-headed Hindu god, Ganesha, who is viewed as an obstacle to be blocked by Mahakala. He is surrounded by a supernova of flames.

All the warriorlike, fearsome implements and graphic symbols that he holds represent the ability of Mahakala to deal with our persistent, unwanted negativities. The chopper grinds them up in the human skull bowl of emptiness that holds the blood of defeated evil and demonic elements. The sword severs the egocentric concepts, and the *khatvanga* wand spears the heads of defeated evil represented as fresh, shriveled and dried heads, again referring to the defeat of ego-centered concepts. A crown of skulls represents the defeat of the five major "poisons" that hinder knowledge of our own enlightenment capabilities: anger, pride, lust, greed, and ignorance.

These objects may appear to be gruesome and horrific, but one needs to keep in mind that they are overly cherished parts of our own bodies or are implements like those used by a warrior against a powerful enemy. In this case the enemy is our own ego, which has no basis in true actuality and only obscures our original pure nature of enlightenment. Once one realizes the unreal fakeness of the ego, one can sever and wear this fake ego (in the form of our head or heart) like an ornament, as Mahakala has done with his garland of fifty severed heads that represent the slaying of the major ego-centered conceptions. Thus Mahakala can be an archetypal instrument through which we can realize and attain enlightenment. Some forms show him with black silken robes in dwarf form, or with the face of a lion, or riding a tiger, among others. Most forms of Mahakala are used by all the Buddhist orders of Tibet, though the six-armed form is most favored by the Gelugpa order, the Panjarnata Mahakala is one of the great deities of the Sakya order, the black-cloaked form is the protector of the Karmapa, and the four-armed form appears prevalent among both the Kagyu and Nyingma.

As protector (*dharmapala*) Mahakala guards the doctrine, the Dharma, particularly in regard to the Hevajra *tantra*, the Vajra Panjara *tantra*, and the Paramasuka Chakrasamvara *tantra*. As archetype he especially serves the advanced Buddhist practitioner, often known as a *tantric* practitioner or adept, in his/her quest for enlightenment. In general, Mahakala is a manifestation of Vajradhara, the essence of all Buddhas, and in his six-armed form he is also considered the fierce and powerful emanation of Avalokiteshvara, the Bodhisattva of Compassion.[8] Though the compassion of the Buddhas and Bodhisattvas is always directed at all living beings over all time, in the archetype form of the Buddhas and Bodhisattvas their compassion is focused in wrathful form with all its immense power toward helping those adepts already advanced on the path of enlightenment and Buddhahood. It is not that the apparent anger of these forms is turned against the practitioner, or is evil or demonic in intent; rather, that the power of wrath with compassionate intent is harnessed to help the practitioner to overcome the stubbornly deep-seated fears hindering true liberation.

Sometimes the power of great compassion is needed to break the iron grip of our clinging to what is thought to be a solid, real, substantial self, ego, or soul. The archetype icon is none other than a representation of the archetypal force that comes from within oneself and is harnessed to overcome the ego. Even though one may recognize the ego to be a false, unreal construction, one is nevertheless primordially deeply loathe to relinquish the idea of its existence supporting us. So Mahakala, the archetype and protector, can be of essential help, like a fearsome warrior ally, if one chooses to wage war with one's ego and negative aspects in the process of opening up the Buddha nature, which is the non-ego, non-self, non-soul, pure and omniscient "clear light" nature of all beings. The wrathful form that we see in these paintings and sculptures of Mahakala is compassion personified and expressed as power that can be harnessed and turned against the incredibly wily, stubborn, subtle, and stealthy enemy—the self-inflicted ego.

EARLY DEPICTIONS OF MAHAKALA IN TIBET

THE ELEVENTH AND TWELFTH CENTURIES

Relatively few examples of Mahakala are known from the early centuries of Tibetan art, but the four-armed seated Mahakala sculpture (fig. 2.1), now in the Tibet Museum, Lhasa, and the *tangka* painting of Mahakala Panjarnata in the Rubin Museum (fig. 2.2) are two such rare examples. In the quite large sculpture, Mahakala looks out at us with enormous, wide, piercing yellow eyes. His expression, rather than horrifically wrathful, appears to have a sense of silent anguish, perhaps a reflection of his compassionate nature as well as a mark of the sensitive, though somewhat naive, realism that is seen in the early Buddhist sculptures of Tibet. His big hands with long fingernails hold his trademark curved knife/chopper and skull bowl in front of this chest. The two outstretched arms probably originally held the sword and *khatvanga*, now lost.[9] With his heavy legs loosely bent, he sits low to the pedestal on a prostrate body, the corpse of ego, which seems stiffly stretched nearly to oblivion under his heavy body. His long garland of fifty miniature severed heads, strung at open intervals, falls over his body and lies in a heavy, limpid semicircle over the corpse and in front of his feet. All his ornaments exactly befit the image; though he wears some beaded strands, most of his adornments are skillfully fashioned, slender wriggling snakes, which twine around his earrings, encircle his arms, wrists and ankles, and loop around his neck and chest. His crown of five skulls is discreet and his tiger-skin loin cloth is very short, with starfishlike incised designs. The wheel of the Dharma (*dharmacakra*) is incised on the palms of his hands and soles of his feet, rarely seen markings for Mahakala. A small Buddha Akshobhya is seated on the top of his hair knot, a reference to Akshobhya as the Buddha of the Hevajra *tantra* of which Mahakala is a main protector.

The care and attention to precise yet amazingly delicate detail also extends to the remarkable pedestal, unlike any currently known. It is practically a semicircle with a straight edge in back and curved sides in front. It is divided horizontally into two nearly equal levels, the lower being a double lotus-petal design, with constricted waist and delicate beaded edging. The upper level has a slightly convex swelling, and the surface is incised with representations of the eight cemeteries. Each is a separate vignette separated by a wave or mountain design and with its own *siddha* adept, stupa, mountain, and various deities. The appearance of the cemeteries, sometimes seen in paintings of Mahakala but not known in other sculptures of this icon, probably relates to the prominence of the cremation grounds in meditation practice and also as a typical abode of Mahakala. In some visualizations of Mahakala the practitioner begins with the pedestal of cremation grounds, then moves to the squashed figure beneath Mahakala's feet, and thence to Mahakala himself.

The *tangka* painting (fig. 2.2) of the Mahakala as Lord of the Pavilion (Panjarnata),[10] though somewhat worn, is nevertheless special as one of the earliest painted portrayals with Mahakala as the main image, probably dating to the twelfth century.[11] In composition and form it relates to paintings of the central regions of Tibet, distinct from the early forms known from western Tibet, such as those from the Sumtsek at Alchi (fig. 2.3). He stands frontally holding his skull bowl and chopper and across his arms lies a simply patterned wooden gong (*gandi*) used in monastic settings to summon the monks. These attributes identify this form of Mahakala as Panjarnata, a major and popular form, especially within the Sakya tradition, which has strong roots in the idea of protecting the scholastic traditions of the Dharma. This form was brought to Tibet by the great translator and propagator of Buddhism in western Tibet, Rinchen Zangpo, who on his last trip to India, had been given the command by his king/monk Yeshe O of the Guge dynasty of western Tibet to bring back a special guardian for the doctrine. At Bodhgaya (site of the enlightenment of the Buddha) Rinchen Zangpo received instruction on how to achieve the manifestation of such a deity. At first unsuccessful in summoning the deity in his meditations, he then went to "the cemetery southwest of Bodhgaya, prepared a circle of offerings and prayed. He heard a fearful sound as though two tigers had leapt on a large human corpse and were devouring it. . . . At twilight on the third day he beheld the form of Mahakala in the act of trampling upon a dwarf and holding a knife and skull, one above the other, level with his heart, and a *gandi* (short length of wood stick to make a sound) held central in his hands." He stayed for three days in contemplation and "when he emerged Mahakala was visible and he said 'Obtain the instructions (from the lama) and then we shall go to Tibet together in order to protect the doctrine.'"[12]

In this early *tangka*, black Mahakala stands frontally with short, chubby, symmetrically bent legs. His head is slightly tilted to one side, and his big feet spread to the sides with heels nearly touching. Like the statue in figure 2.1, the corpse is very flat and almost unnoticeable. The pedestal has a rectangular shape and the lotus petals are broad and simply portrayed in a limited number of colors. Such broad lotus petals are known in eleventh- and twelfth-century paintings, and the appearance of only a single row of down-turned petals is a common early feature.[13] His upper body appears gargantuan, with massive upper arms and shoulders and a big rectangular face. Yet, despite the large proportions, he appears fragile. There is a naively simple patterning to the eyebrows, mustache, and beard. The head of yellow-red hair is more puffy than in the statue in figure 2.1 and begins to have a

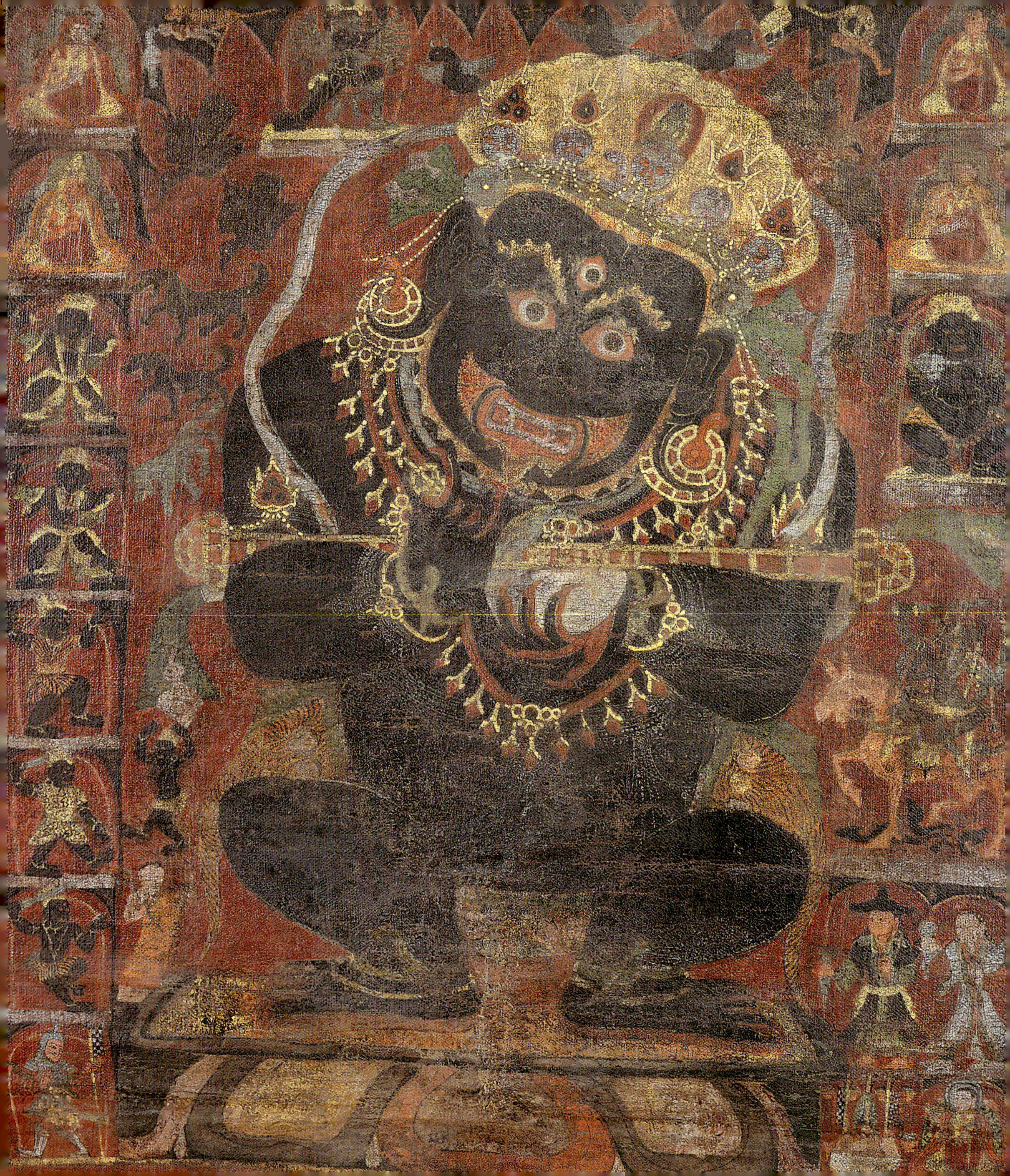

scalloped outline along the top, a feature that develops more clearly in the thirteenth century. The five-skull crown is similar to that in the figure 2.1 statue, but the skulls are slightly larger and the jewels slightly smaller. A seated Buddha Akshobhya is atop the central skull rather than on the top of the hair as in the statue. This Mahakala in the *tangka* has a somewhat sad and wistful expression that gives him a remarkably sympathetic, human appeal. He becomes an empathetic character, seeming to embody the pathos and complex emotions that we associate with the classic sad clown in Western culture. Later renderings do not capture this kind of expression, so this representation, simple as it is, has special appeal. Similar to the sculpture in figure 2.1, this may be an early trait showing a human side to the image, unlike the more masklike iconic and then realistically wrathful appearances seen in later representations.

The ornaments bear some relation to types known in other early *tangkas.* For example, similar spiral earrings are used in a Green Tara of the late eleventh to early twelfth century in the Ford collection and in a Vairocana of the second half of the twelfth century at the Cleveland Museum.[14] Mahakala's gorgeous double-strand necklace of gold-clasped ruby jewels is an unusually prominent feature, actually outshining and dwarfing the garland of severed heads, green snake cord, and tiny delicate white bone ornaments. The fifty fresh heads, representing the severed passions worn as his garland, barely peek out around his legs. Little green flowers appear above his ears, delicate pearl festoons dangle from his crown, and little green snakes are seen here and there as bracelets and anklets. A white silken scarf makes a narrow, floppy, wavering arc behind his head; the green ends curve outward behind each crooked elbow. The fiery flame mandorla (encompassing halo) seems to be a flat orange-red color, only breaking along the top into irregular cone-shaped flames, probably an early rendering of the stronger patterns of flames around the edges of mandorlas seen developing in the thirteenth to fifteenth centuries (see figs. 2.4, 2.7, 2.10, 2.17, and 2.18). Scattered on the fiery red aura around him are ravens, jackals, and dogs, all considered "messengers" of Mahakala and a mark of the cremation-ground setting. Above the points of the flame, in a narrow edge of dark space, appear other cemetery figures: a tiger devouring a corpse (also an allusion to the description in the text quoted above); birds and other animals. A small image of Hevajra Father-Mother (*yab-yum*)[15] is tucked among the flames above Mahakala's right shoulder. This is a clear reference to Mahakala's role as protector of the Hevajra cycle of *tantras.*

In the figure 2.2 *tangka*, Mahakala's area occupies the entire central space from top to bottom; this is quite unusual, as in most *tangkas* from central Tibet of this time there are also small panels for individual figures along the top and bottom. Here there are only smaller side panels, which contain figures belonging to the retinue of Mahakala and are an important part of the whole environment surrounding Mahakala. These attendants are usually portrayed in paintings, but seldom in sculptures of Mahakala. Here the top two panels on both sides have seated lamas: the two at the left with red and yellow hats; the two at the right without hats. These are likely to be Sakya, perhaps both the celibate and lay lamas of the Sakya tradition. The other figures in the *tangka* are those that are associated with the specific form of Panjarnata Mahakala as his entourage and attendants. Below the lamas on the left are probably the five *rakshasas* (fierce *yaksha* protectors) of Panjarnata Mahakala's "Inner Retinue" (that is, the Father, Mother, and three offspring).[16] The figure in the lower left corner in warrior garb with high boots and holding a black-and-white checkered flag is one of the four members of Mahakala's "Outer Retinue." The other three are scattered about. The dark woman and monk appear near Mahakala's

Facing page: Fig. 2.2. Mahakala Panjarnata (Lord of the Pavilion) Central Tibet, Sakya lineage, 12th c. Mineral pigments and gold on cloth; 19 x 17 in. (48.26 x 43.18 cm). F1996.27.2 (HA 497).

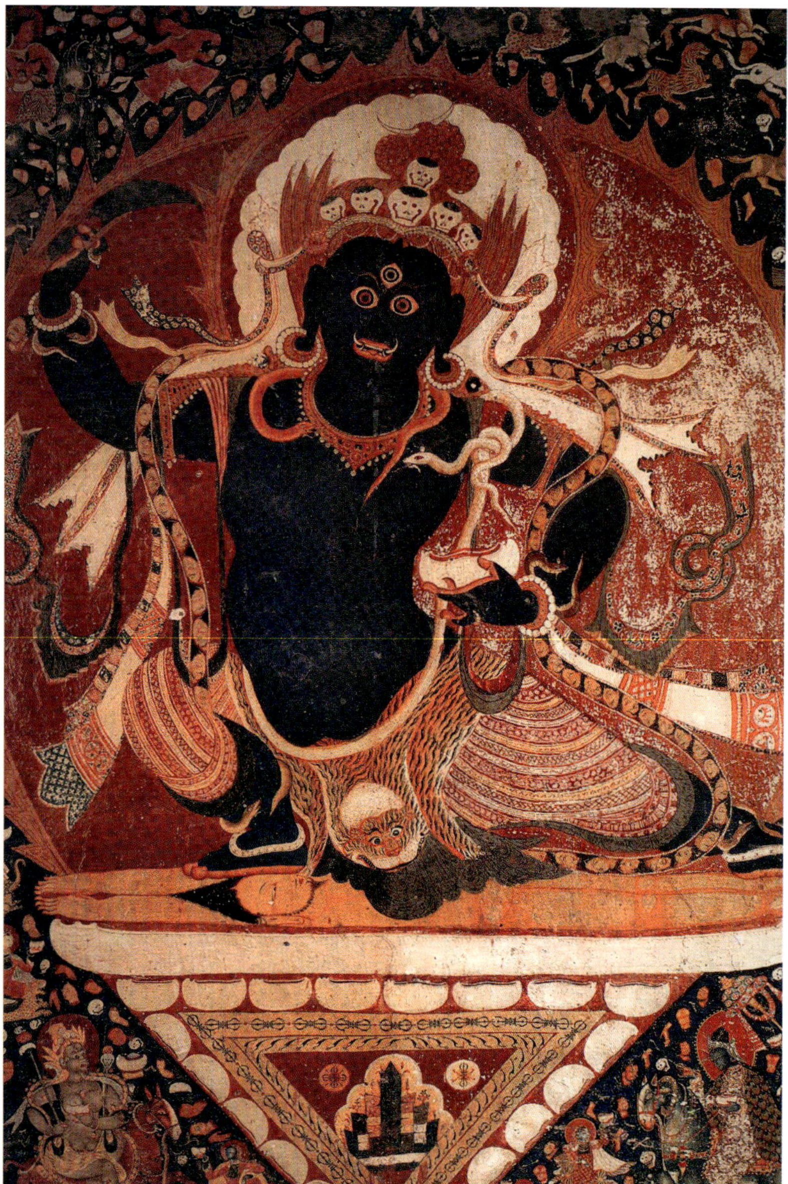

Fig. 2.3.
Two-armed Mahakala
Sumtsek, Alchi, Ladakh,
late 12th to early 13th c.
Mural; 57 1/8 x 39 3/8 in.
(145 x 100 cm).

right leg within his red flaming aura. The third, the holder of the mantras, is probably the black-garbed figure with wide-brimmed black hat standing next to a white-robed secular male (a donor?) on the right side, just above the monk who sits by his consecrating objects that are arranged on a large white tripod with three black-and-white checkered flags behind. In the center of the side panels on the right side (below the lamas) are the goddess Ekajati ("one braid") wearing a white blouse and tiger-skin skirt and holding a pot in front of her chest, and Palden Lhamo (Shri Devi) with four arms holding sword, skull bowl, spear, and trident. This fierce goddess female protector rides a scrawny wild mule through a sea of blood, here suggested by a few jagged dark shapes.[17] All the side figures have plain red body mandorlas with a gold line set in from the edge. On the reverse of the *tangka* is a prayer to Mahakala.

Though lacking the sophistication of the Alchi Mahakala in figure 2.3, which stands in grand form, gorgeously appointed with intricately detailed textiles, including floating and twisting silken scarves, this Mahakala *tangka* has many remarkable early features of the central Tibetan type. It may be counted as one of the earliest known *tangkas* of this form of Mahakala and one related to the Sakya order, which was established in 1073. The painting imparts a special naive charm that gives an endearing human aura to this horrific protector of the doctrine as Lord of the Pavilion.

THE THIRTEENTH CENTURY

The two Mahakalas in figures 2.3 and 2.4 exemplify the finest examples from the two major regions of western Tibet under the Guge dynasty with its Kashmiri artistic lineage (fig. 2.3) and of central Tibet with a predominantly Indo-Nepalese artistic lineage (fig. 2.4). Both are masterworks of their traditions in their respective regions, and each can serve as a model in distinguishing the characteristics in Tibetan painting in these regions around the late twelfth to early thirteenth centuries. Both show the grandeur of form and superbly ornamented figures doubtless inspired by Indian examples. Despite a lack of paintings from India of this time in such scale, we can nevertheless glimpse some of the same quality of massive, sensitively nuanced form and gorgeous ornamentation in the eleventh-century stone sculpture of the standing four-armed Mahakala from Pala dynasty India in figure 2.5.

By pointing out some of the many differences in details between figures 2.3 and 2.4 we can see the wonderfully imaginative artistic sensitivity in these two major schools, each with its own interpretation. The Alchi Sumtsek Mahakala (fig. 2.3) is lively, with spiky hair, large skulls in his crown, a sparkling array of energetic scarves, wriggling snakes, and fine-lined textiles while the Mahakala in the Navin Kumar Collection (fig. 2.4) is more sedate in appearance, with neatly curled up hair, small skull crown, and only one scarf forming an arching semicircular frame around the image and ending in crinkly pleated hems. The textile patterns in figure 2.4 have bolder stripes and the jewelry is more intricate than in figure 2.3. The mandorla and head halo in the Alchi painting are plain red with a saw-tooth flame edge compared to the wavy tongues of flame and relatively naturalistic filling patterns of drawn flamelettes in the figure 2.4 *tangka*. While the pedestal of the Alchi image is distinct, with its large, prone corpse of defeated ego, white moon disk, and triangular cloth bordered by skull bowls, one of the major symbolic attributes of Mahakala, the pedestal in figure 2.4 has a precisely painted lotus pedestal. The setting in both is dark cosmic space, but in the Alchi painting, in addition to attendant figures, various parts of human bodies and animals drift with cemetery-like allusion, while the figure 2.4 *tangka* has star-like flowers and gems.

The four-armed (Chaturbhuja) seated Mahakala in the Rubin Museum (fig. 2.6) is stylistically close to the Kumar Collection *tangka* in figure 2.4, and also probably dates to about the first half of the thirteenth century. From its attributes (sword, *khatvanga*, skull bowl and chopper) it could be the "four-armed wise Gonpo" in the style of Go Lotsava, a famous translator of this early period of Tibetan Buddhism.[18] Though simpler and less elaborated, the ornaments, hair style, filling pattern of the flame mandorla, black space sprinkled with gems, the lotus petals, and general posture and body form closely match those in figure 2.4. In neither of these works, however, is the Buddha image on the head as in the earlier examples in figures 2.1 and 2.2. Surrounding the central image in figure 2.6 is a gridlike formal arrangement of individual spaces, typical of

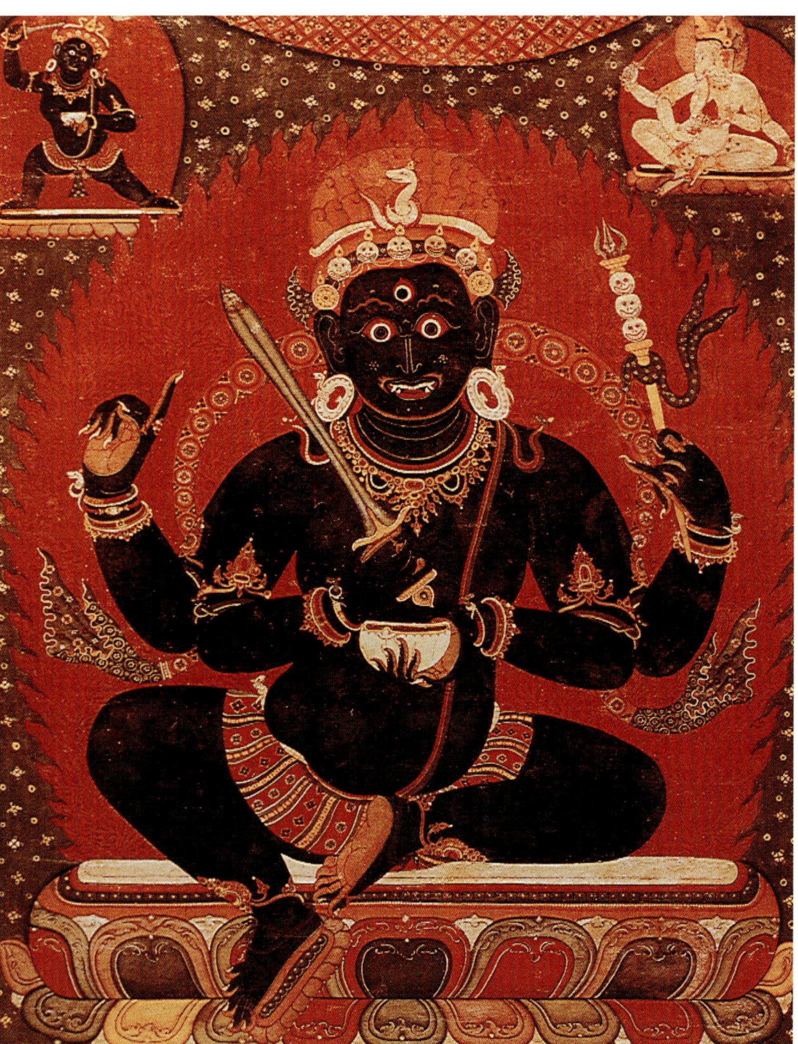

Fig. 2.4.
Four-armed Mahakala
Central Tibet, first half of the 13th c.
Mineral pigments on cloth; 20⅞ x 15¼ in. (53 x 39 cm).
Collection of Navin Kumar, New York.

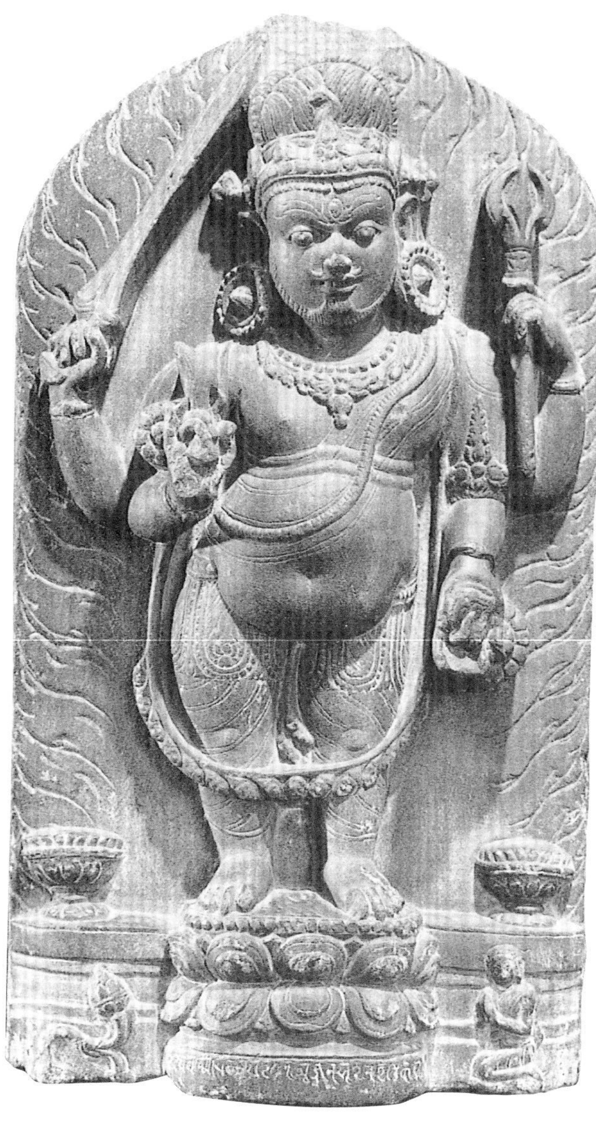

Fig. 2.5.
Four-armed Mahakala
Bihar, India, Pala dynasty,
ca. 11th c.
Black chlorite schist;
H. 14¼ in. (36.2 cm).
Los Angeles County
Museum of Art,
gift of Paul F. Walter
(M. 71.110.3).

this period, containing various smaller figures. Along the bottom are eight bird- and dog-faced demoness-protectors in the retinue of Mahakala. Each side has four other protectors, some with animal heads. Along the top are seven figures (from left to right): Vajradhara (mystical essence of all Buddhas); white and red forms of four-armed Mahakala; two-armed Paramasukha Chakrasamvara (*yab-yum*); and blue, yellow, and green four-armed Mahakalas. The five Mahakalas along the top are a rare example of a set of Mahakalas following the colors of the five cosmic Tathagata (Buddha) families. The presence of Chakrasamvara indicates Mahakala in his role as protector of this cycle of *tantras* and may link this *tangka* to the Kagyu order which particularly valued this form. The sun and moon, *tantric* symbols, appear in the spandrels above the main icon's smoothly curved mandorla filled with a field of delicately drawn flames.

On the reverse are mantras written behind the body of Mahakala. The writing in *ume* script is typical of many inscriptions of the thirteenth century, especially as known from the Taglung (a subsect of the Kagyu order) series of *tangkas*. Though less aristocratic than the Kumar collection Mahakala in figure 2.4, this *tangka* tends to confirm the dissemination of the Indo-Nepalese painting tradition into the wider reaches of Tibetan Buddhist culture, where we clearly see the Tibetan artist at work on the local level. Probably derivative of the great masterworks of the time, such paintings add to the corpus of diffusion and variety in Tibetan art and particularly help with the study of regional and iconographic aspects. Through these we see the workings of the local religious ideas and practices and come into closer touch with the humor, liveliness, and ingenuity of the Tibetan people.

The Panjarnata Mahakala in figure 2.7, also in the Rubin Museum, is probably a painting from the late thirteenth or early fourteenth century from central Tibet. This form of Mahakala became very popular during the thirteenth and fourteenth centuries as that favored by the Sakya order, which attained prosperous status during this period largely because of its mutually supporting relationship with the Mongols of China from the middle of the thirteenth century.[19] The composition used here is one seen in a number of other examples from the thirteenth to fifteenth centuries and can probably be considered the standard for that

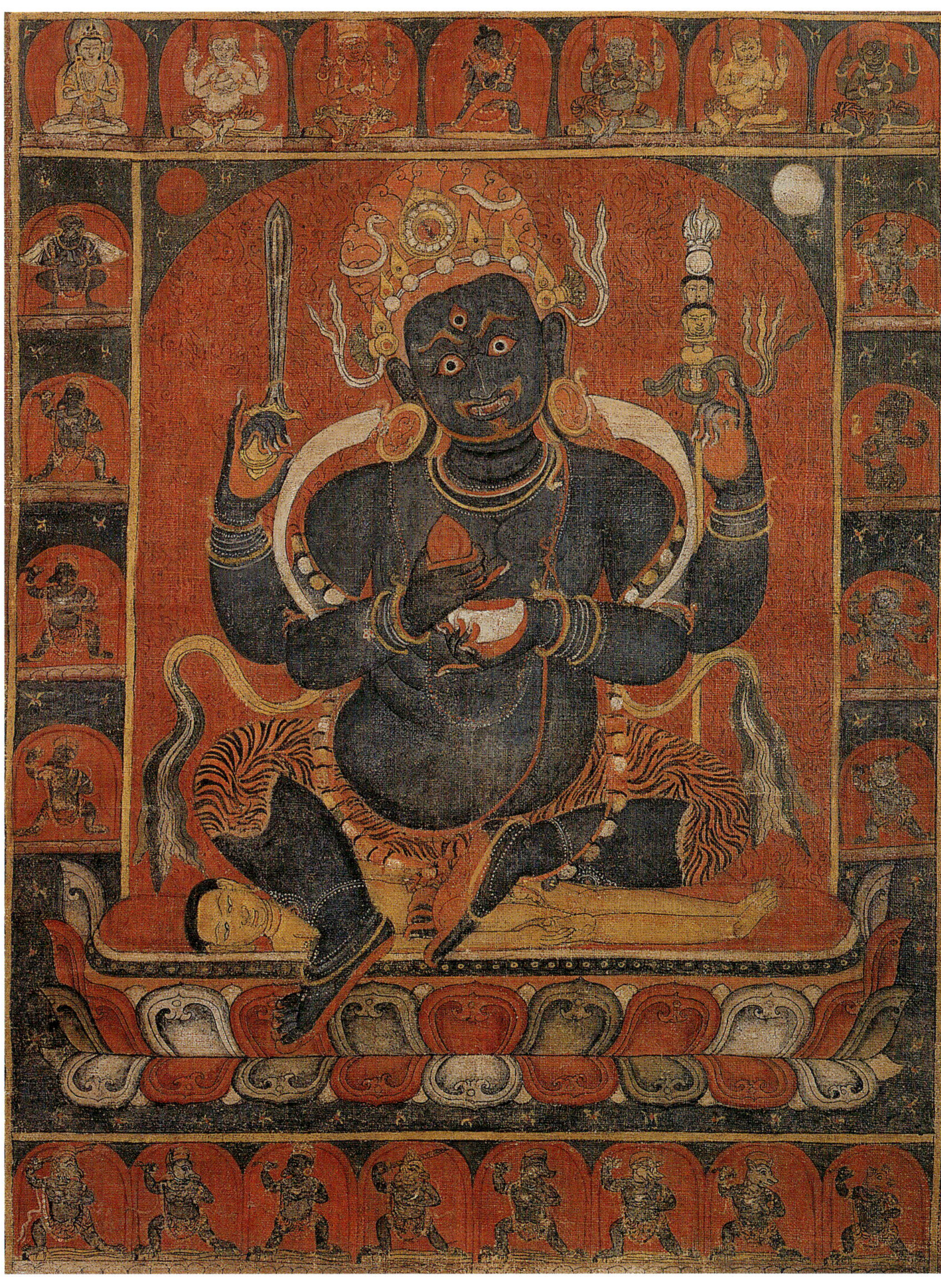

Fig. 2.6.
Four-armed Mahakala
Central Tibet, first half of the 13th c.
Mineral pigments on cloth; 16¾ x 12½ in. (42.55 x 31.75 cm).
F1997.8.1 (HA 104).

Facing page: Fig. 2.7.
Mahakala Panjarnata
Central Tibet, Sakya lineage,
late 13th to early 14th c.
Mineral pigments on cloth;
19 3/4 x 16 1/4 in.
(50.16 x 41.27 cm).
F1997.5.1 (HA 82).

period, derived from the Indo-Nepalese traditions. It shows a relatively smaller central icon of Mahakala than encountered in figure 2.2 of the same iconography. Here the four major accompanying attendants are clearly and prominently displayed within the flaming field of Mahakala himself: Bhutadamara Vajrapani (with *vajra* and *tarjani*—demon subduing gesture) at the upper left; a two-armed Mahakala Kartaridhara (with chopper and skull bowl) at the lower left; Ekajati in white silk blouse in the upper right and Palden Lhamo on her wild mule on the lower right. The large flaming mandorla encompassing them all as a unit is portrayed in soft tongues of flame, not the harsher and more strongly patterned types most typical of the fourteenth and fifteenth centuries. In the upper corners are two *tantric* Buddha forms: Sahaja Heruka Hevajra at the left and Sahaja Heruka Chakrasamvara at the right, both indicating Mahakala's prominent relationship as the protector of the Hevajra and Chakrasamvara *tantras.*[20] Circling around are jackals, black dogs, crows and vultures, and a *kyung* (*garuda* bird) at the top. These are all allusions to the cemetery grounds and are considered messengers of Mahakala. Palden Lhamo is sharp and spiky, sitting on the lanky flayed skin of her son. Her mount, led by *makara* (crocodile)-headed Makarakuti, is unusually static with large ears perked up. The group has halted in a flat, stylized sea of blood in front of a swirling black mass, possibly also the sea, or, less likely, referring to clouds or mountains.[21] Mahakala's lotus pedestal sits on a stylized rocky ground or base—another example of this rather rare depiction.[22]

Blue Mahakala himself has a fairly gentle and calm appearance and is somewhat realistically modeled. His high coiffure and long locks of golden red hair fall loosely onto his shoulders. His beard, eyebrows, and facial features are discreet and mild, though he has strange black frown lines on his forehead.[23] The scarf forms a thin arc of patterned white silk around him; it makes a fancy loop at each side before arching into natural hems that are very similar to those portrayed in a wall painting at Shalu monastery in Tsang datable to around the late thirteenth to early fourteenth centuries (fig. 2.10). The white bone ornaments start to be a bit lavish, a feature that continues to develop with much more enthusiasm in some paintings of the fifteenth century (see fig. 2.17).

The grid pattern around the central icon's panel is indicated by strong, golden demarcation lines. Such patterning is typical of thirteenth-century paintings, as is the dark background with sprinkled flowers at the bottom and lacy gold outlines for the dark green scrolling vines in the upper reaches. Along the top register are twelve seated figures, including lineage holders of the Sakya order. The figures start from the left with Vajradhara, and end with Chogyal Pagpa (1234–80).[24] Down both sides are ten gods, five to a side; they are the "keepers of the ten regions," those on the left side representing the gods of the East and South and on the right the West and North. On the left side from the bottom up, starting just above the warrior, is Indra (East) on a white elephant with a *vajra*; Agni (Southeast) on a blue goat with a rosary; Yama (South), blue on a brown buffalo with a club; Nairiti (Southwest), dark blue, on a corpse, with a sword; and Varuna (West), white on a *makara* (composite creature with crocodile head), with a serpent-noose. On the right side, from the top is Vayu (Northwest), green, on a stag, with a banner; Kubera (North), yellow, on a green bovine; Ishana (Northeast), white, on a bull, with a trident; Brahma (Zenith), yellow, on a swan, with a vase; and Nandikeshvara (Nadir), seen here as white, on a lotus with a flaming gem.[25] They are quite finely represented with their mounts in one of the earliest examples among Tibetan *tangkas*. Beneath them, two on each side, are the guardian gods of the four cardinal directions, with Vaishravana of the North (second from the right) holding a stupa. These four gods must be wearing

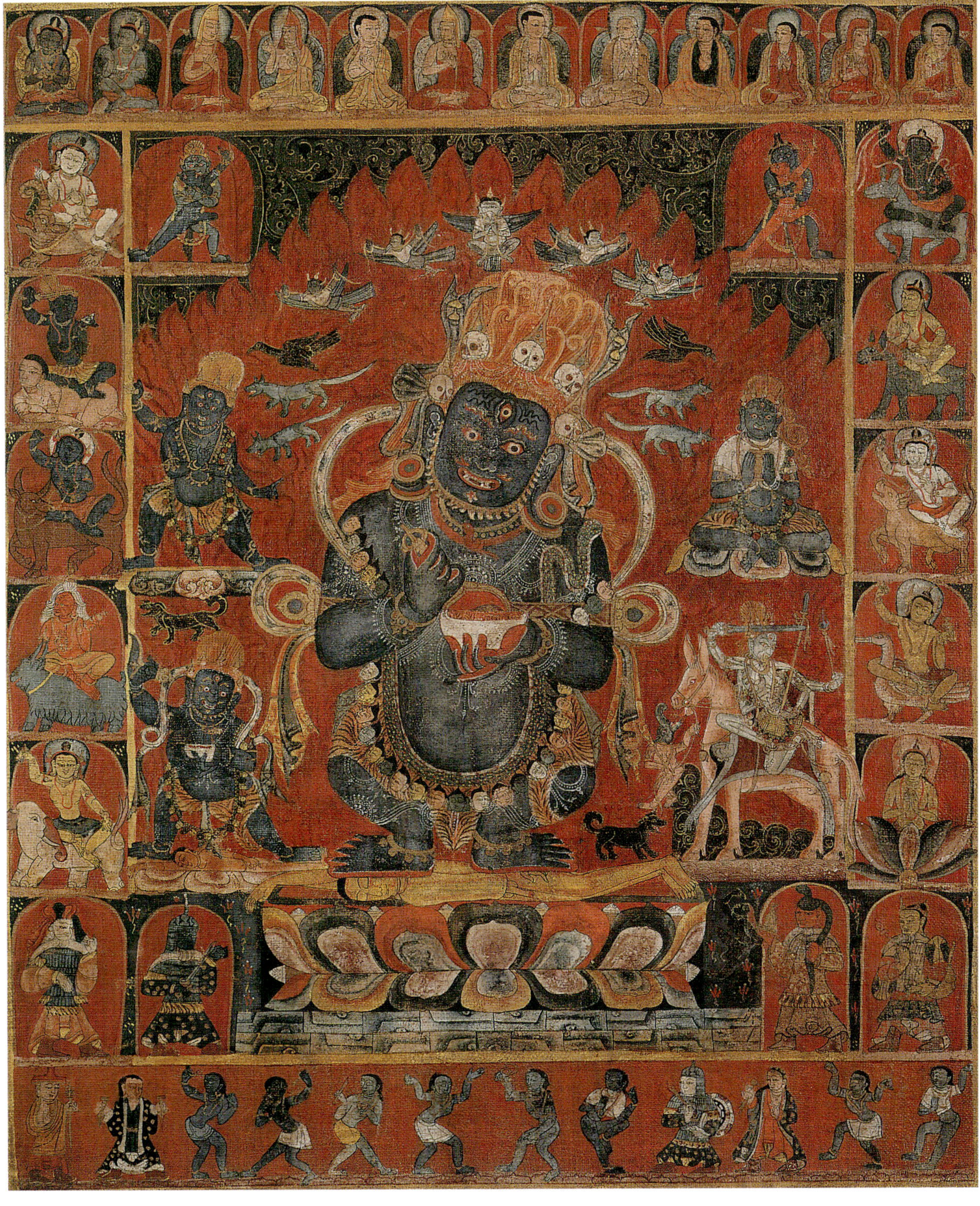

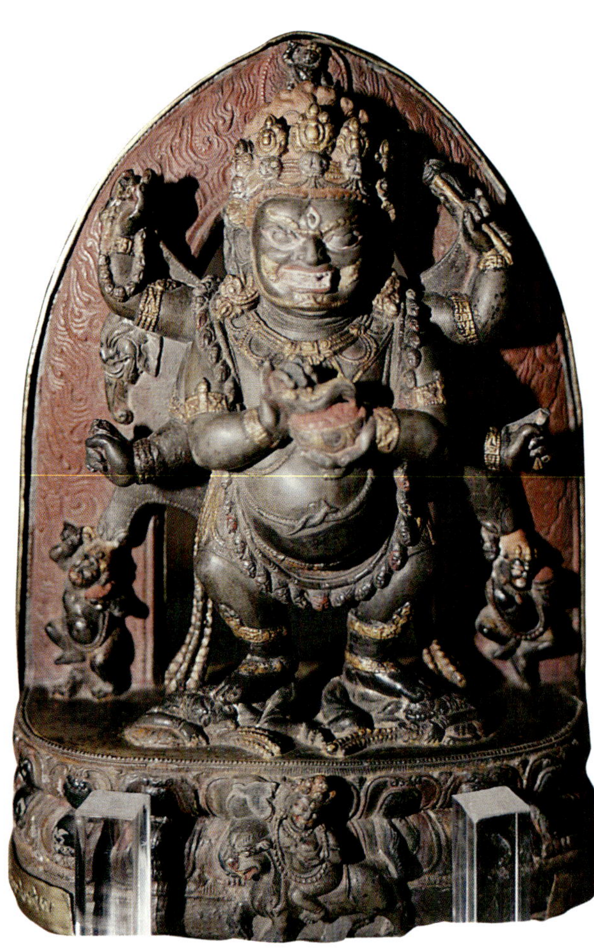

Fig. 2.8.
Six-armed Mahakala
Central Tibet, second half of the 13th c.
Stone with pigments, gold, and gilt copper mount with inscription; H. 7½ in. (19.7 cm).
Carlton Rochelle, New York.

contemporary warrior's garb; each sports an interesting cap or helmet and has the leather-strip (or chain-mail) chest protection. Along the bottom is a row of twelve figures, including the five *rakshasa* demons of Mahakala's Inner Retinue and the four figures of the Outer Retinue plus two others.[26] This *tangka* is especially interesting not only for its iconography, but also as an important work datable to around the late thirteenth or early fourteenth century, a dating upheld stylistically and also suggested by the date of the Lama Pagpa (d. 1280) as the last in the line of figures at the top.

There are notable stone carvings of Mahakala from the twelfth and thirteenth centuries.[27] The thirteenth-century standing six-armed (Shadbhuja) Mahakala in figure 2.8, formerly in the Halpert collection, quite closely matches the Rubin Museum *tangka* of Mahakala in figure 2.7 in body proportions, depiction of the hair, and crown style. It has a rather corpulent body and a large head that begins to have a seriously menacing appearance. Even the flames in the arched mandorla have a pattern somewhat similar to those in figure 2.7 with a relatively naturalistic flavor. The attendant figures are difficult to identify with certainty, as is frequently the case with early images. The two on the pedestal may be two of the four *yaksha* "ministers" that usually accompany the six-armed Mahakala, in this case, probably Jinamitra (right) and possibly Raudrantika (left). Along the bottom of the pedestal is a figure resembling Kshetrapala, another minister, but instead of riding a bear, his customary mount, he appears on a striding lion, so again the identification is in question.[28] Another small figure with flaming halo appears above his head.[29] Mahakala stretches the flayed elephant hide of ignorance behind him and holds implements usual for this form of Mahakala—the rosary of skulls, *damaru* drum, trident, and noose as well as the customary chopper and skull bowl in front of his chest. Most are still intact. There are signs of some opulence and sense of heaviness appearing in this statue, which is probably earlier than the stone Mahakala dated 1292 in the Fournier collection.[30] The statue in figure 2.8 is an early example of the six-armed Mahakala sculptures in Tibet, and as such holds an important place in the history of this specific form of Mahakala.[31]

Mahakala garbed with a "cloak of black silk" occurs in several forms of this deity, one of which is seen in the early stone statue of the dwarf form in the Potala in Lhasa (fig. 2.9). He holds a skull bowl and presumably originally held aloft a chopper, now missing.[32] His outer cloak opens down the front revealing widely pleated robes bound by a sash or belt. He stands in strident pose atop two prone bodies on a pedestal that has curvilinear overlapping mountainous shapes carved around the base—a different style from the rocks in the pedestal of figure 2.7. His face is painted and covered with cold gold; his hair is soft and pulled up, resembling somewhat the hair of the Mahakala in figure 2.7. It is likely that this statue dates from around the same time, that is, around the late thirteenth to early fourteenth century. It may be the form of Mahakala that became favored as a special protector of the Karmapas from the time of the second Karmapa, Karma Pakshi (1206–83), who introduced it into the Karma Kagyu from the Nyingma tradition.[33]

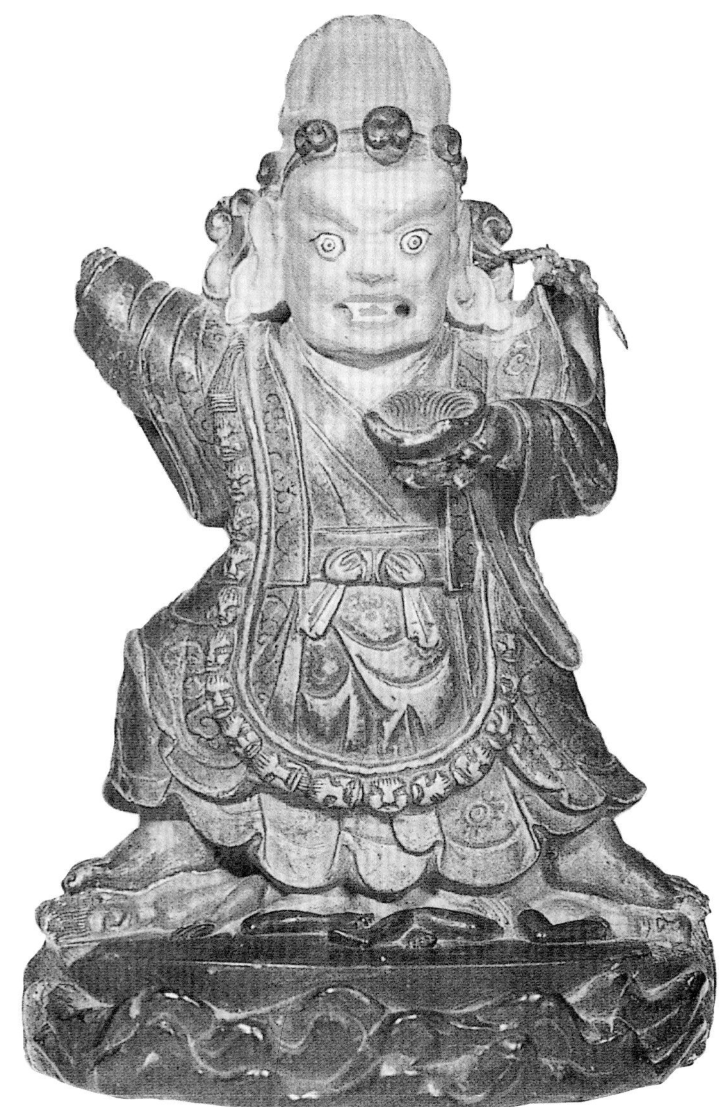

Fig. 2.9.
Mahakala
Lhasa, second half of the 13th c.
Fine-grained yellowish stone, with cold gold and pigments; H. 5⅛ in. (13 cm).
Potala Collection.

THE FOURTEENTH CENTURY

The wall paintings of Shalu Monastery in Tsang are a prime source of central Tibetan paintings of the late thirteenth and first half of the fourteenth century. Among them the image in figure 2.10 is exemplary of the wrathful protector deities, similar to Mahakala, and serves as a datable reference from which to place other early-fourteenth-century paintings, such as the Mahakala as Lord of the Pavilion in the Musée Guimet, Paris, and the one formerly with Rossi and Rossi, London,[34] both of which also show developments with respect to the Rubin Museum painting of the same form of Mahakala as in figure 2.7. They continue the trend toward more elaborate ornamentation, give greater attention to the patterns of the multiple swirling scarves, and present a bolder, tenser, less relaxed body that tends toward abstraction, without the nuances of sensitive naturalistic volume. The energy of patterning begins to dominate and will be heightened in the mid-fifteenth century (see fig. 2.17). This group of Mahakalas represent a primary artistic lineage of the time, which is strongly Nepalese.

Several of the Rubin Museum's Mahakala *tangkas* incorporate elements of the "Shalu style," but also show elements of simplification or imaginative interpretations possibly

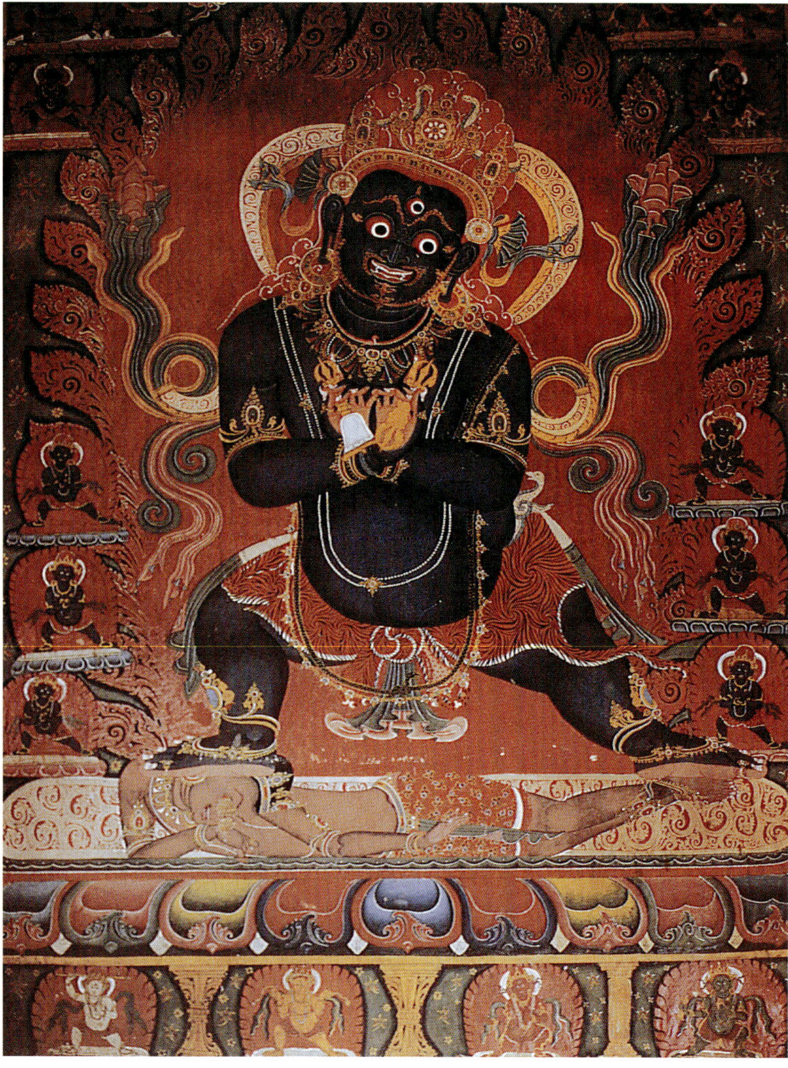

Fig. 2.10.
Wrathful Deity with bell and *vajra*
Shalu monastery, Tsang, first half of the 14th c.
Mural; 130 x 157½ in. (330 x 400 cm).

derived from the high artistic traditions. The Mahakala as Lord of the Pavilion and protector of the Hevajra *tantras*, in figure 2.11, appears to be close to the Shalu style. The painting focuses strongly on the main image by isolating the figure and his red flame mandorla in the dark blue space and by pushing the subsidiary figures to the corners: Hevajra *yab-yum*, two-armed Kartaridhara Mahakala (the Knife Holder) to the left; Ekajati and Palden Lhamo to the right. The edge of the mandorla is patterned with the bold style cone-shaped flames similar to the Shalu mandorlas (fig. 2.10).

Vajradhara and five Sakya lamas line the upper edge of the painting. Along the bottom are the four figures of Mahakala's Outer Retinue (from the right: kneeling warrior, mantra holder, dark woman, and monk) and possibly three of the *rakshasa* figures of the Inner Retinue. Four smaller energetic dark blue figures accompany Mahakala within the flames (possibly two of them being two of the five *rakshasas*), as well as the various dogs, jackals, and crows. Mahakala wears a dark blue scarf that twirls around like a lasso and ends in folded points as in the Kashmiri tradition (fig. 2.3), rather than having the ruffly hems of the Indo-Nepalese tradition (fig. 2.4). This could indicate the mixing of regional stylistic elements in the fourteenth century. His facial features are sharply drawn but retain a simplicity that imparts a more human than iconic, abstract, or masklike appearance. He wears an apron of delicate crisscrossed strings of bone ornament, and the corpse under his feet glowers up at him in the new tendency for expression seen in fourteenth-century trampled figures, as in figure 2.10.

The six-armed Mahakala, one of the major forms of Mahakala in Tibetan art and already seen in an early sculpture (fig. 2.8), appears in the relatively early painting of this form of Mahakala of about the late fourteenth or early fifteenth century from central Tibet in the Rubin Museum (fig. 2.12). Besides his customary chopper and skull bowl held in the two hands in front of his heart, this rather elegant "sky" blue Mahakala holds in his other hands a rosary of skulls, small drum, *khatvanga,* and lasso. In addition, his two uppermost arms stretch the flayed skin of the elephant of ignorance across his back. He strides on the prostrate form of the white elephant god of Hinduism, Ganesha, who looks very displeased with his position.[35]

This painting presents a splendid concoction of figures. It has a loose freedom in

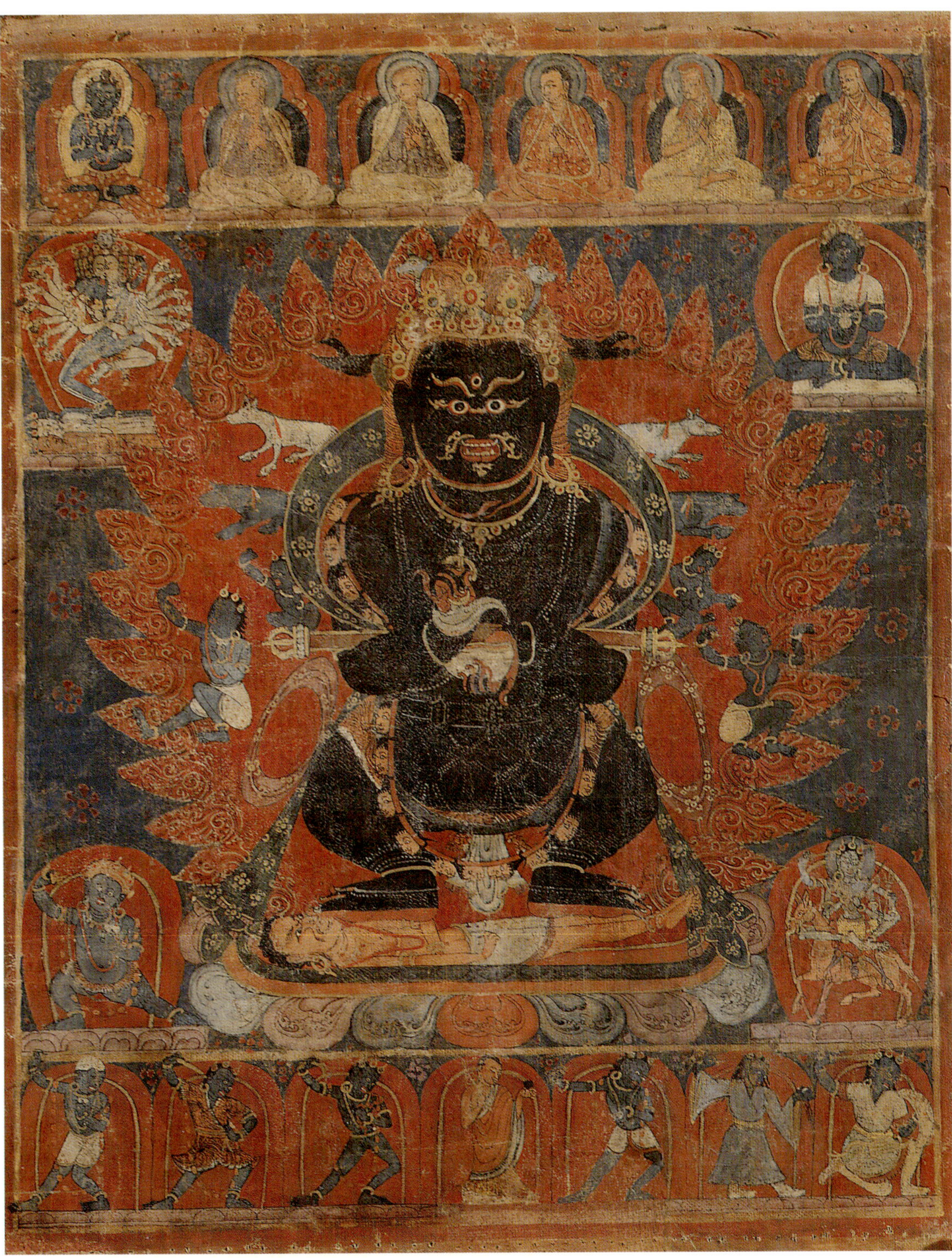

Fig. 2.11.
Mahakala Panjarnata
Central Tibet, Sakya lineage, second half of the 14th c.
Mineral pigments on cloth; 12 1/2 x 9 3/4 in. (31.75 x 24.76 cm).
F1998.11.2 (HA 642).

Facing page: Fig. 2.12.
Six-armed Mahakala
Central Tibet, late 14th to early 15th c.
Mineral pigments on cloth; 18 1/4 x 16 in. (46.4 x 40.6 cm).
Collection of Shelley and Donald Rubin (HA 1039).

the composition which is only held in place by the dominant image of Mahakala, whose arms seem not only to hold but also to create the centrifugal forces of the composition. Tucked into the upper corners are Yama (left) and Vajradhara (?) on the right. A smaller White Padmapani Avalokiteshvara (left) and Red Vajravarahi (right) float between them in the upper reaches of the painting. Members of his entourage cavort within the agitated flame space of his clean-edged mandorla. On the right are Palden Lhamo and Raudrantika (below) holding lance and skull bowl and riding a black horse. On the left is Takkiraja and Jinamitra (below), both leaping on their respective prone corpses. Five other wrathful protectors, mostly other forms of Mahakala, appear in rather large size at the bottom: Lord of the Pavilion; four-armed Mahakala seated on a brown demon; the *yaksha* protector, Krshetrapala, the fourth of the four "ministers" (the others being depicted in the mandorla) seated on a bear; Yama, lord of death and protector; and a two-armed Mahakala standing with a *khatvanga*, skull bowl, and chopper. The mandorlas are all without the patterned tongues of flame at the edges as seen in figures 2.10 and 2.11, following or reviving an earlier mode than that exemplified by the Shalu wall paintings.

This Mahakala in figure 2.12 shows the tendency toward greater elaboration that is a feature of developments in the fourteenth century and the first half of the fifteenth-century. But it is without the startling mask qualities notable in the wall paintings of the Gyantse Kumbum of the second quarter of the fifteenth century such as the splendid mid-fifteenth-century painting of Panjarnata Mahakala in the Philadelphia Museum of Art (see fig. 2.17). In the six-armed Mahakala in figure 2.12 the implements are clearly displayed, and the garland of fifty severed heads shows a touch of greater realism, a feature that began to gain ground in the fifteenth century. Though the face of this Mahakala is close to the Shalu type as in figure 2.10 of the early fourteenth century, certain embellishments suggest a later date, as do the profusion of delicate bone ornaments and the loose twists and modeling of the scarf ends, which relate to techniques noticeable in the Arhat paintings of the late fourteenth and early fifteenth centuries. The flowers and leafy boughs above his well-coifed but rather subdued hair are an unusual touch, possibly also reflect landscape elements that occur in the Arhat paintings of the time.

The *tangka* in figure 2.13, probably a rare early Yogambara,[36] is included here as an example showing forms of Mahakala as a prominent attendant. In this case, at least four side figures at the top appear to be Mahakala: four-armed black at the upper left, four-armed red below; four-armed white at the upper right, two-armed black below. These are variants of Mahakala that document these forms in Tibetan art by around the thirteenth century. They also occur in figure 2.6. A dating for this unusual Yogambara *tangka* around the late thirteenth or early fourteenth century is suggested not only by the arrangement of the surrounding figures, each in its own arched niche, in a looser composition than the grid form typical of the twelfth- to thirteenth-century *tangkas* of this kind, but also by its similarities to an early Kalachakra mandala in the Potala collection (fig. 2.14). Both have similar depictions of the faces of the main images and similar filling patterns. The mandala painting can be stylistically placed in that period partly on the basis of its donor and other figures that relate to the style of the wall paintings in Milarepa's tower at Lhodak (southern Tibet) of about the mid-thirteenth century.[37]

The bronze six-armed Mahakala in the Rubin Museum in the exhibition (cat. no. 28) closely matches the six-armed Mahakala in the *tangka* in figure 2.12 in many ways. This style of sculpture reflects the squat and massive type seen in the stone sculptures of Mahakala from the late thirteenth to early

Increased chased decoration in the border and designs of the robes show this tendency toward elegant and balanced linear ornamentation and may relate to the sculptures from Densatil, a monastery in central Tibet famous for its gilt-bronze sculptures and stupas from this period.

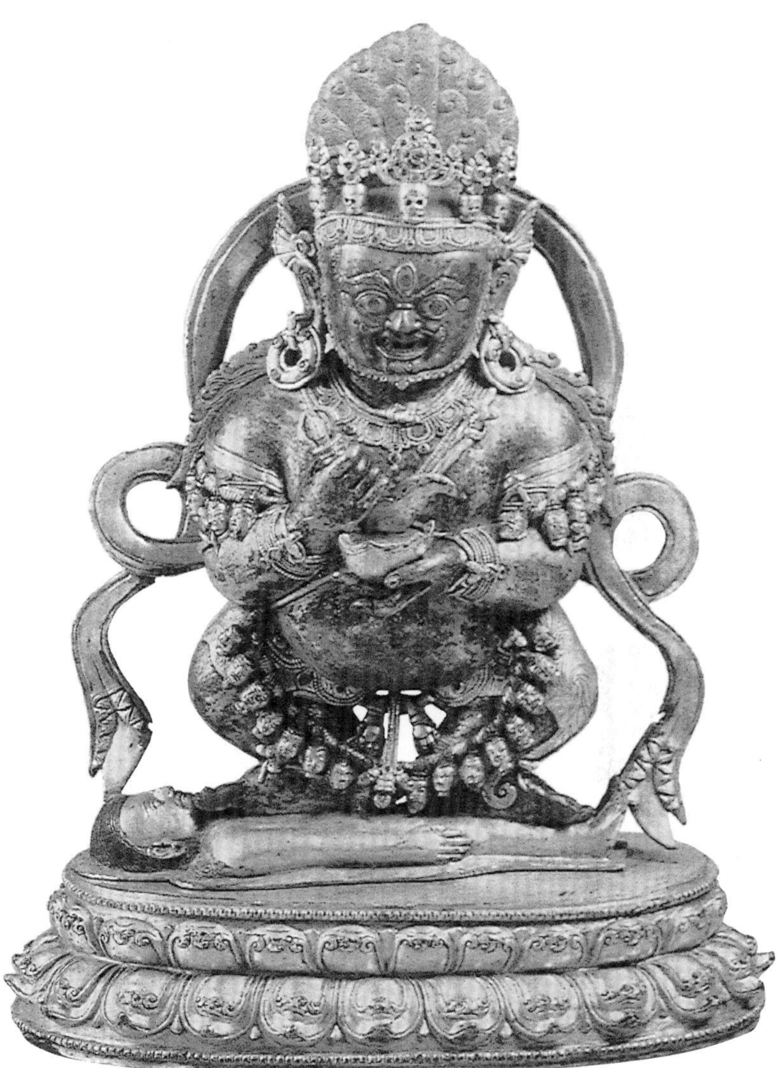

Fig. 2.15.
Mahakala Panjarnata
Central Tibet, mid-14th c.
Copper alloy with inset, parcel gilt and pigments,
H. 15 7/8 in. (40.3 cm).
Collection of Mr. and Mrs. Willard G. Clark.

MAHAKALA IN THE MIDDLE PERIODS OF TIBETAN ART

THE FIFTEENTH CENTURY

The huge painting of black Mahakala Panjarnata (Lord of the Pavilion) in the Museum of Fine Arts, Boston (fig. 2.16), is probably Chinese of fifteenth-century origin, very possibly of the Yongle period (1403–24).[41] Though following the tradition well established in Tibet by this time, there are stylistic variants that suggest a Chinese interpretation, such as in the depiction of the fine jewels, the more floral quality of the flame and filling patterns of the mandorla, the fluid manner of twisting the fluttering ends of the scarves,[42] the soft hair executed with very fine lines on the prostrate body under Mahakala's feet, and the style of robes of the figure riding a tiger in the lower left corner. This latter figure may be one of the earliest appearances of the Mahakala Vyaghra Vahana (Riding a Tiger).[43] He holds a sword high with his right hand and a skull bowl in his left and supplants the form of two-armed Kartridhara Mahakala (Knife Holder) seen in earlier examples, such as figures 2.7 and 2.11. The other three attendants are the customary Vajrapani in the upper left corner, Ekajati dressed in her white silk blouse in the upper right, and Palden Lhamo in the lower right. Images of the Inner and Outer Retinues are conspicuously lacking. Mahakala himself is a monumentally impressive figure, especially as the painting itself is so large. He has a massive form and all the fearsome ornaments. Nevertheless, he still possesses a softness and mild quality not seen in the paintings by Tibetan artists.

The Museum of Fine Arts painting is representative of the important religious contacts around the first half of the fifteenth century between Tibet and early Ming China, which resulted in mutually influential effects in the Buddhist art of both nations. The first half of the fifteenth century is a high-water mark for Tibetan Buddhism,

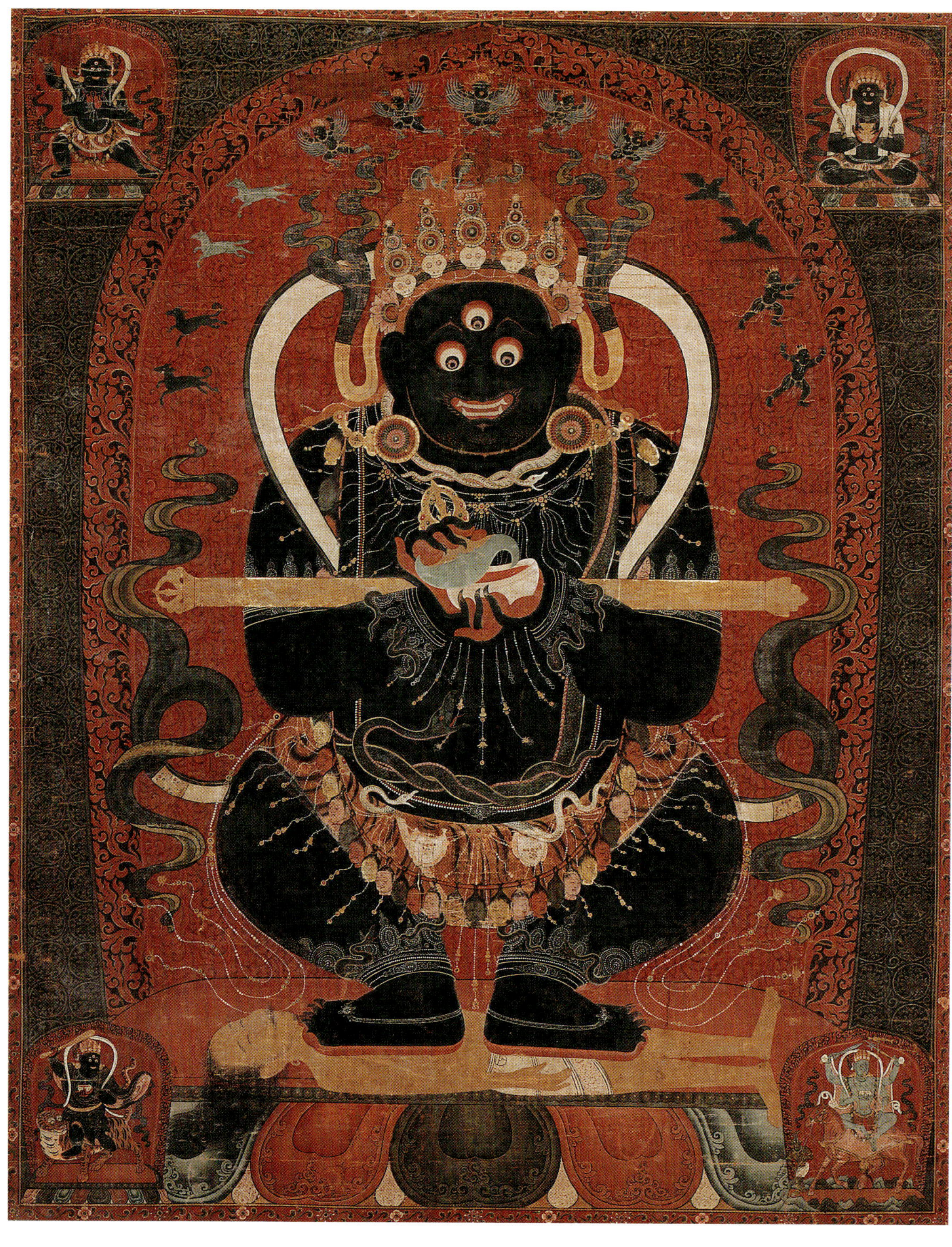

occasioned in large part by the great work of the master Tsongkhapa and the founding of the Gelugpa monasteries around Lhasa and at Tashilhunpo near Shigatse. Buddhist art also reached a crescendo, as witnessed, for example, by the stupendous achievement in the Kumbum at Gyantse in the second quarter of the fifteenth century. The numerous wall paintings and sculptures executed in these monasteries were stimulated by the high quality of the Nepalese artistic tradition and by the contacts with China and its art, which opened up new styles and techniques. These were assimilated by the Tibetan artists, especially in regard to realistic qualities of form and drapery and by the introduction of spatial and landscape elements in painting. The merging of these two powerful influences as they played out in complex ways by various Tibetan artists, such as Menlha Dondrub (ca. 1425–1505, founder of the Menri painting tradition) and Kyentse Wangchug (1420–1500, founder of the Kyenri painting tradition), formed a major turning point and established foundations that profoundly affected nearly all subsequent Tibetan art.[44]

The amazingly patterned Mahakala as Lord of the Pavilion in the Philadelphia Museum of Art (fig. 2.17) probably dates around the second quarter of the fifteenth century. Along with the wall paintings of the Gyantse Kumbum of that same date, the Philadelphia Museum *tangka* represents the culmination of the developments of the Nepalese artistic tradition in Tibetan painting in the central regions of Tibet. The detail of the ornamentation, the cremation grounds at the four corners, the top and bottom rows of numerous lineage and protector images, which are familiar to us from the iconography of the earlier *tangkas* (such as fig. 2.7),[45] reveal the highly advanced decorative concept and painterly skill in this detailed, two-dimensional representation. The brilliancy of color is no less important than the consummate precision of the linear features throughout the painting, which does not slacken for an instant in its heightened intensity of color and pattern used to represent the glorious beauty of these deities of pure visualization.

The Rubin Museum *tangka* of six-armed Mahakala in figure 2.18 is a splendid example from around the third quarter of the fifteenth century. It is generally of the Nepalese artistic lineage, probably executed in central Tibet, but it shows a flexibility in the forms and slightly more humanistic flavor that could suggest influence from the great painters of the time such as Kyentse Wangchug. It is complex and finely detailed, focused on the lively and youthful looking Mahakala while allowing details of great finesse, such as the jewels, flame patterns, shrine pillars, and scrolling arch, to add sophistication and refinement. The five major attendants of this Mahakala's entourage circle around him (clockwise from the lower left): Kshetrapala, the foremost minister on a bear, Jinamitra, Takkiraja, Raudrantika riding a black horse, and four-armed Palden Lhamo riding her pink wild mule. The elegant prone Ganapati (Ganesha) under Mahakala's feet wears a *dhoti* with Nepalese textile patterns typical of this time. The particular foliate tail patterns of the *kinnaras* (half-human, half-bird celestials) on top of the shrine pillars and those flowing from the *nagas* flanking the delicate *kyung* bird at the top are nearly identical to those seen in the wall painting of the Amoghasiddhi Buddha in the Red Temple at Tsaparang under the Guge dynasty, datable to around the third quarter of the fifteenth century.[46] The lotus-petal design also relates to patterns used in the Red Temple, and the bejeweled base has echoes of forms known in the Nepalese-style *tangkas* of the early fifteenth century. The outer borders are filled with tiny, scrolling vine vignettes encircling the lamas, lineage holders of the six-armed Mahakala, Buddhas, and Bodhisattvas, wealth deities (along the bottom), and the "keepers of the ten regions" (five on the lower end of each side).

Facing page: Fig. 2.16.
Mahakala Panjarnata
Tibeto-Chinese, 15th c.
Mineral pigments on cloth; 50 x 36¼ in. (127 x 92 cm).
Museum of Fine Arts, Boston, William Sturgis Bigelow Collection (12.47).

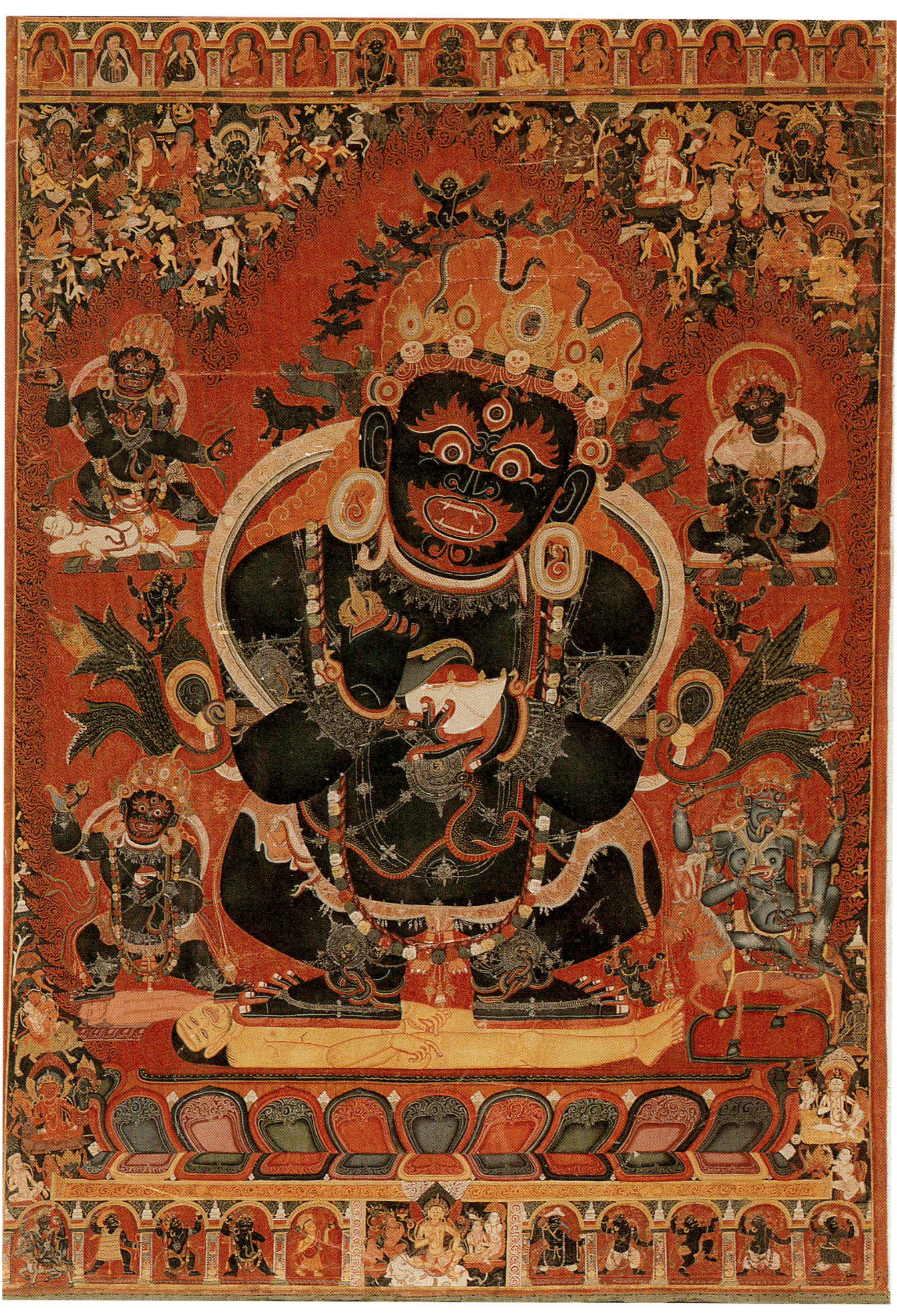

Fig. 2.17.
Mahakala Panjarnata
Central Tibet, Sakya lineage, second quarter of the 15th c.
Mineral pigments on cloth; 38¼ x 26¾ in. (97.2 x 67.9 cm).
Philadelphia Museum of Art, Stella Kramrisch Collection (1994.148.638).

Facing page: Fig. 2.18.
Six-armed Mahakala
Central Tibet, third quarter of the 15th c.
Mineral pigments on cloth; 32¼ x 24¾ in. (81.9 x 62.9 cm).
C2002.34.4 (HA 65165).

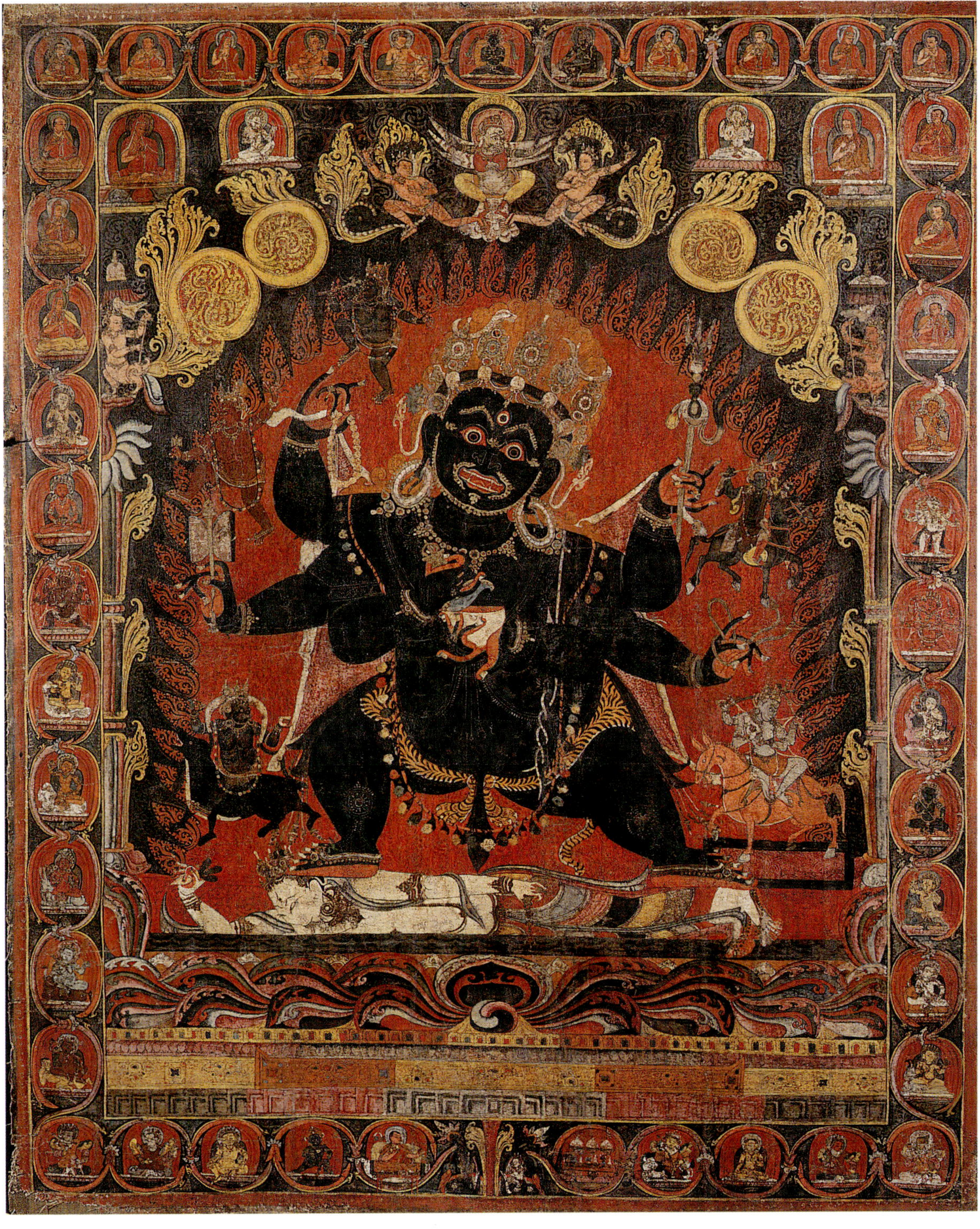

Fig. 2.19.
Two-armed Mahakala
Tibeto-Chinese, ca. mid-15th c.
Gilt bronze; H. 8¾ in. (22.2 cm).
Collection of Marquis de la Willa de San Andres, Spain.

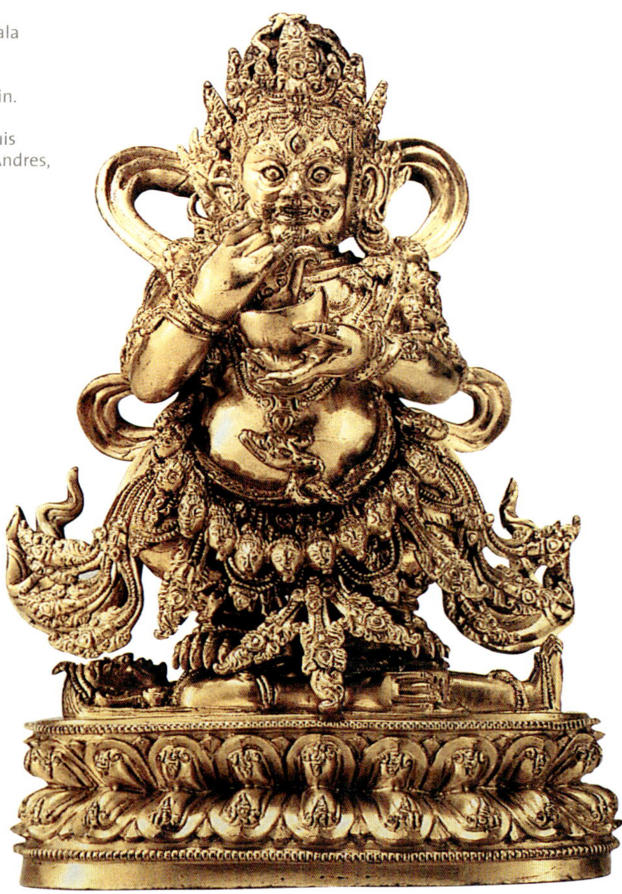

In sculpture, the Tibeto-Chinese[47] examples of the Yongle (1403–24) and Xuande (1425–34) periods of the Ming dynasty (1368–1615) form a major group during the fifteenth century, showing the cross-fertilization tendencies of the time. The Chinese sculptors transformed the Tibetan iconographic forms into a more Chinese interpretation, especially emphasizing rhythmic movements in drapery and ornamentation. Also, typically, the expression is milder and has less sharpness than purely Tibetan works. An example of a fifteenth-century Tibeto-Chinese two-armed standing Mahakala can be seen in figure 2.19. In this gentle rendering he appears almost bewildered and weighed down with excessively elaborate, baroque ornamentation. A small black stone Tibetan six-armed Mahakala in the Rubin Museum (fig. 2.20) may also belong to this same general period, or a bit earlier. Its sympathetic expression imbues the image, somewhat timid and childlike in its stance, with a likable and less grand or heroic aura. The Mahakala Panjarnata and four-armed Mahakala sculptures in the exhibition (cat. nos. 21 and 26) are more typical of the strong realism of much of fifteenth-century Tibetan art. Both show effects of the loose drapery and ornate jewelry that can probably be attributed to Chinese influences occurring at that time and are certainly apparent in the sculptures of the Kumbum at Gyantse around the second quarter of the fifteenth century.

THE SIXTEENTH CENTURY

The large and important Panjarnata Mahakala in the Zimmerman Family collection[48] reveals the tendencies of the late fifteenth into the first half of the sixteenth century. These combined the Indo-Nepalese artistic tradition, which reached its apogée in Tibet in the first half of the fifteenth century, and Chinese elements, which were brought into Tibetan painting by the great artists Menlha Dondrub and Kyentse Wangchug. Kyentse was apparently especially successful in combining the two streams in about equal measure into a style that seems to have served as a model through much of the sixteenth century. While Menlha was known for his peaceful deities, Kyentse was particularly renowned for his wrathful deity portrayals. Landscape becomes a defining change at this time, notably in the paintings of eastern as well as central Tibet. In addition, the Guge dynasty tradition of western Tibet, based largely on the Kashmiri and Indo-Nepalese lineages, lasted well into the sixteenth century, with splendid wall paintings still surviving at Toling monastery, at Tsaparang in the Red and White temples, and at Tabo monastery in Spiti. The six-armed Mahakala in the Los Angeles County Museum of Art shows the consummate style of the Guge Renaissance, which developed during the fifteenth and into the sixteenth century largely under the impetus of the Gelugpa in the region. The painting, which dates to around the second half of the fifteenth century, also shows the inheritance of the Indo-Nepalese artistry, but has the individualistic touches of the western Tibetan region's traditions as well.[49]

Two *tangkas* in the Rubin Museum, probably both from the second half of the sixteenth century, show the effects of the significant changes coming out of the cauldron of the fifteenth century. Figure 2.21 of Mahakala, Lord of the Pavilion of the Sakya tradition, and figure 2.22 of the Mahakala Bernag Chen ("black-cloaked"), the special protector of the Karmapa,[50] who is seen in top center, are both likely to have been painted in eastern Tibet, probably Kham. From the sixteenth century onward this area became a major region for the development of various local schools of Tibetan painting. In both of these *tangkas* the main icon is reduced in size relative to the surrounding space, which begins to resemble our own three-dimensional world, albeit in somewhat simple terms. The element of space and the rudimentary indication of a three-dimensional plane radically change the approach that had been taken in earlier Tibetan paintings that followed the Indo-Nepalese tradition where the icon existed in a basically two-dimensional world. In these sixteenth-century paintings, realism extends to our world as though we coexist with the deities in daily life. This broadens the scope of the images beyond the iconic and brings them into our momentary reality. Although the figures do not lose a spiritual hierarchy and transcendency, they are incorporated easily into our sphere, and we can be expected to assimilate them and all they represent with ease. Rather than the pure beauty of the icon, we now have the reality of the image.

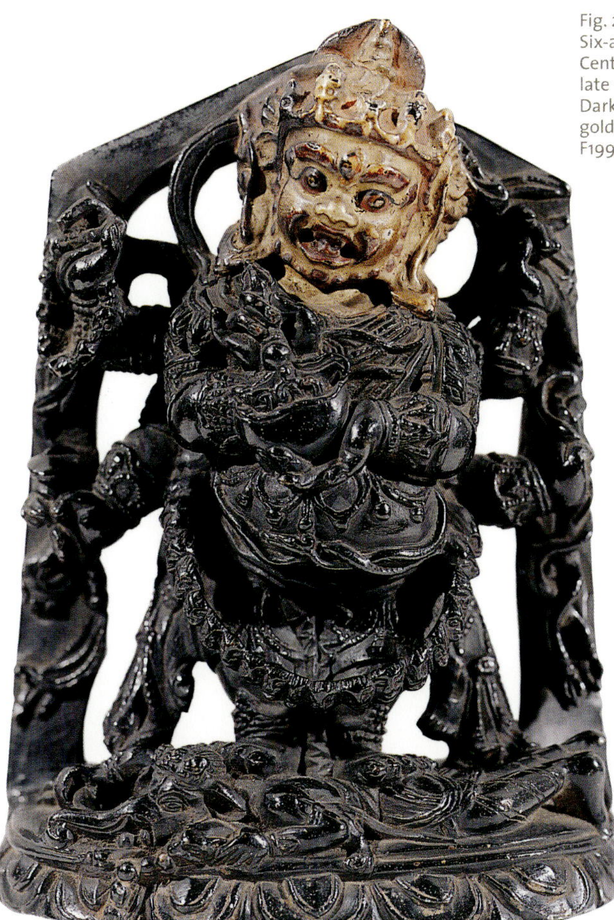

Fig. 2.20.
Six-armed Mahakala
Central or eastern Tibet, late 15th to early 16th c.
Dark gray stone with cold gold; H. 5 1/2 in. (14 cm).
F1997.12.5 (HA 700041).

Though centrally placed with symmetrically arranged figures around him, Mahakala is set back into space in figure 2.21, suggested by the undefined plane of green that imperceptibly fades into the darkish blue of the sky, as if the artist were reluctant to define a clear horizon. Mahakala himself has a simpler rendering than earlier examples; he is without much ornamentation, mainly some snakes and the fluttering ends of his scarf. The embroidered arc of the scarf behind his head is an older feature, but with quite natural floral patterns. His hair is flamelike and a little coarse, without attention being given to piled-up curls as seen earlier. Proportions do not emphasize a large head, but rather a head that is overall more

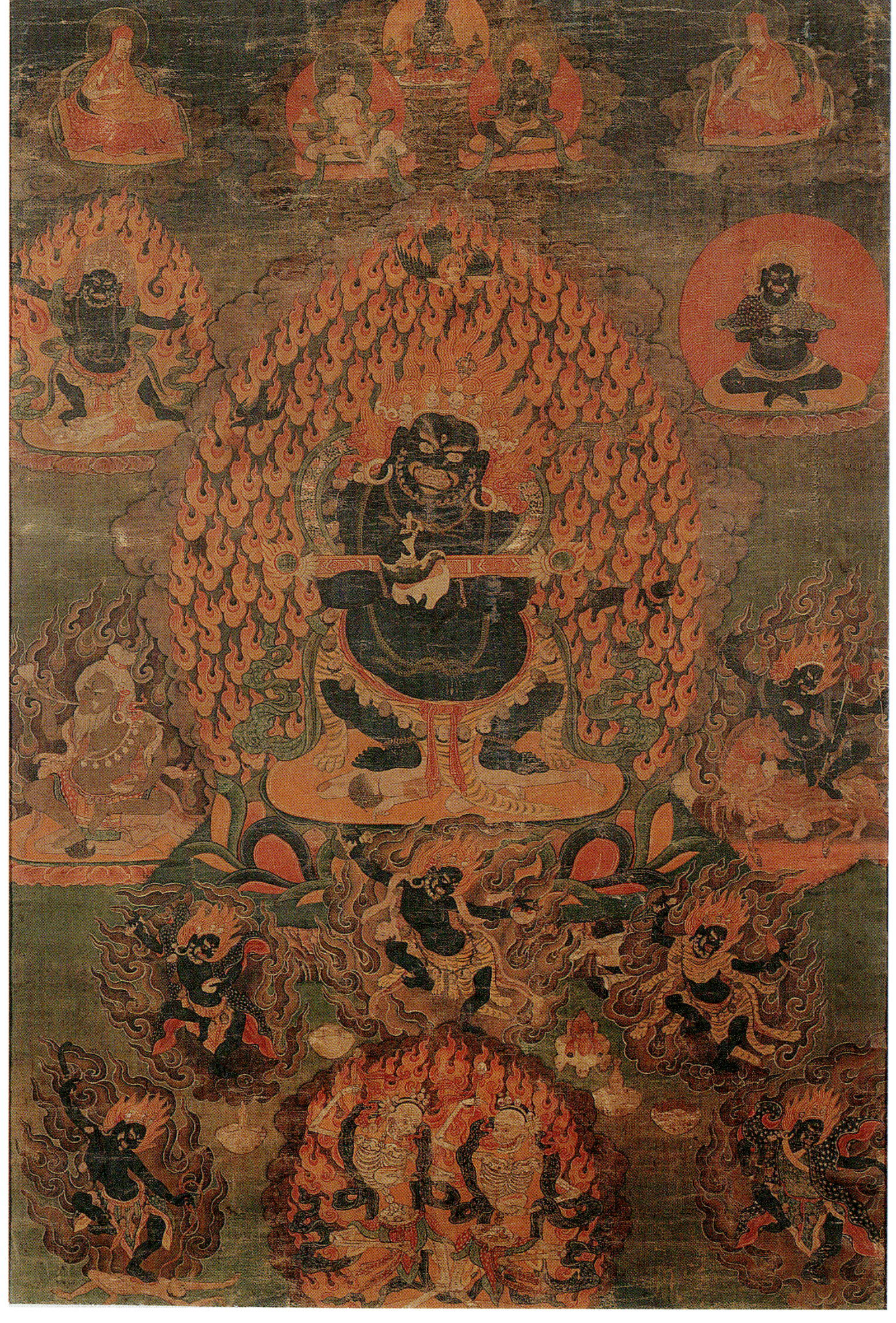

Fig. 2.21.
Mahakala Panjarnata
Central Tibet, second half of the 16th c.
Mineral pigments on cloth; 24 x 16 in. (60.9 x 40.6 cm).
Collection of Shelley and Donald Rubin (HA 312).

normally human in effect. The flames of his mandorla, backed by a smoky billow, are a new type: individually curling flames of strongly orange hue and with modeling lines. The lotus petals are rather plain but have a lyrical rhythm and sense of natural perspective. Some of these elements of naturalism have probably been gradually incorporated since the fifteenth century, partly from Chinese painting as interpreted by the great Tibetan artists who established new directions in Tibetan painting. Though these elements are limited, they nevertheless have a profound effect on the changing modes of Tibetan painting at this time.

The attendant figures now appear to drift individually in the surrounding amorphous space, rather than remain locked into a grid pattern or bound to Mahakala's mandorla. They are supported by dark clouds or lotus pedestals, and the wrathful figures at the bottom all have smoky brown flames outlined in gold. Flanking Mahakala are four major attendants: Ekajati and Palden Lhamo on the right; Bhutadamara Vajrapani and Brahmanarupa (Mahakala in the form of an old Indian Brahman holding a thighbone trumpet) on the left.[51] Interestingly, the Brahmanarupa form of Mahakala, which begins to be seen in Tibetan painting at least by the early fifteenth century, has here supplanted the typical two-armed Knife-Holder form of Mahakala used in most earlier paintings (figs. 2.7, 2.18). Also, the sea of blood under Lhamo's mount has natural eddies rather than the "basketweave" or other abstract patterning of the early styles. Above are two Sakya lamas and in the center is Vajradhara, with two seated figures nearby on the dark clouds.[52] Energizing the lower third of the painting and portrayed more prominently than in any *tangka* we have seen so far are the five prancing *rakshasas* of the Inner Retinue of Mahakala. Conspicuously lacking, however, are the four figures of the Outer Retinue. The five *rakshasas* vigorously dance in a semicircle around a splendid and quite large representation of the pair of dancing skeletons (Chitipati), themselves deities of wisdom and compassion.[53] Their spirited dance and grinning jaws make them seem alive, and their white bones are set off by swirling long blue scarves and orange-red flames backed by brown clouds. As they are normally present in the mandala of Paramasukha Chakrasamvara, they possibly indicate that association in this *tangka*. The whole painting is a clear and effective representation of the icons presented in a new way, completely distinct from earlier versions, as seen in figures. 2.2, 2.7, 2.11, and 2.17.

The *tangka* in figure 2.22 of the dwarf Mahakala wearing a black cloak and holding chopper and skull bowl that contains three hearts, uses much the same compositional technique but adds more details of landscape, including a river and blue-leaved tree. Only indications of the horrific cremation grounds appear: with a jackal eating a corpse; a couple of birds; and a growling tiger at the left, near the river where a serpent deity (*naga*) emerges in homage. A jackal barking at a big blue snake entwined around a tree appears opposite at the right. Below are three fierce forms in Mahakala Bernag Chen's entourage, two also with black robes. In the lower left riding a goat is Damchen Garwai Nagpo, holding hammer and blacksmith's bellows. In the center the protector on a dark horse holds a victory banner and stick. The third, in the right corner holding a skull-topped wand and skull bowl, wears a white robe and appears with a red female. Black spiky flames surround this pair as they each stride on a corpse lying on the rocky cliff. The two black-cloaked figures have orange flames, and their mounts ride through gray clouds. In the upper reaches of the *tangka*, in the center, is the Black Hat Karmapa, flanked on the left by the archetype Guhyasamaja Father-Mother (*yab-yum*) and Danda Mahakala (with club) in a black robe, and on the right by red Shadakshari, Vajrapani, and the wealth god, Vaishravana, sitting on a white snow lion.

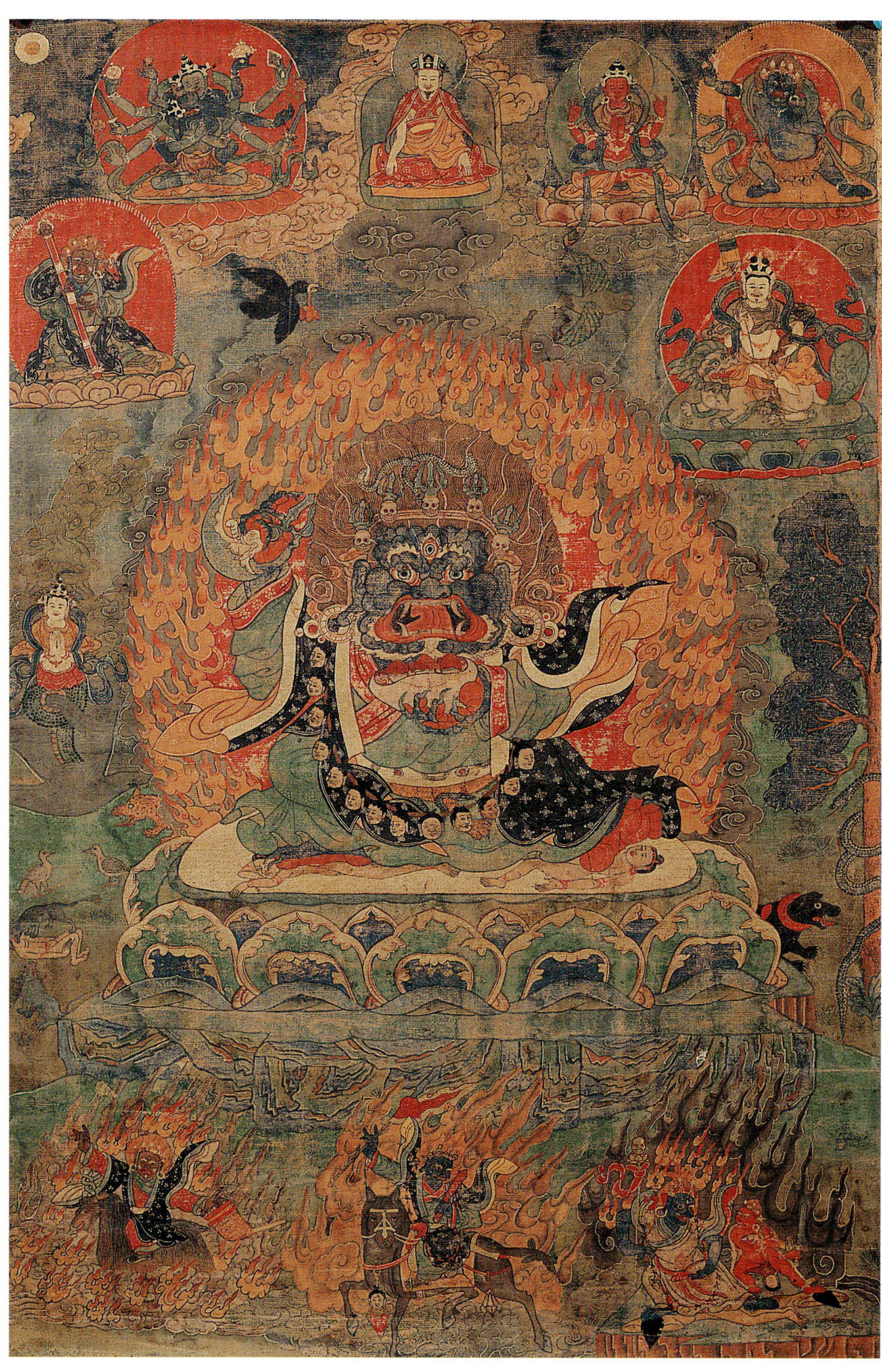

Fig. 2.22.
Mahakala Bernag Chen (black-cloaked)
Central or eastern Tibet, second half of the 16th c.
Mineral pigments on cloth; 22 1/2 x 15 3/4 in. (57.2 x 40 cm).
Collection of Shelley and Donald Rubin (HA 706).

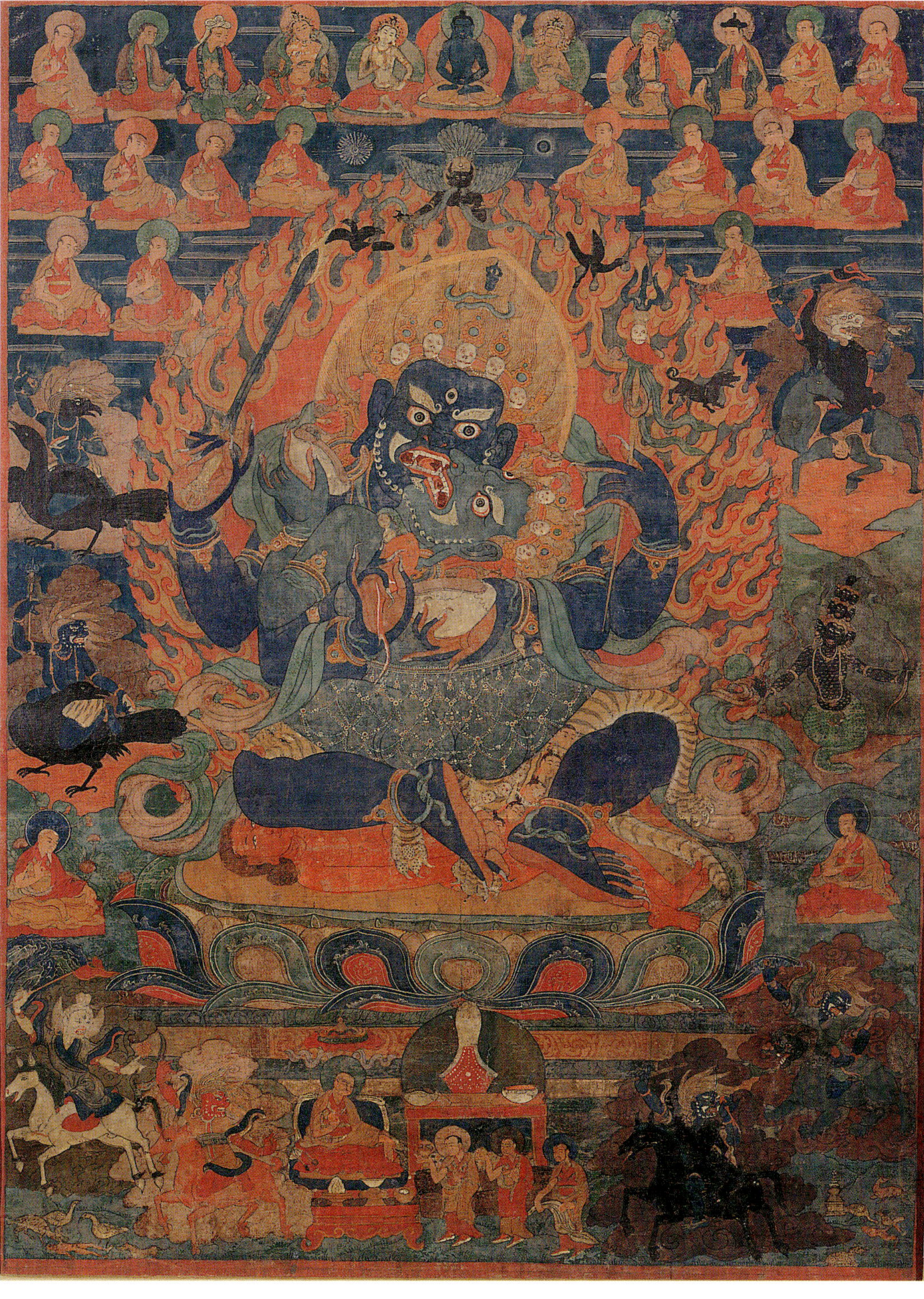

Fig. 2.23.
Four-armed Mahakala
Father-Mother (*yab-yum*)
Central or eastern Tibet,
late 16th to early 17th c.
Mineral pigments on
cloth; 28 1/4 x 20 1/2 in.
(71.8 x 52.1 cm).
F1997.11.1 (HA 170).

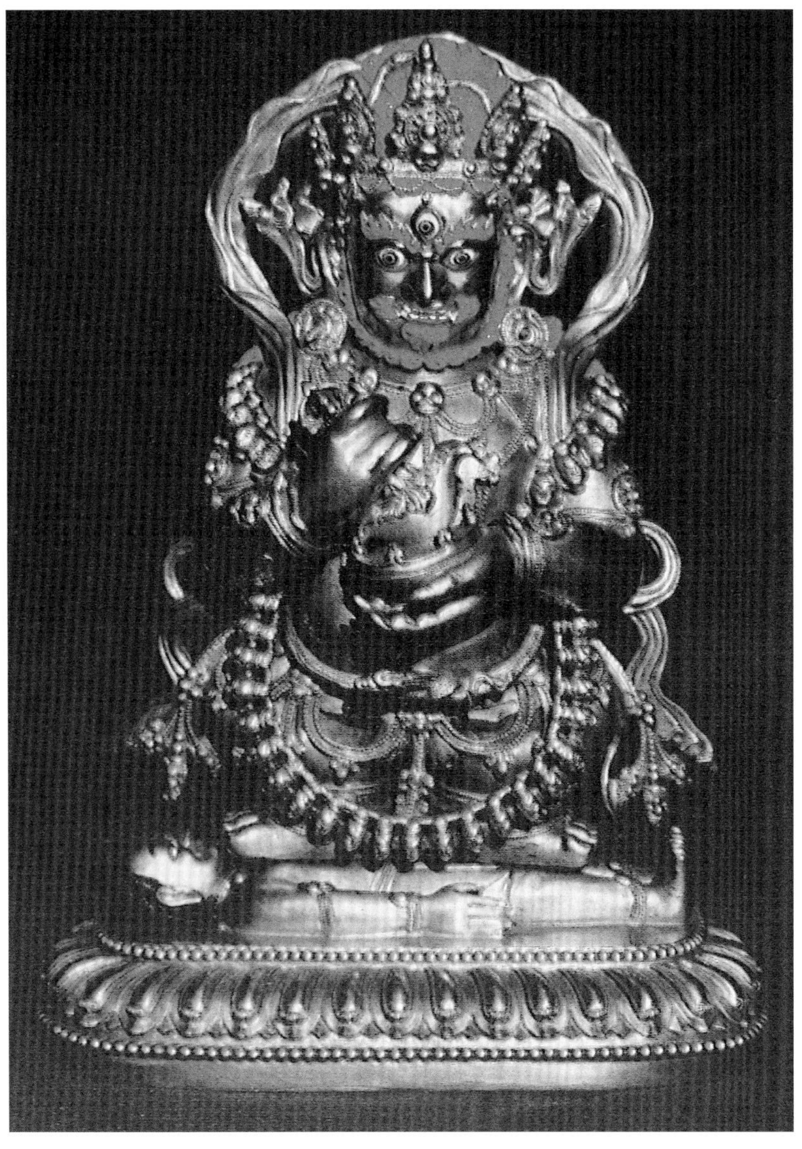

Fig. 2.24.
Two-armed Mahakala (possibly Panjarnata)
Central Tibet, Sakya monastery, 16th c.
Gilt bronze with pigments; dimensions not provided.

As interesting as the landscape and attendant figures are, all focus returns to the bizarre form of the central black-cloaked Mahakala whose lumpy blue-gray face and dwarfish body create quite an impressive and riveting figure, standing on an emerald green and blue lotus pedestal that is lifted aloft by a layer of pale blue rocks. His robes use angular lines, a feature adopted from well-known techniques in Chinese paintings since the Song dynasty (960–1279) and standard style in the Ming dynasty (1368–1644). A flurry of movement and energy is provided by the floppy sleeves and the sizzling, spiky orange flames, but the dominant focus is on the huge monsterlike face directly in the center of the painting. The exaggeration of the features and imaginative craggy "landscape" of his face with its cavernous jaws, giant tongue, and fanlike spread of hair, create a stunningly unique and personalized vision of this Mahakala.

The Rubin Museum *tangka* in figure 2.23 presents a massive, blue four-armed Mahakala, protector of Vajrayana Buddhism. He sits in relaxed pose in the *yab-yum* form in union with his lighter blue two-armed "wisdom" female. Though it is the same four-armed Mahakala as seen in figure 2.1, this later example in *yab-yum* form represents increased powers. This *tangka* probably dates to the late sixteenth or early seventeenth century. There is a split (one side lower than the other) but clear ground/sky demarcation and thin, solid horizontal clouds in the sky. The former is a technique used in sixteenth-century Chinese painting to create tension. The latter motif appears descended from fifteenth-century renderings such as appear in the Gyantse Kumbum wall paintings. The flame mandorla is rather bold, and the main figures are broad and powerful compared with the more delicate images in the previous two *tangkas.* As there is a portrayal of Padmasambhava in the top row of figures above, this work is probably Nyingma, which favors the practice of the four-armed Mahakala.[54] Attendants along the left side are a bird-headed figure (possibly the raven-headed Lekyi Gonpo) as well as a fierce figure, both riding crows; on the right is a lion-headed protector on a horse and nine-headed Rahu with snake body. On each side below them, on greensward flanking the pedestal, is a peacefully seated lama. At the bottom center is a table with offerings to Mahakala. In front are three standing disciples approaching a seated teaching lama who has an offering table in front of him. At the far right is a *yaksha* protector mounted on a snow lion. Three other fierce protector figures mounted on horses of the same color as themselves dash toward the left. This *tangka* is a superb example of the *yab-yum* four-armed Mahakala dating prior to the period when this icon becomes prevalent in the black-*tangka* form of representation.[55]

The sleek, gilded two-armed Mahakala sculpture in figure 2.24 is at the Sakya monastery in Tsang.[56] It appears to be a sculpture from around the late sixteenth or early seventeenth century.[57] He has a similar boldness and static quality of form as seen in the *tangka* in figure 2.23. A creased scarf with fluttering edges lifts up behind his head and frames him at the sides. Fluttering edges have here supplanted the stiff arc form of the scarf, part of the trend toward naturalism that continued to develop after the fifteenth century. The figure is further stabilized by the garland of insistently regular, closely packed, severed heads. This frontal Mahakala appears rigid, majestic, concentrated and determined with a powerful and somewhat smooth form, quite different from the sculptures of the fifteenth century in figures 2.19, 2.20, and catalog number 21.

THE SEVENTEENTH CENTURY

The magnificent, dramatic Mahakala Maning (Black Eunuch) in figure 2.25 stretches boldly across the width of the painted canvas against a superbly rendered red flaming mandorla that seems pocked with swirling holes like a meteorite. In this form he is protector of the Nyingma traditions, and it is likely that the two lamas floating on clouds in the upper part of the painting are Nyingma. Here Mahakala holds a trident with victory banner aloft and grasps a fresh heart in his left hand, which also holds a noose. A huge ornamented club is thrust through his gold and leather-skin belt. His black silk cloak and dark green robes have delicate gold flower designs and geometric ornamental bands and borders. Iron-black snakes slither from the stiff semicircular fan of his gold-strand hair. Golden bracelets and earrings, gold-rimmed boots, and crown add glamour to the form. His face is broad and big and his features continue the gold and red markings that create shimmering color against the darkness dominating the painting. The pedestal, simple in form, by its sheer size serves as a colorful platform for the great black wrathful one. Other figures, though reduced in size, show the same energy and sense of balance in composition. The dark, moonless landscape—islands of jagged brown rocks with dark green tops and brownish lavender smoke and clouds—adds a somber mood to the *tangka*. At the apex is a wrathful red two-armed Hayagriva and in the lower right corner another wrathful red figure wearing a tiger skin. In the lower left corner is a fierce black-cloaked figure, possibly a form of Mahakala, shooting a bow and arrow and crooking a trident in his right elbow as he wildly rides a speeding black horse.[58] This *tangka* has landscape elements consonant with painting of the late sixteenth to early seventeenth century. The realism of the robes with pointed flaring hems and convincingly wrathful face also seems to reflect the continued interest in elements of naturalism in the early seventeenth century.

The two *tangkas* in figures 2.26 and 2.27 of the Panjarnata Mahakala in the Rubin Museum, both probably of the seventeenth century, more exactly fit the category of black *tangkas*, which rose to their height as a genre in the seventeenth and eighteenth centuries.[59] The black *tangka* is a special form of painting with its dark cosmic space emanating figures that seem to glow with ephemeral brilliance. It is especially used for depictions of the *tantric yidam* and protectors, such as Mahakala. In this type of painting, line drawing is of the essence, and the

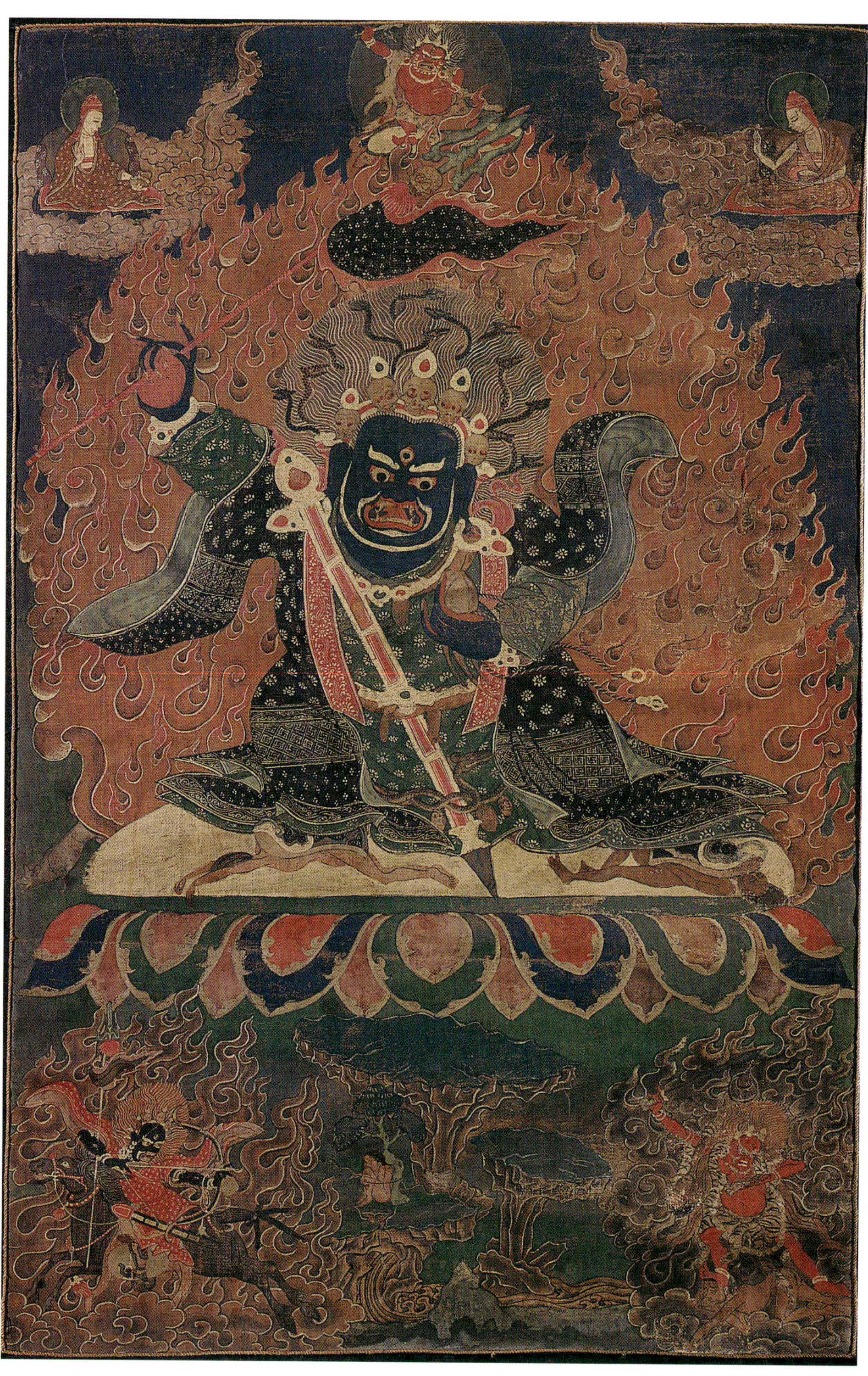

Fig. 2.25.
Mahakala Maning
(Black Eunuch)
Central Tibet, late 16th to early 17th c.
Mineral pigments on cloth; 22 x 14 in.
(55.9 x 35.6 cm).
C2002.26.2 (HA 65131).

brilliance of some colors, such as gold and red as in figure 2.26, probably a painting from the first half of the seventeenth century, or the beauty of blues and greens as in figure 2.27 of the second half of the same century, enhances the dazzlingly transcendent effects.

In figure 2.26 the gold and orange-red colors carry the painting while the large *gandi* (gong) and floral-patterned, arc-shaped flying scarf draw attention to Mahakala, whose facial features reflect the seventeenth-century interest in delicate lines and in breaking up harsh patterns, such as the wispy form of the facial hair, a feature already seen in the sixteenth century in figures 2.21 and 2.23. The flaming mandorla also displays the emerging predilection for using individualized, coiling flames. The entourage of figures drifts discreetly, almost in the shadows. A Hevajra *yab-yum* appears in the upper right corner, a Heruka Vajrabhairava in the left corner and two Sakya lamas flank Vajradhara in top center. A Brahamanarupa is again one of the four main attendants (as in figure 2.21), and at the bottom, instead of the five *rakshasas* of the Inner Retinue, we see three wealth gods: a relatively early appearance of the six-armed White Mahakala (the wealth aspect of the six-armed Mahakala); Yellow Jambhala, the wealth god with jewel-spouting mongoose, and his black, esoteric form (Krishna Jambhala); and lastly, in the right corner, the pair of dancing skeletons. Four little figures of the Outer Retinue can be found in and about the painting: the warrior appears at mid-left, the monk is at mid-right, the mantra holder wearing a Mahakala face on his apron is near White Mahakala, and the "dark" woman (here she is red) stands near the skeleton couple.

Figure 2.27 is a superb black *tangka* of Panjarnata, more beautifully colored in pastel shades than figure 2.26. Also, Mahakala has flying strands of wispy hair and the mandorla has a more pronounced archlike shape, with the flames approaching the patterning that becomes standard in the New Menri artistic school by the eighteenth century.[60] The great clarity and simplicity of this *tangka* mark it as a splendid example of the stage of the black-*tangka* art that occurred in the second half of the seventeenth century, probably during the period of the Fifth Dalai Lama (1617–82).[61] The surrounding figures float like isolated islands in the void, and only touches of clouds and mountains appear in the corners to anchor the scene to the reality of our world. The assortment of attendants, always interesting and changing in some ways from *tangka* to *tangka*, here present the five *rakshasas* dancing in a semicircle around the red warrior *dharmapala* protector, Begtse, at the bottom. At the top are Vajradhara (center), Brahmanarupa (left), and Ekajati (right). At the sides are White Mahakala and the skeleton couple on the left and on the right are two forms of Palden Lhamo. The four members of the Outer Retinue appear as small figures close to Mahakala: the lunging warrior and dark woman on the left and the monk and mantra holder on the right side. Other black *tangkas* in the Rubin Museum help to define the seventeenth century in this genre. They reveal the sublime beauty of well-ordered icons presented with delicate, fluid linearity and deep, smoldering, subdued color that projects an intense but not wild beauty from the cosmic spaces.[62]

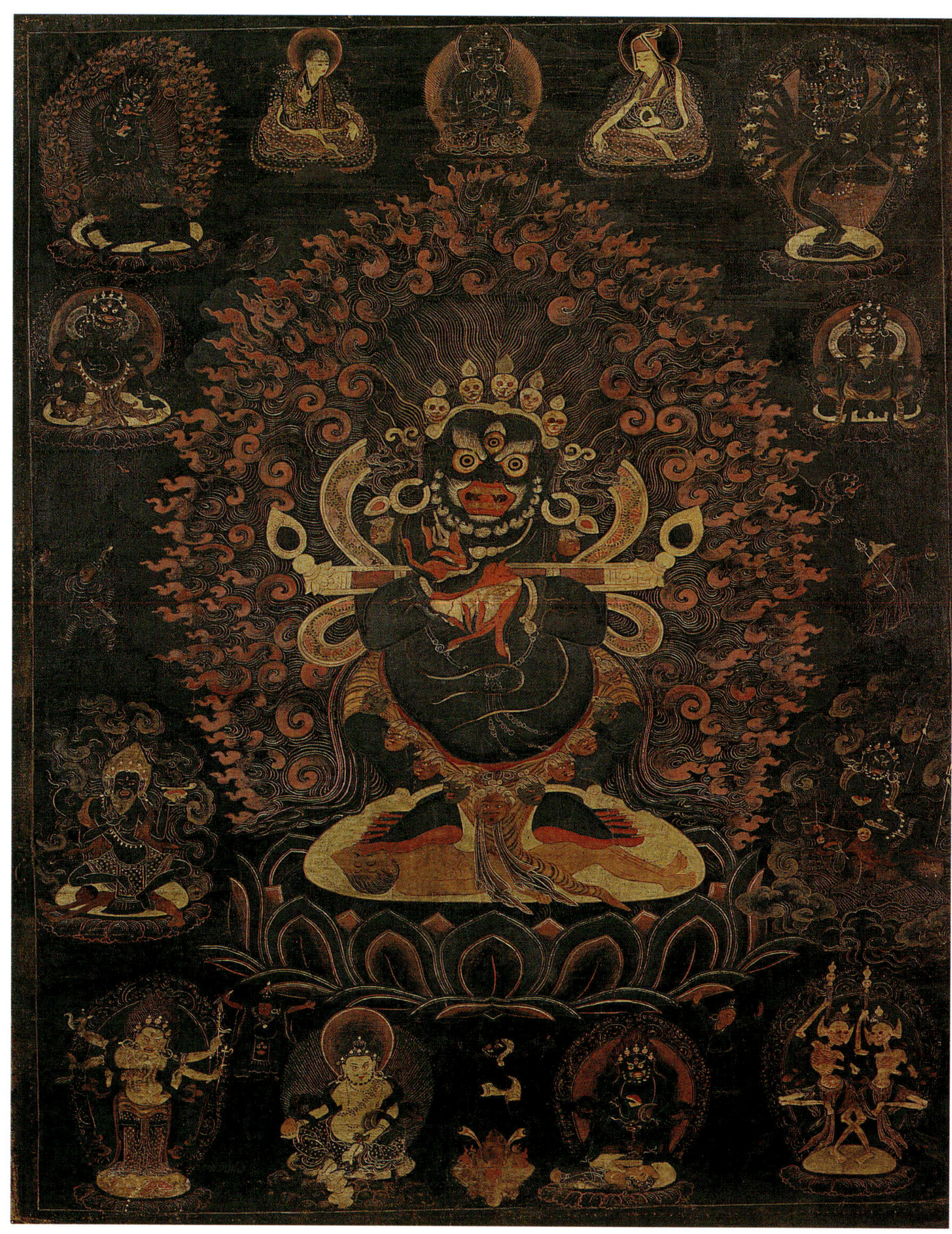

Fig. 2.26.
Mahakala Panjarnata
Central Tibet, first half of the 17th c.
Mineral pigments on cloth; 25 x 19¼ in. (63.5 x 48.9 cm).
F1998.15.1 (HA 649).

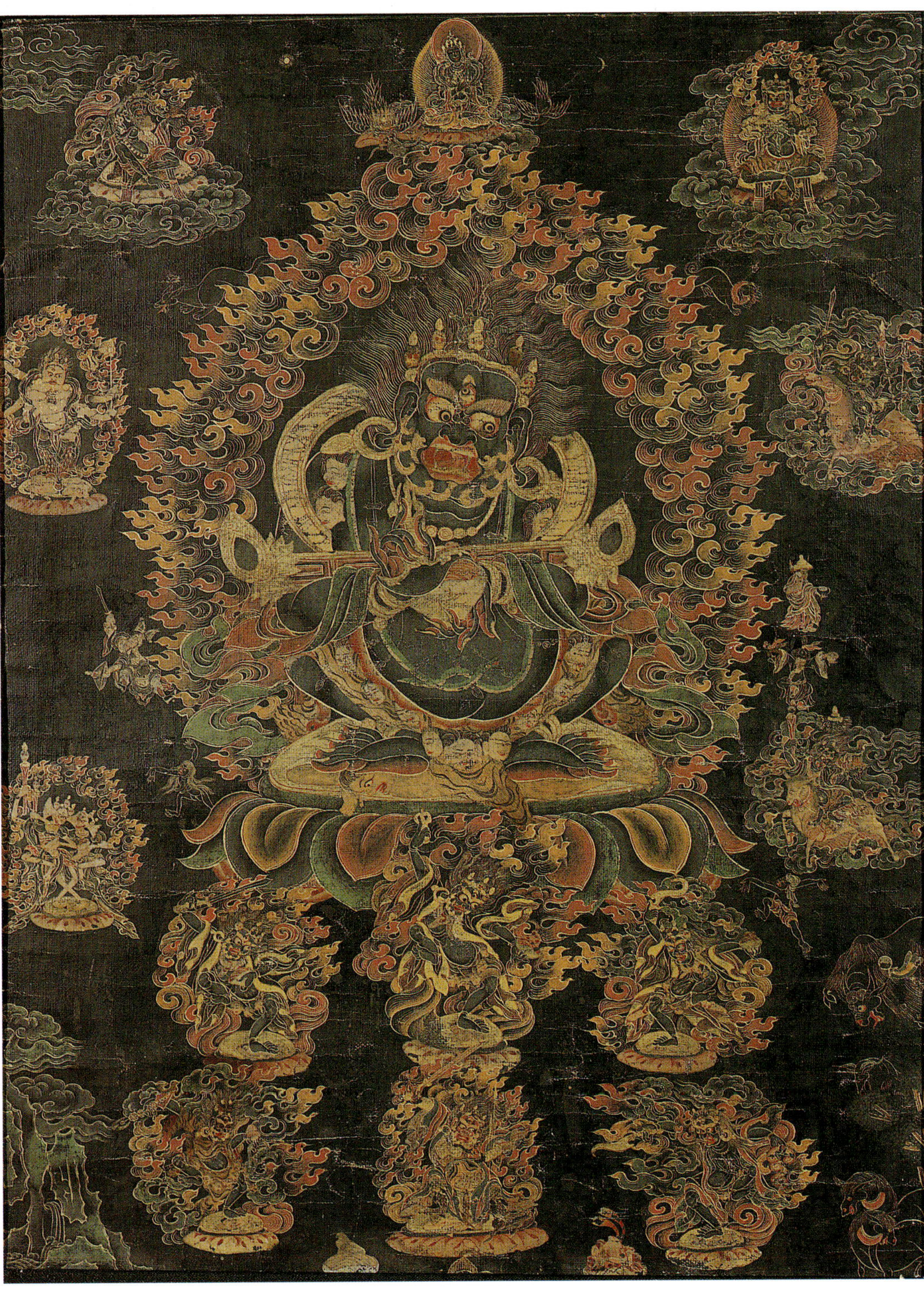

Fig. 2.27.
Mahakala Panjarnata
Central Tibet, second half of the 17th c.
Mineral pigments on cloth; 19½ x 14¼ in. (49.5 x 36.2 cm).
Collection of Shelley and Donald Rubin (HA 92).

MAHAKALA IN THE LATER PERIODS

THE EIGHTEENTH AND NINETEENTH CENTURIES

The evolution of the black *tangka* in the eighteenth century was a marvel of ingenuity by the artists in this genre, which reached its height at this time. The two Panjarnata Mahakalas in figures 2.28 and 2.29 in the Rubin Museum collection take us into that evolving realm. Figure 2.28 of the late seventeenth or early eighteenth century appears to be part of a set, of which the Rubin Museum also has the Palden Lhamo, while the Museum der Kulturen, Basel, has the Begtse (formerly in the Essen collection).[63] This *tangka* shows developments from the great Gelugpa six-armed Mahakala of the second half of the seventeenth century formerly in the Tucci and Ellsworth collections.[64] In figure 2.28 the effects of increased coloration, especially white, produce a less ephemeral and mysterious effect than the earlier *tangka* (fig. 2.26). We can feel the firmer reality of the figures including the cluster of Sakya lamas beside the central Hevajra, small members of Mahakala's Outer Retinue peeking out from his coiling flame mandorla, and three handsome groups at the bottom—dancing Chitipati (the skeleton couple) and Palden Lhamo on either side of a prominent six-armed White Mahakala (Shadbhuja, Sita), the "wish-granting gem" form of Mahakala. The main image of Mahakala, Lord of the Pavilion, seems burdened by his ornaments, especially the giant heads of his garland, which take on a life of their own, but the *tangka* is masterfully executed and brilliant like an embroidered silken tapestry.

The *tangka* in figure 2.29, on the other hand, probably dating into the late eighteenth or even early nineteenth century, develops a compact density of beautifully executed miniature, but more or less equal-sized surrounding figures. This *tangka* brings in a touch of brilliant green and blue to balance the red, orange, and white colors, an indication that it may originate from the eastern regions, possibly around Derge, which developed this stunning coloring in the nineteenth century. The loss of the dark space in this *tangka*, due to the excess of figures, is compensated by the shimmering effects of all the surrounding figures with their clouds, flames, and pedestals. They comprise a virtual pantheon of images. At the top is blue Hevajra *yab-yum*, two *mahasiddhas* (Virupa and Naropa, left and right, respectively), Naro Dakini and Vajrabhairava, another two *siddhas* and two Sakya lamas. The four main attendants to Mahakala (Bhutadamara Vajrapani, Brahmanarupa, Ekajati and Palden Lhamo) flank the left and right sides. Other figures include the marvelous dancing skeleton pair and the red warrior protector Begtse in the lower left corner. On the lower right side appear Yama and the two-armed form of Palden Lhamo. The five *rakshasas* of the Inner Retinue dance in a frenzy below Mahakala's pedestal. Scattered around them are small offerings, cremation ground items, and tiny renditions of the four figures of the Outer Retinue: the warrior, monk, dark woman, and holder of mantras (wearing a big apron with the face of Mahakala, more vigorously portrayed than the earlier example in figure 2.26). All are depicted in the free-fall space of images of this time, markedly different from the earlier representations on a base-line composition as seen in figures 2.2, 2.7, 2.11, and less prominent than those in figure 2.28, which, however, lacks the five *rakshasas*.

The eighteenth century has an amazing production of black *tangkas* connected to all orders. At this time the stylistic development of the black *tangka* is pushed to its limits in a final flourishing phase. Figure 2.30 is likely to be from the first half of the eighteenth century or a little earlier and figures 2.31 and 2.32 from the second half.

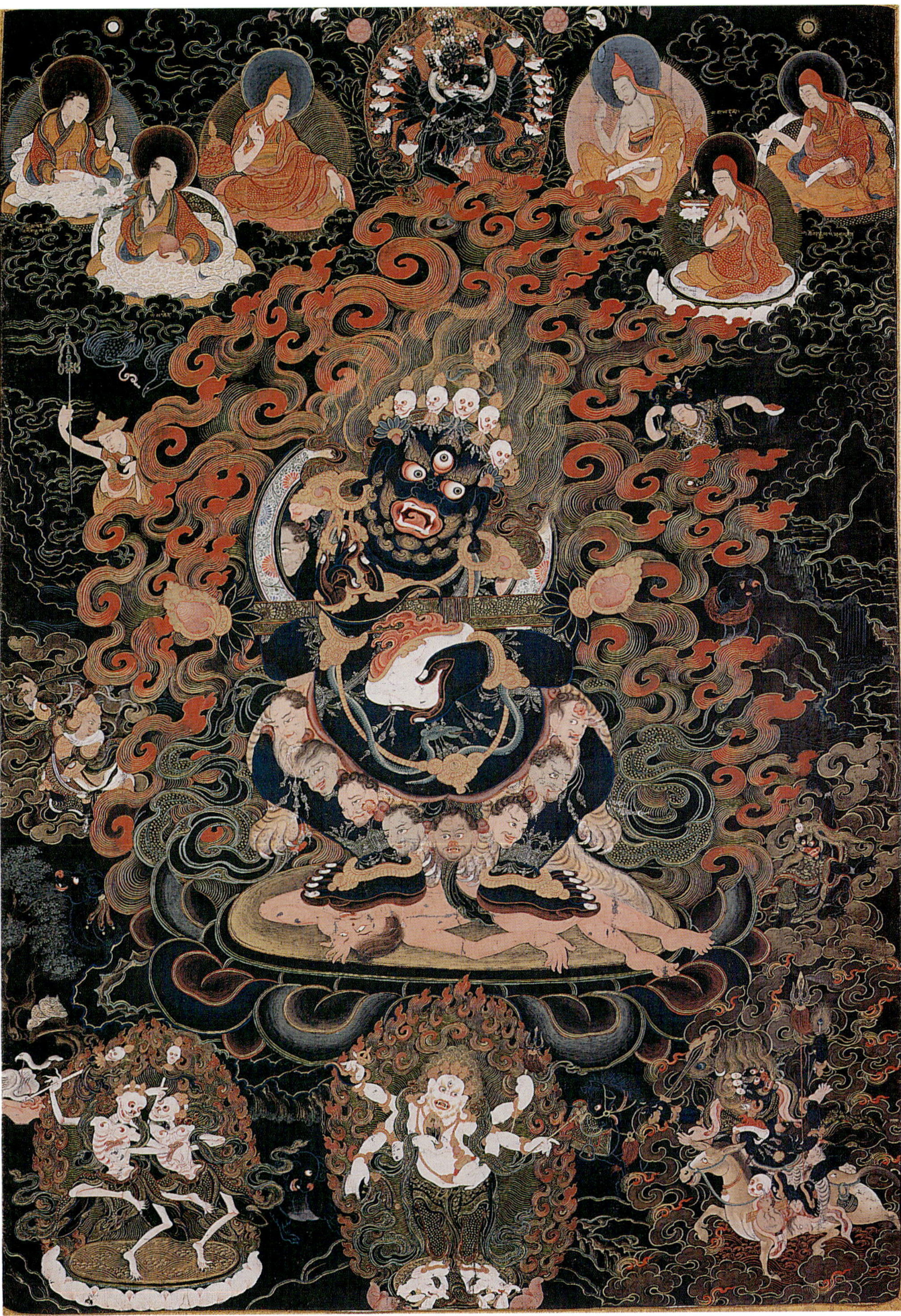

Fig. 2.28.
Mahakala Panjarnata
Central Tibet, late 17th to early 18th c.
Mineral pigments on cloth; 33¾ x 23 in. (85.7 x 58.4 cm).
C2001.1.4 (HA 65004).

Fig. 2.29.
Mahakala Panjarnata
Eastern Tibet (Derge?), 18th to first half of the 19th c.
Mineral pigments on cloth; 28½ x 18 in. (72.4 x 45.7 cm)
Collection of Shelley and Donald Rubin (HA 908).

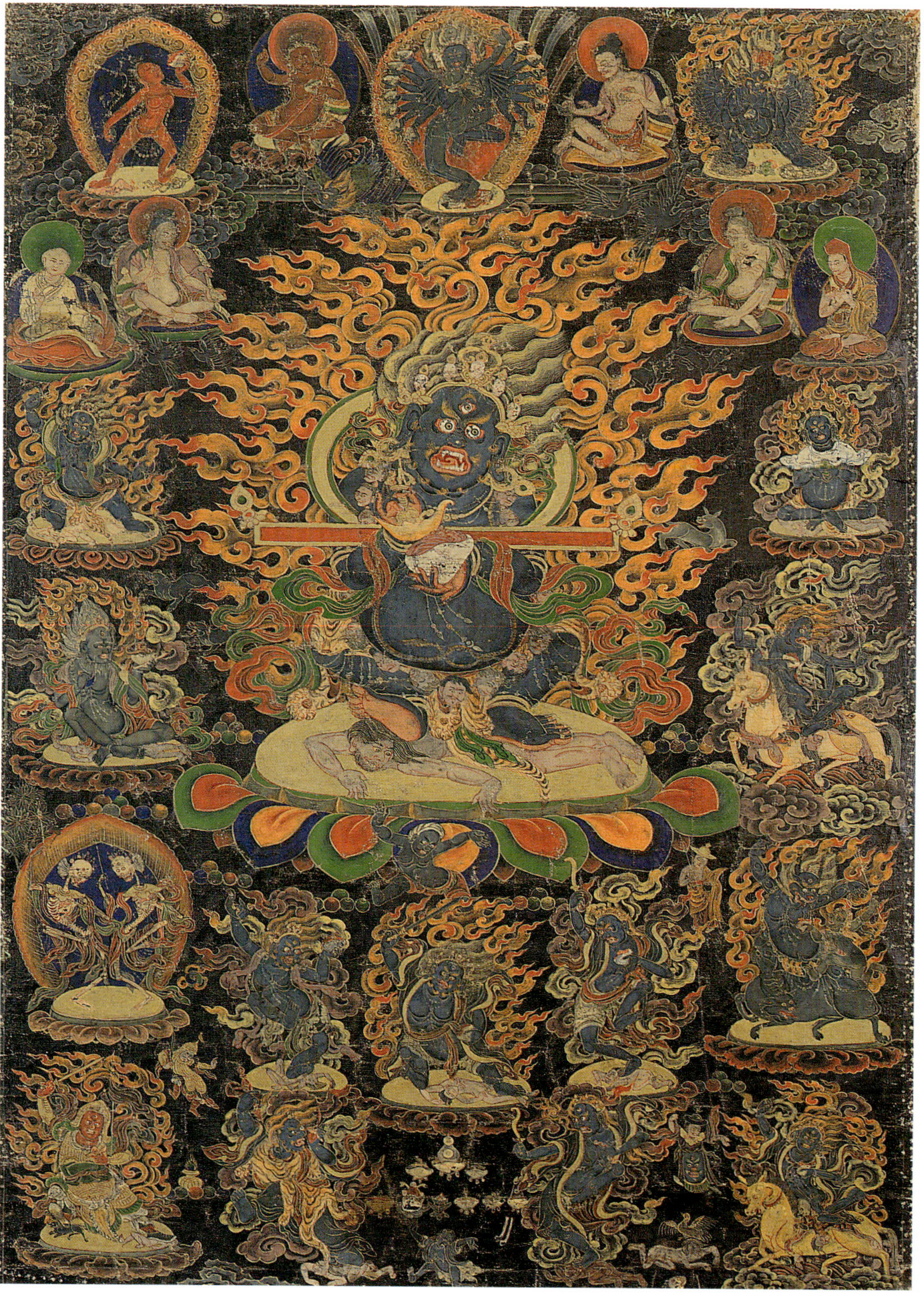

These can represent some of the different forms of Mahakala popular in this period.

The six-armed Mahakala in figure 2.30 is elegant in style. The glowing eyes and mouth of the athletically proportioned Mahakala form the focus—everything else dissolves into golden threads with the lightly touched dark blue mountains and clouds adding some contrast. Though filling the space, one gets caught up in the spider-web delicacy of the various groupings. The four "ministers" of the six-armed Mahakala are present here, as in the earlier tangka in figure 2.12, but they are quite differently portrayed: Takkiraja (right), Jinamitra (left), Raudrantika (in black silk garb holding a lance and skull bowl and riding a horse at the lower right corner), and Kshetrapala (*yaksha* protector of the cemetery, riding the bear in the lower left corner).[65] Two-armed Lhamo and Vaishravana appear right and left just below the main lotus pedestal of Mahakala. Above are two *mahasiddhas* (one likely to be Shavaripa) and a peaceful female deity in the top center. The six-armed Mahakala is an important icon of the Shangpa Kagyu and of the Gelugpa from the fifteenth century.[66]

By contrast, figures 2.31 and 2.32 present a bolder approach, probably consonant with developments in the second half of the eighteenth century. The seated four-armed Mahakala in figure 2.31 is almost swallowed up in the vigorous swirls of gold-red flames and the abstract, surrealistic, imaginative landscape. A small two-armed Paramasukha Chakrasamvara *yab-yum* and two seated lamas are the only other figures in the *tangka*. The black-*tangka* stage is reaching a frenzied climax that propels the whole scene, deity and all, toward the realm of abstraction of dizzying line, a feature also seen in a splendid four-armed Mahakala Father-Mother in *yab-yum* form in the Rubin collection.[67]

More controlled than figure 2.31, the *tangka* of black-robed Mahakala Maning (Black Eunuch) in figure 2.32 has a heightened tension created by steady clusters of attendant figures and the use of horizontal lines in the cloud groups. As also seen in figure 2.29, the surrounding figures are a virtual pantheon of Mahakala and related forms. The somewhat stiff features of the face recall the earlier style physiognomy of Mahakala as seen in figures 2.23 and 2.25, possibly indicating some regional affiliation or a predilection among some Nyingma *tangkas*. Padmasambhava appears in the line of lamas, yogis, and Amitayus Buddha at the top, signifying that this is a Nyingma *tangka*. Compared with figure 2.25 of the late sixteenth to early seventeenth century, there have been remarkable changes from dramatic focus on a powerful figure to the windlike evanescence of the drifting sprays of clouds, fiery auras, and figures that create a truly mystical apparition.

Though the black *tangkas* seem to rule the day in the eighteenth century in terms of depictions of Mahakala and other wrathful deities, new movements in eastern Tibet, especially in Kham during the seventeenth and eighteenth centuries, led to the emergence of important schools of painting, mostly associated with the Karma Kagyu. Notable is the artistic tradition known as the Karma Gardri and that established by Situ Panchen (1700–74) at Palpung monastery in the Derge area of Kham, both of which had an influential impact on eastern Tibetan painting for several centuries.

Figures 2.33, 2.34, and 2.35 illustrate some of the complex variants in eastern Tibetan painting in the eighteenth and early nineteenth centuries. Most of the styles, however, revolve around the use of landscape settings that employ space to a large degree—more so than seen in the sixteenth- and seventeenth-century *tangkas*—while the deity forms, though they remain largely in the styles that had already evolved in earlier centuries, become smaller. For example, the six-armed Mahakala in figure 2.33 is portrayed in rather small scale, set back into the green landscape that stretches to some snow-

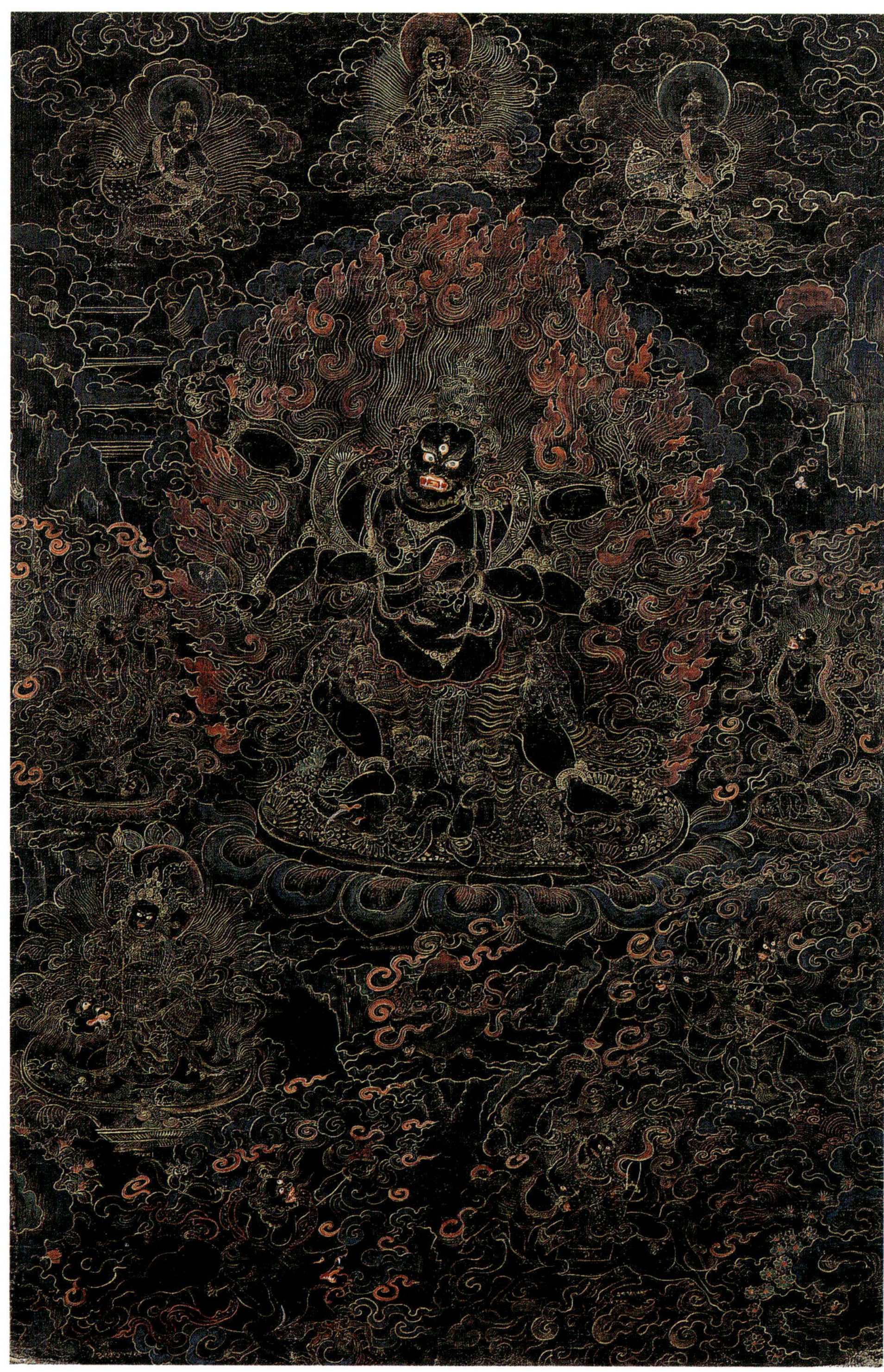

Fig. 2.30.
Six-armed Mahakala
Central or eastern Tibet,
first half of the 18th c.
Mineral pigments on
cloth; 17½ x 12 in.
(55.2 x 36.2 cm).
F1998.15.2 (HA 650).

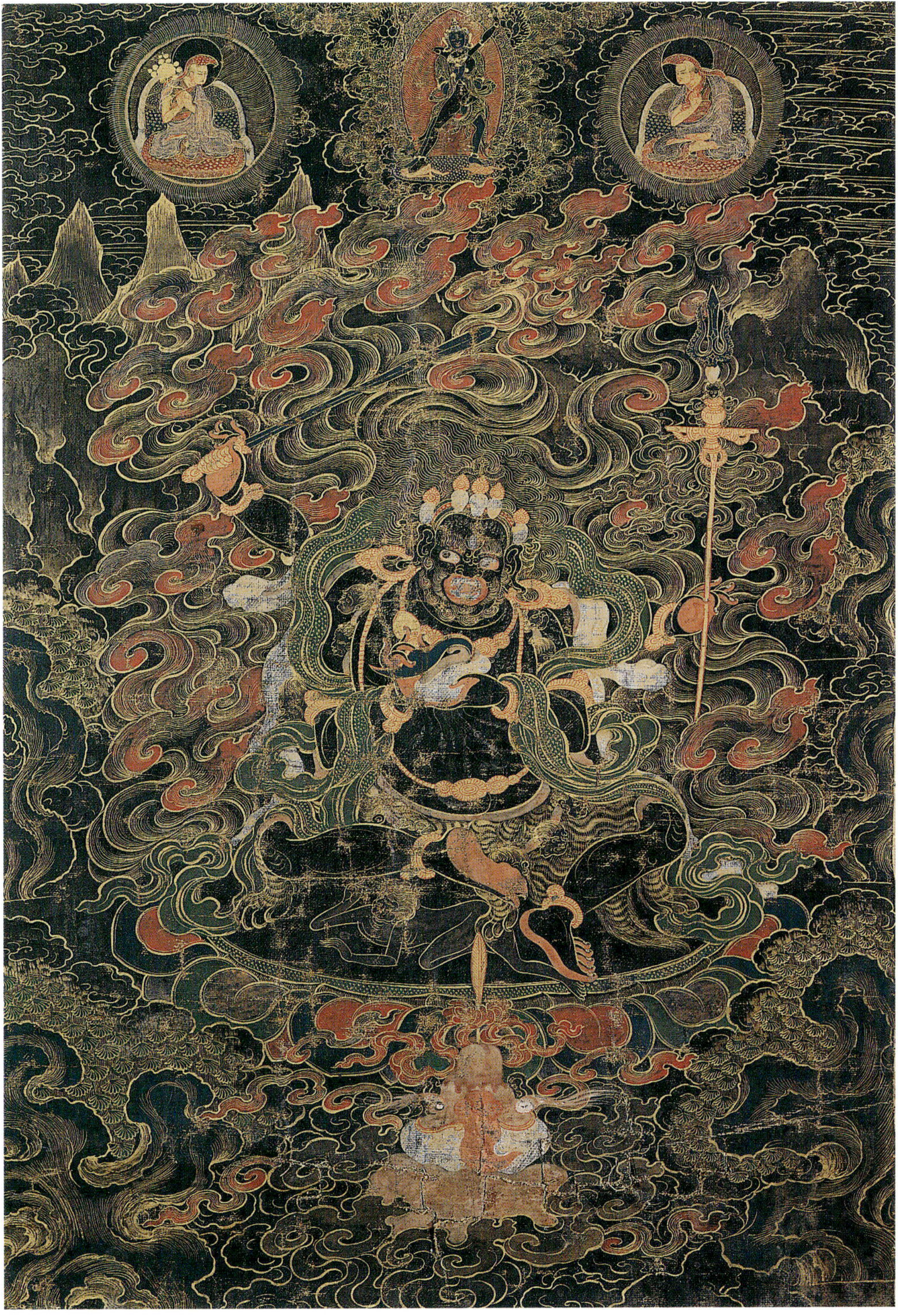

Fig. 2.31.
Four-armed Mahakala
Central or eastern Tibet,
second half of the 18th c.
Mineral pigments on
cloth; 30¼ x 22¾ in.
(44.5 x 30.8 cm).
F1998.1.10 (HA 634).

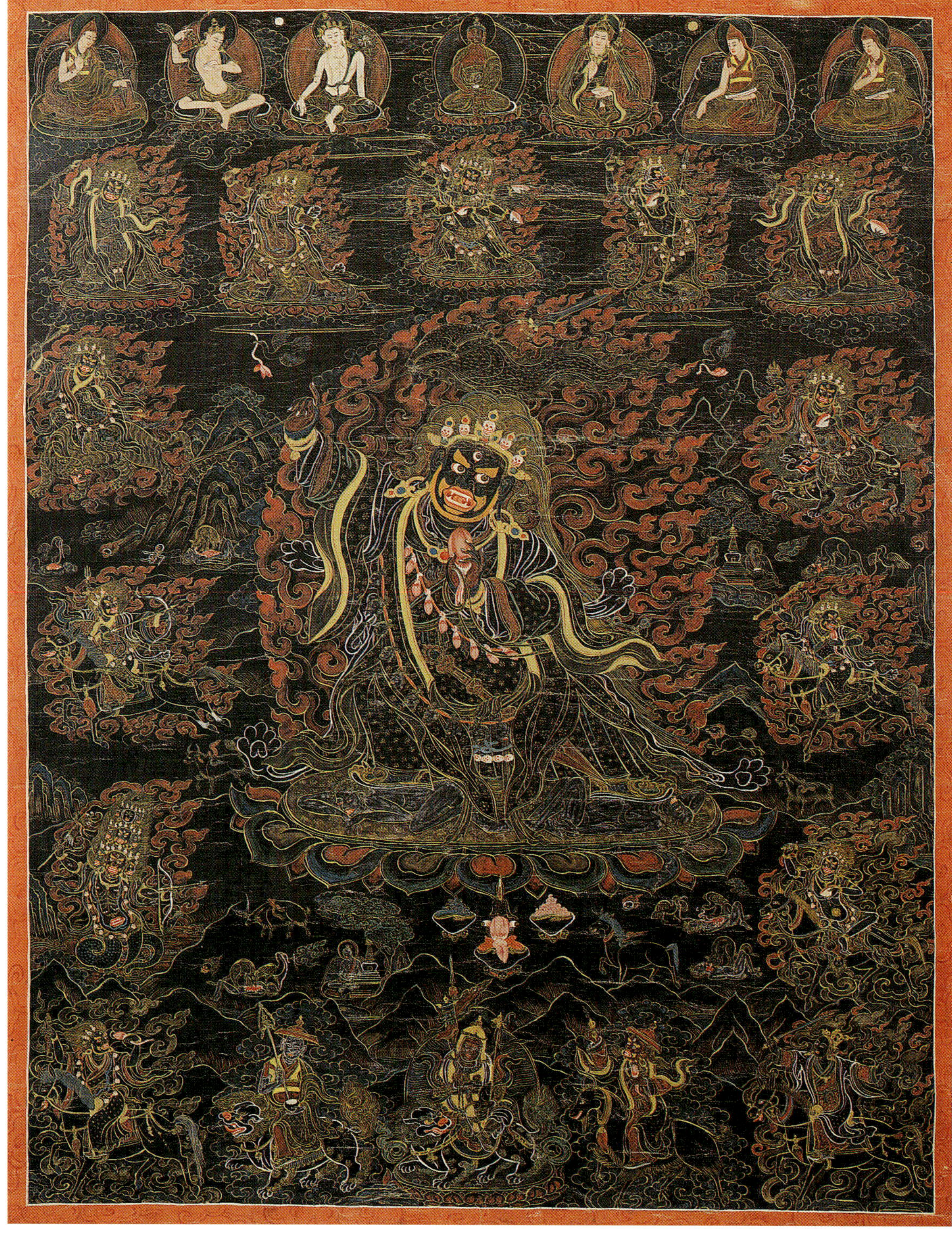

covered peaks near the top edge of the painting. The composition is based on developments already seen in the sixteenth and early seventeenth centuries, but used in a freer manner in this eighteenth- or early-nineteenth-century *tangka* from eastern Tibet. The particular landscape elements appear to be a simplified New Menri style, following the developments in the central regions in the second half of the seventeenth century, especially by the artist Choying Gyatso.[68] At the top of the painting, probably a Gelugpa *tangka*, flanking the Shadakshari Avalokiteshvara are a red Hayagriva and White Mahakala. Down the left side are Vaishravana riding the lion, Jinamitra, and Kshetrapala on a bear. Down the right are Lhamo, Takkiraja, and Raudrantika on a horse with lance and a skull bowl. Below the main Mahakala's lotus pedestal are remnants of cremation grounds, wild yaks, and the "Seven Brothers" riding various beasts and birds.[69] The details are lively and the colors clear and strong, but Mahakala, in becoming more integrated in the setting and closer in scale with other figures in the *tangka*, takes on a rather tamed or subdued appearance, losing the earlier sense of a powerful icon (fig. 2.12) or the shimmering mysteriousness of the black-*tangka* portrayals (fig. 2.30).

In figure 2.34 the landscape has subsumed the deities so that landscape and figures seem closely wedded to one another, creating the interesting illusion of existing naturally in our own world. The landscape is somewhat stylized in its various elements, and it follows the innovations in the depiction of atmospheric space in the school of painting of Situ Panchen in the Derge region of Kham.[70] This is probably a painting from one of the many subschools influenced by the innovations of Situ Panchen that also incorporate elements from Chinese landscape painting, particularly that of the Ming dynasty (1368–1644), such as known in the famous paintings of Qiu Ying (Ch'iu Ying, ca. 1510–51). This painting is quite lovely, using a clear, symmetrical layout of icons and landscape scenes but varying each one to be interesting in its details. The six-armed Mahakala appears set back into the middle-ground area and seems small in size. He is well set off, however, by the spiky flames and puffy clouds of alternating white and lavender. In the golden sky, sharply defined by the horizon line of the river, which one feels is like an ocean without limit, float Vajrayogini, the Black Hat Karmapa, Red Hat Sharmapa, and two attendant lamas. They seem enmeshed in the striations of dark and light horizontal clouds. At the bottom are three protectors: Palden Lhamo on a wild mule (right), and Damchen Garwai Nagpo riding a brown goat and holding hammer and bellows (left). They flank the central dwarf Mahakala Bernag Chen (Black Cloaked), protector of the Karmapa and the same image as seen in figure 2.22, who holds a chopper and skull bowl with a heart.[71] Little piles of jewels, like billiard balls, are found here and there, even in the weathered holes of Mahakala's rocky pedestal. The arrangement of hills in the foreground and midground are skillfully handled to channel our vision into the three-dimensional setting toward the central figure. Interestingly, different clumps of bamboo, trees, and rocks make measured spaces at the far left and right. Overall it is a finely composed work and emits a soothing calm despite the energetic reverberations of the various figures.

The Mahakala Panjarnata in figure 2.35 is also placed in a landscape equally divided between sky and ground, but less attention is given to the landscape and more to the multiple assortment of figures that surround the main image, much like the compositions of the black *tangkas* in figures 2.29 and 2.32. Compared with these, however, the effects of space in figure 2. 35 create a totally different mood; everything seems to exist as a kind of warm tonality. The most exciting element is the beautifully designed and colored flame mandorla of Mahakala. It

Facing page: Fig. 2.32.
Mahakala Maning
(Black Eunuch)
Central or eastern Tibet, second half of the 18th c.
Mineral pigments on cloth; 27½ x 21½ in.
(69.9 x 54.6 cm).
Collection of Shelley and Donald Rubin (HA 878).

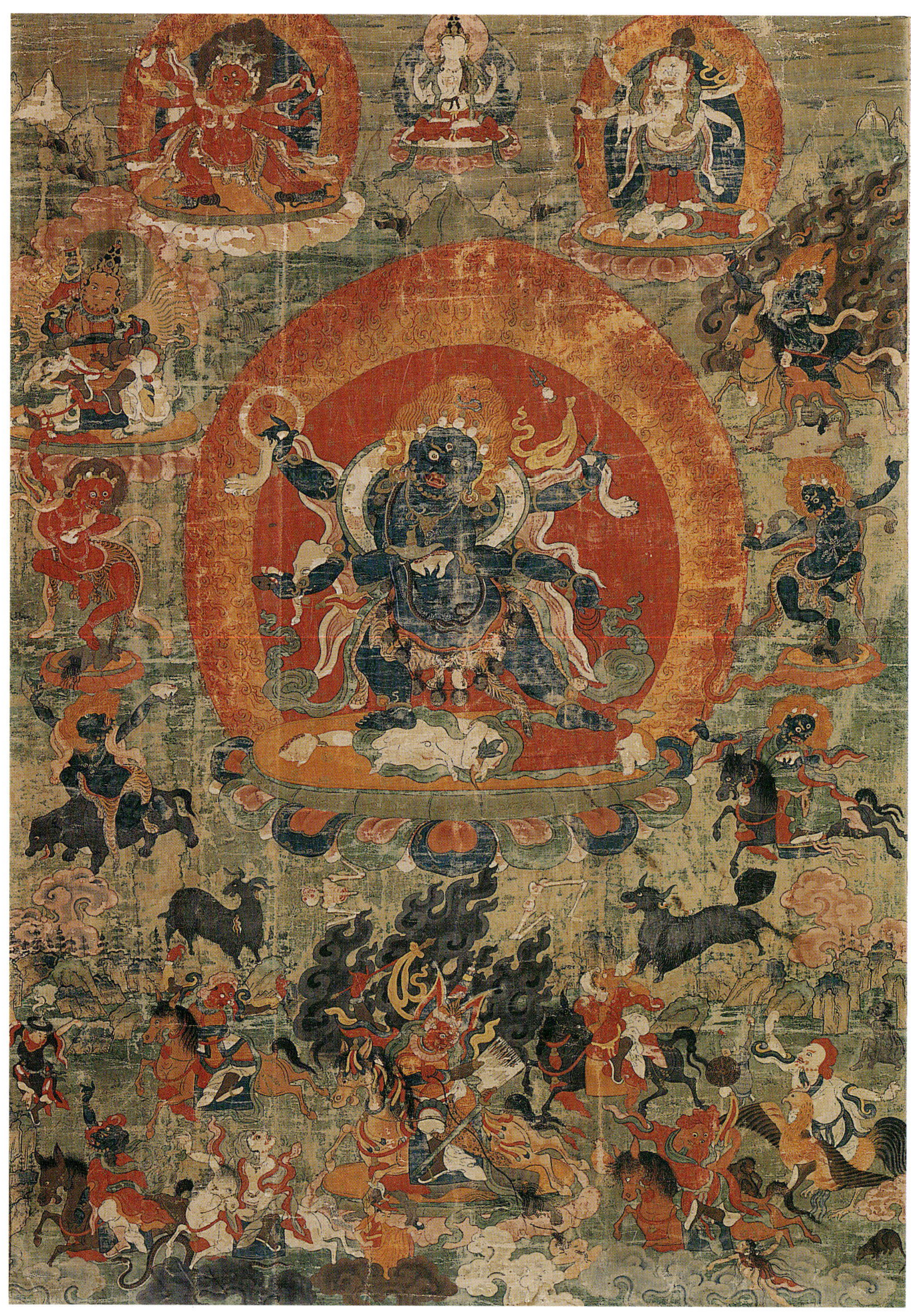

Fig. 2.33.
Six-armed Mahakala
Eastern Tibet, late 18th to early 19th c.
Mineral pigments on cloth; 29 x 19¼ in. (73.7 x 48.9 cm).
Collection of Shelley and Donald Rubin (HA 47).

Facing page: Fig. 2.34.
Six-armed Mahakala
Eastern Tibet, first half of the 19th c.
Mineral pigments on cloth; 22¼ x 18½ in. (56.5 x 47 cm).
F1996.16.8 (HA 465).

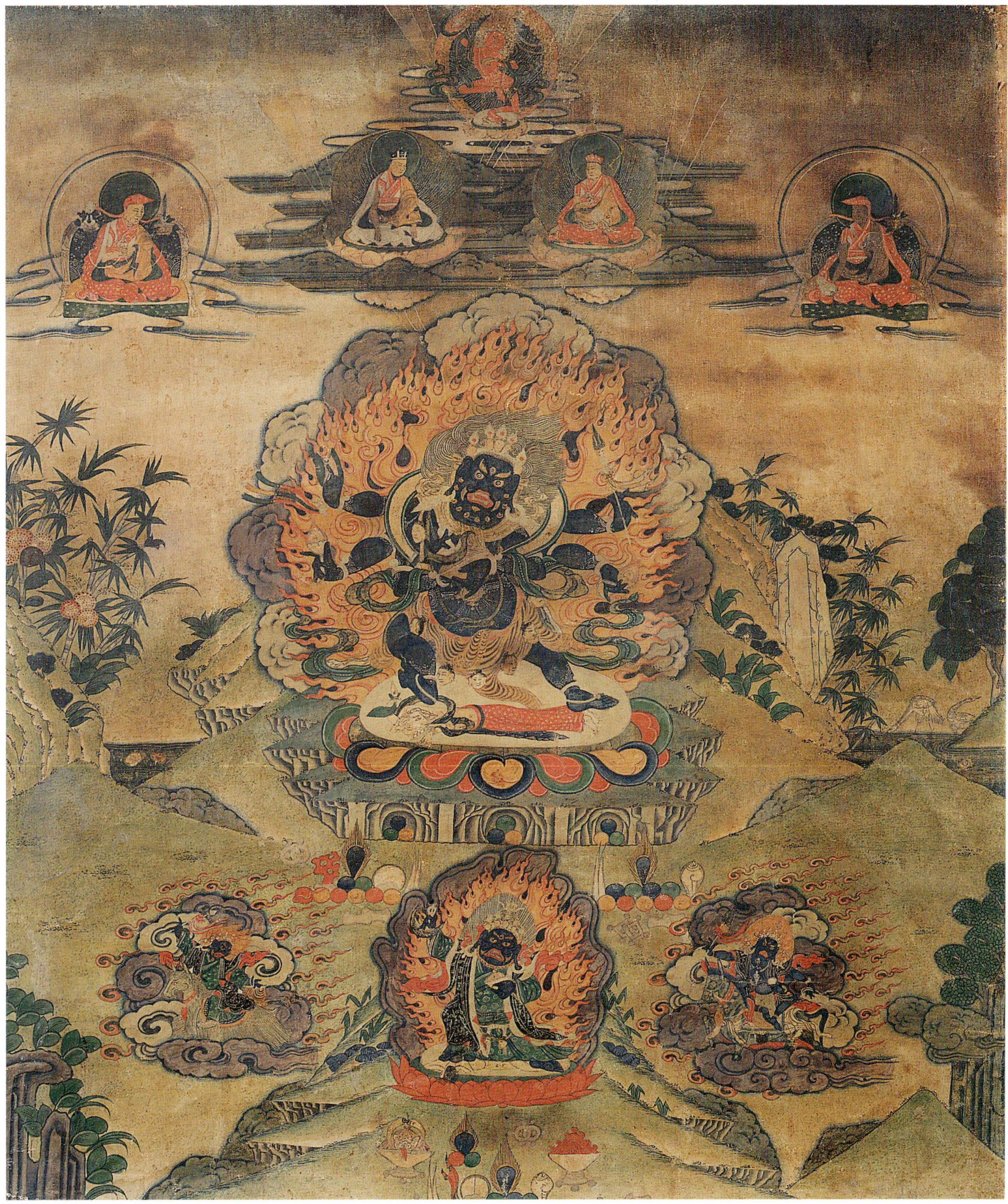

Facing page: Fig. 2.35.
Mahakala Panjaranata
Eastern Tibet, first half of the 19th c.
Mineral pigments on cloth; 30¼ x 22¾ in. (76.83 x 57.78 cm).
Collection of Shelley and Donald Rubin (HA 1086).

outshines all the Sakya lamas, Hevajra at the apex, the five dark blue dancing *rakshasas* at the bottom, the four major attendants at the sides, and the four figures of the Outer Retinue, seen as tiny images in the two puffy clouds in the lower corners—the warrior and mantra holder on the left and the monk and woman (seen here as white) on the right. Other wrathful figures and the skeleton couple fill out the vast entourage of delicately fashioned surrounding icons. This is a far different composition from that prevailing in the thirteenth to fifteenth centuries for Mahakala Panjarnata (see figs. 2.7, 2.11, 2.17) and lacks the transcendent qualities of the black *tangkas* in favor of a believable realism of space and figures.

As a final pair of examples from the Rubin Museum of Art are two *tangkas* showing the white form of the six-armed Mahakala (figures 2.36 and 2.37). This Shadbhuja Sita Mahakala is the wealth aspect of Mahakala (the White Protector Gonkar or "Wish-granting Gem").[72] This form supports the comfort and economic well-being of *tantric* practitioners in particular. The Indian Mahasiddha Shavaripa, the deer hunter tamed by Avalokiteshvara (Bodhisattva of great compassion), was a famous devotee of White Mahakala.[73] Though this form was popular with all orders, it became especially favored by the Shangpa Kagyu and later by the Gelugpa.[74] Also, as a form of the six-armed Mahakala, the White Mahakala has been a major deity of Mongolia since the time of the conversion of Altan Khan by the Third Dalai Lama in the 1570s. In this form he is seen as a playful emanation of Avalokiteshvara (Padmapani), as is clear from his invocation:

> From the Sandalwood Grove deathground,
> like a swirling mass of white clouds of autumn,
> O White Protector, supreme teaching guardian,
> playful emanation of Padmapani,
> please come here pouring rains of jewels![75]

In Tibetan paintings White Mahakala appears somewhat frequently in the middle and later periods of Tibetan art as a small subsidiary figure, such as seen in figures 2.26, 2.27, and 2.28.[76] Two magnificent examples of White Mahakala as a main image in tangkas from the seventeenth century are the one formerly in the Ford collection and a kind of strikingly midsummer's night dream image in a painting in the Rubin collection.[77] The interpretation of White Mahakala in figure 2.36 reveals an elegant and refined image in a vaporous setting portrayed in the artistic style descended from Situ Panchen of Kham. This painting is probably late eighteenth century by a skillful artist working in the Kham region. Here a genteel White Mahakala holds a flaming wish-fulfilling jewel and skull bowl discreetly filled with jewels in his two main hands. The other two right hands hold a chopper and *damaru* drum, and the other two left hands a trident and goad. He is surrounded by small islands of deities, protectors, and lamas: Vajradhara, two lamas,[78] and two seated Bodhisattvas (white Tara and orange Manjushri) at the top; five dancing *dakinis* (celestial "skygoers"; three on the left, two on the right, and one extra at bottom center) below a blue Manjushri and the dark esoteric form of the wealth god, Krishna Jambhala, at the sides; a dancing red Kurukulla, with a white Sarasvati and yellow Vasudhara at the bottom right and yellow Jambhala and Vaishravana on a snow lion at bottom left.

Aside from the offering table and several little clusters of jewels, there is little allusion to the wealth aspect of this deity. The serene landscape of pale nuances of green fading into a dark blue void presents a suitable contrast to the figures and seems to waft them into an idealized setting of space, barely punctuated by a group of trees at the left and mountains at the right. The sense of sublime, ethereal, idealized beauty allows the White Mahakala and his superbly rendered mandorla to become an enticing focus

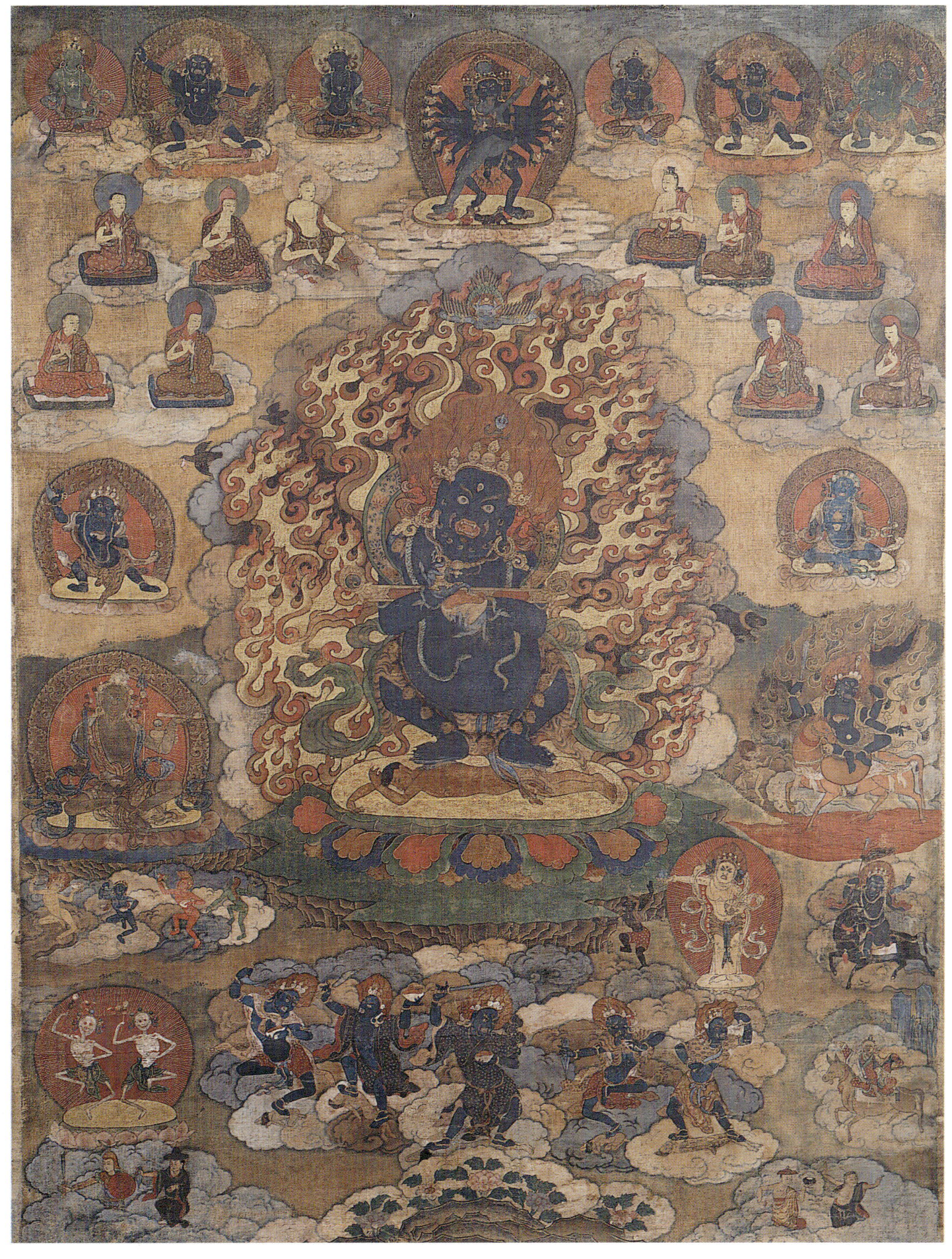

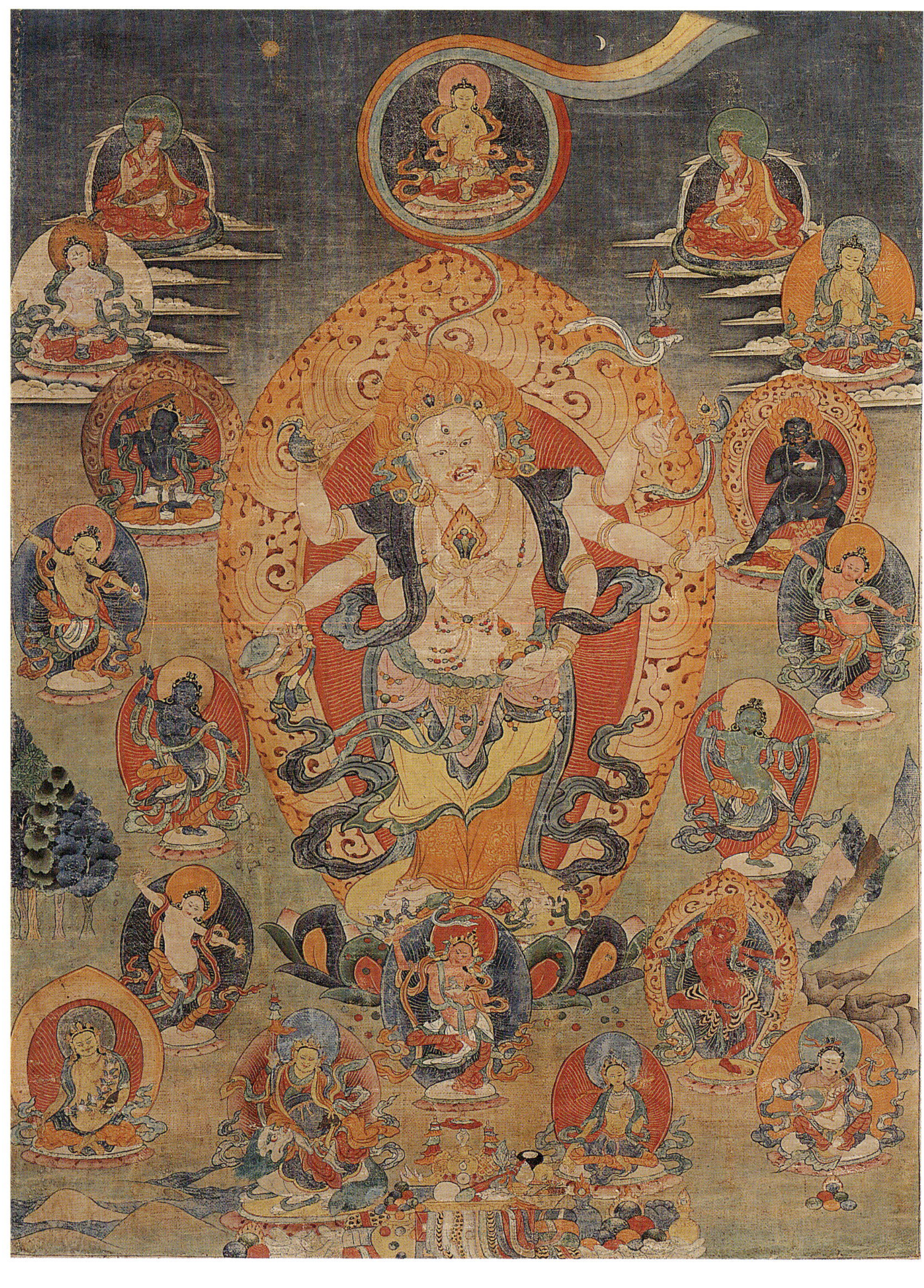

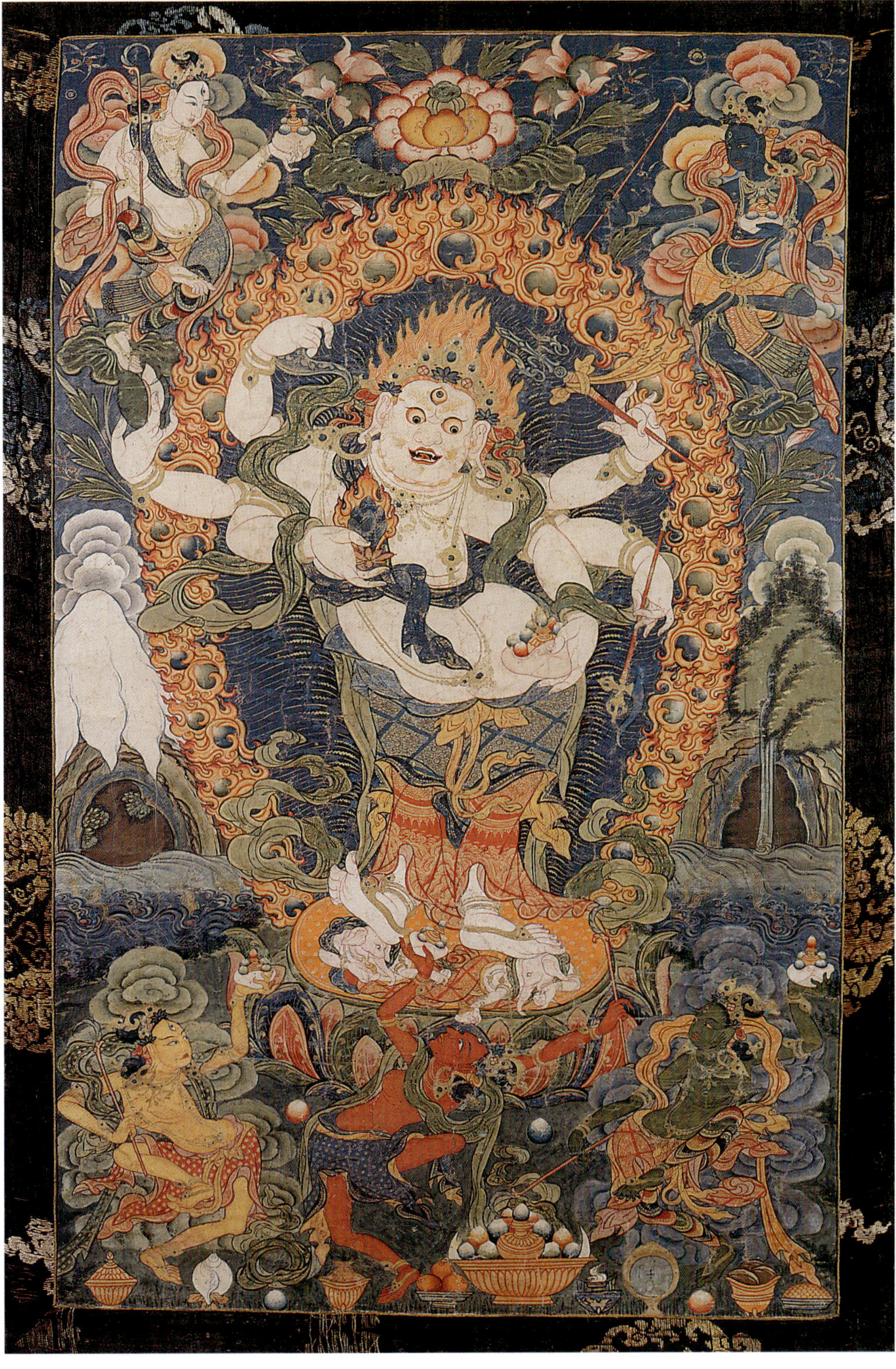

Facing page: Fig. 2.36.
Six-armed White Mahakala
Eastern Tibet, late 18th to early 19th c.
Mineral pigments on cloth; 18 11/16 x 13 3/4 in. (47.46 x 34.92 cm).
Collection of Shelley and Donald Rubin (HA 1026).

Fig. 2.37.
Six-armed White Mahakala
Eastern Tibet (Amdo) or Mongolia, 19th c.
Mineral pigments on cloth; 27 x 17 in. (68.58 x 43.18 cm).
Collection of Shelley and Donald Rubin (HA 813).

with its large body, light silken robes, and nearly childlike expression. We are readily drawn into this lovely world of ideal forms.

By contrast, the six-armed White Mahakala in figure 2.37 seems to bounce around the painting with playful energy and improbable body-bending that thrusts the figure into our space. The style of this *tangka* follows the New Menri school which, unlike that of the Situ Panchen tradition, tends to use profuse landscape and fill up every space with objects in teeming movement. Even though the composition is simple—White Mahakala and five dancing *dakinis* of the five colors, one in each corner and one below—the painting seems brim full, in this case with flowers, gems, snow-peaked and forest-peaked mountains, streaming water and puffy "fungus" clouds. Most elements are executed in a dense, heavy color dominated by a gray-green that grounds all objects to our world. Mahakala is surrounded by a flaming arched mandorla studded with gems, clearly reminding us of the powers of wealth of this emanation. Mahakala himself, with his vigorously bending torso, chubby arms, and perky foot, imparts the playful glee of a child rather than the more characteristic wrathful animation of most Mahakalas. From the mournful expression on the Mahakala of figure 2.2 through the decorative masklike effigies of those in the thirteenth to fifteenth centuries and the more realistically wrathful forms of the sixteenth to eighteenth centuries, we now have yet another expression—the cherubic wealth provider image—of this powerful protector and archetype. Though this gives us another side of Mahakala, it does not supplant the wrathful forms, which also continue in the later centuries.

The Rubin Museum Mahakalas discussed in this essay provide an outline and some idea of the development of this popular icon in Tibetan art. They show not only some of the many incessant stylistic and iconographic changes and variations, but also provide examples of and insights into some of the most prevalent forms of Mahakala known in Tibet—the virtual home of Mahakala. Along with the many other wonderful portrayals of Mahakala in Tibetan art, the Rubin Museum examples reveal the living, vibrant, and continuously changing religious and artistic traditions and genuine veneration of this protector and archetype among the Tibetan people and all the Tibetan Buddhist orders and practitioners. As a result, over the centuries, many potent and skillful paintings and sculptures were made of this favorite form of compassion working in its powerful and multifarious ways. However, we should not forget that, like the Buddhist proverbial raft that is left behind after "reaching the other shore" of wisdom and enlightenment, even the helpful "raft" of the archetype deity is realized as an ephemeral construct of our mind, to be abandoned at the shore of full realization of Buddhahood.

Notes

1. Robert Thurman, the first to use the term *archetype* for the wrathful *yidam* deities of Buddhism, explains it as follows: The archetype deities (*yidam*) "include some of the most beautiful and spectacular of the tantric Buddhaforms, some erotic, some terrific, all benign and compassionate, however fierce the exterior. Previous scholars have tried various terms for *yidam*, and some have retained the Tibetan word. The tendency is to think of them as some sort of external deity, that is, some elaboration of Buddhahood into something utterly alien from the calm, contemplative, humanlike Buddha under the *bodhi* tree. The fact is, these Buddha forms are chosen (*ishta*) by tantric yogis as templates for visualization, forms that artistically express the powerful feelings of insight and breakthrough, exaltation, bliss, and clarity. Jung insightfully discerned the mythic archetypes in the collective mind, archetypes that can serve as vehicles for deep, repressed emotions to surface and be integrated in healthy awareness. The psychological and healing connotations of his term are completely appropriate for the tantric embodiments of enlightenment." And further, the archetype deity is "an embodiment of enlightenment, a Buddha form, used by a tantric practitioner in contemplation to model his or her emotions, insights, and vows into optimal function. Certain such forms were instrumental in the enlightenment experiences of many Great Adepts and have been developed for later use in groups of texts, also called tantras and tantric commentaries." Marylin M. Rhie and Robert A. F. Thurman, *Wisdom and Compassion: The Sacred Art of Tibet* (New York: Harry N. Abrams and Tibet House, 1991; expanded edition 1996), pp. 15 and 389. For Robert Thurman's analysis in detail of the archetype deity with respect to Yamantaka Vajrabhairava, see idem, *Worlds of Transformation: The Sacred Art of Tibet* (New York: Tibet House, 1999), pp. 37–44.
2. *Tangka* is the Tibetan term for paintings, usually executed on sized cotton (but sometimes on silk or linen, possibly without being sized) with mineral pigments mixed with animal glue (similar to distemper). They are generally framed with cotton cloth or, in later centuries, with brocade (mostly imported from China) and are hung by means of a wooden dowel at the top and a wooden roller at the bottom to provide tension and ease of rolling up for storage. Usually the painting is provided with a "dust cover," generally of tie-dyed silk which is attached at the top and allowed to hang over the surface of the painting when it is hanging and not in use.
3. For the suggestion of foreign influences, see Alice Getty, *The Gods of Northern Buddhism* (1912 and 1928; reprint, Rutland, Vt.: Charles E. Tuttle, 1962), pp. 160–61. Rob Linrothe sees the *yaksha* of ancient India as the "ultimate source" of the wrathful destroyers of obstacles, of which Mahakala is one of the important images. He notes the two basics types of these wrathful images: the dwarfish big-bellied type and the heroic warrior type. Rob Linrothe, *Ruthless Compassion: Wrathful Deities in Early Indo-Tibetan Esoteric Buddhist Art* (Boston: Shambhala, 1999), p. 12.
4. Robert Thurman suggests that Nagarjuna "seems to have originated all Mahakala traditions." Rhie and Thurman, *Worlds of Transformation*, p. 386. There is, however, continued, unresolved ambiguity regarding which Nagarjuna, the 1st-century A.D. philosopher, or a later, *tantric* Buddhist, Nagarjuna.
5. Benoytosh Bhattacharyya, *The Indian Buddhist Iconography* (Calcutta: Firma K. L. Mukhopadhayay, 1968), pp. 344–45, mentions the apparent connections of Mahakala with Shiva Mahadeva and calls him a ferocious Hindu god assimilated into the Buddhist pantheon.
6. Rene de Nebesky-Wojkowitz, *Oracles and Demons of Tibet: The cult and iconography of the Tibetan protective deities* (Graz, Austria: Akademische Druck-u. Verlagsanstalt, 1975), pp. 53–54.
7. Ibid., pp. 346–48, notes a sixteen-armed Mahakala with eight faces, but this form must be extremely rare and I have not seen it yet in Tibetan art.
8. I am thankful to Jeff Watt for clarification on this point.
9. Another early example of the seated four-armed Mahakala has these four objects; it is the ca. late-11th-to-12th-century quite perfect and beautiful stone image formerly in the Ellsworth collection. See Rhie and Thurman, *Wisdom and Com-passion*, no. 52.
10. *Panjara* is sometimes translated as "tent" or "canopy." Lokesh Chandra interprets the word to be "skeleton" and this form of Mahakala to be "the god who helps to destroy the corporal cages (*panjara/gur*) in which ignorance keeps us prisoners." Lokesh Chandra, *Transcendental Art of Tibet* (New Delhi: International Academy of Indian Culture and Aditya Prakashan, 1996), p. 63.
11. As a small-sized attendant protector image for a main icon, Mahakala appears frequently, even in the early paintings, but is more rare as a single icon in the early centuries. The single wrathful icon is termed a Phase II phenomenon in Rob Linrothe's study of early wrathful images in India and Tibet. These he finds coexist with the Phase I images (mainly in India), which are wrathful attendants to main Bodhisattvas, etc.; see Linrothe, *Ruthless Compassion*, pp. 13–14.
12. David Snellgrove and Tadeusz Skorupski, *The Cultural Heritage of Ladakh*, vol. 2 (Warminister: Aris and Phillips, Ltd., 1980), p. 99, a translation from the *History of the Gur-mGon ('Canopy God')*.
13. For examples of early paintings with broad, squarish lotus petals, see Steven Kossak and Jane Casey Singer, *Sacred Visions: Early Paintings from Central Tibet* (New York: The Metropolitan Museum of Art, 1998), nos. 6, 9, 10, and 13. For similar lotus petals only in one, down-turned row, see the early Green Tara published in Marylin M. Rhie and Robert A. F. Thurman, *Cibei zhihui* [Wisdom and Compassion] (Taiwan: The China Times, 1998), no. 23, and more recently in Pratapaditya Pal, *Himalayas, An Aesthetic Adventure* (Chicago: The Art Institute of Chicago, 2003), no. 31.
14. Rhie and Thurman, *Wisdom and Compassion* (1996), nos. 24 and 222; Kossak and Singer, *Sacred Visions*, nos. 3 and 13.
15. The *yab-yum* (Father-Mother) form of deities in union represents the union of wisdom (female) and compassion (male).
16. Father Kala Rakshasa, Mother Kali Rakshasi, and offspring Putra, Bhatra,

and Ekajati Rakshasi (see Himalayan Art Website [www.himalayanart.org], Jeff Watt's iconographic outlines of various Panjarnata Mahakala images and description of this particular *tangka* [item 497]).

17. According to Jeff Watt, the eight figures of Mahakala, Ekajati, Shri Devi (Palden Lhamo), and the Five Rakshasas form the so-called popular "Eight Deity Mahakala" of the Sakya, in a lineage that includes Rinchen Zangpo and others up to Sachen Kunga Nyingpo (1092–1158). See J. Watt, Himalayan Art Website item 312, for example.
18. There are a number of four-armed forms of Mahakala described in Nebesky-Wojkowitz, *Oracles and Demons of Tibet*, pp. 44–47, but it is difficult to associate any with this particular *tangka* in regard to the retinue of attendant figures. According to Jeff Watt, the term "Gonpo," meaning "lord" in Tibetan, has a broad application but frequently is used to refer to Mahakala, which, however, literally in Tibetan is Nagpo Chenpo, the Great Black One.
19. Through the priest/patron relationship of Sakya Pandita (1182–1251) and later of Pagpa (1235–80), his nephew, with the leaders of the Mongols in China beginning in the mid-13th century, the Sakya order acquired considerable influence and received many benefits which allowed it to flourish in Tibet in the second half of the 13th century. Though direct relations with the Mongol emperors of the Yuan Dynasty (1279–1368) declined after the death of Kublai Khan in 1294, the Sakya order continued as a strong power, especially in Tsang, and the art production apparently remained quite high. For details, see Tsepon W. D. Shakabpa, *Tibet, A Political History* (New York: Potala Publications, 1984), chaps. 4 and 5.
20. See Jeff Watt, Himalayan Art Website item 82.
21. A similar motif, though larger in scale, appears in the large Palden Lhamo *tangka* in the Pritzker Collection, Chicago, probably of the early 14th century; see Kossak and Singer, *Sacred Visions*, no. 31.
22. Another appears in Pal, *Himalayas*, no. 160.
23. Such frown lines occur in the Hevajra of the ca. 13th- to early 14th-century black *tangka* published in ibid., no. 131, and appear as well in the ca. 11th- to 12th-century stone Mahakala probably from Bihar, India, seen in Susan L. Huntington and John C. Huntington, *Leaves from the Bodhi Tree* (Seattle: University of Washington Press and Dayton Art Institute, 1990), no. 27.
24. Jeff Watt has identified these figures: "Vajradhara, Brahmin Vararuci, Pandita Deva Vajra, Shraddha Karavarma, Lochen Rinchen Zangpo, Drag Tengpa Yontan Tsultrim, Mal Lotsava Lodro Drag, Sachen Kunga Nyingpo (1092–1158), Sonam Tsemo (1142–82), Trakpa Gyaltsen (1147–1216), Sakya Pandita (1182–1251), and Chogyal Pagpa (1235–1280)." J. Watt, Himalayan Art Website item 82.
25. These ten "keepers of the directions" are noted by G. Tucci in the context of discussing Mahakala from texts written by the great 16th-century scholar and historian Taranatha. Guiseppe Tucci, *Tibetan Painted Scrolls*, 3 vols. (Rome: la libreria dello stato, 1949), p. 586. They appear to be the Eight Dikpalas combined with two deities (Brahma and Nandikeshvara) added from the list of ten Brahma deities for the Zenith and Nadir directions.
26. From the left they are: monk, mantra-holder (with a pair of *purba* daggers), the family of five rakshasas, warrior, an unidentified figure in a black cloak, and two dancing figures, of which one is probably the "dark woman" of the Outer Retinue group.
27. One of the most beautiful, probably dating from the 12th century, with original surviving polychrome color and close to Indian forms of Mahakala, was published in Rhie and Thurman *Wisdom and Compassion*, no. 52 (Ellsworth Collection).
28. However, as seen in the side figures riding animal mounts in the figure 2.7 painting, some of the animals seem to be a generic type, not always accurately specific (i.e., the elephant looks like a bovine), so it is possible that there was some confusion or lack of attention in the exact identity of the mounts in the case of this early sculpture as well.
29. In David Weldon and Jane Casey, *Faces of Tibet: The Wesley and Carolyn Halpert Collection* (New York: Carlton Rochelle, Ltd., 2003), no. 7, the authors identify the figure as Vajrapani.
30. Heather Stoddard, "A Stone Sculpture of mGur mGonpo, Mahakala of the Tent, dated 1292," *Oriental Art* 31, no. 3 (1985), pp. 261, 278–82.
31. The inscription on the bottom on the gilt copper mount expresses the wish for virtue to prevail, since this being of pristine cognition has arisen and entered into the crown ornament, heart and so on (paraphrased). For exact translation of the inscription see Weldon and Casey, *Faces of Tibet*, no. 7, note 11.
32. Ulrich Von Schroeder identifies him as probably Tamrakataridhara Krishnacola Mahakala, a form known in the Nartang pantheon. U. Von Schroeder, *Buddhist Sculptures in Tibet*, vol. 2, *Tibet and China* (Hong Kong: Visual Dharma Publications, Ltd., 2001), p. 892, no. 206A.
33. J. Watt, Himalayan Art Website item 544.
34. Published respectively in Giles Béguin, *Les Peintures du Bouddhisme Tibétain* (Paris: Éditions de la Réunion des musées nationaux, 1995), no. 174 (color pl. on p. 37), and Anna Maria Rossi and Fabio Rossi, *Buddhist Art: Sculptures and Paintings from India, Nepal and Tibet* (London: Rossi and Rossi, Ltd., 1999), no. 9.
35. Jeff Watt notes that Tibetan texts refer to this elephant-headed god under the feet of Mahakala as Vignantaka, representing the function and purpose of this god (personal correspondence, November 24, 2003). B. Bhattacharyya notes that in the *Sadhanamala* the word *Vighna* often refers to Ganesha (*Indian Buddhist Iconography*, p. 197).
36. This identification was made by Jeff Watt (Himalayan Art Website item 776), and it is probably accurate, even though the implements he holds do not follow the standard *sadhana* in all respects. The blue-black six-armed, three-headed main image is seated *yab-yum* with a white two-armed female on a recumbent, roaring, white lion. See Bhattacharyya, *Indian Buddhist Iconography*, p. 186, where he mentions that Yogambara is the principal deity of the Yogambara mandala or Nispannayogavali. Yogambara is apparently popular in Nepal, and, according to

Jeff Watt, the practice was popularized in Tibet by Marpa (1012–96) and his student Ngog Lotsava (Himalayan Art Website item 776).

37. For a full view of this splendid Kalachakra *tangka* as well as details of the donor, lama and other deity figures from the borders, see *Precious Deposits: Historical Relics of Tibet, China* (Beijing: Morning glory Publishers, 2000), 3, pp. 81 and 82, no. 43. Though Milarepa's Serkar Gutog Tower at Lhodak was completed by the late 11th century, the wall paintings date stylistically to ca. mid-13th century.
38. See note 35.
39. Jeff Watt in personal correspondence relates that this Buddha is a "special form of Akshobhya used exclusively in the tradition of Six-armed Mahakala."
40. This figure is possibly Lord of the Pavilion, missing the wooden gong. However, two-armed Mahakalas in this same pose and without the gong are known in paintings, such as one in the Museum of Fine Arts, Boston, from the early 15th century.
41. This image has many similarities with the Yongle-period tapestries, such as the one of Mahakala formerly in the Moke Mokotoff collection, New York.
42. The technique of modeling the creases in the twisting scarf ends can be seen in other Tibetan paintings of the first half of the 15th century in particular and occurs in more restrained form in figure 2.12.
43. There is a similar figure in an earlier, ca. 1200, *tangka* of Mahakala Lord of the Pavilion published in Kossak and Singer, *Sacred Visions*, no. 14, where the image is identified as Putra Nakpo. Since Putra Nakpo, as described by Nebesky-Wojkowitz (*Oracles*, p. 50), carries a saber and is not stated to ride a tiger, it may rather be the Mahakala as "lord who rides a tiger" brandishing a lance (ibid., p. 52).
44. See Marylin Rhie, "Tibetan Painting: Styles, Sources and Schools," in Rhie and Thurman, *Worlds of Transformation*, pp. 61–63, and, for a more detailed study, see David Jackson, *A History of Tibetan Painting* (Vienna: Verlag der Osterreichischen Akademie der Wissenschaften, 1996), chaps. 3 and 4.
45. The four main attendants appear at the sides of Mahakala within the flaming mandorla; the four figures of the Outer Retinue are at the bottom left and the five *rakshasas* of the Inner Retinue are at the bottom right. Sakya lamas and others appear at the top, each in their own elaborate niche, as are the figures along the bottom.
46. See *Zhongguo bihua zhuanji*, 32: *Zangzhuan siyuan bihua*, 2 (in *Zhonggui meishu fenlei zhuanji*, (Tianjin: Tianjin Renmin chubansha, 1991), pl. 73.
47. The term *Tibeto-Chinese* refers to art made in China based on Tibetan prototypes and is used in much the same manner as "Greco-Roman" in Western art history.
48. Rhie and Thurman, *Wisdom and Compassion* (1991 and 1996), no. 71.
49. See Tucci, *Tibetan Painted Scrolls*, pl. 195, and Pratapaditya Pal, *Art of Tibet* (Los Angeles: Los Angeles County Museum of Art, 1983), color pl. 16.
50. This "black-cloaked" Mahakala was brought into the Karma Kagyu by the second black-hat Karmapa, Karma Pakshi (1206–83), from an earlier tradition of the Nyingma. Jeff Watt, Himalayan Art Website item 544.
51. There are at least two accounts concerning the origins and/or appearance of this form of Mahakala as an old Brahmin ascetic with thigh-bone trumpet. One account says that he was revealed to the Sakya hierarch Pagpa (1234–80) when Pagpa was in China as preceptor for Kublai Khan. This tradition says that when asked by Kublai Khan to explain the Hevajra *tantra* the next day, Pagpa, who was not familiar with the *tantra* and did not have a copy of the text, was brought one that night by an old Brahmin—Mahakala in his Brahmanarupa form. Getty, *Gods of Northern Buddhism*, pp. 161–62. Another account explains his origins as a black-skinned servant of the four-armed Mahakala that later became incorporated as a form of the four-armed Mahakala of the Guhyasamaja *tantra* and one of the main protectors of the Sakya. See Himalayan Art Website ite, 343. This form as an independent icon also became popular with the Gelugpa following the time of the third Dalai Lama (Amy Heller, in Bazin, *Rituels tibétains*, p. 118). Several splendid *tangkas* of Brahamanarupa are known: in the Zimmerman Family collection (Rhie and Thurman, *Wisdom and Compassion* [1996], no. 201); in the Rubin Museum of Art (Rhie and Thurman, *Worlds of Transformation*, no. 99); and in the collection of R. Kelterborn (Bazin, *Rituels tibétains*, no. 61).
52. Jeff Watt identifies these as: blue Vajrapanjara Dakini and white mahasiddha Brahmin Vararuci. Himalayan Art Website item 312.
53. As noted with earlier, similar representations of Mahakala as Lord of the Pavilion (figs. 2.2, 2.7), the five *rakshasas* along with Mahakala, Ekajati, and Palden Lhamo are, according to J. Watt, the famous "Eight Deity Mahakala" of the Sakya tradition.
54. According to Jeff Watt, there are many "Kama" (Lineage) and "Terma" (Revealed Treasure) traditions of practice in the Nyingma for this form of Mahakala. Himalayan Art Website item 170.
55. For a superb 18th-century form of the same representation, probably of Drigungpa lineage, also in the Rubin collection, see Rhie and Thurman, *Worlds of Transformation*, no. 75.
56. It may be a Panjarnata Mahakala with the *gandi* gong missing, but there are two-armed examples in this posture without the gong (see above, n. 40, in regard to the Willard Clark, two-armed Mahakala sculpture).
57. This sculpture is closely similar to the Mahakala of the same iconography in the *tangka* dating around the late 16th century in the Fournier collection in the Musée Guimet, Paris. See Béguin, *Les Peintures du Bouddhisme Tibétain*, no. 175.
58. The exact identification of the attendant figures is difficult to decipher. For the form of Mahakala in black cloak riding a black horse and shooting the iron bow and arrow, see Nebesky-Wojkowitz, *Oracles and Demons of Tibet*, p. 59.
59. Recent scholarship is pointing toward the existence of the black *tangkas* in Tibet to at least around the 14th century. See Aldo Mignucci, "Tibetan Black Tangkas: New Evidence on the Origins of a Painting Tradition," *Annali di Ca' Foscari*, 39, no. 3 (2000): pp. 317–29. One example with two Mahakalas datable to the 14th centu-

ry was recently shown in an exhibition at the Musée Guimet, Paris: Bazin, *Rituels tibétains*, no. 41. Line drawing on black silk is also known as a type of Buddhist painting in the 9th -century silk banner paintings from Dunhuang.

60. The New Menri school evolved from the painting of the master painter Choying Gyatso (ca. 1615–85), who worked at Tashilhunpo monastery for the First Panchen Lama, Losang Chökyi Gyaltsen, from ca. 1640s. He later was invited to help decorate the Potala Palace in Lhasa under the Fifth Dalai Lama. He is lauded as the artist who revived the Menri style of the 15th century fostered by the artist Menlha. It is a style rich in natural detail, skillfully subtle line, and interesing spatial effects. See Rhie and Thurman, *Worlds of Transformation*, pp. 67–68, and Jackson, *History of Tibetan Painting*, chap. 8.
61. As noted in the entry on this *tangka* in Rhie and Thurman, *Worlds of Transformation*, no. 98, the style is very close to that of the secret Palden Lhamo manuscript of the Fifth Dalai Lama (1617–82) in the Musée Guimet, Paris (Fournier collection). This manuscript is dated to between 1674 and 1681. The complete manuscript is published in Samten Karmay, *Secret Visions of the Fifth Dalai Lama* (London: Serindia, 1988), and some folios are presented in Bazin, *Rituels tibétain*, no. 35. This same exhibition catalogue presents a number of other superbly refined black *tangkas*, some of the 17th and some of the 18th centuries, including some forms of Mahakala, such as the rare lion-headed form (see especially nos. 53–57).
62. For further examples and discussion of the 17th-century black *tangkas*, see Rhie and Thurman, *Worlds of Transformation*, p. 68.
63. See ibid., no. 147; Gerd-Wolfgang Essen and Tsering Tashi Thingo, *Die Götter des Himalaya*, 2 vols. (Munich: Prestel-Verlag, 1989), 1, pl. 140; Rhie and Thurman, *Wisdom and Compassion* (1996), no. 216. All three *tangkas* are of virtually identical measurements (33 x 23 in.)
64. Published in Tucci, *Tibetan Painted Scrolls*, pl. 196, and in Rhie and Thurman, *Wisdom and Compassion* [1991 and 1996], no. 112.
65. For more detail, see Nebesky-Wojkowitz, *Oracles*, pp. 38–42.
66. The Shangpa Kagyu (different from the Kagyupa order) was founded by Kedrub Kyungpo Naljor in the 11th century. Jeff Watt, Himalayan Art Website item 813. According to Jeff Watt, the Second Dalai Lama (1475–1542) was associated with this Shangpa Kagyu tradition, and Tsongkapa's disciple Kedrub Jey (1385–1438) wrote a large volume on all the associated practices of the six-armed Mahakala, thus popularizing the practice of the six-armed Mahakala in the Gelugpa tradition.
67. Rhie and Thurman, *Worlds of Transformation*, no. 75.
68. See above, n. 60, for Choying Gyatso.
69. According to Jeff Watt, this is a group of seven wrathful brothers, led by Tsiu Marpo, the principal worldly protector of Samye Monastery. Personal correspondence and Himalayan Art Website item 47.
70. For more details concerning this artistic school, see Jackson, *History of Tibetan Painting*, chap. 10.
71. Jeff Watt, Himalayan Art Website item 47.
72. Rhie and Thurman, *Worlds of Transformation*, p. 386, no. 145.
73. Jeff Watt provides the lineage of this form of Mahakala: from "Vajradhara, Jnana Dakini, Shri Shavaripa, Lord Maitripa, Mahasiddha Rahulagupta, Khedrup Khyingpo Naljor [11th century], Nyam Med Rinchen Tsondru, Bonton Kyergangpa (famous terton of the Hayagriva cycle of practice), etc." See Himalayan Art Website item 351, where he also notes White Mahakala as a wealth deity of the Kriya class of *tantra*.
74. Ibid., item 351. Also see above, n. 66.
75. The standard invocation of Gonkar translated by Robert Thurman in Rhie and Thurman, *Worlds of Transformation*, p. 386, no. 145.
76. One of the earliest examples of White Mahakala occurs in the wall paintings (east wall, south side) of the Red Temple at Tsparang under the Guge dynasty and datable to ca. third quarter of the 15th century. See *Zhongguo bihua zhuanji*, 32, pl. 81.
77. The Ford collection *tangka* is published in Rhie and Thurman, *Wisdom and Compassion* (1991 and 1996), no. 110. The Rubin Museum *tangka* is published in Rhie and Thurman, *Worlds of Transformation*, no. 145, and in John C. Huntington and Dina Bangdel, *The Circle of Bliss: Buddhist Meditational Art* (Chicago: Serindia Publications and Columbus Museum of Art, 2003), no. 97.
78. Besides clarifying some of the identifications of the various deities in this *tangka*, Jeff Watt identifies the lamas as Sakya Lamas on either side of a special form of Vajradhara (personal correspondence, November 24, 2003).

Catalog

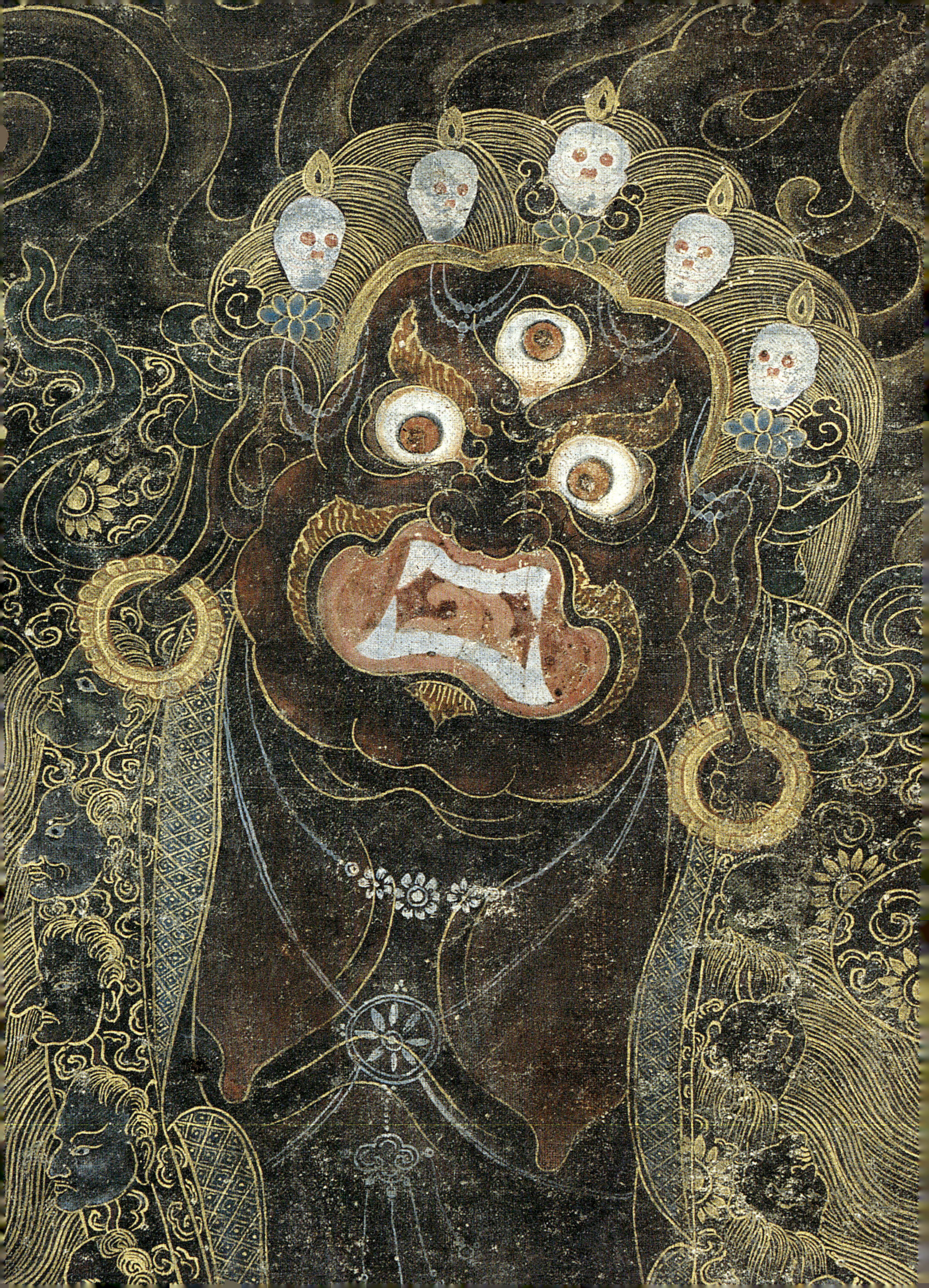

Dangerous Protectors

Dangerous Protectors are typically early nature spirits associated with a specific mountain, lake, animal species, and so on. These primal forces were eventually loosely absorbed into the fringes of the Buddhist pantheon, where their original powers were put into the service of the new faith. According to tradition, these spirits were subdued by powerful teachers, perhaps only partially so. As the name implies, the Dangerous Protectors are notoriously unpredictable and are treated with respect tinged with fear.

Cat. no. 1, detail

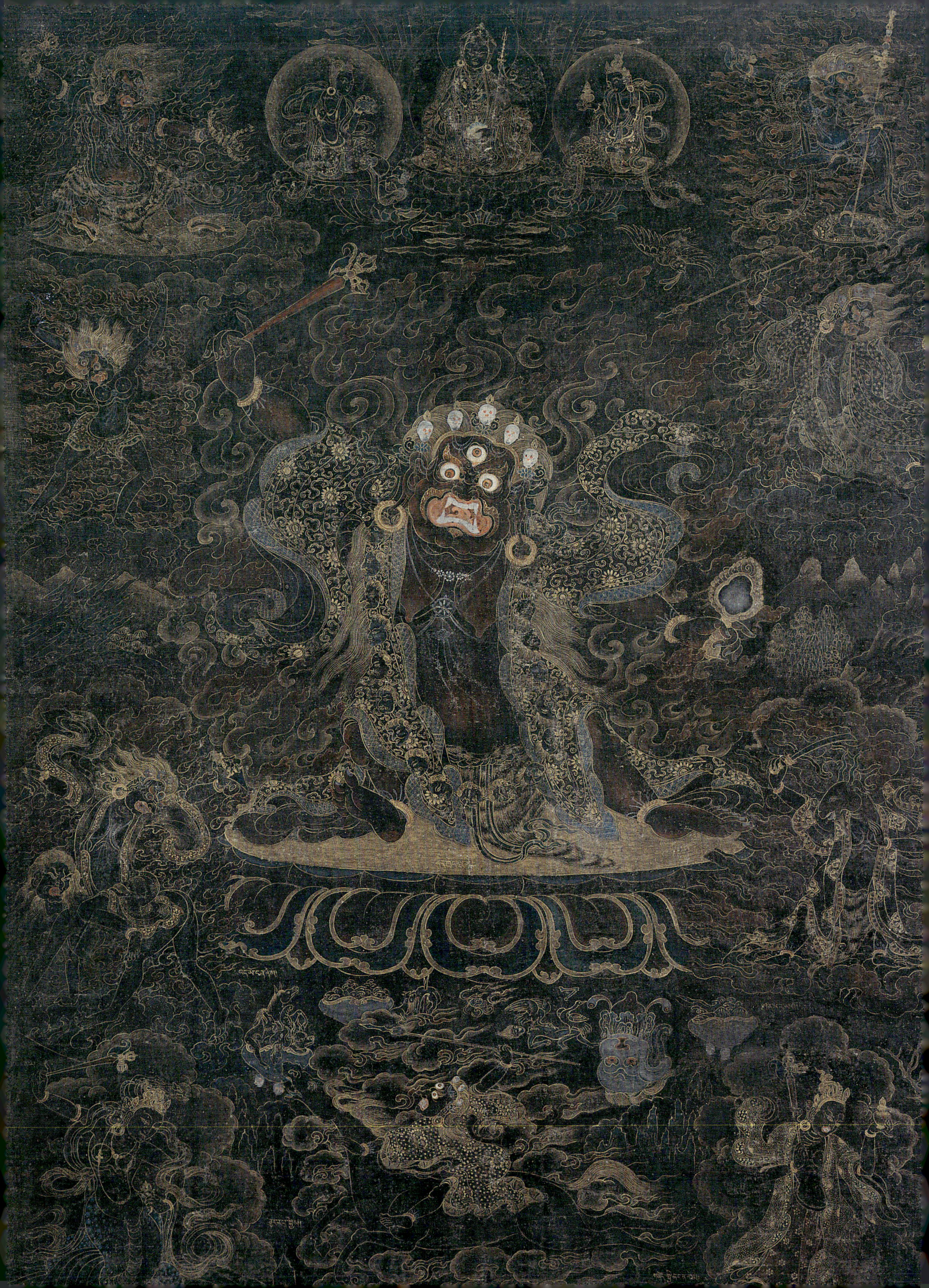

Cat. no. 1

Durtro Lhamo

Protectress of Discovered Texts

An inscription written in gold, barely visible on the yellow sun disk beneath the main figure, identifies this as a painting of Durtro Lhamo, the Goddess of the Charnel Grounds. She is also known as Drogzema, the Powerful (female) Friend. Durtro Lhamo is intimately involved with *terma*, which are the "treasure texts" miraculously discovered in rocks or pillars by teachers with special insights, or revealed to them in dreams or visions and then written down. Those who discover *terma* are known as *tertons*, and Durtro Lhamo protects the *tertons*, the *terma*, the teachings they contain, and the practitioners of those teachings. She is assisted in these tasks by seven female attendants arranged at her sides and below her. One rides a straining, galloping horse, one is goat-headed and waves a cleaver, another rides a naked, crone-faced zombie, and a fourth, the only clearly peaceful one of the group, is a *nagini* with a blue serpent body, emerging gracefully from a pool of water.[1]

Along the lower border of the painting is a large group of weapons, musical instruments, and ritual objects used in ceremonies devoted to Dangerous Protectors. Four skull bowls below Durtro Lhamo's lotus pedestal are understood as offerings to her. The skull with eyes on the right contains the offering of the five senses, while the skull bowl on the left holds the "five meats" (see cat. nos. 10–12). Nearby are tiny but graphic scenes of the devouring of corpses in a charnel ground, over which Durtro Lhamo presides. It seems most likely that a painting of this size, scale, and quality would have been commissioned by an institution such as a Nyingma monastery or a family of lay Nyingma practitioners (*ngagpa*).

Durtro Lhamo, at the center, is a ponderous figure with a large head and ferocious expression. Her tongue is curled up in fury, her teeth and fangs bared, and all three eyes bulge from their sockets. Her flaccid breasts are exposed within the loose robe she wears over a belted tiger-skin skirt. She is two-

(cont. p. 256)

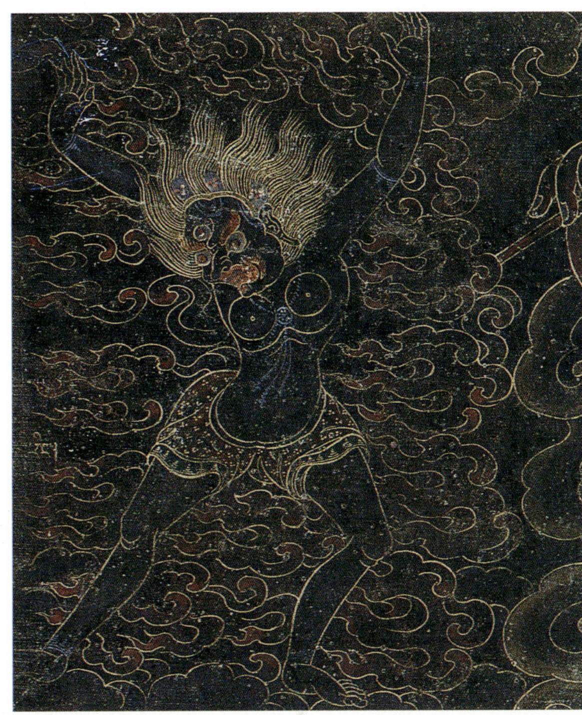

Cat. no. 1 detail

Facing page: Cat. no. 1
Durtro Lhamo
Protectress of Discovered Texts

Tibet, 18th c.
Mineral pigments on cloth
29½ x 20½ in. (74.9 x 52.1 cm)
Collection of Shelley and Donald Rubin (HA 1053)

Cat. no. 2

Dorje Legpa

Protector of Discovered Texts

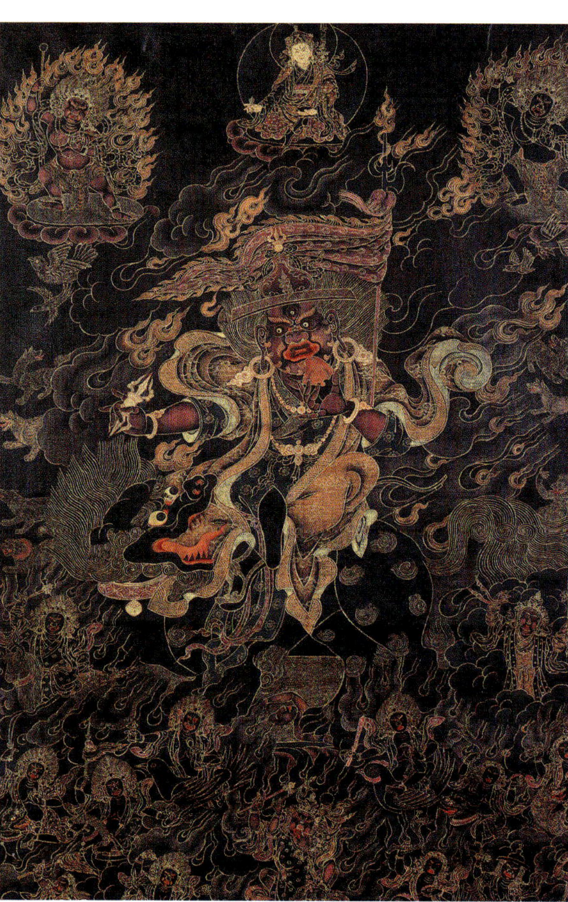

Cat. no. 2
Dorje Legpa
Protector of Discovered Texts

Tibet, 19th c.
Mineral pigments on cloth
17¾ x 11¾ in. (45.1 x 29.8 cm)
Collection of Shelley and Donald Rubin (HA 93)

Thick red lips outlined in black, bared to reveal silvery teeth, and incandescent yellow irises floating in gray eyeballs, give the face of the central figure an eerie, disturbing quality. This is offset to an extent by the comic features of the snow lion on which this figure sits, and the perfect outline of the boot which is pushed out at us in what is nearly the exact center of the painting (see detail). There is no jest, however, in the object the main figure holds up to his mouth: a fresh human heart. His right arm is extended, and he grasps a *vajra*, an attribute that is added to his name: Dorje Legpa (Vajra Renunciant).[1]

Like Durtro Lhamo (cat. no. 1), Dorje Legpa is a Nyingma protector of *terma*, *terton*, and practitioners of *terma* teachings.[2] And like her, he is an oath-bound protector originating in Tibet, converted from his demonic activities by Padmasambhava, who appears directly above Dorje Legpa. In the upper corners are two big-bellied Wrathful Buddhas in aggressive postures. On the left is the red Hayagriva (a small horse's head visible in his hair), and on the right is the blue-black Vajrapani. As a Nyingma liturgical verse describes, Dorje Legpa "performs attentively the commands of Bhagavan Vajrapani."[3] In other words, to ensure that this Dangerous Protector maintains his conversion vows, Vajrapani monitors him so that the violence does not get out of hand and is wisely directed in the furtherance of Buddhist aims. Although Dorje Legpa probably had an additional function as the protector of a localized region, he has become a more general protector within the Nyingma lineage.

The broad hat Dorje Legpa wears is quite distinctive, resembling the so-called riding hats of monks, made of papier-mâché or rattan. It has a *vajra* finial, and the syllable HUM written in *ranjana* ornamental Sanskrit script (also called *lantsa*) on the front. He wears both an inner and an outer robe, but has pushed up his sleeves. In the crook of his left elbow he cradles a pennon-lance, the staff of which terminates

(cont. p. 257)

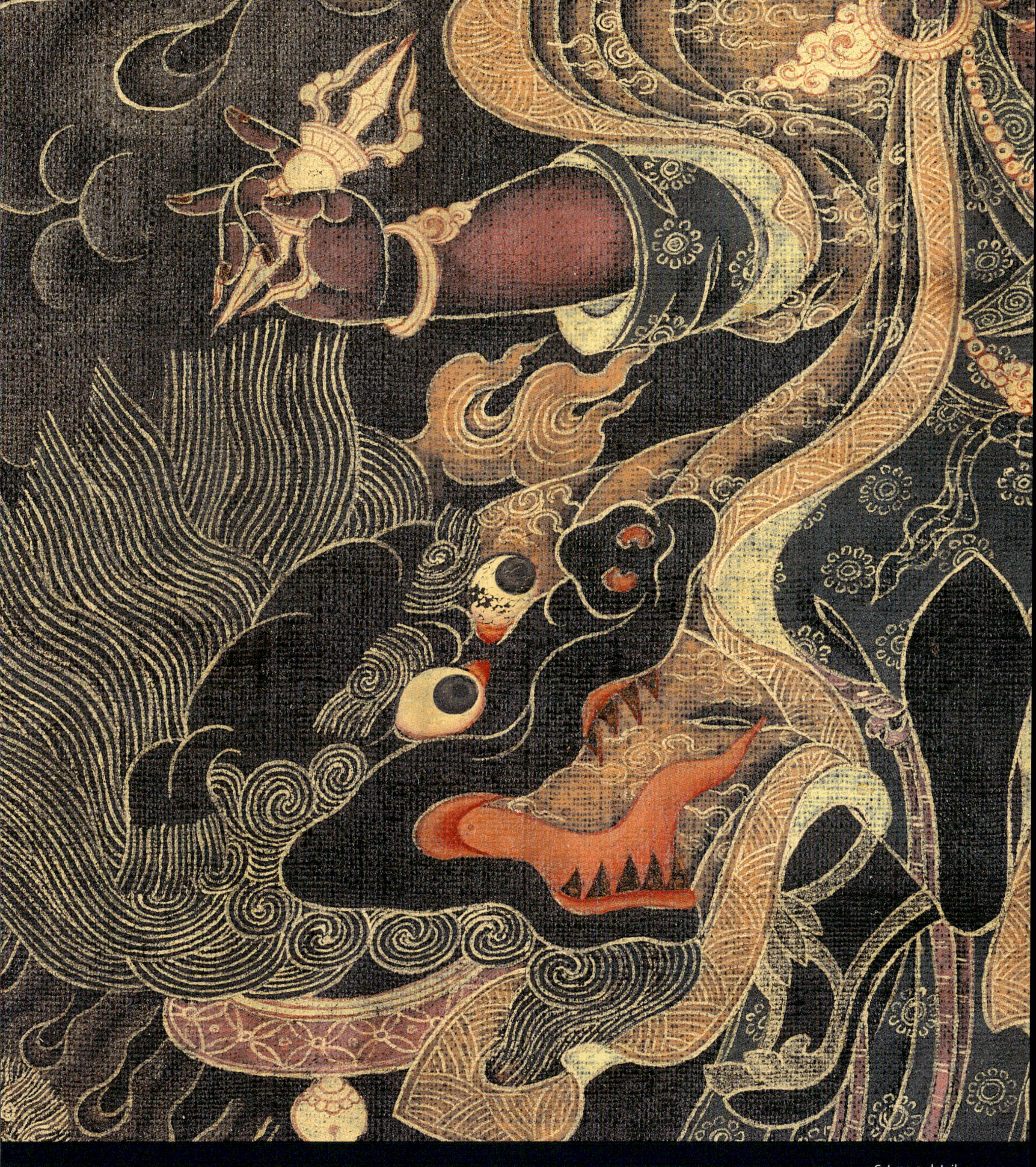

Cat. no. 2, detail

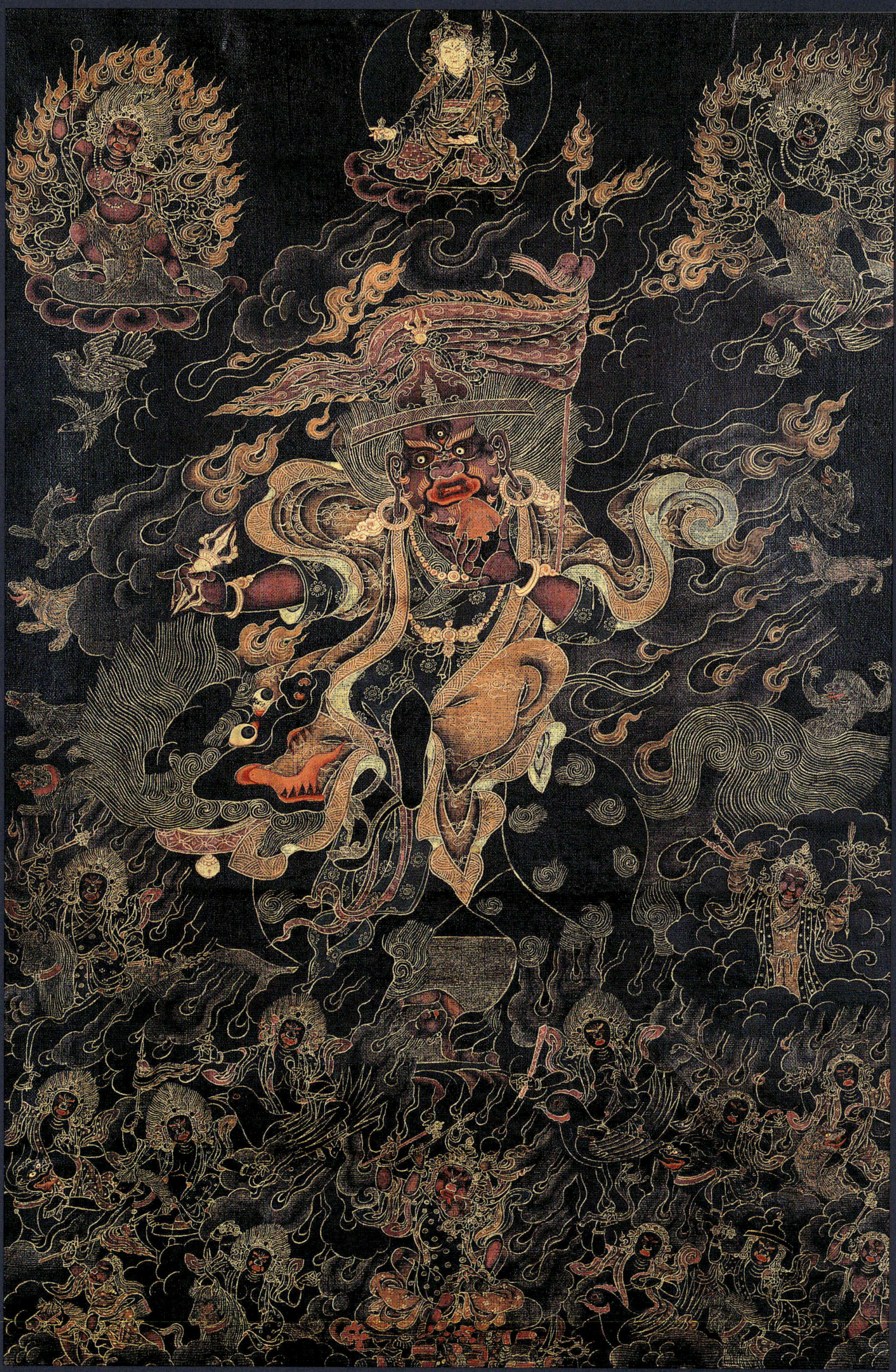

Cat. no.2

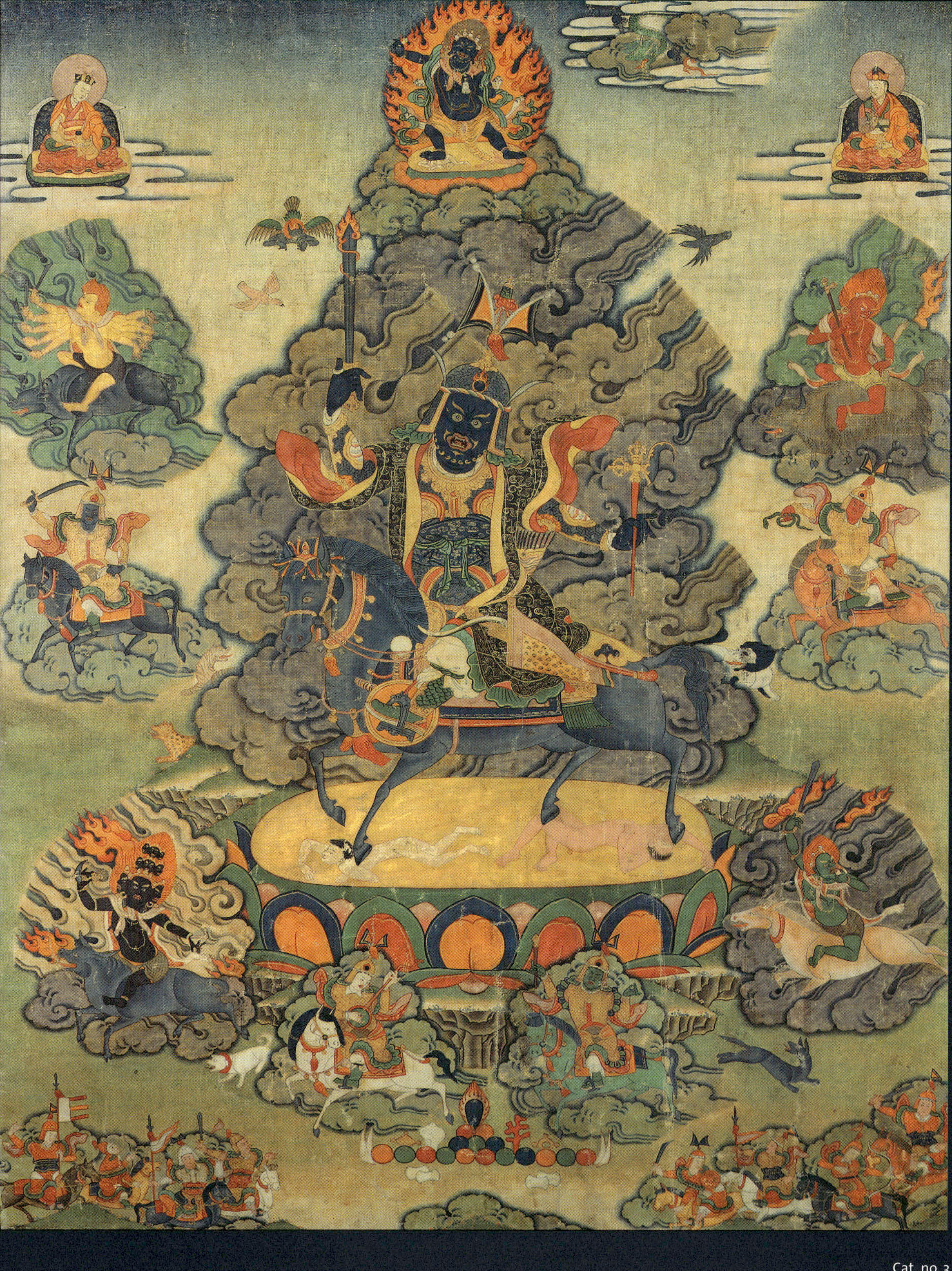

Cat. no. 3

Cat. no. 3

Draglha Gonpo

Protector of Serta and Lhagang monastery

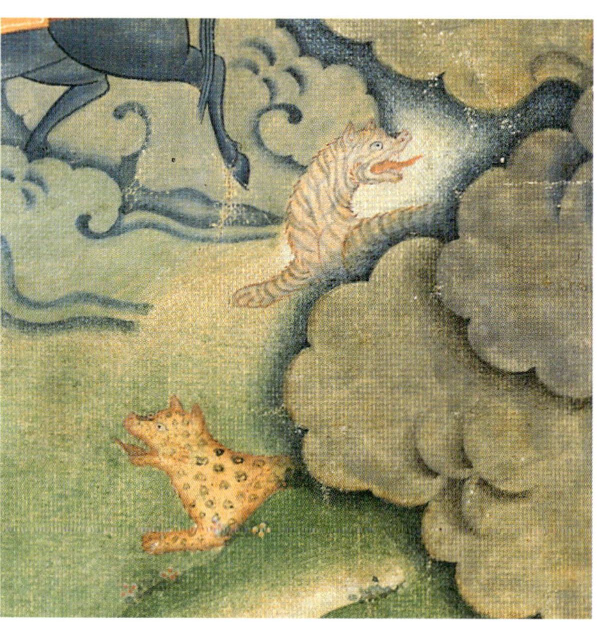

Cat. no. 3, detail

Preceding page: Cat. no. 3
Draglha Gonpo
Protector of Serta and Lhagang monastery

Eastern Tibet, second half of the 19th c.
Mineral pigments on cloth
20¼ x 15½ in. (51.4 x 39.34 cm)
Collection of Shelley and Donald Rubin (HA 862)

Stylistically, this painting is quite clearly Eastern Tibetan, of the Karma Encampment (Gadri) style. Among the features that correspond are: the plain, uncolored background; the uncluttered composition; the sky, which is graded from a medium blue at the top fading quickly; the nearly unmodulated depiction of earth or ground; the hard-edged cloud forms behind wrathful figures that are clipped off at an oblique angle (instead of trailing off); the stylized mushroom-shaped clouds behind peaceful figures; the angular, modeled dark brown eroded earthen banks with gold outlines supporting the green plateau on which the main lotus dais sits; and the dragon emerging out of the clouds, clutching a blue pearl. Many of these features have been absorbed from Chinese landscape painting. Two of the formulators of the style, the Tenth Karmapa Choying Dorje (1604–74) and the Eighth Situ Panchen Chokyi Jungne (1700–74), were both accomplished painters themselves and consciously introduced Chinese aspects into the art they commissioned or created directly.[1] Although this painting is considerably later than their times, they had established a style that maintained a certain "look," even as it continued to develop.

The central figure, Draglha Gonpo, is the principal protector of a region of Eastern Tibet (actually, Kham, now in the Kandze Prefecture of Sichuan bordering Golog) called Serta. It is also the special protector of a monastery called Lhagang in the Minyak region of northeastern ethnographic Tibet.[2] Draglha Gonpo is accompanied by four fully armored warriors who in color and attributes take on the appearance of Kings of the Four Directions. All wear one or another version of a general's helmet with short pennons affixed to the finial. A further retinue of eight figures masses in two groups along the bottom of the painting. In addition, there are four *rakshasa*, female demons who do the protector's bidding. The red *rakshasa* at the right rides a yak, the green one a *khyang*

(cont. p. 257)

Cat. no. 4

Kula Khari

Protector of Lodrak

The Dangerous Protector rides a shaggy, bushy-tailed yak kicking up a cloud of dust that doubles as a smoky nimbus. He is framed by a three-story temple with Chinese-style eaves. Wearing a pennon-tipped helmet and full cuirass that comes down to his boots and helmet, he has a bow in its tiger-skin quiver attached to his belt. As he rides, he carries a spear or arrow and clutches a triple-gem in his left hand. The benefactor aspect of his protector role, suggested by the gems, is reinforced by the small round jewels, one of which has broken off, on the ledge below him. A *naga raja* (serpent king) with a snake body kneels before the yak, offering a bowl of jewels (see detail). On the other side, a woman kneels, proffering or perhaps even receiving another jewel.

The sculpture makes clever use of drop-shaped mountain forms to create a landscape setting for the yak-rider. However out of scale the mountains are to the central figure and temple, they successfully convey the idea of a remote temple in the mountains. Kula Khari is the local protector whose seat was a mountain in Lodrag, south of Lhasa near the border with Bhutan.[1] No doubt he was the subject of an annual ritual of placation. This image might have been found in the local protector's shrine, or in a layman's house-altar. The cult of local protectors is kept at the fringes of Buddhist monasteries, and local protector cults are strongest among laymen and women (see Linrothe essay, part 3). The Himalayan origin of this Dangerous Protector is manifest in the choice of a yak as a mount.

(note p. 258)

Next page: Cat. no. 4
Kula Khari
Protector of Lodrak

Tibet, 19th c.
Painted terracotta
9¾ x 8¼ x 4¾ in. (24.8 x 21 x 12.1 cm)
C2002.7.3 (HA 65079)

Cat. no. 4, detail

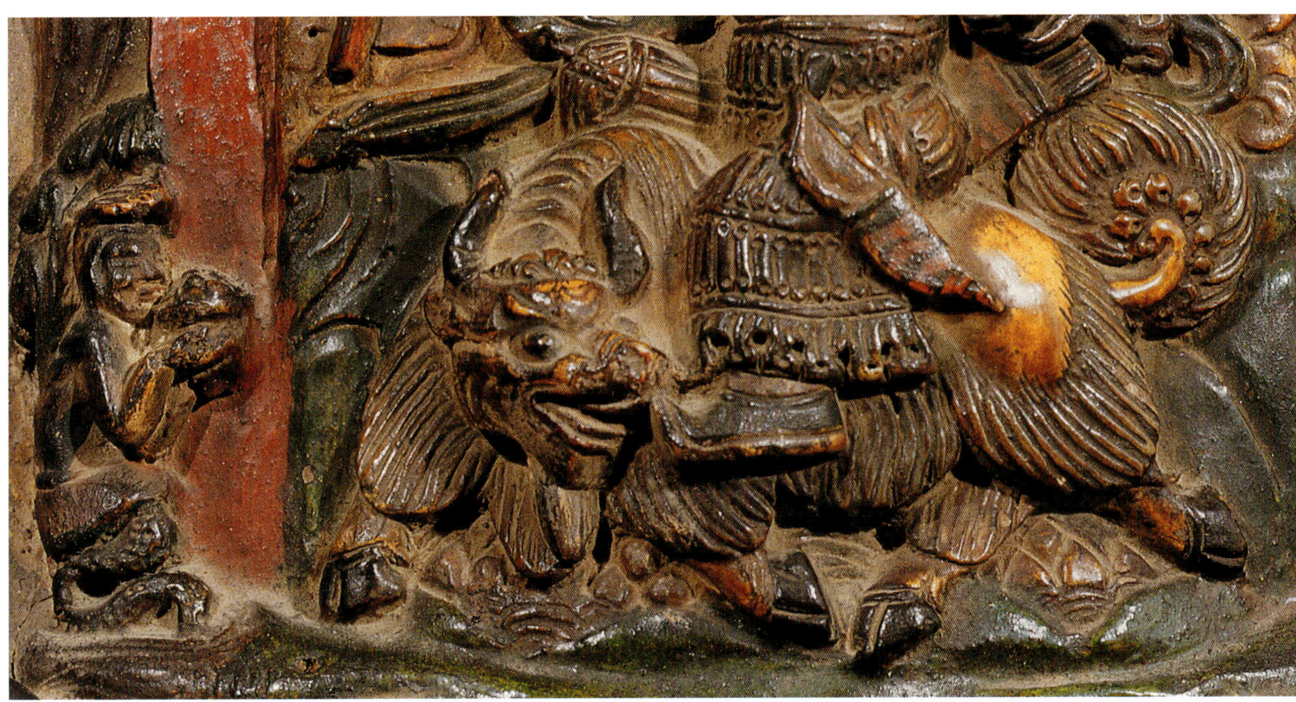

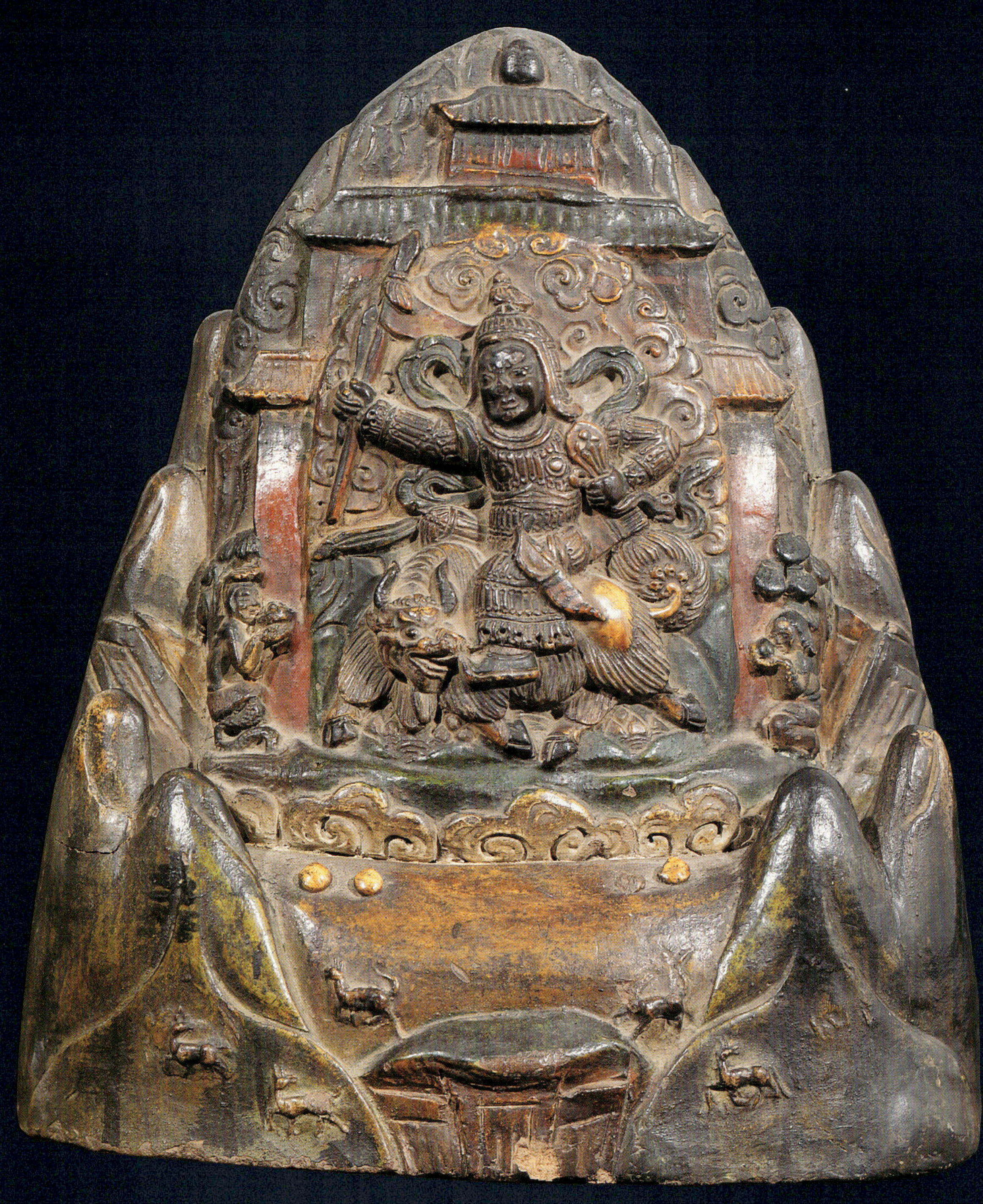

Cat. no. 4

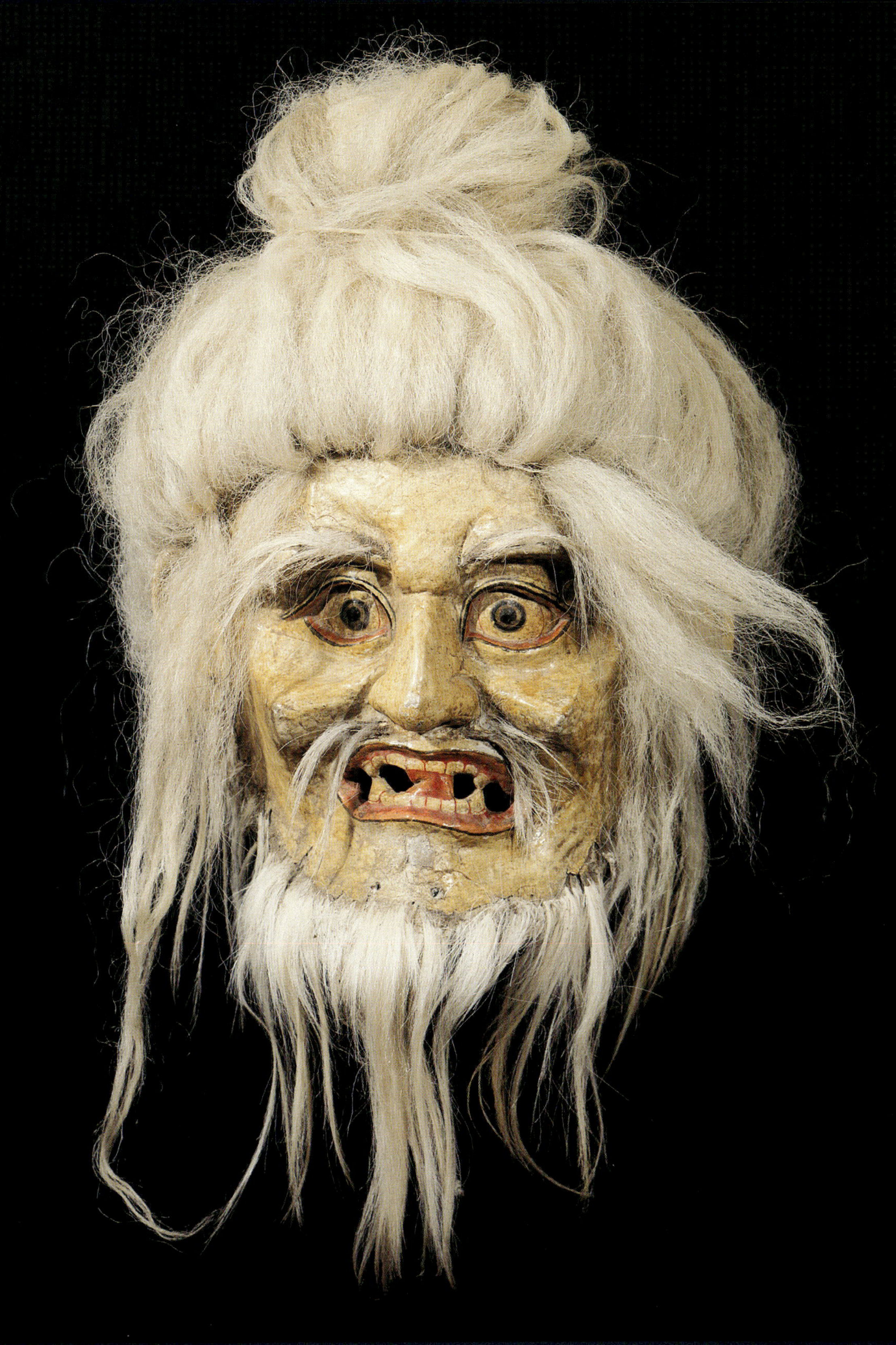

Cat. no. 5

Cat. no. 5

Mask for Ritual Dance

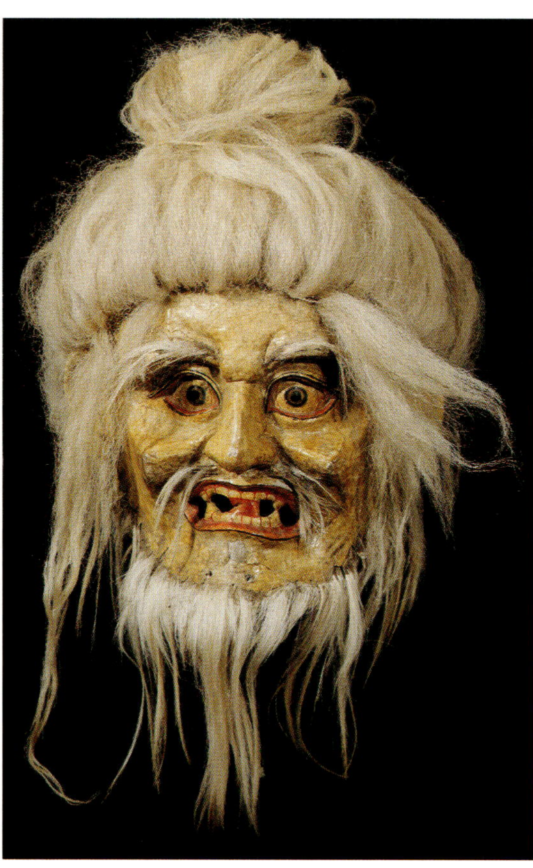

Cat. no. 5
Mask for Ritual Dance

Mongolia, Tibet, or China, 19th–20th c.
Papier-mâché with yak or horse hair
17¾ x 13½ x 11 in. (45.1 x 34.3 x 27.9 cm)
C2003.8.1 (HA 65190)

Masked dances (Cham) are held annually at most larger Buddhist monasteries, from Nepal and Bhutan to Mongolia, from Ladakh and Zangskar to the Tibeto-Chinese temples of Beijing. These performances retell for a lay audience the epic stories of the coming of Buddhism into the larger Himalayan world from India, the conversion of demonic and human opponents, and the ultimate victory of the Buddha's teachings. Monks play all the roles, and dress in elaborate costumes that include masks such as this one. It was worn by a dancer who would see through holes in the open mouth. It probably does not depict a Dangerous Protector, but rather one of the Indian opponents of Buddhism, a Hindu ascetic who is converted through debate or a display of magical power. This would explain the topknot, beard, and long eyebrows, as well as the aggressive expression, corresponding to classical Tibetan depictions of Indian Hindu yogins or *acharyas*.[1] The *yogins* are turned into figures of fun in the masked dance. However, most accounts of the Hindu *acharyas* describe them as having dark hair, so the identification of this mask must be tentative. In Nyingma lineage Cham, as found in the Everest region of Nepal, a Buddhist yogin plays a prominent role as a comic figure who nevertheless gives religious discourses.[2] If it were not for the fact that this character wears a half mask so that he can speak clearly, it would be tempting to identify the mask as depicting him.

It is quite possible that this mask was made for a Cham in Buryatia, Mongolia, or in Chinese-controlled regions of "Inner Mongolia". As a contemporary scholar has pointed out,

> Mask making became one of the greatest art forms practiced by Mongolian monks, who prepared and refurbished masks and dance costumes in the weeks before the performance. They built their masks of papier-mâché and clay. . . . This mixture of materials was formed in

(cont. p. 258)

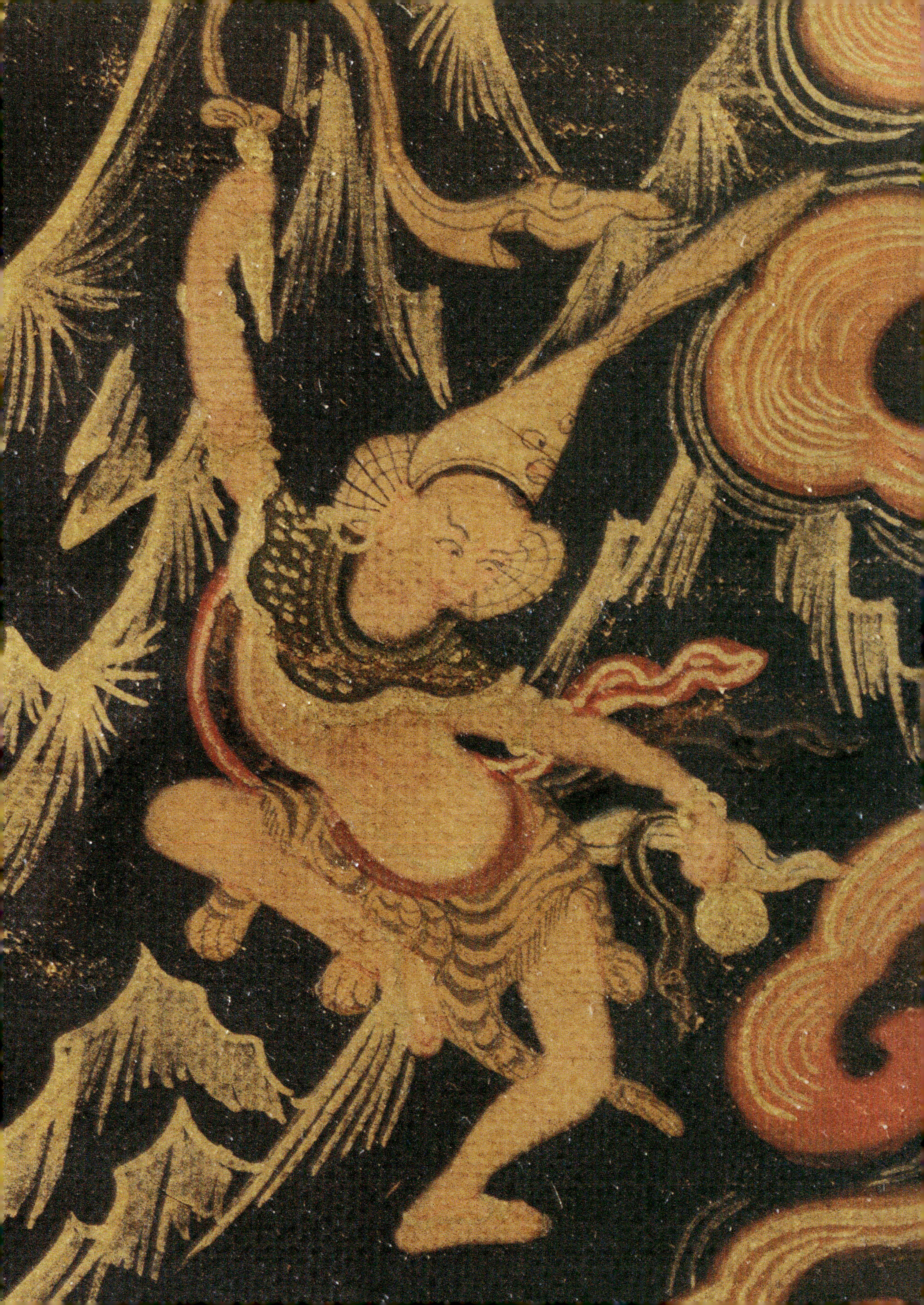

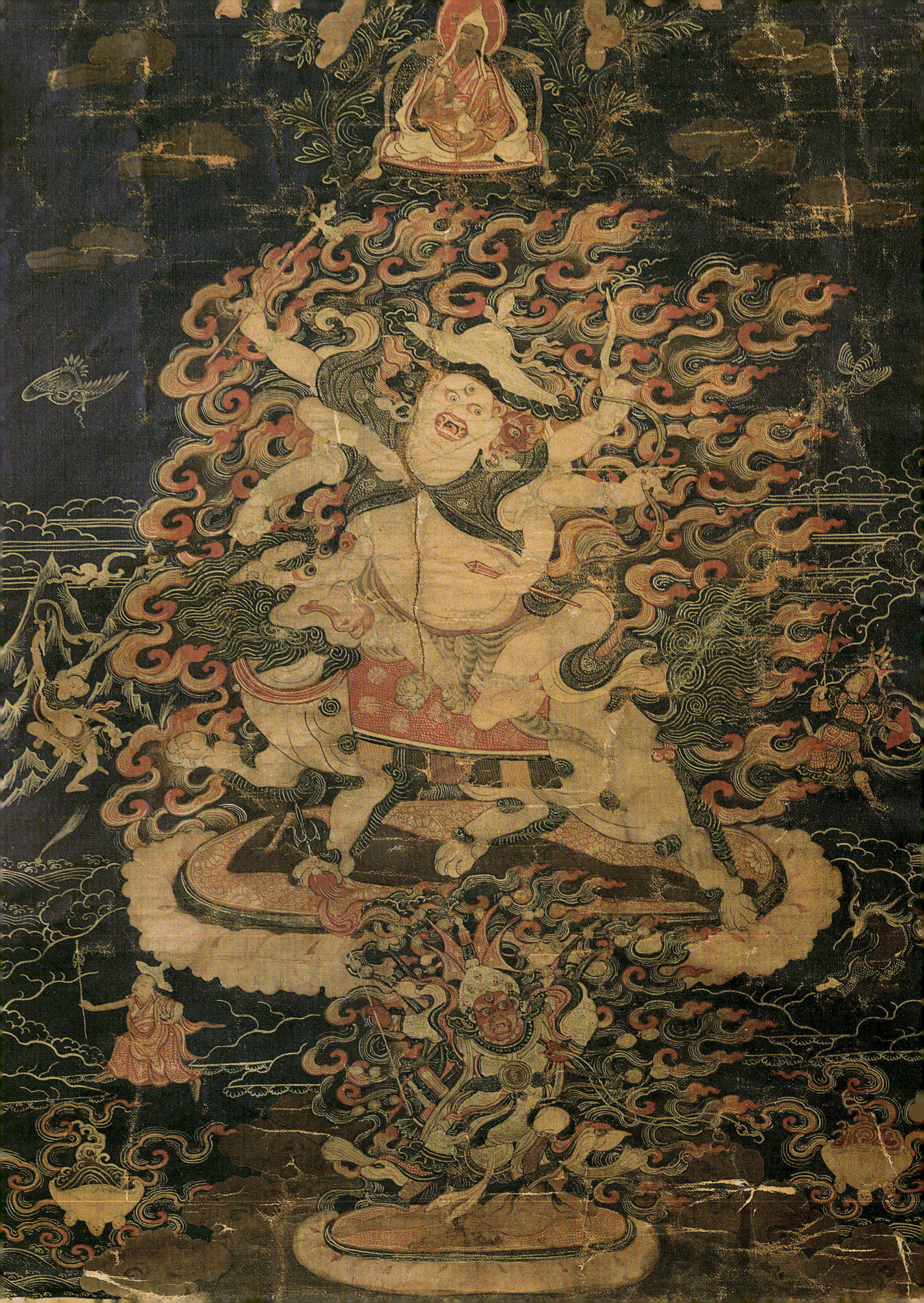

Cat. no. 6

Pehar Gyalpo

Chief Protector of the State

The aesthetic, religious, and political aspects of this fine, small-sized black-ground (*nag-tang*) painting all subtly interlock. The quality of the rendering—the details of garment patterns, delicately painted faces, fully articulated minor characters—and the materials, including the plentiful use of gold, both suggest high level patronage. The presence of the Fifth Dalai Lama Ngagwang Lobsang Gyatso (1617–82) above the head of the main figure, complete with wheel and a *purba* (ritual dagger) in his belt, immediately suggests a possible patron. And the subject matter reinforces a political significance to the painting. King Pehar represents the official protector of a unified Tibetan political state which the Fifth Dalai Lama attempted to create and preside over, bringing "the cult of Pehar and his oracle from Samye monastery to the Nechung monastery near Drepung monastic university outside of Lhasa."[1] Below Pehar is the "chief minister" of Pehar's retinue, Dorje Dragden.[2] Pehar was thought to have been subjugated by Padmasambhava, and was a deity connected most closely with the Nyingma tradition, with which the Fifth Dalai Lama was particularly affiliated by inclination and association, more so, perhaps, than most Gelugpas. The Fifth Dalai Lama's position directly above Pehar in this painting, suggests the role that Padmasambhava plays in Nyingma compositions of Dangerous Protectors (cat. nos. 1–2), as in a sense controlling Pehar and Dorje Dragden.

Pehar has five aspects, signifying his body, speech, mind, qualities (or attributes), and activities.[3] The form of Pehar painted here represents the fifth and principal aspect, that of the "king of Buddha-activities." He has three heads (blue, white, and red), and six arms (carrying an iron hook, sword, knife, butcher's stick, bow, and arrow). He wears a cane "riding hat" and sits astride a snow lion. The four small figures around Pehar include a warrior, dark-skinned old woman, monk, and dancing

(cont. p. 259)

Facing page: Cat. no. 6
Pehar Gyalpo
Chief Protector of the State

Tibet, late 17th or 18th c.
Mineral pigments on cloth
13¼ x 9¾ in. (33.7 x 24.8 cm)
F1997.35.3 (HA 551)

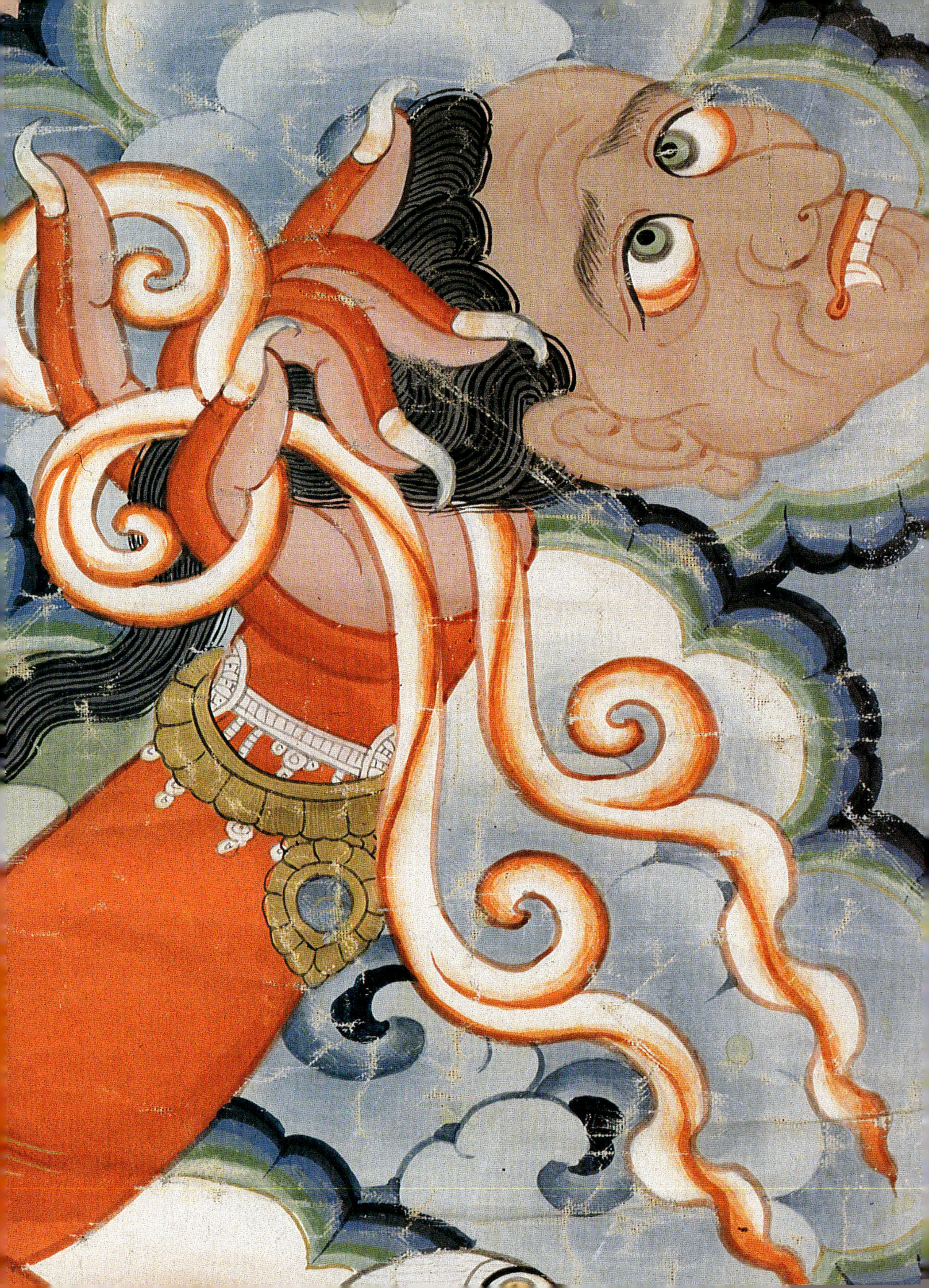

Cat. no. 7

Kandroi Tsomo Chechang Mar

Red Wolf-headed Mistress of Dakinis

Cat no. 8

Sinpoi Tsomo Jigje Mar

Red Zombie-riding Protectress

These two paintings were once part of a set of at least nine paintings centered on Shanglon Gonpo (Minister Mahakala). Collectively, they are the protectors of the four medical *tantras* and derive from the visions or revelations (*nyingtig*, "heart essence") of Yutog Yontan Gonpo (790–1015).[1] The set itself must have been a subset within a larger group, since a third related painting depicts one of the five forms of Pehar, with Yutog Yontan Gonpo above him.[2] In the same place in the composition, catalog number 7 has a depiction of Bhaishajyaguru, the Medicine Buddha. There is an inscription in gold below it, which can be translated as "Buddha, Guru of Medicine," with whom the medical texts are associated.[3] Catalog number 8 includes a portrait of the Desi Sanggye Gyatso (1653–1705) who presided over the group of scholars who produced a commentary on the medical *tantras*, the *Blue Beryl*. An inscription beside the portrait translates as "Homage to the Protector of the World, Sanggye Gyatso."[4] On the back of the cloth mounting of each painting, at the top, are short inscriptions that would be visible when the paintings are rolled up and stacked. They are abbreviated names for the main figures, "The Wrathful Wolf," and "The Demon who Tames the Enemy."

Five of the nine protectors of the medical *tantras*, including the two shown here, have nine-headed animals as mounts and are very large in relation to the picture surface, without attendants. The scale gives room for some surprising nuances, in some instances bordering on the comic. In the painting of Kandroi Tsomo, the "Mistress of Dakinis" (cat. no. 7), there is a witty contrast between the happily ferocious wolf-head and the wide-eyed vapid

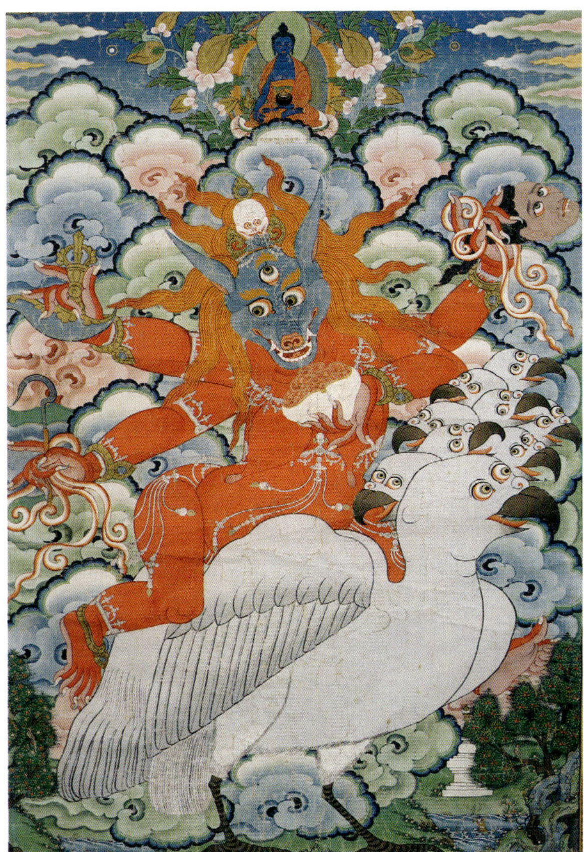

Cat. no. 7
Kandroi Tsomo Chechang Mar
Red Wolf-headed Mistress of Dakinis

Tibet, 19th c.
Mineral pigments on cloth
34¾ x 23½ in. (86.4 x 59.7 cm)
Collection of Shelley and Donald Rubin (HA 192)

On page 119: Cat. no. 8
Sinpoi Tsomo Jigje Mar
Red Zombie-riding Protectress

Tibet, 19th c.
Mineral pigments on cloth
33 x 23¾ in. (83.8 x 60.3 cm)
Collection of Shelley and Donald Rubin (HA 193)

Cat. no. 7, detail

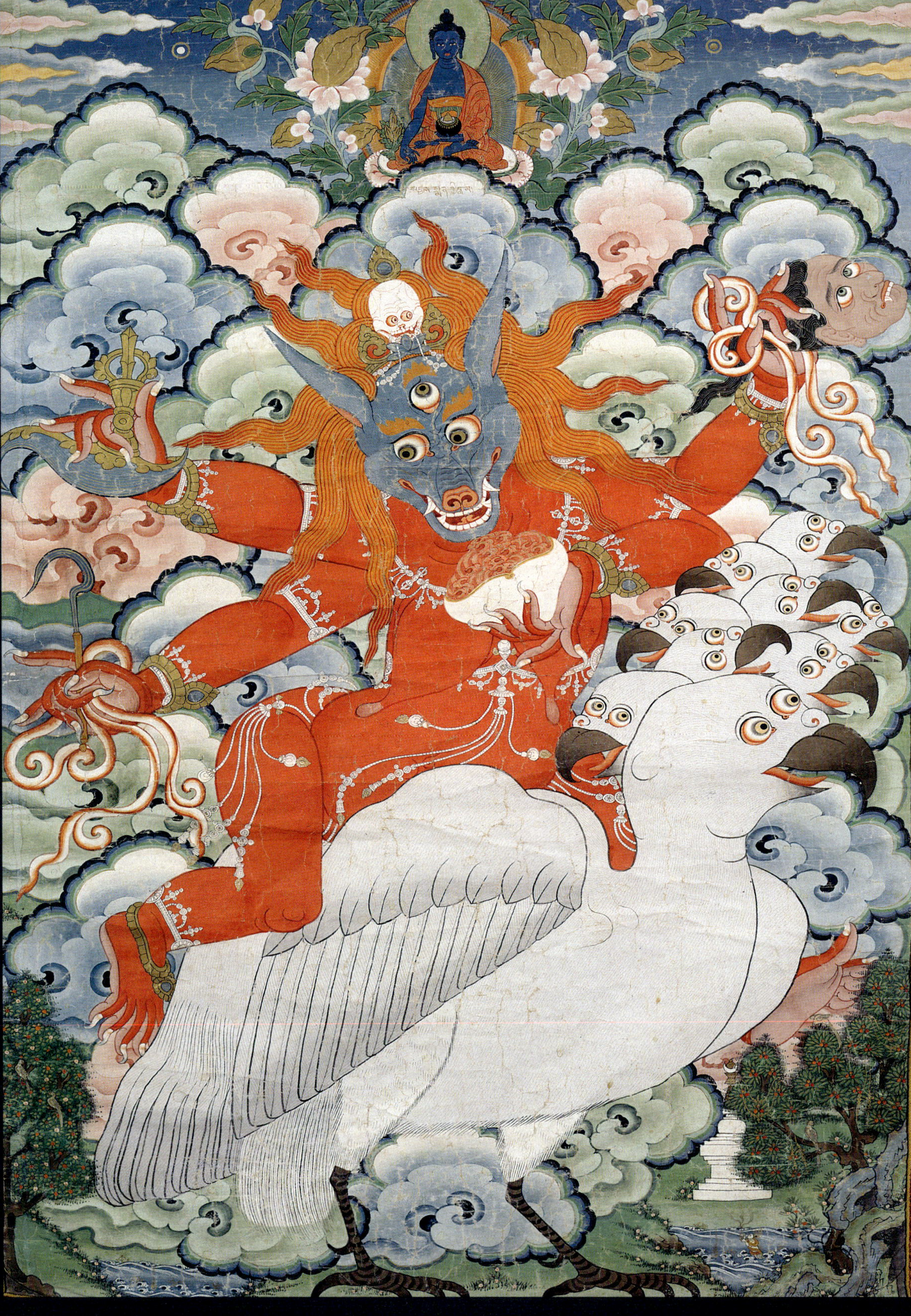

Cat. no. 7

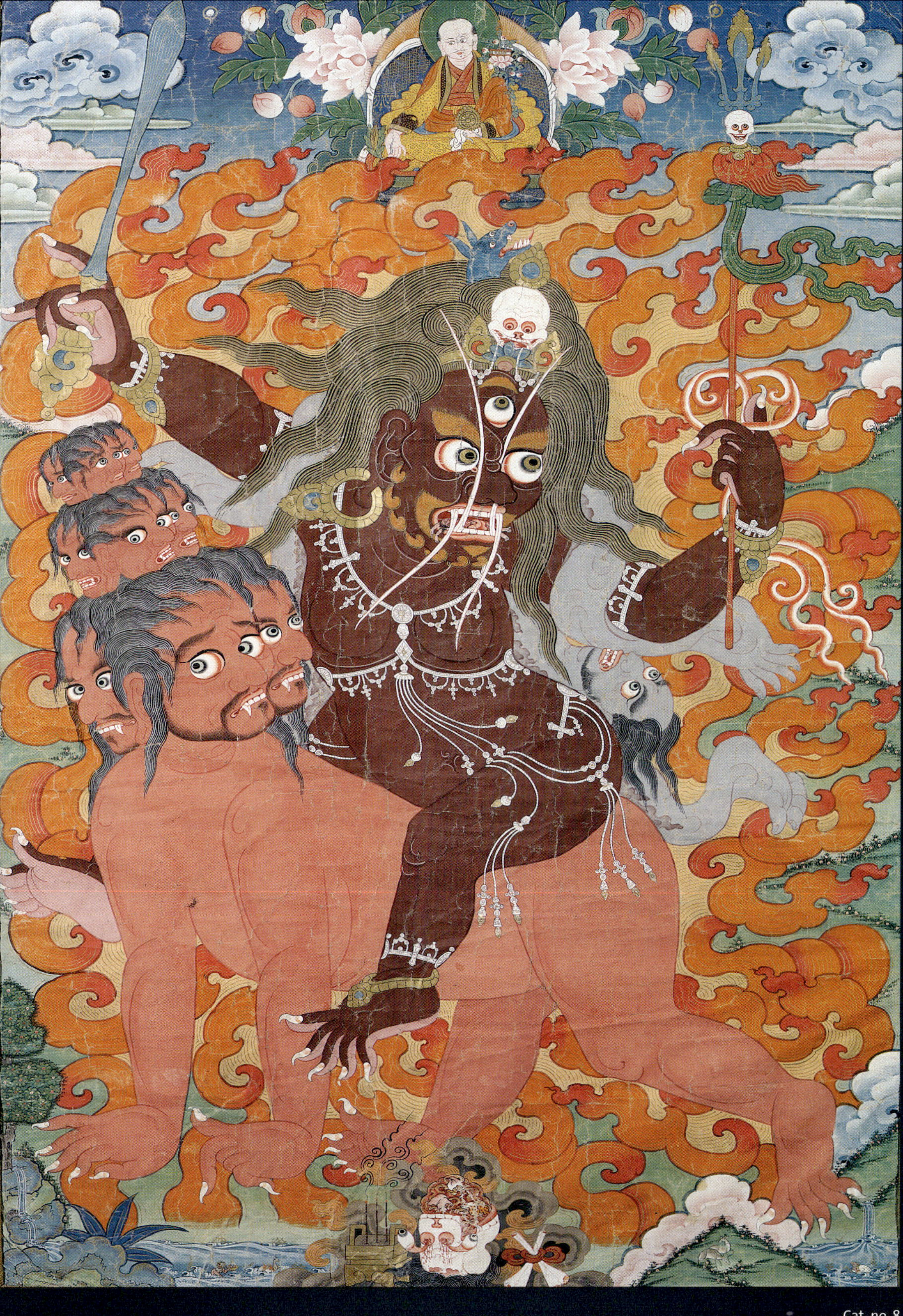

Cat. no. 8

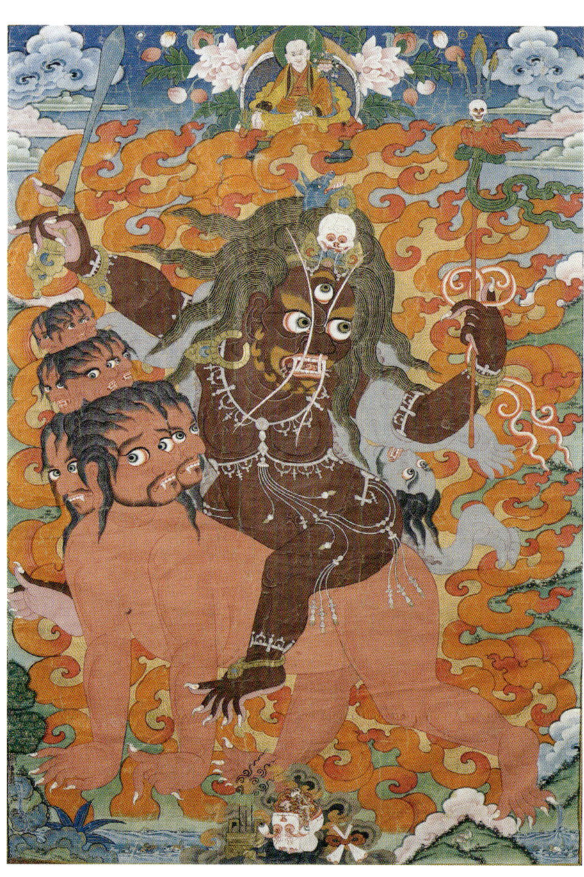

Cat. no. 8

look on the bird heads staring in all directions. There is also a surprising elegance in the hand lifting up the head and intestines of some unfortunate obstacle-creating demon (see detail). In the other painting, of Sinpoi Tsomo, the "Mistress of Demons" (cat. no. 8), there is an expression of almost tender surprise and wonder on the zombie's face, confronted by the bizarre fangs and howling miniature wolf-head of the glowering rider (see detail). An unfeigned embrace of the grisly on the part of the artist(s) is conveyed by, among other discordant notes, the disemboweled corpse which the protectress holds under her tongue and, at the bottom, a skull full of freshly severed organs, next to a pair of shin-bones tied together. Yet along the lower edge of both paintings, there are landscapes with streams, trees, and birds and a most bucolic atmosphere.

(notes p. 259)

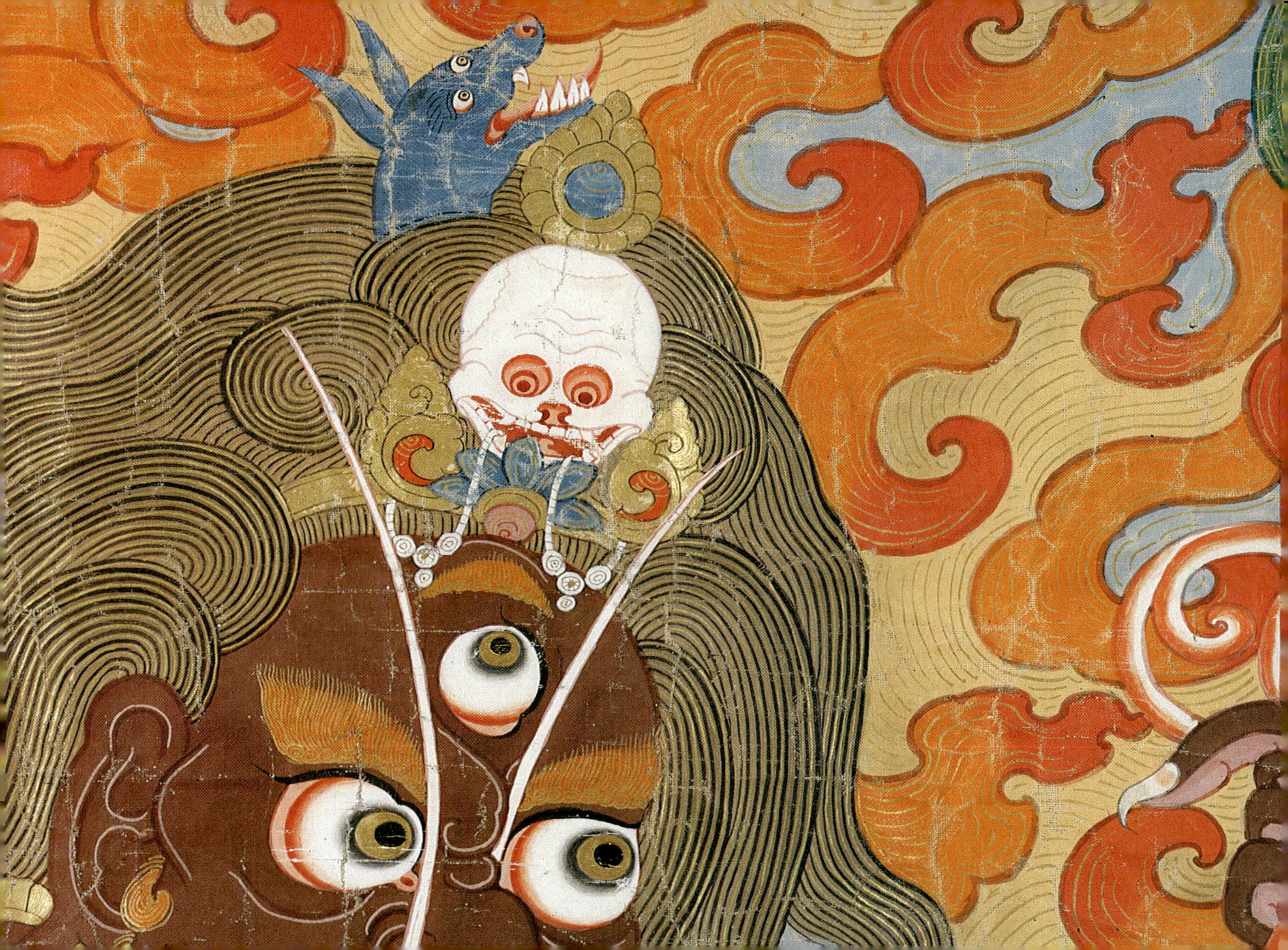

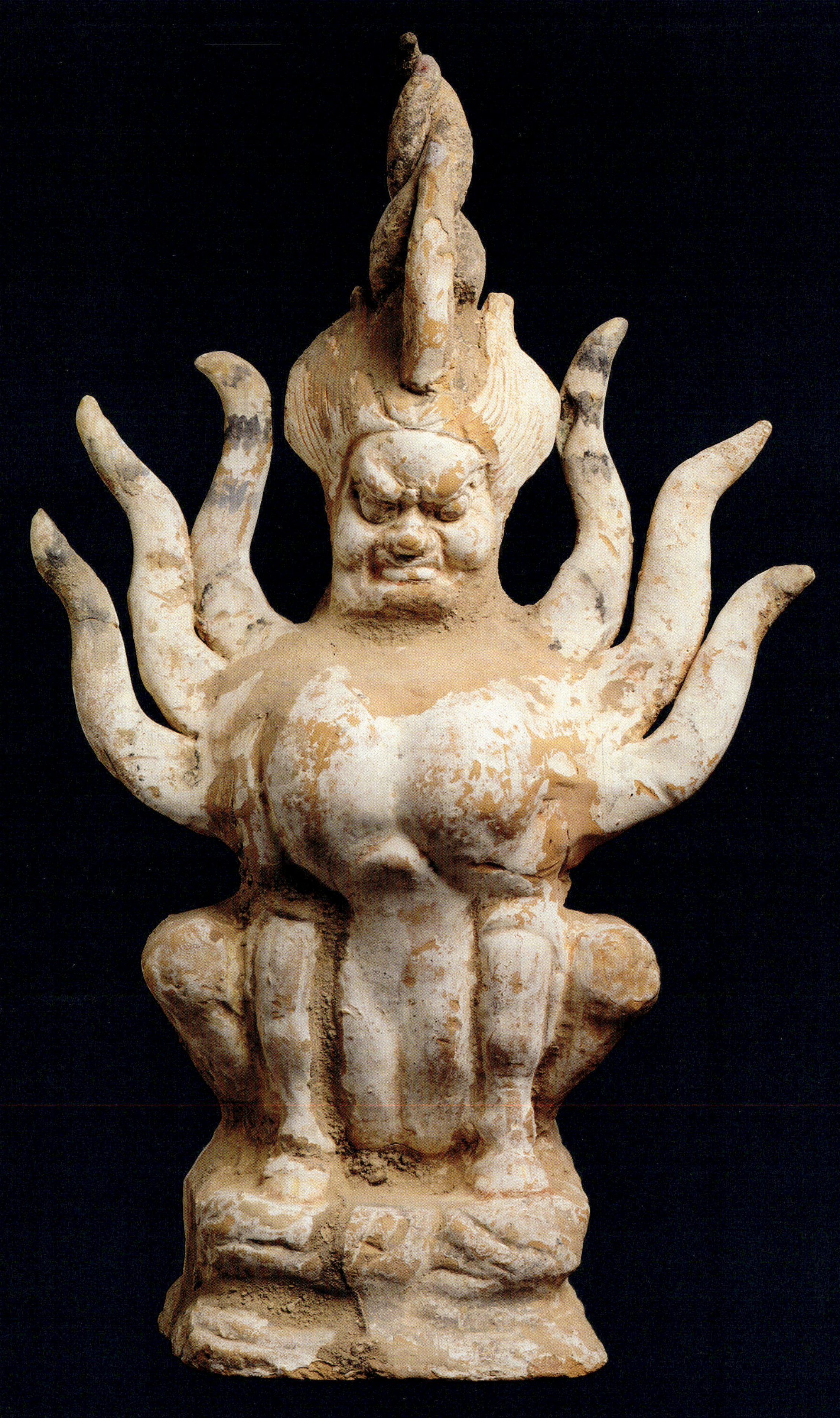

Cat. no. 9

Tomb Guardian

The two Tang dynasty (618–906) tomb figures (cat. nos. 9 and 48) exemplify the enduring tendency in Chinese culture to combine features from different creatures into a fantastic hybrid. Like the Himalayan wrathful protectors, such images were used as apotropaic guardians. In the Tang dynasty, they were created in pairs—one human-faced like the late seventh-century figure, and the other animal-faced—and assembled inside tombs to scare away spirits. Alongside representations of military and civil officials, as well as animals and attendants, a pair of wrathful guardians was one unit within an extensive set of tomb figures employed in upper-class tombs to accompany the tomb's occupant into the afterlife.

This one, which is earlier than catalog number 48, has a scowling human visage, swept-up hair and a high crest. Featherlike spikes emerge from his shoulders, while his bulging chest leads to solid, leonine legs. The red clay is coated with a white slip and fired at relatively low temperatures. The figure was probably painted before placement within the tomb. These terrifying composite defenders are known as *zhenmushou*, or "tomb guardian creature," and though they have deep roots in China's antiquity, "during the Sui and Tang periods, *zhenmushou* become increasingly dramatic and fearsome."[1]

(note p. 260)

Facing page: Cat. no. 9
Tomb Guardian

China, late 7th c.
Red clay with white slip and pigment traces
H. 14 ¾ in. (37.5 cm)
Schloss Collection, New York

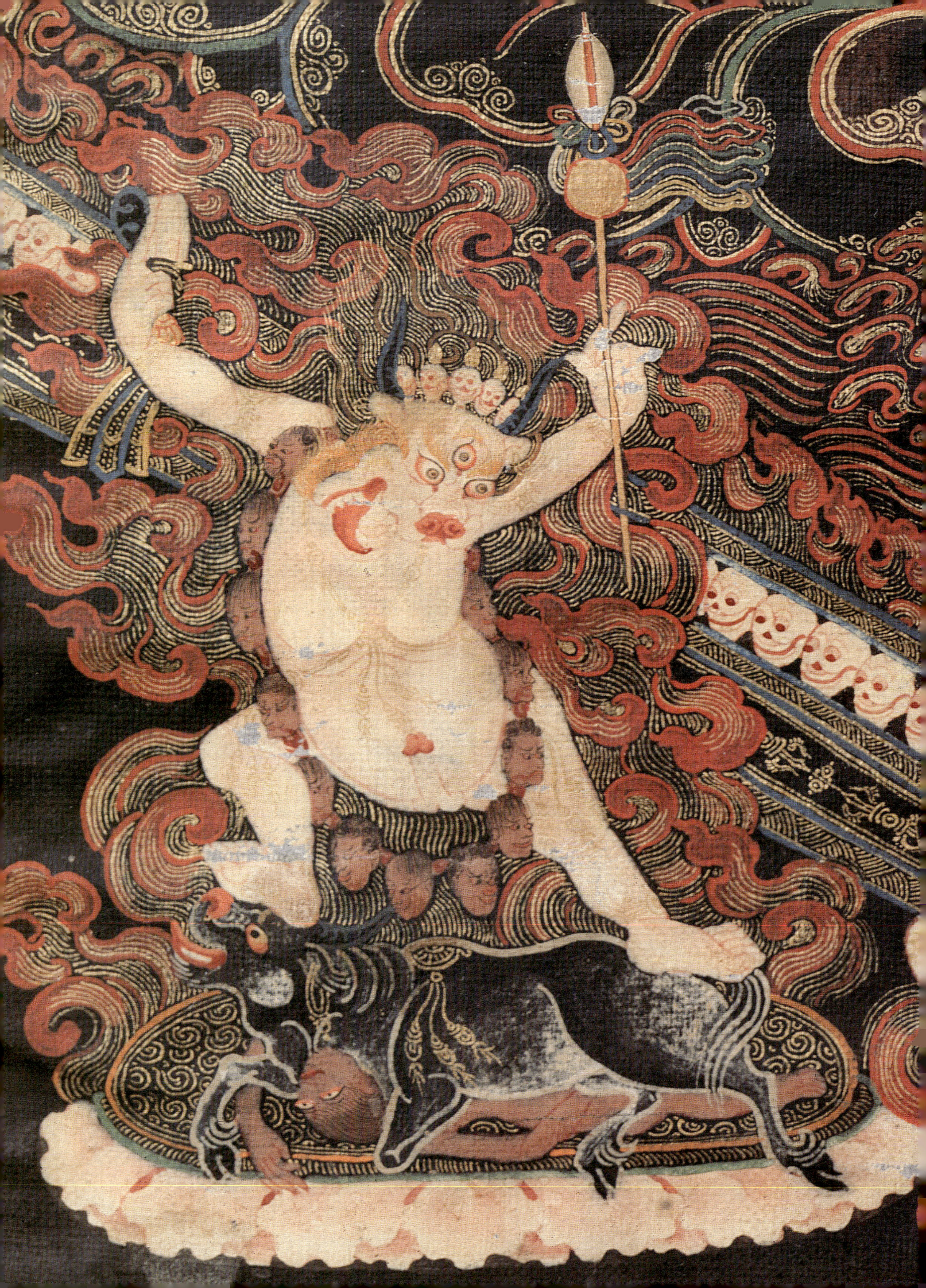

Enlightened Protectors

This broad group of work shows the widest range of emotions and effects, from the wickedly humorous, ghoulish, strange, and unsettling, to the outright horrifying and violent. Paradoxically, the more terrible the central figures look, the more powerful they are considered to be as protectors. Enlightened Protectors are wholehearted supporters of the greater good of those who petition them. Unlike the Dangerous Protectors, who are more limited in what they can do, Enlightened Protectors offer material as well as psychic benefits, protecting spiritual aspirants during times of vulnerability, nourishing religious communities, and safeguarding whole schools of Buddhism. Many of them entered Tibet with Buddhism from India. The two who have, perhaps, inspired the most paintings and sculptures are Mahakala (The Great Black One) and Yama Dharmaraja (Death, the King protector of the Law of Cause and Effect). Each has several different forms, and some of the varieties are surveyed here.

Cat. no. 33, detail

Cat. nos. 10, 11, 12

Smashana Adipati

Lords of the Charnel Ground

Facing page: Cat. no. 10
Smashana Adipati
Lords of the Charnel Ground

Tibet, 15th c.
Mineral pigments on cloth
18 x 14½ in. (45.7 x 36.8 cm)
F1996.16.5 (HA 462)

On page 130: Cat. no. 11
Smashana Adipati
Lords of the Charnel Ground

Tibet, 18th c.
Painted terracotta
6¼ x 5¼ x 1¼ in. (15.9 x 13.3 x 3.2 cm)
C2002.36.1 (HA 65149)

On page 132: Cat. no 12
Smashana Adipati
Lords of the Charnel Ground

Tibet, 19th c.
Mineral pigments on cloth
23¼ x 17 in. (59 x 43.2 cm)
Collection of Shelley and Donald Rubin (HA 302)

Smashana Adipati is one of the Sanskrit names for a dancing-skeleton couple who inhabit and preside over (thus *adipati*, "lords") cremation grounds (*smashana*), where Indian Tantric *yogins* were encouraged to practice. The name used more often in western literature, Chitipati (*chiti*, funeral pyre), has a much more recent pedigree, at least as far as it can be traced at this point.[1] (In this exhibition catalog, "Smashana Adipati" is used for the formal nomenclature of titles, while the more familiar "Chitipati" is used in the text.)

The Chitipati, considered by some to be sibling, and by others to be lovers, have several functions in Esoteric Buddhist practice, including protection for those engaged in the meditation Vajrayogini (see cat. nos. 42, 43 and 57, 58), as well as guarding wealth from thieves. A prayer to the Chitipati compiled by the erudite Tibetan scholar Taranatha (1575–1634) includes the request that they "annihilate all enemies and robbers who would harm or injure us *yogins* and our companions."[2] Indeed, on the back of catalog number 11 is a prayer to ward off thieves. A sense of the variety of their functions can be derived from a request in a Sakya text:

> [G]uard the pledges, do not allow the excellent teachings of the holy gurus, root and lineage, to pass away. For [the sake of] the exceptional Teachings of the Buddha, holders of the teachings, and we, yogis together with retinue, completely eliminate mischief and harm [caused by] all the hosts of enemies, hindrances and harm doers, and bestow longlife, freedom from illness, an increase in resources, and perform the activity of binding all thieves and robbers.[3]

Of the main lineages of Esoteric Buddhist practice in Tibet, it was the Sakyas who first gave the Chitipati a prominent role.[4] Later, around the time of the Fifth Dalai Lama (second half of the seventeenth century), the Gelugpa absorbed the Chitipati into their sys-

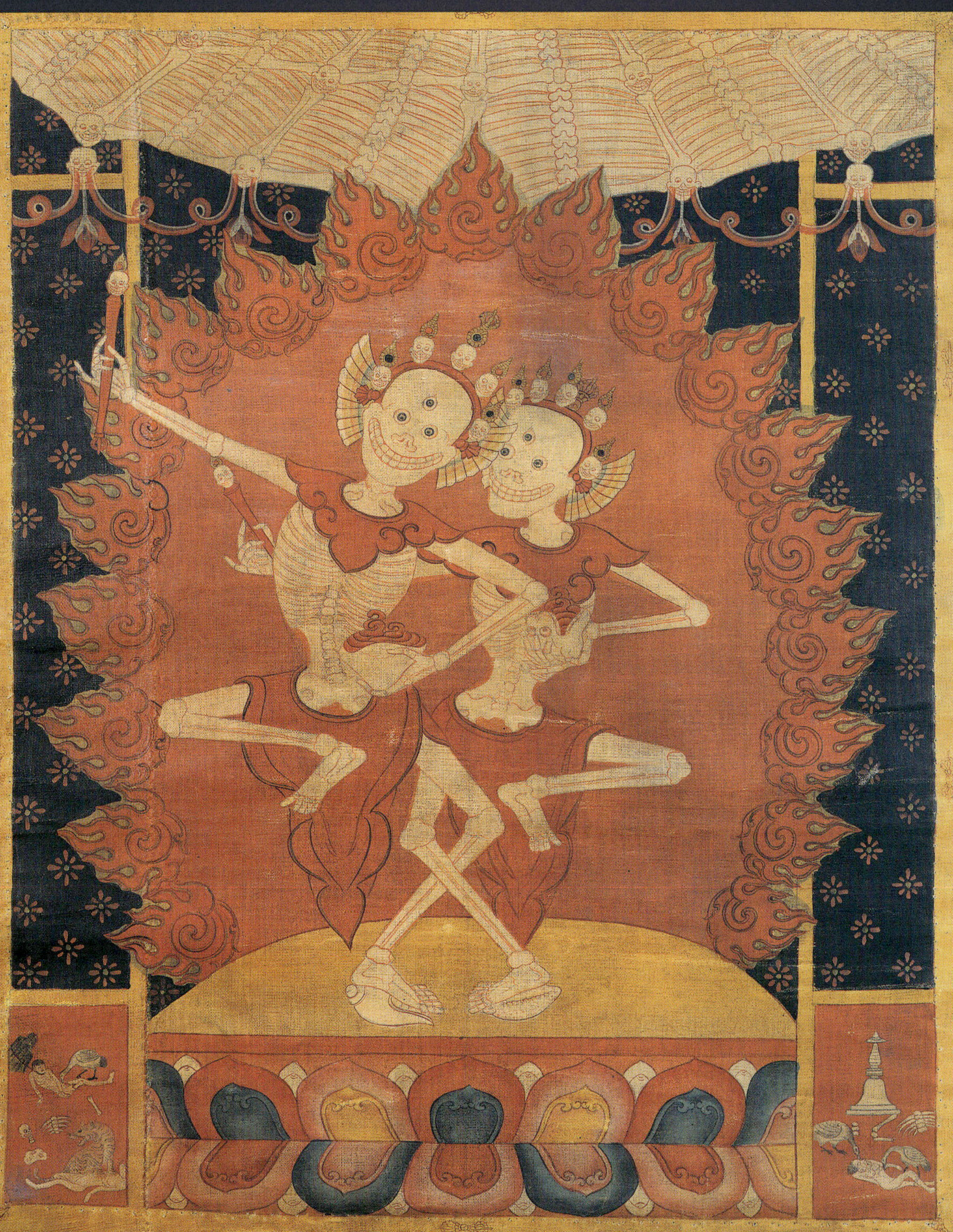

Cat. no. 10

tem, and the couple migrated into Baram Kagyu and Chod lineage paintings as well. There are differences in depictions for the Sakya from those for other lineages. In Sakya texts and paintings (such as cat. no. 10, and fig. 1.6), both figures consistently hold identical objects in their left and right hands: a skull-or skeleton-tipped scepter and a skull bowl containing swirling blood, respectively.[5] By contrast, the Gelugpa images such as catalog number 12 usually give the female a stalk of grain and a vase signifying the bestowal of wealth.[6] Both these attributes may relate to the Chitipati's status as benefactors, an understanding of their roles that traces back to Sakya practice in their function of protecting wealth against thieves. In the case of catalog number 12, a late-nineteenth-century painting, the wealth vase is turned into a long-life vase by the addition on its lid of a tiny image of Amitayus, a Buddha associated with long-life rituals.

Although the artists or patrons of catalog numbers 11 and 12 have changed the attributes held by the female, other crucial distinctions between the pair have been maintained. The male is slightly larger, always appears on the viewer's left, and stands on a conch shell, while the female figure stands on a cowry shell. Another key iconographic characteristic is the crown with skulls.

Compared to other depictions, the painting of catalog number 10, which is among the early extant paintings of Chitipati, is quite clear in its location of the dancing couple in a cremation or charnel ground. Two panels in the lower corners depict vultures and a tiger devouring corpses abandoned there. The tiny human on the right seems still alive, but tethered to a rock as a bird pecks at him. A white *chorten* (*stupa*) on the right panel is a reminder that this ubiquitous symbol of the presence of the Buddha's teaching is also a reliquary built over the ashes and relics of cremated bodies. Another literal reminder of the gruesome habitat of the Chitipati is the canopy of rib cages spread above them, with intestines looped like garlands. Taranatha's text mentions that the Chitipati appear above "a Mount Meru of skeletons" or a "skull-fortress palace," while another text describes it as follows:

> In the sky in front . . . is an ocean of blood . . . a great field of earth . . . a great mountain of piled up skeletons; above that, a dry skull palace saturated with dripping blood; and with half-lattice loops of lung, heart and intestines; the ground covered with spread out skins.[7]

A similar architectural structure constructed of bones and skulls is visible on the right in catalog number 31, though the Chitipati are not depicted within it.

The relish with which painters engaged the theme of these gruesome figures seems to have been shared by sculptors, as catalog number 11 demonstrates. The sculptors have convincingly embodied the paradox of skeletons (which humans inevitably connect with the inert remains when flesh and internal organs have decomposed) animated by ecstatic dance and laughter. This apparent contradiction is an important aspect of the character of the "demonic divine" in general, and the Chitipati theme in particular. As one scholar noted, "Whatever their grisly associations in our minds, in Tibetan art and in dance the [Chitipati] are joyous, even comic figures," who express the "joyful freedom from attachment."[8]

The two main figures of the sculpture are very delicately rendered in low-fired clay, the closely observed physiognomic details recalling Japanese wood or ivory *netsuke* with comparable, but not identical themes. As if stepping together to a syncopated rhythm, the pair emerge off the flat backdrop with angular, interlocking postures, tilting their heads inward toward each other. The two figures are clearly distinguished from each other by the attributes they hold and by the conch and cowry in front of the male and female, respectively. In addition, the male figure wears a garland of freshly severed heads, while the female figure has a dried skulls strung together. Red paint has been applied with care to eye-sockets, tongues, the interior of rib cages, the eyes on the garlanded heads and, mixed with gold, the flames on the backdrop.

Catalog number 12 is the most complex of the Chitipati images in the exhibition. The cremation ground is replaced by a green landscape beneath a blue sky, in which float the wrathful Vajrapani and the peaceful White Tara. On the ground below are Jambhala and Vasudhara, benefactors who reinforce the Chitipati's associations with wealth. In this combination, the four subsidiary deities convey a Gelugpa patronage for the painting, confirmed by the changes made to the attributes held by the female.

In addition to the macabre intensity with which the Chitipati stare into each other's eyes, noteworthy features of the main figures include the floral brocade capes over their shoulders, the tiger pelt wrapped around the pelvis of the male, the female's skirt matching her fluttering scarf, and the rainbow-hued fans attached at the earholes of both figures. These "ear-ornaments" are not found on the Sakya image (cat. no. 10), but do appear on the terracotta sculpture (cat. no. 11). They became so closely associated with the Chitipati that one scholar reported that the Mongolian term for the colorful splayed fans, "butterflies," is also used to designate the Chitipati themselves when they appear in the masked dances (Cham).[9]

Below the lotus dais is a tray with vigorously painted triple *tormas,* representing the

(cont. p. 260)

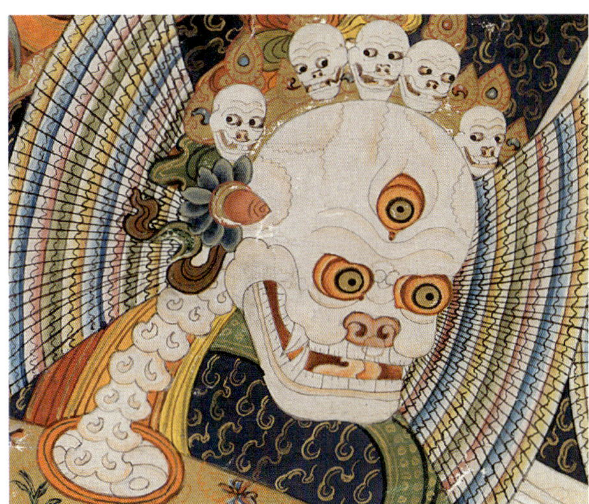

Cat. no. 12, detail

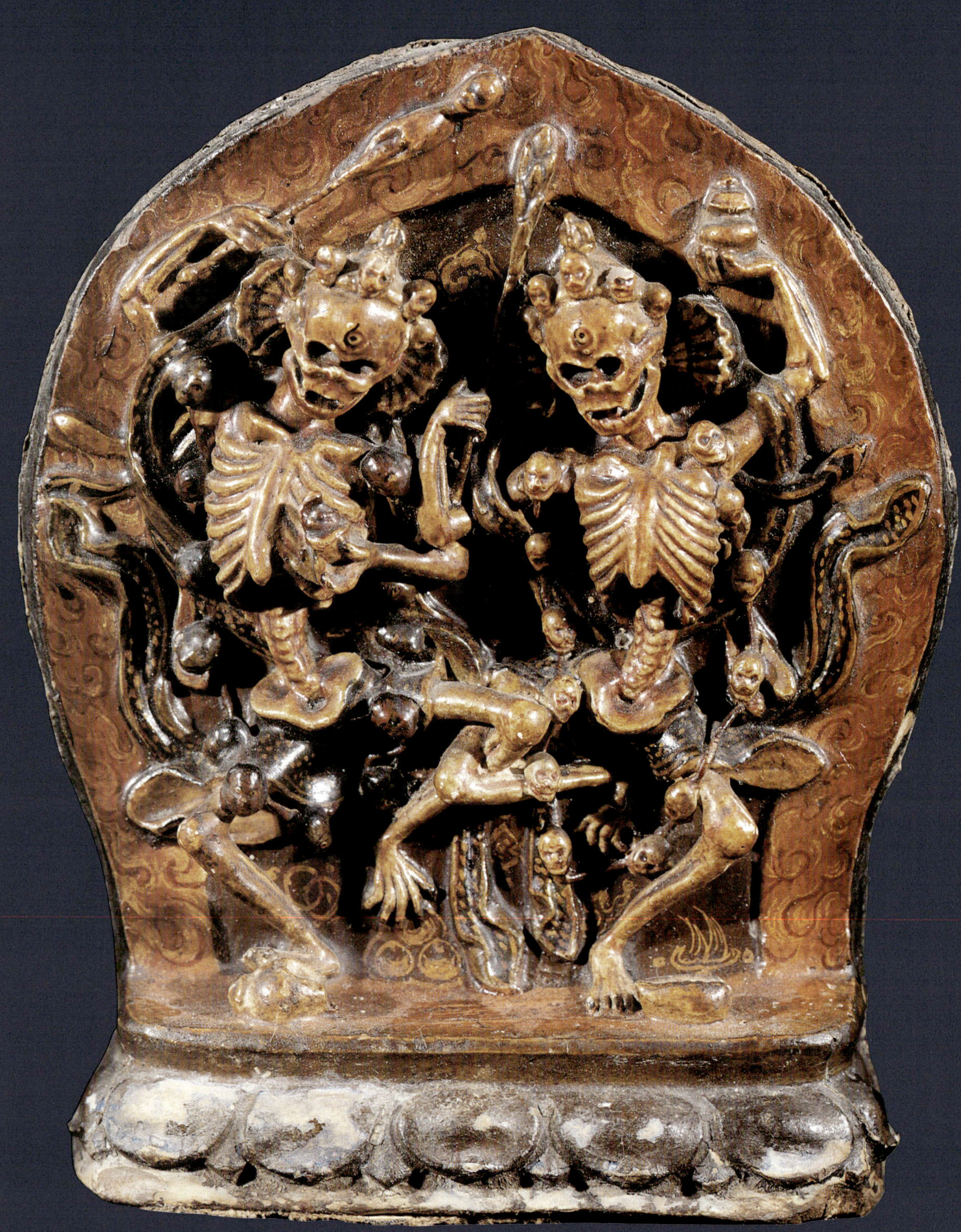

Cat. no. 11

Cat. no. 13

Pareja de Esqueletos

(Skeleton Couple)

Icons of the *memento mori*, skeletons are a cross-cultural reminder that no one escapes death. However, from Goth fetish to laboratory reference, their meaning varies, based on social context. In Mexico, skeletons are closely linked to *Dia de los Muertos* or the Day of the Dead celebration.[1] During this three-day holiday, the spirits of the dead are believed to visit the living friends and families they left behind.[2] In celebration, people decorate altars, graves, and public spaces with a rich display of marigolds, candles, incense, limes, and objects of papier-mâché.[3]

This papier-mâché skeleton couple was made by the popular Mexican artist, Pedro Linares (d. 1992). Festive and bright like the Tibetan Chitipati paintings (cat. nos. 10 and 12), Linares' *esqueletos* are drawn with a stylized line and vivid colors typical of objects made for the *Dia de los Muertos.* Both the Chitipati and the *esqueletos* demonstrate exaggerated facial features—large grinning mouths and well-punctuated eyes. In constrast to Western equivalents such as Albrecht Dürer's skeletal figure of death clothed in tattered garments hanging from the bones, the Linares *esqueletos* are well dressed.[4] Like the Chitipati who are discreetly covered in silks and animal pelts, the female *esqueleto* wears a traditional dance skirt. Cleanly tailored and brightly colored, these garments seem to beautify the skeleton, perhaps demonstrating a more accepting relationship to death than Dürer's macabre Western archetype. Or does this celebration of death deny its inevitable finality?

(notes p. 261)

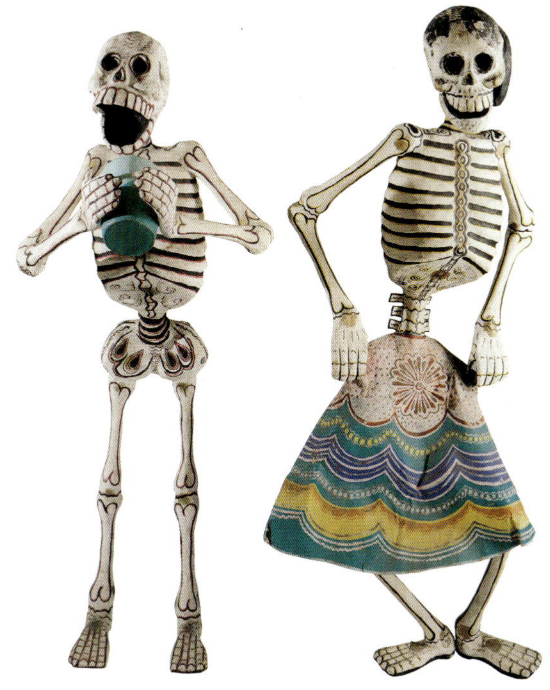

Cat. no 13
Pareja de Esqueletos (Skeleton Couple)

Pedro Linares (1907–1992), Mexico
Painted papier-mâché
Male figure: 69 x 27 x 32 in.
(175.3 x 68.6 x 81.3 cm)
Female figure: 73 x 30 x 15 in.
(185.4 x 76.2 x 38.1 cm)
El Museo del Barrio, New York
Gift of Margery Nathanson

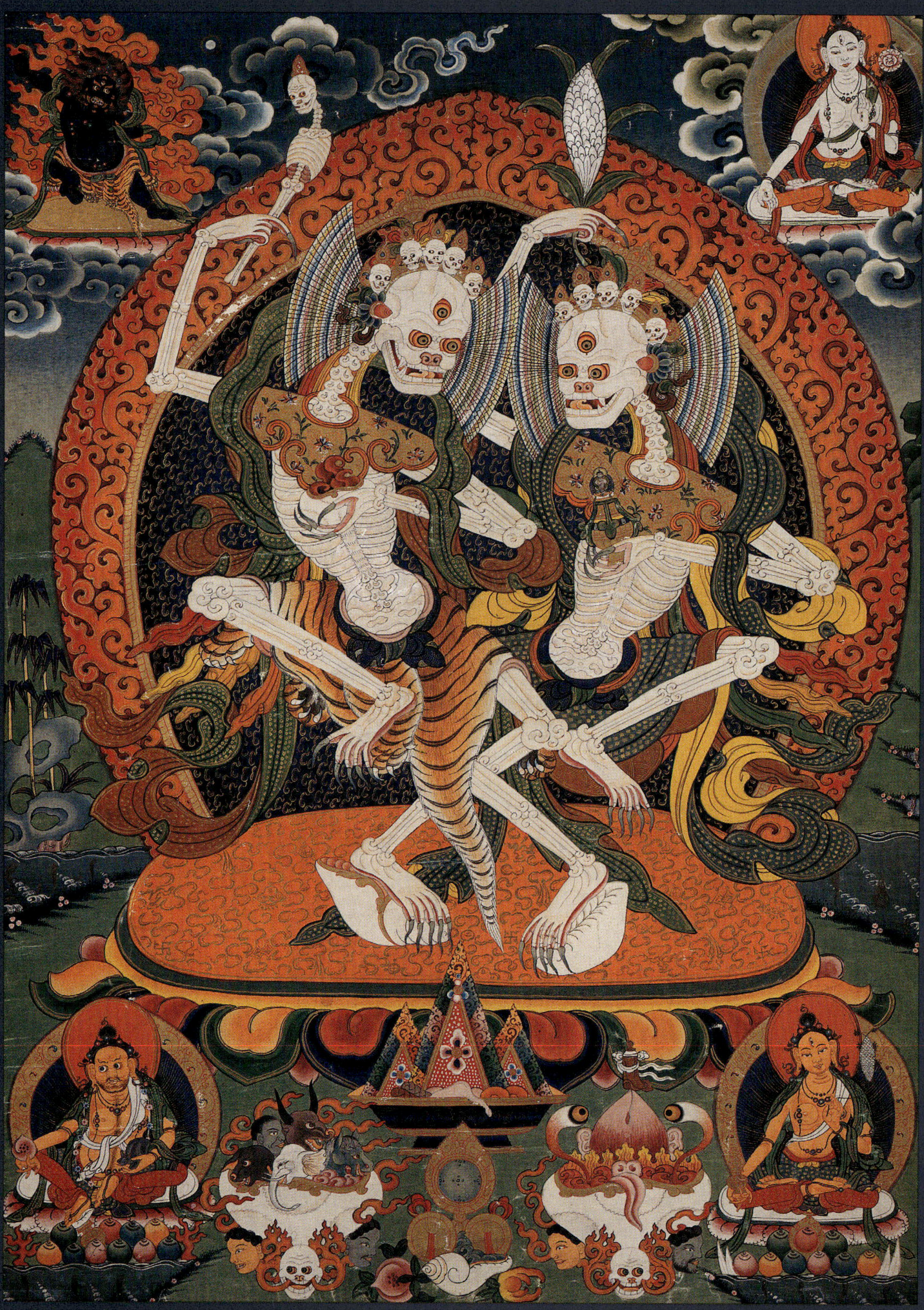

Cat. no. 12

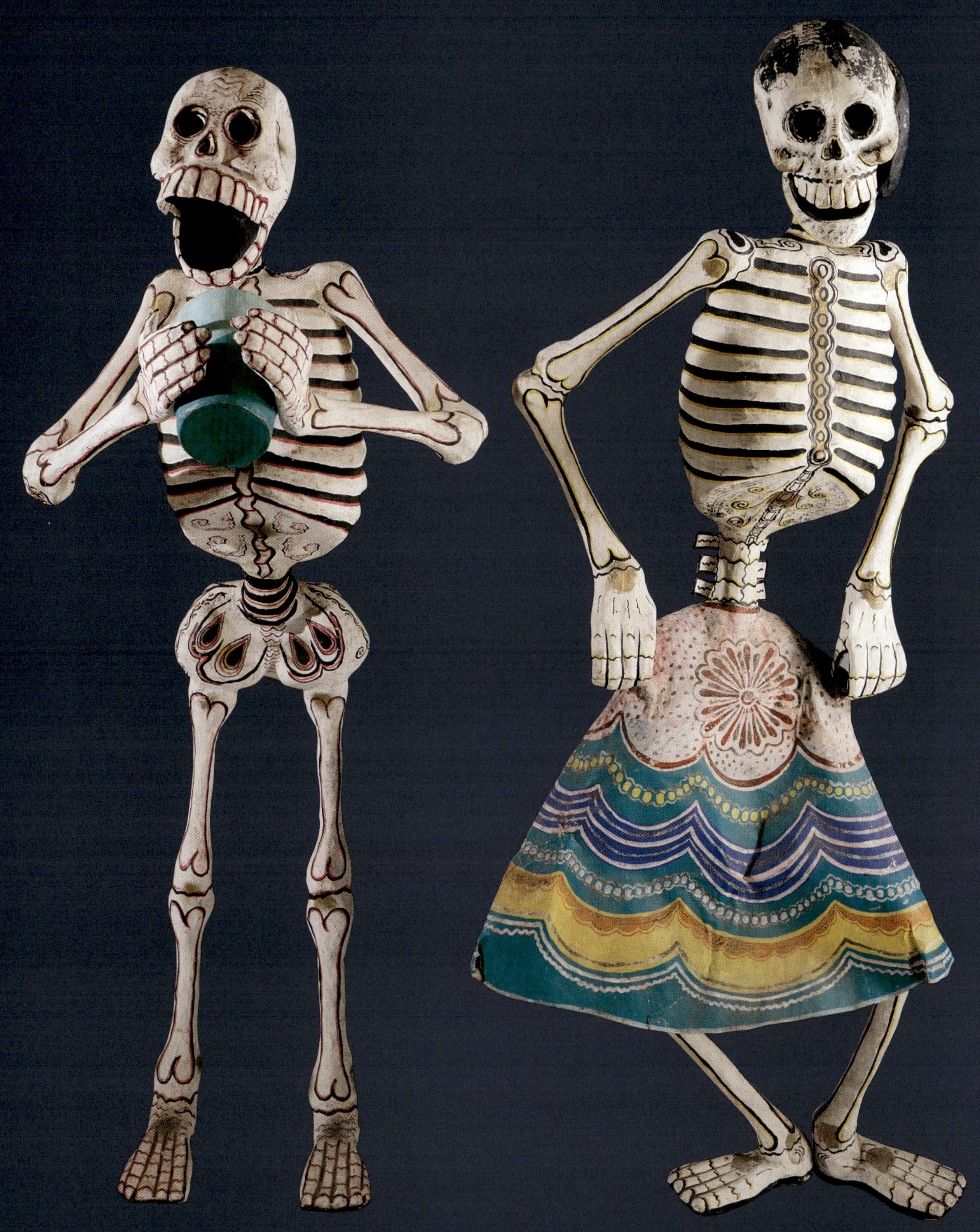

Cat. no. 13

Facing page: Cat. no. 14
One of a Pair of Long Trumpet-horn Stands

Himalayan culture, ca. 17th c.
Metalwork
29 x 13½ x 7 in. (73.7 x 34.3 x 17.8 cm)
Collection of Navin Kumar, New York (HA 70657)

Cat. no. 14

One of a Pair of Long Trumpet-horn Stands

This metalwork figure of a dancing skeleton was one of a pair of stands for the long horns (*dungchen*) used to produce deep lingering bass notes in monastic rituals. The wide end of the trumpet would rest on a metal arc that was attached through a hole in the flat palm of the skeleton's raised hand. A monk stood to blow through the narrow mouthpiece at the other end. In the masked rituals known as Cham, skeletons play minor but visible roles, and it is common for the *dungchen* horns to be played. A stand such as this one would have contributed to the setting in which masked and costumed monks dance in the central courtyard. Comparable stands sometimes consisted of a pair of skeletons.[1]

The visual similarity to the interlocked skeletons known as Chitipati (Smashana Adipati, cat. nos. 10–13) is very close, which has led to much confusion in Western literature. The Chitipati, as Lords of the Charnel Ground, function as protectors and benefactors, requiring initiations for their practice. In Cham dances they are given a certain prominence.[2] There are also hosts of other skeleton figures, who are the minor spirits and ghouls of the charnel ground and subject to the Chitipati. These minor skeleton-types are represented on the trumpet-horn stands.[3]

It is not known when such stands began to be produced or used, or if there was a region or lineage that particularly favored them. Pre-modern painted depictions of monastic rituals commonly include monks playing the *dungchen* horns, but it is rare to find depictions of stands like this one. Instead, the trumpets are suspended with a rope, on the shoulder of another monk, or with other types of painted stands.[4]

The artist here has made a hybrid figure that is neither fully skeletal nor fully flesh covered. The elbows, knees, and ankles are hinged fancifully, and the orbital crests exaggerated as they cross and flow around the sides of the cranium. The legs are thin but not

(cont. p. 261)

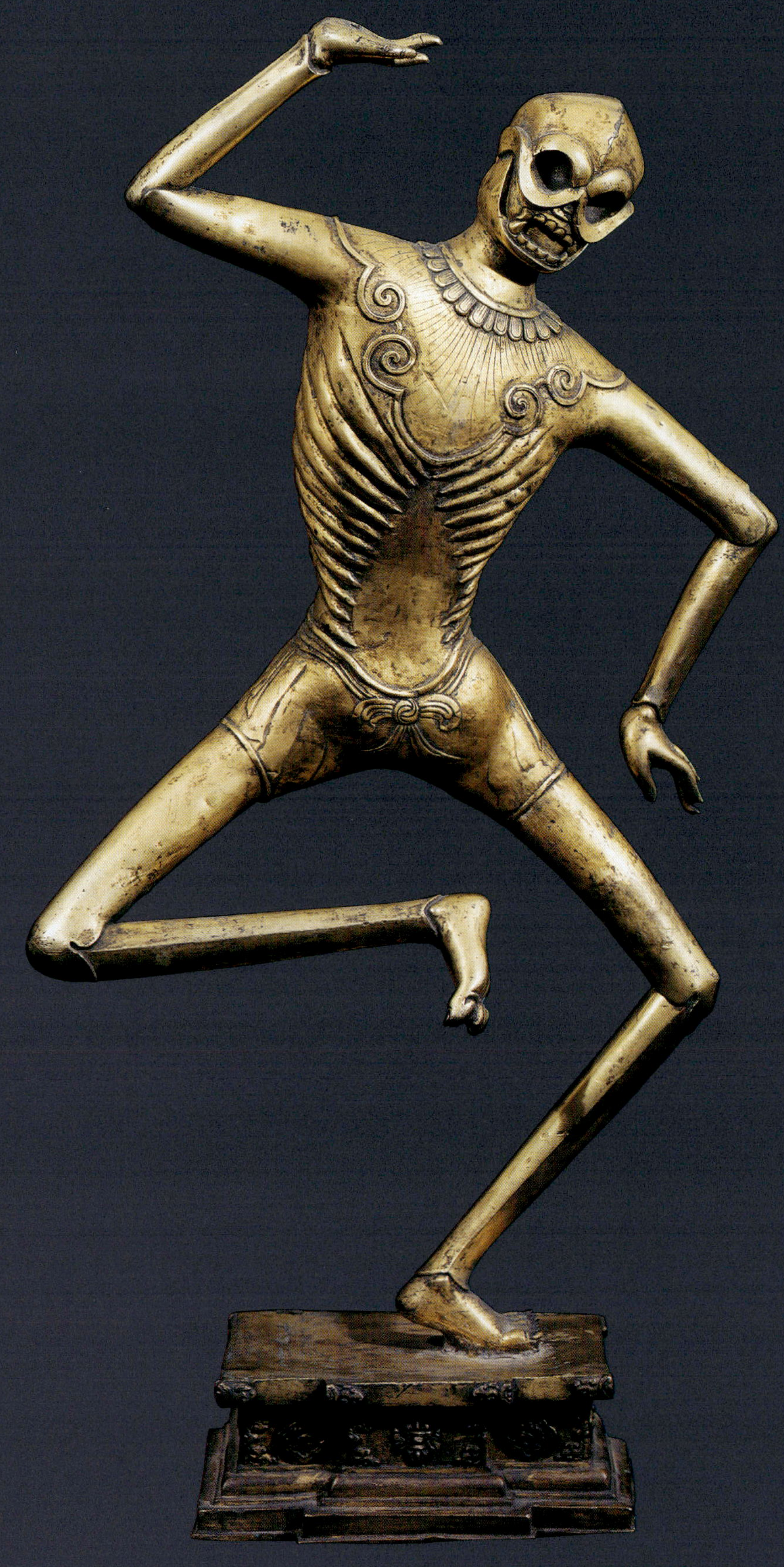

Cat. no. 14

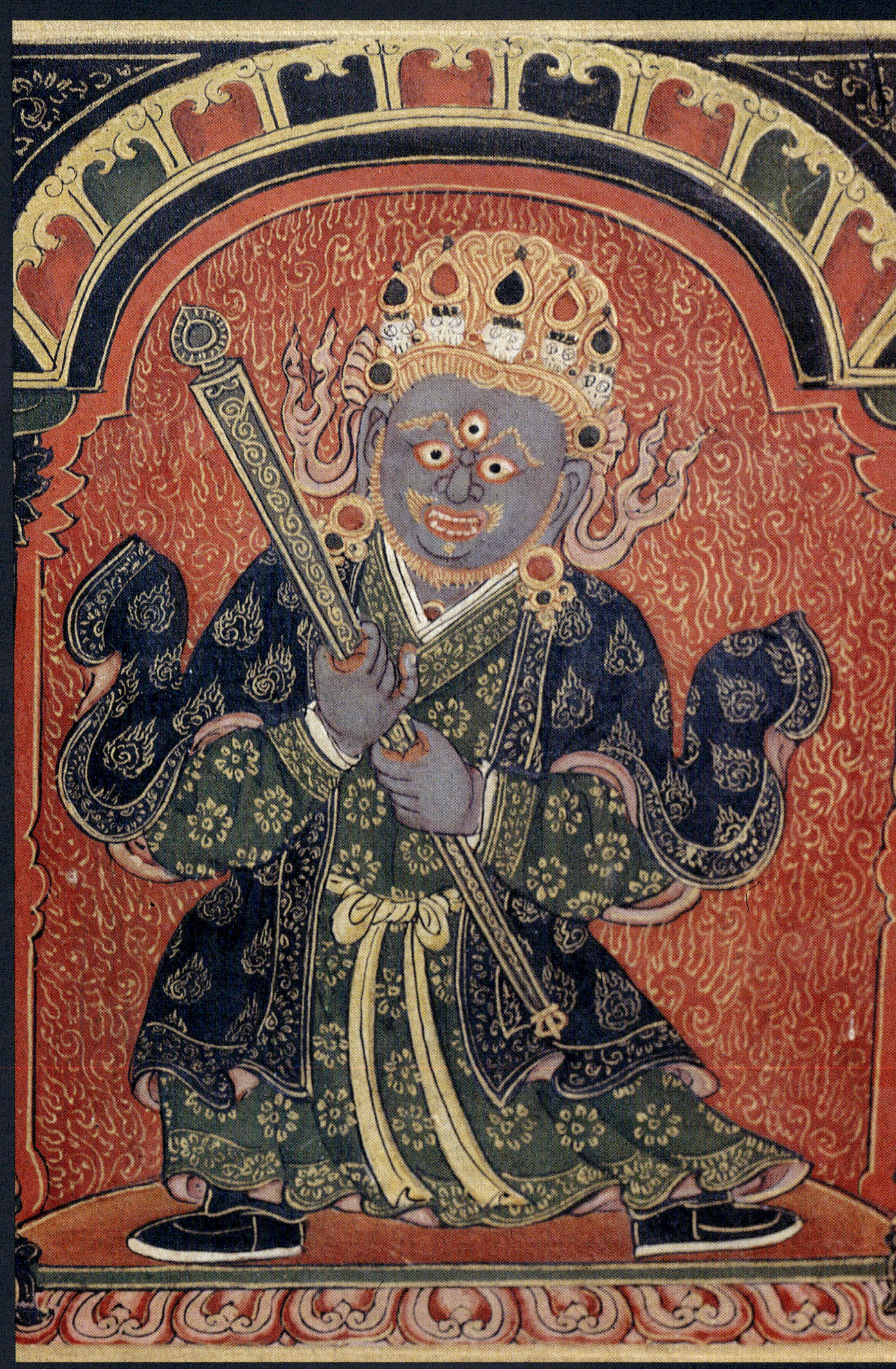

Cat. no. 15

Illuminated Manuscript Page with Four Forms of Mahakala and Vaishravana

This was the back, or bottom, illumination for an elaborately designed and decorated Tibetan-style book. The illustration is inset into a deep rectangular well, or recess, cut into a board made of paper pages glued together. It was at the bottom of the stack of pages, since the front edge has painted decoration consisting of the bottommost tips of petals or medallions, common on some of the more sumptuous books prepared in China. The other three edges were painted plain red. Unfortunately there are no inscriptions on front or back, nor is it possible to determine from the subject matter alone what book this illustrated. It would have been a Buddhist text, most likely from the *tantra (gyu)* sections of the *Kagyur* (collected works accepted as the word of the Buddha by Indo-Himalayan Buddhists) or *Tangyur* (commentaries). Some of the same deities depicted in the painting are known from printed volumes that begin with an illustration of the more important deities described in the *tantras* or commentaries covered in the volume.[1]

The artist was working in a Chinese idiom, as is clear from the faces of the nonwrathful figures, the two corpselike figures under the second and fourth figures, and the central deity. Many such books were produced at court ateliers in the Ming dynasty (1368–1644), particularly in the fifteenth century, for monasteries in the capitals (Nanjing and Beijing) and for visiting Tibetans who received them as gifts.[2] Some of the most elaborate single volumes were profusely illustrated, and perhaps this page was from one of those, rather than part of the larger editions of the complete canon.

The iconography of the main figures is closely based on Tibetan models. At the center is Vaishravana on a lion, a form of the King of the Northern Direction. He holds a mongoose spitting jewels and an umbrella. Here he is both a wealth-bestowing benefactor and a protector of the Dharma (Buddhist teachings) and Buddhists. He is surrounded symmetrically by four forms of Mahakala, each wearing a crown with five skulls, two wearing long green robes on the outside. From the left they are Bernagchen, Chaturbhuja (four-armed), Panjarnata, and Danda Mahakala. Each of the five deities stands on a lotus within his own arch which is supported by decorated pillars, closely related to other paintings of the early Ming Tibeto-Chinese style.[3] The spandrels above the arches have a fine floral pattern of gold on blue, though perhaps not as delicate as the exquisite gold patterns on the red lacquered sandalwood bookcovers prepared for the Ming Yongle Kagyur edition of 1410.[4] Gold lines are applied to the red background against which each figure comes forth, creating a nimbus of swirling flames appropriate to the wrathful theme.

(notes p. 262)

Cat. no. 15
Illuminated Manuscript Page with Four Forms of Mahakala and Vaishravana, King of the Northern Direction
China, 15th c.
Mineral pigments on paper
9½ x 27½ in. (24.1 x 69.9 cm)
F1998.19.2 (HA 700048)

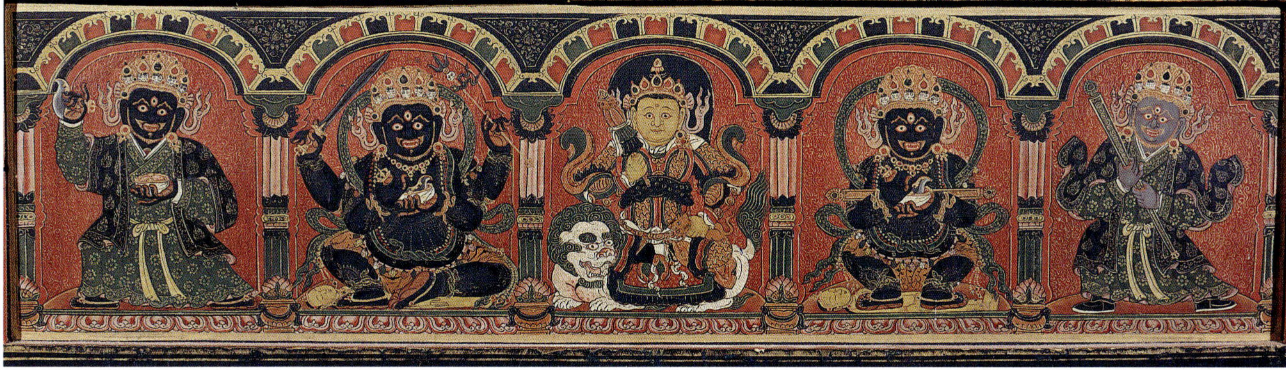

Cat. no. 15, detail

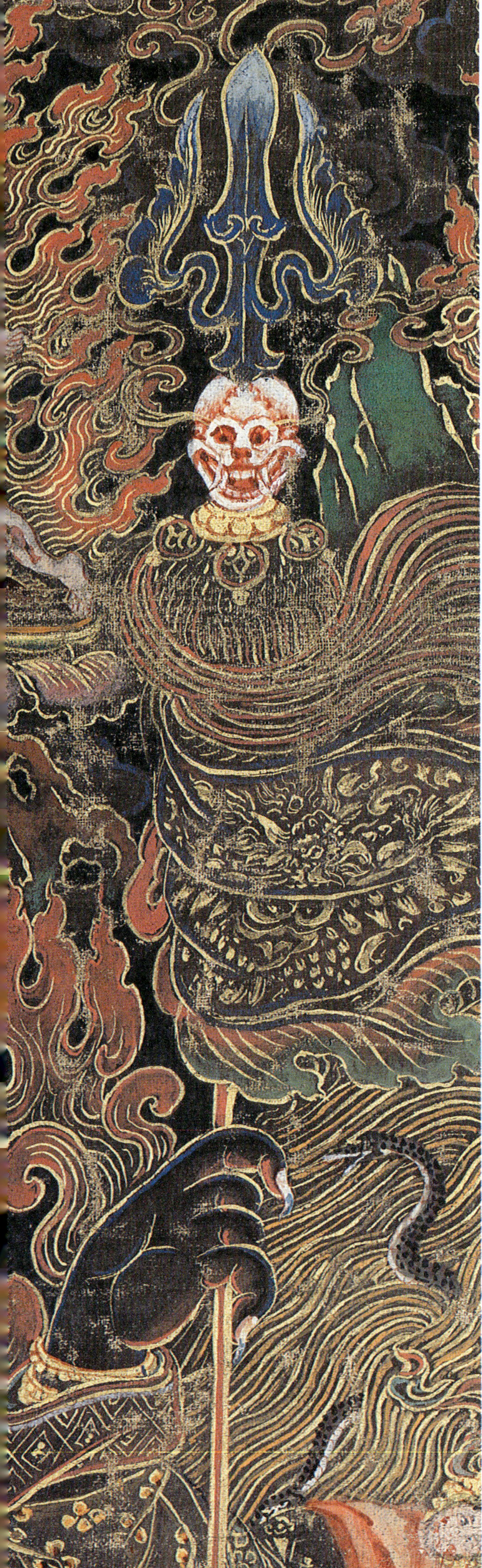

Cat. no. 16

Mahakala

Maning (Eunuch)

This is a relentlessly horrific painting. Out of twenty-five figures (including the two consorts), only three are peaceful deities. The rest form an inventory of the more extreme expressions, activities, and attributes that Himalayan artists working within the Buddhist tradition have created. It is also a compendium of the forms of Mahakala pertinent to the Nyingma school, including some rarely seen versions, nine in all (cat. key 16.1, 16.9–15, 16.19).

The central figure is the Black Eunuch, or Maning Mahakala , with a human heart in his hand and a garland of them around his neck. He carries a *trishula* (trident), with a black pennant. The bottom of the staff sinks into the head of one of the suffering obstacle-enemies underfoot. Maning also drags another demon by a rope held in his left hand. He has his *gandi*-staff pushed through his belt, and human corpses and horses bleeding through the nose and mouth are crushed under his lotus dais. Maning Mahakala presides over all the Dangerous and Enlightened Protectors of the Nyingma school, according to a *terma* from the tradition of Terton Chowang (1212–70).[1] In the context of the exploration of the demonic divine in Himalayan art and beyond, Maning's Medusa-like hair is particularly striking (see cat. no. 20).

The term *maning* (eunuch) used in Mahakala's name requires some explanation. In this context it means without sex or without genitals, but not in the sense of a male who has been castrated. In the past, it has sometimes been translated as "hermaphrodite," as in one with both male and female sexual organs. Since there are words in both Tibetan and Sanskrit for hermaphrodite, one would expect those to be used if that was the intended meaning. The Tibetan word *maning* is explained as the translation for the Sanskrit *napamsika*, which means

(*cont. p. 262*)

(*cat. key p. 263*)

Facing page: Cat. no. 16
Mahakala
Maning (Eunuch)
Tibet or Bhutan
19th c.
Mineral pigments on cloth
33 x 21¼ in. (83.8 x 54 cm)
F1997.30.4 (HA 387)

Left: Cat. no. 16, detail

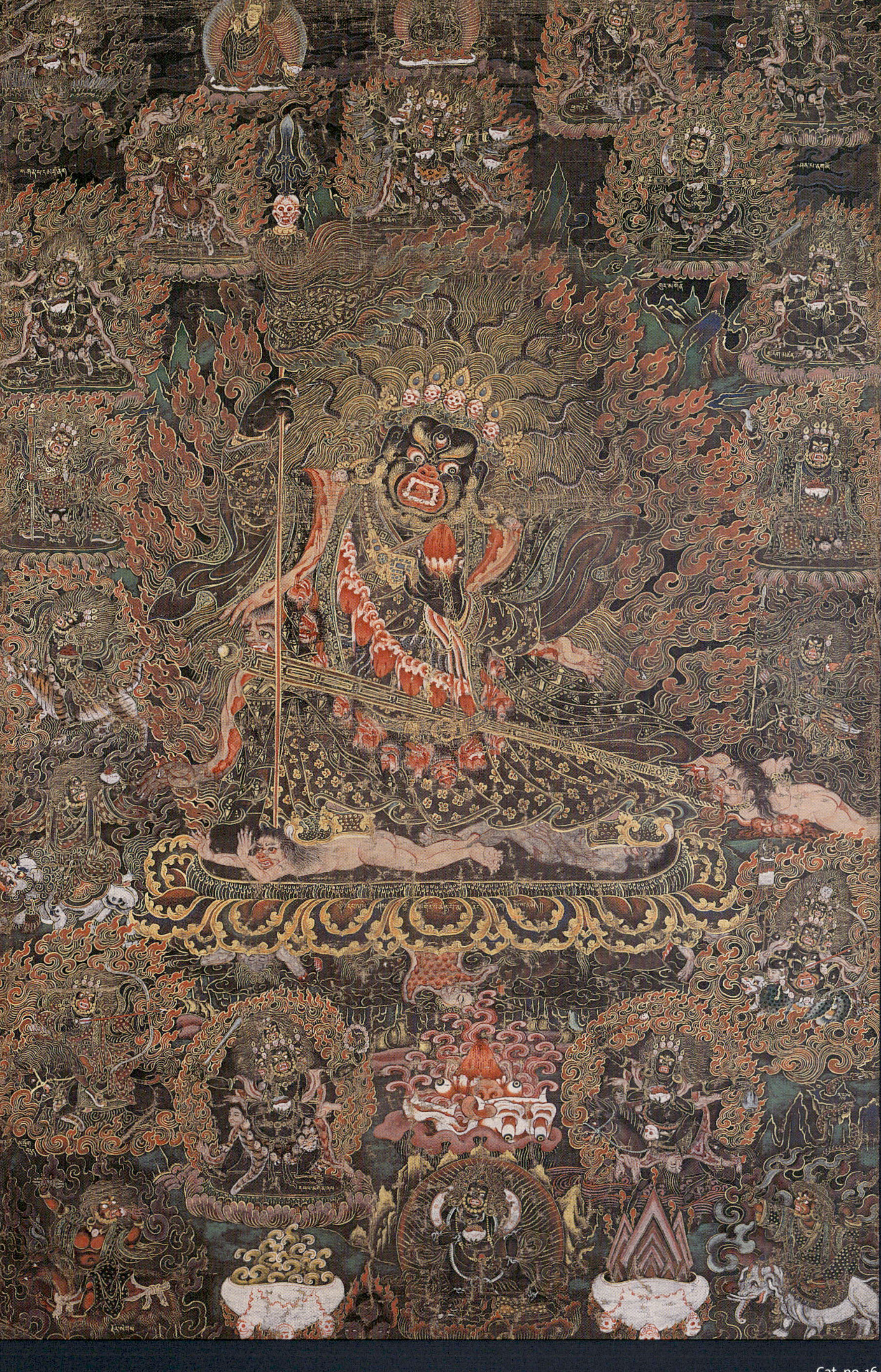

Cat. no. 16

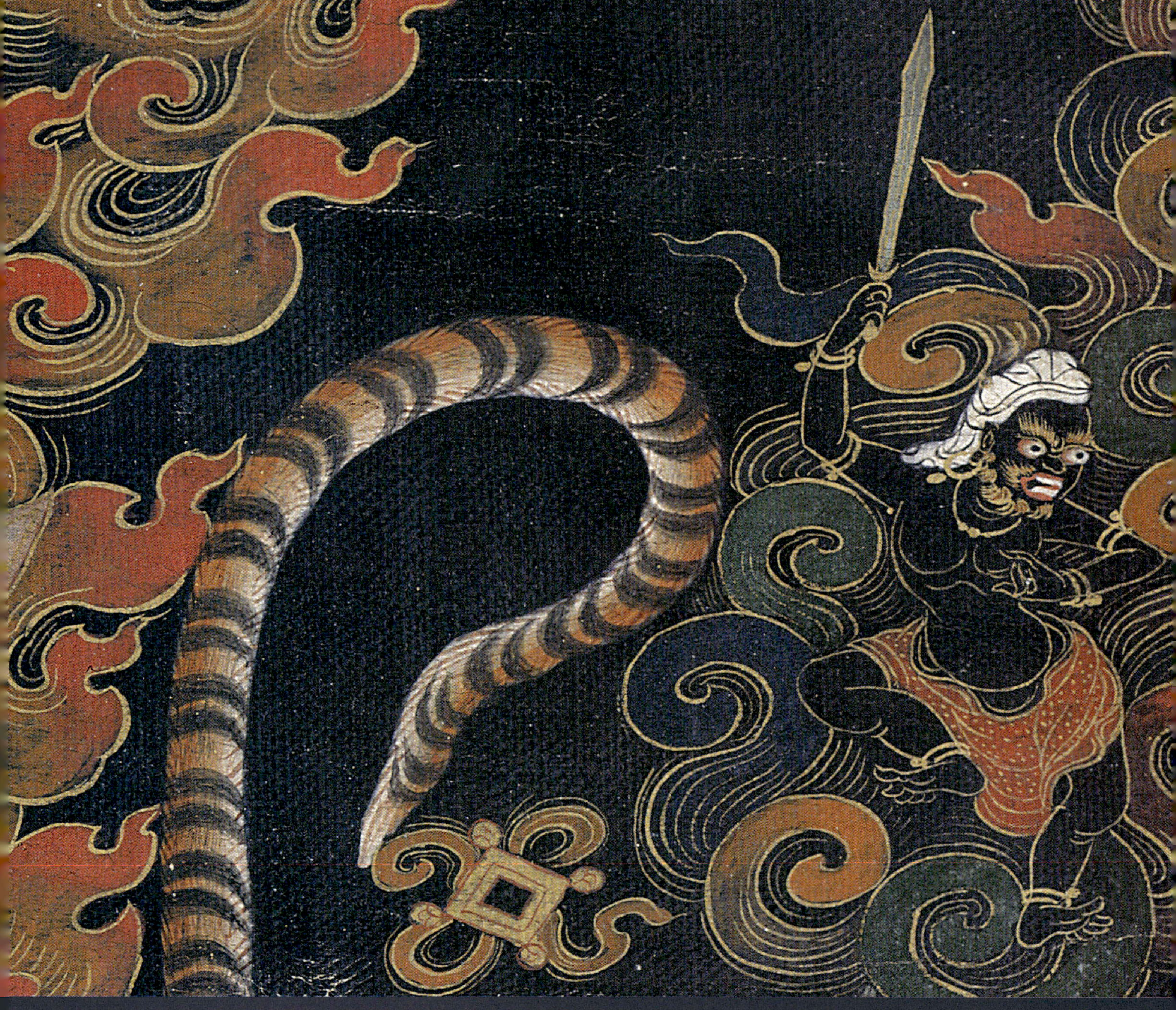

Cat. no. 17, detail

Cat. no. 17

Mahakala

Vyaghra Vahana (Tiger-rider)

This fierce, tiger-riding form of the Enlightened Protector Mahakala is the special protector of one of the four hereditary "houses" of Ngor Monastery, the Thartse. A prominent member of the Thartse house is depicted in the painting—the bearded figure in the upper left, seated directly below the teacher in left corner (cat. key 17.7). Although no inscriptions identify any of the figures, the close resemblance of the bearded figure to an inscribed painting of Ngorpa Thartse Jampa Namka Chime (1765–1820) in the RMA makes the identification secure.[1] Presumably, one of Namka Chime's students (cat. key 17.8) is shown opposite him under the lama in the upper right corner. In that case, the painting must surely be dated to the early nineteenth century.

This is a black-ground painting (*nag-tang*), but a colorful version that seems to be more frequent in the nineteenth century. Earlier black-ground paintings relied more on gold outline alone (compare cat. no. 1). Here, although gold outlining is used generously, there is a full range of colors for the main and attendant deities, as well as for the animals and landscape settings. The vivid red flames behind the main figure are strikingly set off by the black ground. The various attendants are so active, and their nimbi of smoke and flames so eccentrically shaped, that the symmetry of their pairings is disguised. The painter has succeeded in making a painting that is dynamically active and detailed, without becoming excessively busy.

The most active part of the painting is the main figure, with his complicated robes and ornaments. This and many other details correspond with a ritual text describing the main figure and the attendants:

> Shri Mahakala, black in color like a thunder cloud, one face and two hands, wearing a black cloak with nine layers, a radiant face with bared fangs, the tongue flickering shouting HUM PHAT, three-red round eyes very fierce and staring,

(cont. p. 264)
(cat. key p. 265)

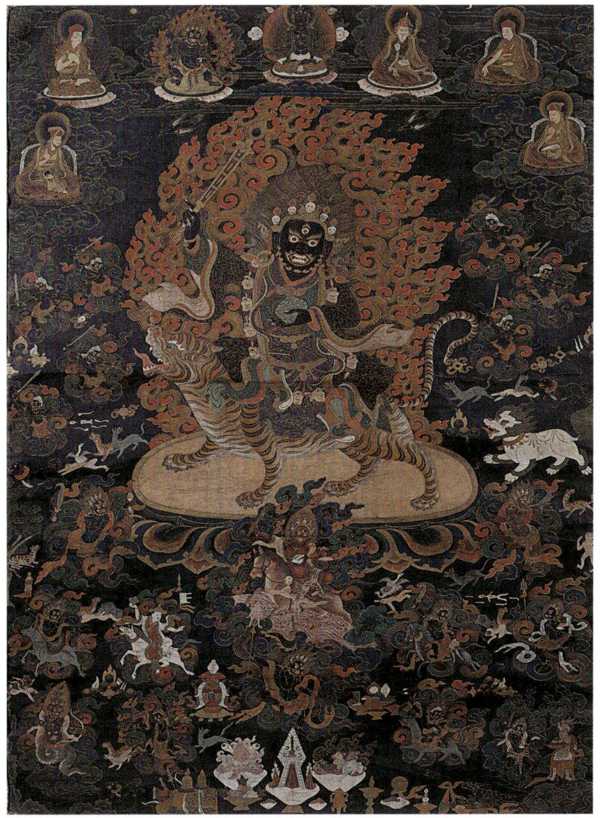

Cat. no. 17
Mahakala
Vyaghra Vahana (Tiger-rider)

Tibet, late 18th–early 19th c.
Mineral pigments on cloth
26¼ x 19½ in. (66.7 x 49.5 cm)
C2002.38.2 (HA 65192)

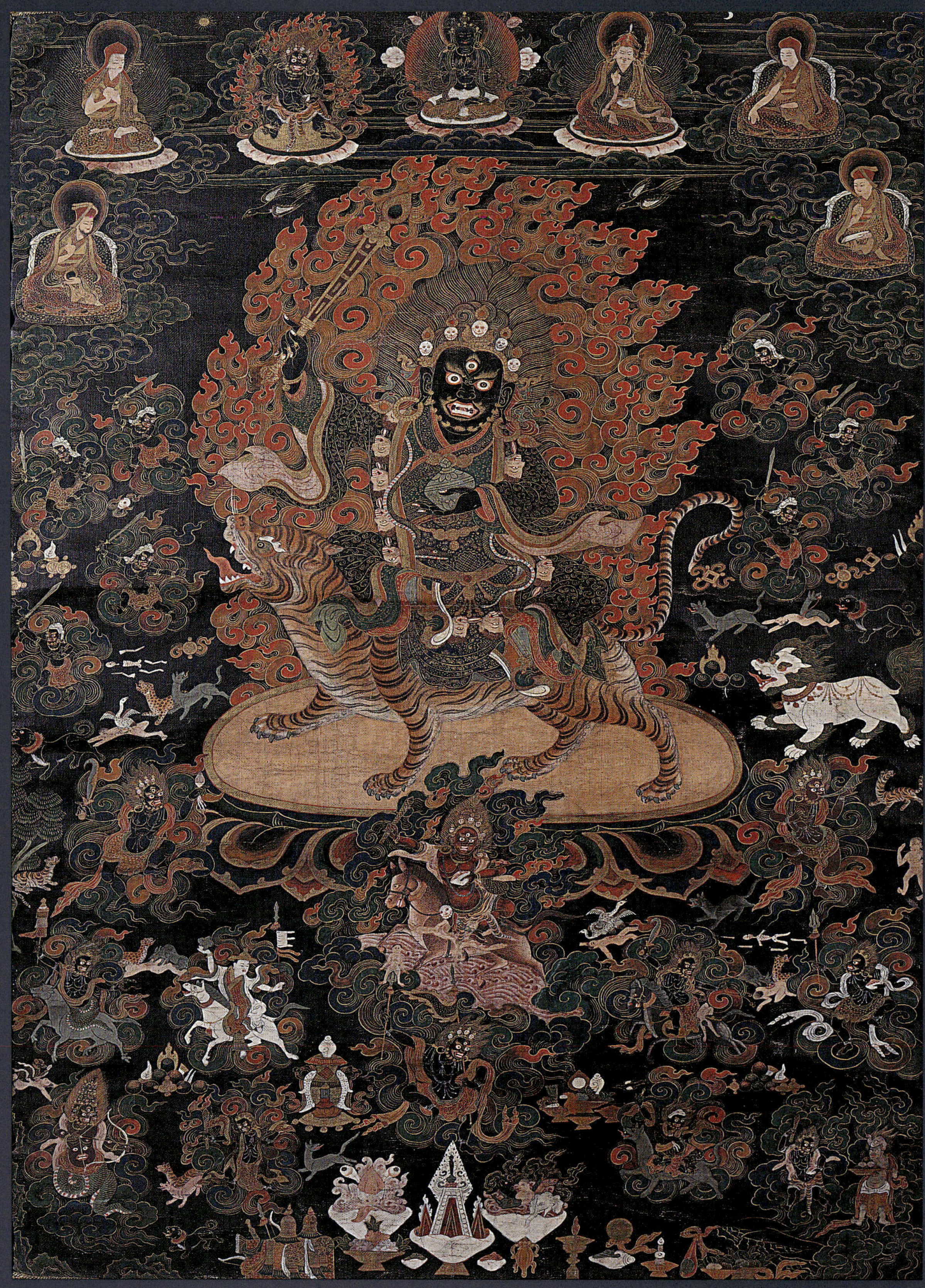

Cat. no. 17

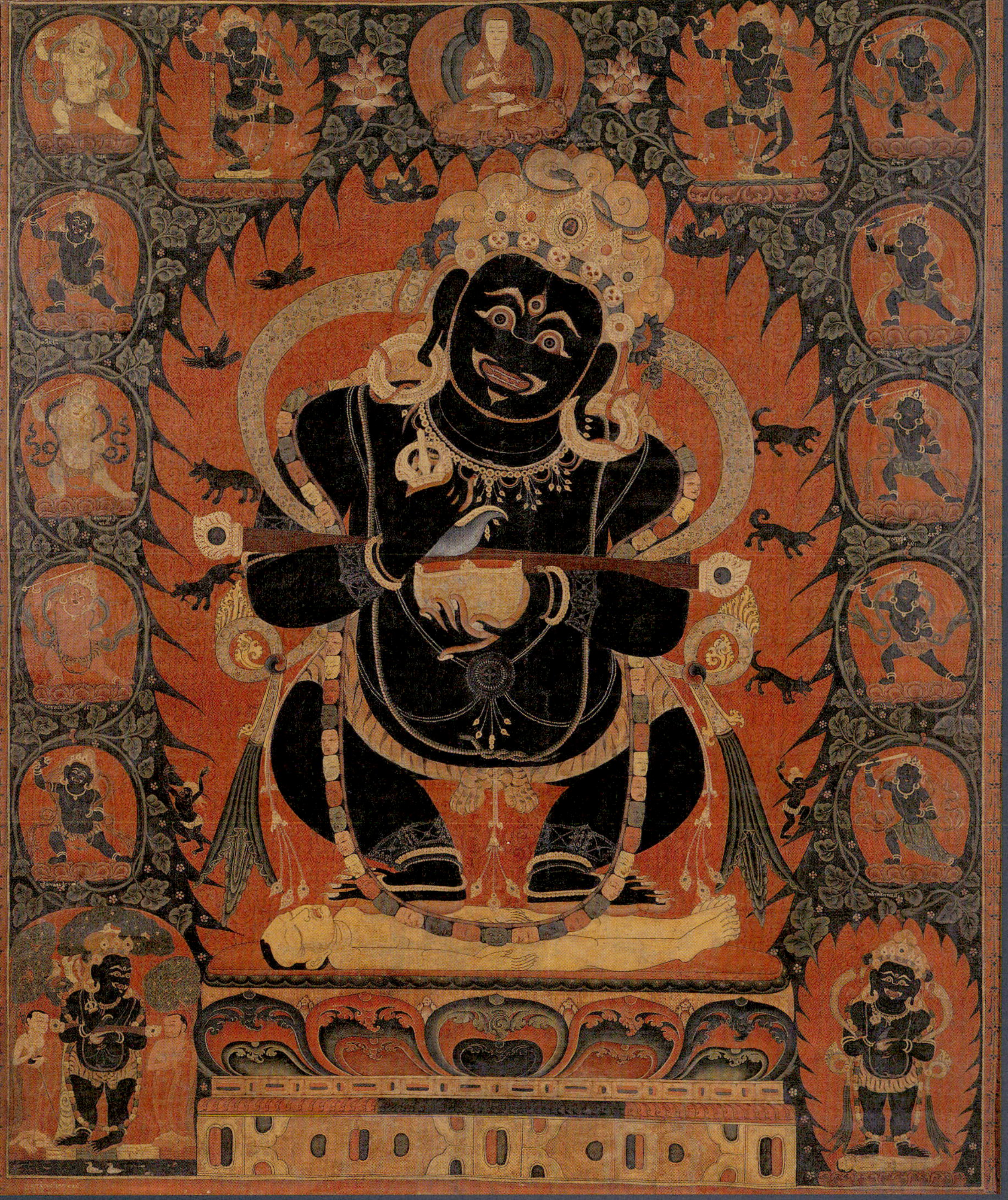

Cat. no. 18

Cat. no. 18

Mahakala

Panjarnata (Lord of the Pavilion)

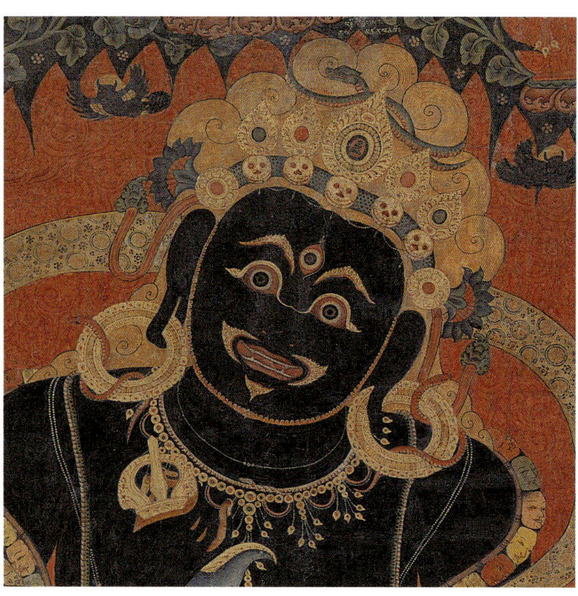

Cat. no. 18, detail

Preceding page: Cat. no. 18
Mahakala
Panjarnata (Lord of the Pavilion)

Tibet, late 15th c.
Mineral pigments on cloth
37⅜ x 31½ in. (94.9 x 80 cm)
Collection of Navin Kumar, New York (HA 90088)

Made at a time when Tibetan art reached one of the crests in its development, this painting effortlessly balances complexity and clarity. The themes are well-engineered to fit together, with nothing extraneous, and the large scale is tailored to the composition. The theme of Mahakala in three different but related forms is presented with precision (cat. key 18.1, 18.5–6). Then, because the one-faced two-armed Mahakala is the protector for those engaged in Hevajra practice, Hevajra and Nairatmya (cat. nos. 44–45) are included at the top (cat. key 18.3–4). Ten protectors who are associated with Hevajra and his consort are painted in two rows of five, beginning at the top left with the yellow Ushnisha Chakravartin (cat. key 18.7–16).[1] Finally, a teacher important to the donor is placed in the premier position at the top center. The importance to the creators of accuracy is demonstrated by the fact that each of the fifteen different deities or scenes around the main figure is identified with a clear reverential inscription underneath it (see catalog key).

The large-scale Mahakala Panjarnata at the center resembles in detail the descriptions of him given in ritual texts.[2] The painting was completed by an accomplished master. Details of the *visva-vajra* in the white "bone" ornament on his belly, the striking faces on the heads in the garland—note the one at bottom center—the snake in the hair (see detail), and the corpse underfoot demonstrate inflections of a personal style. The jewel-encrusted pedestal and the multicolored lotus petals are as lavishly designed as the interlocking iconography. Within the flaming nimbus with its careful pattern of scrolls are two black garudas, two crows, five wolves and dogs, and a black man and woman (compare cat. no. 21).

At the center top is a figure with a small but recognized place in Sakya history, Dragpa Gyaltsen, also known as Guge Pandita Dragpa Gyaltsen (d. 1486). Guge is the name for a kingdom in Western Tibet, and the title

(cont. p. 266)
(cat. key p. 267)

Cat. no. 18, detail

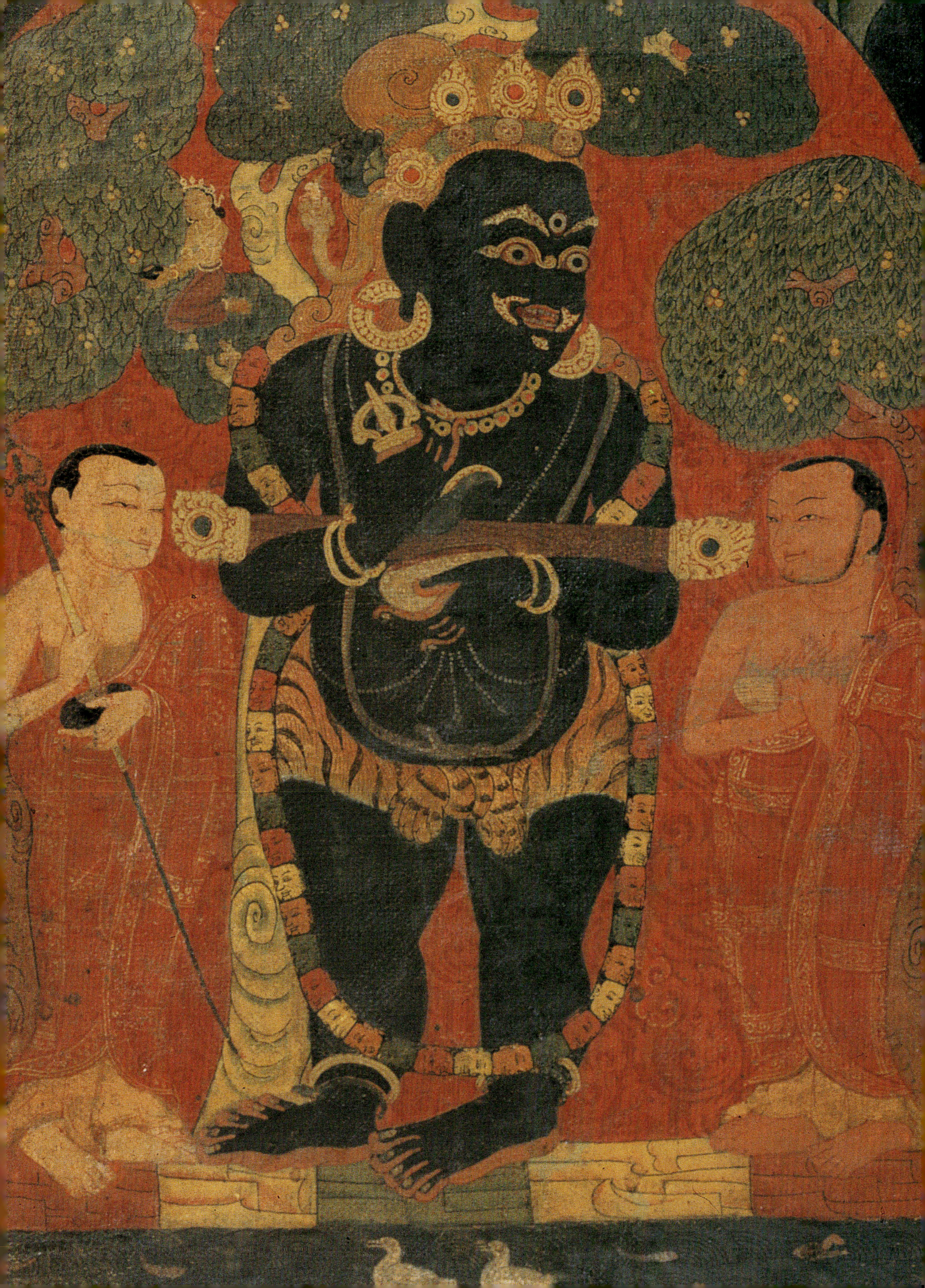

Cat. no. 19

Fragmentary Antefix-Gorgonian

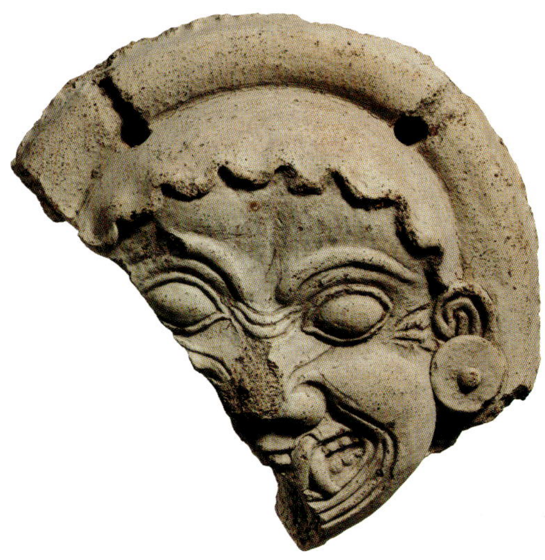

Cat. no. 19
Fragmentary Antefix-Gorgonian

Etruscan or South Italian, 6th–5th c. BCE
Terracotta
H. 8¼ in. (21 cm)
The Metropolitan Museum of Art,
Gift of Mr. and Mrs. Jonathan P. Rosen, 1991

During the Etruscan period (ca. 750–90 B.C.E.),[1] the gorgon figure was used to ward off evil spirits. Greeks and Romans would use the gorgon-face both as a decorative element and to keep their families free from harm. A common motif, the gorgon face was painted on the interior bottom of wine jugs and incorporated into architectural facades. To keep water from spilling down the rows of concave roof tiles unto the unsuspecting passersby, a disk of terracotta called an *antefix* was placed at the end of each row. The central *antefix* on a house or temple was often embellished with a molded design or, as in this example, a gorgon face.[2]

Gorgons are identified by their savage grin, menacing fangs, and penetrating stare. Other common attributes demonstrated by this gorgonian antefix include heavy crease marks around the brow and cheeks, a broad flat nose, circular earrings, tight stylized curls at the forehead, and although it is no longer visible in this example, a protruding tongue.[3] Originally this antefix would have been painted bright colors such as red, blue, and black to heighten its horrible features. It bears a striking resemblance to the Tibetan sculpture of Mahakala (cat. no. 21). Not that they derived from a common source, it is provocative, however, to speculate how two such disparate cultures arrived at such similar illustrations of the demonic.

In later developments, the gorgon image was associated with the Medusa myth. Early literary sources mention Medusa's horrific appearance demonstrated by the Head of Medusa Cameo (cat. no. 20).[4]

(notes p. 269)

Cat. no. 20

Cameo of Medusa with Serpents

This head of Medusa is a small but potent example of the demonic divine. Carved from a single piece of agate, the cameo is heavy to be worn as a brooch and would more likely have been affixed atop a small box. The natural layers of sardonyx quartz (orange in color) and carnelian quartz (mottled and pinkish) create the illusion of a separate surface and base.

According to Roman mythology, the gods stripped Medusa of beauty as punishment for her excessive vanity. She was rendered so unattractive that her gaze alone would transform a man to stone.[1] The common story of Medusa's death states that Perseus, who was the son of Zeus and undaunted by even the fiercest creatures, valiantly decapitated her. Another claims Perseus tricked Medusa into seeing her own reflection, causing her face to ossify in an expression of horror.

Images of Medusa were first used during the Greek period when the gorgon icon became associated with the Medusa myth. Gorgons (see cat. no. 19) were popularly used to ward off evil as it was thought that one fierce and ugly face could effectively repulse another. With this in mind, early incarnations of the gorgon-type Medusa image appear more beast than woman—a style referred to as the *horrible* type. In later years, the Medusa gorgon icon developed a human likeness *(beautiful* type). Often, the feminine vulnerability of the *beautiful*-type Medusa was emphasized by rendering Medusa's hair as a wild mess of serpents—a victim of her own vanity.[2]

Although this cameo was fashioned after the Late Roman *beautiful* type, when it was crafted is uncertain. Roman glyptics were of high value during the Renaissance and generated widespread reproduction throughout Europe for centuries.[3] Ironically, by the late twentieth century, the Medusa image was appropriated for use in the logos of luxury commerce and remains one of the few mythological figures still identifiable today.[4]

(notes p. 269)

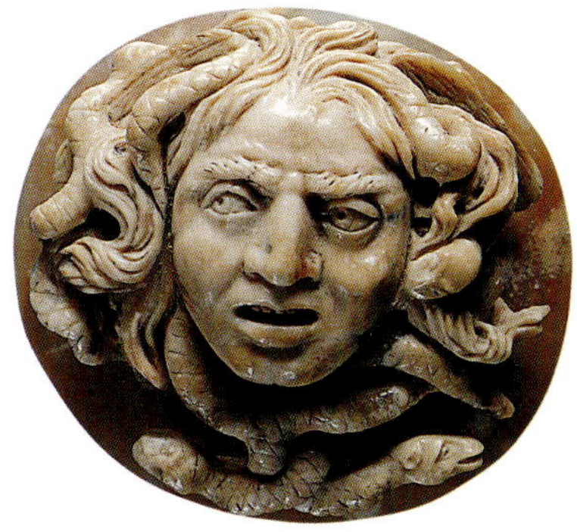

Cat. no. 20
Cameo of Medusa with Serpents

Western Europe, Post-Classical (after 4th c. CE)
Grey stone, carnelian with sardonyx back
2 x 1⅞ in. (5.1 x 4.8 cm), shown approximately actual size
University of Pennsylvania Museum of
Archaeology and Anthropology

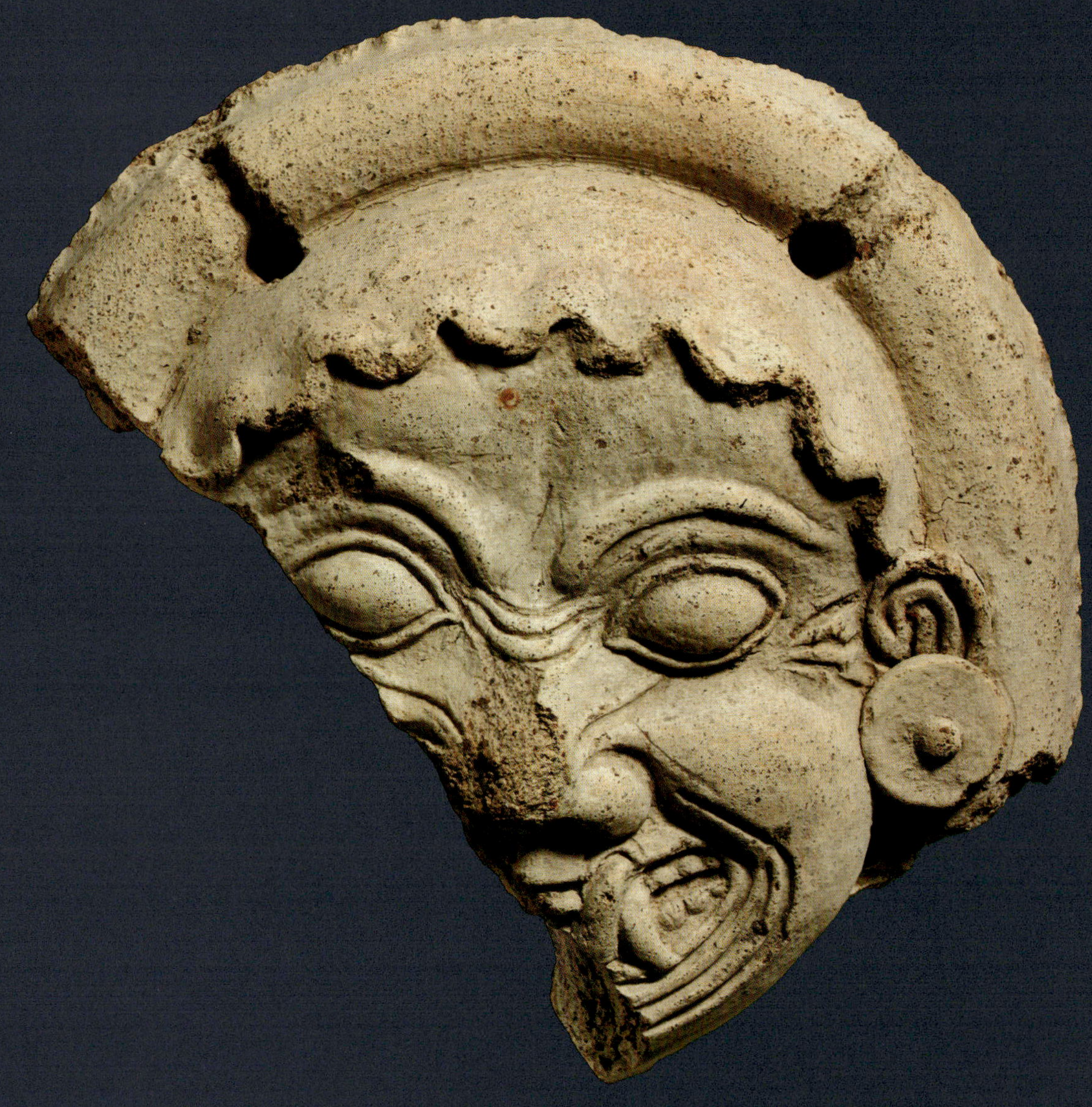

Cat. no. 19

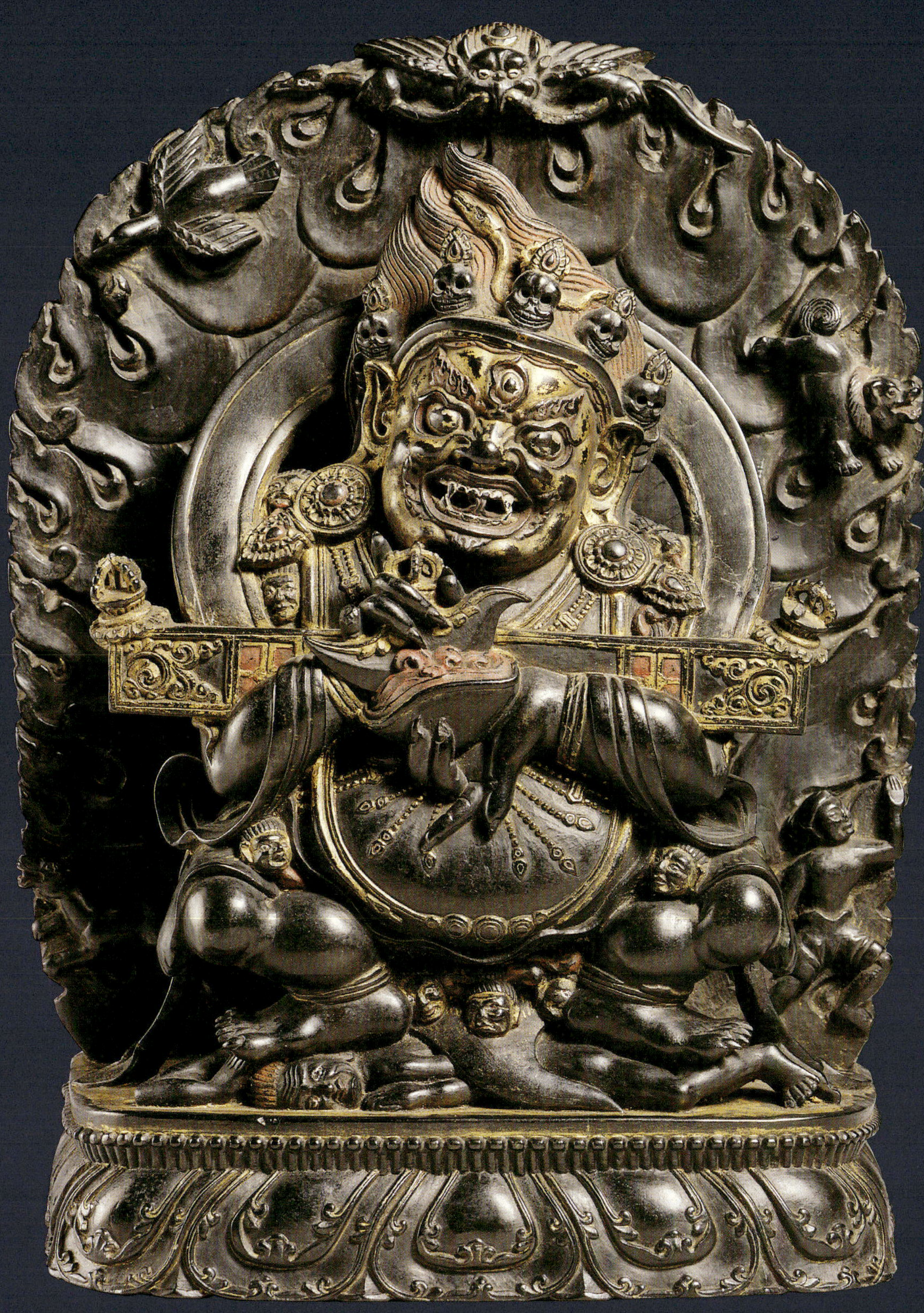

Cat. no. 20

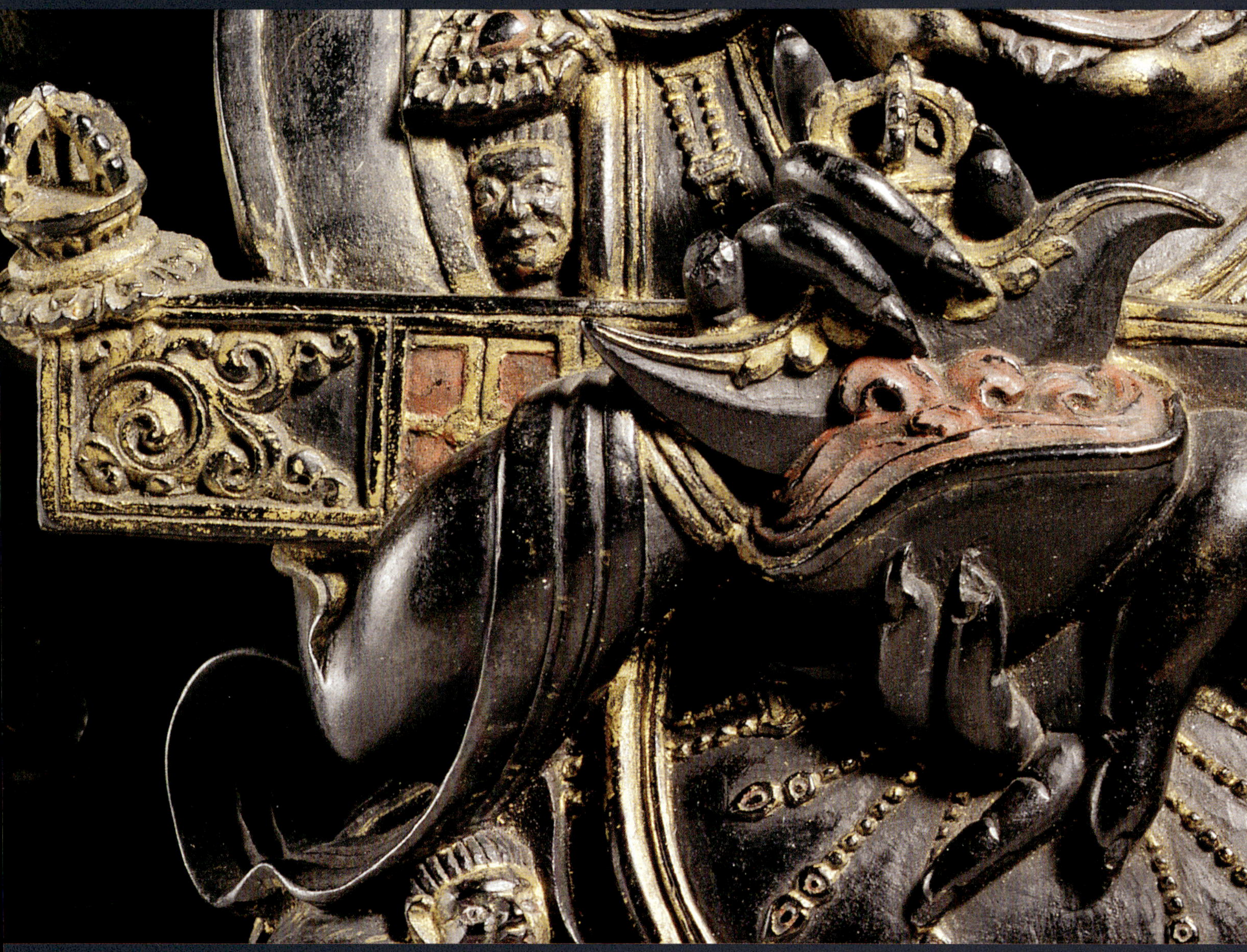

Cat. no. 21, detail

Cat. no. 21

Mahakala

Panjarnata (Lord of the Pavilion)

This stone carving of Mahakala is one of the most intensely fierce and detailed sculptures of an Enlightened Protector that has come to light. There are some startling details. The curved flaying knife, delicately held by fingers with clawlike nails, is not just suspended above the skull bowl, as is usual (cat. nos. 20, 22), but is actually plunged into the bowl causing blood and brains to splash out (see detail). The corpse underfoot is so thoroughly crushed that his face is pressed into the top of the lotus platform and his arm bent backward. The depth of the carving allows the Mahakala to step away from the backdrop, giving him, in all his grotesque dimensionality, a lifelike power. The hard stone allowed the carver to create the fine beading above the lotus petals, which are particularly well designed and executed. The sculptor has also alternated dense areas of varied relief with smooth curved surfaces such as the starched scarf rising from Mahakala's shoulders, and his bulbous knees and calves.

Perhaps the most intriguing, and meaningful, part of the sculpture is the fully rendered stick held horizontally in the crook of Mahakala's elbows. This is the "*gandi*-stick of Emanation," carried only by this form of Mahakala. What emanates from the stick are all Mahakala's other forms. They are thought to emerge into the world from two sets of doors, which are so carefully carved and painted in red and gold on the sculpture (see detail). Panjarnata Mahakala, who can be thought of as the fundamental or original form of Mahakala, is the source for all the others forms, including the four- and six-armed forms. On the backdrop of flames are carved (starting at the lower right) a black wolf, black crow, black *garuda*, barking black dog wearing a red collar, and gesturing black human. Except for the *garuda*, all of them are running outward, away from Panjarnata. He is emitting them as well, and they are his "messengers."

Panjarnata Mahakala is the main protector of the Sakya School, deriving from the

(cont. p. 269)

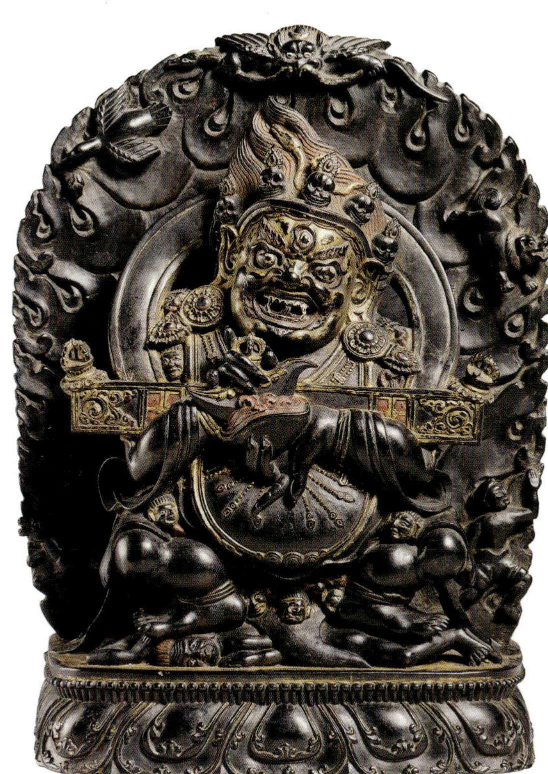

Cat. no. 21
Mahakala
Panjarnata (Lord of the Pavilion)

Tibet, 15th c.
Stone
10¼ x 6¾ x 3½ (26 x 17.1 x 8.9 cm)
C2002.10.2 (HA 65085)

Cat. no. 22

Mahakala

Panjarnata (Lord of the Pavilion)

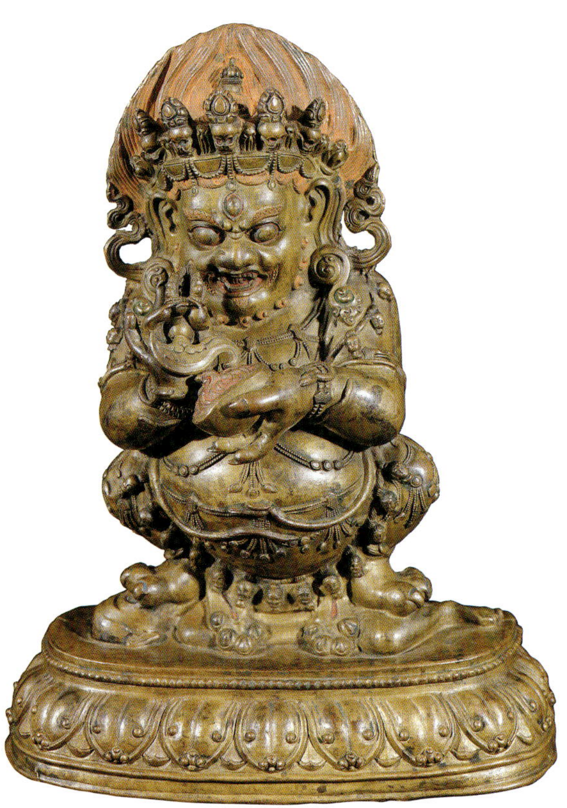

Cat. no. 22
Mahakala
Panjarnata (Lord of the Pavilion)
Nepal or Tibet, 18th c.
Metalwork
11 x 10 x 4½ in. (27.9 x 25.4 x 11.4 cm)
C2001.7.1 (HA 65018)

Sculptures of wrathful deities were enhanced with pigments. They are still visible in this work depicting the Enlightened Protector Mahakala. The long hair standing up is given an orange hue, as are the curls of beard, mustache, and flaming eyebrows. His bulging eyeballs are rimmed with red, and his gums and curling tongue are also red. The brains and blood in the skull bowl is similarly colored, and traces of red are visible on the cord to which human heads were tied. His three eyeballs were painted white, though this has turned gray, and the black irises and pupils have flaked off. The missing *gandi*-stick was probably painted red and gold, and the green paint adheres to crevices in the jewelry.

Mahakala has an oversized head and belly, typical of Panjarnata images of the seventeenth through nineteenth century and apparent in both sculpture and painting (see figs. 2.26–29, 2.35). The fleshy parts of the body have become almost doughy, and the legs squatting in his distinctive posture seem overwhelmed, pushed outward by the spreading flesh of the rounded stomach. One can well imagine the obstacle-creating corpse beneath his feet being thoroughly crushed. Details of the snake ornaments, hair, skull crown, and implements are crisply rendered. The face is finely contrived, and care was taken with the clawlike finger- and toenails. The back is more cursorily done, though it is still finished. An eighteenth-century date is warranted by the fluent S-shaped curves of the ribbons tied to the ends of his crown, a fluttering conceit derived probably from Chinese art, which had become standard among Himalayan artists by that time.

The bulkiness of the image of Mahakala prepares one for a heavy piece of metal, but in fact, it is surprisingly lightweight. The metalwork process combined extraordinarily thin lost-wax casting with repoussé for which the Newaris are famous. It was cast in two pieces (front and back) and probably hammered from the inside of each half to shape and thin

(cont. p. 270)

Cat. no. 23
Bes-image

Cat. no. 24
Finial with Bes-image

The Bes-image actually represents a number of Egyptian gods.[1] At least some of them acted as protectors of children and new mothers. Such a specialized function is not apparent from the dwarfish, grotesque imagery of the Bes-image. The association may derive from the fact that since infants born with achondroplasian (short-limbed) dwarfism rarely survived infancy, Egyptians imagined survivors to be a potent symbol of the vanquishing of premature death in infants.[2] They thus adopted a god with dwarfish proportion for its apotropaic uses.

The Bes-image achieved a relatively stable, recognizable set of characteristics, but only after a long history and many changes. This form has been called the Bes-image, "one of the most protean of all Egyptian religious images."[3] By the tenth century BCE, the high, vertically arranged plumed headdress, furrowed brow, rounded leonine ears, beard and mustache, flattened nose, bowed legs and dwarfish features were standard. On the turquoise-colored faience plaque (cat. no. 23), the tongue protrudes noticeably, something also frequently found on Himalayan wrathful deity images. There is also a miniature duplicate Bes-image between the main figure's legs, and a oryx antelope with its legs bound on the back of the headdress, as if to suggest Bes's power over the natural world. Small holes in the plaque indicate that objects—perhaps feathers?—were attached to the plaque. The bronze finial (cat. no. 24) would logically be used for a processional or ritual purpose, though the exact function of both objects is not known.

Figures with broad, short proportions are frequently found in Himalayan images of the demonic divine. They too capitalized on the conjunction of physical ugliness and protective power. Bulging eyes, flattened noses, animal features (notably the ears), and leering

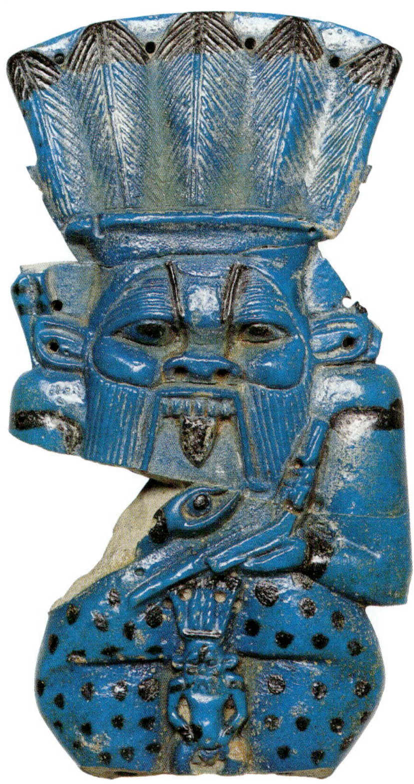

Cat. no. 23
Bes-image

Egyptian, 22nd–25th dynasty (ca. 945–656 BCE)
Faience with turquoise glaze
6⅞x 3⅝ x ⅞ in. (17.5 x 9.2 x 2.3 cm)
Brooklyn Museum of Art

Cat. no. 24 (p. 156)
Finial with Bes-image

Egyptian, 22nd–25th dynasty (ca. 945–656 BCE)
Bronze
16 x 2⅞ in. (40.6 x 7.3 cm)
Brooklyn Museum of Art

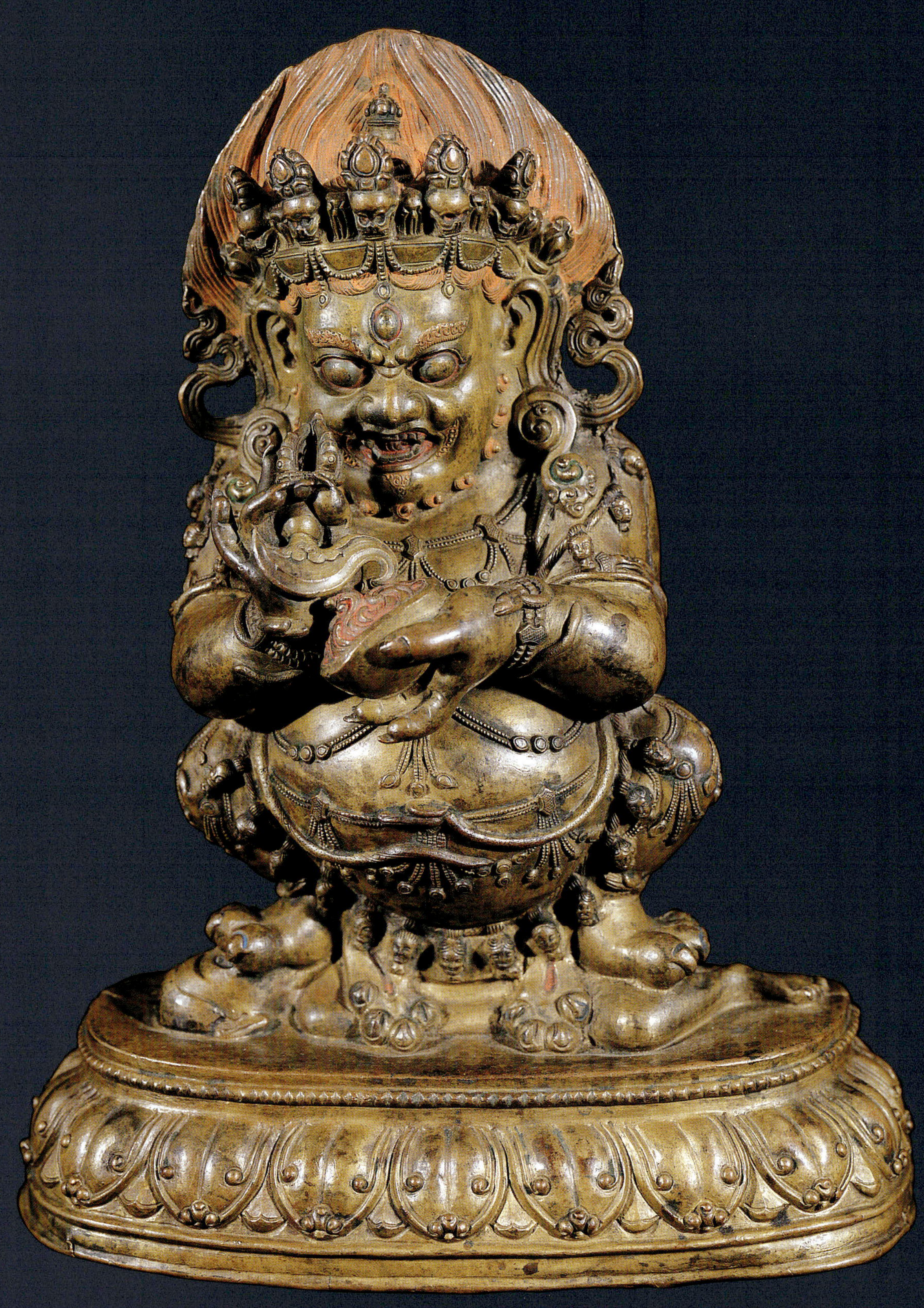

Cat. no. 22

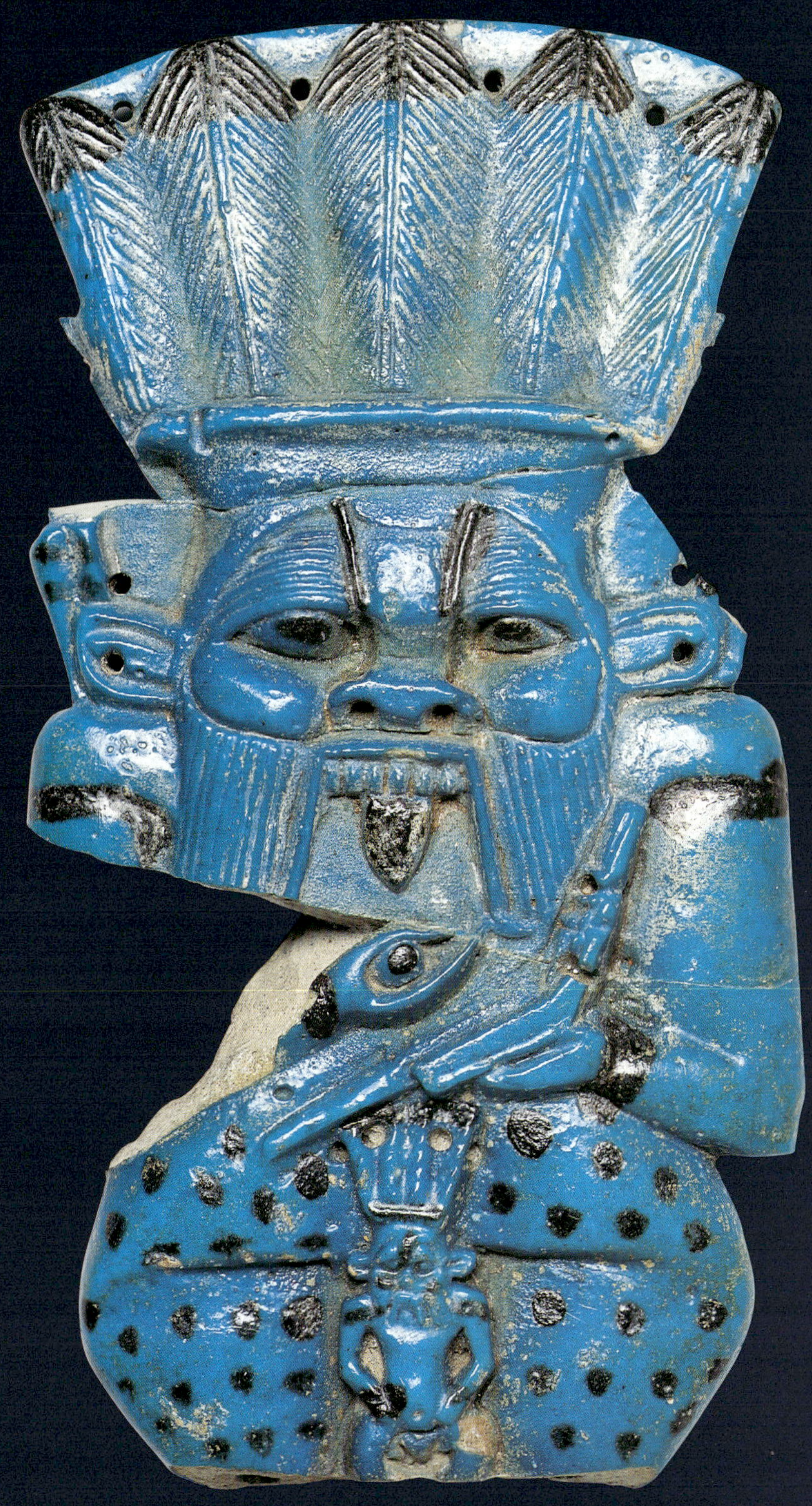

Cat. no. 23

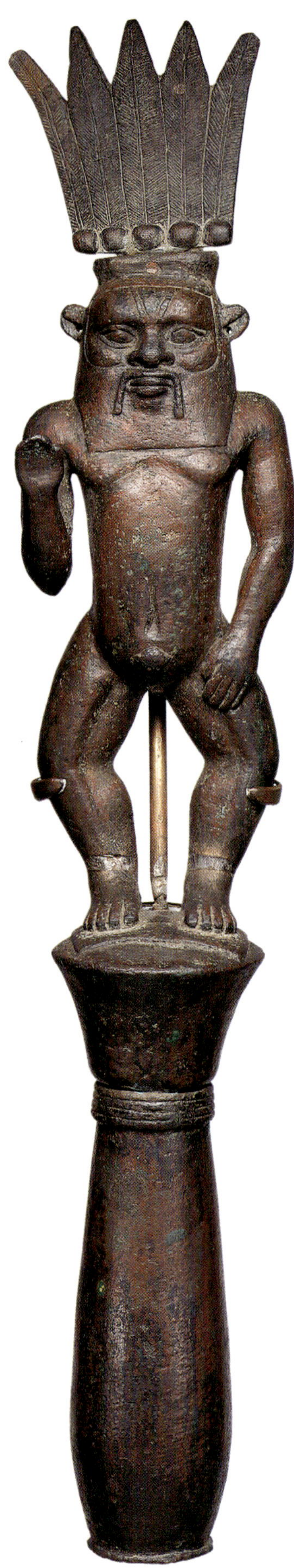

faces are also shared. It suggests artists in Egypt and the Himalayas recognized that relatively contained violence or the violation of norms of appearance and behavior—nakedness, an offensive expression, odd proportions—can also be perceived as unsettling, eerie, and suggestive of supernatural powers.

(notes p. 270)

Cat. no. 24

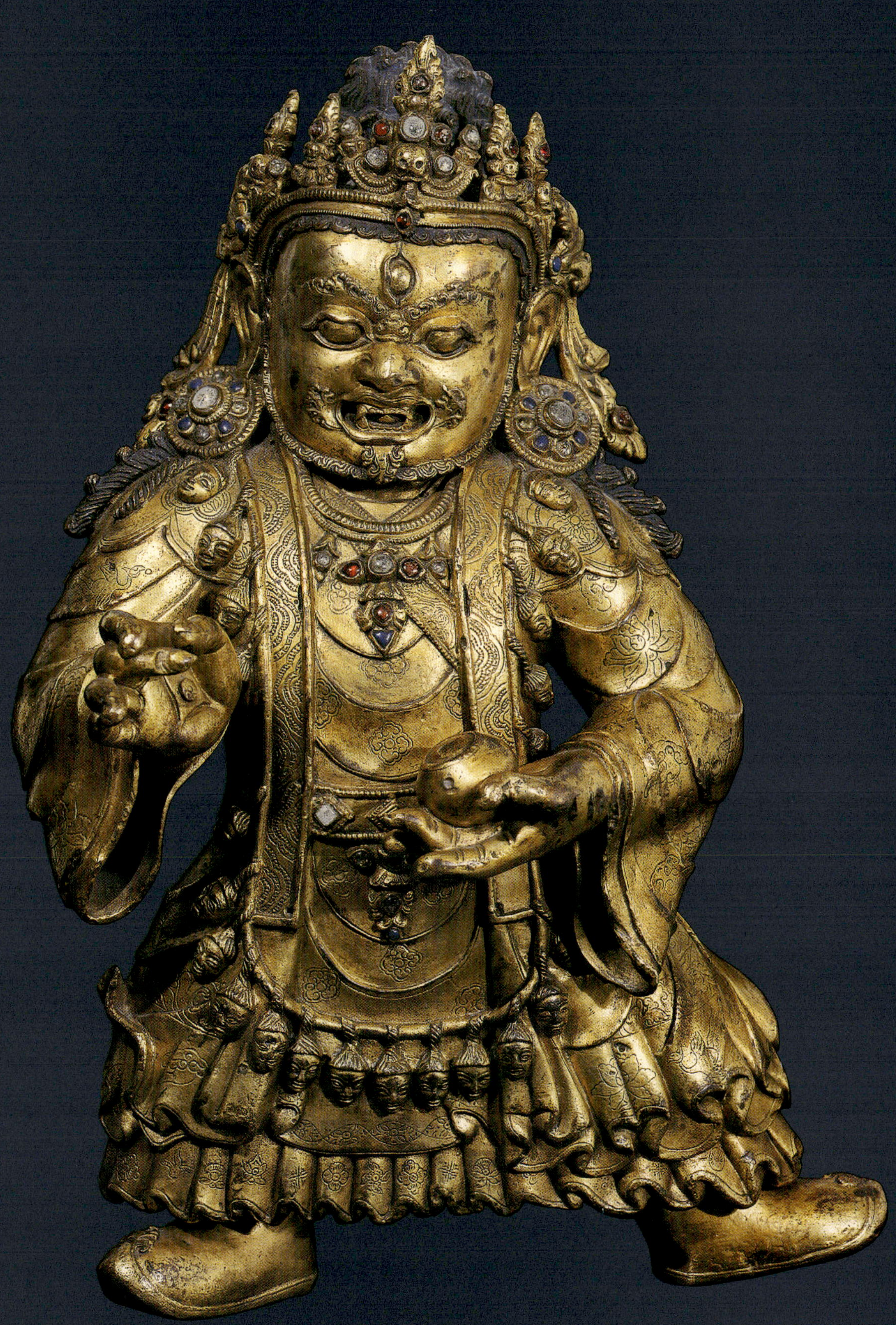

Cat. no. 25

Cat. no. 25

Mahakala

Legden (Excellent One)

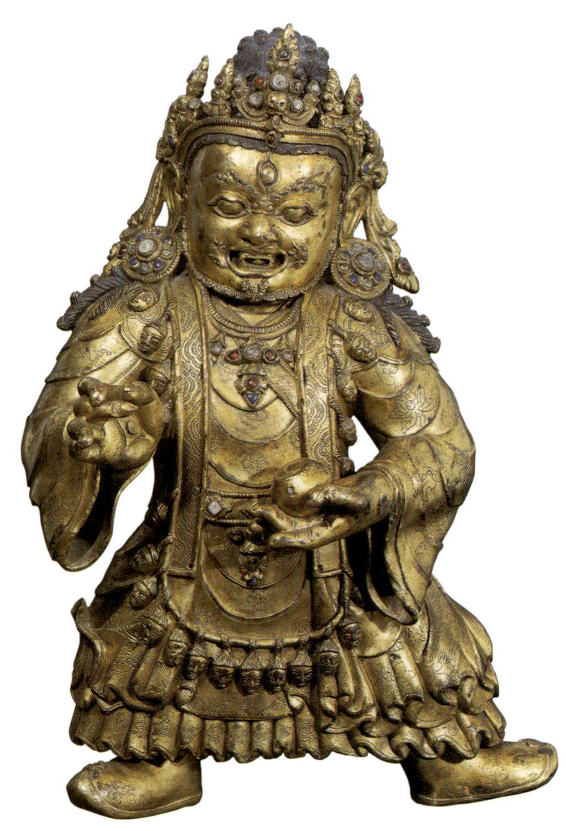

Cat. no. 25
Mahakala
Legden (Excellent One)

Tibet, ca. 15th c.
Metalwork with inlaid stones
13½ x 9 x 5¾ in. (34.3 x 22.9 x 14.6 cm)
C2003.10.3 (HA 65208)

This sculpture of an Enlightened Protector was solid cast in one piece. As much time and effort went into finishing the work as went into the design and casting. After the metal sculpture was removed from the mold assembly and rough-polished, it was then decorated with chased ornaments. The robe was attentively engraved with a variety of patterns. Quartered concentric medallions define the stole. A scrolling foliage pattern imitates a band of brocade near the hem of the robe. A *visva-vajra* (crossed *vajra*) medallion decorates the shawl, and lotus, cloud and phoenix motifs were carefully chiseled onto the outer robe (see back view). On the lower pleats of the front skirt are six different alternating floral and geometric motifs.

The sculpture was inlaid with shaped semiprecious stones such as quartz crystal cabochons and lapis lazuli, along with an unidentified red stone imitating ruby. None of these are missing, but some may be replacements. Finally, it was gilded, fine-polished and then at least partially painted—there is still blue paint adhering to the piled-up hair. The impressive scale allows for all the detail without losing the strength of the figure's upright bearing.

The identity of this figure is confirmed to be Legden Mahakala, based on a *terma* (discovered treasure text). It describes him as follows:

> Legden Nagpo, Desire Free Son, with a body blue-black in color, one face, two hands, three eyes. The right [hand] holds a large sandalwood *gandi*-stick marked with a jewel. From the upper [portion] of the *gandi* fire blazes and from the lower [portion] water flows. From inside the *gandi* a great army of *asuras* issue. The left [hand holds] at the side an iron [bowl] filled with various diseases. Wearing a thick upper cloak and tied with a gold belt, wearing boots, a crown of five dry skulls and having a necklace

(cont. p. 270)

Cat. no. 26

Mahakala

Chaturbhuja, Four Hands

Unlike other four-armed Mahakala images, such as the one depicted in catalog number 15, in which in his first right hand he carries a curved flaying knife, this form of the four-armed Mahakala carries a stemmed flower that is very heartlike in appearance.[1] The other three hands carry a skull bowl, sword (the blade of which is broken here), and *katvanga*, a long staff with streamers (also broken).[2] Wearing a tiara with five skulls to which other decorations were attached, Mahakala also has a long garland of heads and serpents as ear ornaments. He sits in a characteristic relaxed pose, with one knee partly raised, and wears a tiger pelt as a loincloth. The flattened face of the tiger is visible on Mahakala's right thigh, the tail or one of the tigers' legs on the left thigh. A human corpse serves as a cushion, his head just visible at the left and one foot at the right side.

This work was very solidly cast, and is quite heavy for its size. The head scarves, nimbus, and garment-ends at the lower sides were cast separately and attached with pins. On the back, which is fully finished, three holes were made on the horizontal part of the lotus pedestal to accommodate a larger outer nimbus.[3]

(notes p. 270)

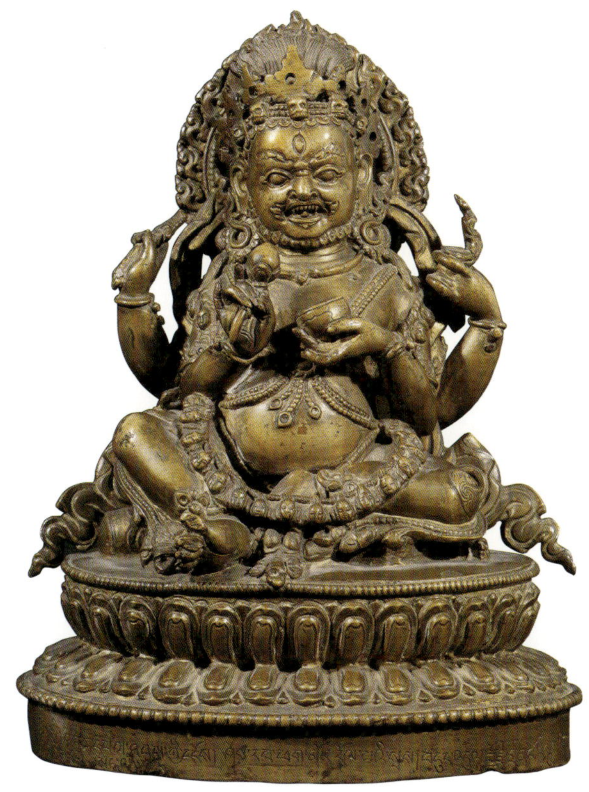

Cat. no. 26
Mahakala
Chaturbhuja, Four Hands

Tibet, ca. 17th c.
Metalwork
8½ x 6 x 4 in. (21.6 x 15.2 x 10.2 cm)
Collection of Navin Kumar, New York (HA 90059)

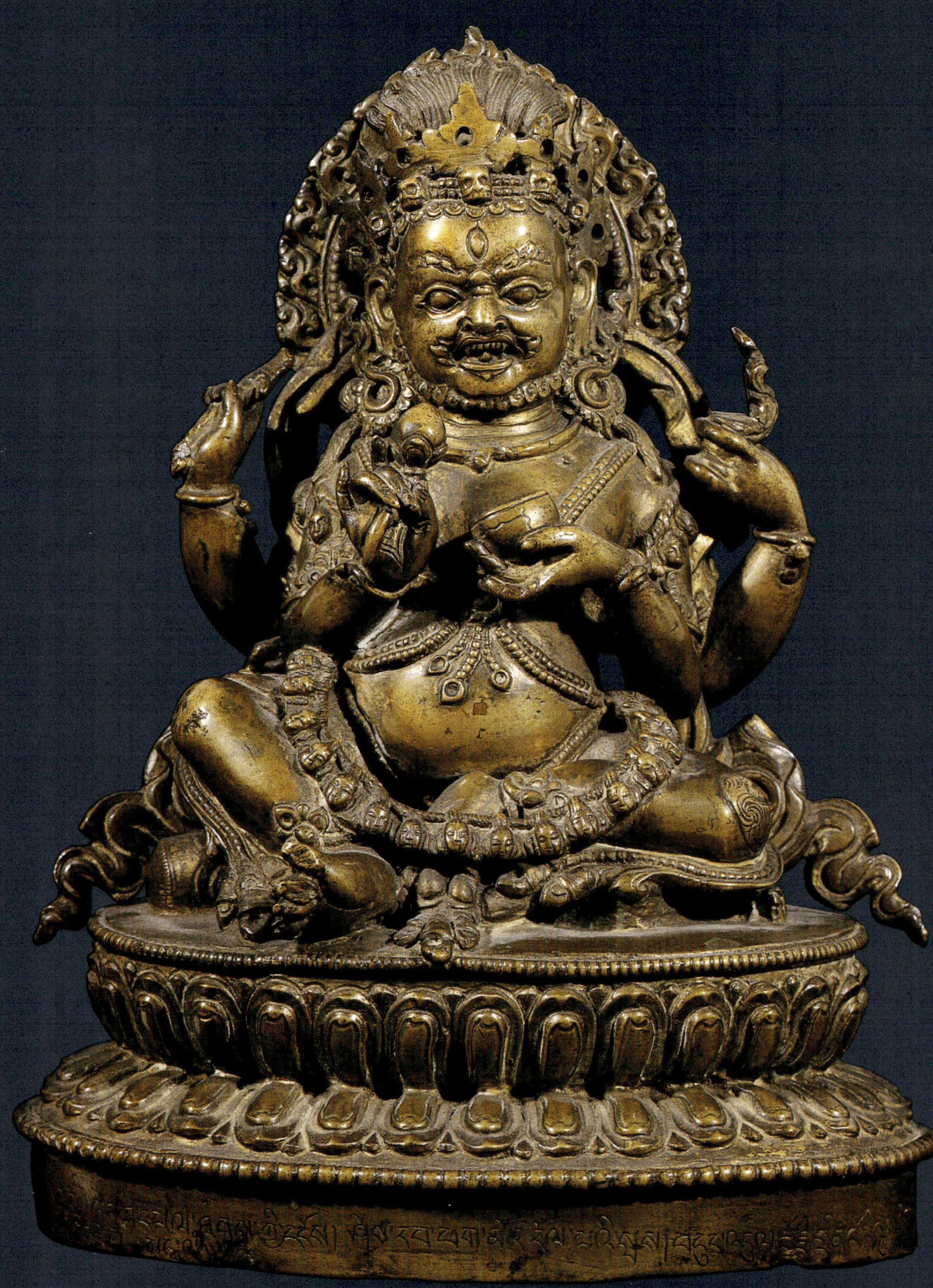

Cat. no. 26

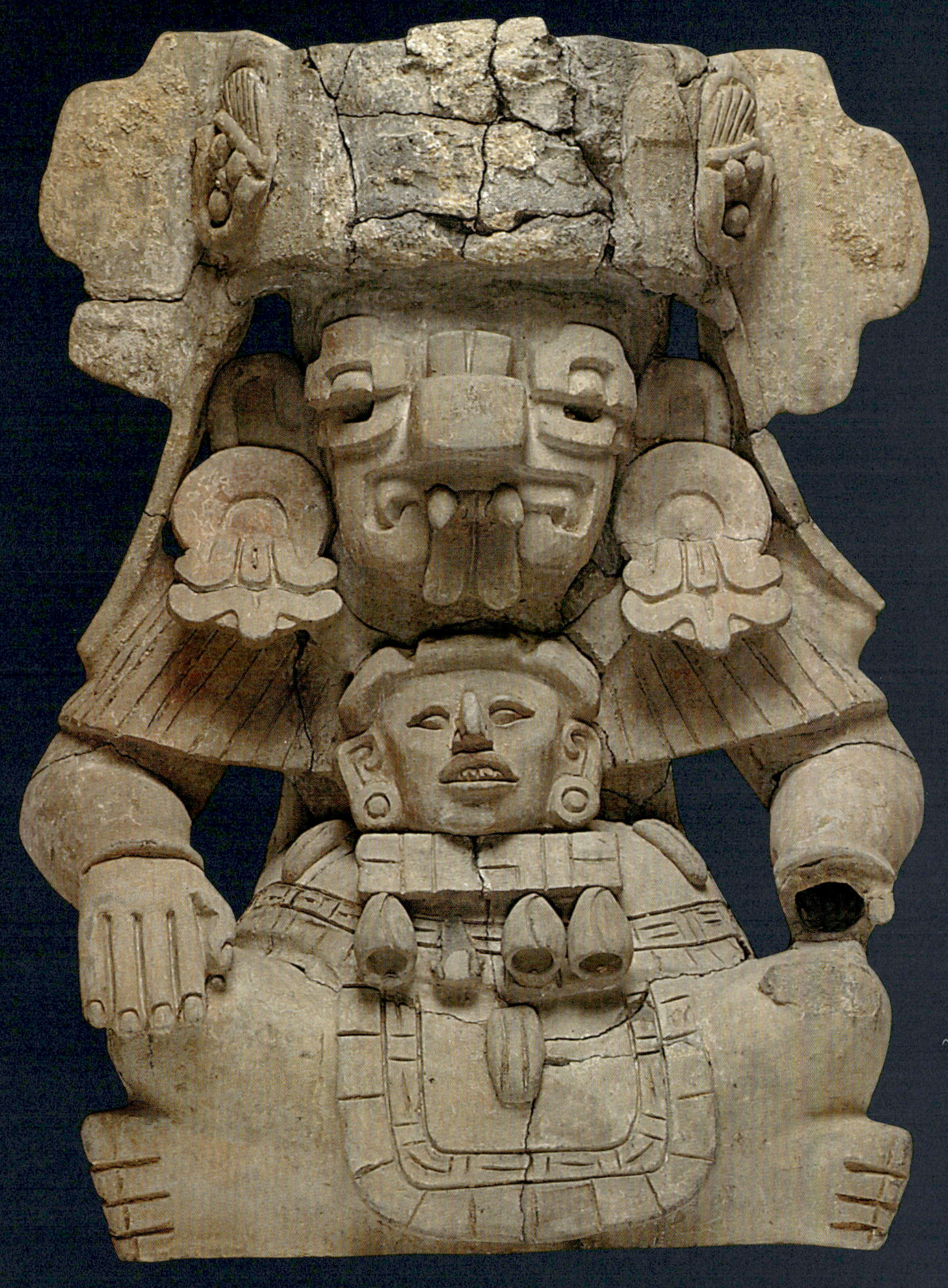

Cat. no. 27

Cat. no. 27

Funeral Urn

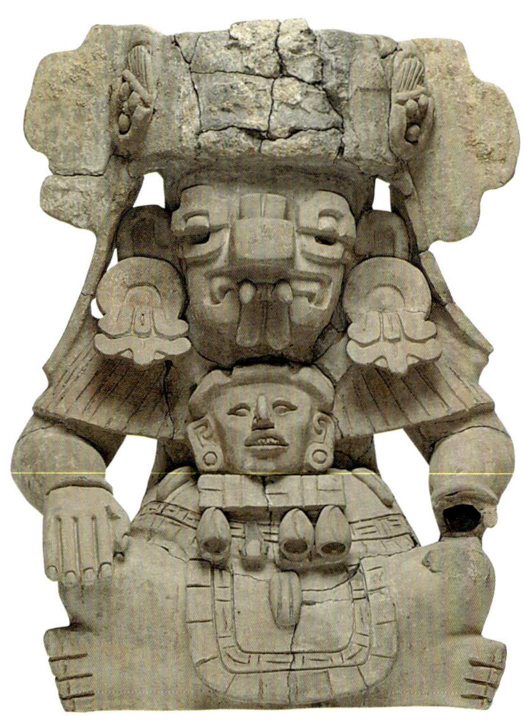

Cat. no. 27
Funeral Urn

Mexico, Oaxaca, Xoxocotlan (Zapotec culture)
ca. Monté Alban III (250–500 CE)
Clay
23⅝ x 19¾ x 13¾ in. (60 x 50.2 x 34.9 cm)
American Museum of Natural History, New York

The Zapotec people believed that shortly after death, leading members of society became semi-divine.[1] In this state, a dignitary would continue his service by appealing to the gods on behalf of the living for good fortune, large families, and healthy crops. Great effort went into Zapotec funerals. Family members would work to provide food and festivities for the community to last several weeks. It was hoped that through these efforts, the living could convince the gods of the departed's merit.[2] For further emphasis, funerary urns were sculpted for the dead in the forms of their patron deities.[3] The choice of deities was intended to reflect venerable aspects of the deceased's personality.[4] Once placed inside the tomb, the urns would create a "portrait" of the dead based on his or her virtue.

The back of this Zapotec urn is cylindrical, plain, and hollow in form.[5] However, the front is elaborately molded into the form of Cocijo, the Zapotec god of lightning, rain, and fertility. Not surprisingly Cocijo became a popular subject for funerary urns. He can be identified by his prominent nose, goggled eyes, and the pointed teeth framing his forked tongue. The cult of Cocijo derived from his ancient pledge to bring forth the earth's water in return for man's sacrificial gifts.

Although there are no direct historical connections, it is interesting to compare how Cocijo's broad flat nose, wide fanged grin, circular earrings, and bushy eyebrows parallel both the Greek gorgon antefix (cat. no. 19) and the Tibetan Mahakala sculpture (cat. no. 28).

(notes p. 270)

Cat. no. 28

Mahakala

Shadbhuja, Six Hands

Painted versions depict this Mahakala with a blue-black color, as in figure 2.12. Rather than holding up an elephant skin with his two uppermost arms, as most painted versions show, the elephant skin is draped over his back. The flattened head of the elephant, looking particularly floppy and lifeless, is visible on the back. The head and trunk of an elephant-faced demon, the creator of obstacles, lies prone beneath Mahakala. This is Vinayaka or Ganapati, and like the Ganesha of Hinduism, he clutches a white radish. A square opening was cast into the back of the sculpture to insert consecration materials. The plate closing the hole has been lost, but paper scrolls and silk cloth remain inside.[1] Although the hair on the back of the head is finished, and the elephant skin is completely rendered, the back of the base is left in a rough state.

This form of the six-armed Mahakala is known as the Swift-Acting Lord of Pristine Awareness with Six Hands.[2] He is considered a wrathful manifestation of the bodhisattva Avalokiteshvara, and is the principal protector of the Shangpa Kagyu and Gelugpa lineages. In a text by Tsarchen Losal Gyatso (1502–56), an abbot of Shalu monastery and a "brilliant [Sakyapa] scholar and monk," this type of Mahakala is described in detail:

> In the middle of the great charnel ground of Sitavana, above a multicolored lotus, sun, and layered Ganapatis, white with elephant heads, is the Quick Acting Lord of Pristine Awareness with a body blue-black in color, one face and six hands. Pale yellow hair flowing upward, three round red eyes, bared fangs and curled tongue, a crown of five dry skulls, having a necklace of fifty blood-dripping wet [heads], the first right hand holds a curved knife, second a skull *mala* [prayer beads], third a *damaru* [drum]. The first left holds a blood [filled] skullcup, second a trident, and third a *vajra* lasso; adorned with the

(cont. p. 271)

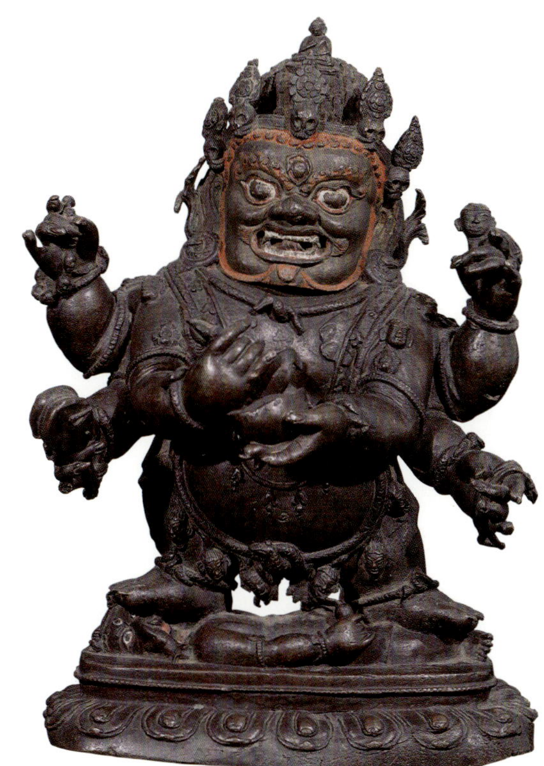

Cat. no. 28
Mahakala
Shadbhuja, Six Hands

Tibet, 14th c.
Metalwork
12⅜ x 8⅜ x 5¼ in. (31.4 x 21.3 x 13.3 cm)
Collection of Shelley and Donald Rubin (HA 700065)

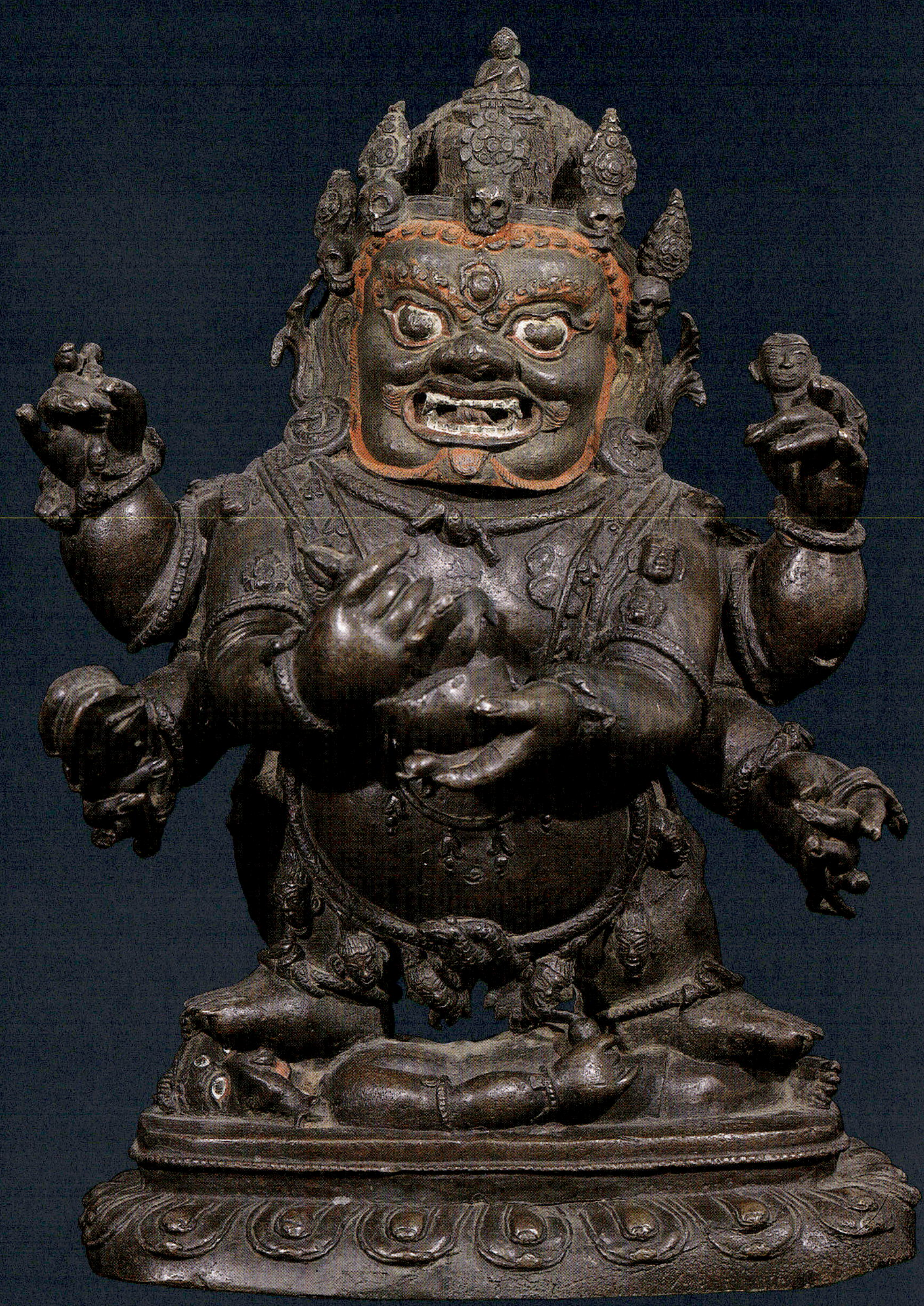

Cat. no. 28

Cat. nos. 29, 30

Masks

Surrounded by dense layers of vegetation and living beings, the Liberian world is filled with spirits. Occasionally, during periods of transition, adversity or celebration these spirits take on a physical presence through the use of masks.[1] Featured here are two different types of masks given to twentieth-century traveler, Tina Rolff, during her extended stay among the Krau, Guere cultures of Liberia in 1951–52.[2]

Catalog number 30 shows what Rolff referred to as a Krau "devil mask" due to its fierce appearance and the unsettling demands it could impose upon a village. It is not unusual for Krau masks to include materials that enhance its other worldliness. Five antelope horns protrude from the brow line. A beard of dried grass extends from the nose and chin. Sideburns of horse hair, bushcat fur, and patches of iguana skin below the eyes form a composite face drawn from the dangers of the bush.[3] The spirit animated by this type of mask would play a role in initiation ceremonies, appearing to the young men and women when taken deep into the forest. In Rolff's narrative account, she cites the spirit's request for sacrifice of cows, goats, chickens, and even human beings, to which the Krau would steadfastly oblige.[4]

In contrast to the "devil mask," catalog number 29 housed a more jovial spirit. Appearing during times of celebration, the spirit of this dance mask performed to amuse. However, due to the thin metal disks outlining its circular eyes, full grin of carved teeth painted white, and semicircular incising at the brow, it shares visual commonalities with more wrathful figures, such as the Greek gorgon face (see cat. no. 19) and the Tibetan wrathful Vajrapani (see cat. no. 56).[5]

(notes p. 271)

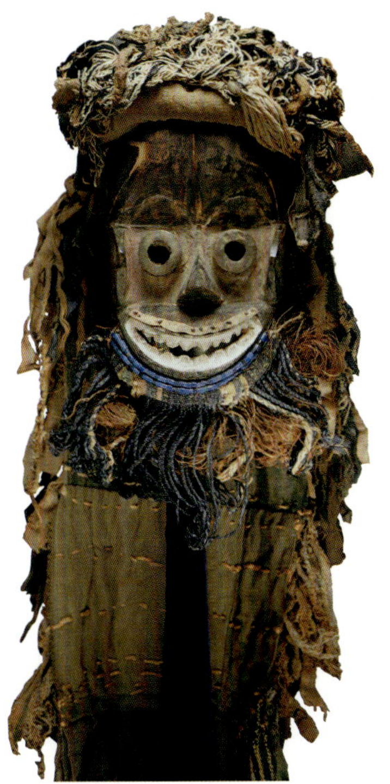

Cat. no. 29
Mask

Liberia, Africa (Krau, Guere culture), 20th c.
Mixed media (including wood, brass, beads, grass fibers, imported cotton cloth, raffia, cotton thread, and mud pigment)
24 x 15 x 117 in. (61 x 38.1 x 297.2 cm)
American Museum of Natural History, New York

Next page: Cat. no. 30
Mask

Liberia, Africa (Krau, Guere culture), 20th c.
Mixed media (including wood, plant fiber, cowrie shells, aluminum, antelope horns, iguana skin, bushcat fur, horse hair, porcelain shards, and mud pigment)
30 x 24 x 12 in. (76.2 x 61 x 30.5 cm)
American Museum of Natural History, New York

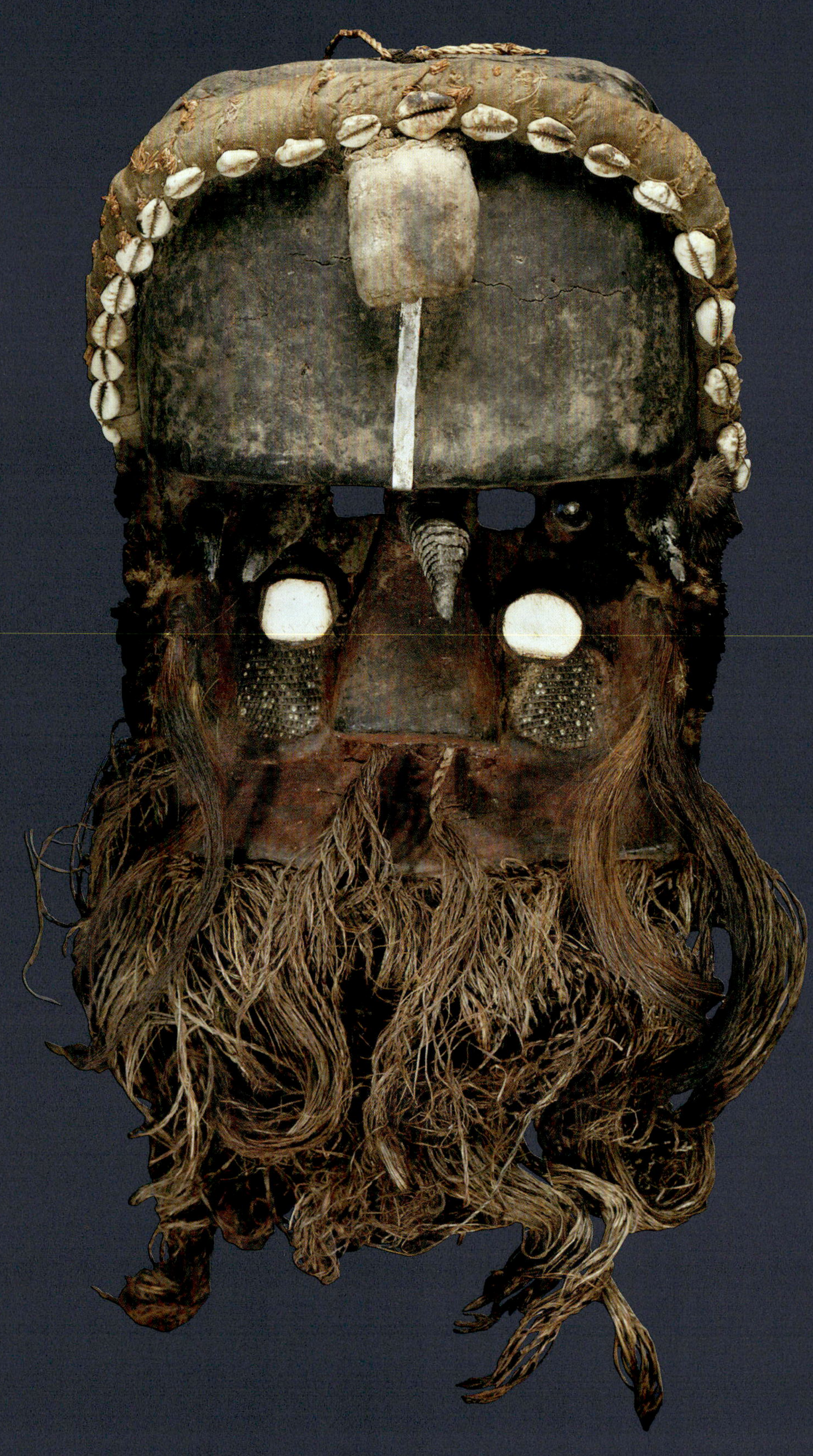

Cat. no. 30

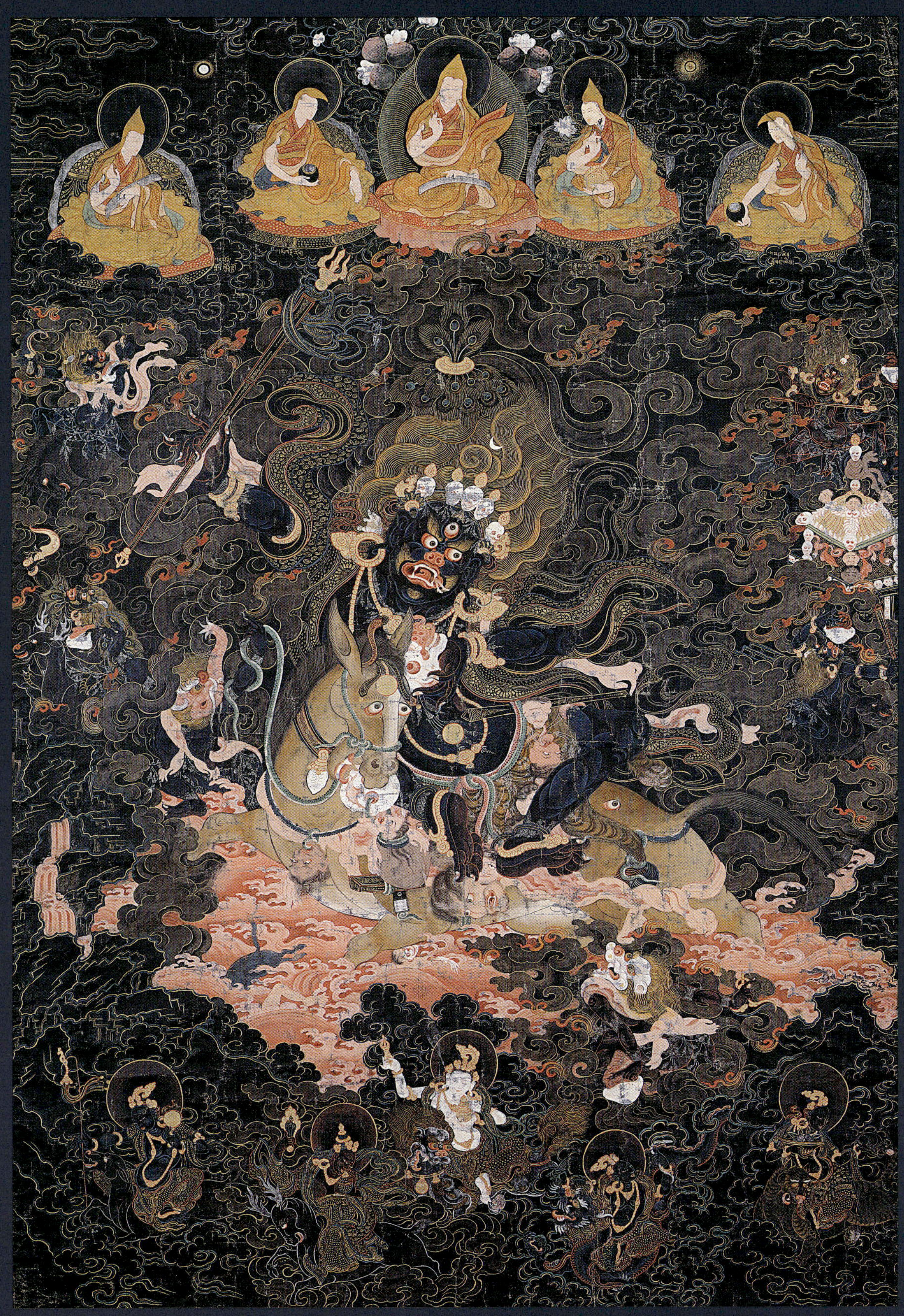

Cat. no. 31

Cat. no. 31

Shri Devi, Magzor Gyalmo

Queen who Has the Power to Turn Back Armies

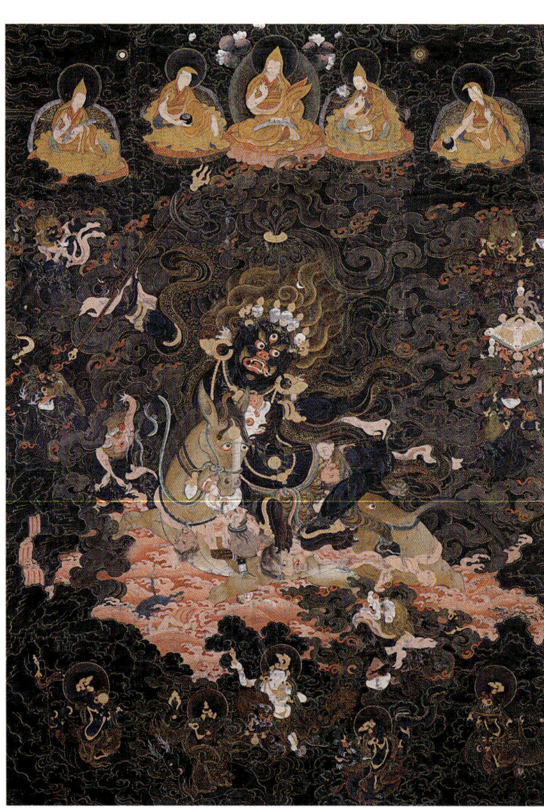

Cat. no. 31
Shri Devi
Magzor Gyalmo
Queen who Has the Power to Turn Back Armies

Central Tibet, mid-18th c.
Mineral pigments on cloth
33¼ x 22¾ in. (84.5 x 57.8 cm)
Collection of Shelley and Donald Rubin (HA 105)

From political, religious, aesthetic, and methodological perspectives, this is one of the most fascinating paintings in the exhibition. Art historically, it is remarkable for marrying the idealizing realism of portraiture to graphically fantastic visions of violent themes. As a historical document, its provenance is impeccable: it belonged to a set of seven paintings produced for persons at the highest reaches of the monastic culture centered on Lhasa in the second half of the seventeenth and the first half of the eighteenth century. The painting provides a rare window onto behind-the-scenes debates and disputes that changed the course of Tibetan history. The portraits and inscriptions on the back are the keys to unlocking this painting. Some of the most famous teachers in Tibetan history (notably the Fifth Dalai Lama) are portrayed, along with some whose history has been—and continues to be—officially marginalized due to political and theological struggles, but whose memory is kept alive in Tibetan vernacular culture. Finally, the inscription on the back has been found in an eighteenth-century book, in a genre of Tibetan literature in which a lama records the inscriptions he composes for the backs of paintings. This discovery helps to validate the utility of such literature for the study of Tibetan painting.

The painting's principal subject is Shri Devi Magzor Gyalmo (Queen who Has the Power to Turn Back Armies), the wrathful aspect of the peaceful goddess Sarasvati (Yang Chenma) (cat. key 31.6).[1] She is the main attendant to Shri Devi Paldan Lhamo and though they are iconographically distinct (two versus four arms), had independent origins and affiliations in Hindu India, and had different histories and personalities, they are often confused.[2] Magzor Gyalmo is always a protector and is also used for divination rituals. Any serious undertaking of the practice of "The Queen who Has the Power to Turn Back Armies" is always done with a self-

(cont. p. 271)
(cat. key p. 274)

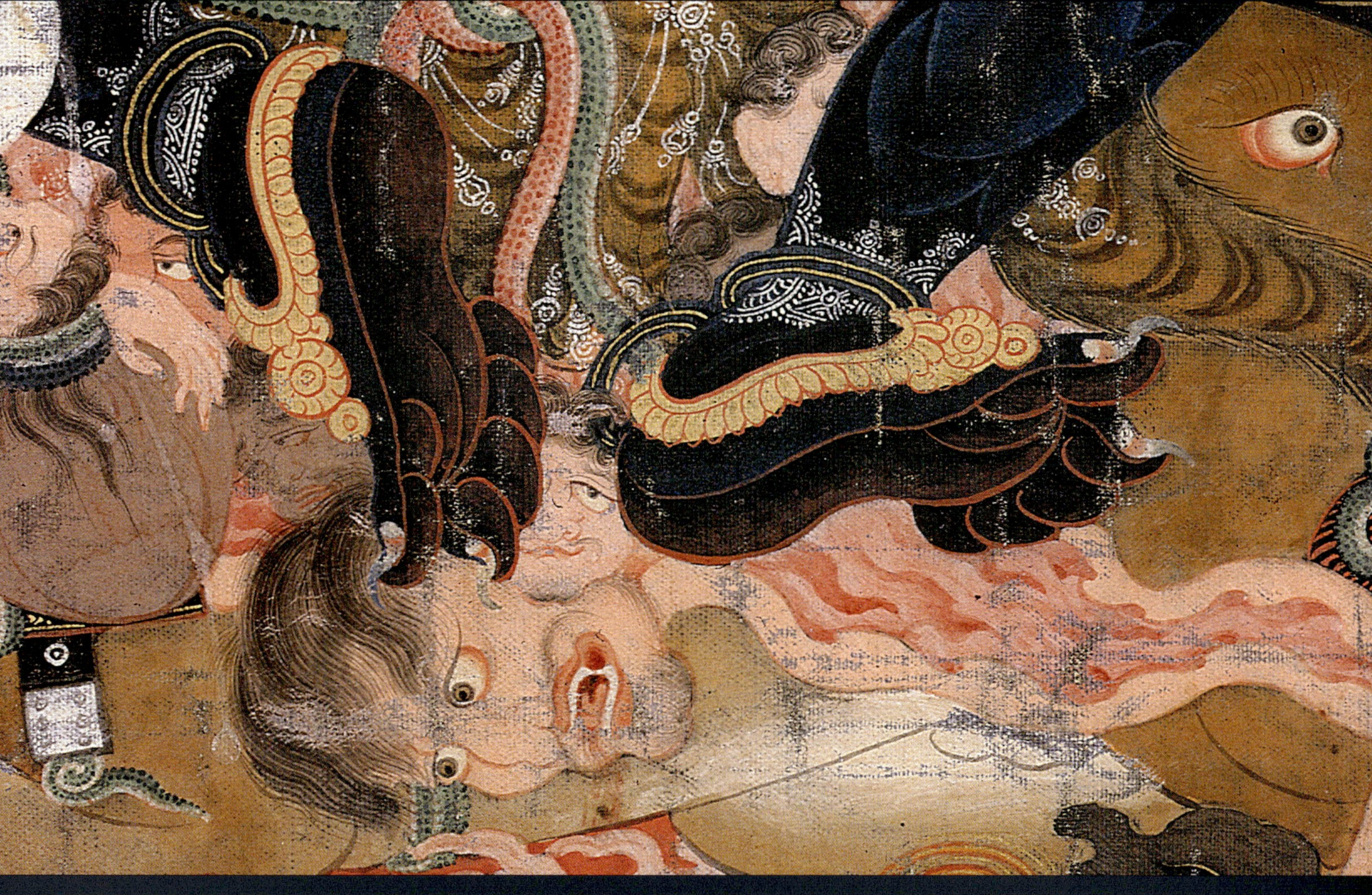

Cat. no. 31, detail

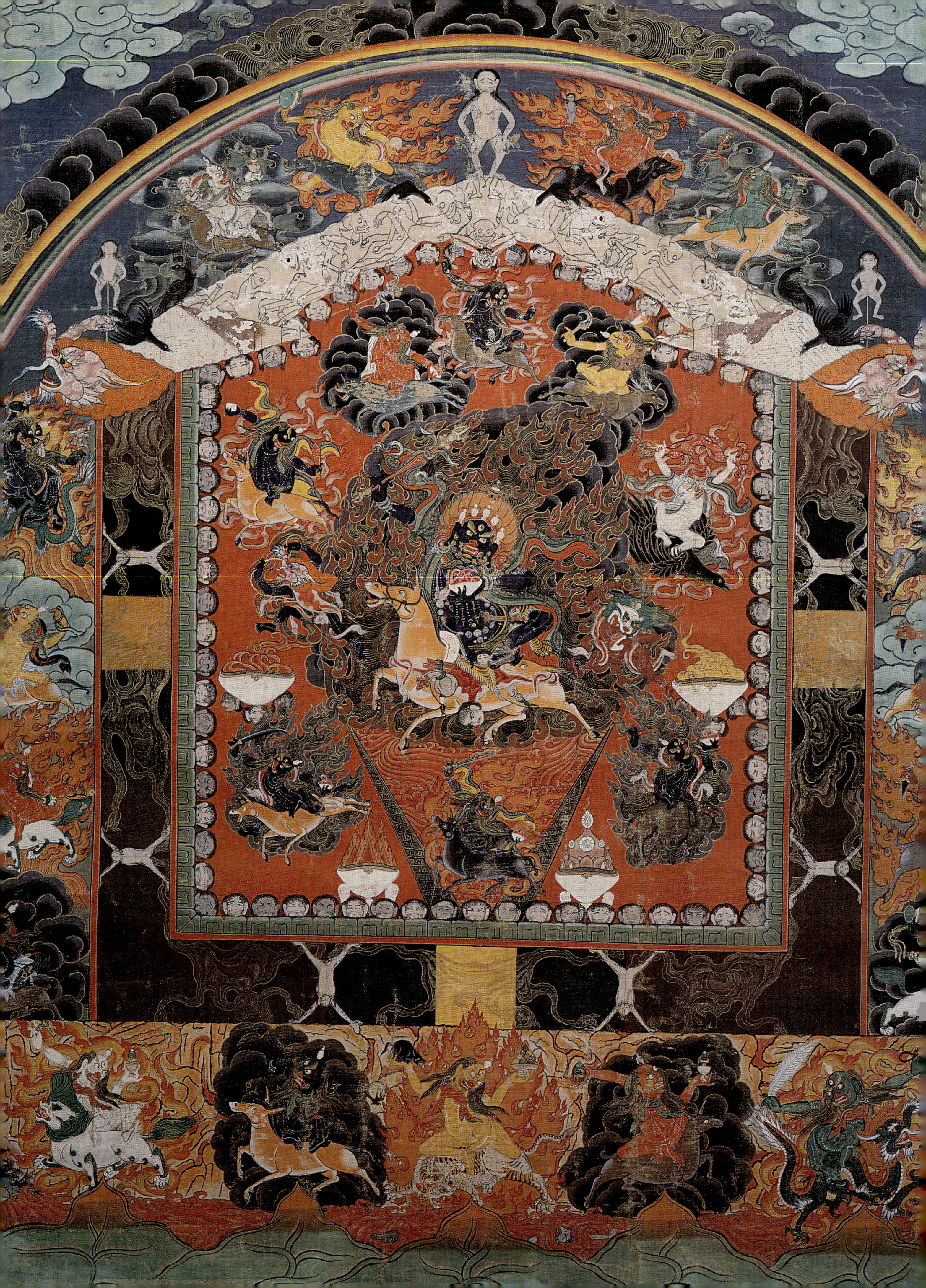

Cat. no. 32

Shri Devi, Magzor Gyalmo

Queen who Has the Power to Turn Back Armies

Although commonly misidentified as Palden Lhamo, the wrathful central figure is actually a particular form of Shri Devi called in Himalayan contexts Magzor Gyalmo. Magzor Gyalmo is two-armed while Palden Lhamo has four arms.[1] Usually shown beneath a canopy of peacock feathers, Magzor Gyalmo is depicted within a palace, or "the mansion from which the ferocious goddess is summoned during her rituals of protection."[2] In a configuration of concentric circles that is reminiscent of a mandala, the wrathful queen is surrounded by inner (within the palace) and outer retinue figures numbering twenty-seven (cat. key 32.2–28). The palace, which is synoptically represented as if in both plan and section, has a roof of skeletons and is protected by borders of a rainbow and dark flames giving off black smoke. The outer walls, on which flayed skins and fresh corpses are suspended (see detail), are shown as if each is viewed head on. Only three of the four outer walls are shown, suggesting that one sees the roof held up by two walls in a section view.[3] The parapet of the outer wall is lined with severed heads, and the whole palace floats in a sea of blood and fat.

We peer through the walls into the inner chamber where Magzor Gyalmo rides a mule with a poisonous-snake bridle, its reins held by the *makara*-headed female groom (cat. key 32.1, 32.2). A second lion-headed attendant runs after the mule (cat. key 32.3). The queen, who is chewing on a corpse, wields a sandalwood club with a *vajra* finial in one hand and what has been identified as the skull of a child born of incestuous union in the other. Her saddle is made from the flayed skin of one of her children, and tied to it are a sack of diseases, pair of dice, and magical thread ball.[4]

Eight more wicked-looking female attendants are arranged around her. These are associated with the four directions (cat. key 32.4–7) and the four seasons (cat. key 32.8–11).[5] Supporting the mounted queen in the inner chamber is a tetrahedronal *homa* (fire ritual) altar filled with blood and fat, a veritable ocean of blood. The three sides represent three types of emptiness in Buddhist philosophy, reinforcing that Magzor Gyalmo, like all Buddhist wrathful deities, arises from emptiness and, however revered, ultimately has no inherent existence.

(notes p. 275)
(cat. key p. 276)

Facing page: Cat. no. 32
Shri Devi, Magzor Gyalmo
Queen who Has the Power to Turn Back Armies

Tibet, 19th c.
Mineral pigments on cloth
25 x 20⅜ in. (63.5 x 51.8 cm)
Collection of Shelley and Donald Rubin
(HA 140)

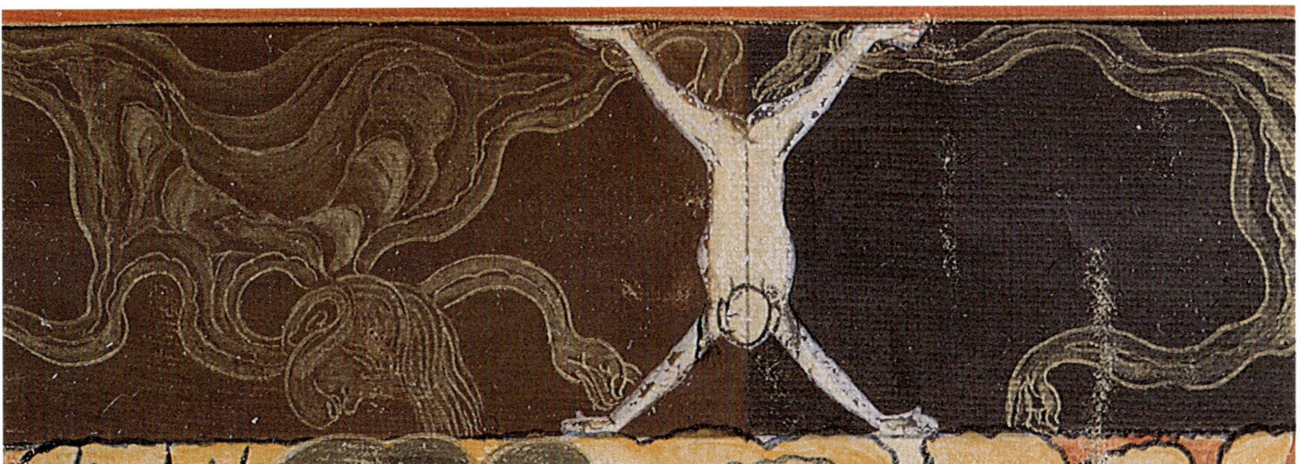

Cat. no. 32, detail

Cat. no. 33

Yama Dharmaraja

With Demon Head

Destroyer of the King of Hell

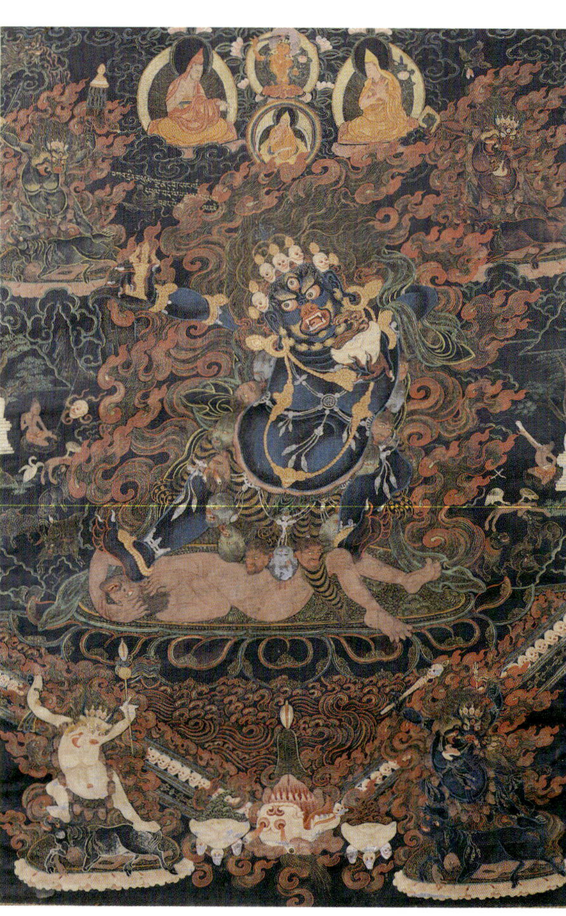

Cat. no. 33
Yama Dharmaraja with Demon Head
Destroyer of the King of Hell

Central Tibet, second half of the 18th c.
Mineral pigments on cloth
16¾ x 11 in. (42.5 x 27.9 cm)
Collection of Shelley and Donald Rubin (HA 159)

The "wisdom bodhisattva" Manjushri emanates Enlightened Protectors who represent the power of the Buddhist teachings to overcome the endless cycle of birth, death, and rebirth. Yama, the King of Hell, or Lord of Death, is a convenient symbol for this cycle of misery, and Yama Dharmaraja, a symbol for its vanquishing.[1] In the process of overcoming Yama, some emanations manifest the attributes of Yama, including his buffalo head, buffalo mount (cat. no. 34), and even his name, to which is added Dharmaraja, or "King of the Law of Cause and Effect."[2] However, there are three forms of Yama Dharamaraja: Outer, Inner, and Secret. This concentrated, detailed black-ground (*nag-tang*) painting shows the Inner form of Yama Dharmaraja.[3]

The bodhisattva Manjushri is depicted at the top center of the painting, holding aloft a sword, with the Wisdom text on a lotus flower. The Inner Yama Dharmaraja has a demon (*rakshasa*) head and carries a skull bowl and *vajra*-handled, curved flaying knife, the attributes also held by the Wrathful Buddha Vajravarahi (cat. nos. 57, 58) and by some forms of the Enlightened Protector Mahakala (cat. nos. 18, 21, 22, 28). Yama Dharmaraja is depicted in an extreme version of the archer's pose, leaning far to his left, but tilting his head back and to his right. His four retinue figures reverse the direction of the archer's pose. As white, yellow, red, and blue Yama-conquerors, they share Yama's pose, buffalo head, and mount (see detail, p. 124).[4] Reinforcing the connection to death are two charnel grounds at the middle sides of the painting, complete with *chortens* (architectural reliquaries), corpses being pecked by birds, bones and skulls, and other wild animals nearby. Two Mahasiddhas perform their *tantric* practices in these lonely spots, amid reminders of the decomposition of all physical phenomena.

Yama Dharmaraja's lotus pedestal is set into a triangular altar lined with skulls and *vajras* and containing a sea of blood. Three

(cont. p. 275)

Cat. no. 33, detail

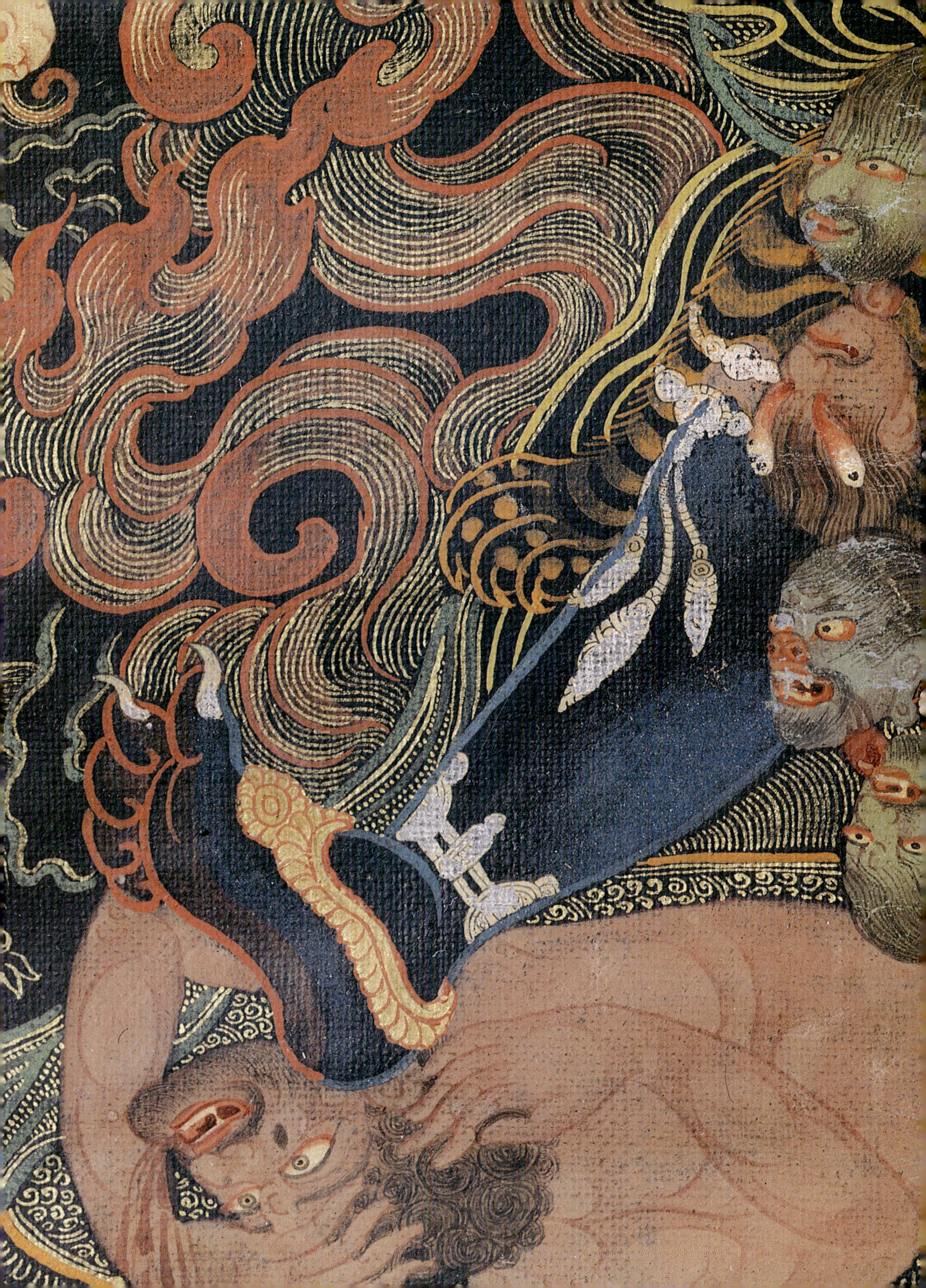

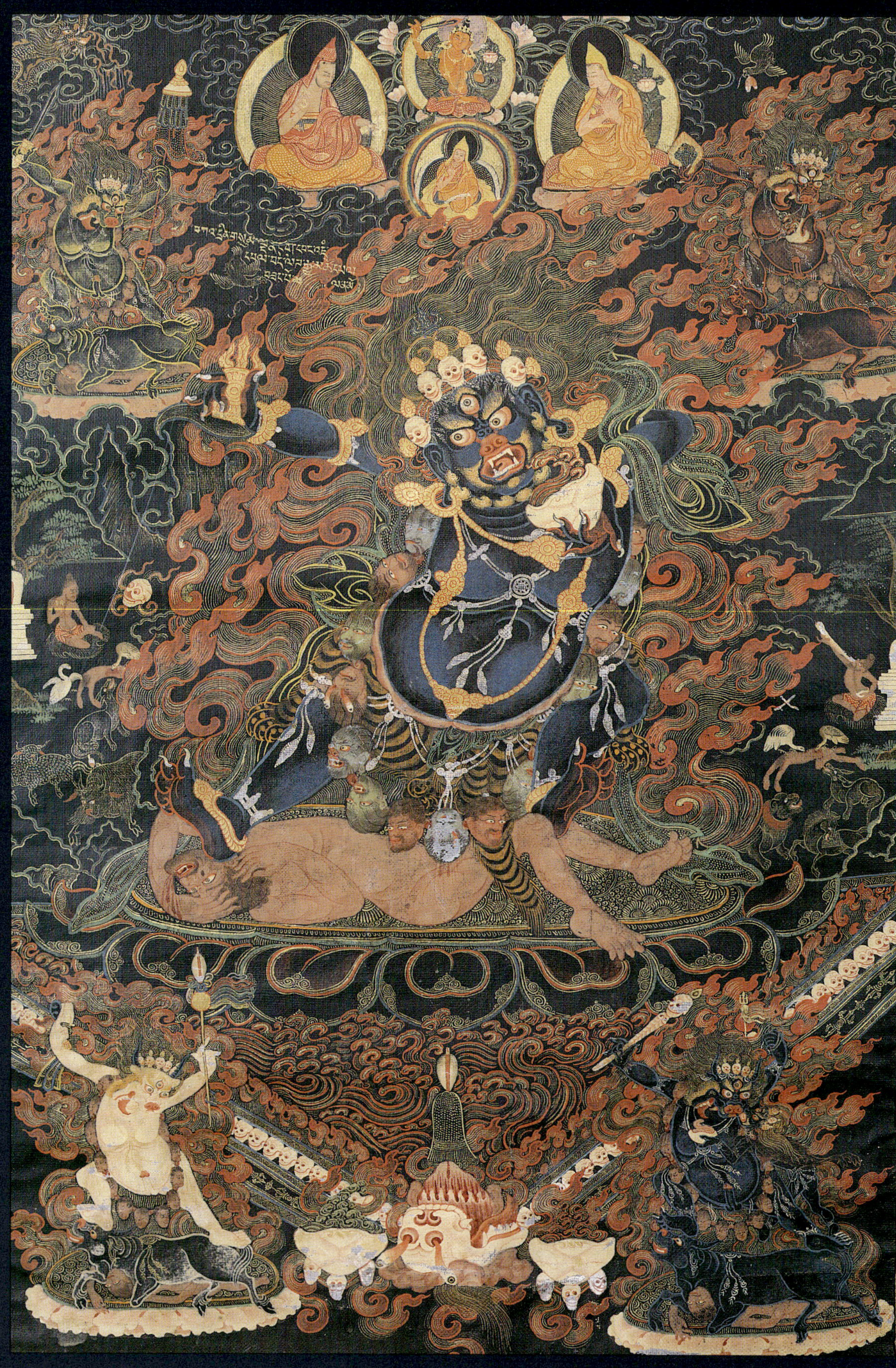

Cat. no. 33

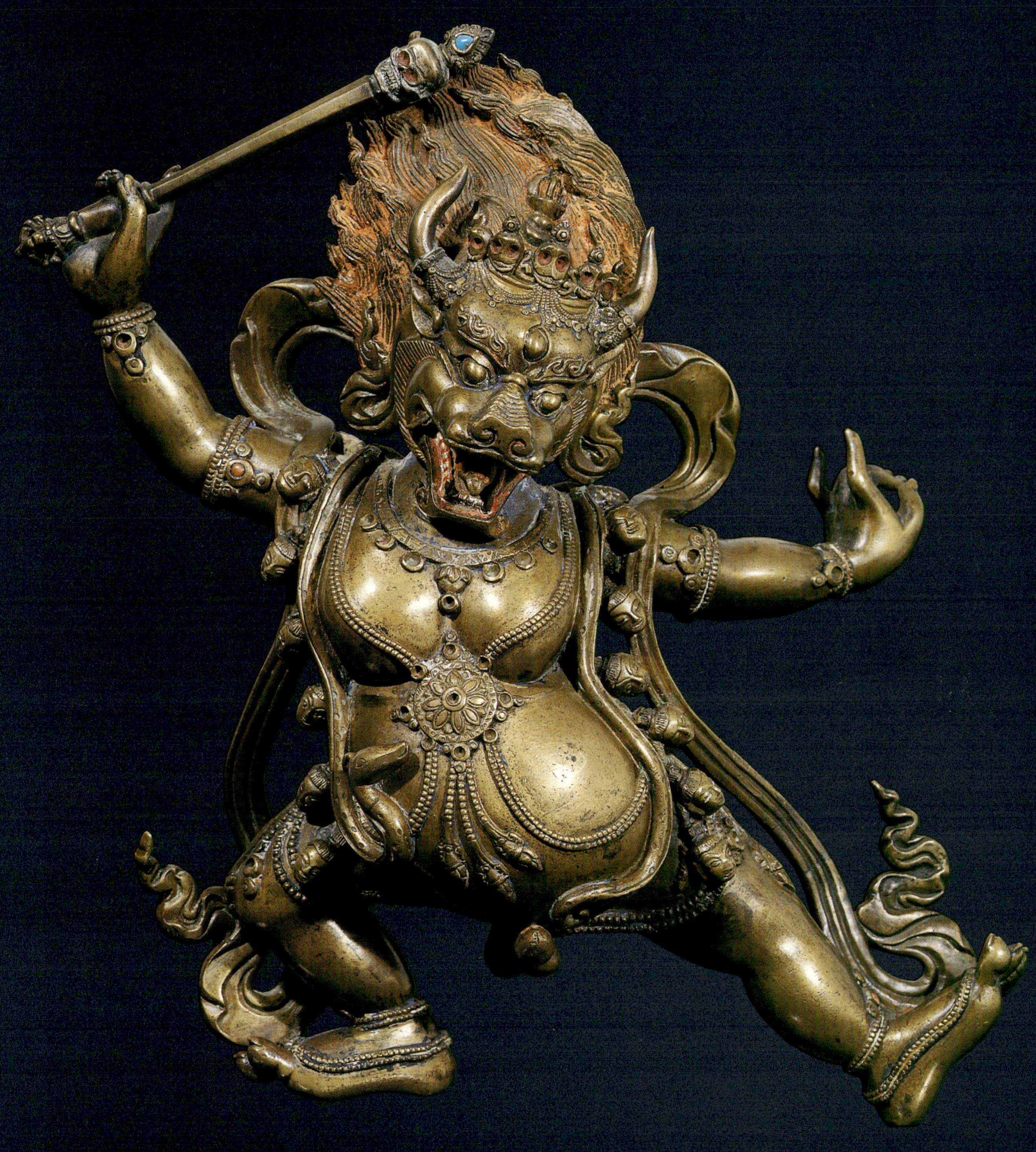

Cat. no. 34

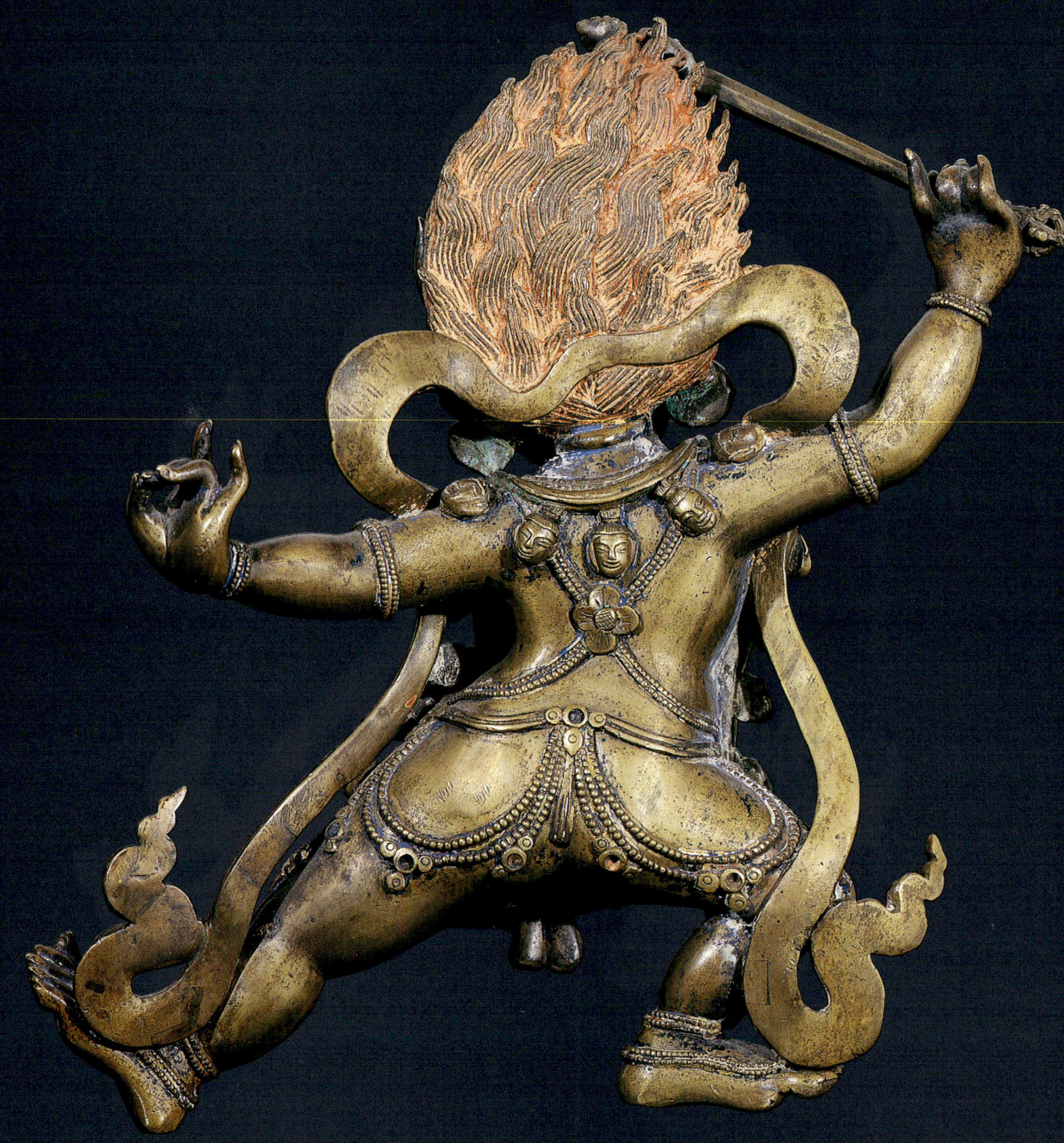

Cat. no. 34, back

Cat. no. 34

Yama Dharmaraja

With Buffalo Head

Destroyer of the King of Hell

The dynamism and grace of Yama Dharmaraja's pose is almost balletic. Both arms are flung to the sides, fully outstretched, with rounded limbs. He towers over his enemy, glaring down furiously with his grotesque buffalo head. One expects the raised right arm to swing the skull club three times around his head and then sweep it down across his big body, while he shifts its weight and pivots like one of the masked dancers of the *cham*. The artist has used flamelike hair that is swept to the side to convey the force with which Yama Dharmaraja moves. Even the scarves ripple with energy, their ends undulating in fluid patterns. Fiercely terrifying, this work conveys the quintessence of the Enlightened Protector type.

There are a few other exceptional features of the solid cast bronze. The expression on the faces tied to his garland are all peaceful, even smiling. The beaded swags attached to his crown and his horns are extremely delicate and fine, as is the post-cast chasing on his necklace. Unfortunately, most of the coral and turquoise beads that once ornamented his jewelry are gone. So too is the lasso once held in his left hand, the blue buffalo on which he stood, and the human corpse under the buffalo. (For these elements, see fig. 1.1.)

Yama Dharmaraja, also known as Kalarupa, is an Enlightened Protector employed by those who have been initiated in and practice Vajrabhairava practices in Kagyu, Sakya, and Gelugpa traditions.[1] The Gelugpa tradition holds Yama Dharmaraja in a special regard as one of the three main Dharma protectors of the Gelugpa along with the Shadbhuja Mahakala (cat. no. 26) and Vaishravana. These three were the special protectors of Lama Tsongkapa, Lobzang Dragpa (1357–1419), founder of the Gelugpa tradition.

(note p. 276)

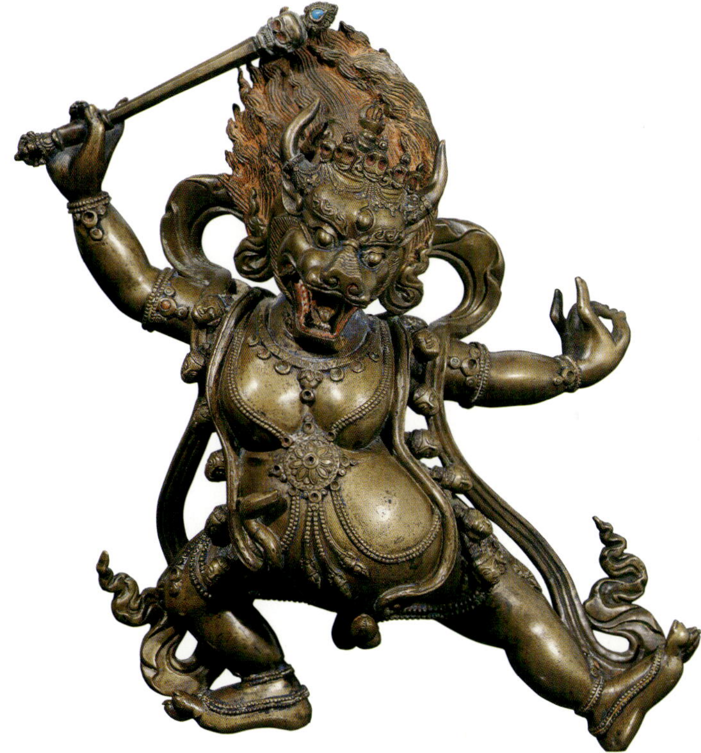

Cat. no. 34
Yama Dharmaraja with Buffalo Head
Destroyer of the King of Hell

Tibet, 17th–18th c.
Metalwork, inset coral and turquoise
10½ x 8 x 3 in. (26.7 x 20.3 x 7.6 cm)
Collection of Shelley and Donald Rubin (HA 700009)

Cat. no. 35

Symbol Mandala of Yama Dharmaraja and Chamunda

Facing page: Cat. no. 35
Symbol Mandala of Yama Dharmaraja and Chamunda

Tibet, 18th c.
Mineral pigments on cloth
12 x 12 in. (30.5 x 30.5 cm)
F1996.11.1 (HA 436)

This painting appears at first glance to be a colorful and beautifully designed series of abstract shapes, lacking obvious characteristics of the "demonic divine." A close second look, however, reveals its underlying structure and meaning. Symbols of Yama Dharmaraja, conqueror of the God of Death, and of his demonic consort Chamunda (see cat. no. 64), rest on a lotus inside the central circle. His skull- and *vajra*-tipped cudgel is on the left, along with his snare or lasso, while Chamunda is represented by her trident with skull finial and a skull bowl sloshing with blood and fat (also see cat. key 50.19). The attributes are seen on or through an eight-pointed whirling blade. Yama's eight primary minions are similarly represented by their ritual attributes on the eight spokes of the blade weapon, with an additional four in the T-shaped gates: an *ankusha* (elephant goad, at the bottom, the East), noose (left), club (top), and fang-shaped object (right). The mandala setting has been expressively described:

> The eight-pointed blade wheel containing the principals and their retinue lies in the circular mandala palace on a jewel floor with a wall of stacked skulls. The palace doors are surmounted by simple curved gateways with a skull spire and skin pennants. The parapets of the building are made of compressed bones and eaves adorned with intestines. The building sits on an island in a moat of boiling blood, encircled by the eight [charnel grounds] with the usual world gods present (a form of Yama himself stands on a white bull in the southern [left side charnel ground]). The [charnel grounds] themselves are contained by a vajra wall and a ring of flames.[1]

In *tantric* rituals performed by initiated practitioners for protection, benefaction, and transformative spiritual experience, deities are often visualized, invited, and requested to perform tasks, through the manipulation of

(cont. p. 277)

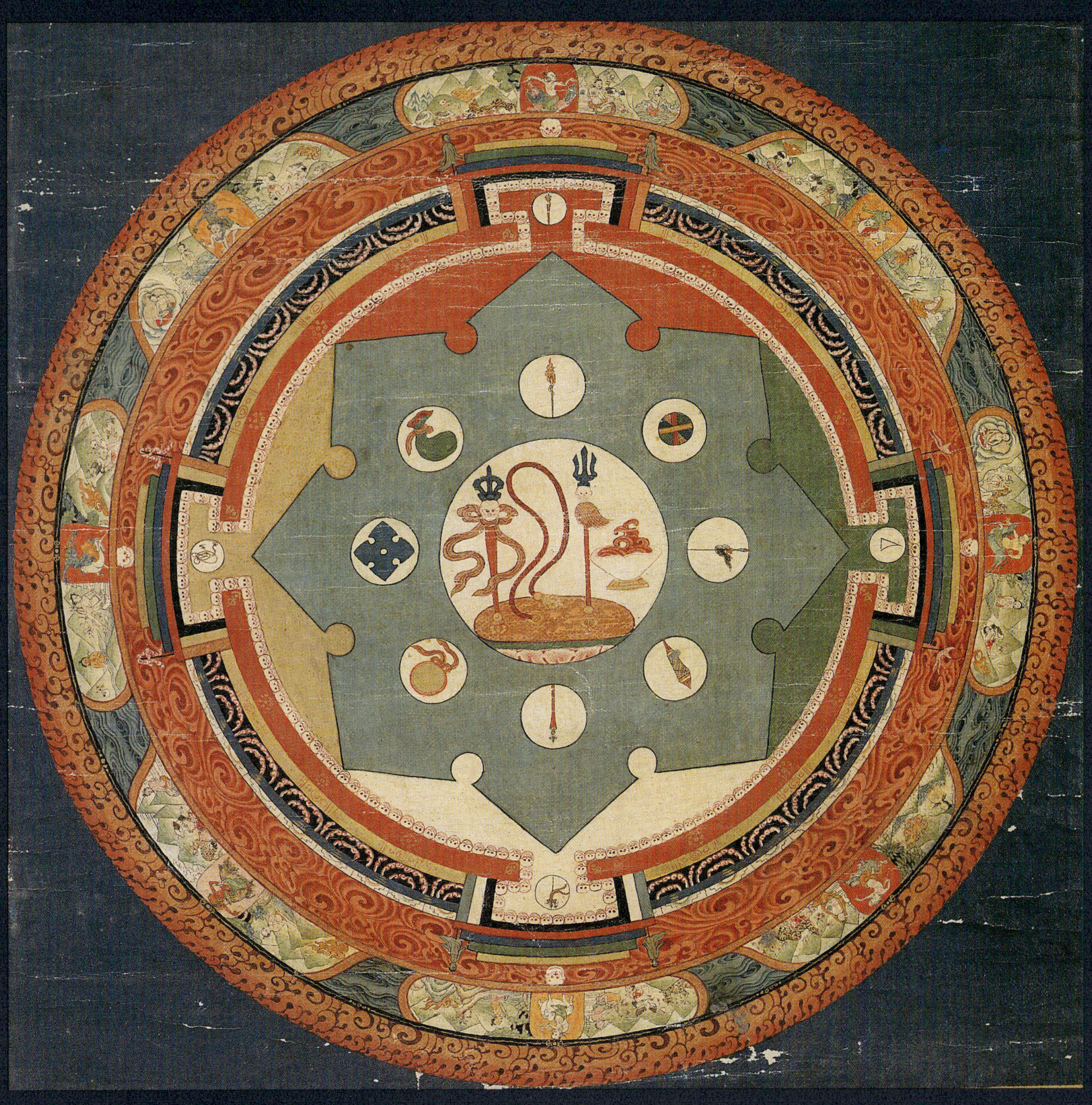

Cat. no. 35

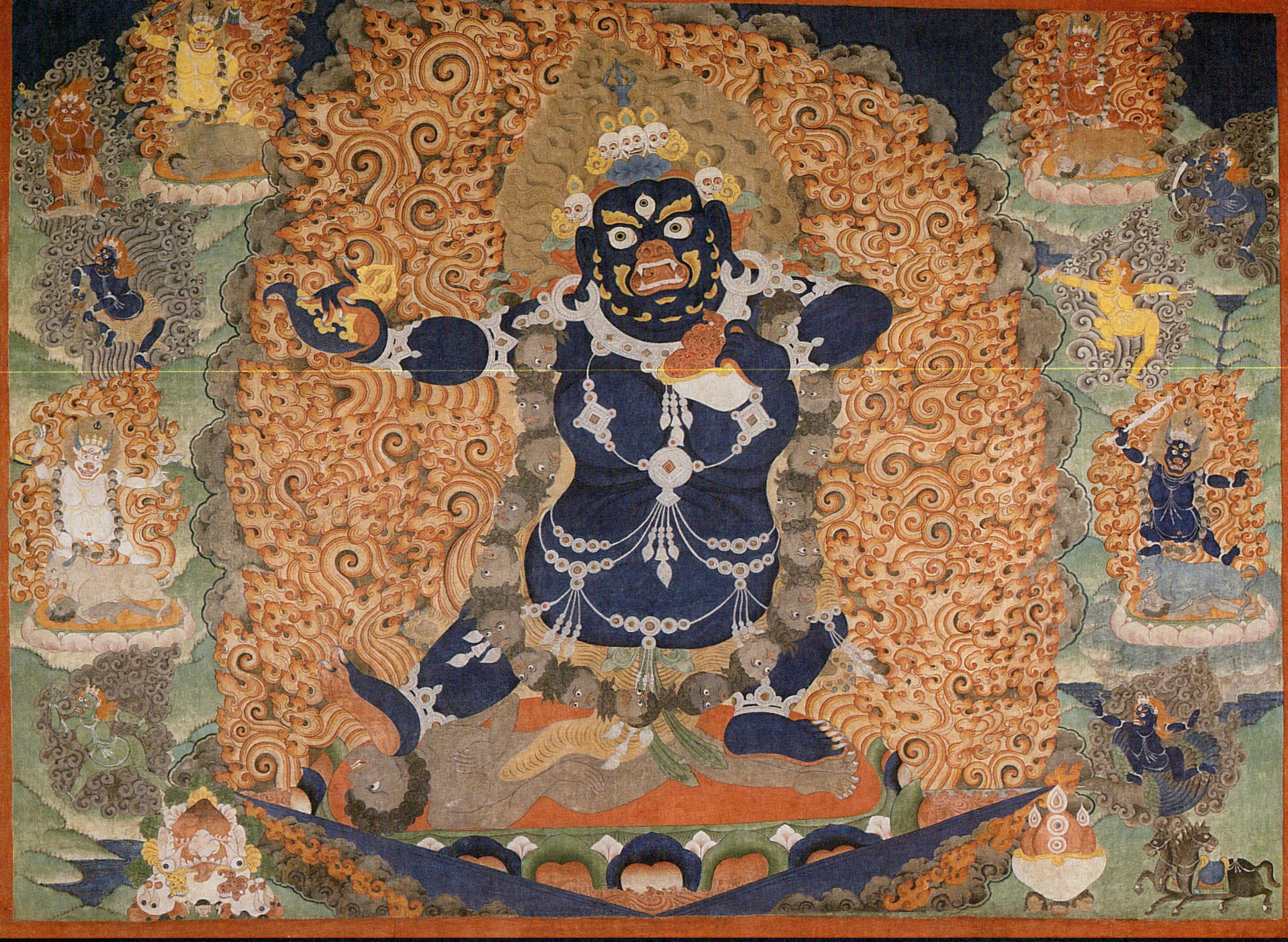

Cat. no. 36

Cat. no. 36

Yama Dharmaraja

With Demon Head

Destroyer of the King of Hell

In Esoteric Buddhism in India and Tibet, the *gaze* of the deity, and of the practitioner, has the power to overthrow, subdue, summon, and petrify.[1] The Indian Tantric master Amoghavajra (705–74), who taught in China in the eighth century, had even more evocative terms for the *chatur-drishti*, the four gazes: blazing gaze, hook-summoning gaze, angry gaze, and gaze of subjugation.[2] Purely from an expressive point of view, all of these gazes fit this Yama Dharmaraja, but given the blinding flash of flames behind him, perhaps the blazing gaze is most appropriate.

The Kumar painting is by far the largest work of art in the exhibition. It was not a *tangka* hanging in silk brocades the way most of the rest of the paintings originally were. Instead it was a mural hung in front of a wall inside a monastery. It is most common for murals to be painted directly on prepared walls within the various buildings of a Buddhist monastery. In recent times, particularly in eastern and western Tibet, in order to preserve older murals that have become darkened or damaged, large cloth paintings are sometimes suspended in front of the walls. This preserves the older murals, but satisfies popular demand for colorful, new-looking murals that better express the living sentiment. It also allows the artists to work more conveniently within their own quarters. While it is not known how long this mode of mural painting has been in practice, it is quite possible that it is pre-nineteenth-century.

The mural was probably hung on the inside entrance wall of a Dukhang (Assembly Hall) possibly in Northeastern Tibet. (See part seven and appendix of Linrothe's essay, on placement within monasteries of wrathful imagery.) Like catalog number 33, it depicts the Inner Yama Dharmaraja standing on a corpse within a triangular enclosure (Sanskrit: *dharmadayo*). He is again accompanied by his four retinue figures standing on buffalo of matching colors and leering comically.[3]

(cont. p. 278)

Facing page: Cat. no. 36
Yama Dharmaraja with Demon Head
Destroyer of the King of Hell

Tibet, 18th–19th c.
Mineral pigments on cloth
73⅞ x 96½ in. (185.4 x 245.1 cm)
Collection of Navin Kumar, New York

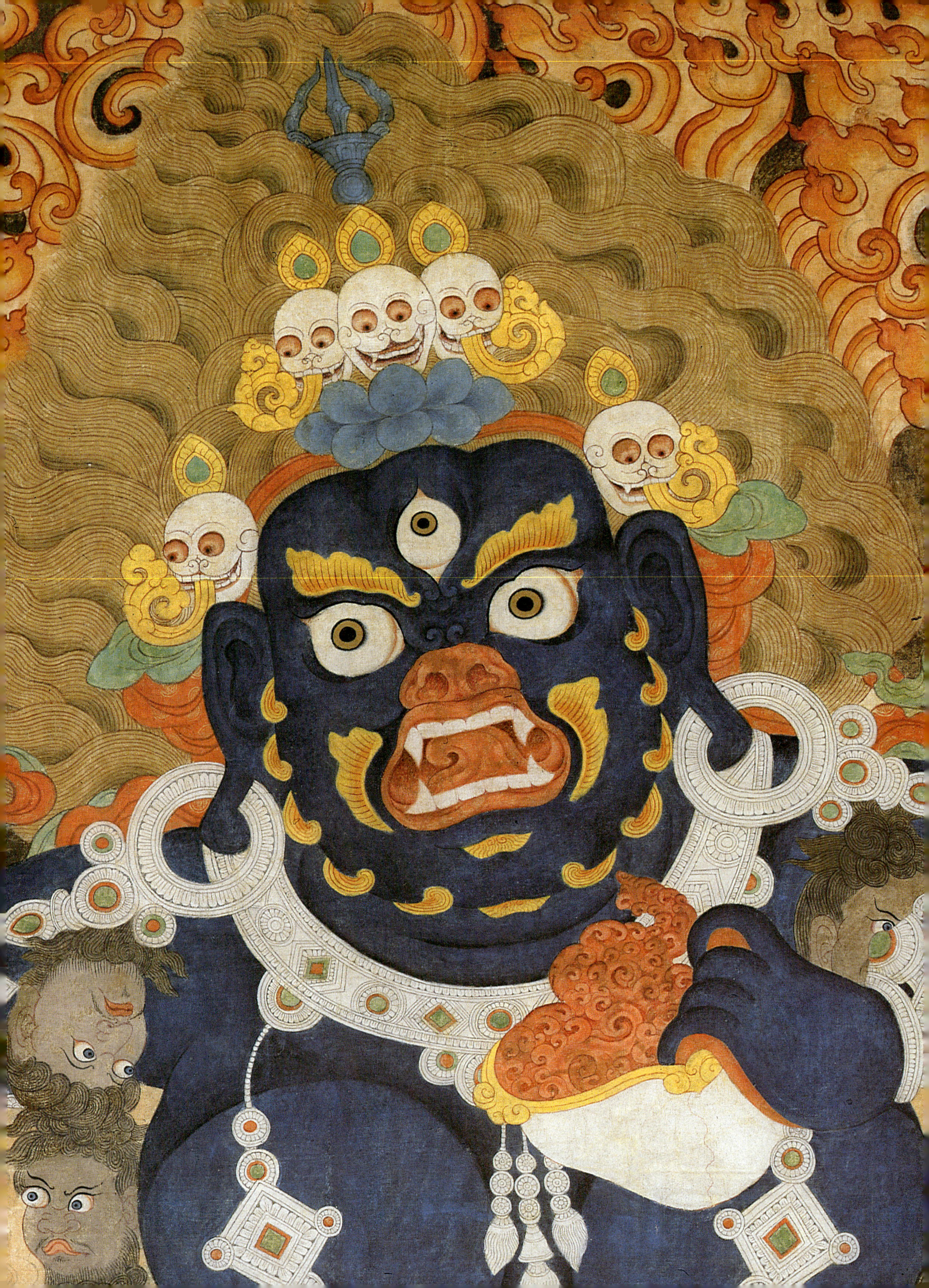

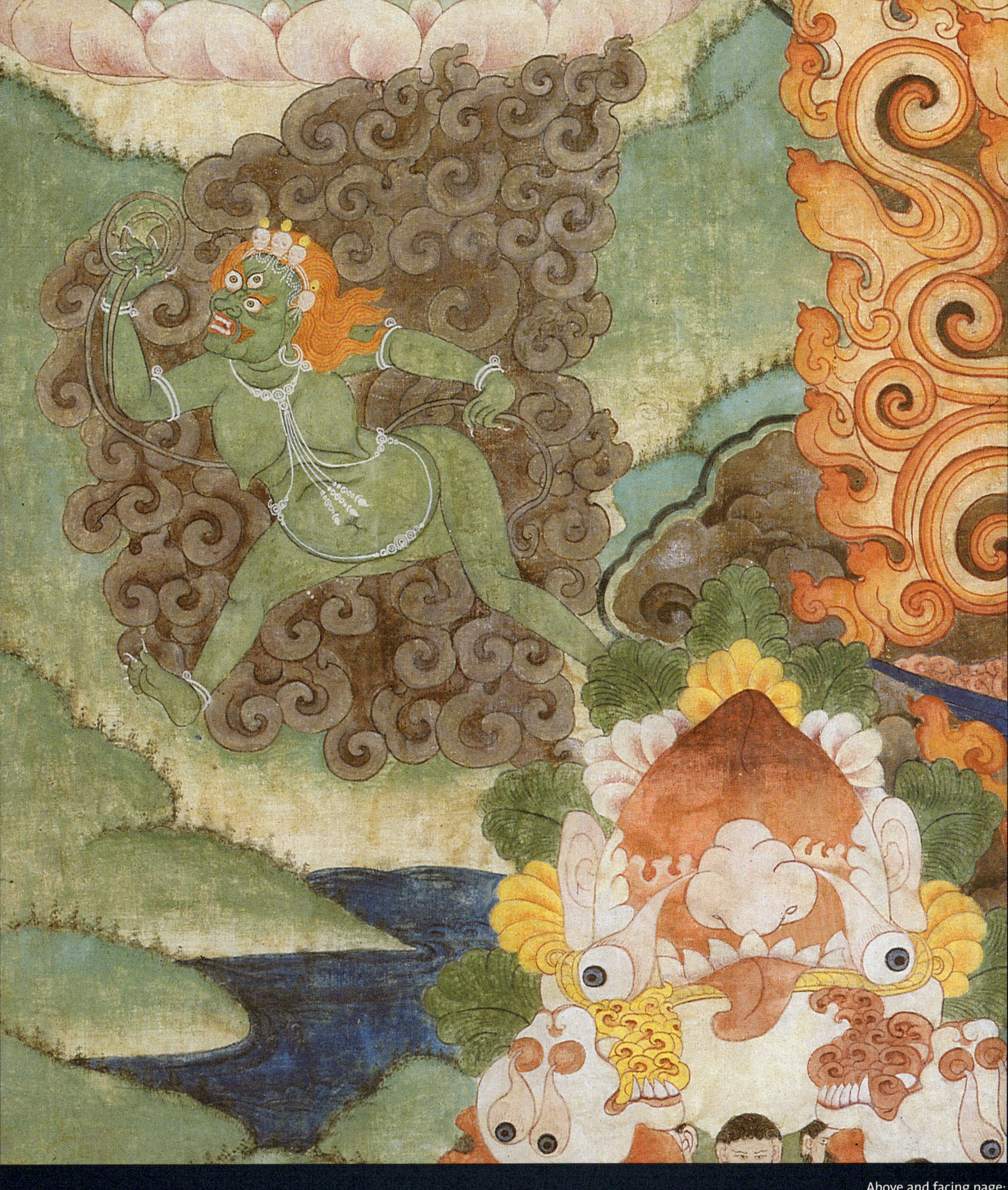

Above and facing page:

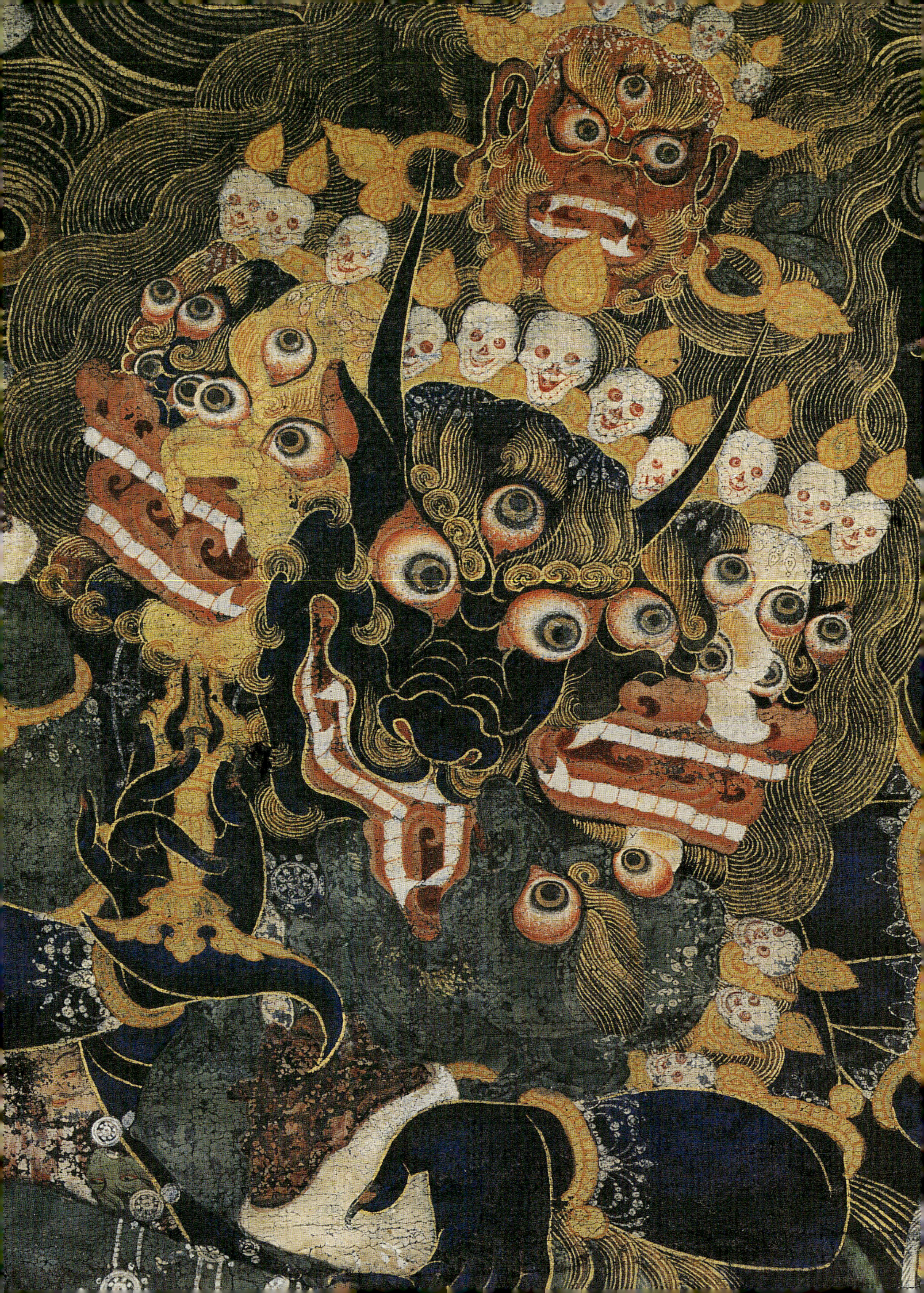

Wrathful Buddhas

Within Himalayan Buddhism, Wrathful Buddhas are understood to be totally enlightened Buddhas, even though they do not look like the traditional robe-clad figure of a monk. They form an important component of the set of paramount deities in the pantheons of Esoteric Buddhism, Bön, and Hinduism. Large cycles of teachings, including ritual texts, commentaries, and the liturgies to support them, are dedicated to these deities. Wrathful Buddhas take on terrifying forms in order to subdue the most tenacious, deeply rooted, and powerful inner and outer demons. Ultimately, their images are of the enlightened mind itself.

Cat. no. 50, detail

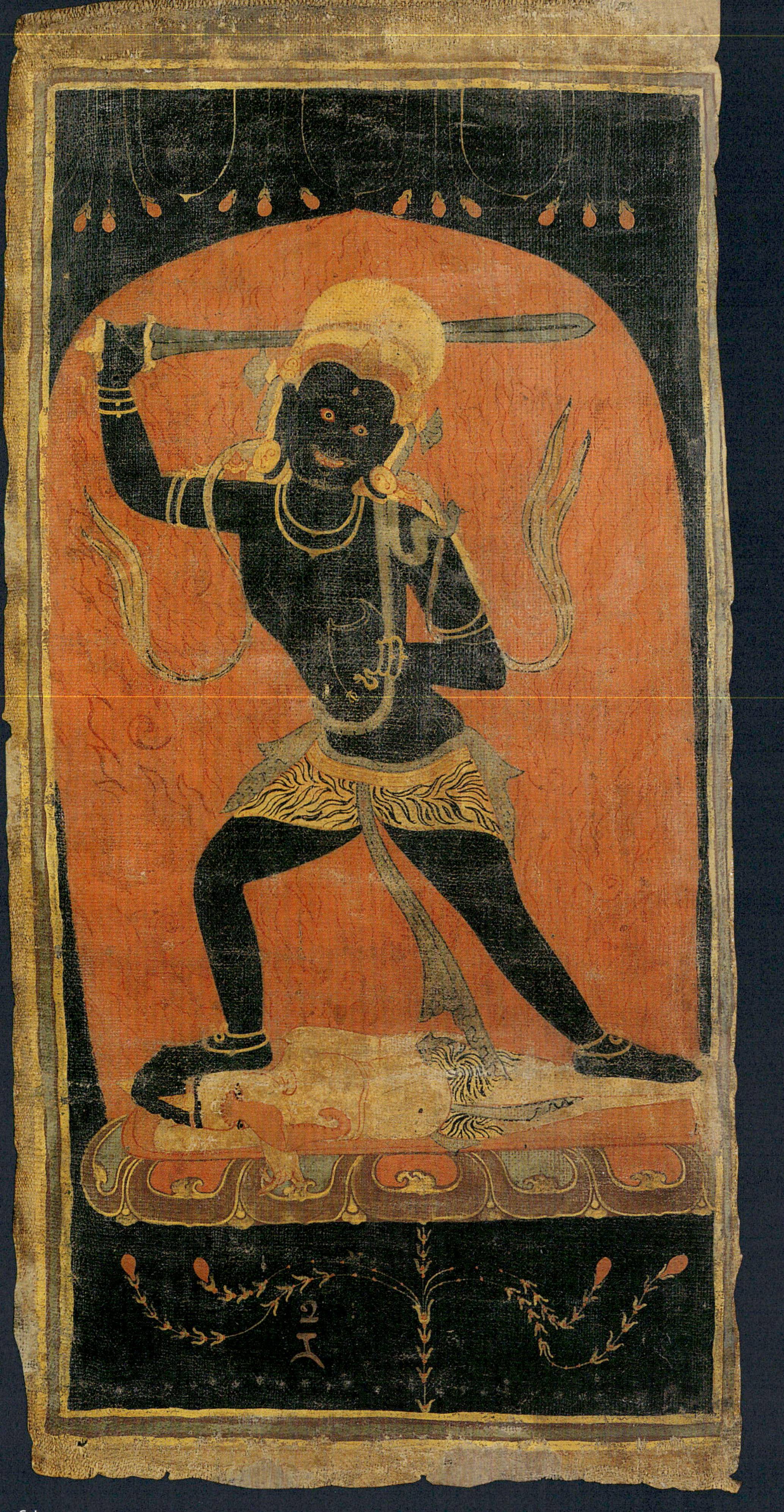

Cat. no. 37

Cat. no. 37

Achala

(The Immovable One)

This small painting is one of the most intriguing in the personal collection of Shelley and Donald Rubin. It can be placed at the center of a controversy in the field of Tibetan art history. Thematically, it is a painting of Achala (also: Achalanata), an important deity in Indian Esoteric Buddhism who inspired art in all the cultures to which this form of Buddhism was transmitted, even in Japan (see cat. no. 41). The Immovable One holds up a convincingly rendered sword, makes a gesture of admonition and threat while grasping a lasso, and is ready to tie up and slice through any and all delusions and obstructions. He tramples on an elephant-headed demon, the Lord of Obstacles.[1] Stylistically, there is general agreement that the painting is done in what is known as Gyalug, "meaning the style that had been evolving in India during the late Pala dynasty."[2]

But is the painting Tibetan or Eastern Indian? Since no large-scale murals or paintings on cloth survive in Eastern India, the only comparisons are with Indian sculptures and manuscript illuminations, which do survive in great numbers. In addition, Burmese wall paintings of the eleventh and twelfth centuries provide another body of evidence, since they too were "directly related to India."[3] There is no question that early painting in Tibet (tenth–thirteenth centuries) was strongly and directly affected by Indian painting. There were a number of avenues by which Indian paintings arrived in Tibet. Indian artists may have traveled to Tibet to paint for Tibetan patrons, just as we know Newari artists did. Tibetans such as Rinchen Zangpo (958–1055), who went to India and Kashmir more than once, surely commissioned Indian artists in India and brought works back with him. It is well known that he also brought Kashmiri artists back with him on at least one occasion. The many revered Indian teachers who came to Tibet, such as Atisha (982–1054), must just as surely have brought paintings with them.

(cont. p. 278)

Facing page: Cat. no. 37
Achala
(The Immovable One)

Tibet or Eastern India, 11th–12th c.
Mineral pigments on cloth
6¾ x 14 in. (17.1 x 35.6 cm)
Collection of Shelley and Donald Rubin (HA 594)

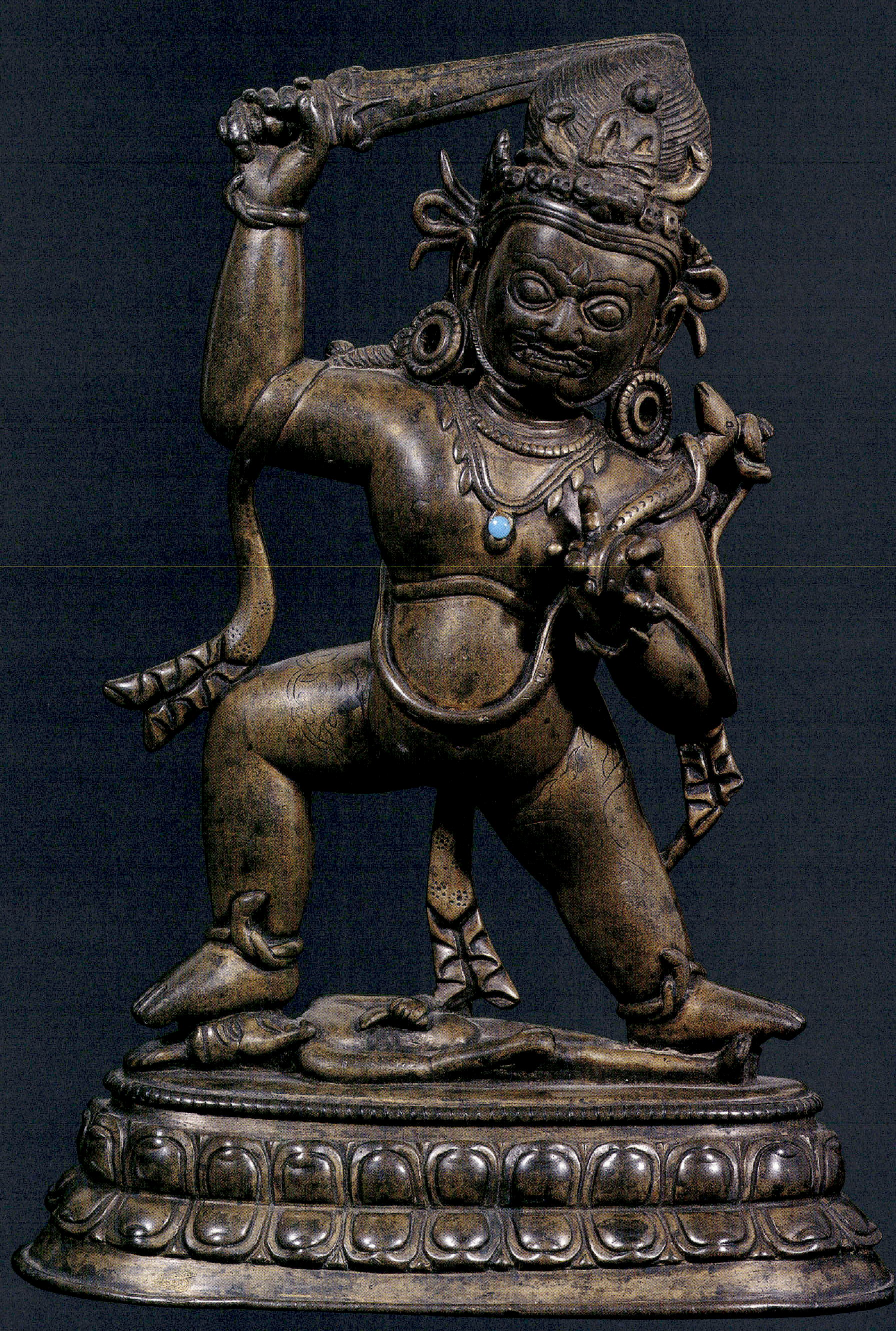

Cat. no. 38

Cat nos. 38, 39

Achala

(The Immovable One)

Both these metal sculptures show a determined Wrathful Buddha ensuring the submission of the Lord of Obstacles. A small image of Akshobhya Buddha sits in front of the high chignon above the crown of both works. These Achalas are in the so-called Atisha style, like catalog number 37. Despite the similarity of the theme, there are considerable differences between the two sculptures (cat nos. 38, 39), more than the difference in date would seem to imply. Catalog number 38 is the older of the two, though perhaps only by fifty or seventy-five years. If taken as representative of their respective times, they indicate that Tibetan sculptors had gained in skill, moving away from the Eastern Indian style (Gyalug), toward a more distinctly Tibetan mode. However, this is too simple a scenario, since some earlier images are much more accomplished than either one of these two. The differences are more easily explained with reference to patronage levels than to the evolution of Tibetan sculpture at a macro level.

The earlier piece is a bit more provincial, the rotund body and limbs held at a stiff angle, the back finished, but with metal struts undisguised (cat. no. 38). The deity seems tipped to one side because his left leg is shorter than the bent right leg, and the sword rests on his hair so it almost looks like he is slicing his own head. There is an attempt at embellishing the surface by adding chiseled decoration on the scarves and animal skin around his waist. Compared to the later one, the crown is much simpler, with five beadlike skulls, three to the left of center, and two to the right. The snakes on the wrists, ankles, hair, and around the torso all have the same simplified head. Achala's face follows a well-established protocol. He bites down on his lower lip with his upper teeth, the fangs protruding. He has clear mustaches, and the beard that edges his jaw turns up over his chin to the bottom of his lower lip. The eyebrows, which are quite wavy, closely resemble other thirteenth-century

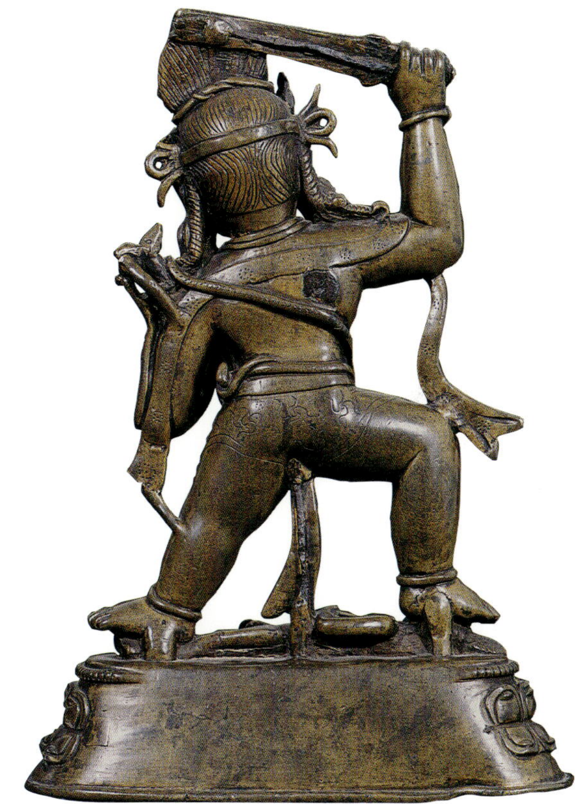

Cat no. 38, back

Facing page: Cat no. 38
Achala
(The Immovable One)

Tibet, 13th c.
Metalwork, inlaid turquoise
9 x 6¼ x 2½ in. (22.9 x 15.9 x 6.4 cm)
F1998.19.1 (HA 700047)

Page 191: Cat no. 39
Achala
(The Immovable One)

Tibet, ca. 13th–14th c.
Metalwork
13¼ x 9½ x 4¼ in.
(33.7 x 24.1 x 10.8 cm)
F1997.50.1 (HA 700044)

examples.[1] There is a charming sense of naive intensity to the work, enhanced by the flattened Vighnaraja (Lord of Obstacles) underfoot, grasping his radish and looking out at the viewer, a little wide-eyed and fearful.

The necklace worn by the thirteenth-century Achala (cat. no. 38), with simple, almond-shaped drops hanging from a double strand or chain, is closer to Eastern Indian models than the one worn by the later Achala (cat. no. 39), the artists of which displays a more refined touch. The figure balances more steadily over the prostrate Ganesha, and holds up the sword in a more natural gesture.[2] While the decoration of the crown and jewelry moves away from an Eastern Indian prototype, the artist's understanding that the Lord of Obstacles was directly related to the Hindu god Ganesha is much richer. That is, the artist seems to know who Ganesha is and what he looks like, and to model Vighnaraja on the images he is familiar with. Even as Vighnaraja is submitting to Achala, he lolls across on the lotus base like the sensualist he is portrayed as being in Indian imagery. His belly is swollen with sweets, the leafy stalks of his radish are splayed out on the lotus base, his crown is prominent, and one tusk is broken, just like Ganesha.[3]

The jewelry of this Achala takes a more elegant turn, with a greater variety of surfaces, treatments, and detailing. Note the snakes that slither out of the hollow core of the earrings. The swallow-tail scarf-ends are more elegantly asymmetrical than those of the earlier Achala, and flowers are added above the ears. The noose in his right hand has a clearly formed *vajra* finial, though the other end is broken off.[4] The base, too has been built up, and feels more proportionate to the scale of the main figure. The third eye, mentioned in most of the visualization descriptions (see cat. nos. 37 and 40), is much more fully understood and worked out in catalog number 39 than in 38 where it is merely scoredonto the forehead.

(cont. p. 281)

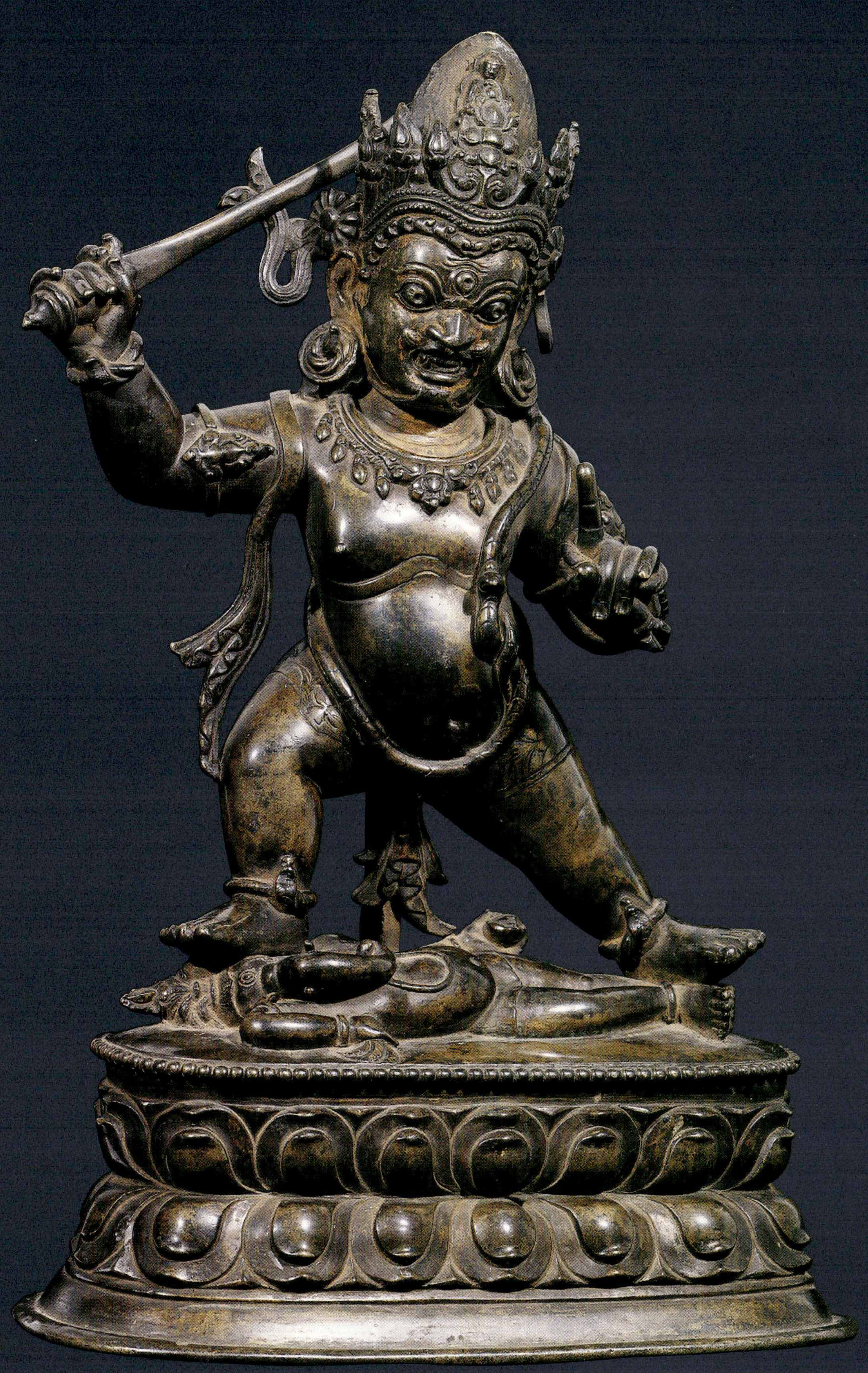

Cat. no. 39

Cat. no. 40

Achala

(The Immovable One)

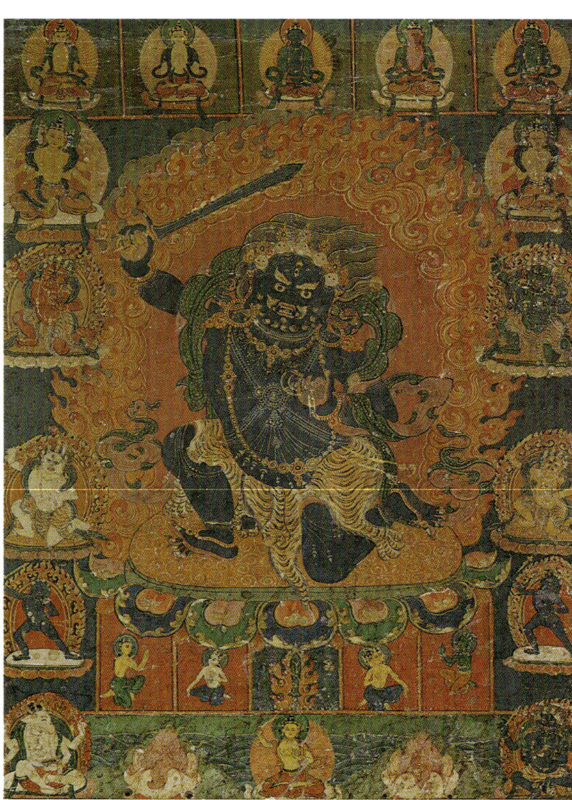

Cat. no. 40
Achala
(The Immovable One)

Nepal, dated 1871
Mineral pigments on cloth
17¼ x 14 in. (43.8 x 35.6 cm)
Collection of Shelley and Donald Rubin (HA 100045)

This painting testifies that Achala's importance as a Wrathful Buddha was not limited to a specific time. Remarkably, the painting demonstrates that the theme was current for Buddhists in *both* the thirteenth and the nineteenth centuries, for it bears a date on the back indicating that it was made in 1871, after a famous painting of 1275. Copying older works was a frequent practice among artists throughout the Himalayan region.[1] These pious copies were not meant to deceive—however much they now complicate the issue of dating—nor do they indicate a paucity of imagination on the part of the artists. Instead they demonstrate an admiration for earlier styles of art, and the characteristics of special images that became icons.

The posture is different from that of the "Atisha-style" Achala of catalog numbers 37–39. This Nepalese Achala assumes the pose that is most common in early images made in India, with one knee down, but this form was not unusual in Tibet and other regions of the Himalayas. There are many textual descriptions of this type of Achala, which help to define his role as a remover of obstacles and the special protector for the practices of Manjushri, a small image of whom is found at the center of the lowest register.[2] One of the ritual texts that fits this image describes him:

> Lord Achala. The body is blue in color, one face, two hands, the right brandishing to the sky a sword fiercely flaming with a mass of wisdom fire. And the left at the heart, in a wrathful gesture, holds a *vajra* lasso wound [around the index finger]. . . . With bared fangs, biting down on the lower lip, possessing three eyes, the right gazes upward completely eliminating [planetary demons]. The left gazes down, destroying *nagas*, spirits of disease and earth lords. The middle gazes forward completely eliminating all types of obstacles. Wearing a white snake as a necklace, gathering the power of *nagas*,

(cont. p. 282)

Cat. no. 41

Fudo Myo-o (Achala Vidyaraja)

With Two Attendants

Images and texts related to Achala spread with Esoteric Buddhism from India to China in the eighth century and then to Japan in the ninth. At around the same time, they were brought to Nepal and Tibet. Buddhism has died in India (apart from the exiled Tibetans and small numbers of recent converts), and Chinese Buddhists no longer revere Achala. Buddhists in Japan, Nepal, Tibet, and other Himalayan cultures, however, continue to make powerful images of Achala and use them in rituals and meditations. In Japan, Achala has become something of a cult figure within popular religion, even beyond the boundaries of the original Esoteric Buddhist context.

This magnificent painting captures the deity's "immovable" quality, of not bending to convenience or bowing to entrenched enemies of enlightenment. Achala sits locked in the lotus posture, his broad torso as erect and upright as his *vajra*-handled sword. His left hand holds a noose, just as in the Himalayan forms. These weapons of noose and sword are used to bind illusion and cut through errors. He bites down on his lower lip, two short fangs protruding. His red-rimmed eyes glare intently over the heads of his two diminutive acolytes who carry *vajras* of different kinds; one is pestle-like. Achala's long hair is gathered into a braid that hangs down the left side of his chest. His gold ornaments glow against the dark blue of his skin. Such drama married to fierceness is enhanced by the halo of flames behind him and compares well with the kinds of effects Himalayan artists sought and achieved in developing the theme of the demonic divine. In fact, among Buddhist artists, probably only the Japanese can rival the Himalayan for expressive effect.

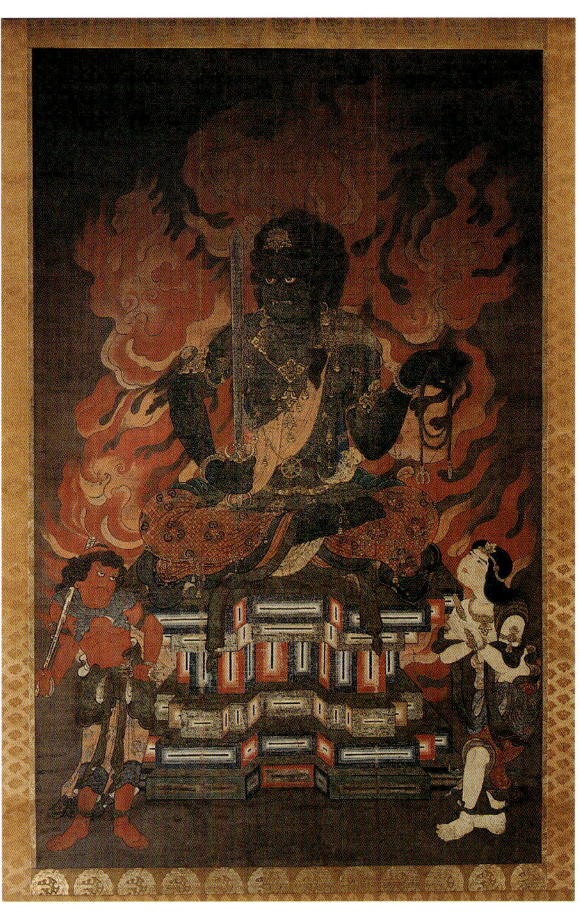

Cat. no. 41
Fudo Myo-o (Achala Vidyaraja) with Two Attendants

Japan, Kamakura period, early 14th c.
Hanging scroll; ink, color, and gold on silk
72 x 45 in. (182.9 x 114.3 cm)
Asia Society, New York

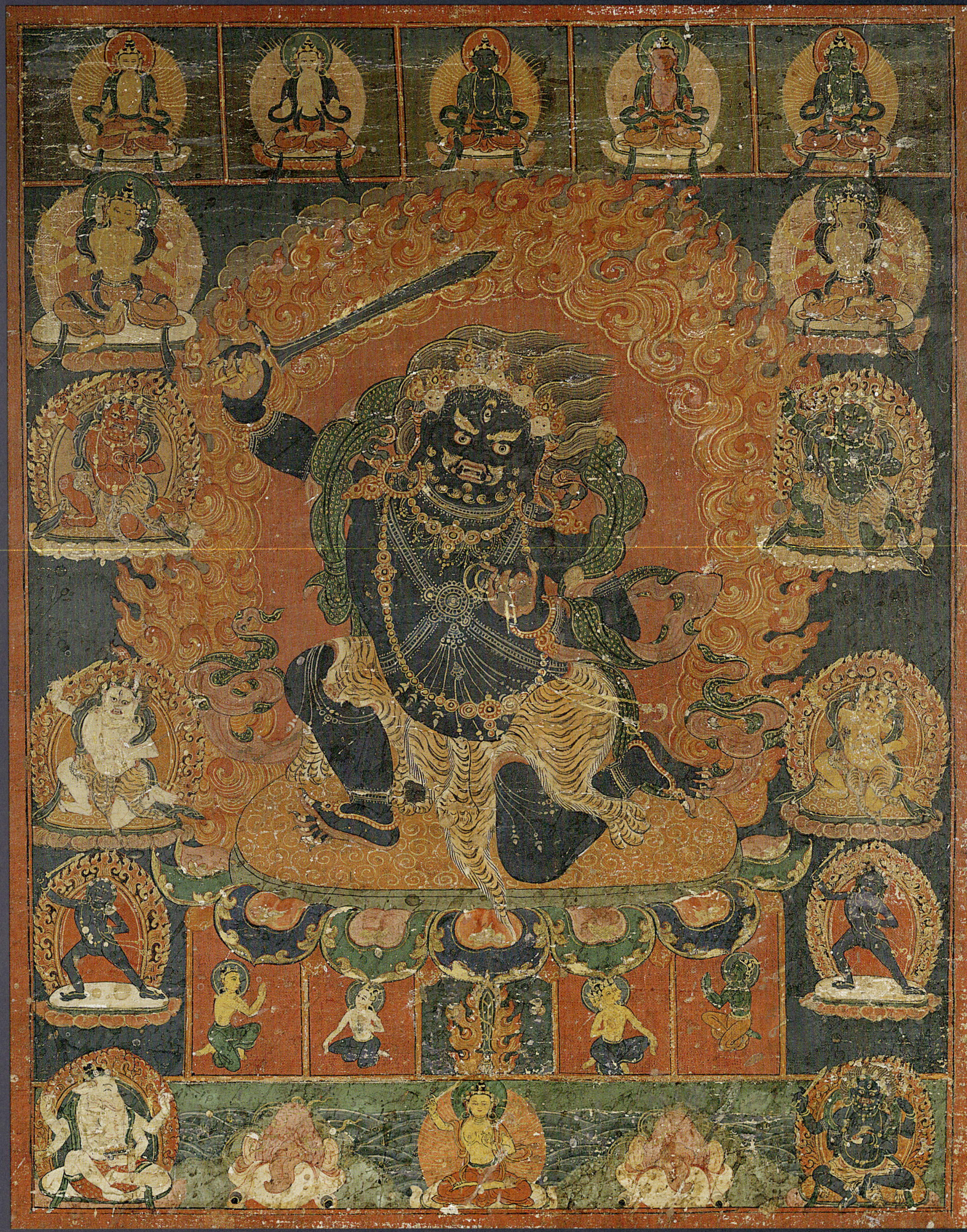

Cat. no. 40

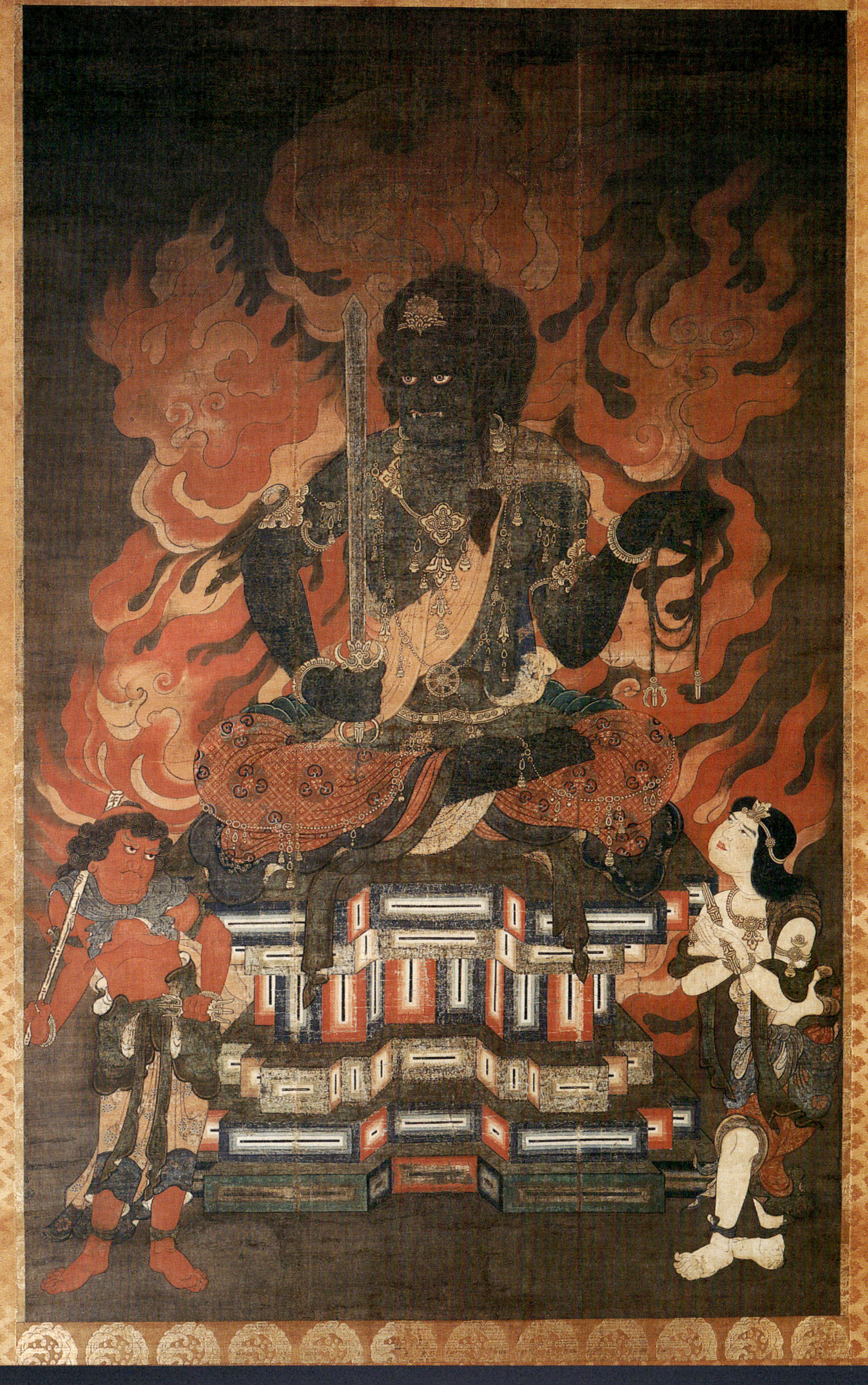

Cat. no. 41

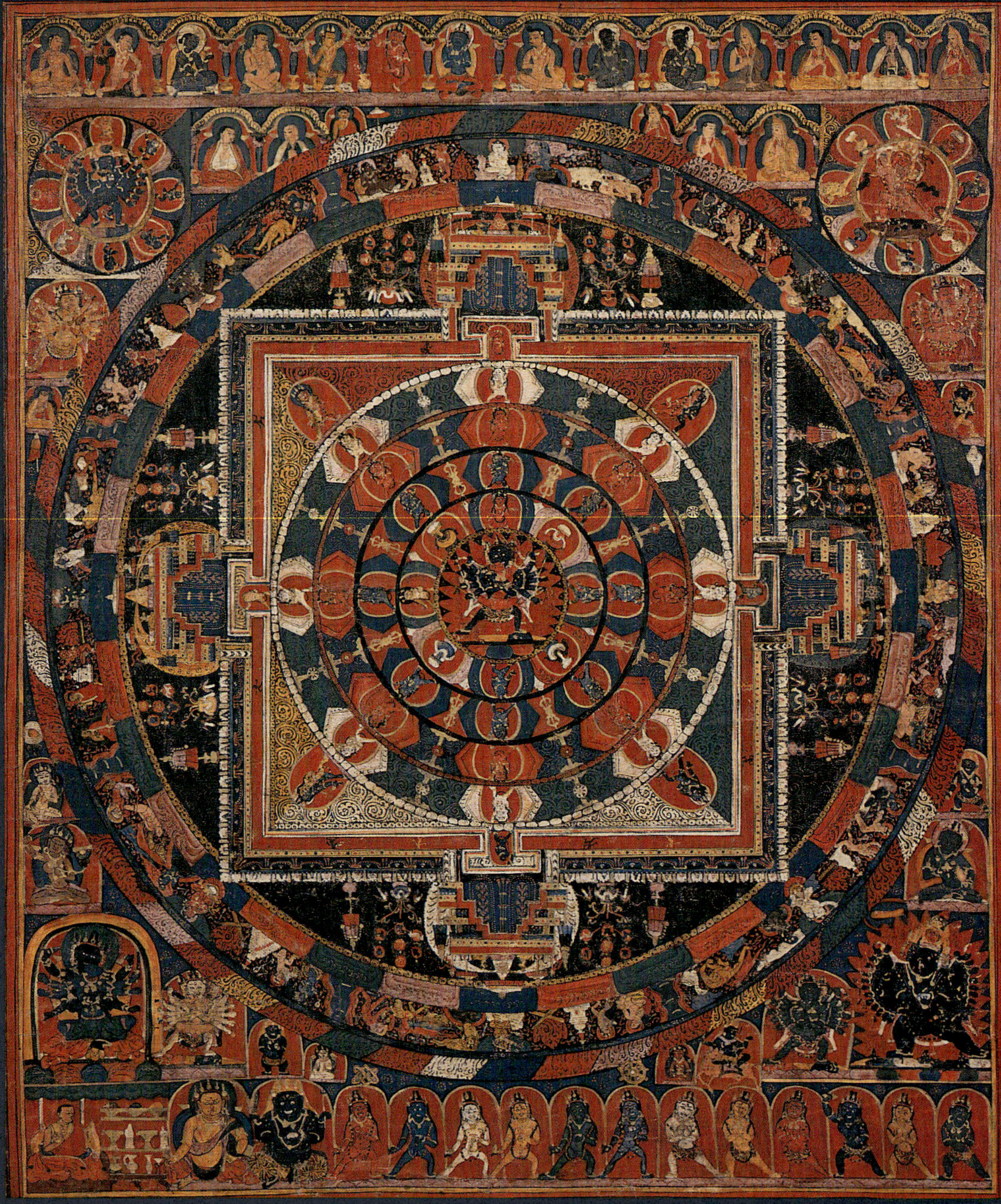

Cat. no. 42

Cat. no. 42

Chakrasamvara

With Twelve Hands and Vajrayogini Mandala

A Wrathful Buddha couple are the core of this mandala. They appear to radiate explosively a universe of retinue figures and auspicious objects such as vases, *vajras*, flowers, and wheels. The square palace with four gateways is barely contained within its concentric circles of lotus petals, charnel grounds, *vajras*, and flames. At its corners, it actually overlaps onto the lotus circles more than is usual. The feeling of overflowing energy is continued in squinches outside the mandala proper, which are crowded with figures. Although the top register is set off from the mandala space, the lower register is continuous with it. Only the probable patron or donor, in the lower left, has a discrete, curtained-off space. He sits in front of an altar table and two shelves that are loaded with lamps, pitchers, water containers, tripod stands, and other offering containers. Next to him is the wealth benefactor Jambhala, who appears about to pick up one of the cups on monk's table. Beside Jambhala to the right is four-handed Mahakala, the special protector of the Chakrasamvara teachings (see also cat. no. 26).

This is the sixty-two-deity Chakrasamvara mandala as transmitted by the Mahasiddha Luipa, though in the version associated with Ghantapada.[1] In one of two variant postures, the red Vajrayogini has both legs encircling the hips of the blue, twelve-armed Chakrasamvara. In form and style the painting resembles Sakya paintings of the sixteenth century, but in a more cursory, less polished manner. Alternatively, the intermittent clarity and detail may be due to extensive but uneven restoration. It is unusual that the Vajrabhairava at the lower right, in his *ekavira*, or solitary, consortless form, is done in the mode favored by Gelugpa, with three stacks of seven, one, and one heads, instead of the three-three-three stack seen in most non-Gelugpa paintings (see cat. nos. 46, 47, 50).

Instead of beginning the teaching lineage at the far left of the top register, as in other mandalas in the exhibition (cat. nos. 43, 46),

(cont. p. 283)

Facing page: Cat. no. 42
Chakrasamvara
with Twelve Hands and Vajrayogini
Mandala

Tibet, late 15th–16th c.
Mineral pigments on cloth
26½x 22 in. (67.3 x 55.9 cm)
Collection of Shelley and Donald Rubin (HA 97)

Cat. no. 43

Chakrasamvara

With Six Hands and Vajrayogini Mandala

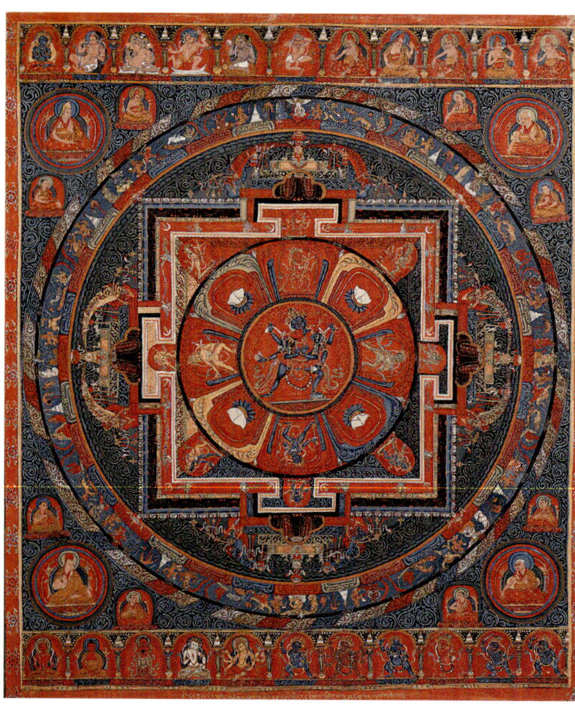

Cat. no. 43
Chakrasamvara with Six Hands and Vajrayogini Mandala

Tibet, ca. 1500
Mineral pigments on cloth
21½ x 17½ in. (54.6 x 44.5 cm)
C2001.9.1 (HA 65020)

One of the pleasures of this painting is the impressive characterizations of the teachers—yogis and monks—in the top register, and the expressive facial portraits of the monks in the corners. Then there is the exacting precision of the geometrical divisions of nestled circles and squares to admire (see detail). The inscription carefully added to the lower border of the painting gives a sense of the circumstances under which this, and many other paintings, were made.[1] It was commissioned by one monk for the longevity of his teacher, meaning that the merit derived from commissioning an artist to make such a detailed painting with sumptuous materials, was dedicated to the long life of the teacher. The painting probably also played a role in a long-life ritual performed for the recipient. Since the individual portraits are not inscribed, it is not known whether one of the twelve monks in the squinches of the mandala is the teacher, Konchog Pelwa (1445–1514), or his student, Lhachog Sengge (1468–1535), who commissioned this painting.[2] Lhachog Sengge "was a major figure at Ngor [monastery] in the early sixteenth century who commissioned many paintings during his abbatial tenure (1524–1535)."[3] The long-life purpose explains, perhaps, why Amitayus, the Buddha of Long Life (red in color and holding a vase with the nectar of longevity) appears at the far left, the first deity in the bottom register. Beside him are two forms of Amitabha Buddha. The inscription also provides a rough date, since long-life rituals would most likely be performed late in the life of the teacher. Thus a date around 1500 seems reasonable.[4]

The central deities are Chakrasamvara embracing Vajrayogini. Chakrasamvara is one of the most important Wrathful Buddhas, and this prominence can be traced back through eleventh-century Eastern Indian monumental stone images.[5] This particular form, however, is extremely unusual, in that it has six arms instead of twelve. In other respects, this

(cont. p. 283)

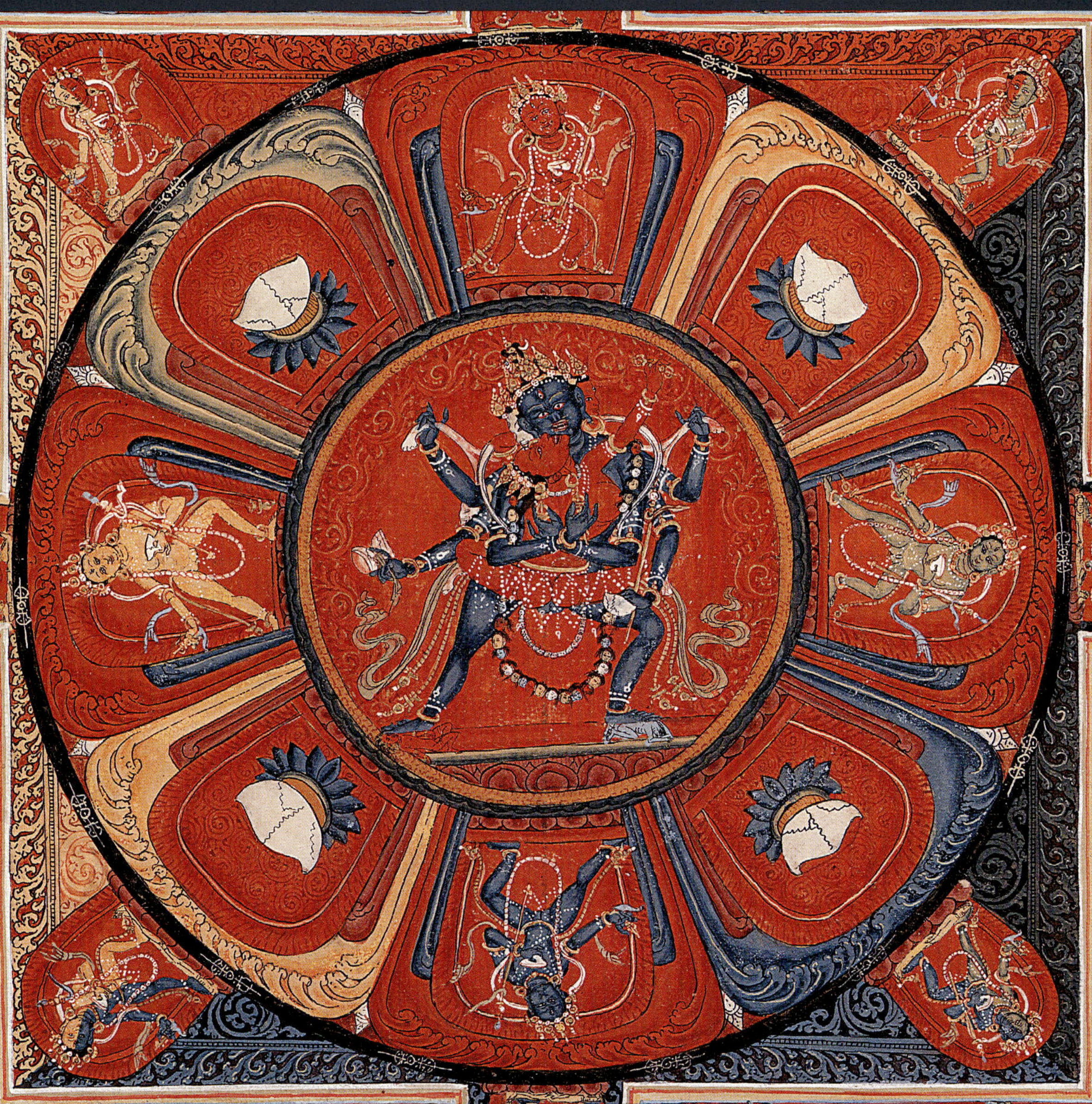

Cat. no. 43, detail

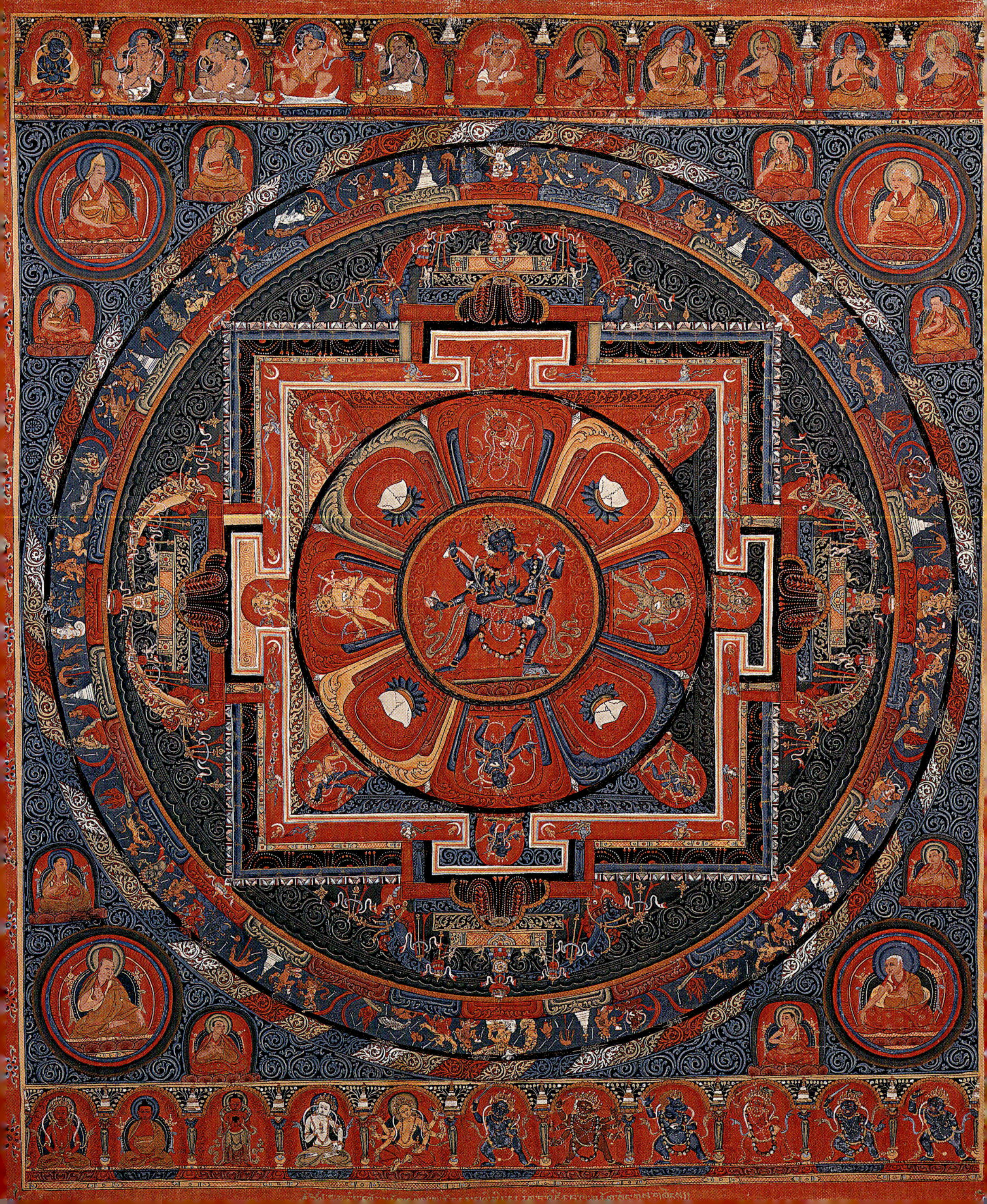

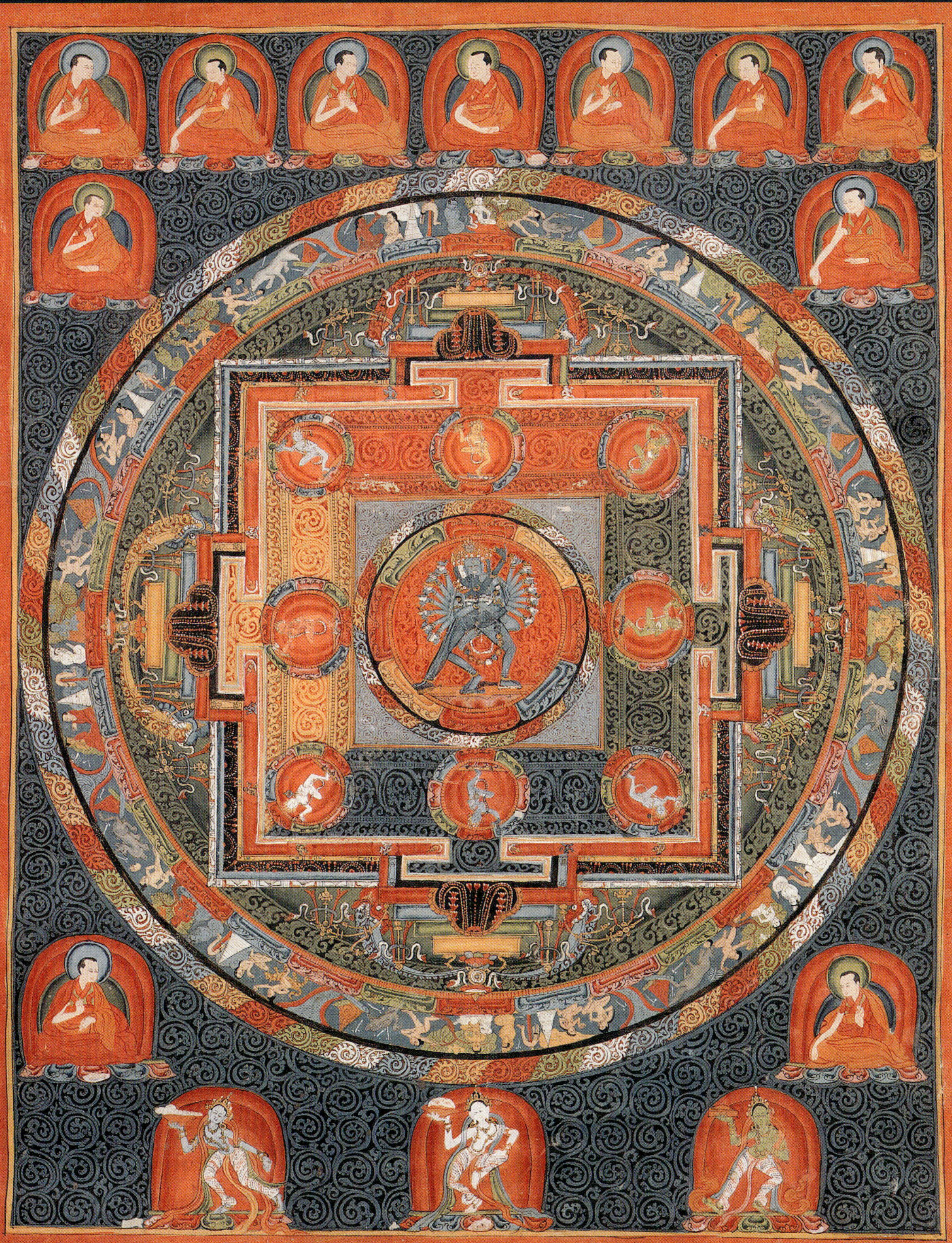

Cat. no. 44

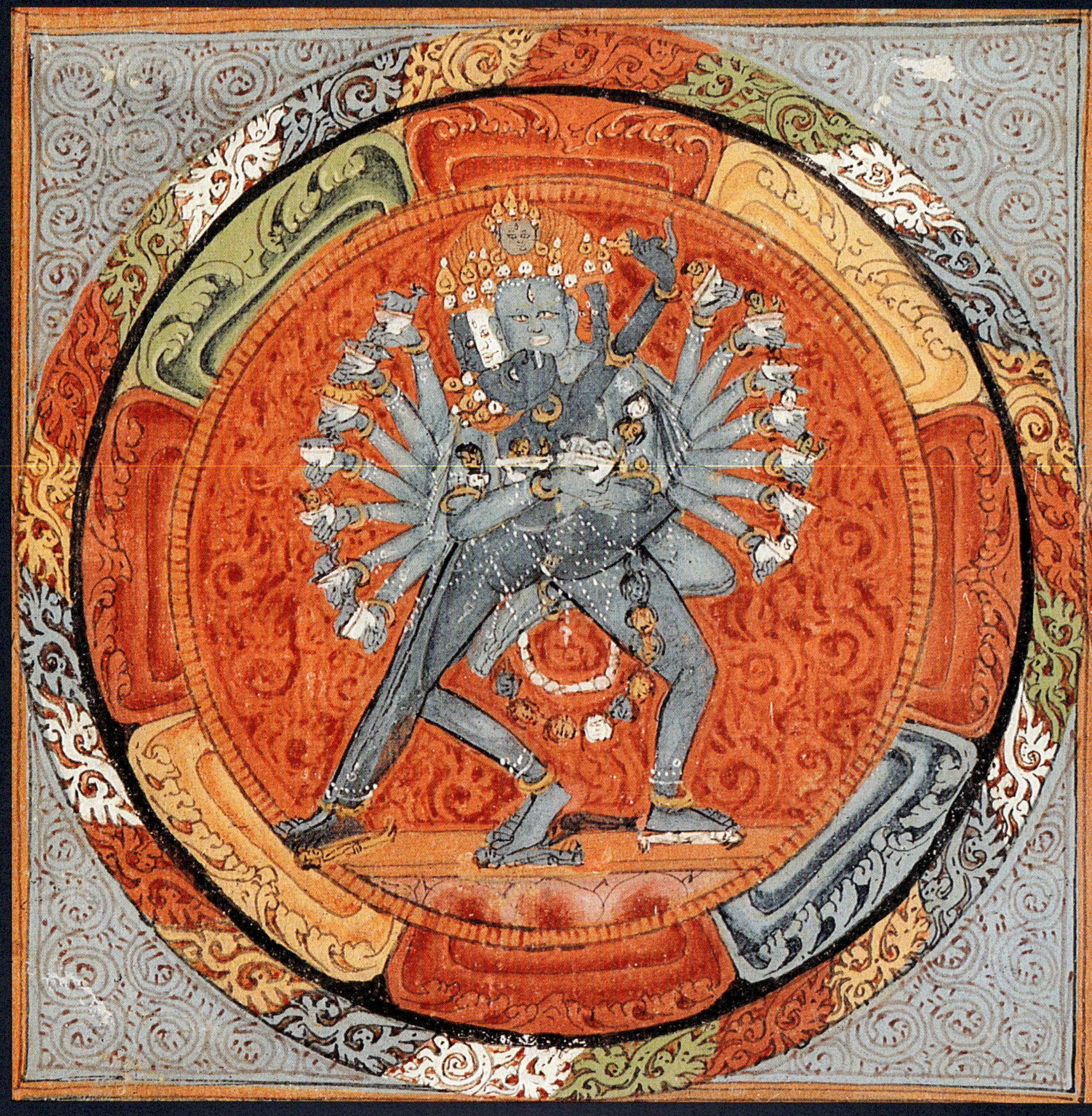

Cat. no. 44, detail

Cat. no. 44

Hevajra

With Nairatmya Mandala

At the center of a painting alive with dynamic whorls, a Wrathful Buddha couple in ecstatic embrace presides over a celestial mansion. The lotus on which they stand is eight petalled, and it can be simultaneously viewed from above and from the side (see detail). Outlined in black like a pupil's iris, it resembles an oculus or round mirror, reflecting the enlightened self as the image of pure mind. Enclosed by smaller lotus-circles that radiate from the central square, eight goddesses attend the main figures in the eight directions.[1] The details of the mansion, the tiny figures in and above the walls, the gateways with their elaborate decoration are all done with a burnished perfection, belying the modest size of the painting.

This mandala corresponds to the nine-deity *hrdaya* (essence) Hevajra mandala as transmitted by Kanha.[2] The important physical distinctions for the Kanha Hevajra mandala are the postures of Hevajra and Nairatmya (compare cat. no. 45), and the fact that each of the eight goddesses stands on her own lotus flower, whereas in the normal Hevajra mandala as transmitted from Virupa, they each stand on a petal with Hevajra in the middle of the lotus flower.

Based on its close resemblance to published examples with inscriptions, this painting was produced by a monastic patron belonging to the Ngor branch of the Sakya lineage.[3] The visualization and meditation practice of Hevajra and Nairatmya is of primary importance among Sakyapa, and the Ngorpa have become renowned for the sets of mandalas produced for the main monastery and its many satellite temples. This painting belonged to the *kabab nam shi*, a subset within the *kabab nam dun*, the seven principal oral transmissions of Hevajra in the Sakya school.[4] This explains why the top register portrays only Tibetan monastics, since when hung together, the lineage would presumably carry across or be related in some way to the top of the paintings adjacent to this one in the series. It also explains

(cont. p. 284)

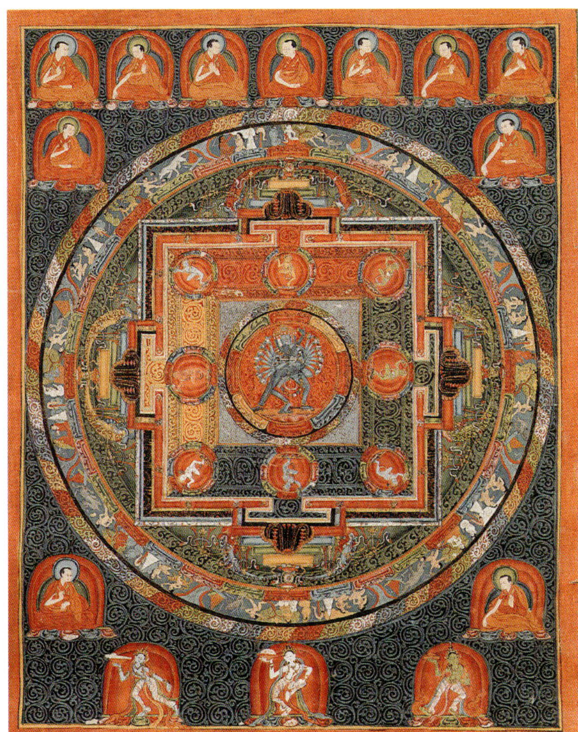

Cat. no. 44
Hevajra
with Nairatmya
Mandala

Tibet, ca. late 16th c.
Mineral pigments on cloth
14½ x 11½ in. (36.8 x 29.2 cm)
Collection of Shelley and Donald Rubin (HA 964)

Cat. no. 45

Hevajra

With Nairatmya

Facing page: Cat. no. 45
Hevajra with Nairatmya

Nepal, 14th c.
Copper
7¾ x 6½ x 3 in. (19.7 x 16.5 x 7.6 cm)
Collection of Shelley and Donald Rubin (HA 700066)

Like many of the Indian Hindu wrathful deities, this Nepalese Wrathful Buddha couple adopts relatively neutral, almost tender, expressions that belie their violent action. Even as they stand embracing each other, they trample underfoot the Hindu gods (Indra, Brahma, Shiva, and Vishnu). In Himalayan Buddhism, Hevajra and Nairatmya are classed as "semi-wrathful," not as fearsome in appearance as Durtro Lhamo (cat. no. 1), for example. Yet even among Hevajra images, this one is less wrathful than is typical. None of Hevajra's eight heads grimaces or glares.[1]

An unusual image, it is also a fascinating one. The tenderness of the expressions, softened by wear, is itself quite riveting. What is also unusual is the way the arms appear in a nearly horizontal splay, instead of the usual vertical arrangement common to both Indian and Tibetan versions. This fanlike arrangement is actually more faithful to the *Hevajra Tantra* description, suggesting this was made by or for someone very involved in actual practice. In time, this mode was abandoned even by sculptors who were apparently influenced by the painted versions in which the horizontal arrangement would have rendered some of the arms invisible. Each of Hevajra's hands is canonic in what it holds. As far as can be determined from the tiny, abbreviated details, seven of the left hands properly hold skull bowls with worldly gods looking outward, but the animals in the right hands' skull bowls, who represent eight different diseases and afflictions which Hevajra takes in, are also looking outward, while they should be looking toward Hevajra. The gods in the left skull bowls represent eight special powers which are emanated or given out by Hevajra, so it is proper that they look outward. The eighth pair embraces the consort. Nairatmya, the Vajra Egoless One, responds by putting both arms around his neck, and clutches a curved knife in her right hand, visible only on the back.

Hevarja, again canonically, has four legs.

(cont. p. 285)

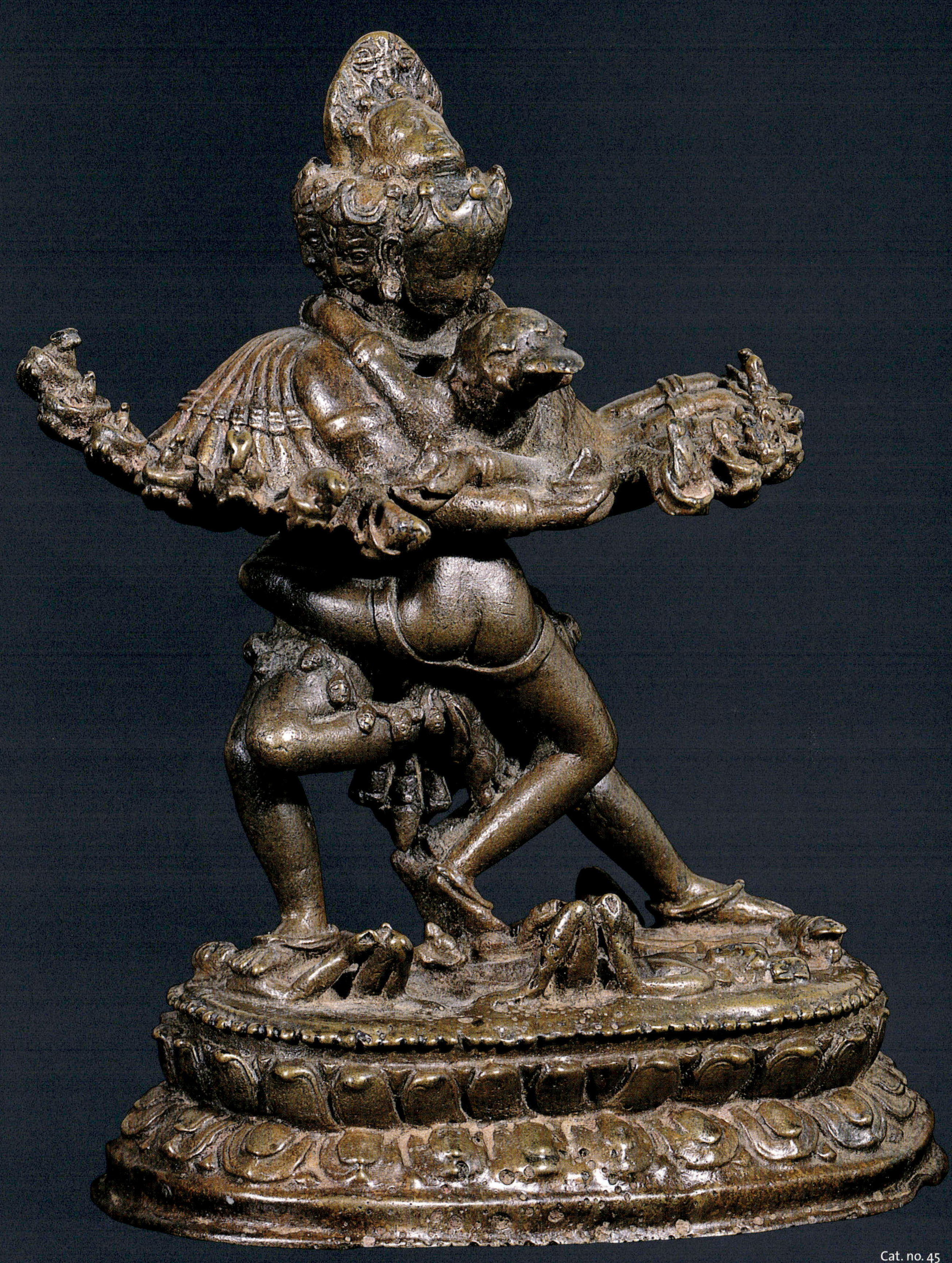

Cat. no. 45

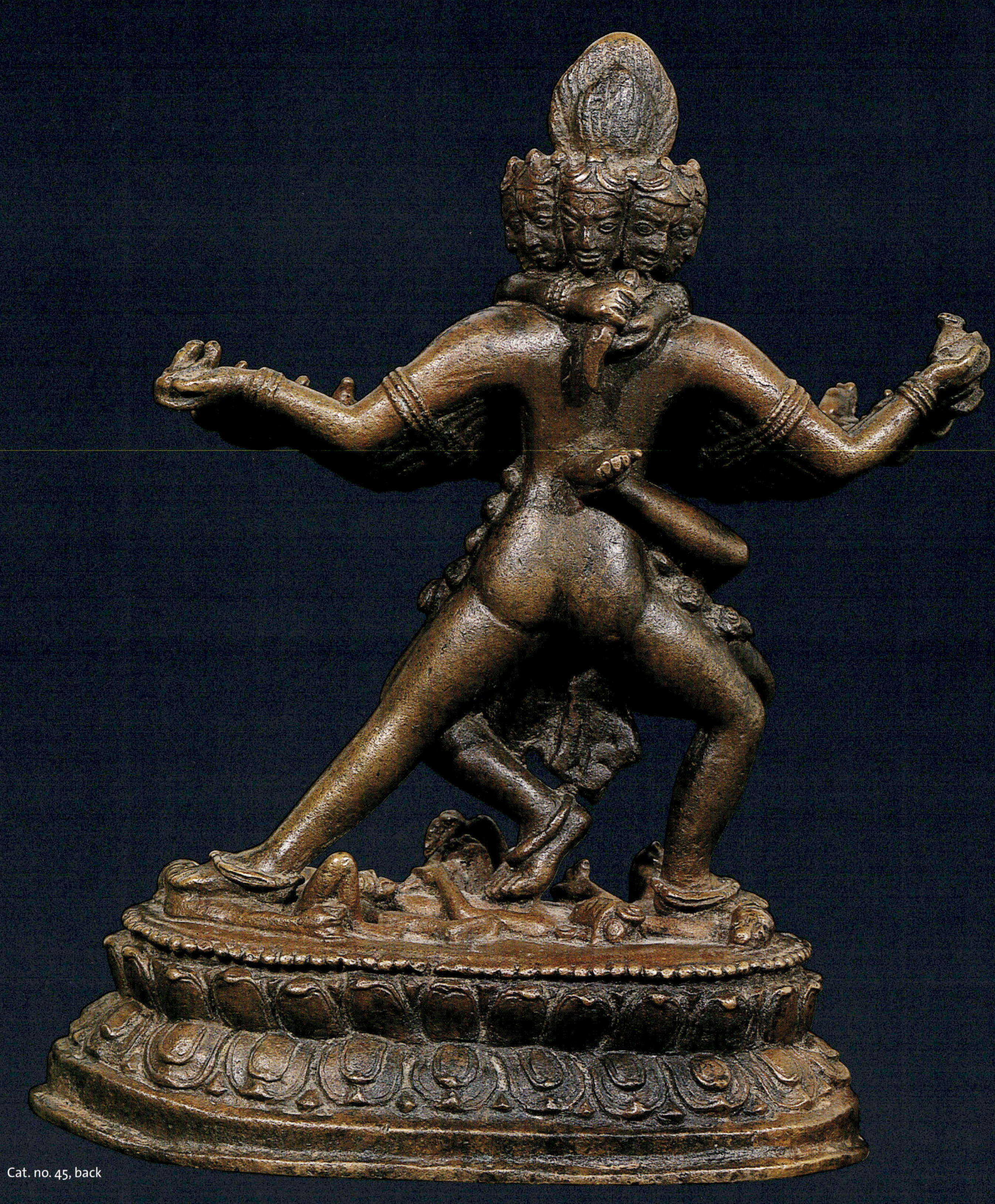

Cat. no. 45, back

Cat. no. 46

Vajrabhairava Mandala

This large, complex mandala is a thirteen-deity Vajrabhairava mandala transmitted through Rwa Lotsava Dorje Drag (1016–98). Rwa Lotsava is depicted in the top register, the eighth figure from the left (cat. key 46.29), this seminal teacher transmitted most of the active Vajrabhairava mandala traditions.[1] The ithyphallic Vajrabhairava is depicted in the early, pre-Gelugpa manner, with three tiers of three heads (compare cat. no. 50). He seems barely contained within the central chamber of the mandala, bursting its boundaries. Above his head, as if hanging on the interior walls of the dark chamber, is a valance of skeletal torsos, suspended upside down.[2]

Surrounding Vajrabhairava are eight personifications of primary attributes (cat. key 46.2–9), while twenty-four more attributes are placed at the top, inside each wall, six per wall, each with a red flaming nimbus. The total number of attributes is thirty-two, two short of the total number of his hands. In the T-shaped gates are four gate-guardians (cat. key 46.10–13).

As the mandala text indicates, Vajrabhairava is oriented so that he faces south, the direction of the bottom of the painting. Most mandalas have east at the bottom. The artist has not only rotated the corresponding colors—the red color of the west, for instance, is usually at the top but here it is on the left—and also the *dikpala* (directional protectors of the eight charnel grounds) and the corresponding Mahasiddhas.[3]

There is one anomaly, however, and it is a significant deviation from the thirteen-deity Vajrabhairava mandala as preserved and maintained in the Sakya and other traditions. In the painting, the central deity Vajrabhairava is depicted in the *ekavira* form, that is, without a consort, while normally he is shown embracing his consort. The Ngor mandalas are a collection of the common Vajrabhairava mandala in Gelug and Kagyu practice, but not this one is not included among them. The painting

(cont. p. 285)
(cat. key p. 286)

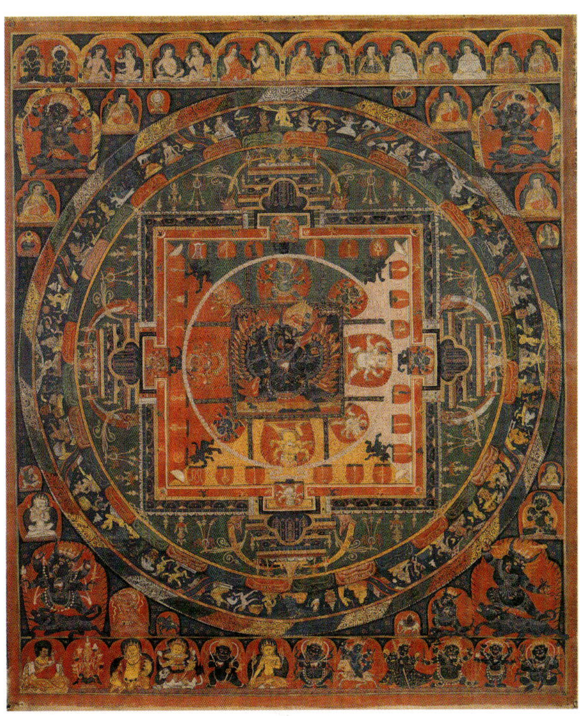

Cat. no. 46
Vajrabhairava Mandala
Tibet, late 15th–16th c.
Mineral pigments on cloth
29½ x 24½ in. (74.9 x 62.2 cm)
Collection of Navin Kumar, New York (HA 900095)

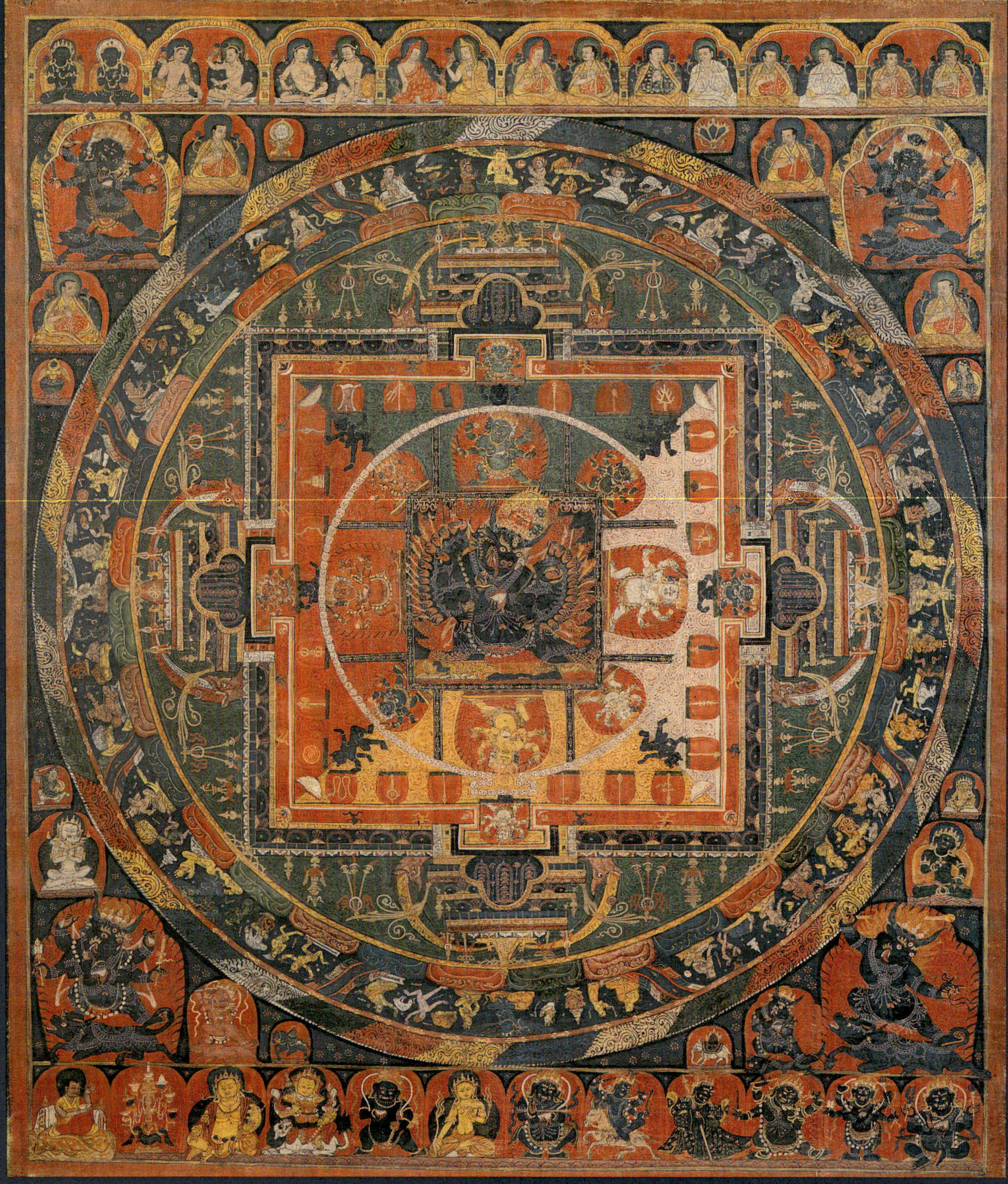

Cat. no. 46

Cat. no. 47

Vajrabhairava

Fragment

This gilt copper head is so powerful that it spurs one to imagine what the rest of the sculpture looked like. Even in the absence of the body below the neck, and another six heads above, the existing heads push in all directions into the space around it. No viewpoint is definitive, and it inspires movement around the object to see it from various angles, even the back, which was as finely cast as the front. So many details reward careful looking. The earring piercing the soft, hairy flesh of the right ear on the main buffalo head is a brilliant naturalistic gesture. The stubbly texture of the muzzle is another. The noses of the side heads appear to protrude more sharply due to the bulge at the top of the bridge of the nose, consistent with the expression of furious outrage. On the central head, the sculptor finesses the ends of the crown of five grinning skulls by encircling the base of the horns with chains from which hang stone-studded beaded swags. Some of the finest touches were mandated by the iconography of Vajrabhairava, such as the flames surrounding the tips of the horns, and the curling tongue, visible most clearly behind the bared teeth of the buffalo.

Originally there were two more rows of three heads, all but the top central one wrathful, as in the central figure of catalog number 46. The hole on the crown of the head where these were affixed is clearly visible. They would have fit between the two horns, and the flat splay of hair would have been less prominent.[1] There were two main conventions for depicting the nine heads of Vajrabhairava. The most common mode for the last few hundred years, certainly in Gelugpa paintings and sculptures and in Nepal, is to show a main register of seven heads, including the central buffalo head, with one head on the second and third registers.[2] This mode was used for catalog number 50. The convention that appears to have been employed earlier was the one used here, with three registers of three heads (see also cat. no. 46). Unfortunately, Indian

(cont. p. 287)

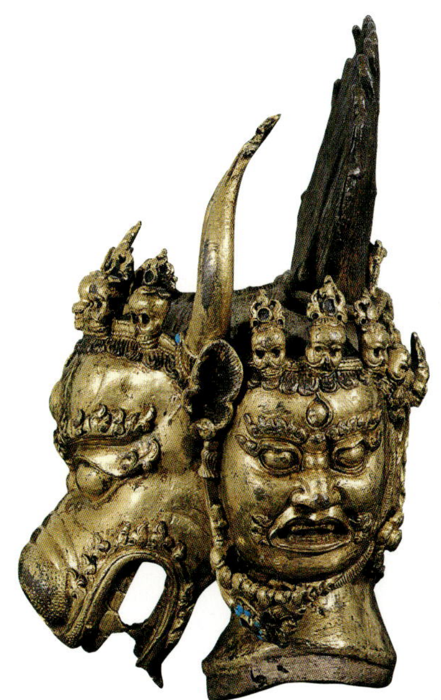

Cat. no. 47, side view

Page 210: Cat. no. 47
Vajrabhairava
Fragment

Tibet, 15th–16th c.
Metalwork with inlaid stones
8¼ x 6¼ x 4¾ in. (21x 15.9 x 12.1 cm)
C2002.40.1 (HA 65160)

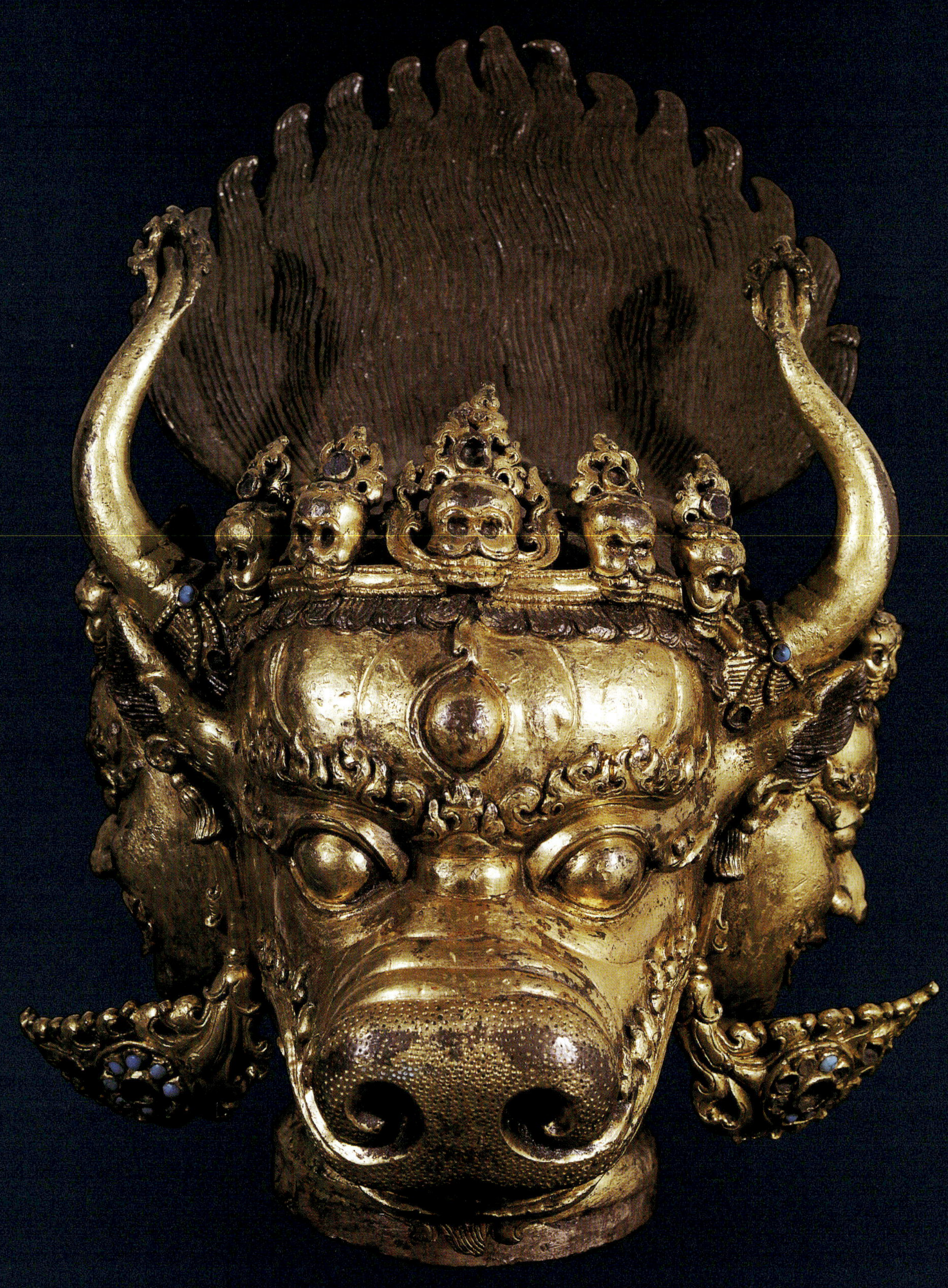

Cat. no. 47

Cat. no. 48

Tomb Guardian

The two Tang dynasty (618–906) tomb figures (Cat. nos. 9 and 48) exemplify the enduring practice in Chinese culture to combine features from different creatures into a fantastic hybrid. Like the Himalayan wrathful protectors, such images were used as apotropaic guardians. In the Tang dynasty, they were created in pairs—one human-faced, like the late seventh-century figure, and the other animal-faced—and assembled inside tombs to scare away spirits. Alongside representations of military and civil officials, animals and attendants, a pair of wrathful guardians was one unit within an extensive set of tomb figures employed in upper-class tombs to accompany the tomb-occupant into the afterlife.

The later guardian is dramatically glazed in what is called *sancai* (three color glaze): green, orange, and white. Capping the grotesque face, with its oversized eyes, open maw with fangs, and flattened nose, are a pair of exaggerated horns and a crest. The wings terminate in sharp feathers, and the mane juts out into a halo of spikes. These terrifying composite defenders are known as *zhenmushou*, or "tomb guardian creature" and, though they have deep roots in China's antiquity, "during the Sui and Tang periods, *zhenmushou* become increasingly dramatic and fearsome."[1]

(note p. 288)

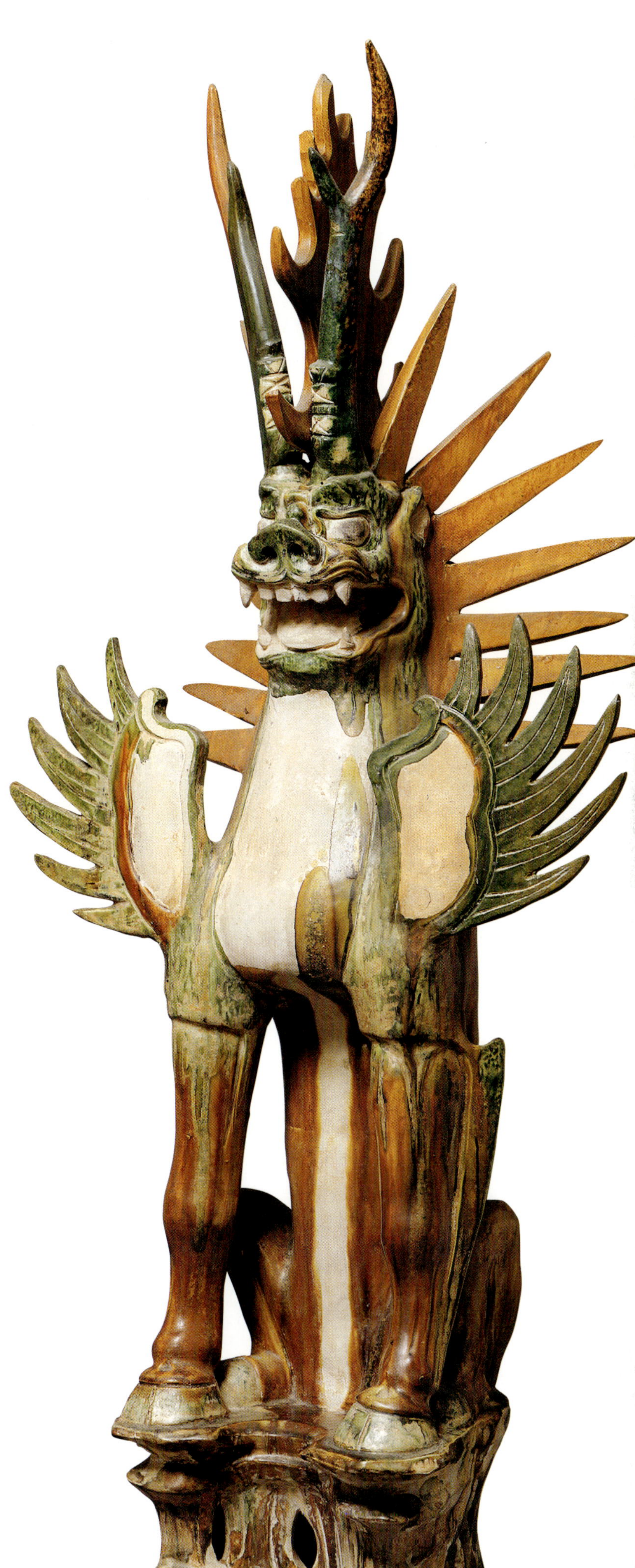

Right: Cat. no. 48
Tomb Guardian

China, early 8th c.
White pottery with *sancai* glaze and pigment traces
H. 37½ in. (95.3 cm)
Schloss Collection, New York

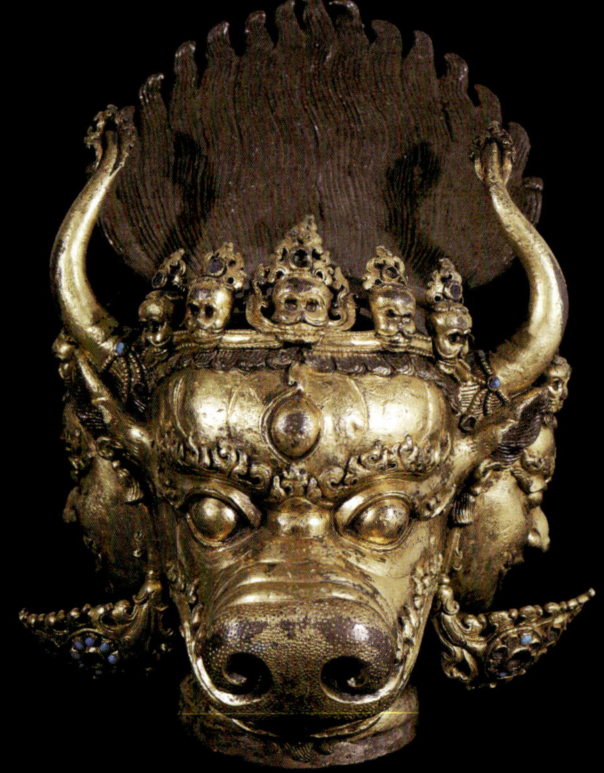

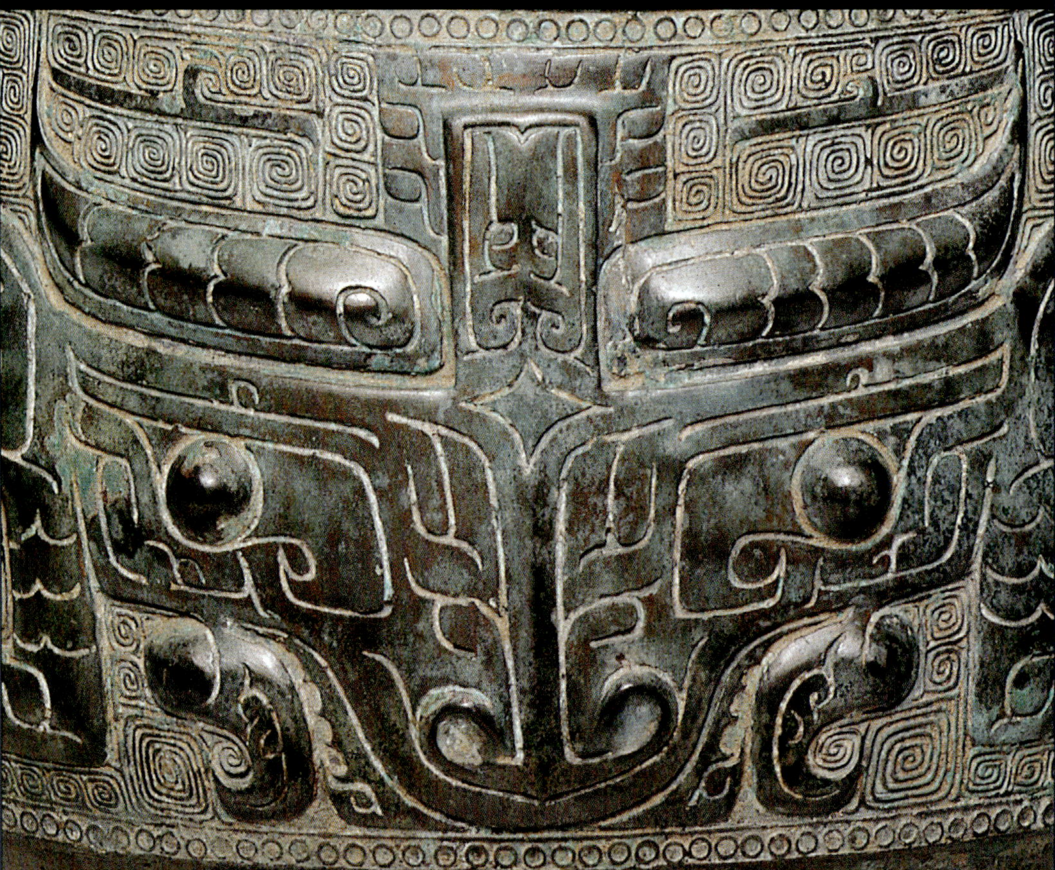

Top: Cat. no. 47

Bottom: Cat. no. 49, detail

Cat. no. 49

Wine Vessel: *You*

Although the exact significance of the mask-like forms (*taotie*) decorating Shang and Zhou dynasty bronze ritual vessels is not known, they are certainly expressively wrathful. The fangs, horns, bulging eyes, and claws suggests an implied threat, yet their placement on the surface of vessels used in ancestor ritual implies a protective or apotropaic function. The spiky outline of this *you* vessel with its hooked flanges is also formidable.

Three of the four bands of decoration (counting the foot and removable lid) are centered on a *taotie* that emerges off the dense spiral background as a hybrid creature. The horns, nose, bent legs, and hooves appear bovine, but the long fangs are closer to those of tigers, while the central crest seems avian. Himalayan artists also combined elements from different animals to create a being that is neither of this world, nor completely alien to it. The result is a personification of the unseen, powerful forces that control our lives and, in the Chinese funerary ideology, the afterlife of the ancestors to whom rituals using such vessels were devoted. Another parallel is that both Himalayan and bronze-age Chinese artists worked simultaneously in fantastic and naturalistic modes of representation. On the *you* vessel, the heads on the ends of the bail-handle are recognizable as buffalo, and one likewise finds animals and people naturalistically rendered in many Himalayan paintings and sculptures.

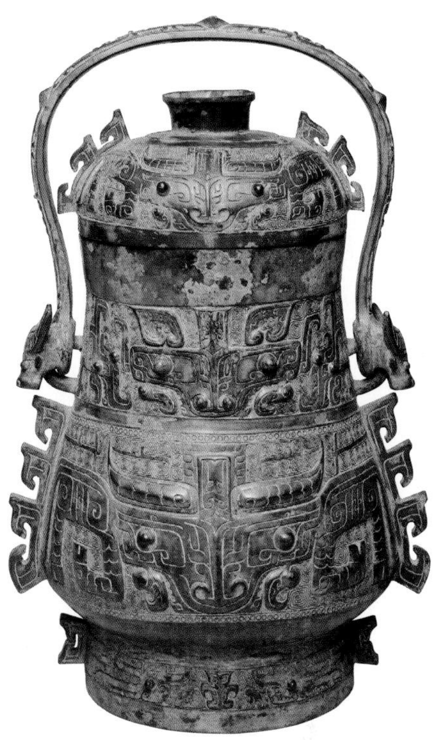

Cat. no. 49
Wine Vessel: *You*

North China: Western Zhou period, ca. late 11th c. BCE
Bronze
H. 14⅞ (37.8 cm), including handle; W. 8¾ (22.23 cm), across flanges
Asia Society, New York

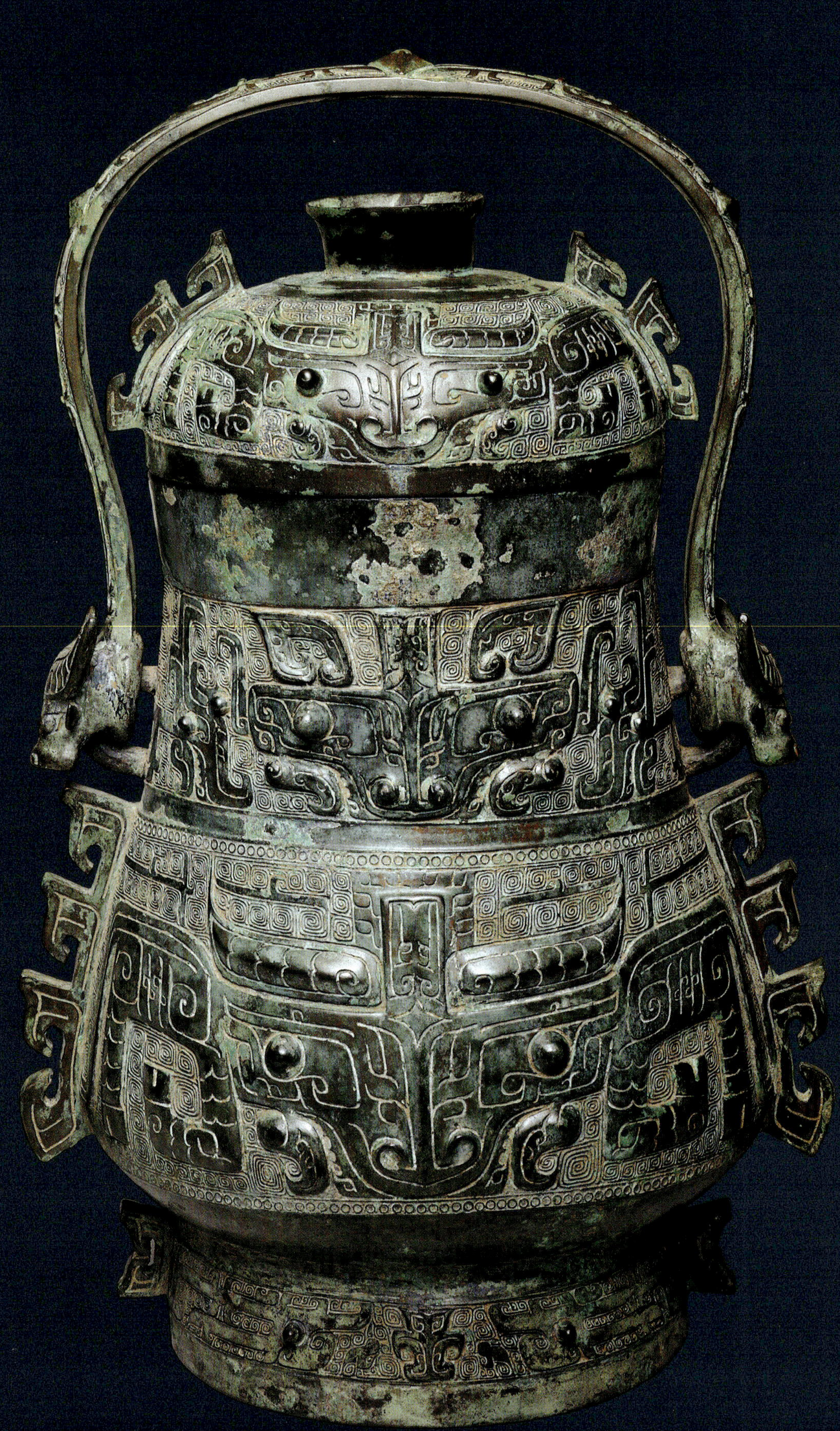

Cat. no. 49

Cat. no. 50

Vajrabhairava

With Vajravetali

Against a sea of reddish flames, the dark buffalo-headed Vajrabhairava embraces his fearsome consort, the "Vajra-zombie." His thirty-four arms and sixteen legs are lightly blushed with a velvety midnight blue. Underneath her lacy girdle and other bone ornaments, her slate blue skin color is the marbled tone of decomposing flesh, in keeping with the overall grotesque flavor. There are dozens of references to physical death, and three charnel grounds scattered through the composition. The skull bowl at the bottom center containing the "five meats" shows the corpses in a sharply observed style, the heads and necks lolling, the legs in lifeless suspension. Vajrabhairava himself holds aloft weapons for cutting, clubbing, and piercing, along with severed limbs, a body impaled by a stick, a flayed elephant skin, entrails, and the like. Even the Hindu gods are trampled under the feet of the couple. The point of Vajrabhairava's gleeful ire is the destruction of death itself, or, as a contemporary Gelugpa scholar-practitioner interprets it,

> the Exterminator of death . . . is created in imaginative samadhi in order to navigate the deep, deep spaces of dying and death in order to accelerate the development of one's compassionate side. . . . Vajrabhairava embodies full enlightenment adamant in confrontation with the most profound demons of the individual and collective unconscious.[1]

As an emanation related to Manjushri, the bodhisattva associated with discriminating knowledge and penetrating wisdom (whose peaceful yellow face is at the top of the nine heads), Vajrabhairava is the "preferred" Wrathful Buddha for Drepung monastery and, it is fair to say, for the Gelugpa in

(cont. p. 288)

(cat. key p. 289)

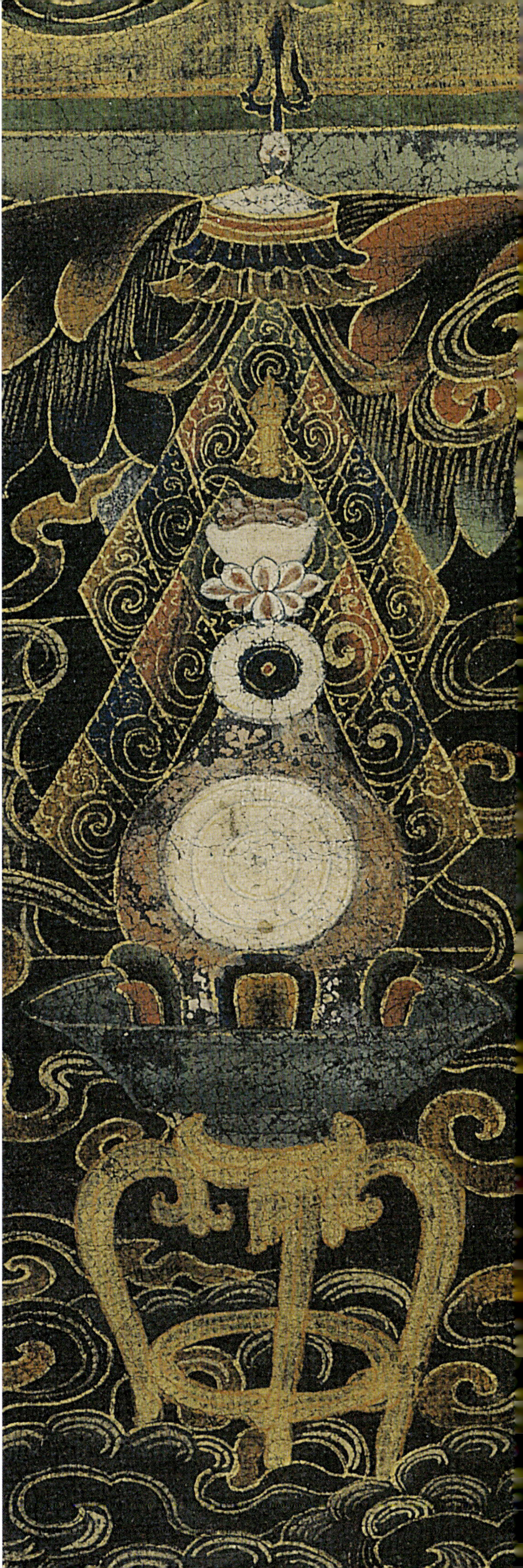

Right: Cat. no. 50, detail
(Page 216: Cat. no. 50, over all view)
Vajrabhairava with Vajravetali

Tibet, 18th c.
Mineral pigments on cloth
26 x 17 in. (66 x 43.2 cm)
C2002.21.2 (HA 65113)

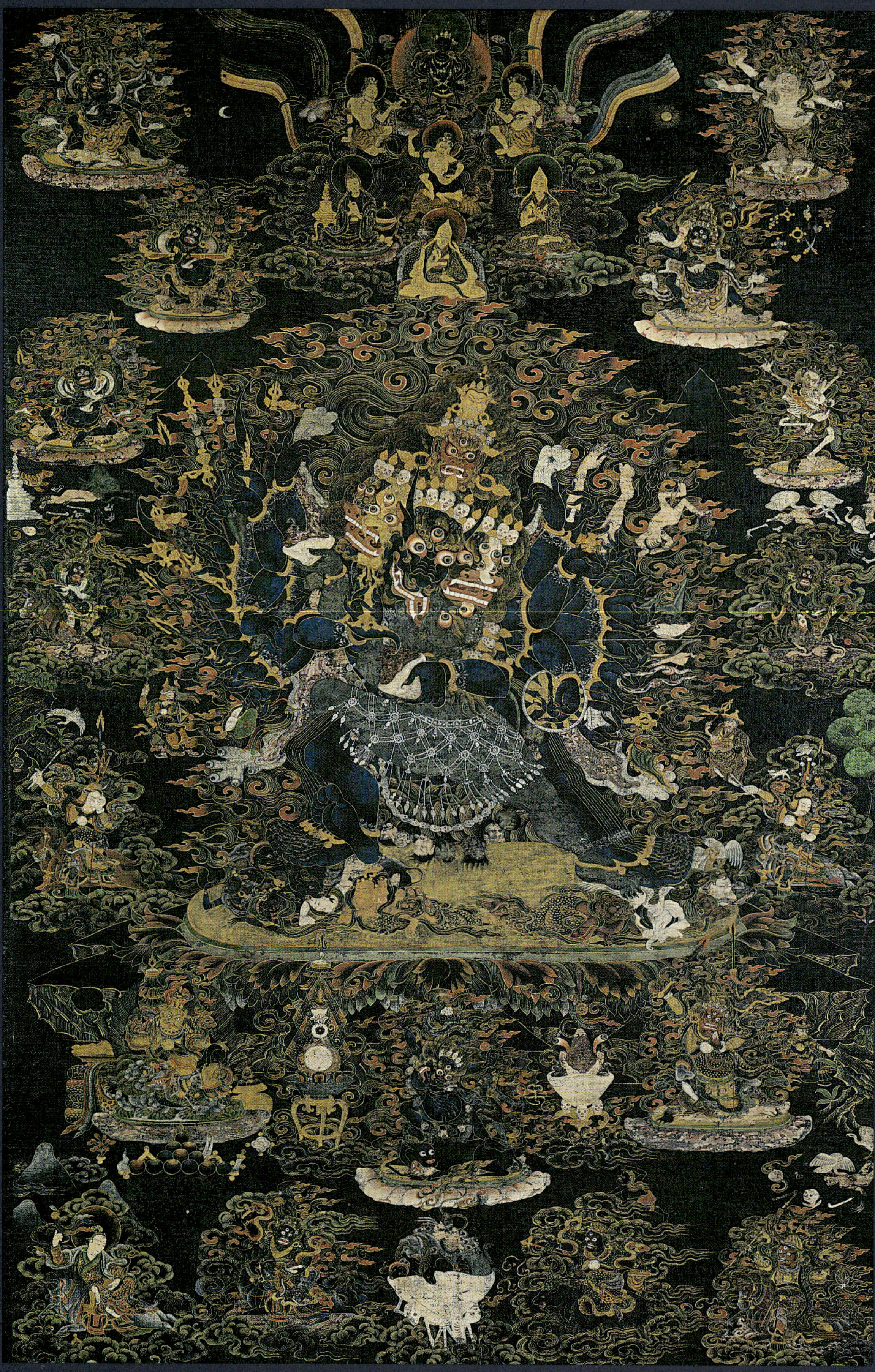

Cat. no. 50

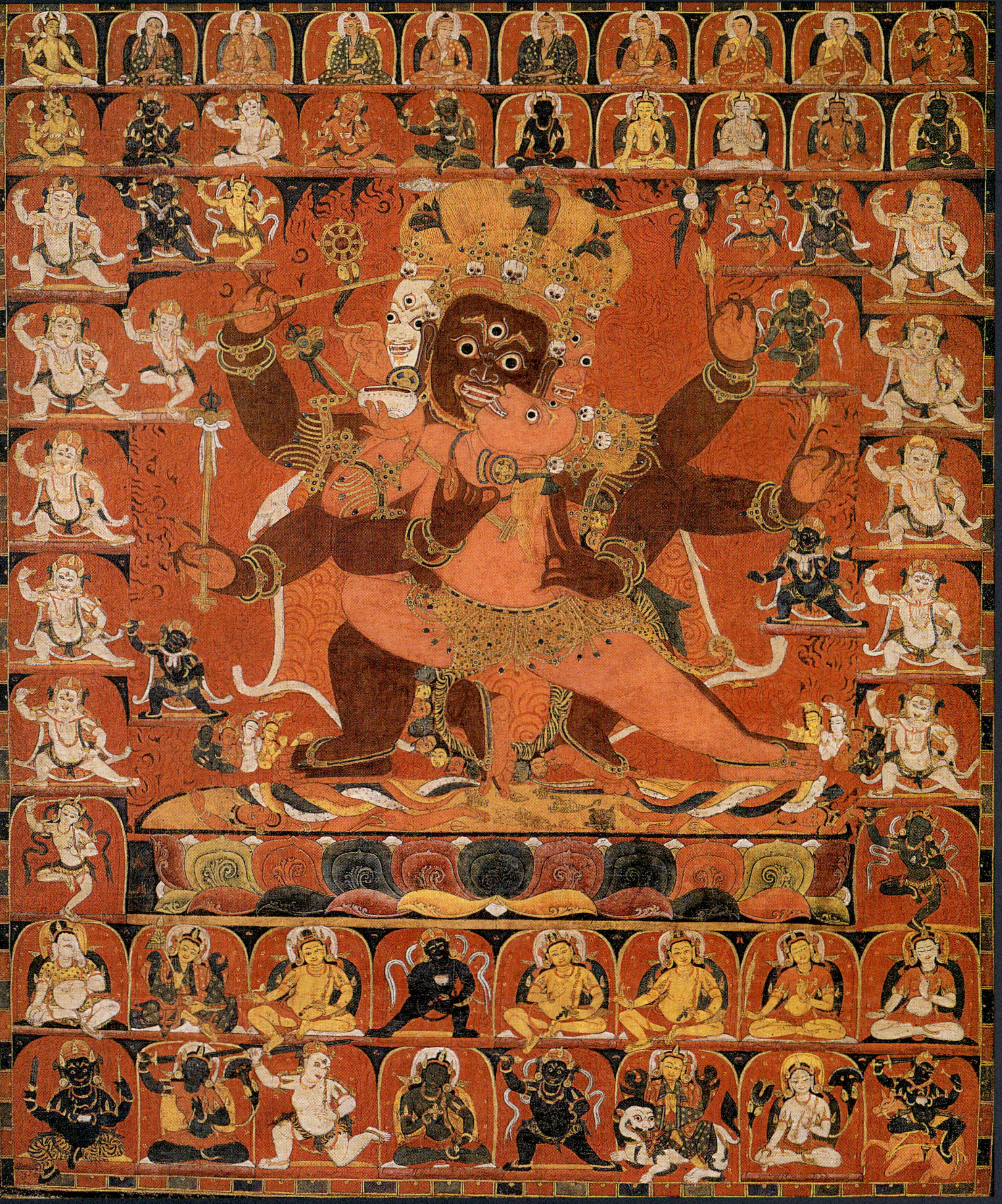

Cat. no. 51

Cat. no. 51

Hayagriva

With Six Hands and Consort

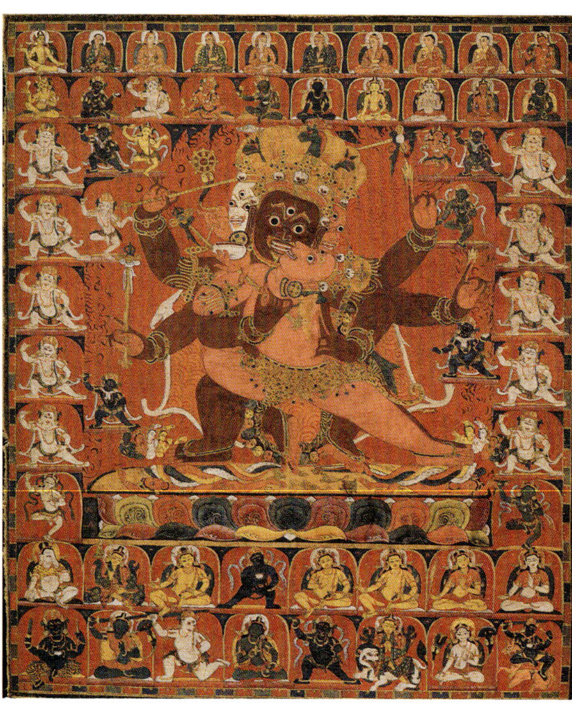

Cat. no. 51
Hayagriva with Six Hands and Consort

Tibet, ca. 1300
Mineral pigments on cloth
26 x 21¼ in. (66. x 54 cm)
Collection of Navin Kumar, New York

The central figures of this painting represent Hayagriva Liberating All Hindrances (Tibetan, Tamdrin Dregpa Kundrol) and his consort, Krodhishvari (The Wrathful Goddess). This is based on a *terma* (revealed treasure text) form of Hayagriva, the horse-necked one, discovered by Drugu Yangwang (ca. late 11th–mid 12th century).[1] Although this *terma* text was not preserved in the standard Tibetan Buddhist canons, in the nineteenth century, and may even have been lost, it was rediscovered, gathered with others, edited and commented on by the great polymath, Jamgon Kongtrul (1813–99).[2]

Hayagriva is three-faced, six-armed, and four-legged. His skin is a dark reddish brown color, while she is one-faced, two-armed, in a pinkish-orange color, and, in accord with the *terma* source, carries a skullcup and a wheel. The *terma* also confirms the authenticity of the flames shooting from Hayagriva's index fingers. Hayagriva and Krodhishvari wear tiger- and leopard-skins, respectively, wrapped around their waists.

From Hayagriva's long hair emerge three green horse heads with orange manes. A key iconographic feature for Hayagriva outside of India, here they can be correlated to the eight snake-bodied *naga*-kings on which Hayagriva and Krodhishvari are trampling. In the Nyingma tradition, Hayagriva is especially lauded for his subjugation of nagas, controlling them through his neighing.[3] The artist seems to have understood this control clearly. On the pedestal between the two groups of nagas, the artists has drawn outlines of the "messengers" of the naga-kings: a frog, salamander, spider, and two unidentified creatures, along with shells. Three garudas, the traditional enemies of serpents, are painted directly above Hayagirva's head, in white, red, and blue, just as the *terma* text specifies.[4]

The sonic aspect of Hayagriva, controlling the demonic sources of obstacles through the

(cont. p. 290)

(cat. key p. 290)

Cat. no. 51, detail

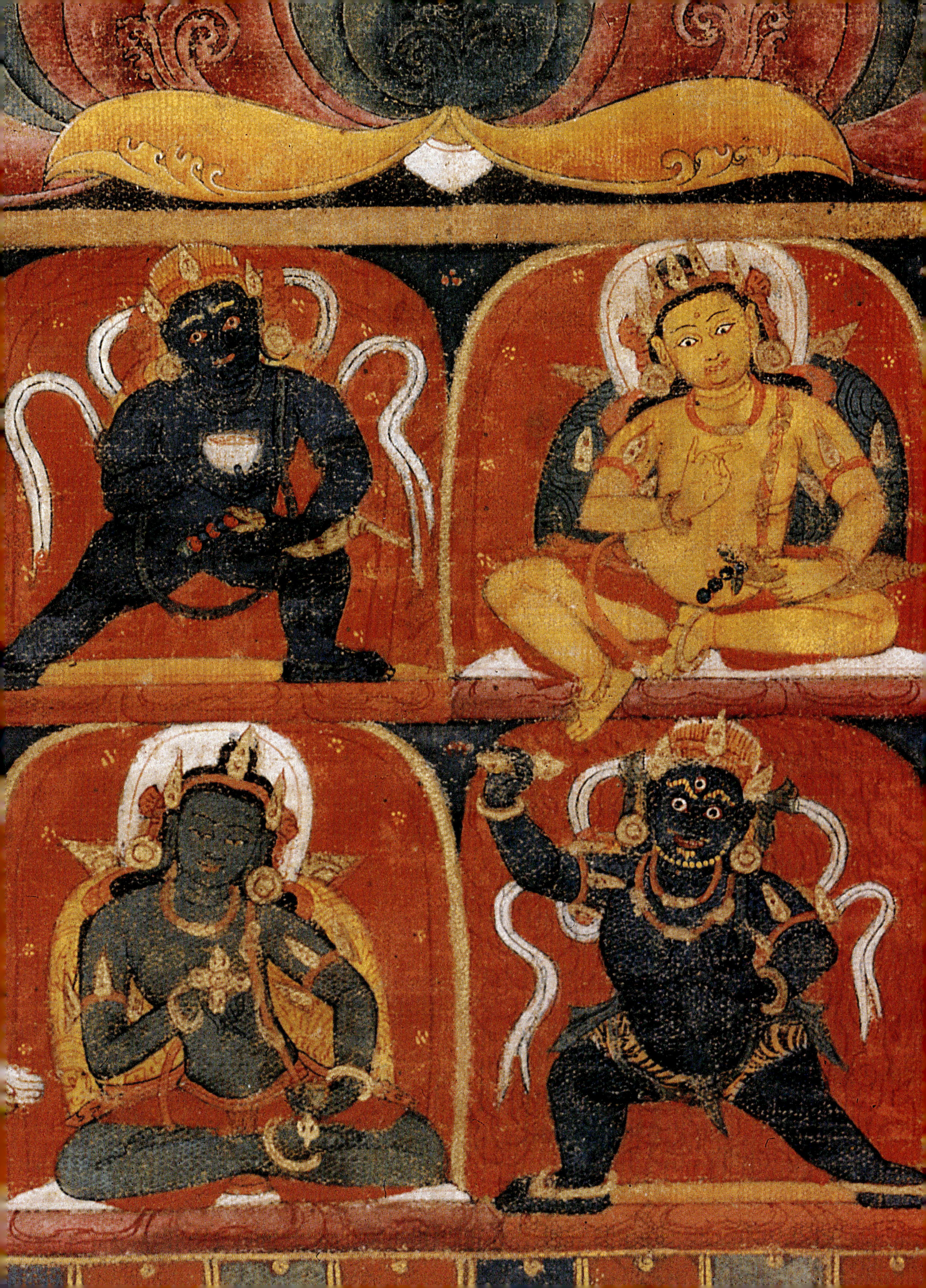

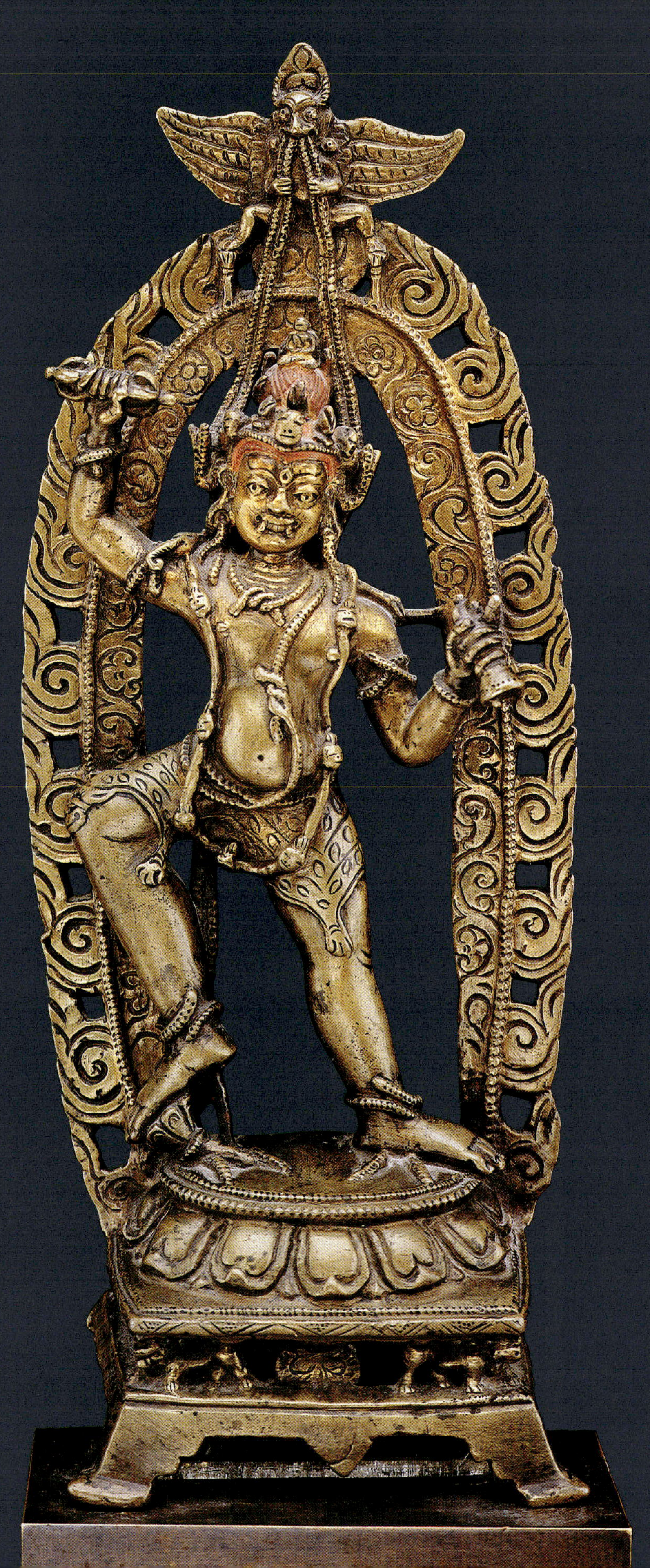

Cat. no. 52

Vajrapani

Trampling Snakes

The *vajra* and bell held in the right and left hands by a big-bellied wrathful (*krodha*) figure suggests this is a form of Vajrapani. He holds the *vajra* up, grasping its center in a fist. The bell is held lower, and he extends his index finger, an expressive gesture of admonition. What distinguishes this particular sculpture is the combination of snakes and the bird-headed, winged *garuda* at the apex of the fiery nimbus. The *garuda*—traditionally pitted against snakes in Indian visual iconography—is biting down on the heads of four snakes.[1] The bodies of the snakes hang down behind the figure (which is only roughly finished on the back) until the tips of their tails emerge beneath Varjapani's feet. Snakes bind themselves to Vajrapani's body as necklaces, wrist-, arm-, and anklets, in his earrings, and around his red hair. (For more on the iconography of these *nagas* in the form of snakes, see cat. no. 56.) He wears a headdress adorned by three skulls, and a garland with six human heads tied by their hair. A spotted leopard skin is wrapped around his thighs, cinched with a snake belt. In contrast to these terrifying elements, a lotus flower delicately props up his right leg in a version of *alidha*, the archer's posture. Two tiny lotus flowers similarly prop up the splayed legs of the *garuda* at the top. Vajrapani bites down firmly over his lower lip, his fangs protruding, in a grimace that recalls a standard iconographic feature of Achala. One anomaly is the presence of a Buddha making the gesture of meditation usually associated with Amitabha in his headdress. For Vajrapani one would expect Akshobhya Buddha, but perhaps this is a special form of Akshobhya. (See cat. no. 28 for another variant form of Akshobhya.)

Where this was made is as difficult to pin down as the precise iconography. It was published as Western Tibetan, a reasonable suggestion.[2] However, in the last twenty years, a great deal more material is available for comparison, and von Schroeder's recent two-volume work provides an excellent corpus of material from

(cont. p. 292)

Facing page: Cat. no. 52
Vajrapani Trampling Snakes

Eastern India or Western Tibet (?), ca. 10th–11th c.
Metalwork
10½ x 4 in. (26.7 x 10.2 cm)
Collection of Michael and Beata McCormick, New York

Cat. no. 53

Mahachakra Vajrapani

Great Wheel Vajra Holder

Facing page: Cat. no. 53
Mahachakra Vajrapani
Great Wheel Vajra Holder

Tibet, ca. 12th c.
Mineral pigments on cloth
27 x 19¾ x 6¾ in. (68.58 x 50.2 x 17.1 cm)
C2002.25.1 (HA 65128)

This is one of the oldest Buddhist paintings in the exhibition. It shares that honor with the Achala of catalog number 37, with which also it shares a darkened palette dominated by red on blue, a simplified composition which focused on a single deity, and elements derived from Tibet's contact with flourishing Buddhist painting traditions in Eastern India and Nepal.[1] The six-armed, three-faced deity carrying a *vajra* and a *vajra*-handled bell is in the big-bellied (*lambodara*) form found also in Indian examples of wrathful deities, among whom Vajrapani plays an important role, particularly in the early stages of the evolution of Esoteric Buddhism.[2] Distinctive to Mahachakra Vajrapani is the horrific action of biting down on the heads of snakes, the bodies of which emerge from—in this case—his three mouths.[3] As in catalog numbers 52 and 58, Vajrapani has many snakes as ornaments, in his hair, arms, wrists, and ankles and around his neck.

The separate rectangular panel below the main deity is especially interesting, with unquestionably archaic elements. In the center, lined up between two vases, is a set of seven offering vessels on tripod stands of an antiquated style.[4] In the background, a rain of flowers continues on slightly smaller scale from the area behind Vajrapani's fiery nimbus. To the left of the offering vessels is a seated monk wearing a yellow outer meditation cloak and a broad-brimmed hat like those found in some of the earliest surviving Tibetan paintings.[5] Both the monk with the hat and the kneeling monk in the right corner wear an early style of monastic robes associated with Indian habits, with one shoulder bare and the hems outlined in a lighter color. The kneeling monk seems to offer reverence both to Vajrapani above and his teacher (?) on the left.

There are no inscriptions on the painting. Its cloth ground, while not yet scientifically tested, appears convincingly old, comprised of two pieces of cloth stitched together, with a

(cont. p. 292)

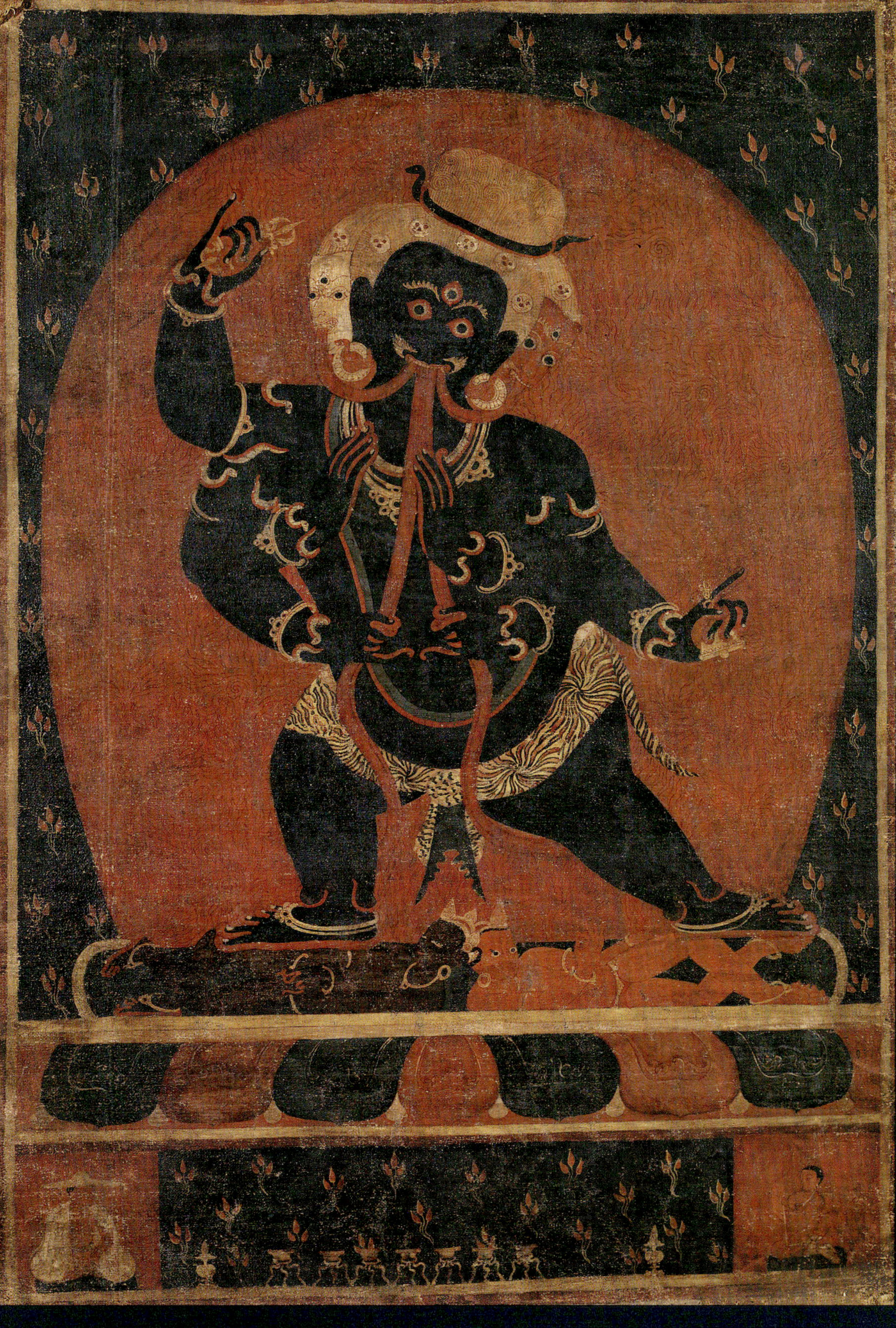

Cat. no. 53

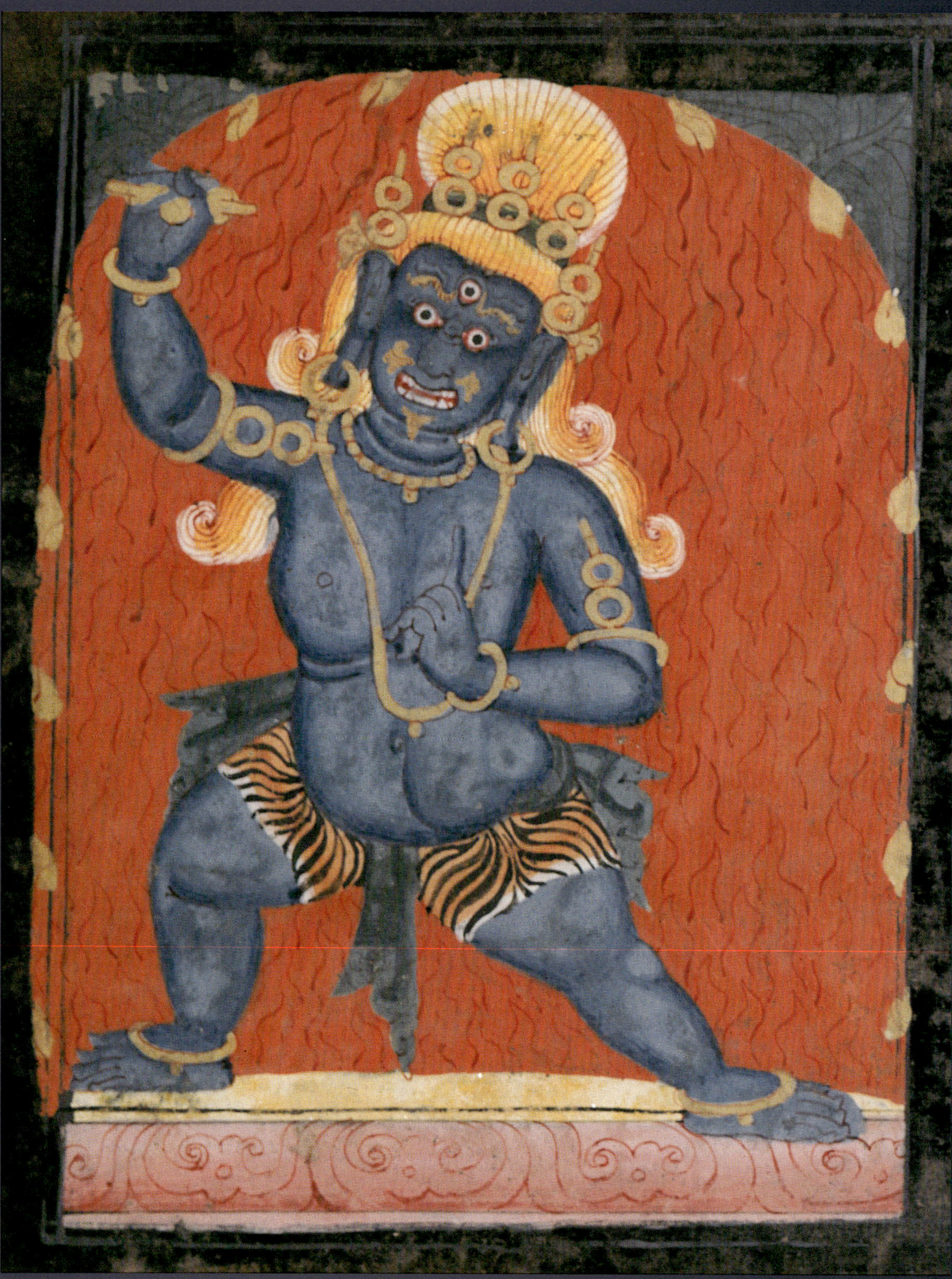

Cat. no. 54, detail

Cat. no. 54

Vajrapani and Vaishravana

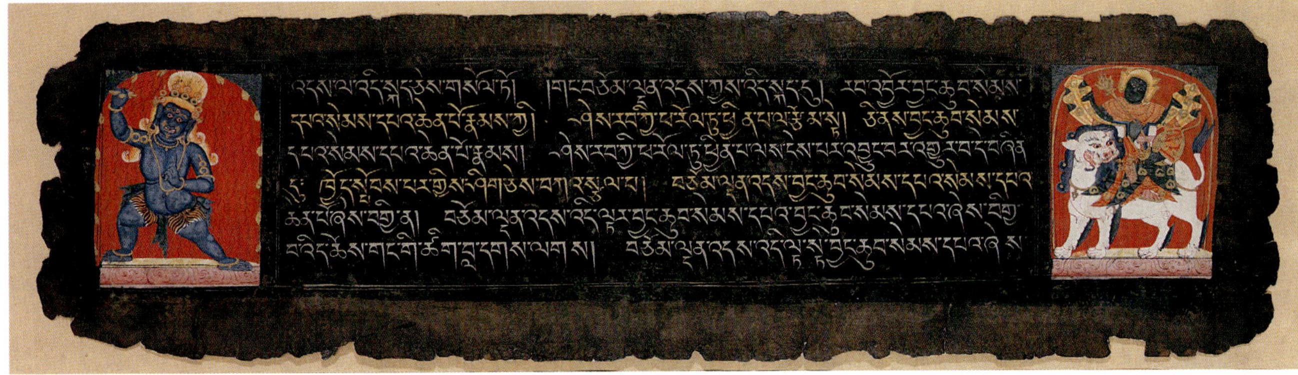

This page was once part of a Tibetan illuminated manuscript, a philosophical (Prajnaparamita) text. Larger in size than Indian and Nepalese books, Tibetans books of an early period were made of paper instead of palm leaves. Tibetans bookmakers did, however, retain the South Asian format of a stack of sheets, rather than the Chinese style of books on a continuous scroll or with accordion folds.[1] As a consequence of increasing the size of each sheet, Tibetan illuminations are often considerably larger than those on Indian or Nepalese manuscripts. This manuscript is quite large even by contemporary Tibetan standards.

This folio belonged to a book that was very carefully produced in a costly and time-consuming manner. Each page was sized, painted blue-black, and then burnished. Reserved rectangles, marked out by double lines of silver, define and enclose the illustrations on either end of the text. The illustrations were identified by brief inscriptions, no longer visible except under infrared light. The text of this folio (the fourth in the manuscript) is in six lines, two of which are in gold ink, the other four in silver. The tops of the letters are aligned horizontally with a fine straight line etched into the paper through the burnished surface.

The side illustrated is actually the back of the folio page. The recto begins a section of the text which flows continuously onto the verso shown here. It also has six lines of writing. Although spaces at the ends of the text are also reserved on the recto, no illuminations were added, other than a decorative border at the ends of rectangle of script, perhaps to ornament the beginning of a section of text. Unfortunately, before it was acquired by the Rubins, in order to mend tears in the paper, a heat-activated thermal plastic was applied to the recto, leaving a nearly opaque film over the entire surface, rendering it un-exhibitable. However, infrared examination revealed the page number to be the fourth folio of the text. The Rubins also own the second and third folios of the same text, and these also have two illuminations on the verso, none on the recto. The text of the *Prajnaparamita Sutra* begins on the second folio with four lines, continued on the verso with five lines. The illustrations are of Vajradhara and the Buddha making the teaching gesture (*dharmachakra mudra*). The third folio, acquired at a different time from a different source, is not treated, so both sides are clear. It has five lines of writing on both sides and depicts the bodhisattvas Manjushri on the left and Avalokiteshvara (Chenrezig) on the right.[2]

The fourth folio, catalog number 54, depicts a wrathful Vajrapani (see detail) and Vaishravana on a snow lion. These figures were important Protectors and Benefactors. Vajrapani is also considered a Wrathful

(cont. p. 293)

Cat. no. 54
Vajrapani, Vajra Holder (left) and Vaishravana, King of the North Direction (right)

Tibet, ca. late 13th c.
Pigments, gold, silver, and ink on paper
8 x 28 in. (20.3 x 17.1 cm)
Collection of Shelley and Donald Rubin
(HA 700115)

Cat. no. 55

Vajrapani Nilambaradhara

Vajra Holder

Three images of the Enlightened Buddha Vajrapani are featured in this wooden relief panel, each standing on a lotus base. The larger one in the center is Vajrapani Nilambaradhara (Vajra Holder Wearing Blue), and it is his Sanskrit name and abbreviated *mantra* which, in the lower half of the panel, Tibetan letters transliterate.[1] All three Vajrapanis have big bellies and assume the identical aggressive posture, a variant of what is known as the archer's pose. They each hold up a *vajra*—Vajrapani's eponymous attribute—in the right hand but in slightly different ways. The gestures of the left hand may also be distinguished among them, at least between the left figure, who holds a bell against his thigh and the other two who make a gesture of threat or admonition, their index fingers erect. Within the Sakya lineage, the central Vajrapani Nilambaradhara is regarded as the main form of Vajrapani, and visualization of this image continues to be practiced today. In fact the image is so associated with Sakya that other Sarma (i.e. non-Nyingma lineages) schools refer to it as "Sa Lug" Vajrapani, an abbreviation for "Sakya Tradition" Vajrapani.

Stylistically, one of the features that places this work in late thirteenth or early fourteenth century is the use of the rinceau to enclose the three deities. The complexly rendered floral scrolling, including the elegant stems that branch into sprays of leaves (see detail), is found in paintings datable to this period. The carver appears to be working within a Newari idiom, and was able to render a rich surface with many different levels of relief. There is a surprising amount of detail in the central figure, including the snake hair-tie and diagonal band running down from his left shoulder, the bulbous earrings, necklace, and structure of the *vajra* in the raised right hand.

(cont. p. 294)

Cat. no. 55
Vajrapani Nilambaradhara
Vajra Holder

Tibet, 14th c.
Wood
9 x 17¾ x 1½in.
(22.9 x 45.1 x 3.8 cm)
Collection of Shelley and Donald Rubin (HA 700005)

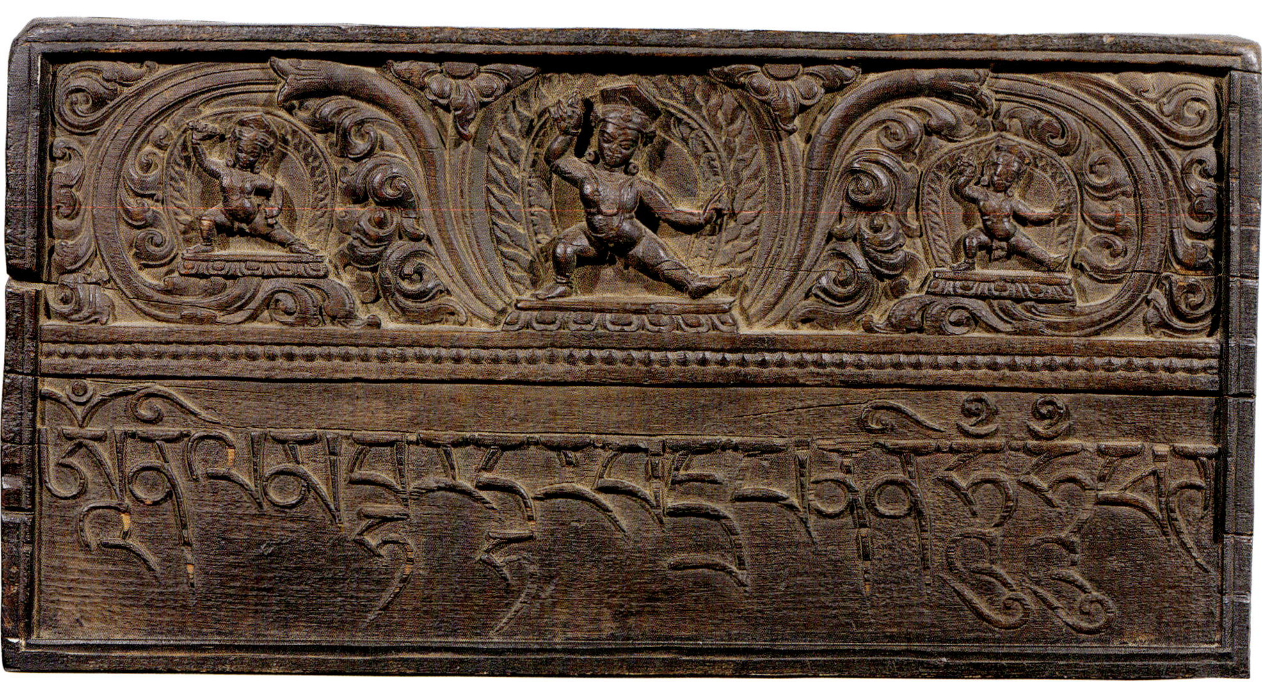

Facing page: Cat. no. 55, detail

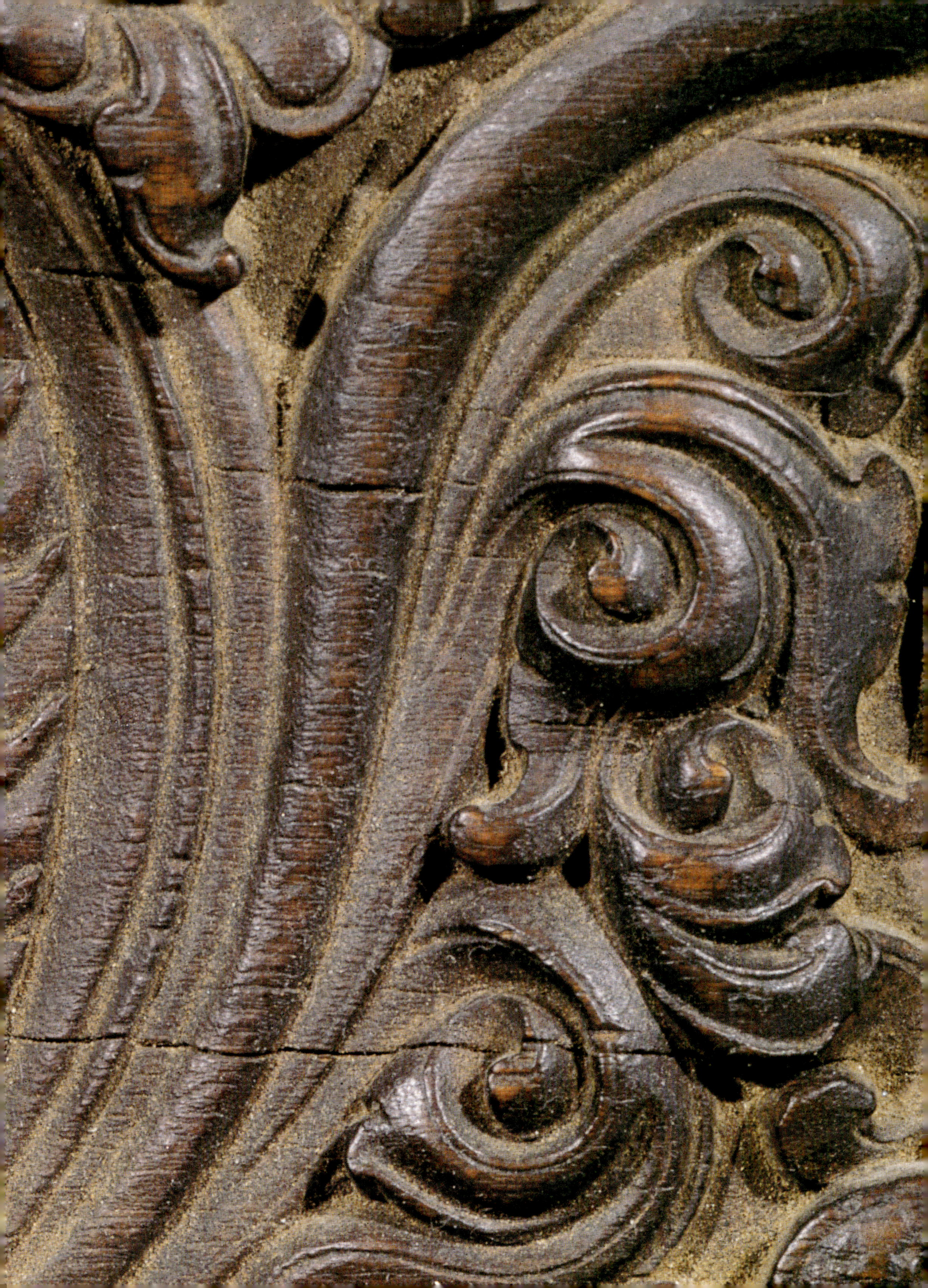

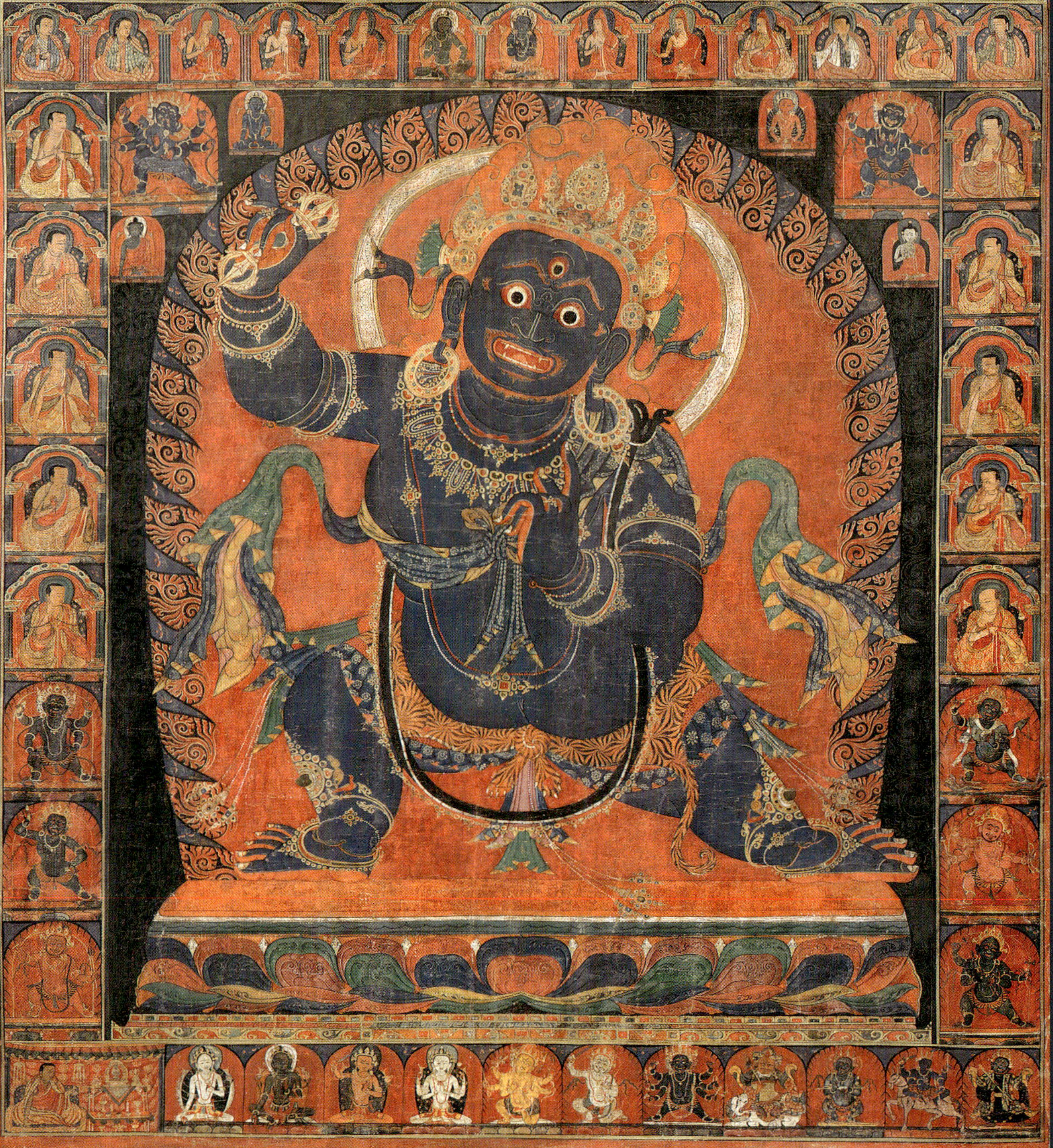

Cat. no. 56

Vajrapani

Lord of Secrets

The midnight blue skin of the main figure in this large-scale painting was chosen with care and precision. Visually it is set off from the crimson on the flaming nimbus, and enriched by the presence nearby of a much blacker background. The blue is just a shade darker than the blue scarf tied across his chest and fluttering at his sides. This cloth and the *vajra* held in the raised right hand give his name: Nilambara Vajrapani, "the Vajra-holder of dark-blue raiment."[1] He is also marked by the fact that unlike other Vajrapani images (cat. nos. 52, 53, 65), he does not carry a bell. Nor is he shown embracing a consort (cat. no. 65). Another characteristic is the presence of eight great *nagas* in the form of snakes. A blue pair is tied to the top of his hair above his crown; a red one curls around his neck like a choker; dark ones with red undersides act as clasps on his wrists and ankles; and a thick black one with a rainbow underside loops around his torso like a brahmin's cord, its head on his left shoulder.[2] Having them as live ornaments demonstrates his mastery over the various obstacles that they represent. At the same time, they contribute to his awe-inspiring appearance.

The snake theme continues in the upper left corner of the inner rectangle, with an image of Mahachakra Vajapani with consort, biting down on two snakes (see also cat. no. 53). In the right corner is an unusual variant of Bhutadamara, also a form of Vajrapani. This image makes the canonical gestures with his four hands, but has three heads instead of one prescribed head. Four Buddhas are also found within the inner rectangle, two near Bhutadamara (Amitayus Buddha and Shakyamuni or Vairochana Buddha in *nirmanakaya* form, making *dharmacakra mudra*) and two near Mahachakra Vajrapani (Akshobhya Buddha in *sambhogakaya* [crowned, bejeweled form] and a blue-green Buddha [Amoghasiddhi?] in *bhumisparsha mudra*). All of them are overwhelmed by the

(cont. p. 294)

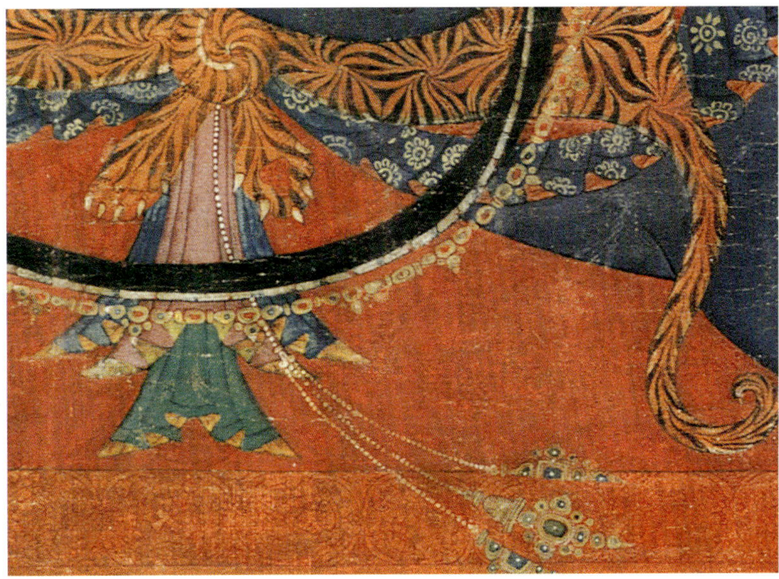

Cat. no. 56, detail

Facing page: Cat. no. 56
Vajrapani
Lord of Secrets

Tibet, early 15th c.
Mineral pigments on cloth
36 x 32 in. (91.4 x 81.3 cm)
Collection of Michael and Beata McCormick, New York (HA 90135)

Cat. no. 57

Vajravarahi

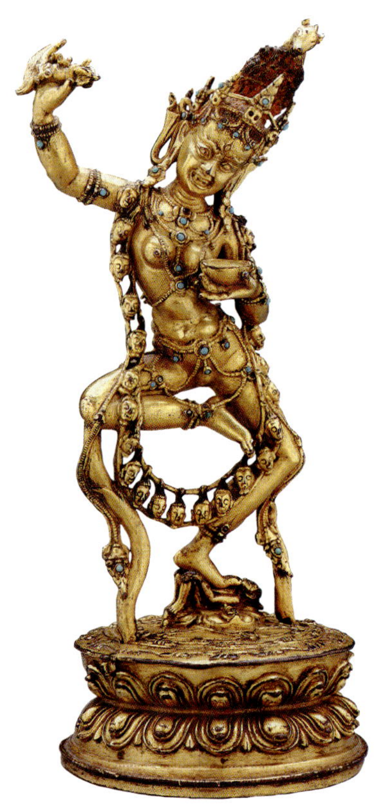

Cat. no. 57
Vajravarahi
Tibet, 15th c.
Gilt metal
9½ x 3½ in. (24.1 x 8.9 cm)
Collection of Michael and Beata McCormick, New York (HA 90164)

If, to paraphrase the lyric poet Rainier Maria Rilke, any angel is terrible, it is this one. Beautiful in and through the terror she emanates, this Wrathful Buddha takes the notion of the demonic divine in a new direction. Where the female Dangerous and Enlightened Protectors in the exhibition (cat. nos. 1, 7, 8, 31, 32) demonstrate that the female can be horrifying, this fierce Vajravarahi shows that the terrifying can be feminine. The gracefulness with which she holds her elegant pose, the stateliness of her elongated proportions, the network of jewel-studded chains (understood to be bone) that do nothing to obscure her unabashed nudity, all work together to create a new kind of paradox, conjoining allure and fearful awe. An explanation that attempts to come to terms with a beautiful, feminine, Wrathful Buddha, has been recently offered:

> [Vajravarahi] is beautiful, the most heavenly of all women. But it is not her beauty that attracts. Rather, it is her promise, the potential of controlling the ego and its cravings, that draws the practitioner. Her relative beauty is but a metaphor for that which is absolutely beautiful—the Void State (*shunyata*).[1]

Vajravarahi is the most renowned female meditational deity.[2] She is named for the sow's head that emerges from the right side of her hair or, as here, from the top of her high-piled hair. She holds up a *vajra*-handled curved flaying knife, and a skull bowl. The long staff (*katvanga*) that she once held inside her left forearm is missing (compare cat. no. 58). A garland of freshly severed heads hangs down almost to the ankle of her left leg. The right leg is bent and brought up to her inner thigh in a dancer's pose. In her red form, she is the consort of Chakrasamvara and is shown clinging to him at the centers of the mandalas featured in catalog numbers 42 and 43. In this sculpture she is standing in the center of her own mandala, formed on the base

(cont. p. 295)

Cat. no. 58

Vajravarahi

Krodha Kali (Fierce Black One)

This small painting is a *tsagli*, a card used in initiations and individual practice. It is extremely finely done for its size, with lavish gold for the flames and accents. It is part of a group of small paintings that have recently come to light. They share an intense red and blue palette, wrathful themes of a Nyingma variety, small size with complex compositions and/or dense detail, and an archaistic painting style that relates to the fourteenth century. Indeed, two of them have been published as being from the fourteenth century, though a third published example has a portrait which has been identified as Ratna Lingpa (1403–79), the famous *terton* (treasure-text discoverer) and compiler of *terma* teachings.[1] Two other paintings, about twice the size of this *tsagli*, and belonging to the same group, feature Orgyan Pema Lingpa (1450 1521), the reincarnation of Longchenpa, and Chokyi Gocha (1542–85), the fourth Tai Situ.[2] They place the date of the painting of this group to no earlier than the second half of the sixteenth century. The painting with the Pema Lingpa portrait includes a nearly identical image of the fierce blue form of Vajravarahi that is depicted in this *tsagli*.[3] According to a Nyingma liturgical verse, she is, in true Wrathful Buddha fashion, a "treasure of all excellent and common attainments," one who "performs [for] the benefit of beings."[4]

A later Nyingma practitioner, Terdag Lingpa (1646–1714), renowned as the founder of Mindroling Monastery and contemporary of the Fifth Dalai Lama, co-authored with his brother Minling Lochen (1654–1718) wrote a visualization and interpretation of this form of Varjavarahi that matches in all details:

> Bhagavani [Krodha Kali] with a great radiance at the time of darkness, fierce and raging. The main face is wrathful, the very pure relative truth, and the upper face of a sow is the pure ultimate truth, gazing upward; [both] having

(cont. p. 296)

Cat. no. 58
Vajravarahi
Krodha Kali (Fierce Black One)

Tibet, second half of the 16th c.
Mineral pigments on cloth
5 x 4¼ in. (12.7 x 10.8 cm)
Collection of Michael and Beata McCormick, New York

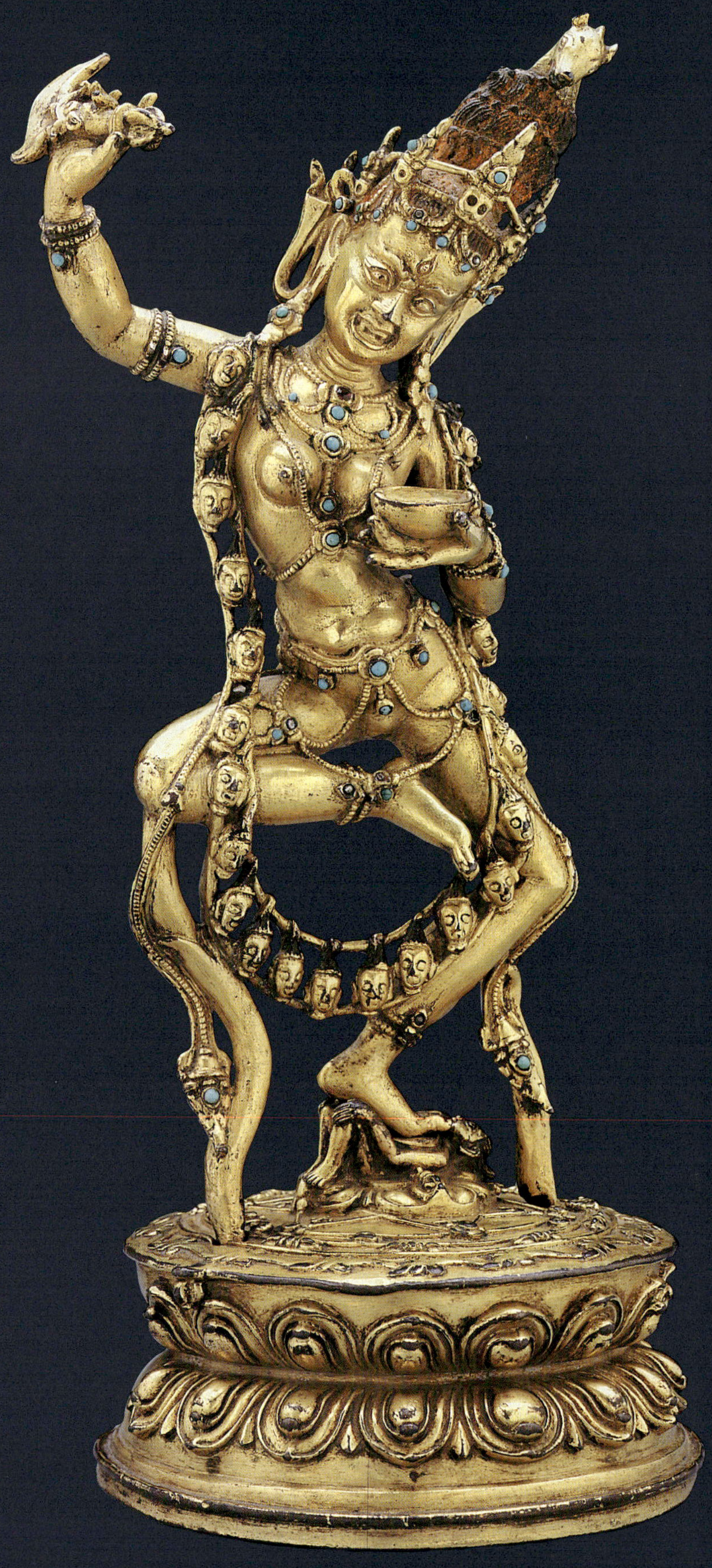

Cat. no. 57

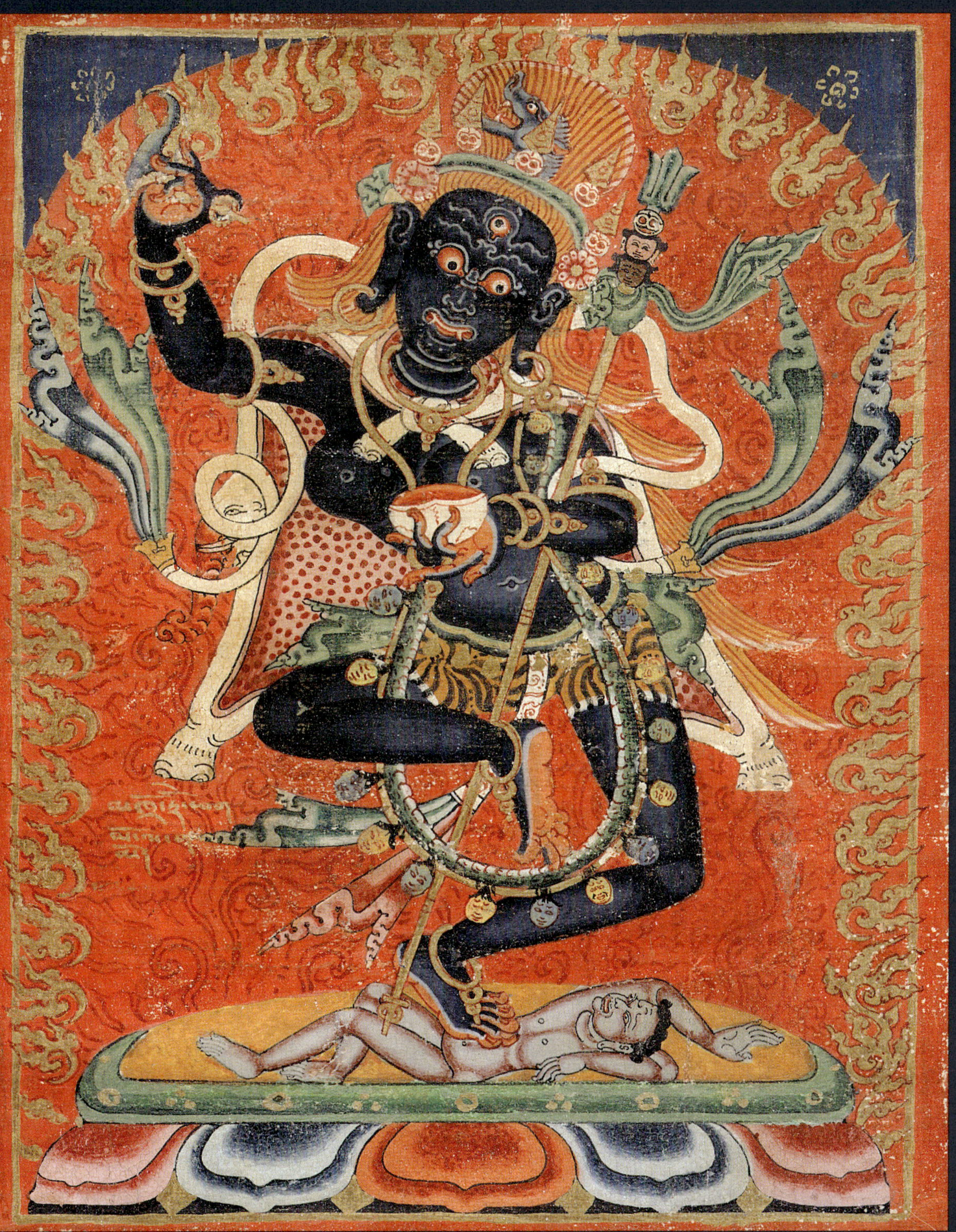

Cat. no. 58

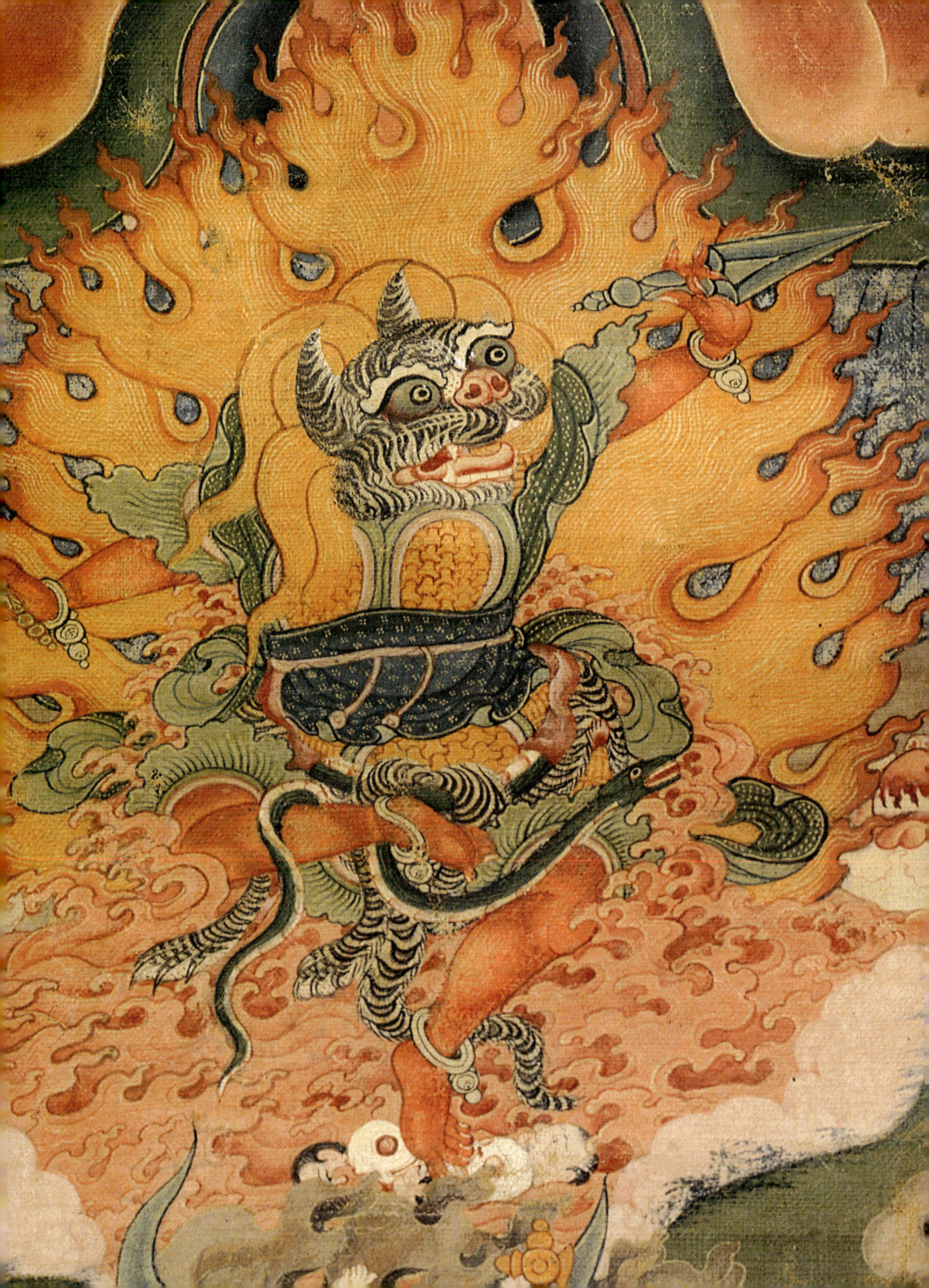

Bön Wrathful Deities

Wrathful imagery in Himalayan and Tibetan art is very much based on the *raksha* demon figure of classical Indian literature. A massive face with three large staring eyes, gnashing teeth, and a flickering tongue, hair flowing upward, thick limbs and torso, adorned with fearsome ornaments, skins, weapons, and the like. This is all standard imagery used in the sacred art of the Himalayas by the Hindu, Buddhist, and Bön religions. Because of this standard imagery it is very difficult to tell the difference between a Bön wrathful deity and a Buddhist wrathful deity.

Fortunately, there are a number of uniquely Bön iconographic characteristics and conventions not found on the Buddhist paintings. First and foremost is the varied use by the Bön of animal imagery. Animal faces are commonly found on many of the important Bön wrathful deities.

Several different animals are also grouped beneath the thrones of Bön deities, instead of a pair of the same animals as in most Buddhist art. The animals of the four directions, commonly found on prayer flags, often appear in paintings of wrathful deities such as Tagla Membar (cat. no. 59). Animals in Bön art are not just the animals inherited from Indian observations and imaginations. Claiming their own origins in the land of Tazik to the west of the Himalayas, Bön artists freely incorporate all of the wildlife of the Tibetan Plateau and Central Asia. Finally, where Buddhist art tends toward symmetrical balance in grouping retinue figures, Bön paintings are looser and sometimes appear to be purposely asymmetric.

Cat. no. 59, detail

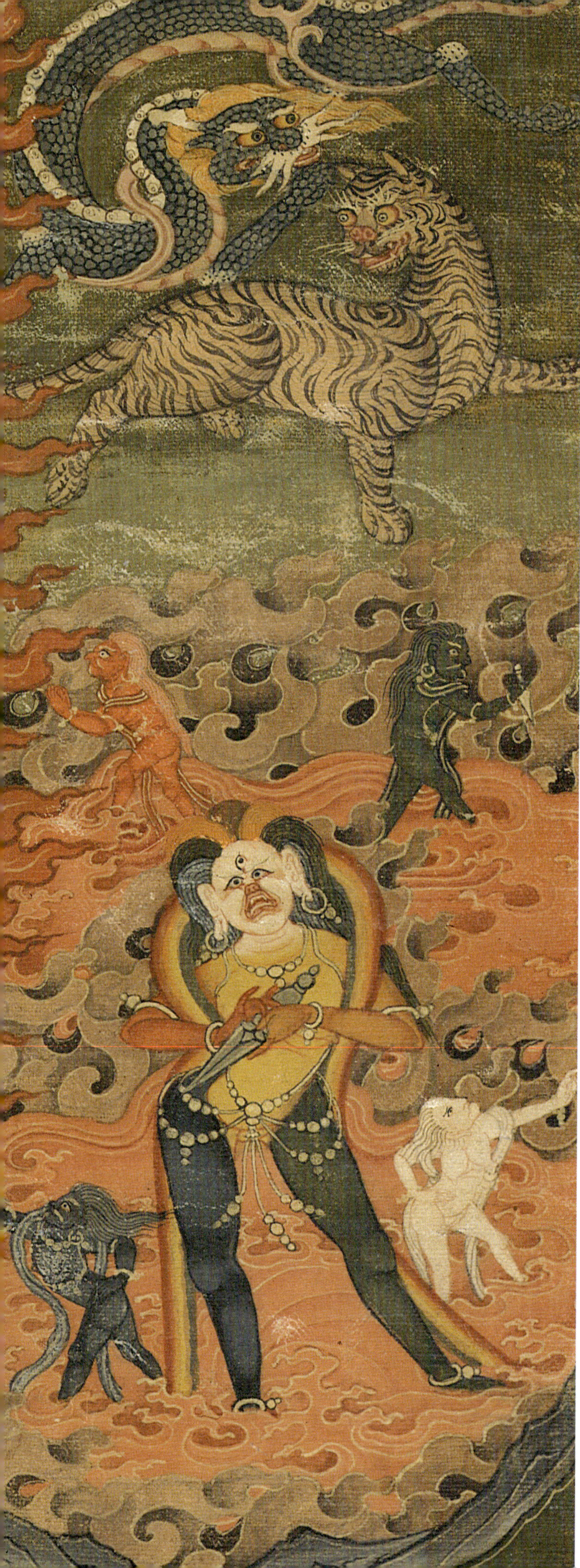

Cat. no. 59

Tagla Membar

(Flaming Tiger-God)

Tagla Membar is an important Bön deity with three different appearances collectively known as the Three White, Black, and Red Ones, the red being the most important.[1] Although primarily employed as a meditational system and a complete teaching, leading the practitioner to Bön enlightenment, Tagla Membar is also referred to as a "doctrinal weapon" because of its use against Buddhists whenever the Bön religion is being suppressed.[2] Although no specific geographic location is special for Tagla Membar, a cave called *walrong* on the side of Mount Kailash, well known among the Bönpo, is dedicated to his practice.[3]

The actual appearance of Tagla Membar is not very much different from Buddhist wrathful deities and it is clear that there is more in common here than there are differences. The upraised right hand holds what looks like an eight spoked wheel common to Buddhism. A small Buddha-like figure, Tonpa Shenrab, the founder of the Bön religion, sits peacefully atop the upward flowing hair of Tagla Membar.[4] The left hand holds a symbolic weapon unique to Bön iconography, nine crossed swords.

Directly below the central deity is the Red Tiger-faced One, holding a sword and peg, dancing wildly above a sea of blood and surrounded by orange flames (see detail, p. 234).[5] Filling the landscape at the sides of the painting are small clusters of figures, some grouped around a slightly larger figure, and others simply uniform in appearance standing together. Most visually striking, on Tagla Membar's left are the Five Female Mamo Mind Emanations with the leader, multicolored and wearing a rainbow shawl, accompanied by four smaller female figures (see detail). Other clusters

(cont. p. 297)

Facing page: Cat. no. 59
Tagla Membar (Flaming Tiger-God)

Tibet, 19th c.
Mineral pigments on cloth
39 x 25¾ in. (99.1 x 65.4 cm)
Collection of Shelley and Donald Rubin
(HA 200041)

Left: Cat. no. 59, detail

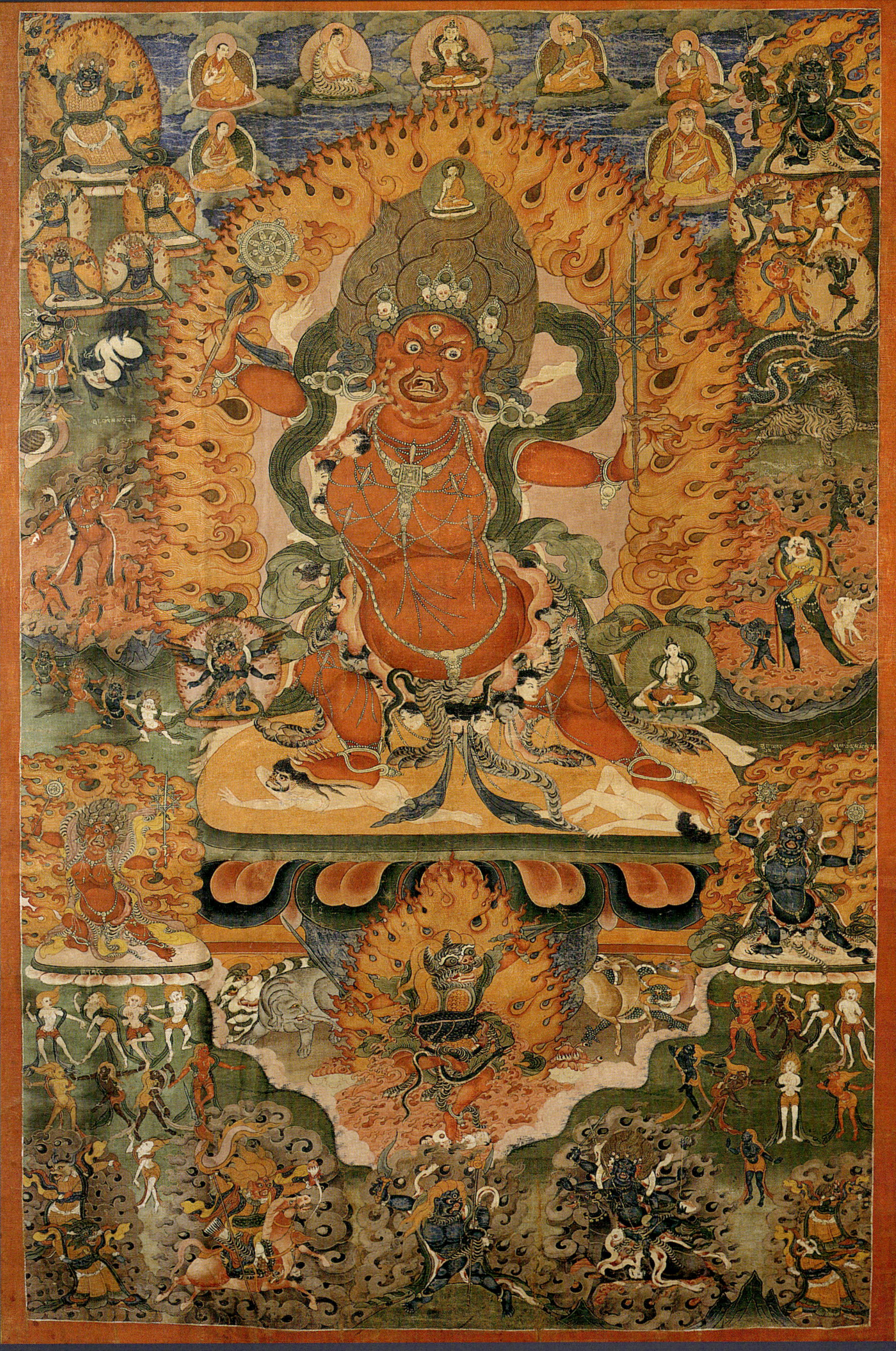

Cat. no. 59

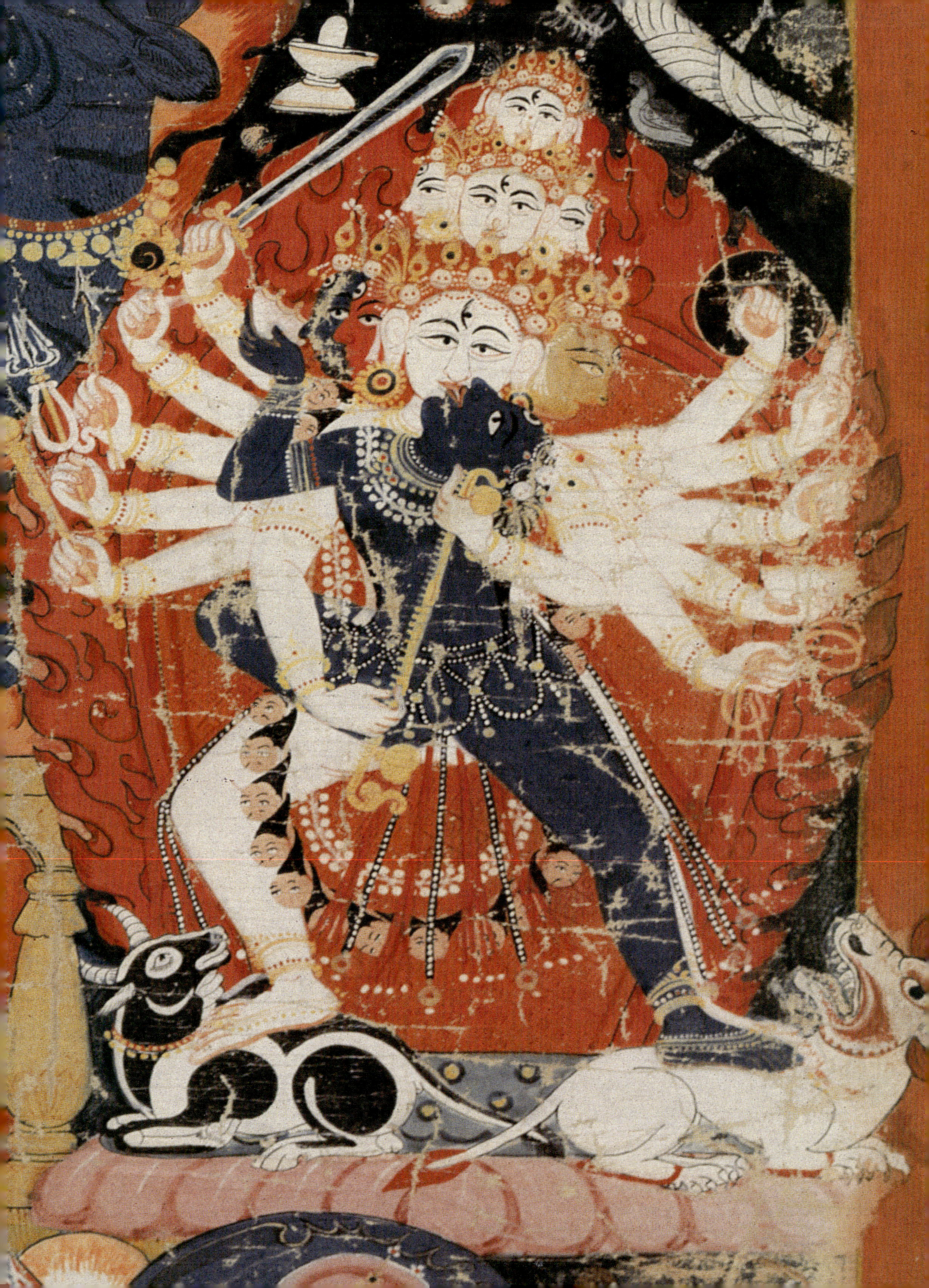

Hindu Wrathful Deities

The theme of the "demonic divine" seems to be a mode of religious art in many artistic traditions, both visual and literary, including the Hindu. While Hinduism was not transplanted to quite as many different cultural contexts as Buddhism, it did spread to Southeast Asia, and continues to thrive all over India and Nepal. Wherever it took root, wrathful deities are prominent, from Kali in Calcutta, Bhairava in Western Sumatra, to Chamunda in Rajasthan, Narasimha in Karnataka in South India, Mahishashura Mardini in East Java, Vishvarupa Vishnu in Nepal, and the monumental *kirtimukha* in Bali.

Many Hindu paintings and sculptures of the demonic divine use a slightly different visual paradox than the one found in Buddhist and Bön work in the Himalayas. Instead of matching violent behavior, such as spearing demons, with an equally aggressive facial expression, often the deities appear completely neutral, passive, almost disengaged. In Southeast Asia, sometimes the wrathful deities positively seem to be dreaming with their eyes closed. On the other hand, there are many instances where the facial expressions are eerie or frightening. Both types are included here.

Cat. no. 61, detail

Cat. no. 60

Vishnu Vishvarupa

Universal Form

Facing page: Cat. no. 60
Vishnu Vishvarupa
Universal Form

Nepal, 17th–18th c.
Clay
20 x 14½ x 4 in. (50.8 x 36.8 x 10.2 cm)
C2003.12.3 (HA 65214)

The awe-inspiring form of Vishnu depicted in this clay sculpture relates to the episode in the *Bhagavad Gita* in which Krishna reveals his cosmic form to the warrior Arjuna. Overwhelmed, Arjuna begs Krishna to return to his human form. Hindu artists of Nepal have used this episode as a warrant to exercise their imaginations for a form expressing sacred terror.[1] Two of the principal hands hold the sun and moon, standard visual shorthand for a cosmic deity. Among the twenty visible heads are those of gods and animals representing Vishnu's *avatars* (manifestations). On the second register of heads are a fish and tortoise, representing Mastya and Kurma; the third register has a lion and boar, Narasimha and Varaha respectively; and the fourth, an elephant, eagle, and bull, possibly referring to the mounts of Indra, Vishnu, and Shiva. Presumably, some of the human heads in the stack of twenty represent Parusurama, Rama, and Krishna who are Vishnu's human incarnations. In Hindu accounts, Vishnu's ninth incarnation was Shakyamuni Buddha, and he is represented here as well on the third tier of heads, first on the left, identified by the tight hair curls and the *ushnisha* (cranial protuberance).

Along with the twenty heads are ten visible legs and three concentric rings of hands, fifty-eight in all. Other Nepalese depictions of Vishnu Vishvarupa vary the number of visible heads, hands, and legs, so these numbers were apparently not iconographically fixed. The attributes held in the prominent hands are paired, such as the sun and moon (already mentioned), the arrow and bow, *vajra* and bell, sword and shield, umbrella and canopy, and flaying knife and skull bowl. This last pair is one of the distinctive attributes of Mahakala and Bhairava, and it is clear from comparison with Nepalese sculpture from the same period that the sculptor has adapted the look of Mahakala for Vishnu. Related features include the big belly (note the human being swallowed

(cont. p. 297)

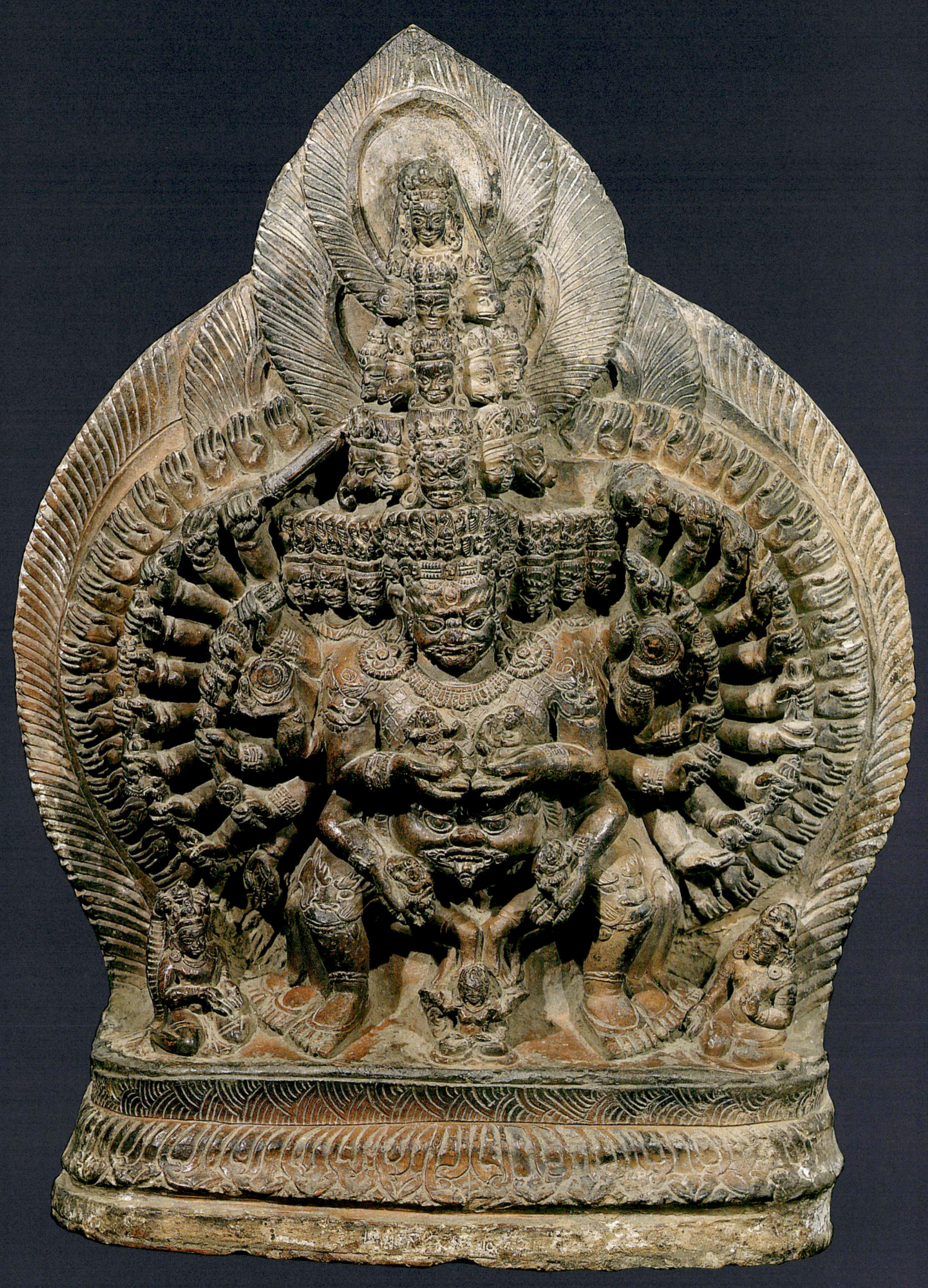

Cat. no. 60

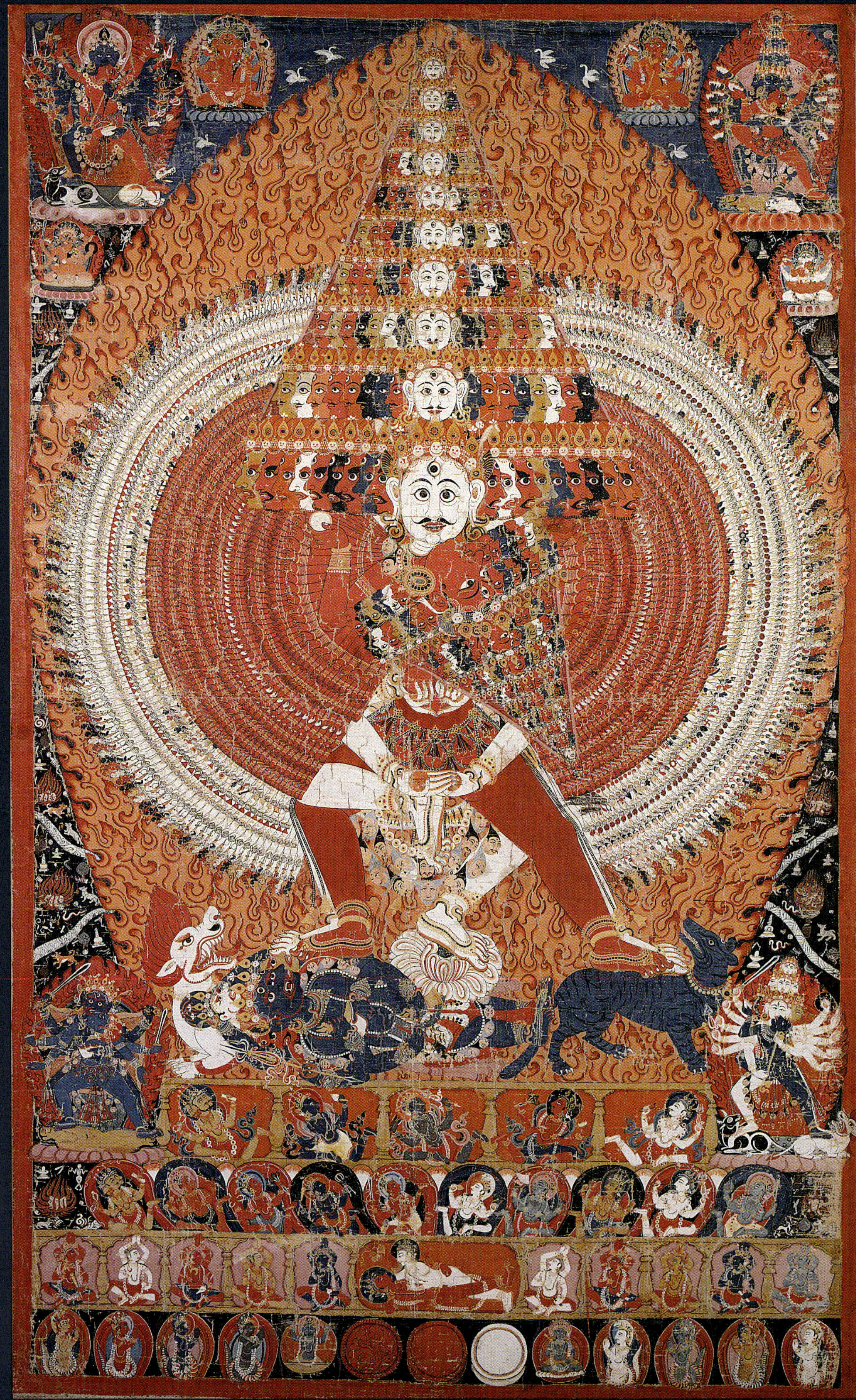

Cat. no. 61

Cat. no. 61

Shiva Vishvarupa

Universal Form with Consort

Although the principal faces of Shiva and his consort are peaceful or neutral, the painter has employed all the devices developed over two millennia in the Hindu and Buddhist traditions to convey the tremendous power of the primordial deity in its universal form. To indicate its all-seeing nature, both the white Shiva and his red consort have a multitude of heads and arms, indicating an infinite vision and reach. For all intents and purposes, the idea is successfully conveyed that the hands are innumerable. Shiva bears the orbs of the sun and moon in his two main hands, as if the cosmos itself was in his grasp. His six-armed blue form, Bhairava, is trampled underfoot, together with a ferocious lion and vicious dog or jackal striped like a tiger. Multiarmed gods including Brahma and Vishnu underneath Shiva's dais reel back even as they make the gesture of obeisance, holding aloft joined palms.

These visual metaphors are all based on the concrete figurations of the artist. Shiva's tower of heads has ten registers, the one to the sides of the main head having nineteen, the next one up seventeen, the next fifteen, and so on to the top register with one head, totaling 100 in all. His consort has 108, another auspicious number. Both main figures have multiple concentric rings with hands, hers turned away from the viewer, his hands palm out. The hands in his outermost ring hold 228 small beings, some who are snake-hooded *nagas*, some animal-headed spirits, and a large number of Shaiva ascetics.

The Nepalese artist is also drawing on themes that would have been familiar to a nineteenth-century audience acquainted with Buddhist forms as well as Hindu. The tower of heads and thousand-armed conceit is conventional for Buddhist depictions of Ushnisha Sitatapatra and Sahasrabhuja-sahasranetra Avalokiteshvara. The latter was transformed into Shrishtikanta Lokeshvara, "unique to Nepal . . . [who] emanates the entire

(cont. p. 297)

Cat. no. 61, detail

Facing page: Cat. no. 61
Shiva Vishvarupa
Universal Form with Consort

Nepal, mid-19th c.
Mineral pigments on cloth
63 x 38 in. (160 x 96.5 cm)
C2003.20.2 (HA 65250)

Cat. no. 62

Shiva Andhakashuramurti

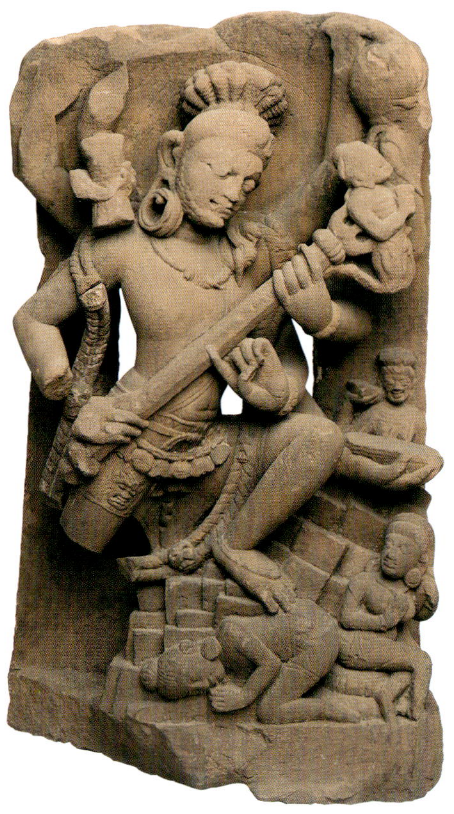

Cat. no. 62
Shiva Andhakashuramurti

Rajasthan, India, late 8th c.
Red sandstone
27¼ x 16⅜ x 11¼ in. (69.2 x 41.6 x 28.6 cm)
Brooklyn Museum of Art

Originally, the figure of Shiva, who dominates the composition, was eight-armed. The most prominent of the attributes he holds is a trident (*trishula*) with which he spears the demon, the *ashura* Andhaka. Shiva holds up a flayed elephant skin, symbol of ignorance and obstacles, the head of which is visible at the upper right. One of his right hands also holds a two-sided, hourglass-shaped drum (*damaru*). Other objects, carried by this form of Shiva in different representations, are broken off, though the gesture of admonition, with the index finger on one of his left hands extended, is quite prominent in this example.[1] With another left hand, Shiva proffers a skull bowl to an emaciated female figure, Yogeshvari, who must drink up the blood shed by Andhaka before he can be defeated. Below her is an image of a beautiful female, figure, next a small figure bowing before Shiva as the latter tramples him.

This stone sculpture of a form of Shiva is a particularly clear expression of one of the distinctive Hindu treatments of the theme of the demonic divine, at least compared to Himalayan ones. That is the combination of violent activity with a passive, neutral expression. Shiva looks on impassively as he spears Andhaka with the sharp prongs of his *trishula*. Shiva's face is curiously absent of emotion, as if acting out of impersonal motives, though Hindu worshipers would have recognized that the narrative behind the icon gives several good reasons why Shiva would take revenge on Andhaka. Andhaka's arrogance, hubris, and lust after Shiva's consort brought Shiva's wrath upon him. After being speared by Shiva, the demon realizes the errors of his ways and is revived or reborn as a properly obedient servitor. The sculptor shows both moments—being pierced by the trident, and bowing underfoot, next to Shiva's beautiful consort who seems to move away from him in revulsion. Once the stories are recognized, it is obvious that, like Himalayan artists, Indian

(cont. p. 297)

Cat. no. 63

Devi

This eight-armed female deity sits with her legs splayed on top of an owl with outstretched wings, between two rampant lions. Unfortunately, four of the goddess' arms are broken off, but one of them probably held up a sword, and two may have rested on her legs. Of the four that remain, one holds an hourglass-shaped drum (*damaru*) while the other grasps a shield. The main pair of arms is raised and originally made one of two possible gestures. Her index fingers may have been inserted into the corners of her mouth in a gesture of astonishment or, more likely, wrath. This gesture is close to that of another horrific female deity, Chamunda, who picks out of her teeth the blood and flesh of sacrifices she has consumed. Alternatively, like other known sculptures of Hindu female deities, she may have been holding entrails up to her mouth.[1] The owl is the vehicle of Chamunda (cat. no. 64) and of other Hindu Tantric female deities.[2] Whichever form of the goddess this represents, the sculpture demonstrates that wrathful imagery was not confined to male deities. Both Himalayan and South Asian art (as well as Southeast Asian) include many examples of the female demonic divine.

(note p. 298)

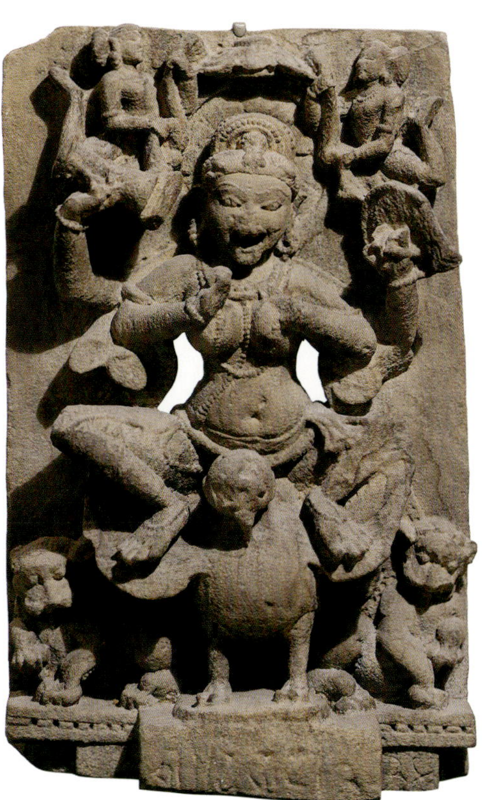

Cat. no. 63
Devi

India, 10th c.
Stone
H. 19¼ in. (48.9 cm)
Collection of Michael Cohn, New York

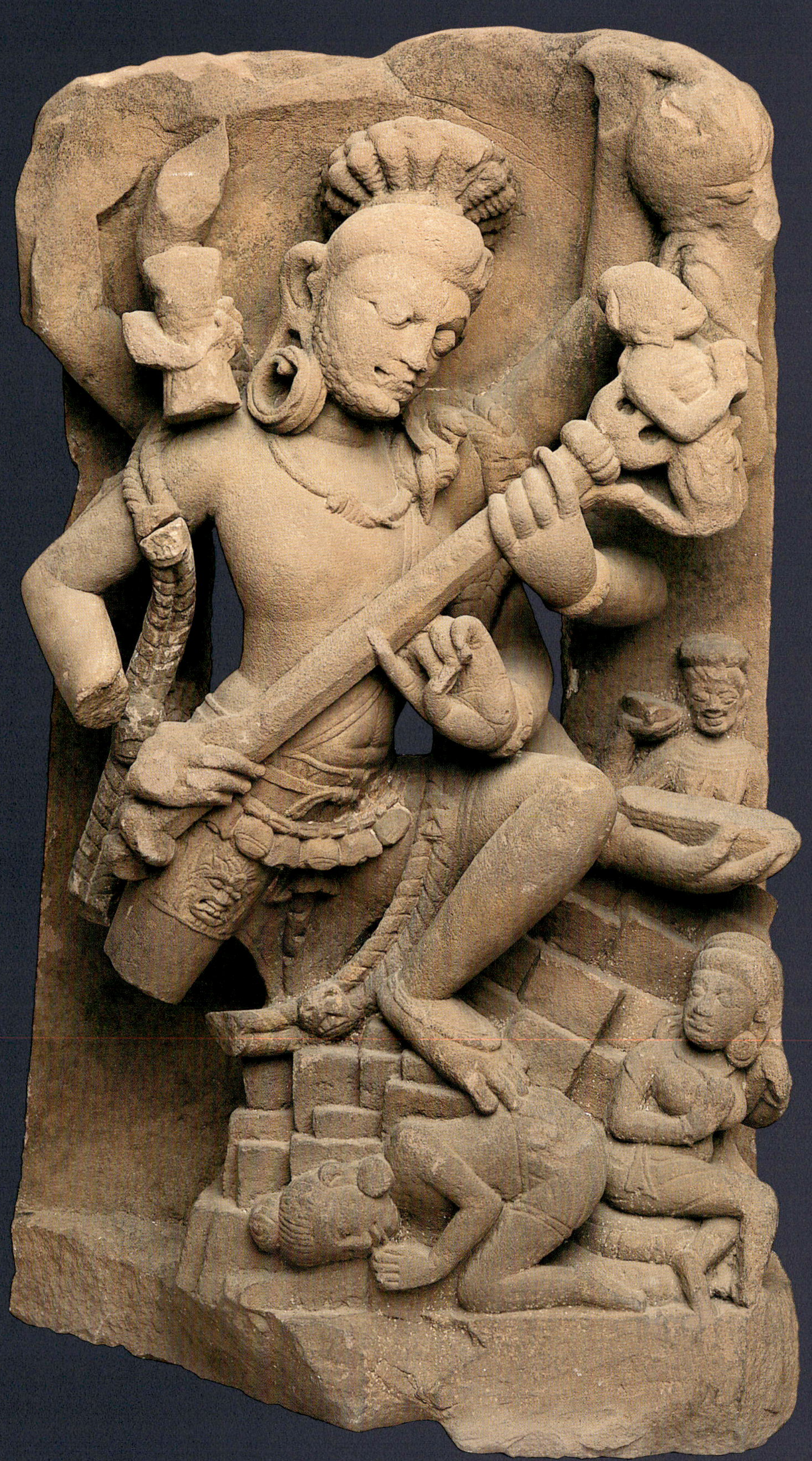

Cat. no. 62

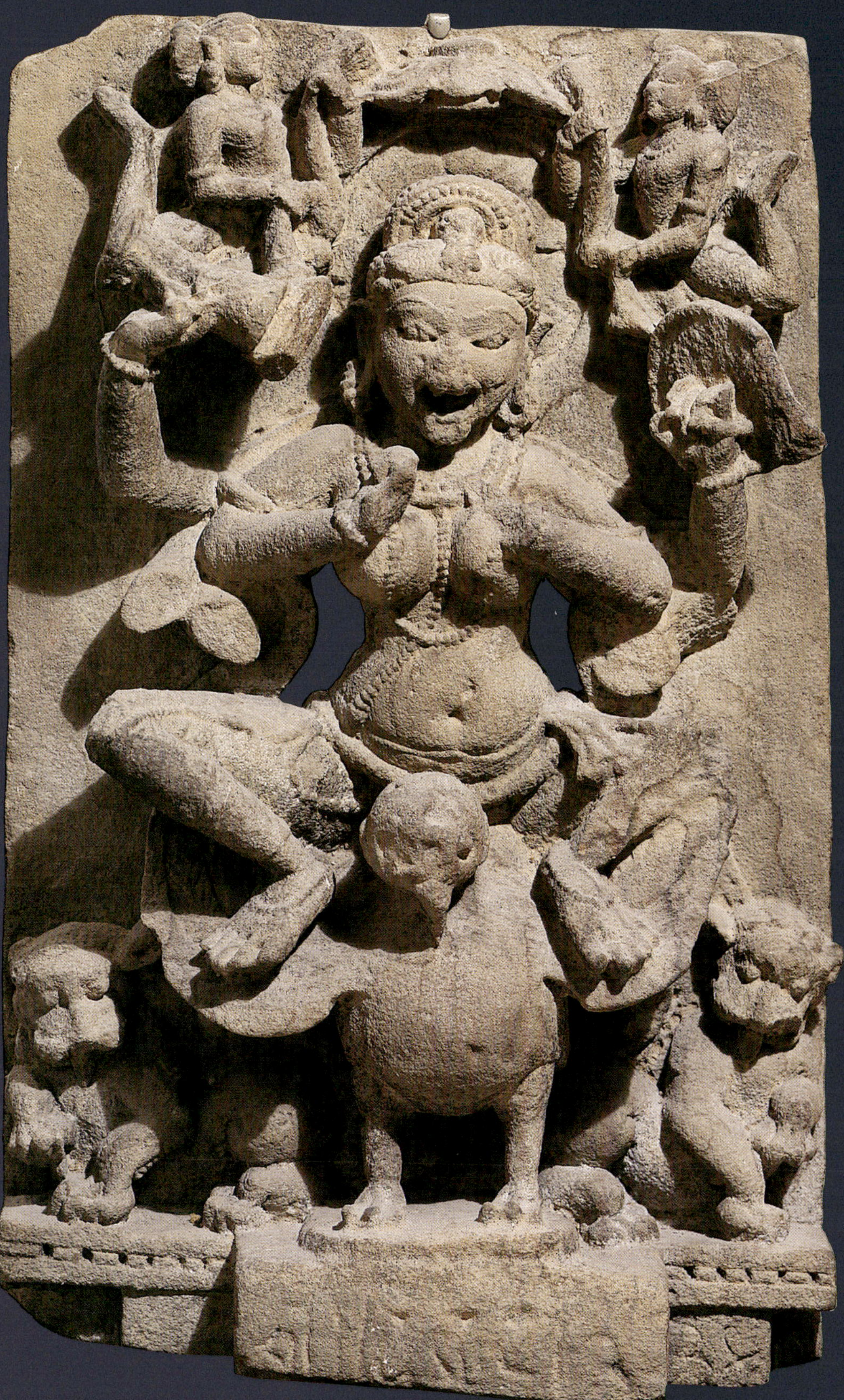

Cat. no. 64

Page from an artist's manual

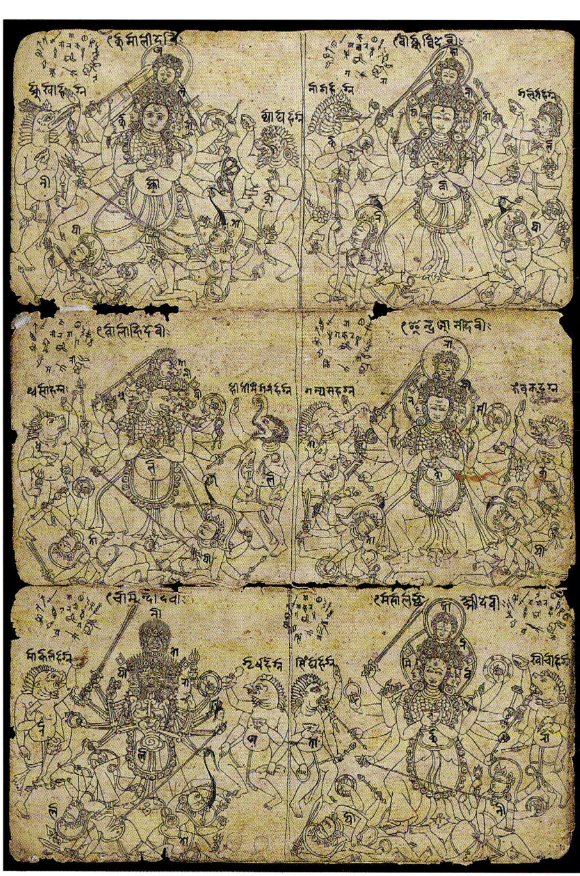

Cat. no. 64
Page from an artist's manual

Nepal, 18th–19th c.
Ink on paper
16¾ x 11½ in. (42.5 x 29.2 cm)
C2003.10.1 (HA 65238)

This Nepalese artist's manual is constructed of accordion-folded paper leaves, and contains drawing made with a pen in sooty black ink.[1] The figures are oriented so that two or more leaves can be unfolded to form a continuous composition of two or three pages. Almost all the images are of Hindu deities (one composition bears a Buddha image), arranged in sets, so if an artist is called on to reproduce relatively obscure iconography, these drawings could act as an aide-mémoire. The Rubin Museum of Art has seven leaves in all, with drawing on both sides.

The three leaves exhibited catalog the iconography of six Hindu goddesses, all ten-armed and five-headed with animal-headed attendants. Each tramples what appear to be the same demon-warriors. Above and to the left of each drawing of a goddess is an abbreviated sketch plan of the attributes held in the goddess's hands, corresponding only roughly to the actual drawing. Short titles identify the names of the gods, while the single letters of *devanagari* script on or next to the various figures are no doubt color notations, abbreviations of words signifying the color in which the figure should appear.

The drawing of Chamunda (see detail) is one of the most vivid of the group, which includes Varahi, the sow-faced goddess who is, like Chamunda, one of the Sapta Matrika, or seven mothers. Chamunda is frequently found as an independent goddess in the Kathmandu Valley, as well as in other regions of India. She is "the personification of the Goddess' wrath in the *Devimahatmya* and fights on her behalf; she is also the personification of death."[2] Here she pulls out the ropelike intestines of the four-armed demon under her left foot, reinforcing the ghoulish thirst for blood that her origin stories recount.[3] The two demons being trampled are either Chanda and Munda, or Sumbha and Nisumbha, both pairs of whom figure in those same *puranic* accounts. Like the Lords of the Charnel

(cont. p. 298)

Cat. no. 64, detail

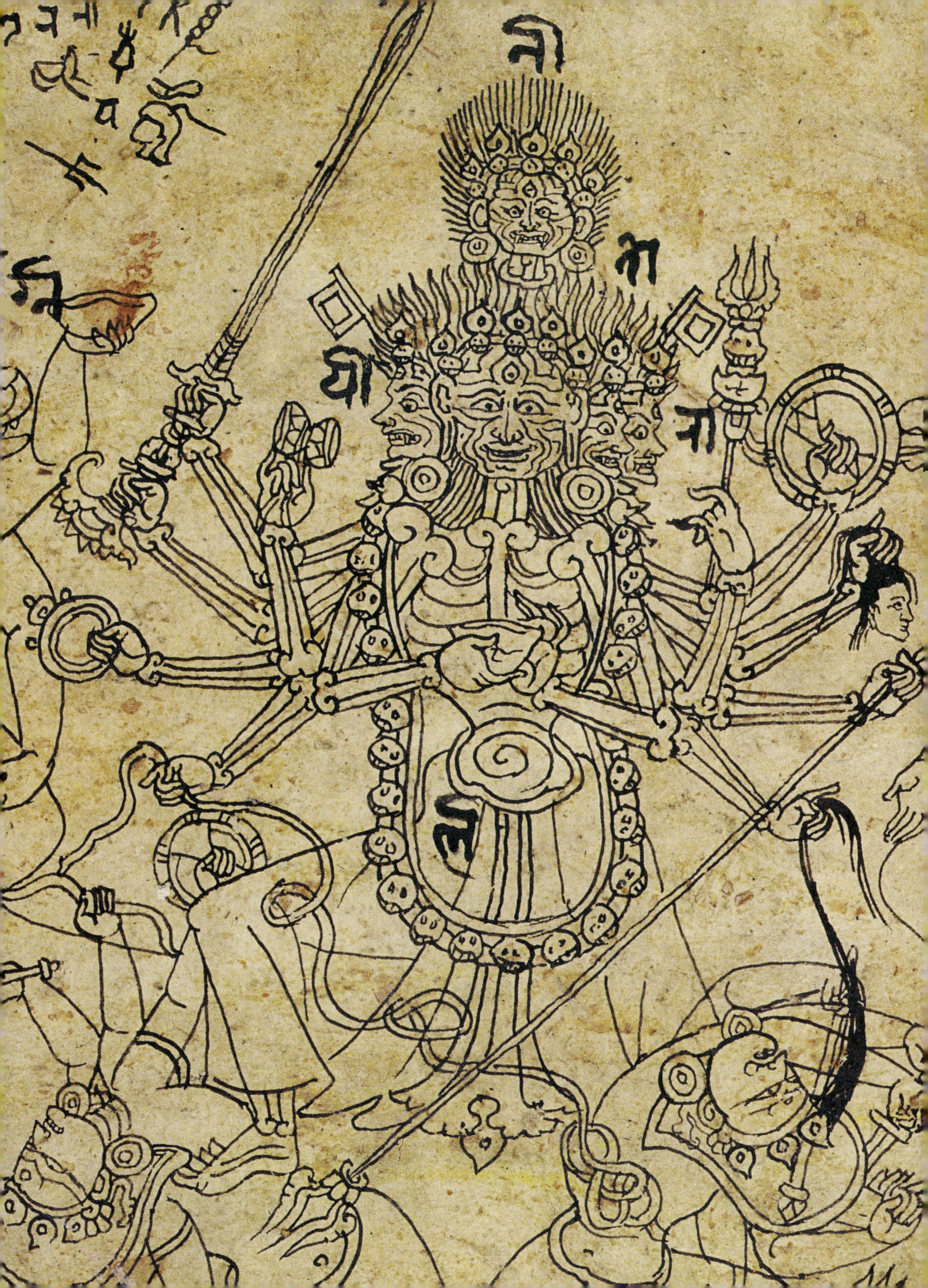

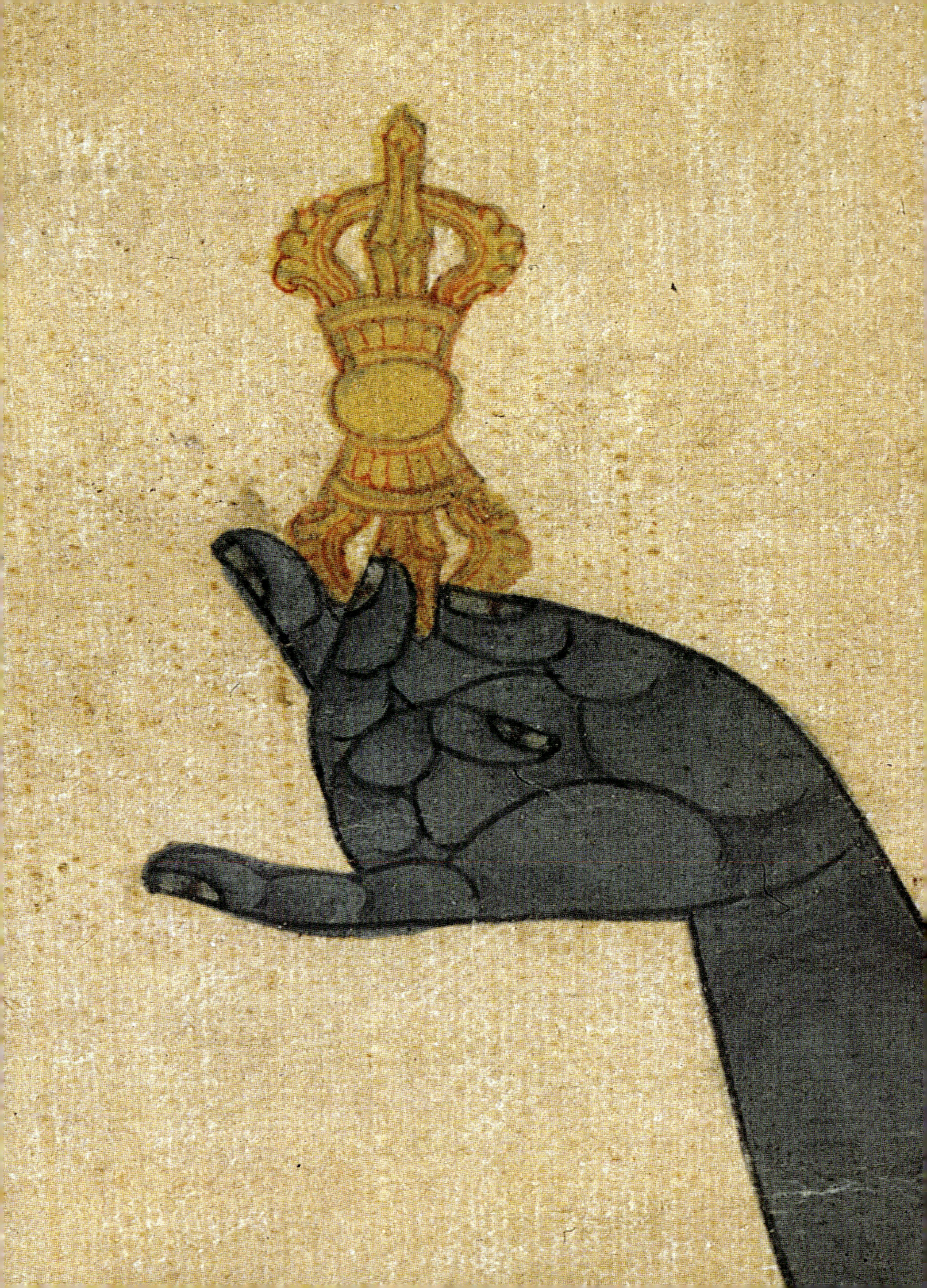

Equivalence of Form: Beyond Wrathful and Peaceful Identity

A crucial feature of Himalayan art is most liable to be misunderstood by those unfamiliar with the theme of the demonic divine. Wrathful qualities do not convey demonic identity. Wrath is directed against the enemies of enlightenment, not against the faithful. Wrathful deities are not malignant, but are pacific and ultimately benign in intent. Therefore, deities such as the bodhisattva Vajrapani have both a peaceful and a wrathful form. Neither form is necessarily "truer" than the other. One emphasizes compassion, and another emphasizes wisdom or power, but both are aimed at the same goal. The appearances of pacific and wrathful are not binaries indicating "good" and "evil." As discussed in part 5 of the introductory essay by Linrothe, many other deities, including Padmasambhava, Manjushri, and the Buddha Amitabha, have both peaceful and wrathful forms.

Cat. no. 66, detail

Cat. no. 65

Vajrapani

This is the same bearer of the *vajra* as the modest figure who sits placidly beneath a tree on a rock (cat. no. 66), the Bodhisattva Vajrapani. The two visions could not be more different. The wrathful one is naked but for scarves turbulent from the energy radiating from within him, the flayed skin of a tiger tied insouciantly around his hips, and the scraped skin of a white elephant draped over his shoulders like a cape. Corpulent instead of slender, bearded and aggressive instead of almost androgynously gentle, the two visions are fundamentally identical in conveying wisdom in action.

The dark blue wrathful Vajrapani holds his green consort to him with his left arm. She is dark green, wearing only jeweled chains around her waist, a fillet, anklets, armlets, and bracelets. With a furrowed brow, her open mouth revealing her curled tongue, her left leg hooked around his right thigh, she stares up at him with gleeful intensity. One of the most significant features in the painting is the group of twenty-one white, blue, yellow, red, and green *garudas*, flying off in all directions. In ritual descriptions, Vajrapani is said to emanate *garudas* as his messengers from his pores, exactly what we see here.[1]

The flaming nimbus enclosing them overlaps with the second of two upper registers featuring deities and teachers dressed in early, Kadampa-style hats usually associated with Atisha Dipamkara Shrijnana (b. 972/82). Vajradhara at the center has Vajrayogini on his right and the solitary Vajrapani on his left. There are a number of resemblances between this painting and Rechungpa's five-deity Vajrapani mandala, of which it might be an "implied" version.[2] If that is the case, then the white-robed figure, second from the left, is Rechungpa himself (twelfth century). Each of these two upper registers floats on a shared ground line, and the side figures are similarly ruled off from the central figure with a thin line. The blue background, with thin gold lines, continues "behind" the line, so the figures are both abstractly set off from the main

(cont. p. 298)

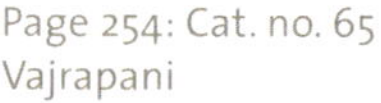

Page 254: Cat. no. 65
Vajrapani

Tibet, early 15th c.
Mineral pigments on cloth
17¼ x 16¼ in. (43.8 x 41.3 cm)
Collection of Shelley
and Donald Rubin (HA 11)

Cat. no. 65, detail

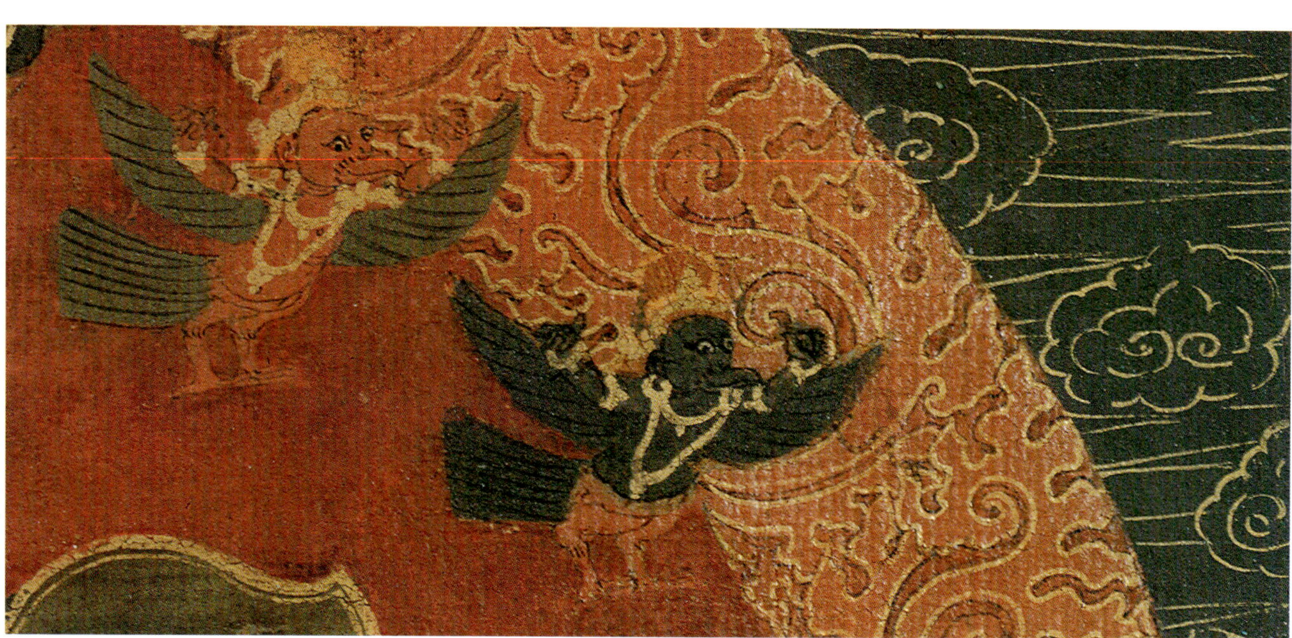

Cat. no. 66

Vajrapani

With a richly contrasting scarlet *dhoti* (wrapped skirt) and dark blue skin, the bodhisattva sits calmly on a blue-and-green rock beneath a tree with overhanging branches. His hair is pulled onto the top of his head in a *chignon*, and in his right hand he holds up a golden *vajra* (see detail), the other palm resting lightly on the rock. The posture is very relaxed and the setting peaceful, with his torso silhouetted against the blank background. The treatment of the background and the landscape features are transformations of Chinese painting elements by Tibetan artists.

A contemporary scholar has suggested that the composition of this painting probably belongs to a painted set of eight great bodhisattvas commissioned by Situ Panchen Chokyi Jungne (1700–74) about 1732.[1] This painting is a later rendition based on the earlier set, maintaining the basic composition, coloration, and posture of the bodhisattva. However, the landscape elements have become stiffer and more hard-edged.

In the art of Esoteric Buddhism (Vajrayana), particularly in the Himalayan region, the wrathful forms of Vajrapani are perhaps more frequently encountered than the peaceful ones. In India, however, peaceful forms are found in the major Mahayana caves such as Aurangabad and Ellora, as well as in free-standing sculpture in Eastern India. As in this painting, the form typically holds up a *vajra* in the right hand, or it rests on top of a lotus the stem of which is held in the hand.[2] The resort to a peaceful form of Vajrapani reveals something of an antiquarian knowledge and experience on the part of Situ Panchen, as well as intimate knowledge of a variety of texts, both *sutra* and *tantra*. It is no wonder he is described as a "great scholar and connoisseur . . . he is said to have designed and sponsored more than one hundred major tangkas, often executing the layouts and rough sketches himself."[3]

(notes p. 299)

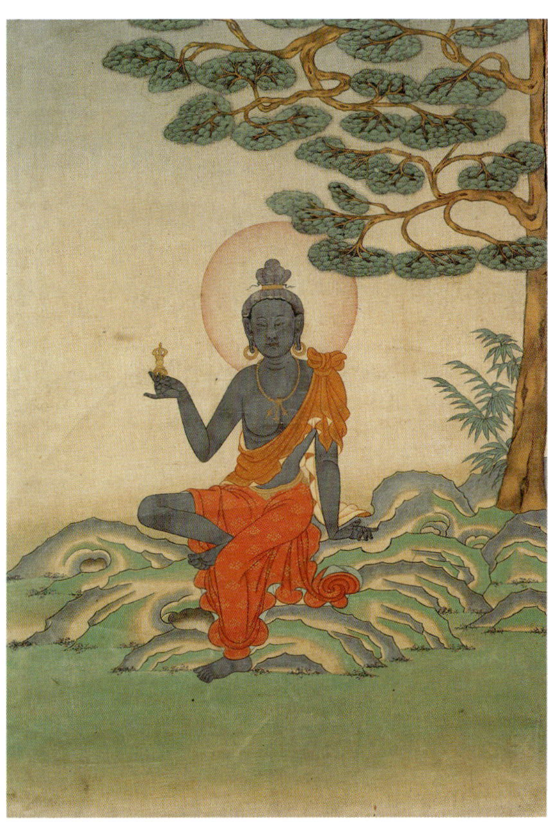

Cat. no. 66
Vajrapani, Lord of Secrets

Eastern Tibet, 19th c.
Mineral pigments on cloth
31¼ x 20½ in. (80.6 x 52.1 cm)
F1997.40.5 (HA 586)

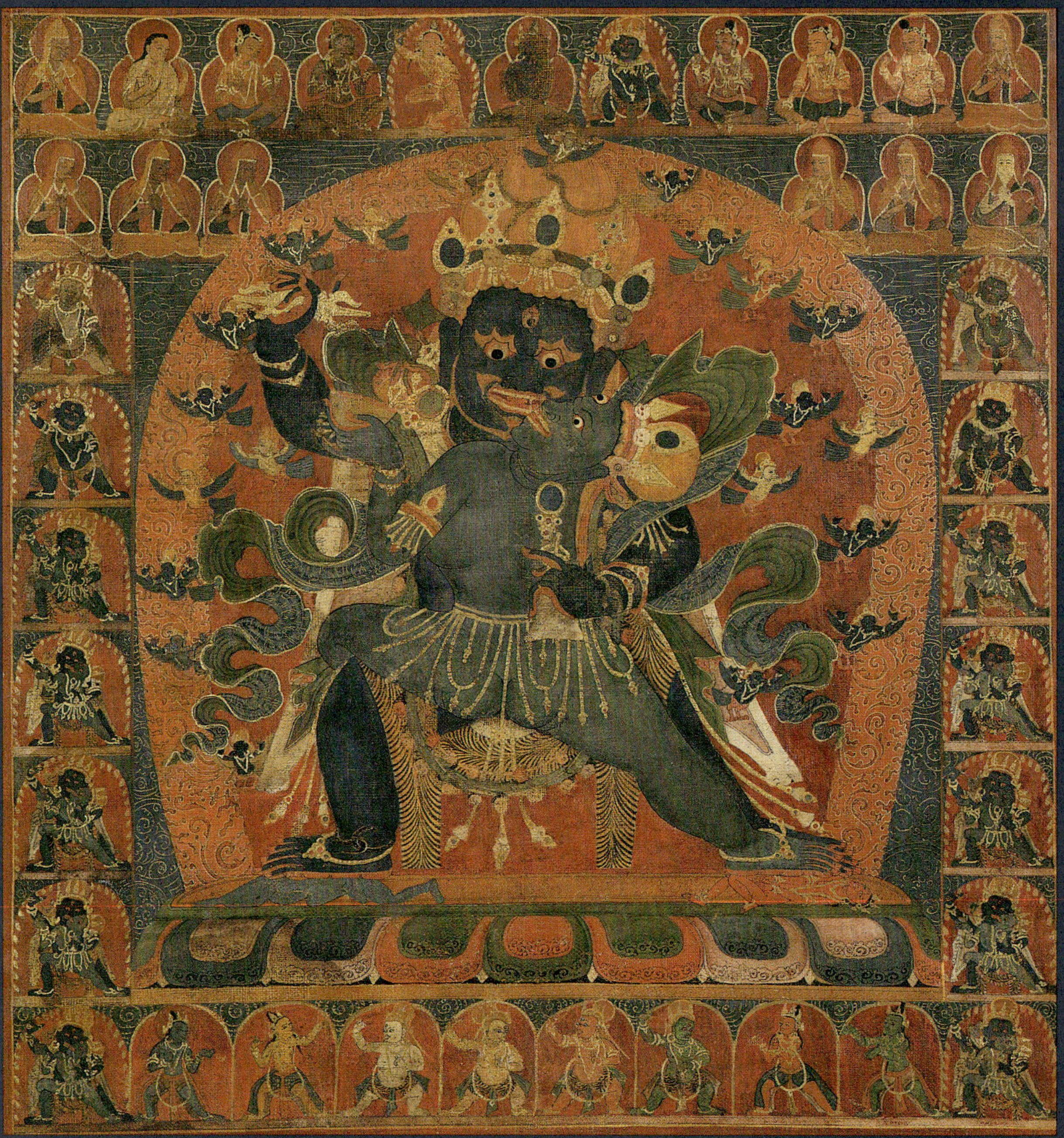

Cat. no. 65

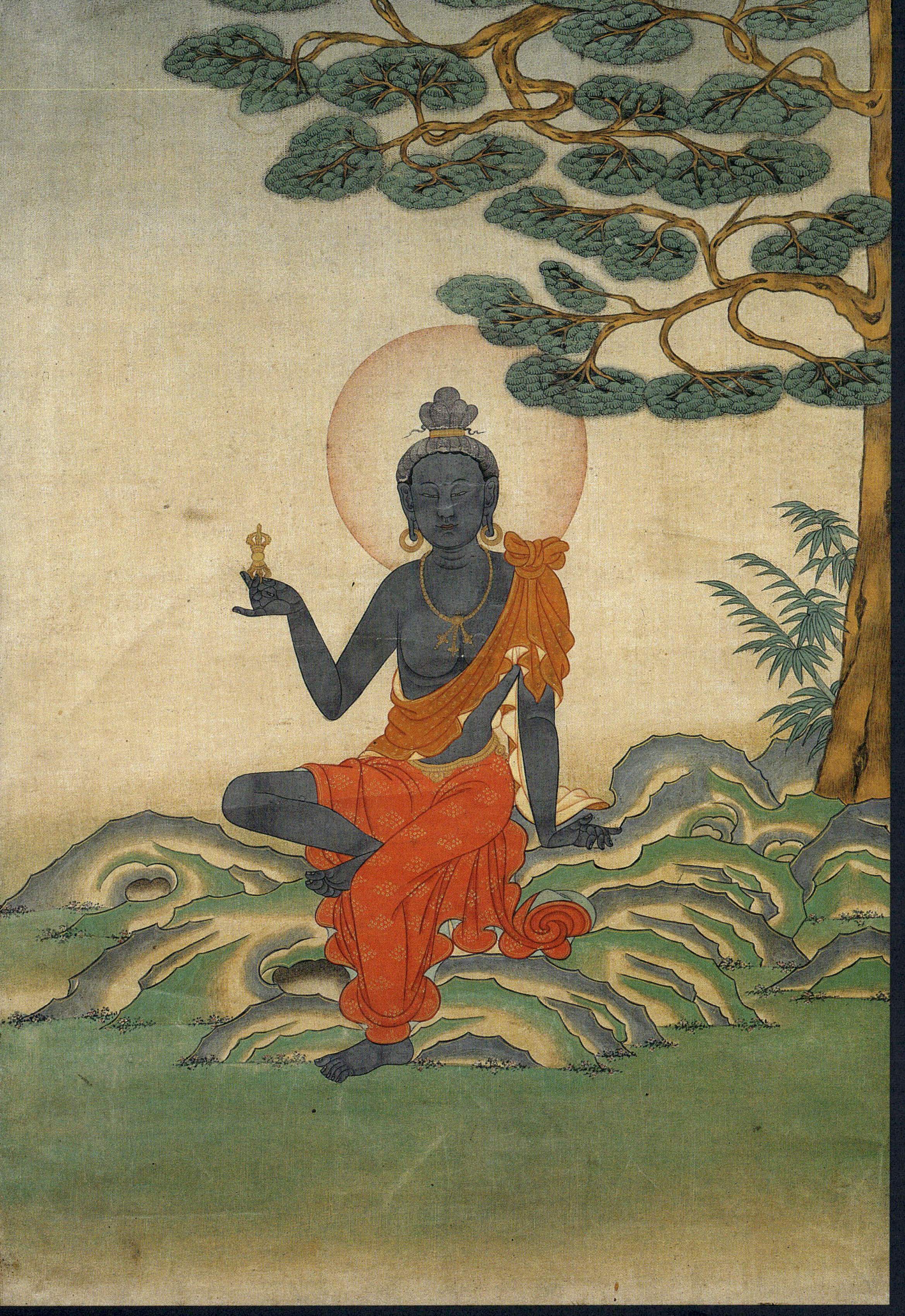

Cat. no. 66

Catalog continued

Cat. no. 1

(Cont. from p. 103) armed, and in her right hand she holds up a red-handled, *vajra*-tipped curved hook, known as an elephant-goad (*ankusha*). With the use of such an instrument, obstacles in the form of demons are summoned and dragged forth.[2] With the other hand she exposes them to a mirror, in which their villainous deeds will be reflected back at them, along with the natural, or true, state of being.[3] Interestingly, Durtro Lhamo herself is an oath-bound protector who has been converted from her formerly demonic behavior. This conversion was accomplished by the great teacher and wizard, progenitor of the Nyingma lineage, Padmasambhava, who lived in the eighth century. He appears in the top register, directly above Durtro Lhamo, accompanied by his two consorts who appear as if within golden orbs. Yeshe Tsogyal, his Tibetan consort, appears on his right holding a skull bowl, and Mandarava with a long-life vase containing *amrita*, the nectar of longevity, is on his left.

Reinforcing the connection with Padmasambhava is the maroon wrathful figure in the upper left corner, holding a *vajra* and scorpion. This is Guru Dragpo, one of the meditational forms of Padmasambhava. In the other corner is a blue-skinned female figure with a lion head, whose name, Simhamukha, simply describes that fact: "lion face." Simhamukha is frequently encountered in Sakya, Kagyu, and Gelug lineage contexts, where she is considered an important Wrathful Buddha. Although her form and attributes there are identical, in this Nyingma context she represents instead the secret form of Padmasambhava. Thus, the triad at the top of Padmasambhava, Guru Dragpo on his right and Simhamukha on his left represent the outer, inner, and secret forms of Padmasambhava, respectively.

This is a black-ground painting (*nag-tang*; see Linrothe essay, part 6), on which most of the drawing is in gold lines. A few dark-hued colors have been added to model or create highlights. The skin of Durtro Lhamo and Guru Dragpo, for instance, has been shaded with a deep maroon-brown, as have the flames surrounding most of the figures. White has been applied to the skulls on crown, teeth and eyes of Durtro Lhamo and the horse-riding retinue figure, as well as to the bowl in Padmasambhava's (but not Yeshe Tsogyal's) hand. The use of blue is particularly subtle and adept. It is applied effectively on the hem of Durtro Lhamo's robe to create the illusion of a silvery mirror, on the skull bowls below the lotus dais, and as spots or scales on the *nagini*'s serpent body. The landscape setting is another noteworthy feature of this painting. A wide repertoire of mountain types—jagged peaks, snow-capped hills, flat-topped mesas—are scattered here and there between the figures, suggesting a hallucinogenic world flashing from one scene to the next in nightmarish intensity.

Notes

1. "Zombie" is a translation of the Sanskrit term *vetali*, which means a corpse that has been partially revived through supernatural power. The names of the main figure and the seven retinue figures were originally inscribed next to them. Some of the inscriptions are no longer legible. The central figure was inscribed with "*dur khrod lha mo*." Only the last letter of the name of the goddess at upper left (see detail) remains: ". . . ring." Below her, the figure riding the zombie holding two *purba*s (ritual daggers) is inscribed "*de mo ngan ne ma*" (The Exultant Awful Female); the figure riding the horse at the lower center is inscribed "*zur ra ra skyes*;" the one in the right corner, "*gnod spyin ngan ne ma*," (The Awful Yakshi); the one with a sheep's head near Durtro Lhamo's left foot, "*shan pa ra mgo*" (The Sheep Headed Butcher).
2. For instance, in an early Nyingma text on Vajrakila, the "messenger goddess" Vajrangkusha is described as "the messenger with the iron hook drags the obstacles by their hearts; think (of them) as definitely summoned . . ."; quoted in Robert Mayer and Cathy Cantwell, "Reprint: A Dunhuang Manuscript on Vajrakilaya," *Tibet Journal* 19 no. 1 (1994): 59.
3. Except for the attribute in her right hand, Durtro Lhamo's appearance in the painting corresponds well to the descriptions found in Tibetan source texts, such as that by Minling Lochen Dharmashri (1654–1718): "One Mother, Mistress of the Three Realms, with a body maroon in color, ferocious and frightful in appearance, with one face and two hands. In the right, eating the heart of an enemy, blood dripping and warm. Reflecting the Three Realms, the left holds a mirror. Wearing an upper garment of white silk, a tiger-skin lower garment and a fresh human skin cloak. Dark brown hair hanging downward, earrings, a crown of five dry skulls and a necklace of fifty fresh, a garland of bones and a long necklace; standing haughtily with the left leg extended." Minling Lochen Dharmashri, *sgrub thabs 'dod 'jo 'bum bzang* (TBRC item W18), part 2, pp. 261–62, trans. Jeff Watt. An even more relevant description from a *terma* is found in the *Rinchen Terdzo* vol.

62, pp. 91–164. The rediscovered *terma* is by Nyang Ral Nyima Ozer (1136–1204) and Padma Lingpa (1450–1521), on whom see TBRC items P364 and P1693. For quotations from other related texts for this painting, see Himalayan Art Website item 1053.

Cat. no. 2

(Cont. from p. 104) with a hook and a yak-tail fluttering in the same direction as the pennon itself.

Surrounding Dorje Legpa are his messengers: an owl, raven, dog with a red collar, wolves, and, partly obscured by the snow lion's tail, an odd-looking creature which might be a black bear or, possibly, a Yeti, the "abominable snowman." At the level of the snow lion's front legs is Dorje Legpa's principal assistant and emanation, Damchen Garwai Nagpo. He carries a blacksmith's hammer and bellows, and rides on a shaggy goat with its horns distinctively intertwined.[4] On the right, placed as a pendant to Damchen Garwai Nagpo, is the female Dorje Yudronma (She of the Vajra Turquoise Lamp) holding up a mirror and an arrow with ribbon streamers.

Below Dorje Legpa are twelve more figures, some with very imaginatively rendered mounts. Two ride on roosters, one on a crow, two more on goats, two on horses or mules, one on a lion, and one on a striped wolf. At the bottom center is a seated Damchen Nordrub Dorje Legpa with his consort. He is red, with three eyes, holding upraised in the right hand a hook (elephant goad) and in the left, a mongoose. The consort holds aloft in the left hand a long-life arrow with a white ribbon, and in the right a gold mirror with a red ribbon. With the pile of jewels, bolts of silk, coral tree, and other treasures below the seat, this couple reinforces another aspect of Dorje Legpa as Protector: that of benefactor, dispensing prosperity.

Compared to catalog number 1, and other black-ground paintings (*nag-tang*) in the exhibition, this one has considerably more color. Except for the sole of the boot, which is reserved in the black of the ground, the main figure is completely painted, albeit in a less colorful palette than a normal painting. Red and reddish-brown are used quite liberally throughout the painting, as is the somber blue. The artist has contrived the flames and clouds to move diagonally toward the upper right, as if whipped by the movement of the snow lion on the left. The one prominent exception is the pennon fluttering above Dorje Legpa's head, which blows contrarily in the same direction that the snow lion walks. There are no indications of landscape or setting whatsoever, nor are there any inscriptions on the front or the back.

Notes

1. This identification refines the provisional designation of "Protector, perhaps Pehar," in Marylin M. Rhie and Robert A. F. Thurman, *Worlds of Transformation: Tibetan Art of Wisdom and Compassion* (New York: Tibet House, 1999), cat. no. 81. Compare the image with that of a contemporary painting in Do Khyentse Hungkar Dorje et al., *Tangkas in Golog: The Tangka Album of Lung-ngon Monastery* (Beijing: Encyclopedia of China Publishing, 2001), pp. 202–03.
2. Dorje Legpa "is one of the three foremost protectors of the Dzogchen teachings maintained by the Nyingmapa tradition, and has particular importance as a custodian of treasure-doctrines (*gter-chos*). In geographical terms, [Dorje Legpa] has associations with the Oyuk region of Tsang . . ." (Gyurme Dorje, "A Rare Series of Tibetan Banners," in Nigel Allan, ed., *Pearls of the Orient: Asian Treasures from the Wellcome Library* [London: Serindia, 2003], p. 174).
3. Translation by Jeff Watt. For more of the verse, see the Himalayan Art Website item 93.
4. For Damchen Garwai Nagpo and the rest of Dorje Legpa's retinue, see Rene de Nebesky-Wojkowitz, *Oracles and Demons of Tibet: The Cult and Iconography of the Tibetan Protective Deities* (The Hague: Mouton & Co., 1956), pp. 154–59.

Cat. no. 3

(Cont. from p. 108) (Tibetan wild ass), and the other two are mounted on buffalo.

The most interesting historical aspects of the painting are the two portraits in the sky above. On the left is the Fourteenth Karmapa Tegchog Dorje (1798–1868). Wearing his characteristic black hat, he sits on a pillow against a blue bolster holding a wealth vase with a blue pearl on its lid.[3] On the right is a long-haired lay figure wearing a blue and red hat associated with Padmasambhava and the Nyingma lineage. He holds a *terma* (treasure text) casket in his left hand, and makes the teaching gesture with his right. This is probably the famous Terton Chogyur Lingpa (1829–70) who was invited to Tsurphu, the seat of the Karma Kagyu, by the Fourteenth Karmapa.[4] It is possible that this painting was commissioned while one or both of the teachers were still alive, or perhaps shortly after their passing. At any rate, by celebrating teachers from both Karma Kagyu and Nyingma lineages, the painting hints at the ecumenical attitude for which the Fourteenth Karmapa was famous. He and Chogyur Lingpa both had an important influence on Jamgon Kongtrul (1813–99), one of the key figures in the so-called nonsectarian movement of Rimé.[5]

Notes

1. For Choying Dorje, see the section on paintings in Ulrich von Schroeder, *Buddhist Sculptures in Tibet*, vol. 2: *Tibet & China* (Hong Kong: Visual Dharma, 2001), pp. 808–19; Karl Debreczeny, "The Buddha's Law Among the 'Jang: The 10th Karma-pa's Development of his 'Chinese-Style Thangka Painting' in the Kingdom of Lijiang," *Orientations* 34, no. 4 (2003): 46–52. For Chokyi Jungne and his self-described interest and exposure to Chinese style art, see David Jackson, "Si tu Pan chen and the Thangka Treasures of Palpung: The Great Eighteenth-Century Lama Connoisseur and His Revival of Buddhist Painting in Eastern Tibet," in press, mss. June 2003.
2. This information was kindly provided by Tudeng Nima Rinpoche (Alak Zenkar Rinpoche). Personal communication, April 2004.
3. Compare the portraits of the Fourteenth Karmapa in Kagyu Thubten Chöling Publications Committee, *Karmapa: The Sacred Prophecy* (Wappinger Falls: Kagyu Thubten Chöling, 1999), p. 40; and Himalayan Art Website item 687.
4. For short biographies of Tegchog Dorje, see Karma Thinley Rinpoche, *The History of the Sixteen Karmapas of Tibet* (Boulder: Prajna Press, 1980), 121–22; Nik Douglas and Meryl White, *Karmapa: The Black Hat Lama of Tibet* (London: Luzac & Company, 1976), pp. 99–100; and Kagyu Thubten Chöling, *Karmapa*, p. 41. For an image of Chogyur Lingpa that is close in many respects to the one in cat. no. 3, see Himalayan Art Website item 15531.
5. For Jamgon Kongtrul, see E. Gene Smith, "Jam mgon Kong sprul and the Nonsectarian Movement," in E. Gene Smith, *Among Tibetan Texts: History & Literature of the Himalayan Plateau* (Boston: Wisdom Publications, 2001), pp. 235–72; Jamgon Kongtrul Lodo Thaye, *The Autobiography of Jamgön Kongtrul: A Gem of Many Colors*, trans. Richard Barron (Ithaca: Snow Lion, 2003), esp. pp. 122–25, 146–49 (relationship with Chogyur Lingpa); and "Translators' Introduction" in Jamgon Kongtrul Lodro Thaye, *The Treasure of Knowledge, Book One: Myriad Worlds*, trans. Kalu Rinpoche Translation Group (Ithaca: Snow Lion, 2003), pp. 15–35. The Rimé movement is succinctly defined.

   Although Buddhist scholars speak of a Rimé (ris-med), or nonsectarian, movement in connection with Kyentsé, Kongtrul, Chogling and other masters of eastern Tibet, it is unlikely that these masters intended to create a movement that encompassed the various Tibetan traditions. These master were, however, unbiased in their approach to the teachings in that their interest were not directed exclusively toward the traditions to which they belonged. They collected, committed to writing, taught, and thereby preserved, revitalized, and propagated instruction lineages that encompassed every aspect of Buddhist teaching. Significantly, they did so at a time when, as a result of the policy of strict adherence to particular teachings that was followed by various schools and traditions, there was a real danger that many instruction lineages would disappear (ibid., p. 27).

   For a complete bibliography of Jamgon Kongtrul, see TBRC item P264.

Cat. no. 4

Note *(Cont. from p. 109)*

1. This identification is based on the drawing included in Sle-lung Rje-drun Bzad-pa'i-rdo-rje (b. 1697), *Dam can bstan srun rgya mtsho'i rnam . . .* (Leh: T.S. Tashigang, 1979), vol. 2, fig. 12, captioned "lho.brag.sku.lha.mkha.ri." See TBRC items W3966 and P675. Earlier editions of this source have not been checked to confirm this identity, nor has a precise textual description been found. Nevertheless, the iconography of the inscribed drawing and of the sculpture is identical, down to the position of the yak's head. This deserves further study.

Cat. no. 5

(Cont. from p. 112) kaolin clay molds and, when dry, the mask was sanded, painted, gilded, jeweled, and wigged with horsehair.[3]

The interior of this mask is lined with scraps of paper that appear to be from the twentieth century and have Chinese characters written and printed on them. It is possible that the mask was reinforced and used in dance performances in the frontier regions where the Chinese, Mongol, and Tibetan cultures overlapped.

Notes

1. Nebesky-Wojkowitz points out, "they represent Hindus. Accordingly their masks are dark brown or black, with prominent noses, often bearded and with long hair or with a hair-knot on top, as customarily worn by Indian mendicants . . . [designed to] ridicule the priesthood of Hinduism" (Rene de Nebesky-Wojkowitz, *Tibetan Religious Dances* [Delhi: Paljor Publications, 1997], p. 82).
2. Richard J. Kohn, *Lord of the Dance: The Mani Rimdu Festival in Tibet and Nepal* (Albany: SUNY Press, 2001), pp. 220–27.

3. Patricia Berger, "Buddhist Festivals in Mongolia," in Patricia Berger and Terese Tse Bartholomew, *Mongolia: The Legacy of Chinggis Khan* (San Francisco: Asian Art Museum, 1995), p. 151.

Cat. no. 6

(Cont. from p. 115) wizard or Mantradharin (see detail). They appear to be adopted from the set of four "outer retinue" figures of Panjarnata Mahakala (see Rhie's essay).[4] In this context they are Pehar's messengers, dispatched to execute his bidding. In the lower corners are two skull bowls. The one on the left contains a brown substance meant to be nectar (*amrita*), while the one on the right has red blood (*rakta*). In Esoteric Buddhist rituals and meditation, these offerings represent the transformation of the mundane into the supramundane.

Unlike some *nag-tang* that have no landscape elements (cat. no. 2), this painting shows landscape clearly. However, except for the brown clouds, the scene is relatively restrained in the use of added color. While other paintings have colored shading to enhance the impact of the landscape elements (see cat. no. 16), here only gold line and gold shading are used. A clear chronology that would allow a dating based on the presence or absence of landscape and its color in *nag-tang* has yet to be formulated. The presence of landscape, however restrained in coloration, does seem to distance the painting from most Karma Gadri-style paintings.[5] The shapes of the gold clouds, however, with cumulous puffs supported by horizontal lines, are much more like those found in the Old Menri. The gold-lined azurite green leaves surrounding the Fifth Dalai Lama at the top of the painting particularly recall Old Menri painting of the late seventeenth century.[6] A Central Tibetan attribution fits best with the thematic, religious and political aspects touched on already.

Notes

1. Marylin M. Rhie and Robert A. F. Thurman, *Worlds of Transformation: Tibetan Art of Wisdom and Compassion* (New York: Tibet House, 1999), p. 399. There are a number of accounts of the earlier origins of Pehar. See Réne de Nebesky-Wojkowitz, *Oracles and Demons of Tibet: The Cult and Iconography of the Tibetan Protective Deities* (The Hague: Mouton & Co., 1956), pp. 94–133.
2. An impressive silk appliqué featuring Dorje Dragden is found in Patricia Berger and Terese Tse Bartholomew, *Mongolia: The Legacy of Chinggis Khan* (San Francisco: Asian Art Museum, 1995), cat. no. 86, where he is described in a Tibetan inscription as "king of the gods of war."
3. Gyurme Dorje, "A Rare Series of Tibetan Banners," in Nigel Allan, ed., *Pearls of the Orient: Asian Treasures from the Wellcome Library* (London: Serindia, 2003), p. 171. For an image of the "King of Qualities" Pehar, see Himalayan Art Website item 377. It belongs to the same set as cat. nos. 7–8.
4. Examples include Himalayan Art Website items 82, 92, 135, and 497.
5. With the exception perhaps of the 18th- and 19th-century hybrid Gadri/Menri in Kham (Eastern Tibetan) painting identified by David Jackson. David Jackson, "Painting Styles in the Rubin Collection: Identifications and Clarifications," www.himalayanart.org/exhibits/david/davidj.thml, consulted 4/8/04.
6. See ibid. and Himalayan Art Website item 380.

Cat. nos. 7, 8

Notes *(Cont. from p. 120)*

1. For this "Yuthog the Elder," see TBRC item P4333. For an introduction to his role in the transmission (or creation) of the medical *tantras*, see Yuri Parfionovitch et al., *Tibetan Medical Paintings: Illustrations to the* Blue Beryl *treatise of Sangye Gyamtso (1653–1705)* (London: Serindia, 1992), p. 4. The teaching lineage for the eight protectors around Hayagriva is in Himalayan Art Website thematic set 761. For all nine members of the subset of wrathful protectors, see the upper cartouche of painting fourteen in ibid. A version of their names is given in ibid., p. 199. They can be collated with items on the Himalayan Art website, and their locations within a nine-deity mandala, as follows (direction, name, Himalayan Art Project item number):
   1. Center: Zhanglon (Shanglon Gonpo; Mahakala Nujin Chenpo Dorje Dudul), 77909
   2. East: Ekajati, 77910, 52448774
   3. South: Rahula, 77911, 52448752
   4. West: Chejangma (Chechang Mar, Kandroi Tsomo Che Chang), 77912, 52448769, and 192 (cat. no. 7)
   5. North: Nujin Shanpa Marpo, 77913, 52448770
   6. Southeast: Soki Putri (Damchen Soggi Putri), 77914, 52448773
   7. Southwest: Jigche (Jigje Mar, Sinpo Dradul), 77915, 52448771, and 193 (cat. no. 8)
   8. Northwest: Shanti Rozenma (Du Shanti Rozendu), 77916, 52448768
   9. Northeast: Hab-se (Sogdag Hose), 77917, 52448772, 90186
2. Himalayan Art Website item 377.
3. The inscription reads: "*snga yas sman kyi bla ma.*"
4. The inscription reads: "*srid skyong snga kyas brgya mthso na mo.*" Although the portrait resembles in many respects other known depictions of Sanggye Gyatso, and the inscription actually names him, the use of the term *si kyong* is not common for him. E. Gene Smith has suggested that this is probably an abbreviated form of a longer title (personal communication, April 2004.) For portraits of Sanggye Gyatso, see

the frontispiece to Parfionovitch, *Tibetan Medical Paintings*, p. viii, and Himalayan Art website item 74196. Cat. no. 8 was also published and discussed in Marylin M. Rhie and Robert A. F. Thurman, *Worlds of Transformation: Tibetan Art of Wisdom and Compassion* (New York: Tibet House New York, 1999), cat. no. 150, pp. 394–96; both cat. nos. 7 and 8 were published by Glenn H. Mullin, *Female Buddhas: Women of Enlightenment in Tibetan Mystical Art* (Santa Fe: Clear Light Publishers, 2003), pp. 194–97. Another unusual feature of the portrait is the depiction of Sanggye Gyatso as an emanation of Manjushri, where normally he is considered an emanation of Vajrapani.

5. Catalog number 7: "*mkhro' ci spyang.*" Catalog number 8: "*srin po dgra 'dul.*" On the back of catalog number 7: "*pad dkar star bsngags pad 'byung gyu thug pa'i' thugs rje'i las byung phan gde'i bstan pa'i srog min nub phyog bcur kun tu rgyas mdzad pa mkha' gro yongs kyi pho nya rten 'dir bzhugs.*" On the back of catalog number 8: "*zhi ba rnyes kyang drag po'i rnam rol 'bar byams sdang bral yang tshar bcad rjes 'dzin gyi gtum drag ros pa'i mo las mdzad phyogs bcur nyul srin po'i dbang phyug rten 'dir brtan par bzhugs.*"

Cat. no. 9

Note (Cont. from p. 123)

1. Janet Baker, *Seeking Immortality: Chinese Tomb Sculpture from the Schloss Collection* (Santa Ana, Cal.: The Bowers Museum of Cultural Art, 1996), p. 53.

Cat. nos. 10, 11, 12

(Cont. from p. 129) painted and decorated offering cakes made of barley flour and butter presented to wrathful deities in Buddhist rituals. To either side are offerings of the sense organs and objects to delight the senses. Each of the skull bowls is propped up by three heads, one freshly severed, one that is blue to indicate decomposing flesh, and one dried skull. The bowl on the right is filled with sense organs (eyes, ears, tongue, nose, and heart), while the left bowl contains the "five meats" (buffalo, elephant, horse, human, and dog). The offerings of the five meats are understood as representing five psycho-emotional states which are transformed into the five wisdoms. Between the two skull bowls are offerings of objects delighting the senses (mirror, cymbals, conch with scented water, fruit, and flower). Together, they represent outer, inner, and secret offering sacraments.[10]

The landscape setting of catalog number 12 incorporates a pierced, foraminate rock with blue bamboo, overhanging the bank of a stream, a theme common in Chinese paintings, carpets, and other media. The sky color is gradient, from dark at the top to a much lighter shade above the tips of the mountain forms. The blue and dusky-green clouds on which Vajrapani and White Tara sit are hard-edged and set up a repeating pattern. It is difficult to locate the painting regionally. It could have been painted in Central Tibet or Amdo, and most likely dates from the late nineteenth or even early twentieth century.[11] The faces of the two peaceful deities, White Tara and Vasudhara, are a little slack or bland. By contrast, the wrathful deities are painted with verve and imagination, as if the artist was inspired by the dramatic wrathful themes. For instance, the eyes of the skulls in the crowns are synchronized in the direction in which they look, creating an alternating rhythm, admittedly a stock feature for skull garlands. Nevertheless, the painting demonstrates that there is still much to admire in later paintings.

Notes

1. The name *Chitipati* can be traced as far back as a Sanskrit version in the pantheon of 300 by Rolpai Dorje (1717–86). See Himalayan Art Website item 78353.
2. Martin Willson and Martin Brauen, *Deities of Tibetan Buddhism* (Boston: Wisdom Publications, 2000), p. 373.
3. From *Sakya Kangso*, (folios 44a to 46a), translated by Jeff Watt, Vancouver, B.C., August 1992.
4. The Sanskrit text titled *Shri smashana adhipati guhya chitta chakra tantra* is accepted by the Sakya lineage as a translation from Sanskrit and has been in use since teachings on Chitipati were conveyed to Sachen Kunga Nyingpo (1092–1158) by Gwa Lotsava (1110–1170). The *tantra* seems to have been transmitted to Tibet by the Indian Vairochana Rakshita and written down by Dzim Lotsawa. A *sadhana* related to the *tantra*, *Smashana adhipati sadhanam nama*, comes from the same sources. A third text includes notes for practitioners on the *sadhana*. These three texts were taught to Sachen Kunga Nyingpo, who himself wrote a commentary, as did, much later, Zhuchen Tsultrim Rinchen (1697–1774), editor of the Dege Kangyur who wrote on the *tantra*, *sadhana*, and composed notes on how to do a practice and retreat on Chitipati. As the editor of the Dege Parkhang Tangyur, he knew Sachen Kunga Nyingpo's commentary, and probably the *sadhana* by Taranatha. In the Palace Monastery Dzongsar edition, Sachen Kunga Nyingpo's text is included immediately following the other three (*tantra*, *sadhana*, notes). The lineage of these teachings begins as follows: Vajradhara, Vajrayogini, Padmavajra, Shri Vajra Rahula, Lalitavajra, Jnanasiddhi, Shri Samayavajra, Chime Lodro Zangpo,

Vairochana, Khampa Gwa Lotsawa, Lama Sakyapa Chenpo, etc. The root *tantra* has eight chapters: History, Root *Sadhana*, Activities, Reversal, Receiving Attainments, Extreme Activities, Inducing with Praise, and Conclusion. The second chapter contains instructions for the creation of a painting of Chitipati, and deserves fuller study.

5. See the description from *Ngor Kangso:*

   From a transformation of that are the two, Shri [Smashana Adipati], Father Mother, with bodies white in colour and having a very frightful skeleton form, shining forth with rays of light; staring eyes, curled tongue, faces with bared fangs. The right hands hold aloft to the sky sticks of dry bone, and the left hold skullcups of blood to the heart; [they are] drinking, [and wear] a crown of five dry human skulls, twisted jewel earrings, with a lower garment of various silks. The two feet are in dancing postures standing in the middle of a blazing fire of pristine awareness.

   From *Ngor Kangso*, (folios 35a to 38b), trans. Jeff Watt, Vancouver, B.C., August 1992.
6. An exception, in several respects, is found in catalog number 50, a Gelugpa painting in which the Chitipati appear to be holding identical attributes. See cat. key 50.14.
7. For Taranatha's text, see Willson and Brauen, *Deities*, p. 373; the other text is *Sakya Kangso*, (folios 44a to 46a), trans. Jeff Watt, Vancouver, B.C., August 1992.
8. Richard J. Kohn, *Lord of the Dance: The Mani Rimdu Festival in Tibet and Nepal* (Albany: SUNY Press, 2001), p. 205.
9. Rene de Nebesky-Wojkowitz, *Tibetan Religious Dances* (Delhi: Paljor Publications, 1997), p. 78.
10. As explained in Gyurme Dorje, "A Rare Series of Tibetan Banners," in Nigel Allan, ed., *Pearls of the Orient: Asian Treasures from the Wellcome Library* (London: Serindia, 2003), p. 163. See also Robert Beer, *The Encyclopedia of Tibetan Symbols and Motifs* (London: Serindia, 1999), pp. 194–203, 325–33.
11. The only inscriptions on the back of catalog nunber 12 are the usual "OM–AH–HUM" syllables.

Cat. no. 13

Notes *(Cont. from p. 131)*

1. *Dia de los Muertos* begins on the evening of October 31 and continues through November 2.
2. *Dia de los Muertos* is thought to have derived from a confluence of traditions including that of pre-Columbian Meso-Americans, 15th-century African slaves, and colonizing Spanish Catholics. Coordination with the Christian All Saints Day is not coincidental, but it is likely an effort to integrate indigenous holidays with the Christian liturgical calendar. Deborah Cullen, "Popular Traditions" in *Voces y Visiones: Highlights from El Museo del Bario's Permanent Collection* (New York: El Museo del Barrio 2003), p. 52.
3. Further common offerings (*ofrendas)* include money, cigarettes, chocolate bones, marzipan skulls, water, roasted corn cobs, photos, avocados, and special breads, although this list is not exhaustive.
4. See Albrecht Dürer, *Four Horsemen of the Apocalypse,* 1497–98, woodcut; www.metmuseum.org/toah/hd/durr/ho_19.73.209.htm, consulted April 2004.

Cat. no. 14

(Cont. from p. 134) as bony as those of Chitipati (cat. nos. 10–13). Belted shorts modestly clothe the pelvis, and the figure wears a crenellated cape with a necklace. Instead of the wide grin usually found on painted or sculpted skulls, the mouth is rectangular, baring enlarged, fanglike incisors. The back is fully finished, with the vertebrae indicated and cranial sutures inscribed. One of these sutures opens up into a cavity at the back of the head. The three-dimensional quality of the work is enhanced by the angular posture, balancing on one foot and extending the body into the space well beyond the dimensions of the base.

Notes

1. Zla-ba-tshe-ring et al., *Precious Deposits: Historical Relics of Tibet, China,* vol. 4, *Qing Dynasty* (Beijing: Morning Glory Publishers, 2000), pl. 62.
2. See, for instance, Richard J. Kohn, *Lord of the Dance: The Mani Rimdu Festival in Tibet and Nepal* (Albany: SUNY Press, 2001), pp. 204–6.
3. This distinction is clearly made in Rene de Nebesky-Wojkowitz, *Tibetan Religion Dances* (New Delhi: Paljor Publications, 1997), pp. 78–79.
4. Examples of Tibetan paintings with clear depictions of *dungchen*-playing include a painting from the 15th-century set of biographical paintings of Chogyal Pagpa (1235–1280) in Yang Shuwen et al., *Buddhist Thang-ka Art of Tibet: The Biographical Paintings of 'Phags-pa* (Beijing: New World Press, 1987), p. 95, and the paintings in a 17th-century set of Sakya portraits, especially the Sakya Tridzin in the Rubin collection (Himalyan Art Website item 932). A photograph probably taken in 1954 in Lhasa shows a pair of silver trumpets resting on an elaborate gilt stand with floral decor; Vladimir Sis et al., *On the Road Through Tibet* (London: Spring Books, n.d.), fig. 127. See also the images in Luther G. Jerstad, *Mani-Rimdu: Sherpa Dance-Drama* (Seattle: University of Washington Press, 1969), fig. 1, and photographs opp. pp. 112 and 128; Mario Fantin, *Mani Rimdu Nepal: The Buddhist Dance Drama of Tengpoche* (New Delhi: English Book Store, 1976), pls. 48, 101; and Clare Harris and Tsering Shakya, *Seeing Lhasa: British Depictions of the Tibetan Capital 1936–1947* (Chicago: Serindia, 2003), pp. 30–31.

Cat. no. 15

Notes (Cont. from p. 137)

1. Josef Kolmas, *The Iconography of the Derge Kanjur and Tanjur* (New Delhi: Mrs. Sharada Rani, 1978), pp. 158, 202.
2. The Palace Museum, *Cultural Relics of Tibetan Buddhism Collected in the Qing Palace* (Beijing: Forbidden City Press, 1992), cat. 83; the 15th-century Amitayus ritual text in *Tibet: Treasures from the Roof of the World*, the Tibet Museum, Lhasa, and Bowers Musuem of Cultural Art, (Santa Ana, Cal.: Bowers Museum, 2003), cat. no. 39. The most likely periods for the RMA painting is the Yongle era (1403–24), which produced an edition of the *Kangyur*, as did the Wanli period (1573–1620), the Xuande (1425–36) or the Chenghua era (1465–87), all of which had deep and direct connections with Tibet and its Buddhism. The size of this work is exactly (within millimeters) that of the Yongle edition of the Kanjur, which was 69.5 x 24.3 cm according to rGya mtsho, Karma, Phun tshogs et al., "Lasa xianzang de liangbe Yongle ba "Gan zhu er," *Wenwu* 1985, no. 9, p. 86. This reference is courtesy of Arthur Leeper. For color photographs of the Yongle edition pages, see Tsewang Rinchen, *Sera Thekchen Ling* (Beijing: Nationalities Press, 1995), p. 84. Comparison of a Panjarnata Mahakala painting of the 15th century in the Museum of Fine Arts, Boston, which should also be attributed to the Yongle period, shows many similarities of style; see Himalayan Art Website item 87211. Many features relate to Ming Yongle depictions. Compare the Panjarnata and Chaturbhuja Mahakalas in the painting with the metal sculptures of the same themes dated by inscription to the Yongle period; see Ulrich von Schroeder, *Buddhist Sculptures in Tibet*, vol. 2, *Tibet & China* (Hong Kong: Visual Dharma Publication, 2001), pls. 348A, 347A; figs. 20-3 and 20-8. An even closer comparison is between the painted Chaturbhuja Mahakala and a woodblock illustration on paper of the same theme from the printed canon of 1410; fig. 20-5.
3. Compare the arches in the 15th-century Chinese Vajrayogini in a Swiss private collection; see Jane Casey et al., *Divine Presence: Arts of India and the Himalayas* (Barcelona: Casa Asia, 2003), cat. no. 52.
4. This is the assessment of Arthur Leeper, who has made a specialized study in the book covers and whose comments and suggestions along with those of E. Gene Smith, were very helpful in considering the possible context for this painting (personal communications, April 2004). For a pair of lacquered bookcovers from the 1410 Yongle *Kangyur*, see Valrae Reynolds, *From the Sacred Realm: Treasures of Tibetan Art from the Newark Museum* (Munich: Prestel, 1999), pl. 2.

Cat. no. 16

(Cont. from p. 138) without organs, which in Indian Buddhism makes one unable to join the *sangha* as either a monk or a nun. Why this is used for a form of Mahakala is a matter of speculation. A sexless deity, neither male nor female, points in the direction of transcending duality, an apparent feature of enlightened mind.

Extraordinary details pack the painting (see detail and figs. 1.7–8, 1.10, 1.23–24). They include eerie landscapes bathed in strange light, bizarre creatures, graphic violence, and lively patterning. The artist compresses the composition tightly and then proceeds to fill the intervening space with more details. For a black-ground painting (*nag-tang*) it is quite colorful, also suggestive of a later date. So too are some of the naturalistic details such as the modeling on the skulls of the crown and amulet box (*gau*) worn by Maning. The application of color on the landscape areas is distinctive. Particularly noticeable on the lower half of the painting, the pigment is not applied solidly, stopping short of the edges or enclosing unpainted areas, allowing the ground color to come through. This, and the banded treatment of the pool of blood through which Remati's donkey walks (cat. key 16.20) resembles Bhutanese *nag-tang*, prompting the provisional attribution to Tibet or Bhutan. (Compare figs. 1.37 and 38; and see Linrothe essay, section 6, on Bhutanese *nag-tang*.)

A long lineage for this form of Mahakala begins with Samantabhadra, Chemchog, Palgon, and Padmasambhava with a consort. Samantabhadra with his consort Samantabhadri is depicted at the top center of the painting (cat. key 16.2). He is the Primordial Buddha for Nyingmapa, something like Vajradhara in other lineages. The Nyingma Wrathful Buddha, Chemchog Heruka (cat. key 16.5), is depicted just below in the role of the controller of Maning Mahakala, a role Guru Dragpo and Vajrapani play in other paintings (see cat. nos. 1–3, 17). Padmasambhava, though shown without a consort, is found both in the lineage and on the painting (cat. key 16.3).[2]

Aside from the embracing couple in the top center (cat. key 16.2), each of the figures is identified by a brief inscription beneath or beside him or her. On the reverse of the painting, behind each deity are consecration inscriptions of mantras including OM-AH-HUM written in *ranjana* (ornamental Sanskrit script, also called *lantsa*). Three of the deities (cat. key 16.12,

16.14, 16.22) have mantras transcribed in Tibetan script below the *ranjana*.

Notes

1. The full title of the central figure is The Glorious Lord of Pristine Awareness, Black Eunuch (Tibetan: *pal ye she gyi gon po ma ning nag po*). A textual description of him corresponds well to the painting:

   > Glorious Lord of Pristine Awareness, Black Eunuch, with a body blue black in color, one face and two hands. Holding aloft in the right, pointed to the sky, a flaming lance, and in the left a poisoned heart and lasso. With three round red eyes, a curled tongue and hanging black snakes for hair. Having a crown of five dry skulls and a necklace of fifty fresh. Adorned with a garland of hearts and piles of snakes, dressed in silk cloaks, black and layered. Having a gold belt and a girdle of fresh human skin. From the three doors of a great stick of sandalwood, fastened at the waist, an army of snakes is dispersed. Decorated with varieties of colorful flowing streamers and all the frightful ornaments. Standing with the left leg extended atop a corpse seat.

   From a text by Terdag Lingpa Gyurme Dorje (1646–1714) and Minling Lochen Dharmashri (1654–1718), Part II, page 121–23; TBRC item 18, trans. Jeff Watt, July 1999.
2. According the *sgrub thabs 'dod 'jo 'bum bzang*, p. 20, the lineage begins: Samantabhadra (Kuntu Zangpo), Chemchog, Palgon, Orgyan Yab yum, Terton Chowang, Manlungpa, Dagton, Nyenton, Sedingpa Khupon, Paljor Wangchug, Chokyi Wangpo, Karma Guru, Nyadag Trulku, Chowang Kunzang, Rigdzin Tinle Lhundrup, etc. Also see the variant lineages of Dorje Lingpa, Ratna Lingpa, Pema Lingpa and Jatson Nyingpo.

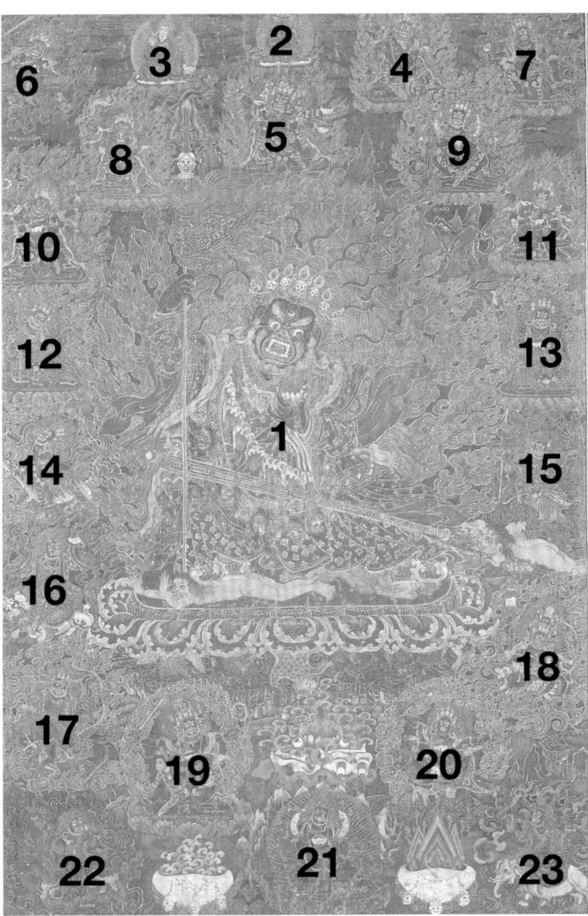

Cat. Key 16, with inscriptions under or near each figure where provided

1. Maning Mahakala, *dpal ye shes kyi mgon po chen po ma ning nag po la na mo* (Homage to the Glorious Great Lord of Pristine Awareness, Black Maning) 2. Samantabhadra (Tibetan: Kuntu Zangpo) with consort Samantabhadri, no inscription 3. Padmasambhava, *ayon* (Urgyen) 4. Vajrapani, *phyag rdor(je)* 5. Chemchog (Wrathful Blooddrinker) Heruka, *che mchog he ru ka* 6. Maroon Butcher, *gshan pa dmar nag* 7. Black Butcheress, *shan pa nag mo* 8. Ekajati, *ral cig ma* (She of the One-braid) 9. Panjarnata Mahakala, *gur mgon* 10. Shadbhuja Mahakala, *phyag drug pa* 11. Chaturbhuja Mahakala, *bya rog mtshan* (Raven-marked) 12. *Gandi*-holding Mahakala (with *phurba*), *beng can*; part of retinue of Maning 13. Kartridhara Mahakala, *gri gug* 14. Vyaghra Vahana (Tiger Riding) Mahakala, inscription no longer visible; part of retinue of Maning 15. Raudrantika Mahakala, *trag [shad]*; part of retinue of Maning 16. Legpa Nagpo, inscription no longer visible; reconstructed on basis of text: *leg pa nagpo* 17. Activity Lord Life Demon, *las mgon srog bdud*; part of retinue of Maning 18. Rahula, *ra hu la* 19. Chaturmukha Mahakala, *dpal mgon zhal* 20. Remati, *re ma ti* 21. Black Jambhala, *dzam bha la* 22. Dorje Legpa, *rdor legs [pa]*; part of retinue of Maning 23. Pehar, *bhi har*

Cat. no. 17

> *(Cont. from p. 141)* orange hair, moustache and eyebrows blazing upward, a crown of five dry human skulls, a necklace of fifty fresh blood dripping heads. Wearing a jeweled belt and a snake hanging below the stomach. Wearing felt boots . . . riding a large tall tiger with a white snow lion running behind. The right hand holds aloft a sandalwood stick (*gandi*) adorned with jewels; waving calling forth a host of heavenly soldiers. The left hand holds an iron bowl to the heart.[2]

Directly above Mahakala is Vajradhara (cat. key 17.2), his forehead just blushed with blue pigment. To Vajradhara's right is the wrathful Vajrapani holding a *vajra* and bell (cat. key 17.3). On Vajradhara's left is Padmasambhava, the eighth-century teacher and wizard, who helped to establish Buddhism in Tibet and is revered as the progenitor of the Nyingma lineage (cat. key 17.4). The transmission lineage of the text begins with these three figures.[3] In the upper left corner is Sakya Pandita Kunga Gyaltsen Pal Zangpo (1182–1251; cat. key 17.5), the Sixth Throne holder of Sakya Monastery. His presence helps to establish that this teaching which was originally Nyingma, became part of Sakya practice. The figure in the upper right corner is definitely a Sakya lama, because of the hat; he has not yet been identified (cat. key 17.6). As already mentioned, the teacher below Sakya Pandita is probably Thartse Jampa Namka Chime (cat. key 17.7), and opposite him is another unidentified lama, probably Namka Chime's student (cat. key 17.8).

Vajradhara, Vajrapani, Padmasambhava, and Sakya Pandita sit on lotus pedestals (cat. key 17.2–5). The other three lamas sit on cushioned seats and have head nimbi but not body aureoles, which may suggest that they are all living (cat. key 17.6–8). If the figure in the upper right corner (cat. key 17.6) is Namka Chime's principal teacher, the three lamas on cushioned seats would represent three direct generations of teachers and students.

Beneath Mahakala, riding on an ass through "an ocean of clotted blood with turbulent waves," is the red Shri Devi, holding a butcher's stick and a skull bowl filled with blood (cat. key 17.9). Her importance relative to most of the other attendant figures is indicated by the way her nimbus actually overlaps with the peach-colored lotus pedestal on which the tiger stands. The visualization text almost seems to be describing the other figures on this painting:

> In front of that [Shri Devi] is the Body Black Monpa holding in the right hand a trident upraised and marked with an impaled human corpse [cat. key 17.10]. The left holds aloft a spear with the black flag of the army causing terror for the demons and enemies. At the right is Mind Black Monpa, blue black, the right [hand] holding a razor and left a heart upraised, in a manner looking towards the Lord [cat. key 17.11]. . . . At the left is Speech Black Monpa, maroon, the left [hand] holds a lasso leading the [figure] of enemies and demons [cat. key 17.12]. The right blows a buffalo horn gathering the army and defeating the hosts of enemies and hindrances. . . . Behind that are seven demon Monpa [cat. key 17.20a–g) with knives and skull bowls leading a demon army of 100,000.[4]

In the lower left corner is the serpent-bodied nine-headed Dangerous Protector, Rahula (cat. key 17.19). He is part of the outer retinue, who are also identified in detail. The text refers to the seven white-turbaned black figures beside Mahakala, each waving a sword aggressively, as Monpa Nagpo, or Black Monpa (cat. key 17.20a–g). They are named after the tribal villagers in southeast areas of Tibet. In a familiar pattern of demonizing those with whom one has conflicts, Tibetans have stereotyped the Monpa as fearsome savages and project their image as minor demon-warriors of the tiger-riding Mahakala under control of three Monpa "officers" (cat. key 17.10–12).[5]

There are a noteworthy number of animals in the painting. Besides the central tiger on which Mahakala rides, leopards, panthers, a snow lion, wolves, two red-collared dogs, and black and white birds animate the charnel grounds strewn with decomposing corpses. There is even what looks like a brown rat with horns feasting on a human carcass just behind and above Rahula (cat. key 17.19).

At the bottom center of the painting is an elaborate *torma* (offering cake), which depicts the two attributes of Mahakala (*gandi*-stick and iron bowl) in miniature. To either side are skull bowls with wrathful offerings of the sense organs (left) and the "five meats" of the inner offering (see cat. no. 12). Farther to the left are offerings of the clothes, armor, helmets, and weapons for wrathful protectors, and to the right are peaceful sense offerings of sound (musical instrument), fruit (taste), and so on. Just above the skull bowl with the sense organs is a design of the eight auspicious objects (conch, vase, endless knot, pair of fish, lotus, parasol, umbrella, and wheel), symbolizing the *dharma.* Above the skull bowl with the "five meats" are offerings known as the eight auspicious substances (mirror, medicine, *durva* grass, *bilva* fruit, right-spiraling conch, bowls of curd, vermillion powder, and mustard seeds).[6]

Sustained examination of the painting reveals a subtle implied purpose which goes beyond protection. One begins to notice how many objects of wealth and treasure there are scattered throughout the background, objects such as round and square earrings, flaming jewels, rhinoceros horns, elephant tusks, and the like. In the lower right is an ugly demon, with a red gash for a mouth and *makara*-head hat bearing a tray of jewels (cat. key 17.21).

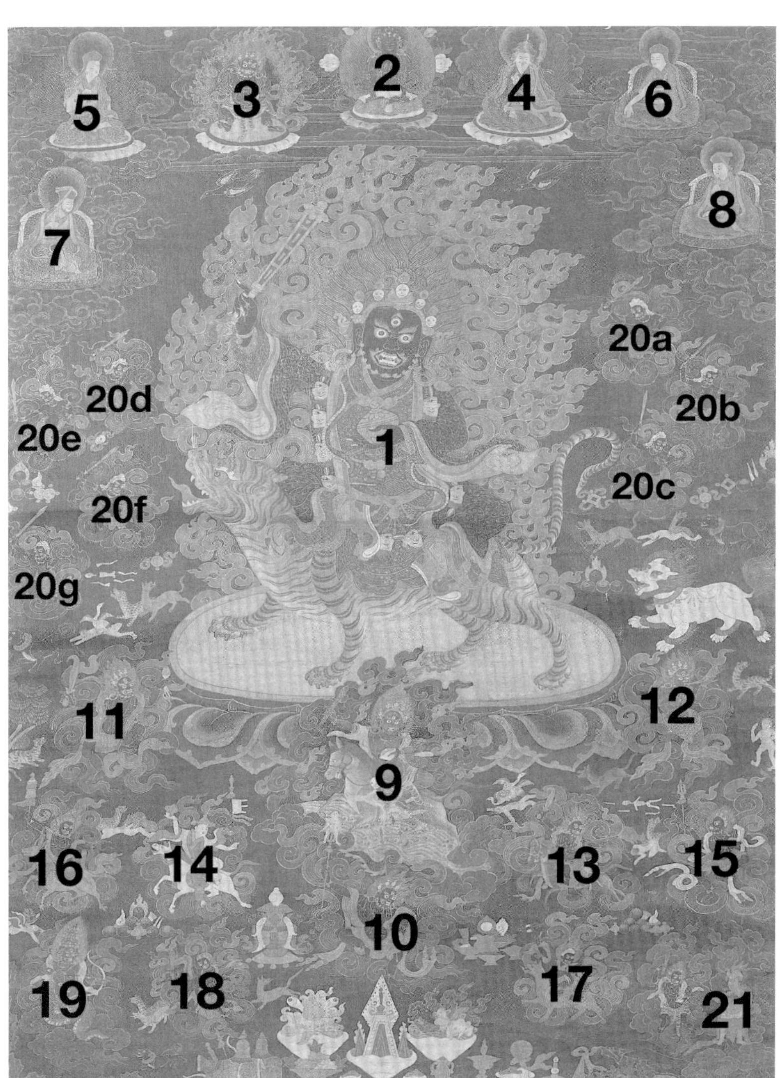

Cat. key 17

Note: retinue figures are identified by name where possible, on the basis of the text in the *Drubtab Kuntu*, not by inscriptions.

1. Vyaghra Vahana Mahakala 2. Vajradhara 3. Krodha Vajrapani 4. Padmasambhava 5. Sakya Pandita (1182–1251) 6. Unidentified Sakya lama 7. Ngorpa Thartse Jampa Namka Chime (1765–1820) 8. Unidentified Sakya Ngorpa lama 9. Shri Devi 10. Body Black Monpa 11. Mind Black Monpa 12. Speech Black Monpa 13. Dugon 14. Sogdag Odlha 15. Chagshu 16. Lugon 17. Gying Gon Dorje Legpa (see cat. no. 2) 18. Magon Dorje Derchen 19. Yangon Rahula 20a–g. Seven demon Monpa 21. Yaksha with offering jewels

With the help of the visualization text, one discovers that there is a hidden wealth deity whose presence as a retinue figure in the meditation is made explicit: "Behind [Mahakala] is the Lord of Wealth Black Jambhala holding in the right [hand] a skull bowl of blood to the heart and in the left a mongoose."[7] Since he is placed "behind" Mahakala, the frontal view of Mahakala blocks our vision of Black Jambhala, but those initiated into this practice would know he is there. The artist has indicated his hidden presence and the implied purpose of benefaction, through the rain of treasures that accumulate in the background. Nevertheless, the many graphic images of subjugation and destruction, such as the Black Monpas (17.10–12) holding up the heart of an enemy-obstruction as a trophy, impaling a corpse on a trident, and dragging a captured enemy by a rope around the neck, suggest that protection and the destruction of enemies are the paramount purposes.

Notes

1. Compare the portrait of Namkha Chime in this painting with another in the RMA collection, Himalayan Art Website item 545. He was the abbot of Ngor monastary in the late 18th century and was also a previous incarnations of Jamyang Kyentse Wangpo (1820–92).
2. *Drubtab Kuntu* (sgrub thabs kun btus), TBRC item W19221, vol. 14, pp. 355–77 on Gonpo Tagshon, the Tiger-riding Lord, trans. Jeff Watt, April 2004. See also Rene de Nebesky-Wojkowitz, *Oracles and Demons of Tibet: The Cult and Iconography of the Tibetan Protective Deities* (The Hague: Mouton & Co., 1956), p. 52. This form of Mahakala, though rare, does appear as an attendant figure on other forms of Mahakala. See cat. no. 16 and fig. 1.24; as well as Himalayan Art Website items 878, 87211, and 90553. A chapel in the Gyantse Kumbum is devoted to him; see Franco Ricca and Erberto Lo Bue, *The Great Stupa of Gyantse: A Complete Tibetan Pantheon of the Fifteenth Century* (London: Serindia, 1993), p. 239.
3. Two transmission lineages are provided in the *Drubtab Kuntu*, indicating that it was both a *kama* (oral) teaching coming from Padmasambhava, and a *terma* (treasure text). The first lineage starts: Vajradhara, Krodha Vajrapani, Acharya Padmasambhava, Shantigarbha, Rombuguhya Chanda, the Indian Krishna Heruka, Lilavajra, the Nepali Vasudhara, Drubchen Sanggye Yeshe, Terton Drawa Kunga Drag, Sei Bande Bumdrag Sumpa, Kyo Bande Tuchen, Chetsun Dode Sengge, Rongpa Galo, Che Loden Sengge, Lama Leu Chungwa, Jamyang Rinchen Gyaltsen, Kunkyen Chogyal Palzang, Ponchen Chokyong Gyaltsen, Pago Rinchen Gyaltsen, Tsarchen Losal Gyatso (1502–1566), etc. The second lineage is the Buddha, Manjushri Mitra, and continues with Chetsun Dode Sengge and the rest of the names after him in the first lineages. See *Drubtab Kuntu*, vol. 14, pp. 374–75.
4. *Drubtab Kuntu*, p. 359.
5. "Our contemporary suspicion of and antipathy for the Other, the Stranger, goes back to the fear our tribal ancestors felt towards the Outsider, seeing him as the carrier of evil, the source of misfortune." Ryszard Kapuscinski, *The Shadow of the Sun*, trans. Klara Glowczewska (New York: Alfred A. Knopf, 2001), p. 188.
6. Robert Beer, *The Encyclopedia of Tibetan Symbols and Motifs* (London: Serindia, 1999), pp. 187–92.
7. *Drubtab Kuntu*, p. 359.

Cat. no. 18

(Cont. from p. 144) Pandita indicates a scholar. He was a disciple of Ngorchen Kunga Zangpo (1382–1456) and the author of a biography of the latter.[3] Dragpa Gyaltsen does not appear in any of the common Panjara Mahakala lineages, which signals that his presence here in so prominent a position is probably due to a personal connection with the donor of the painting. That was likely to be one of his direct students, to whom he gave the Mahakala empowerments and initiations. Because he is seated on a lotus, not a cushion, it suggests he is already dead. That would provide a date of the late fifteenth century, which fits with the stylistic evidence.

The widely scrolling rinceaux enclosing the ten protectors, and flowing around the others, is reminiscent of the use of foliage in murals at the Gyantse Kumbum. However, here its use is more controlled and rationally patterned—at Gyantse it sometimes appears randomly distributed, cropping up here and there.[4] The flames at the tips of the nimbi are also more tightly constrained to the main body of flames, and are not distinguished by color or a different scrolling pattern as at Gyantse. Nevertheless, the overall look and feel of the painting, as well as the specific details of Panjarnata can be closely related to the same theme, in sculpture and painting, at Gyantse.[5] The treatment of the stiff scarf with a medallion design, closely resembles those found in the

Kumbum murals.[6]

The three versions of the standing two-armed Panjarnata Mahakala deserve comment. The two in the bottom corners (cat. key 18.5–6) stand straight legged, not in the squatting position which is more common today for Panjarnata images (compare cat. nos. 21–22). The one on the right (cat. key 18.6) does not carry the *gandi* emanation stick. Identified by inscription as the Lord of the Gayadhara lineage, he is the "original" Panjarnata, as he derives from the eighteenth chapter of the *Vajra Panjara Tantra*, which is concerned with Hevajra (cat. key 18.3). Gayadhara brought the Lamdre Virupa teachings to Tibet in 1041.[7] He and Drogmi translated the *Hevajra Tantra* and two explanatory *tantras*, including the *Vajra Panjara* in 1043.[8]

The Mahakala in the bottom left corner (cat. key 18.5 and see detail) accompanied by two monks is identified by inscription as the Vision of Nagarjuna. Himalayan Buddhists accept that there was a single Nagarjuna, a very long-lived one. Historians find this question quite vexing, as it appears to them that there were several Nagarjunas after the great Madhyamika philosopher of the second–third centuries, including ones that were more Tantric in orientation. It is not clear whether this is a vision of Nagarjuna or by Nagarjuna, but it shows the two armed Mahakala, with the *gandi* emanation stick, curved flaying knife, and skull bowl accompanied by two monks. The triad resembles many images of Shakyamuni with two disciples,

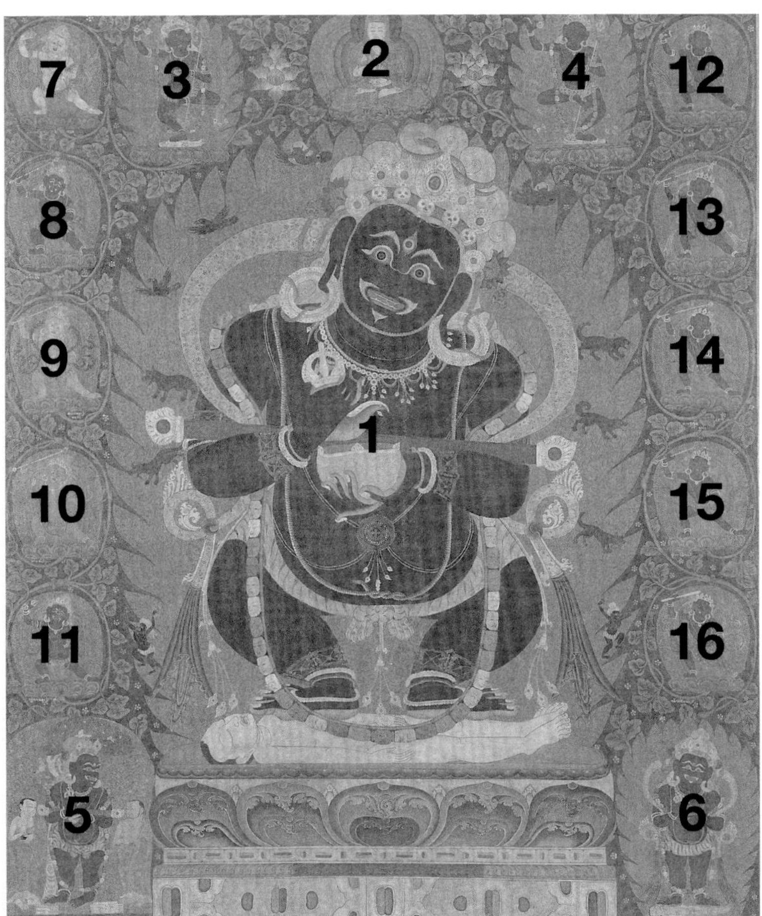

Cat. key 18, with inscriptions under each figure

1. Mahakala Panjarnata 2. Pandita Dragpa Gyaltsen, *pan di ta grags pa rgyal mtshan la na mo* 3. "Body" Hevajra, *sku rdo [rje] la na mo* 4. Nairatyma, *bdag med ma la na mo* 5. Vision of Nagarjuna, *klu grub gyi zhal zigs la na mo* 6. Mahakala Panjarnata, Lord of the Gayadhara lineage, *ga ya da ra'i lugs kyi mgon po la na mo* 7. Ushnisha Chakravartin (yellow, holds wheel), *mkhor lo sgyur ba la na mo* 8. Yamantaka (blue, holds hammer), *gshin rje'i gshed la na mo* 9. Prajnantaka (white, holds *vajra*-staff), *shes rab mthar byed la na mo* 10. Padmantaka (red, holds lotus-staff), *pad ma mthar byed la na mo* 11. Vignantaka (blue, holds *vajra*), *dgyegs mthar byed la na mo* 12. Achalanata (blue, holds sword), *mig yo ba la na mo* 13. Takkiraja (blue, holds *ankusha*-hook), *mdod rgya[l] la na mo* 14. Niladanda (blue, holds staff) *gyug sngon can la na mo* 15. Mahabala (blue, holds *trishula*), *stobs po che la na mo* 16. Shumbharaja (blue, holds cudgel), *gnod mdzes la na mo*

which accurately indicates the important role held by Mahakala in the Sakya system. The scene is also of interest in that it depicts a vignette in which four figures (including the kneeling offering goddess in the tree above the left monk) share the same space. The monks are standing on the same colorful rocky ledge (done in an archaic manner) as Mahakala, above a pool of water in which fishes swim and ducks float. Three tree trunks are interrupted by the standing figures but curve behind or around them. This little module is distinct from the larger abstract composition, even as it is integrated within it. Each of the other deities inhabits his or her own space (though the corpses underneath the main deities demonstrate a relative relationship) and are conceptually juxtaposed more than spatially composed. This early attempt at a naturalistic landscape, albeit limited to a small corner in a large composition, is the direction in which Tibetan painting developed over the course of the sixteenth and seventeenth centuries, stimulated no doubt by Chinese landscape painting in general and by Arhat painting in particular.[9]

The central Mahakala Panjarnata with the *gandi* emanation stick derives from the *Mahakala Tantra,* in its twenty-five and fifty chapter iterations, and is alleged to have come into Tibet with Lochen Rinchen Zangpo (958–1055).[10] Since the two-armed form occurs first in the *Mahakala Tantra,* and if one moves logically from simplest to most complex, this form is accepted as the fundamental form of Mahakala, from which all the others emerge. While the form without the *gandi* emanation stick (cat. key 18.6) is essentially a protector for the Hevajra practice, with the stick, he is looked on as a major protector. There are teachings on him as a tutelary deity, a Wrathful Buddha, with his own inner yoga.[11] His dominating presence in the Kumar painting is indicative of his importance already in the late fifteenth century.

Notes

1. The ten protectors, slight variants of the ones also found in catalog number 51, are part of a mandala surrounding the protector Ushnisha Chakravartin, making eleven in all. Ushnisha Chakravartin is the first on the left (cat. key 18.7). They follow closely the order found in a text by Ngorchen Konchog Lhundrub (1497–1557), except that, presumably in order to maintain symmetry and an even number, they omit Humkara:

    Inside the chakra, at the center and ten directions is a lotus and sun disc. On the middle sun is . . . yellow Ushnisha Chakravartin holding a wheel, in the east blue Yamantaka holding a hammer, south white Prajnantaka holding a mace, west red Padmantaka holding a lotus, north blue Vighnantaka holding a vajra, northeast blue Achala holding a sword, southeast blue Takkiraja holding a hook, southwest blue Niladanda holding a stick, northwest blue Mahabala holding a trident, above blue Humkara holding a vajra and bell crossed at the heart in his own gesture, below blue Shumbharaja holding a wooden club. Excluding Humkara, all the others each hold their own objects with uplifted right hands and with the left hands perform the wrathful gesture at the heart. The central and four direction Wrathful Ones are flaming wrathful, with three red eyes, round and staring, bodies fat and short, large bellied, and wearing a lower garment of tiger skin, adorned with snakes, yellow hair, eyebrows and beards twisting upwards. The other Wrathful Ones are beautiful wrathful, slightly peaceful and slightly wrathful, with bodies thin and straight, black hair, a lower garment of various silks, adorned with jewel ornaments. Also, all are standing in the middle of a blazing fire of pristine awareness with the left leg extended.

    From *The Beautiful Six Branched Ornament* by Ngorchen Konchog Lhundrub (1497–1557) written in 1551; transcribed in *Lamdre Collection,* vol. 18, fol. 375–98, *sGrub Thabs Kun bTus,* vol. 10, fol. 400–42, TBRC item W23681; *Gyu De Kun Tus,* vol. 18, fol. 128–50. Draft copy, trans. Jeff Watt, Vancouver, B.C., September 1995. Rev. July 1998.

2. Compare the following description (from ibid.):

    [The] great Vajra Mahakala, blazing, with one face, two hands. In the right is a curved knife and left a skullcup filled with blood held above and below the heart. Held across the middle of the two arms is the "*Gandi* of Emanation," having three eyes, bared fangs, yellow hair flowing upward, with a crown of five dry human skulls and a necklace of fifty wet, blood dripping, adorned with six bone ornaments and snakes, having a lower garment of tiger skin, flowing with pendants and streamers of various silks, in posture dwarfish and thick, standing above a corpse. To the right is a black crow, left a black dog, behind a wolf, in front a black man, above a garuda, emanations of messengers issue forth; with Akshobhya as a crown; standing in the middle of blazing fire of pristine awareness.

3. E. Gene Smith, *Among Tibetan Texts: History & Literature of the Himalayan Plateau* (Boston: Wisdom Publications, 2001), p. 302 n. 368.
4. For example, in a mural in the Ratnasambhava Chapel; see Xiong Wenbing et al., *The Kumbum of Gyantse Palcho Monastery in Tibet* (Chengdu: Tibet People's Publishing House & Sichuan Nationalities Publishing House, 2001), pl.

170; and on a mural in the Sarvavid Vairochana temple; Franco Ricca and Erberto Lo Bue, *The Great Stupa of Gyantse: A Complete Tibetan Pantheon of the Fifteenth Century* (London: Serindia, 1993), pl. 63.

5. Xiong Wenbing et al., *Kumbum*, pls. 32, 41.
6. Ibid., pls.48, 111, 115; Ricca and Lo Bue, *Great Stupa*, pls. 40, 42, 44,53, 66. Another similarity visible on most of the same examples is the treatment of the scarves that attach the crown above the ears. They end in a little foliate flourish.
7. For Gayadhara see Cyrus Stearns, *Luminous Lives: The Story of the Early Masters of the Lam 'bras Tradition in Tibet* (Boston: Wisdom Publications, 2001), pp. 46–55.
8. Ibid., p. 56.
9. For further discussion of this issue, see Rob Linrothe, *Paradise and Plumage: Chinese Connections in Tibetan Arhat Painting* (New York: Museum of Art; Chicago: Serindia, 2004). The *yin-yang* buckles on the looping scarf ends also suggest a Chinese origin for minor motifs in the painting style.
10. The various Mahakala *tantras* have all been translated and retranslated over a several-hundred-year period. It is the oral history and commentary which asserts that Rinchen Zangpo brought these texts and teachings from India, though the question is complicated given the earliness of his activity and the reworking of historical sources since then.
11. There are four lineages for Panjarnata, in Sakya and others in Kagyu, which is appropriate since the seminal teacher of Kagyu, Marpa (1002/12–97), had Hevajra as his main practice. One of Marpa's students, Ngog Lotsava (TBRC item P5514), is associated with a Ngoglug tradition of Panjarnata without a stick.

Cat. no. 19

Notes *(Cont. from p. 146)*

1. "Etruscan Period" as defined by the Metropolitan Museum of Art, New York, 2004; http://www.metmuseum.org/toah/ht/04/eust/ht04eust.htm, consulted May 12, 2004).
2. "Antefix" from *The Perseus Digital Library*, www.perseus.tufts.edu, consulted February 2004.
3. Lillian May Wilson, "The Gorgon in Greek Art," Ph.D. diss., University of Chicago, 1918; michrofiche ed., New York Public Library, pp. 3, 14.
4. "*se tamen horrendae clipei, quem laeva gerebat, aere repercusso formam adspexisse Medusae*," Ovid, *Metamorphoses* Bk IV, Lines 782–84, http://latein-pagina.de/ovid/ovid_m4.htm#22, consulted May 12, 2004. English: "nevertheless, he had himself looked at the dread form of Medusa reflected in a circular shield of polished bronze that he carried on his left arm," trans. A. S. Kline, www.tkline.freeserve.co.uk/Webworks/Website/Metamorph4.htm#Bkfour663, consulted May 12, 2004.

Cat. no. 20

Notes *(Cont. from p. 147)*

1. "Gorgone bis centum riguerunt corpora visa," Ovid, *Metamorphoses* Bk V, Line 209, www.latein-pagina.de/ovid/ovid_m5.htm#5, consulted May 12, 2004. English: "two hundred bodies were turned to stone at the sight of the Gorgon," tran. A. S. Kline,www.tkline.freeserve.co.uk/Webworks/Website/Metamorph5.htm#_Toc64106312, consulted May 12, 2004.
2. Lillian May Wilson, "The Gorgon in Greek Art," Ph.D. diss., University of Chicago, 1918; michrofiche ed., New York Public Library, pp. 3, 14.
3. Franca Maria Vanni, "The Rennaissance Glyptic: and their view of antiquity," in *Out of the Opulent Past: Italian Treasures from the Etruscan Age to the Renaissance*, exhib. cat., Grey Art Gallery, New York University (New York, 1992), p. 199.
4. The fashion house Versace uses an adaptation of the late-Roman *beautiful*-type Medusa for their company logo; The icon-of-vanity's-evil has thus become a 21st-century object-of-vanity. It is also evident in other areas of contemporary popular culture. A song by Kanye West, "Get Em High," performed by Common, criticizes another artist's work by making a loose reference to the Medusa myth. "Video hard to watch like Medusa. Even your club record need a booster," *College Dropout* (Talib Kweli and Common) CD, Roc-A-Fella Records, New York, Feb. 2004.

Cat. no. 21

(Cont. from p. 151) *Vajrapanjara Tantra.* That is an exclusive "explanatory *tantra*" for the *Hevajra Tantra* the root text for the most important meditation practice in Sakya, on the Wrathful Buddha Hevajra (cat. nos. 44–45). He is the special protector for the whole cycle of Hevajra *tantras*, and for the practitioners. (See fig. 1.27 where Hevajra appears above Panjarnata.) This form of Mahakala can also be found in the twenty-five–chapter and fifty–chapter *Mahakala Tantras.* Panjarnata and Brahmarupa Mahakala, associated with the *Guhyasamaja Tantra*, are known as the "Greater and Lesser Mahakalas" of the Sakya School (Tibetan: *gon po che chung*).[1]

Note

1. The lineage for this form of Panjarnata Vajra Mahakala (Tibetan: *gur gyi gon po dor je nag po chen po*; English: the Great Vajra Black One, Lord of the Pavilion [or Canopy]) begins: Vajradhara, Vajrapanjara Dakini, Brahmin Vararuci, Pandita Deva Vajra, Shraddha Karavarma, Lochen Rinchen Zangpo, Drag Tengpa Yontan Tsultrim, Mal Lotsawa Lodro Drag, Sachen Kunga Nyingpo (1092–1158), etc.

Cat. no. 22

(Cont. from p. 152) it even more. There is also post-cast chasing on the snakes and the tiger pelt wrapped around his loins. Given the technical proficiency of Newari metalworkers, it is tempting to suggest that it was made in Nepal for Tibetan patrons.

Cat. nos. 23, 24

Notes *(Cont. from p. 156)*

1. James F. Romano, "Notes on the Historiography and History of the Bes-image in Ancient Egypt," *The Bulletin of the Australian Centre for Egyptology* 9 (1998): 89–105. Dr. Romano's article serves as the main source for the account of the Bes-image. During the period over which this catalog was prepared, James F. Romano died tragically in an automobile accident. His enthusiasm and encouragement for this project were greatly appreciated, and his passing deeply regretted.
2. Ibid.
3. Ibid.

Cat. no. 25

(Cont. from p. 158)

> of fifty wet heads, adorned with snakes, three staring eyes, bared fangs and a curled tongue, black flowing eyebrows, moustache and hair, standing with the right leg bent and the left straight in the middle of a blazing mass of fire.[1]

Based on this, it is obvious that the *gandi* staff he once held in his right hand is missing.

A few stylistic features recall sculpture done in Tibet under Newari inspiration in about the fifteenth and sixteenth centuries. These features include the split-leaf jewel drop on the necklace, plentiful stone inlays that are distributed to different areas of the sculpture, hair beneath the crown arranged into curls directed symmetrically away from the center, wavelike garment folds, hems falling into swallow-tail patterns, and chased floral ornament. A sixteenth-century example from Southern Tibet with comparable features is the Maitreya in the Berti Aschmann collection in Zurich.[2]

A piece of the metal on the back was pried up, and the metal below this area was dented in the process. It is hard to imagine that such serious damage to thick metal could have been done by accident. Probably it was caused by unscrupulous persons trying to extract the consecration materials in the hollow interior, which sometimes can include valuable items. Originally, these materials were inserted through a hole on the underside between his two boots. It was later sealed with a plate, which is still intact.

Notes

1. Terdag Lingpa Gyurme Dorje (1646–1714) and Minling Lochen Dharmashri (1654–1718), *sgrub thabs 'dod 'jo 'bum bzang,* Part 2, page 149–50, TBRC item W18.
2. Helmut Uhlig, *On the Path to Enlightenment: The Berti Aschmann Foundation of Tibetan Art at the Museum Rietberg Zürich* (Zurich: Museum Rietberg, 1995), cat. no. 40, pp. 84–85.

Cat. no. 26

Notes *(Cont. from p. 159)*

1. Known as beta fruit, the plant belongs to the family Elaeocarpaceae, *Crinodendron hookeranum.* For images of this scarlet flower, see: http://caliban.mpiz-koeln.mpg.de/~stueber/BioSearch/bioinfo/getimage.cgi?whattodo=showfamily&family=Elaeocarpaceae. Consulted April 2004.
2. This form of Mahakala is known as 'Tshal lugs kyi ye shes mgon po phyag bzhi pa, "The four-handed wise *mGon po,* according to the style of 'Tshal;" Rene de Nebesky-Wojkowitz, *Oracles and Demons of Tibet: The Cult and Iconography of the Tibetan Protective Deities* (The Hague: Mouton & Co., 1956), p. 47. See also Martin Willson and Martin Brauen, *Deities of Tibetan Buddhism* (Boston: Wisdom Publications, 2000), p. 343, and the Rhie essay in this volume, esp. introduction to Mahakala and discussion of figs. 2.1, 2.4, 2.6, and 2.23. The same form of Mahakala is portrayed in the Bhutanese painting in the Rubin personal collection (Himalayan Art Website item 113), illustrated in the Linrothe essay, fig. 1.38.
3. The inscription, with many mispellings, encircles the lowest register of the base. It reads:
   Om sva sti
   He ru ka dpal thabs kyi dngos
   shes rab phag mor rol pa'i sras
   bdung 'dul rdo rje srin po'i skur
   legs sdom ye shes mgon por 'ngup bas dad bas
   na 'dzin srung skyob ces
   rgyal ba'i spyan sngar tam bcas bzhin
   dus 'dir gnod bying gsang ba'i dgra
   myur du gzhol ba'i phrin las mdzod
   mang alam.

Cat. no. 27

Notes *(Cont. from p. 162)*

1. Zapotec culture began around 2,500 years ago in Oaxaco, Mexico, which is located roughly 250 miles southeast of present-day Mexico City. See John Paddock, ed., *Ancient Oaxaca: Discoveries in Mexican Archaeology and History* (California: Stanford University Press, 1970).
2. Arthur G. Miller, *The Painted Tombs of Oaxaca, Mexico: Living with the Dead* (New York: Cambridge University Press, 1995), p. 242.

3. This type of funerary urn was not intended to hold cremation ashes. See Kent V. Flannery and Joyce Marcus, eds., *The Cloud People: Divergent Evolution of the Zapotec and Mixtec Civilizations* (New York: Academic Press, 1983), p. 144.
4. Miller, *Painted Tombs*, p. 12
5. Richard E. Blanton et al., *Ancient Oaxaca: The Monte Albán State* (Cambridge: Cambridge University Press, 1999), p. 105.

Cat. no. 28

(Cont. from p. 163) eight great *nagas* [serpent beings], an elephant skin as an upper garment and a tiger skin as a lower garment tied with a sash of green silk. The forehead is anointed with a drop of *sindura* and Akshobhya adorns the crown of the head. All the arms and legs are decorated with small bells. [He is] standing in a manner with the two legs striding forth in the middle of a blazing fire of pristine awareness.[3]

Aside from the trident which has been broken off, the only apparent deviation is the fact that in the sculpture, the Buddha in his crown makes a gesture often associated with Amoghasiddhi, not Akshobhya. However, this is a special appearance of Akshobhya associated with Mahakala in the Shangpa Kagyu school. Thus, the close conformity between image and text, despite the relative earliness of the sculpture, suggests they share a common source.[4] The root *tantra* for the six-armed Mahakala is the *Mahakala Tantra in Eight Chapters.*[5]

Notes

1. All but one of the paper scrolls are tightly wrapped and sealed; they have not been opened. They are printed Tibetan texts. Four are approximately 3½ inches in length (the height of the unrolled paper), the diameter of the roll being ¾ of an inch. Two are approximately 2 inches in length. A seventh is much smaller and can be unrolled and read. It consists of several lengths of paper fixed together, with the printed names of Indian pandits and Mahasiddhas. In addition there are several pieces of yellow silk wrapped around mandala outlines printed on paper rolls. This material has not been scientifically tested, and it cannot be assumed that they date from the time of the manufacture of the sculpture or its first consecration.
2. Tibetan: *pal ye she gyi gon po nyur du dze pa chag drug pa.*
3. Tsarchen Losal Gyatso, in the *Drubtab Kuntu*, vol. 10, folios 557–61 (TBRC item 23681), trans. Jeff Watt, Vancouver, July 1998. The quote about Tsarchen Losal Gyatso is in E. Gene Smith, *Among Tibetan Texts: History & Literature of the Himalayan Plateau* (Boston: Wisdom Publications, 2001), p. 242. On Tsarchen, see also Cyrus Stearns, *Luminous Lives: The Story of the Early Masters of the Lam 'Bras Tradition in Tibet* (Boston: Wisdom Publications, 2001), pp. 41–43.
4. Tucci makes an even stronger statement about the dependence of two paintings of six-armed Mahakala on the "liturgical pattern" provided by two texts by Taranatha (1575–1634); see Giuseppe Tucci, *Tibetan Painted Scrolls* (Rome: Libreria Dello Stato: 1949), p. 586.
5. *Nag po chen po'i rgyud le'u brgyad pa,* TBRC item W25655. See also Himalayan Art Website thematic set 85.

Cat. nos. 29, 30

Notes (Cont. from p. 165)

1. Spirits may come alive through the use of masks worn by members of the *Poro* (a secret male society). See William C. Siegmann and Cynthia E. Schmidt, *Rock of Ancestors* (Liberia: Cuttingham University College and Africana Museum, 1977), p. 2.
2. Both masks are made from a single piece of local wood that is light in both weight and color. To achieve the dark tone, the wood was treated with a mud stain. In use, the masks include a back veil of cloth strips and raffia that helped conceal the performer's head beneath. Catalog number 58 provides a clear example of how this system worked. See Tina Rolff, original catalog description for the *Collectie Koninklitjk Instituut Voor de Tropen* (Amsterdam: Afeling Culturele en Physiche Anthropology, March 8, 1956; trans. New York: American Museum of Natural History, 2000).
3. Cowrie shells are sewn to the roll of grasses encased in cloth. Aluminum strips, both down the mask's center and directly under the protruding brow are used to fasten the mask to the wooden base with a style of wire nails developed post-1890. Two pieces of polished porcelain serve as the lower eyes; and at the top center of forehead sits a pouch of medicinal/magical substances.
4. Tina Rolff, "Parts of Bitter Paradise: Living in the Interior of Liberia," narrative transcript, 1951–52 (reprinted, 1994 by Tina Rolff).
5. Strands of vibrant blue beads are strung below the mouth; a metal strip is nailed to the wood base above the mouth; a roll of grasses is encased in cloth at top of forehead; and the beard is made from cotton and grass fibers.

Cat. no. 31

(Cont. from p. 168) visualization of some wrathful form of Manjushri, bodhisattva of wisdom. Most Tibetan lineages have some form of this deity. It is commonly found on Gelugpa and Sakya paintings. This practice was adopted early on as the special protector for the Dalai Lamas and the Namgyal College of the Tse Potala Palace.

Magzor Gyalmo is two-armed and has a sun disk at her navel and a crescent moon in her hair—Palden Lhamo has both at the navel (see fig. 1.37). Under a canopy of peacock flowers, she lifts up her trident-tipped staff, and holds a skull bowl at the level of her heart. She is swallowing a tiny demon-obstacle whose legs still dangle from her mouth. She rides a male mule, through a lake of blood. The blood cascades like a waterfall down craggy rocks on the left, pooling and splashing in the center. A leg emerges from the surface of the pool at left, as if someone is struggling to stay afloat in the turbulent liquid, which tosses up a limp blue animal carcass.

Beside the mule (left), holding its reins, is a blue female servitor with a pink *makara* head (cat. key 31.7). She grasps the green snake serving as the bridle and reins. Below the mount (right) is a lion-headed attendant (cat. key 31.8). Surrounding Magzor Gyalmo are the Queens of the Four Seasons, riding a mule, buffalo, stag, and camel (cat. key 31.9–12). Below are the Five Long Life Sisters, headed by Tseringma at the center (cat. key 31.13–17), astride snow lion, stag, dragon, mule, and tiger. To the right of Magzor Gyalmo, between the Queens of Summer and Winter (cat. key 31.10, 31.12), is a two-story construction with a golden roof, pillars of skulls, and walls adorned with skulls, heads, and flayed skins. This is probably meant to depict Magzor Gyalmo's palace or mansion, the one she is shown standing within in catalog number 32. A similar, though not identical structure, is found in the same relative location in the Begtse Chen painting that belongs to this set.[3]

The portraits of Gelugpa lamas in the upper part of the painting are all identified by inscriptions, and other inscriptions on the back include the names of the donors. Chief among the group of portraits, at top center, is Je Drubkang Rinchen [i.e., Rinpoche] Geleg Gyatso (1641–1713), one of the most learned and deeply respected monks of his age, a recognized incarnation (*tulku*) whose current title-holder is one of the most influential teachers in Lhasa (cat. key 31.1). To his right is his student [Kardo] Rinchen Zopa Gyatso (1672–1749), a prolific author trained at Sera monastery (cat. key 31.2). On the other side is the Fifth Dalai Lama Ngagwang Lobzang Gyatso (1617–82), arguably one of the most powerful men in the history of Tibet (cat. key 31.3), who oversaw the systematic concentration of political power and religious prestige into the hands of the Dalai Lamas and of an inner circle in Lhasa. On the far left is a portrait of Ponlob Drago Rabjampa Puntsog Gyatso (d. before 1682; cat. key 31.4), author of a lost spiritual biography of Tsongkapa (1357–1419), the founder of the Gelug tradition. A fifth portrait on the far right depicts a student of the Fifth Dalai Lama, the Second Panchen Lama Lobzang Yeshe (1663–1737; cat. key 31.5). The reason these five are painted at the top of this painting is because they were all teachers of the principal donor, Purbu Chog Ngagwang Jampa (1682–1762) The inscription on the back give his name, along with those of three other donors: the Forty-ninth Ganden Tripa Lobzang Dargye, Jampa Yeshe, and Lozang Trinle (1697–1761).

Of these influential people, perhaps the most intriguing is Drago Rabjampa. He and the donor Purbu Chog were theological conservatives, or traditionalists. Drago Rabjampa, a strong supporter of the Gelug tradition, was a friend, colleague, and friendly competitor with the Fifth Dalai Lama. He was active in a hermitage called Drago at the foot of the Potala (Red Palace), and the two men, the Fifth Dalai Lama and Drago Rabjampa, visited, had informal poetry exchanges, and knew each other well. In fact, when Drago Rabjampa died, the Fifth Dalai Lama built a *drubkang* (retreat house) near the Chagpo Ri and the Red Palace, in the place where Drago Rabjampa meditated, in his memory.

On some issues, however, Drago Rabjampa was also in direct conflict with the Fifth Dalai Lama and his regent, Sanggye Gyatso (1653–1705), who famously covered up the Dalai Lama's death for many years and ruled in his place. (Sanggye Gytaso is shown at the top of cat. no. 8). The basis of the conflict revolved around two intertwined issues, one political, the other religious. Drago Rabjampa objected to the attempt of the Fifth Dalai Lama and his regent to create a dynastic state in which transfer of authority was to be by direct inheritance. (Much evidence exists that Sanggye Gyatso was the Dalai Lama's son by the sister of the regent Trinle Gyatso.) Another issue of contention was the emphasis among some Gelugpa on the Nyingma revelations of the Avalokiteshvara cult as espoused in the *Mani Kabum.*

As background to this issue, it must be remembered that before the Fifth Dalai Lama, the status of the Dalai Lamas was not nearly as high as it is now, not only among all the other lineages, but even within the Gelug tradition itself. In the late sixteenth and first half of the seventeenth centuries, the Dalai Lama was not the highest Gelug *tulku.* Before the Third Dalai Lama went to Mongolia and received that title, the lineage was a relatively minor *tulku* line from Drepung monastery. Until the Potala Palace was built, the Dalai Lamas lived in the Ganden Podrang of Drepung monastery. The Mongols took advantage of an opportunity to exert influence in Tibet when the Fourth Dalai Lama was recognized as the grandson of the Mongol Altan Khan. Mongol troops came with the boy to Lhasa, and it was naturally in the Mongol interest to promote the status of the Dalai Lamas. After the early death of the Fourth Dalai Lama, and a disputed selection process, the Fifth Dalai was installed and continued to make use of a Mongol army. Although he did not succeed in creating a dynastic rulership, he did catapult the Dalai Lama into spiritual and political preeminence in many regions of the Tibetan ethnographic world.

Drago Rabjampa challenged the authenticity of the *Mani Kabum,* the basic text of the Avalokiteshvara cult of the Dalai Lamas. He was among a group of traditionalists who objected to the acceptance into Gelugpa standard practice of Nyingma traditions. The Fifth Dalai Lama was in the vanguard of absorbing Nyingma practices and forming a state cult of Padmasambhava. The Dalai Lama had been exposed to Nyingmapa magic ritual as a young man and "became very fond of these rites which left a strong imprint on his personality in later years and indeed on his secret visionary experiences."[4] Drago Rabjampa resisted movement in these directions, unsuccessfully, and has been almost completely erased from the history written by the victors.[5] Although his writings seem to have been purged in the eighteenth century—perhaps as part of a campaign led by the Mongols or after the Seventh Dalai Lama—the memory of Drago Rabjampa has lived on in popular culture. Even today, he is remembered for his wit, the elegance of his extemporaneous speaking, his spontaneously composed poetry, and his pranks, some of which were scatological.

Purbu Chog, the principle donor of this painting, was a productive writer and scholar. Among his compositions is a biography of his teacher Drubkang, whose portrait is at top center of the painting (cat. key 31.1). Both of them are included consecutively in the lineage of Lamrim philosophy pictured in woodblock prints.[6] Purbu Chog kept a record of the inscriptions he wrote for the backs of paintings, including this one. It was part of a set of seven paintings, listed with the subject matter, and one of the other works in the Essen Collection in Basel, has also been identified.[7] The fact that an authentic painting has been discovered with a text matching one recorded in eighteenth-century literature has important methodological implications. It suggests that this underutilized genre of literature which can be termed "recorded inscriptions" may be a dependable source of information about paintings, providing a historical context which is often sadly lacking in the discussion of Himalayan painting among Western art historians.[8]

This painting of Magzor Gyalmo must have been done when the controversies surrounding some of the subjects of the portraits were still fresh. All were personally linked to the donor, and they all knew each other. Except for the Fifth Dalai Lama, the group, including Purbu Chog, represent a very orthodox, or conservative group of teachers. It might seem ironic then, that a painting depicting opponents of the "Nyingmacization" of Gelug should include the Queens of the Seasons (cat. key 31.9–12) and the Sisters of Long Life (cat. key 31.13–17), who are certainly derived from local cult deities, and probably more Nyingma or Bön, than they are strictly orthodox inheritances from Sanskritic Buddhism. By the seventeenth century, however, they had long been incorporated into the major traditions without sectarian distinctions.

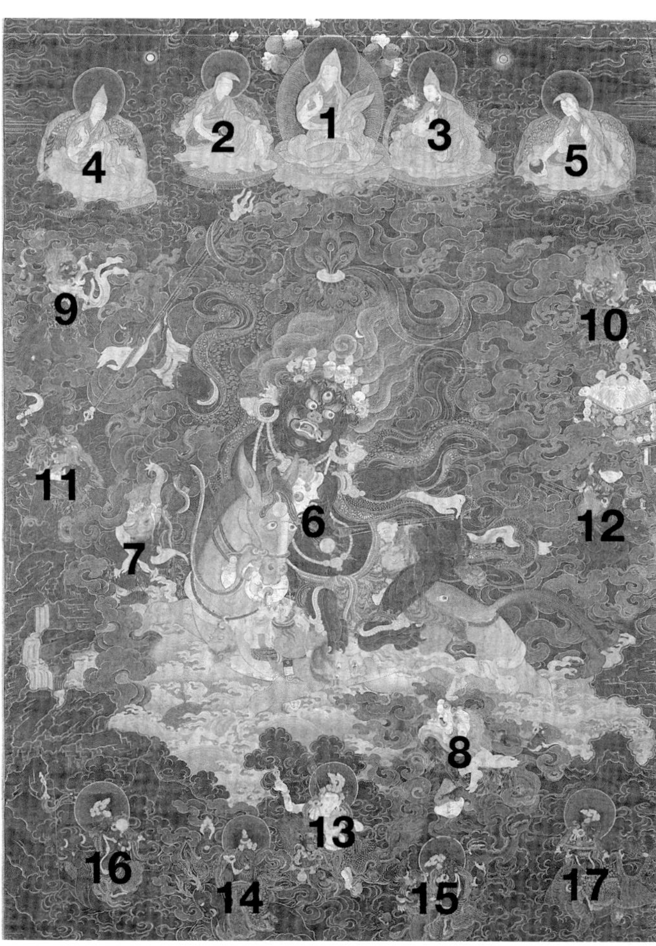

Cat. key 31 , with inscriptions

1. Je Drubkang Rinchen Geleg Gyatso (1641–1713; TBRC item P1005), rje sgrub khang rin chen **2.** Khardo Rinchen (1672–1749; TBRC item P38), mkhardo rin chen **3.** Fifth Dalai Lama Gyalwa Ngapa Chenpo (Ngagwang Lobzang Gyatso; 1617–82; TBRC item P37), rgyal ba lnga pa chen po **4.** Ponlob Drago Rabjampa Puntsog Gyatso (17th c., TBRC item P3435), dpon blob phun tshog rgya tsho **5.** Second Panchen Lama Lobzang Yeshe (1663–1737; TBRC item P106), pan chen blo bzang ye shes **6.** Shri Devi, Magzor Gyalmo **7.** chu srin gdong can (*makara*-headed attendant) **8.** seng ge'i gdong can (lion-headed attendant) **9.** Queen of Spring (dpyid kyi rgyal mo) **10.** Queen of Summer (bbyar gyi rgyal mo) **11.** Queen of Autumn (ston gyi rgyal mo) **12.** Queen of Winter (dgun gyi rgyal mo) **13.** Tseringma (Auspicious Mistress of the Five Long-life Sisters) **14.** Chopen Drinzangma **15.** Tekar Drozangma **16.** Ting gyi Shal Zangma (Fair Blue-faced One) **17.** Miyo Lozangma (Immovable Noble Mind)

Notes

1. Magzor Gyalmo (Tibetan: *pal den lha mo, mag gyi zor le, gyal mo*), "Queen who Has the Power to Turn Back Armies." Her Sanskrit names are Shri Devi and Yakshi Remati.
2. For a *purana*-like retelling of the origins of both Magzor Gyalmo (Remati) and her mistress Palden Lhamo, see the *Dakini agni jihvajvala tantra* (Toh. 842 folio 223–53), in English in Giuseppe Tucci, *Tibetan Painted Scrolls* (Rome: Libreria Dello Stato, 1949), pp. 218–19.
3. This painting is in the Essen Collection of the Museum der Kulturen, Basel; see Gerd-Wolfgang Essen and Tsering Tashi Thingo, *Die Gotter des Himalaya: Buddhistische Kunst Tibets, Die Sammlung Gerd Wolfgang Essen,* 2 vols. (Munich: Prestel-Verlag, 1989), 1:227–28, pl. 1-140; Clara B. Wilpert with Maria Angela Algar, *Tibet: Buddhas, Gods, Saints* (Munich: Pretel-Verlag, 2001), p. 142. The Essen painting depicts the protector Begtse Chen with his retinue. At the top center is the Buddha Amitabha with two lamas on the right, Jetsunpa and Sera Kunkyenpa. On the left side are the second and third Dalai Lamas, Gyalwa Gendun Gyatso (1476–1542) and Gyalwa Sonam Gyatso (1543–88).
4. Samten Karmay, *Secret Visions of the Fifth Dalai Lama: The Gold Manuscript in the Fournier Collection* (London: Serindia, 1988), p. 7.
5. The historical summary in this entry is deeply indebted to Gene Smith; any errors are the authors' responsibility. Smith points out that none of the biographical dictionaries mention Drago Rabjampa Puntsog Gyatso, nor have any of his works—his biographies of Tsongkapa and the Buddha and his polemical works—been seen since the 19th century. *Dungkar's Desk Encyclopedia* (*Dung dkar tshig mdzod chen mo (Pe cin : Krung go'i bod rig pa dpe bskrun khang,* 2002, p. 1495, TBRC item W26372) does mention that Drago Rabjampa lived at the hermitage below the Potala, and alludes to his difficulties with the Fifth Dalai Lama. The story is also supported by Longdol Lama (1719–94) who in his list of important books describes a set of Gelug refutations of the Nyingmapa, including an argument

against the thoughts and positions of the Nyingmapa master Dodrag Rigdzin Pema Trinley (1642–1718). Lokesh Chandra, comp., *Materials for a History of Tibetan Literature*, 3 vols. (New Delhi: International Academy of Indian Culture, 1963), 3:673ff. The *Gazetteer* of Lhasa mentions the Drago *drubkang*, though not Drago Rabjampa, pp. 1495–97. Gene Smith, personal communication, April 2004.

6. Lokesh Chandra, *Buddhist Iconography, Compact Edition* (New Delhi: Aditya Prakashan, 1991), nos. 1266 and 1268; in addition Drubkang is included in the practice lineage for the same teachings, no. 1277.
7. For a list of Purbu Chog's writings, see TBRC item P108. Among them are the *Collected Works (gsun 'bum) Phur bu lcog Nag dban byams pa*, 4 vols., TBRC item W1229, reproduced from a set of tracings from prints from the Phur bu lcog Hermitage blocks by Ngagwang Sopa, New Delhi, 1973), vol. 4, 43 PI. *Thang sku'i rgyab yig le tshan dang mchod rdzas gsar bskrun gyi 'dod gsol smon lam gyi rim pa*, pp. 284–364. For the subsection listing inscriptions composed by Purbu Chog for various paintings, see ibid., pp. 312–24, and within that subsection are seven paintings relevant here. The Rubin inscription on the back of catalog number 31 and the text on page 319 match exactly. It has not yet been possible to check the inscription on the back of the Essen painting, but presumably it will match as well. (For reproductions of the Essen painting, see Essen and Thingo, *Gotter des Himalaya*, 1:227–28, pl. 1-140.) A third painting which probably belonged to the same set is the Vaishravana in a European collection; see Pia and Louis Van der Wee, *A Tale of Thangkas: Living with a Collection* (Antwerp: Ethnographic Museum of Antwerp, 1995), p. 108, pl. 53. The following list is a concordance of page numbers from Purbu Chog's text and the subject matter for each of the seven paintings, and, where applicable, catalog numbers from this exhibitions of works with the same theme:
318: Begtse inscription (Essen collection).
318: Panjarnata Mahakala; cat. nos. 18, 21–22
319: Shri Devi Magzor Gyalmo (Rubin collection); cat. nos. 31–32.
319: Vaishravana (Van der Wee collection).
320: Shadbhuja Mahakala; cat. no. 28.
320: Yama Dharmaraja; cat. nos. 33–36.
321: Vajrabhairava; cat. nos. 46–47, 50.
The group of seven must have been arranged with the Vajrabhairava in the center, and the others on either side. These are the principal protectors of the Gelug, along with the most important Wrathful Buddha, Vajrabhhairava.
8. The known examples of the "Recorded Inscription" genre of literature is impressive, including works by the Fifth and Seventh Dalai Lamas, and Mindrol Lingpa authors. Among them are:
Fifth Dalai Lama, three volumes
Panchen incarnations, TBRC item W2042, etc.
Yondzin Yeshe Gyaltsen, TBRC item W1105, W1114
Kyisho Shabdrung, TBRC item W9872
Yeshe Chopel, TBRC item W6068
Ngagwang Chophel, TBRC item W7233
7th Dalai Lama, TBRC W2621
Ngagwang Kedrup of Urga, TBRC item W16860
Purbuchog Ngagwang Jampa, TBRC W1199 (P108)
Getse Maha Pandita, TBRC item W22684
(Information generously provided by Gene Smith, personal communication, April 2004.)

Cat. no. 32

Notes *(Cont. from p. 171)*

1. Shri Devi as Palden Lhamo can be considered the wrathful form of Lakshmi, while Magzor Gyalmo, the wrathful form of Sarasvati. The latter is thought of as the younger sister, or sometimes the servant, of the Palden Lhamo. In catalog number 50, both forms are present in the same painting (see cat. key 50.15–16).
2. Marylin M. Rhie and Robert A. F. Thurman, *Worlds of Transformation: Tibetan Art of Wisdom and Compassion* (New York: Tibet House, 1999), p. 445.
3. A similar impulse to visualize the three-dimensionality of a mandala-palace is found in 19th-century paintings of the Vajrayogini mandala. See Himalayan Art Website items 318, 334, 86931, 90725.
4. Rhie and Thurman, *Worlds of Transformation*, p. 445. This provides an account of how she came to butcher her own children.
5. The retinue figures correspond very well to a text which has been summarized in Rene de Nebesky-Wojkowitz, *Oracles and Demons of Tibet: The Cult and Iconography of the Tibetan Protective Deities* (The Hague: Mouton & Co., 1956), pp. 24–31; the directional and seasonal deities are described on pp. 29–30. The seventeen outer retinue figures (cat. key 32.12–28) correspond with only minor variations to the description of other deities found in the same text.

Cat. no. 33

(Cont. from p. 172) skull bowls with wrathful offerings of sense organs, *amrita* (nectar), and blood are at bottom center. On the lotus base, trampled by Yama Dharmaraja's red-outlined feet, a body is in the throes of agony, though whether it is physical pain or mental anguish is impossible to determine. His head, and the varicolored garland of heads were painted with particular care (see detail).

The figures directly above the main figure, along with inscriptions on the front and back, help to identify the date and patronage. The Indian monk with a pandit's red pointed hat is the Mahasiddha Lalitavajra, who played an important role in the transmission of Vajrabhairava and Yama Dharmaraja teachings. Across from him is a figure who has been tentatively identified as the Seventh Dalai Lama (1708–57), while the small monk under Manjushri is most likely the patron of the painting, the Seventh Demo Rinpoche,

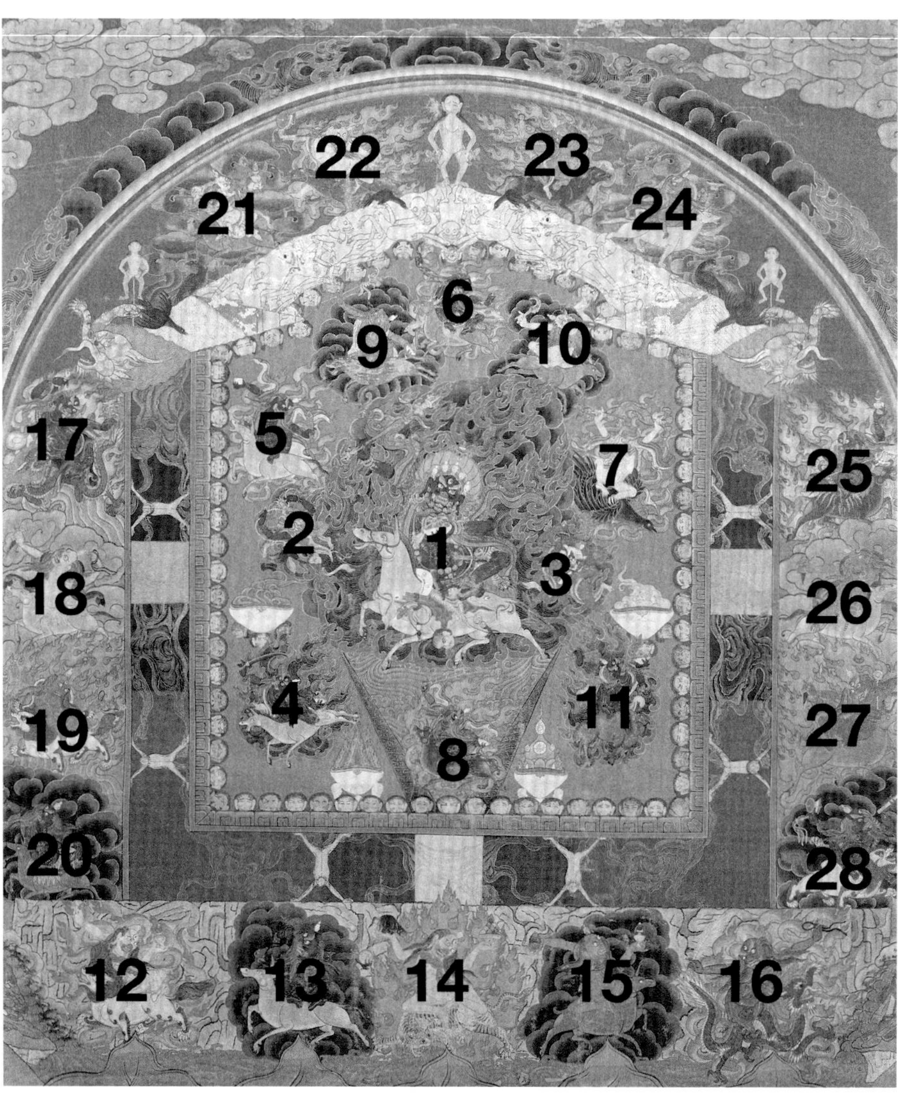

Cat. key 32

Names based on Nebesky-Wojkowitz, *Oracles and Demons*

1. Magzor Gyalmo **2.** Chu srin gdong can **3.** Seng ge'i gdong can **4.** bDud mo remati **5.** Nad kyi bdag mo **6.** sKye mthing ma **7.** Khri sman sa le ma **8.** dPyid kyi rgyal mo **9.** dByar gyi rgyal mo **10.** sTon gyi rgyal mo **11.** dGun gyi rgyal mo **12.** bKra shis tshe ring ma **13.** mThing gi zhal bsang ma **14.** Mi g.yo blo bzang ma **15.** Cod pan mgrin bzang ma **16.** gTad dkar 'gro bzang ma **17.** rDo rje kun grags ma **18.** rDo rje g.ya' ma skyong **19.** rDo rje kun bzang ma **20.** rDo rje bgegs kyi gtso **21.** rDo rje spyan gcig ma **22.** rDo rje dpal gyi yum **23.** rDo rje klu mo **24.** rDo rje drag mo rgyal **25.** rDo rje dpal mo che **26.** rDo rje sman gcig ma **27.** rDo rje g.ya' mo sil **28.** rDo rje dril bu gzugs legs ma

Ngagwang Jampal Deleg Gyatso (d. 1777), who was regent between 1757 and 1762, during the minority of the Eighth Dalai Lama, Ngagwang Jampal Gyatso (1758–1804). The painting was created as an antidote to the obstacles and enemies threatening the Demo Rinpoche.[5] It was certainly painted during his lifetime, but exactly when is not known. It was possibly made during the narrower period of his regency. This high level of patronage is in accord with the high quality of the painting and the luxurious gold and silver brocade mounting. The silk is Chinese, possibly of the seventeenth or eighteenth century. The brocade and elaborate fringe at the top (not visible in the photograph) show the special treatment this painting received.

Notes

1. Yama, the "Lord of Death," is conceived as a sentient creature and the King of the Pretas (ghosts), arising in early Buddhist literature, adopted later into Sutra and Esoteric Buddhist systems. Yama Dharmaraja is based exclusively on the Bhairava Root Tantra where Manjushri assumes a variety of terrifying (*bhairava*) forms to subdue Yama and uses the theme of death as a metaphor for an entire cycle of *tantric* practice.
2. For a discussion of the pattern of the conqueror adopting the form of the conquered as a kind of trophy, see Linrothe's essay, part 1. The Wrathful Buddha Vajrabhairava, who develops in *Anuttara Tantras*, shares many features with Yama Dharmaraja, Yamantaka, Rakta Yamari, including the connection with Manjushri; see catalog numbers 46–47, 50. The Inner form of Yama Dharmaraja is the inner protector for the Vajrabhairava cycle *tantra*.
3. In Tibetan, Inner Yama Dharmaraja is *shin je cho kyi gyal po, nang wa.* See also

Rene de Nebesky-Wojkowitz, *Oracles and Demons of Tibet: The Cult and Iconography of the Tibetan Protective Deities* (The Hague: Mouton & Co., 1956), pp. 82–83. Gelugpas maintain outer, inner, and secret forms of Yama Dharmaraja. It is alleged that they all come from the Rwa tradition. The inner and secret forms are likely to be considered suspect by Sakya and Kagyu teachers.

4. At the lower left is white Peaceful Yamaraja with two hands, holding a *damaru* drum and a divination arrow with the left. Above that is yellow Increasing Yamaraja holding a sword and banner. To the right is red Powerful Yamaraja holding a wishing jewel and a skullcup to the heart. Below that is blue black Wrathful Yamaraja holding a bone stick and a lasso, embraced by the consort Chamundi, black in color, offering a skull bowl to the Lord. Each of the Yamas has a buffalo head, is ithyphallic, adorned with various wrathful ornaments and stands upon a buffalo of similar color, above a corpse, sun disc and lotus surrounded by the flames of pristine awareness.
5. The closeness of the personal names of the Seventh Demo and Eighth Dalai Lama, Ngagwang Jampal Deleg Gyatso, and Ngagwang Jampal Gyatso, respectively, has led to confusion. Rhie and Thurman translated the inscription on the front as "Homage to the thrice kind Ngagwang Jambel Delek Gyatso Pelsang" and suggest that it refers to the Eighth Dalai Lama; see Marylin M. Rhie and Robert A. F. Thurman, *Worlds of Transformation: Tibetan Art of Wisdom and Compassion* (New York: Tibet House, 1999), p. 380. E. Gene Smith, however, after reading both the front and back inscriptions, understood the front inscription as referring to the Seventh Demo, acknowledging there are other alternatives (personal communication, April 2004). He pointed out that the regent would have named the Eighth Dalai Lama, and it was not unusual in the naming process to bestow parts of his own name. The inscription on the front reads: *bka' drin gsum ldan ngag dbang 'jam dpal bde legs rgya mtsho dpal bzang po la na mo.* Its slanted orientation is unusual. One letter, *la* has been crossed out, and then rewritten in an open space, as part of the final *la na mo.* However, the spelling is very proper in inscriptions on the front and back. The longer inscription on the back, in nine-syllable verse, reads:
dge sdig las kyi me long ngos gnyis par
dkar nag shan 'byed 'chi bdag gshin rje'i rgyal
rdor rje'i rwa ldan ma he khros pa'i steng
bskyang bskum gar gyis brjid ldan 'khor bcas
pas rje btsun bla ma'i sku la bar gcod bgegs
bsam sbyor ngan par brtsegs pa'i brag ri'i steng
drag sbyor thog gi bu yug dpal phab pas
ming gi tha mar bshig la ma g.yel zhig

Cat. no. 34

Note *(Cont. from p. 177)*

1. Yama Dharmaraja (Tibetan: *shin je cho gyal*; English: the Lord of Death, King of the Law of Cause and Effect) is an Enlightened Protector of the father class of *anuttarayoga tantra.* The lineage for his practice begins: Vajradhara, Shri Vajrabhairava, Jnana Dakini, Lalitavajra, Vajrasana, Amoghavajra, Jnana Sambhava Bepa, Padmavajra, Dipamkara Shrijnana (the Nepali), Bharo Chag Dum (the Tibetan) Ra Lotsawa Dorje Drag, etc.

Cat. no. 35

(Cont. from p. 178) emblems that represent them. Manuals that aid in the memorization or performance of these rituals sometimes are created by master artists and have great aesthetic value. This work resembles some of the best of such paintings, in overall composition, choice of plain background, and aniconic use of attributes.[2] It is not uncommon, however, in Esoteric Buddhist traditions from Tibet to Japan to find finished mandalas using symbols, attributes, or *mantras* to represent the deities.[3] In the Himalayan context these would include the Kalachakra sand mandalas made by contemporary Gelugpa monks in a variety of settings (including museums), Arhat mandalas, and Medicine Buddha mandalas in which the center is Prajnaparamita represented by the book.[4] In this case, the painting would have been used for initiation into the Yama Dharmaraja and Chamunda teachings. It would have been laid flat on a table, not hung on the wall, and implements used in the ritual arranged around it.

Notes

1. Marylin M. Rhie and Robert A. F. Thurman, *Worlds of Transformation: Tibetan Art of Wisdom and Compassion* (New York: Tibet House, 1999), cat. no. 177, p. 442.
2. See, for example, the "Gold manuscript," in Samten Karmay, *Secret Visions of the Fifth Dalai Lama: The Gold Manuscript in the Fournier Collection* (London: Serindia, 1988), esp. pl. 38.
3. In Japanese Shingon Esoteric Buddhism, two of the nine mandalas of the Vajradhatu "Diamond World" mandala are of attributes only, and in some versions, the complete mandala is done with *mantras* only. See Sawa Ryuken et al., *Kobo Daishin and the Art of Esoteric Buddhism* (Tokyo: Tokyo National Museum, 1983), cat. nos. 60, 71; and Rolf W. Giebel, "The *Chin-kang-ting ching yü-ch'ieh shih-pa-hui chih-kuei*: An Annotated Translation," *Journal of the Naritasan Institute for Buddhist Studies* 18 (1995): 132–33.
4. Laura Scanlon, "Mandalas in Museums: The Kalachakra Particle Mandala," in *Embodying Wisdom: Art, Text and Interpretation in the History of Esoteric Buddhism*, ed. Rob Linrothe and Hernik H. Sorensen (Copenhagen: Seminar for Buddhist Studies, 2001), pp. 229–46; Denise Patry Leidy and Robert A. F. Thurman, *Mandala: The Architecture of Enlightenment* (New York: Asia Society Galleries, 1997), pp. 148–56; Himalayan Art Website items 420, 146, 868, 74273.

Cat. no. 36

(Cont. from p. 181) In addition, there are six more messengers of Yama Dharmaraja, three male and three female, the latter among the group known as the *mamo chenmo*, the "Great Mothers."[4] The female with medium-blue skin and bright orange hair near the top on the right holds a tusk; the darker male one near the bottom flies on a huge bird clutching a snake. The red male at the top left chews on an intestine pulled out of the corpse he stands on, while the blue male beneath him eviscerates a second corpse. The scholar Giuseppe Tucci has described the demonic figures surrounding a different Yama Dharmaraja painting in phrases that are as dynamic as their poses:

> [Around Yama Dharmaraja] a crowd of terrific creatures hovers weirdly; they brandish weapons, they twist their muscular bodies in violent contortions, as if swept away by a hellish fury; they rush off as though a hurricane scattered them about. But it is their inner fierceness which moves them and flings them into space with a sort of devouring frenzy. Some of them are female figures, although their monstrous aspect all but abolishes any distinction of sex: all the images are mingled in the same horror.[5]

The tentative attribution to Northeastern Tibet is based on the simplified green landscape. It has a noticeably high horizon line, some lakes or streams, and a comparatively dark sky. However, in the last few centuries, there has been a certain artistic homogenization within Gelugpa monasteries. Artists move from outlying Gelugpa monasteries to central ones, and vice versa, spreading and integrating regional styles. A Central Tibetan origin cannot be ruled out.

Notes

1. These are terms found in English translations of the *Hevajra Tantra*; Snellgrove has overthrowing, subduing, conjuring, petrifying; Farrow and Menon, overthrowing, subduing, attracting and paralyzing. See David Snellgrove, *The Hevajra Tantra: A Critical Study* (London: Oxford University Press, 1959), pp. 84–85; G. W. Farrow and I. Menon, *The Concealed Essence of the Hevajra Tantra* (Delhi: Motilal Banarsidass, 1992), p. 139. The gazes are the subject of an entire chapter in the *Hevajra Tantra*.
2. As found in Rolf W. Giebel, "The *Chin-kang-ting ching yü-ch'ieh shih-pa-hui chih-kuei*: An Annotated Translation," *Journal of the Naritasan Institute for Buddhist Studies* 18 (1995): 132–34; the reconstructed Sanskrit is *dipta-dristi* (blazing gaze); *akarsana-dristi* (hook summoning); *krodha-dristi* (angry gaze); *abhicaraka-dristi* (subjugation).
3. For the four retinue figures, see entry for catalog number 33. The white Yamaraja carries a *damaru*-drum and long noose; the yellow Dharmaraja has a sword; the red Dharmaraja has wish-fulfilling jewels and a skull bowl; and the blue Yamaraja has a bone *danda*-club, made from the fused spine and skull.
4. See Giuseppe Tucci, *Tibetan Painted Scrolls* (Rome: Libreria Dello Stato, 1949), p. 582; Rene de Nebesky-Wojkowitz, *Oracles and Demons of Tibet: The Cult and Iconography of the Tibetan Protective Deities* (The Hague: Mouton & Co., 1956), pp. 85–86.
5. Tucci, *Tibetan Painted Scrolls*, p. 582.

Cat. no. 37

(Cont. from p. 187) Some Indian paintings could have been preserved in Tibetan monasteries, alongside the large number of Eastern Indian metalwork sculptures still in the monastic treasuries.[4] Tibetan painters, however, may have quickly absorbed the Eastern Indian style from Indian artists working in Tibet, or by traveling to Nepal or India itself to study with Indian artists, or by copying the art that was brought to Tibet. The difficulty lies not so much in identifying the Indian style, but in determining which surviving works are Tibetan (painted by a Tibetan painter) and which are Indian (painted by an Indian painter in either Tibet or India). This is a task of connoisseurship, the difficulties of which are deepened by the lack of *pata* (paintings on cloth) preserved in India. Some scholars are relatively generous in assigning an Indian provenance, while others are more skeptical and reticent to do so.[5]

This painting is one of a very few paintings that might actually be an Indian painting, despite the fact that a Tibetan syllable, *ram*, is written in Tibetan script on the lower portion of the black ground.[6] This could have been added later or included in the brief given an Indian artist. Based on textual descriptions, paintings of this scale were recommended by an early Esoteric Budhdist text, the *Manjushrimulakalpa* (MMK) which describes three sizes of paintings: large, measuring 6 by 12 feet; medium, measuring 2 by 5 feet; and small, measuring approximately 3 by 9 inches.[7] The Achala painting is 6¾ by 14 inches. The difference in size can easily be explained by the difficulty in translating early medieval measurements into modern ones, as well as by acknowledging that what the texts state as ideal, and what artists actually produce, are not always identical.[8] At any rate, according to the sixth chapter of the MMK, small-sized *pata* like this one were used for rituals that involve "the pacification of hindrances (*shantika*), the increase of wealth, health, happiness, and so forth (*paustika*), and the expulsion of terrific forces (*daruna*)."[9] By this token, the size, format, and subject matter of the painting are generally compatible with what Indian texts describe as *pata*.

Scientific testing of the cloth ground, pigments, and sizing might be helpful in this case, but without a significant pool of comparative data on Indian cloth painting, even this might not be definitive. Stylistic evidence remains almost our only recourse in establishing the origin of this painting, since the iconography is certainly shared across the borders of India and Tibet.[10] To indicate the fidelity of this painting to Indian art, links are suggested between specific elements of the painting and features of Indian painting and sculpture. Admittedly, artists worked holistically. Separating elements individually and finding connections to other works is thus a purely heuristic art historical method, not an artistic one. These connections are offered not to prove conclusively that the painting is Eastern Indian, although the evidence could be used to support that conclusion. The evidence can also be used to show how thoroughly Tibetan artists in the eleventh and twelfth centuries had assimilated, absorbed, and integrated the Gyalug as their own. Until much more is known about Indian cloth painting, it is sufficient to leave the question open, acknowledging the possibility that the Rubin painting might have had an Indian origin.

Visual Elements Shared by the Rubin Achala painting and Eastern Indian Art

Individual elements in the Rubin painting are followed by abbreviated citations of illustrations of Eastern Indian manuscript illuminations (P) and sculptures (S) dating from the tenth to twelfth century, and Burmese mural paintings (BP) of the late eleventh to early twelfth century. A key to the source citations precedes the notes for this entry.

Nimbus of flames

with overall rounded shape, individual licks of flame outlined in a darker color:

P: Huntington and Huntington, *Leaves from the* Bodhi *Tree*, pl. 60; Jamieson, *Perfection of Wisdom*, pp. 95, 32, 41.

S: Saraswati, *Tantrayana Art*, nos. 177, 119.

Dark blue background

against which flowers are rendered in red with silver stalks:

P: Jamieson, *Perfection of Wisdom*, pp. 30, 35, 42, 52, 56, 67, 96, 99, 103.

Shape of the lotus

wide and flat, with a single layer of downward turning petals, their tips embellished; calyx given a rim or border either with a color change, a line, or both:

P: Jamieson, *Perfection of Wisdom*, pp. 73, 103.

S: Linrothe, *Ruthless Compassion*, 185, 206.

Jewelry

around ankles, wrists and upper arms, unusual gold coil wrapped around the joint or limb:

S: Saraswati, *Tantrayana Art*, nos. 22, 25.

Large earrings of cylindrical shape:

BP: Bautze-Picron, *Buddhist Murals of Pagan*, pls. 102–06, 109–13, passim.

P: Huntington and Huntington, *Leaves from the* Bodhi *Tree*, pls. 57–60.

S: Linrothe, *Ruthless Compassion*, figs. 118–19, 164–65.

However, the spoollike shape, with the earlobes sandwiched between the outer whorls is found more often in Tibetan images than in Eastern Indian.

Tibetan painting: Bowers Museum, *Tibet Treasures*, cat. no. 78.

Crown

with triangular pendants, pleated splayed ribbons above ears:

BP: Bautze-Picron, *Buddhist Murals of Pagan*, pls.103–106, passim.

P: Jamieson, *Perfection of Wisdom*, pp. 15, 17, 32, 39, 88, passim; Pal and Meech, *Buddhist Book Illuminations*, p. 81, top; S. Huntington, *"Pala-Sena" Schools of Sculpture,* pls. 72, 215, 226; Saraswati, *Tantrayana Art,* nos. 203–06.

S: Bhattasali, *Dacca Museum,* pls. XII, XXI; Linrothe, *Ruthless Compassion,* fig. 60.

Cobra

as "sacred cord," with its head just over the proper left shoulder:

P: Huntington and Huntington, *Leaves from the* Bodhi *Tree,* pl. 58c, lower left; Saraswati *Tantrayana Art,* no. 260.

S: Linrothe, *Ruthless Compassion* fig. 59, late 11th century; Saraswati *Tantrayana Art,* no. 170.

Suspended decorative vine-like swags

(upper part of the composition) a favored ornament in Eastern Indian sculpture to decorate belts, girdles, and crowns as well as pillars:

P: Bowers Museum, *Tibet Treasures,* cat. no. 37.

S: Linrothe, *Ruthless Compassion,* figs. 193, 195, 198, 199, 203, 213–14, 219–20; Saraswati, *Tantrayana Art,* nos. 15, 44, 104, 172.

Floral support for lotus pedestal

leafy vines with red flowers sprouting from central stem:

BP: Bautze-Picron, *Buddhist Murals of Pagan,* pl. 1.

S: Bhattasali, *Dacca Museum,* pls. 15, 16; Saraswati, *Tantrayana Art,* nos. 33, 43, 151, 160.

Elephant with red trunk:

BP: Bautze-Picron, *Buddhist Murals of Pagan,* pl. 60

P: Huntington and Huntington, *Leaves from the* Bodhi *Tree,* pl. 58c, middle right; Saraswati, *Tantrayana Art,* no. 229.

Scarf ends

floating up and/or with split-ends (swallow-tail):

BP: Bautze-Picron, *Buddhist Murals of Pagan,* pls. 21, 103–6.

S: Bhattasali, *Dacca Museum,* pl. 7(b); S. Huntington, *"Pala-Sena" Schools of Sculpture,* pl. 187; Linrothe: *Ruthless Compassion,* fig. 175. However, they are more split than usual.

Belt end

hanging down from between the legs with split-ends (swallow-tail):

S: S. Huntington, *"Pala-Sena" Schools of Sculpture,* pl. 215.

In the Rubin painting, this feature is rather odd in that the scarf acts as a belt tied around the waist, then goes under another belt, and hangs down in front of the tiger skin.

Long slender torso

"bent" pose and undulating belt-line:

BP: Bautze-Picron, *Buddhist Murals of Pagan,* pls. 31, 105–6.

P: Huntington and Huntington, *Leaves from the* Bodhi *Tree,* pls. 58b, middle left and lower left.

S: Saraswati, *Tantrayana Art,* no. 82.

Hair style

flowing upward, tied at crown, tiara above hairline:

S: Bhattasali, *Dacca Museum,* pl. 12; Linrothe, *Ruthless Compassion,* figs. 1, 59.

P: Jamieson, *Perfection of Wisdom,* p. 40; Linrothe, *Ruthless Compassion,* pl. 13; Pal and Meech, *Buddhist Book Illuminations,* p. 80, top; Saraswati, *Tantrayana Art,* no. 221.

Sword held aloft, behind head:

S: Bhattasali, *Dacca Museum,* pls. 47(a), 66; Linrothe, *Ruthless Compassion,* figs. 162, 165; Saraswati, *Tantrayana Art,* no. 25.

P: Huntington and Huntington, *Leaves from the* Bodhi *Tree,* pl. 60, top.

Archer's pose

right leg bent, left leg straight:

P: Huntington and Huntington, *Leaves from the* Bodhi *Tree,* pl. 60, bottom center and right.

S: Linrothe, *Ruthless Compassion,* figs. 160, 162, 167, 217

The citations are from the following sources:

Bautze-Picron, Claudine. *The Buddhist Murals of Pagan: Timeless vistas of the cosmos.* Trumbull, CT: Weatherhill, 2003.

Bhattasali, Nalini Kanta. *Iconography of Buddhist and Brahmanical Sculptures (In the Dacca Museum).* 1929. Reprint, New Delhi: Aryan Books International, 2001.

Bowers Museum of Cultural Art. *Tibet Treasures from the Roof of the World.* Santa Ana, CA: Bowers Museum, 2003.

Huntington, Susan L. *The "Pala-Sena" Schools of Sculpture.* Leiden: E. J. Brill, 1984.

Huntington, Susan L. and John C. Huntington. *Leaves from the* Bodhi *Tree.* Dayton: Dayton Art Institute, 1990.

Jamieson, R. C. *The Perfection of Wisdom: Extracts from the Astasahasrikaprajnaparamita.* London: Frances Lincoln, 2000.

Linrothe, Rob. *Ruthless Compassion: Wrathful Deities in Early Indo-Tibetan Esoteric Buddhist Art.* London: Serindia, 1999.

Pal, Pratapaditya and Julia Meech-Pekarik. *Buddhist Book Illuminations.* Hong Kong: Ravi Kumar Publishers, 1988.

Saraswati, S. K. *Tantrayana Art, an Album.* Calcutta: The Asiatic Society, 1977.

Notes

1. The specific iconography here, of Arya Achala trampling Vinayaka (Vighnaraja), is associated with Atisha Dipamkara Shrijnana (982–1054).

   Arya Achala has a body dark blue in color with one face and two hands. The right hand holds aloft a sword and the left performs the wrathful gesture at the heart. Above a lotus and sun seat [he] stands with the right leg bent and the left straight [atop] Vighnaraja [Lord of Hindrances—the elephant-headed Ganesha-like figure]. Wearing a lower garment of tiger skin, having three eyes, red and round, orange hair flowing upward, all the limbs adorned with snakes, [he] stands in the middle of a blazing mass of fire."

   From the *Narthang Gyatsa, Drubtab Kuntu* (TBRC item W23681) vol. 13, pp. 759–61, trans. Jeff Watt, January 1999. See also Amy Heller, "On the Development of the Iconography of Acala and Vighnantaka in Tibet," in *Embodying Wisdom: Art, Text and Interpretation in the History of Esoteric Buddhism*, ed. Rob Linrothe and Hernik H. Sorensen (Copenhagen: Seminar for Buddhist Studies, 2001), 209–28.
2. Heather Stoddard, "The 'Indian Style' *rGya Lugs* on an Early Tibetan Book Cover," in *The Inner Asian International Style 12th–14th Centuries*, ed. Deborah E. Klimburg-Slater and Eva Allinger (Vienna: Österreichischen Akademie der Wissenschaftern, 1998), p. 124.
3. Claudine Bautze-Picron, "The Elaboration of a Style: Eastern Indian Motifs and Forms in Early Tibetan (?) and Burmese Painting," in *Inner Asian International Style*, ed. Klimburg-Slater and Allinger, p. 41.
4. For the documentation of well over a hundred Eastern Indian metalwork and stone sculptures still surviving in Tibetan monasteries, see Ulrich von Schroeder, *Buddhist Sculptures in Tibet,* vol. 1, *India & Nepal* (Hong Kong: Visual Dharma, 2001), pp. 210–405.
5. For a number of works assigned to Eastern India, or either Tibet or Eastern India, see Steven M. Kossak and Jane Casey Singer, *Sacred Visions: Early Paintings from Central Tibet* (New York: Metropolitan Museum of Art, 1998). For a review of this issue, see Dan Martin, "Painters, Patrons and Paintings of Patrons in Early Tibetan Art," in *Embodying Wisdom*, ed. Linrothe and Sorensen, pp. 139–84. Kossak and Singer are sympathetic to the possibility of an Eastern India origin for the "Ford Tara," which is refuted by Martin and by Allinger in Eva Allinger, "The Green Tara in the Ford-Collection: Some Stylistic Remarks," in *Inner Asian International Style*, ed. Klimburg-Slater and Allinger, pp. 107–19.
6. The reading of "RAM" is derived by taking the mark above the RA to be a stylized chandra bindu thus changing the sound to RAM.
7. Glenn Wallis, *Mediating the Power of Buddhas: Ritual in the* Manjushrimulakalpa (Albany: SUNY Press, 2002), p. 121.
8. Matthew Kapstein, "Weaving the World: The Ritual Art of the Pata in Pala Buddhism and Its Legacy in Tibet," *History of Religions* 34, no. 3 (1995): 241–62.
9. Wallis, *Mediating the Power*, p. 123. The text goes on to say that even small paintings, when created using the correct rituals, instantly free one from the most extreme negative karma and have the same merit as worship of all the Buddhas in person.
10. A note on iconographic distinctions: known Indian versions of Achala depict him with one knee down, not standing as here, a posture that was popularized in Tibet by Atisha. On the other hand, the fact that Achala is depicted in a slender, *vira* (warrior) mode, instead of the big-bellied *lambodara* type, shows an adherence to the older Indian model. Most Achala figures in Tibet are in the big-bodied type (e.g., cat. nos. 38, 39). See the metalwork inscribed with the version of Achala's name in anuttara *tantras*, Chanda Maharoshana, *Indian and Southeast Asian Art*, sale cat., Christie's New York, 27 March 2003, sale 1212, lot 79 (sold for $83,650); also Heller, "On the Development," in *Embodying Wisdom*, ed. Linrothe and Sorensen, fig. 3. Curiously close to the Rubin Achala is one in a "banner painting" dated 11th/12th century, in *Indian and Southeast Asian Art*, sale cat., Sotheby's New York, 24 March 2004, Sale N07975, lot 54 (unsold).

Cat. nos. 38, 39

(Cont. from p. 190) In fact, that mark may be taken as nothing more than a frown's furrow on the forehead. The expression of the later Achala looks less grim, but more sinister, since he now has a wicked grin as he bares his fangs, and one can see both upper and lower teeth. Stylistically, the work seems to fit somewhere between some sculptures credited to the thirteenth century and others to the fourteenth.[5] The late thirteenth or fourteenth century is a reasonably accurate date.

Notes

1. See the metalwork Achala dated 13th century in the sale catalog, *South and Southeast Asian Art*, sale cat., Christie's New York, 25 March 2004, Sale 1355, lot 60 (sold, $35,850). Similar eyebrows and earrings are shown in a seated wrathful big-bellied figure dated also to the 13th century in the Jokhang; see Ulrich von Schroeder, *Buddhist Sculptures in Tibet*, vol. 2, *Tibet & China* (Hong Kong: Visual Dharma Publication, 2001), pl. 289E. Though identified as Vajrasattva, it seems more likely to be Vajrapani.
2. The blade of the sword may be a repair or replacement.

3. The Ganesha-like figure underfoot is even more relaxed than the similarly depicted figure underfoot in the important Achala sculpture of the ex-Kipniss collection, *Indian and Southeast Asian Art*, sale cat. Christie's New York, 27 March, 2003, sale 1212, lot 79 (sold for $83,650); also Amy Heller, "On the Development of the Iconography of Acala and Vighnantaka in Tibet," in *Embodying Wisdom: Art, Text and Interpretation in the History of Esoteric Buddhism*, ed. Rob Linrothe and Hernik H. Sorensen (Copenhagen: Seminar for Buddhist Studies, 2001), fig. 3.
4. The other end of the noose probably rested above his left shoulder, like the one depicted in David Weldon and Jane Casey Singer, *Buddhist Art in the Nyingjei Lam Collection* (London: Laurence King, 1999), cat. no. 17.
5. See von Schroeder, *Buddhist Sculptures in Tibet*, vol. 2 pl. 291, for a comparable 13th-century Achala, and ibid., pls. 326B–C for comparable 14th-century Vajrapani; one has similarly looped scarves above the ears.

Cat. no. 40

(Cont. from p. 192) spirits of disease and earth lords; with black hair, tied in a black tuft on the crown of the head; with jewel ornaments and various silks as a lower garment. The heel of the right foot and the left knee are pressing down on the seat in a manner of rising; dwelling in the center of a flaming mass of pristine awareness fire.[3]

Seated at the top are the Five Tathagatas representing the five Buddha families, with the blue Akshobhya in the middle.[4] Just as there are white, red, yellow, and green Buddhas around the central blue Buddha, so too at the blue Achala's sides are red, white, green, and yellow forms of protective deities adopting his pose. The five of them are in one sense the emanations of the wrathful compassion of the five Buddhas. Directly below the Buddhas on the ends of the first register are two goddesses, each with three faces and six hands. Parallel to the throne are two standing wrathful black goddesses, naked, each with one face and two hands. One holds a sword in the upraised right hand, and the other a stick. Both have a lasso in the left hand. Directly beneath the lotus, on either side of a flaming sword, are Indra and Shiva (left), Brahma and Vishnu (right).[5] In Nepal, Hinduism and Buddhism thrive alongside each other, a phenomenon that manifests itself in signs of both sectarian rivalry and syncretism.

At the bottom left is the elephant-headed wealth deity Ganapati of the Atisha Lineage, white in color, with one face and four hands. As already mentioned, Manjushri, the bodhisattva of wisdom, is in the bottom center. To either side of him are skull bowls filled with wrathful offerings of the five senses (see cat. nos. 10–12). To the right is the wrathful protector Chaturbhuja Mahakala, blue black, with one face and four hands, seated in a relaxed posture (also see cat. nos. 15, second from left; 26; and cat. key 50.9).

The painting at one time acquired a resinous layer, presumably to preserve it, which has caused serious flaking of pigment.[6] Nonetheless, the painting retains much of its power, drawing on centuries of depictions of Achala. It also remains a powerful testament to the enduring life of Buddhist images, Achala in particular. In many ways, he is the primordial Wrathful Buddha.

Notes

1. David Weldon, "Tibetan sculpture inspired by earlier foreign sculptural styles," *Oriental Art* 46, no. 2 (2000): 47–56; published with the same title in the *Tibet Journal* 27 nos. 1–2 (2002): 3–36; Ian Alsop, "Copies in Tibetan sacred art: Two examples," *Oriental Art* 46, no. 2 (2000): 4–13; Ulrich von Schroeder, "Tibetan Imperial Period Revival School," in *Buddhist Sculptures in Tibet*, vol. 2, *Tibet & China* (Hong Kong: Visual Dharma Publication, 2001), pp. 796–819; Michael Henss, "13th or 18th Century? Original and Copy, Stylistic Conventions and Derivatives in Himalayan Metal Sculpture," paper delivered at the Lempertz Symposium, Dating Tibetan Art, 17–18 November 2001, Cologne, summarized in Michael Henss, review of *Dating Tibetan Art*, ed. Ingrid Kreide-Damani (Wiesbaden: Dr. Ludwig Reichert, 2003), the volume of the proceedings of the Lempertz Symposium; Henss review will appear in the *Tibet Journal*, currently in press.
2. The root Tantra for Krodharaja Achala is the *Siddhaikavira Tantra*, commonly known as the *White Manjushri Tantra* of the *kriya* classification, though Achala also plays a role in the *Mahavairochana Sutra*. In *anuttarayoga*, Achala is also known as Chandamaharoshana from the *tantra* of the same name, and has the same appearance with an added consort and nine deity mandala. The *kriya tantra* practice of Achala was popularized by Atisha (982–1054), founder of the Kadampa School, and also by Lobpon Sonam Tsemo of Sakya (1142–82).
3. From a Tibetan text written by Ngorchen Konchog Lhundrup (1497–1557), trans. Jeff Watt, June 1998.
4. From left: Ratnasambhava, Vairochana, Akshobhya, Amitabha, and Amoghasiddhi.

5. Compare a painting of Achala with his consort, trampling on the same Hindu gods, dated to the early 18th century in Hugo E. Kreijger, *Kathmandu Valley Painting: The Jucker Collection* (London: Serindia, 1999), no. 19.
6. Conservation report no. 04.561, March 2004, Alan M. Farancz Painting Conservation Studio, Inc.

Cat. no. 42

(Cont. from p. 197) this painting at first appears to adopt the lineage-depiction convention of starting in the center with Vajradhara and alternating to his right and left, a convention used more often in later paintings.[2] Curiously, Vajradhara is not placed in the exact center, but slightly to the left. Moreover, the figures on either side are unbalanced, six on the left and seven on the right, unusual but not unprecedented. Some of the figures in the upper register can be identified more fully than in the past. To the left of Vajradhara is the red Vajravarahi. To the left of her is Ghantapada, with one knee down, just as he appears in the charnel ground in the Southeast direction. The fourth figure from the left, next to Ghantapada, is the latter's student, Kumarapada, sitting on a faintly visible tortoise. The next must be Jalandhara, followed by Krishmacharin, holding the hair of a zombie with his other hand raised as if to strike her, and finally on the far left, Guhyapa.

Unexpectedly, despite the fact that Vajradhara is in the center, the painting does not use the alternating convention of lineage depiction. It starts from the center and moves toward the left, then returns to the center and moves to the right. All the Tibetan monastic and lay recipients of the teachings are on the far right, while the Vajradhara through Guhyapa section of the lineage are set out consecutively to the left of Vajravarahi. This is an unusual variant combination of the two conventions of depicting a chronological chain of teachers and students. There are several possible explanations: the artist didn't fully understand the system; this is a regional variation not so far attested; the painting has been wrongly restored; or this variant was transitional between the use of the two conventional systems.

Notes

1. This type of mandala has been explained in detail, making it unnecessary to explicate here. For the identification of all the mandala deities, please refer to bSod nams rgya mtsho, *The Ngor Mandalas of Tibet*, 2 vols. Revised by Musashi Tachikawa et al., (Tokyo: Centre for East Asian Cultural Studies, 1989/91), mandala no. 62. Many of the other deities are identified in Marylin M. Rhie and Robert A. F. Thurman, *Worlds of Transformation: Tibetan Art of Wisdom and Compassion* (New York: Tibet House New York, 1999), cat. no. 170, pp. 430–31. The Ghantapada lineage for Chakrasamvara is Vajradhara, Vajravarahi, Ghantapa, Kumarapada, Jalandhara, Kanha, Guhyapa, Nampar Gyalwai Shap, Barmai Lobpon, Tilopa, Naropa, etc. The most recent, and no doubt the fullest discussion in English to date is John C. Huntington and Dina Bangdel, *The Circle of Bliss: Buddhist Meditational Art* (Columbus: Columbus Museum of Art, 2003), pp. 240–52, 260–69, passim.
2. David Jackson, "The Identification of Individual Teachers in Paintings of Sa-skya-pa Lineages," in *Indo-Tibetan Studies, Papers in honour and appreciation of David L. Snellgrove's contribution to Indo-Tibetan Studies*, ed. Tadeusz Skorupski (Tring: Institute of Buddhist Studies, 1990), p. 138.

Cat. no. 43

(Cont. from p. 198) thirteen-deity mandala closely resembles a well-known mandala transmitted through Maitripa.[6] The crow-, boar-, dog-, and owl-faced gate guardians are especially pertinent to the exploration of the hybrid-grotesque aspect of the "demonic divine."

The upper and lower registers have well defined roles on a painting such as this one. The upper register gives an abbreviated pictorial account of the chain by which the teachings associated with the main mandala arrived in Tibet. Starting on the left with the meta-deity Vajradhara, there are five Indian yogi-Mahasiddhas, followed by five Indian monastic pandits. Several are arranged in pairs, as if the teacher was imparting the teachings to the student. The monks within the squinches wear a different style of monastic robe than the Indian pandits who are bare-chested, except for their outer robe. One of the monks in the central area (top left with yellow hat) is robed like the pandits and may be a Jonangpa lama, but the rest are in the Tibetan style, thus representing the teachers closer in time to the commissioning of the painting, compared with the yogi-Mahasiddhas who are generally given dates between the seventh and tenth centuries.

The three Mahasiddhas on the left side of the top register can be identified due to conformity with standard iconographic conventions for Ghantapada (fourth from the left, with one knee down), Kumarapada (fifth, seated on a tortoise), and Jalandhara (sixth, in a dancing posture). Since they are found in that order in the standard Luipa Chakrasamvara teaching lineage, it seems that a collapsed version of that was used rather than the Maitripa lineage.[7] In that case, after Vajradhara it should be Luipa and Darikapa before Ghantapada.

The lower register, as on many other paintings, includes deities who are benefactors and protectors. As already indicated, the Buddhas on the left have to do with longevity: starting at the far left, Amitayus, Amitabha (seated), Amitabha (standing), Vajrasattva, Vasudhara, Achala, Bhurkumkuta, unidentified wrathful deity,[8] Hayagriva, Black Hayagriva, Vajrapani. Bhurkumkuta is a little-known deity whose meditation is practiced among Sakya and Nyingma lineages.[9] He is specifically employed in the eradication of sickness and disease, and may have been included for the specific purpose of ensuring the longevity of Konchog Pelwa.

Notes

1. The inscription is *rje btsun bla ma dam pa dkon mchog 'phel sku tshe brnyan pa'i phir du/ rig pa 'dzin pa lha mchog seng ges gzhengs.* It translates, "For the purpose of increasing the life span of the holy teacher, Lord Konchog Pel, [this painting was] sponsored by the knowledge holder Lhachog Sengge"; see Denise Patry Leidy and Robert A. F. Thurman, *Mandala: The Architecture of Enlightenment* (New York: Asia Society Galleries, 1997), pp. 92–93. The inscriptions on the back include only OM–AH–HUM written thirty-nine times behind the five central deities, the eleven figures in the top register, and the eleven figures in the bottom register. The painting appears to have had some repainting, particularly in the lower area.
2. For Lachog Sengge (lha mchog sen ge) see TBRC item P2509; he was a nephew of Ngorchen Kunga Zangpo (ngor chen kun dga' bzang po,1382 1456), the found of the Ngor subschool of Sakya. For Konchog Pelwa (dkon mchog 'phel ba) see TBRC item P1873.
3. David Jackson, "The Dating of Tibetan Paintings is Perfectly Possible—Though Not Always Perfectly Exact," in *Dating Tibetan Art: Essays on the Possibilities and Impossibilities of Chronology from the Lempertz Symposium, Cologne,* ed. Ingrid Kreide-Damani, (Wiesbaden: Dr. Ludwig Reichert, 2003), p. 98.
4. Among a number of paintings in a very similar style that could be cited, see the Krishnayamari mandala, Hugo Kreijger, *Tibetan Painting: The Jucker Collection* (Boston: Shambhala, 2001), no. 63, pp. 158–59.
5. Rob Linrothe, *Ruthless Compassion: Wrathful Deities in Early Indo-Tibetan Esoteric Buddhist Art* (London: Serindia, 1999), pp. 276–94. Indeed, Chakrasamvara has recently been the focus of a major exhibition and catalog; John Huntington and Dina Bangdel, *The Circle of Bliss: Buddhist Meditational Art* (Columbus: Columbus Museum of Art, 2003).
6. *Khor lo dem chog lha chu sum gyi kyil kor* from the *Abhidhana Tantra* according to the tradition of Maitripa. See bSod nams rgya mtsho, *The Ngor Mandalas of Tibet,* 2 vols., revised by Musashi Tachikawa et al. (Tokyo: Centre for East Asian Cultural Studies, 1989/91), mandala no. 65. The central pair is counted as one deity.
7. The standard Chakrasamvara lineage of the Sakya tradition (to which the patron of this painting belonged) begins as follows: Vajradhara, Vajrapani, Saraha, Nagarjuna, Shavaripa, Luipa, Darikapa, Ghantapa, Kumarapada, Jalandhara, Kanha, Guhyapa, Nampar Gyalwai Shap, Barmai Lobpon, Tilopa, Naropa, etc. The Maitripa lineage for the thirteen-deity Chakrasamvara begins: Vajradhara, Mati Ratna, Shavaripa, Maitrigupta, Tipu Drime Shenyen, Bareg Lotsawa, Rechung Dorje Drag, Gyalwa Lore, Sumpa Repa, Ling Repa Padma Dorje, Tsangpa Gyare Yeshe Dorje, Ganden Sonam Dar, Ging Pub Nyejung Dar, Ozer Gyatso, Sanggye Repa, etc. The Maitri lineage came down through Maitripa, the direct teacher of Marpa, then to Rechungpa, student of Milarepa, and then into the Drugpa Kagyu School. After several generations it went into the Jonang School and from there eventually went into the Ngor School. This is not a common form of Chakrasamvara found in the Sakya School. Another lineage is the so-called Drugpa lineage, beginning Vajradhara, Vajrapani, Tailopa, Naropa, Marpa, Mila, Dagpo (Gampopa), Tatsawa, Ling Re, Gyare, Sanggye On Re, Shon Seng, Nyi Seng, Sengge Sherab, etc. See *Gyu de kun tu* (TBRC item W21491), fol. 120–21.
8. This blue two-armed deity is a little unusual. It is not absolutely clear is it has a lion's head or a buffalo head. If it is a lion's head, it holds the correct attributes (skull bowl and curved flaying knife) for Simhamukha, but is not in the right pose for her. If it is a buffalo head, the attributes are wrong for "outer" Yama Dharmaraja (cat. no. 34); they fit with Vajrabhairava Heruka but are held in the wrong way, and it would be unusual to find him in this position. Finally, the attributes and pose are correct for the "secret" form of Yama Dharmaraja (cat. no. 33), but the latter usually does not have a buffalo head. Perhaps it has been restored incorrectly.
9. Himalayan Art Website thematic set 564.

Cat. no. 44

(Cont. from p. 203) why the lineage portraits do not include Vajradhara, Nairatmya, or the Indian Mahasiddha Kanha, through whom this form of Hevarja was transmitted to Tibet. Another unusual element explained by the fact that the painting was intended to be seen in the context of a set of

seven paintings, is the inclusion of three of the eight offering goddesses at the bottom. They are beautifully painted in exotic, rainbow-striped pants.[5]

Notes

1. Beginning at the top and placed in a clockwise direction is yellow Vetali, multi-colored Dombini, green Ghashmari, blue Pukkasi, blue-black Gauri, white Shavari, red Chauri, and purple Chandali.
2. bSod nams rgya mtsho, *The Ngor Mandalas of Tibet*, 2 vols., revised by Musashi Tachikawa et al. (Tokyo: Centre for East Asian Cultural Studies, 1989/91), mandala no. 104. This is confirmed by an inscription on the back of the cloth mounting at the top: *nag po lugs kyi snying po kyai rdo* (i.e., *do rje*).
3. See the Krishna Yamari mandala in the Jucker collection, of nearly the identical size (39 x 31 cm); Hugo Kreijger, *Tibetan Painting: The Jucker Collection* (London: Serindia, 2001), no. 63; see also a related Pancharaksha mandala; Blanche Christine Olschak with Geshé Thupten Wangyal, *Mystic Art of Ancient Tibet* (Boston: Shambhala, 1987), pl. 110.
4. The *kabab nam shi* of Kanha, part of the set of *kabab nam dun*, include the Hevajra from Virupa, Saroruhavajra, Kanha, and Dombi Heruka; see bSod nams rgya mtsho, *Ngor Mandalas,* nos. 99–105, respectively. Some of these are also in a grouping known as the *kabab dun*, the seven transmissions of Ngor which are the Guhyasamaja Akshobhyavajra, Nagarjuna lineage, Guhyasamaja Manjuvajra, Jnanapada lineage, Chakrasamvara, Luipa lineage, Chakrasamvara, Krishnacharin lineage, Hevajra, Virupa lineage, Hevajra Panchadaka, and Vajra Samputa; bSod nams rgya mtsho, *Ngor Mandalas,* nos. 42, 44, 62, 63, 99, 109, 111, respectively.
5. An offering goddess with identically painted pants is found in a painting of five mandalas from the *Vajravali*; John Huntington and Dina Bangdel, *The Circle of Bliss: Buddhist Meditational Art* (Columbus: Columbus Museum of Art, 2003), cat. no. 90, key D10, identified as the earth goddess Prithvi.

Cat. no. 45

(Cont. from p. 204) His back legs are in the archer's pose, the second left one hangs parallel to her left leg, his second right leg brought up into the dancer's pose like Vajravarahi (cat. nos. 57–58; compare the different pose of Hevajra's second pair of legs in cat. no. 44). Nairatmya, who has one head, two arms, and two legs, entwines her left leg around his right side, clinging to him with arms and leg. Although the Sakya tradition maintains this form of Hevarja as a minor variant, it is the primary form among Kagyu and Gelugpa. This may indicate a Kagyu patron. Unlike paintings or relief sculptures in which the artists project the other faces to the sides, in this work seven of the heads form an encircling ring, a treatment common to Eastern Indian Hevajra sculptures.[2] The eighth head seems to stare upward, again an exceptional feature. At the tip of Hevajra's flame-shaped hair is a *visva-vajra* (crossed *vajras*).[3]

Notes

1. Shri Hevajra is known in Tibetan as *pal gye pa dor je*; Vajra Nairatmya as *dor je dag me ma*. Hevajra is the principal Sakya school Wrathful Buddha and was the tutelary deity of Marpa the Translator, founder of the Kagyu School. According to the Kagyu system of *tantra* classification Hevajra belongs to the "Wisdom mother" *Anuttarayoga tantra*. According to the Sakya system, Hevajra belongs to the "Nondual" *Anuttarayoga*. Among the various forms of Hevajra, this figure is known as the "Essence Hevajra" as taught in the root *Tantra of Two Sections*. The transmission lineage begins as follows: Vajradhara, Jnana Dakini, Bodhivajra Garbha, Arya Nagarjuna, Aryadeva, Chandrakirti, Matangipa, Tailo Prajnabhadra (Tilopa), Naro Jnana Siddhi (Naropa), etc.
2. For Eastern Indian images of Hevajra, see Rob Linrothe, *Ruthless Compassion: Wrathful Deities in Early Indo-Tibetan Esoteric Buddhist Art* (London: Serindia, 1999), pp. 268–71; Ulrich von Schroeder, *Buddhist Sculptures in Tibet*, vol. 1, *India & Nepal* (Hong Kong, Visual Dharma, 2001), pl. 102C–E. For an example of a thirteenth-century stone Hevajra with projecting heads to either side, see ibid., vol. 2, *Tibet & China*, pl. 208B.
3. Interpretations of what each of the features "represents" in the Esoteric Buddhist systems are available, based mainly on the *Hevajra Tantra*. See John C. Huntington and Dina Bangdel, *The Circle of Bliss: Buddhist Meditational Art* (Columbus: Columbus Museum of Art, 2003), pp. 454–57.

Cat. no. 46

(Cont. from p. 207) thus preserves a variant tradition that may have died out at some point.[4]

In each of the four squinches beyond the flaming outer border of the mandala are five more figures. The two smallest ones comprise the seven treasures of the ideal Buddhist king—wheel, gem, faithful queen, elephant, horse, warrior, vase—with the addition of a wealth deity to keep the symmetry. In the four corners (cat. key 46.14–17) are three forms of Krishna Yamari (one with a buffalo head), and the buffalo-headed Yama Dharmaraja without consort (or possibly Krishna Yamari). In addition, beside the lower corners are Rakta Yamari (cat. key 46.18) and Vajrabhairava Heruka (cat. key 46.19). In the lowest register is a monk who is probably either the patron of the work or

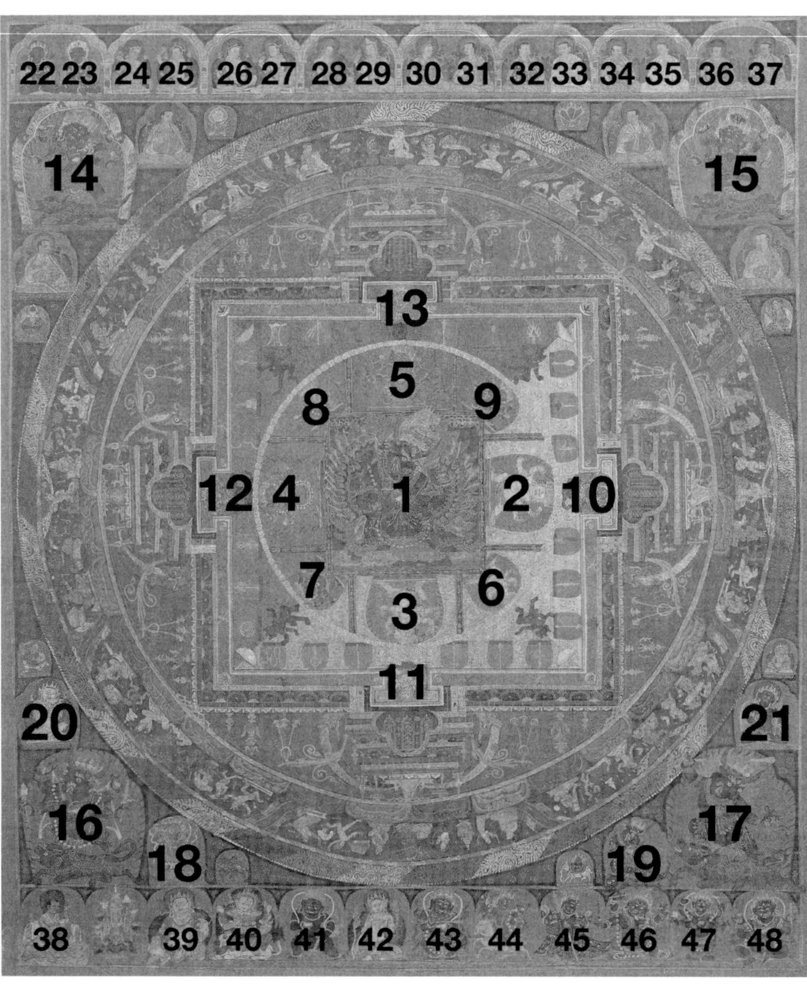

its intended consecrator (cat. key 46.38), and beside him, a group of wrathful protectors and wealth deities.

Dating mandalas is challenging since so many elements are iconographically determined, and the composition is conservative and resistant to change. The inscriptions on the back of this painting are no help. The usual OM–AH–HUM is behind each deity, but otherwise the short inscription at the center in *lantsa* (*ranjana*) script is only a *mantra*. One of the keys to help determine the date of the painting is the structure of the arches, which are a kind of framing nimbus for the members of the lineage in the top register (cat. key 46.22–37) and for two of the deities in the squinches (cat. key 46.14, 46.15). In the upper register, the arch is trilobate in shape and golden in color, supported by short pillars which are as if inlaid with gems alternating in color. The arches surrounding the upper deities are not as wide in span and form an outer gem-studded border to the

Cat. key 46

1. Vajrabhairava [2–9 are personifications of eight prominent attributes held in Vajrabhairava's hands.] 2. Head of Brahma 3. Hand 4. Intestines 5. Foot 6. Skull bowl with blood 7. Head of a human corpse 8. Shroud 9. Impaled human body [10–13 are guardian deities] 10. Mudgara (hammer) Yamantaka 11. Danda (club) Yamantaka 12. Padma (lotus) Yamantaka 13. Khadga (sword) Yamantaka 14. Three-faced Krishna Yamari 15. Six-faced Krishna Yamari 16. Krishna Yamari with buffalo head 17. Yama Dharmaraja or Krishna Yamari 18. Rakta Yamari 19. Vajrabhairava Heruka 20. Vajrasattva with Vajragarvi 21. Vajravidarana 22. Vajradhara 23. Jnana Dakini 24. Lalita Vajra 25. Amogha Vajra 26. Yeshe Jungne Bepa (Jnanakaragupta) 27. Padma Vajra 28. Dipamkara Rakshita 29. Lama Rwa Dorje Drag 30. Rwa Lotsawa Chorab 31. Rwa Yeshe Senge 32. Rwa Bum Seng 33. Lama Lok Kyapa Wangchug Dragpa 34. Lama Ngong 35. Lama Chokyi Gyalpo (?) 36. Unidentified teacher 37. Unidentified teacher 38. Unidentified patron or consecration sponsor 39. Yellow Jambhala 40. Vaishravana 41. Black Jamabhala 42. Vasudhara 43. Panjarnata Mahakala 44. Shri Devi Palden Lhamo (?) 45. Legden Mahakala 46. Four-armed wrathful deity, unidentified 47. Shadbhuja Mahakala 48. Chaturbhuja Mahakala

flaming nimbus. Similar arches are found in portraits of teachers and deities in several sixteenth-century paintings, though it is rare to find two teachers sharing the same arch.[5] It is fairly usual, however, to find paintings in which two teachers are depicted next to each other, each within his own frame.

Another indicator of style and date is the flame patterns. Around the four wrathful figures in the squinches (cat. key 46.14–17), the outer edge of flames is distinguished from the main mass by being formed into tongues of flame, but still subordinate to the overall shape. They are more restrained than those in fifteenth-century works. Additionally, even without the golden arch, the flames are molded into a trilobate shape (cat. key 46.16, 46.17). Some of the monks and other peaceful figures within the squinches (including cat. key 46.20, 46.21) have no flames but are also shown with a trilobed backdrop, surely a phenomenon not earlier than the late fifteenth century.

Notes

1. For the identification of the other twelve deities, please refer to bSod nams rgya mtsho, *The Ngor Mandalas of Tibet*, 2 vols., revised by Musashi Tachikawa et al. (Tokyo: Centre for East Asian Cultural Studies, 1989/91), mandala no. 54. For Rwa Lotsawa Dorje Drag, see TBRC item P3143; Hubert Decleer, "The Melodious Drumsound All Pervading: Sacred Biography of Rwa Lotsawa," *Tibetan Studies, Proceedings of the 5th Seminar of the International Association for Tibetan Studies, Narita, 1989* (Narita: Naritasan Shinshoji, 1992), 1:13–28. The root text for most of the Vajrabhairava mandala still in practice is the *Shri Vajrabhairava nama tantra,* Toh 468. For depictions of Rwa Lotsawa, see the Kalachakra mandala in the R. R. E. collection; John C. Huntington and Dina Bangdel, *The Circle of Bliss: Buddhist Meditational Art* (Columbus: Columbus Museum of Art, 2003), cat. no. 148. See also Himalayan Art Website item 79875. The lineage is also discussed in David Jackson, "The Identification of Individual Teachers in Paintings of Sa-skya-pa Lineages," in *Indo-Tibetan Studies, Papers in honour and appreciation of David L. Snellgrove's contribution to Indo-Tibetan Studies*, ed. Tadeusz Skorupski (Tring: Institute of Buddhist Studies, 1990), pp. 137–38.
2. In this and a few other ways the mandala resembles the great painting in the Los Angeles County Museum of Art; see Himalayan Art Website item 85722.
3. Starting from the east, the viewer's right (at 3 o'clock) the Mahasiddhas are: Saraha, Dombhi Heruka (NE), Nagarjuna, Ghantapada, Virupa, Luipa, Kukkuripa. This maintains the usual order but shifts them all two stops counterclockwise.
4. One can speculate that it may be a Jonangpa mandala, part of the Rwa tradition itself, or a variant tradition by Mitra Yogin.
5. See for example, Himalayan Art Website items 203, 1041, 87225, 90902; see also cat. no. 42.

Cat. no. 47

(Cont. from p. 209) images of Vajrabhairava are not known, as his practices apparently circulated privately before being transmitted to Tibet.[3] Therefore, monastic institutions did not create and install large images, which would have been more likely to survive, making it impossible to compare them to the Vajrabhairava images of the Himalayan regions. There is comparable Indian material, however, for Yamantaka, who, like Vajrabhairava, is related to Manjushri and is also closely associated with the destruction of buffalo-headed Yama, the god of death. Yamantaka has six faces, six hands, and six legs and rides on a buffalo, while Vajrabhairava has nine faces, thirty-four hands, and sixteen legs and takes the head of the buffalo. Indian artists creating Yamantaka images were also faced with the challenge of showing six heads, and since Tibetan artistic traditions certainly drew directly on the Indian ones at a formative stage, how the Indian artists handled the six heads of Yamantaka may be of relevance here.

Among the few known Eastern Indian images of Yamantaka as the central figure, once again two modes were used. Most have one register of six heads, but some have two registers of five and one heads.[4] Outside of India, the record is similarly mixed: the site of Mangyu in Ladakh of about the twelfth century, with its strong connections to Kashmiri artists, features a Yamantaka with two rows of three heads each, the same is true at the Alchi Sumtsek, and from the ninth century onward, in Shingon contexts of Japan.[5] On the other hand, Zhang Shengwen's image of Yamantaka datable to 1180 from southwest China shows him with two registers of five and one.[6] In a loose sense, then, the ambiguity found in the Tibetan conventions for depicting Vajrabhairava can be traced to India. It was a matter of artistic conventions that became accepted as correct, but without the warrant of a clear textual authority, could be changed.

Notes

1. For a sense of how it looked, apart from matters of style and size, see Ulrich von Schroeder, *Buddhist Sculptures in Tibet*, vol. 2, *Tibet and China* (Hong Kong, Visual Dharma, 2001), pl. 265B–C. Closer in style, perhaps, but again, not in scale is the ex-Pan Asian sculpture in Ulrich von Schroeder, *Indo-Tibetan Bronzes* (Hong Kong: Visual Dharma Publications, 1981), pl. 123E.
2. For an 18th-century Nepalese example of this type, see John C. Huntington and Dina Bangdel, *The Circle of Bliss: Buddhist Meditational Art* (Columbus: Columbus Museum of Art, 2003), cat. no. 146.
3. An exception to this may be the odd-looking, provincial metalwork Vajrabhairava tentatively attributed to an 11th-century "provincial atelier in Kashmir proper, or it could be the handiwork of an artist in western Tibet" (Pratapaditya Pal, *Bronzes of Kashmir* [New York: Hacker Art Books, 1975], cat. no. 63). It has three registers of three heads each.
4. For examples, see Rob Linrothe, *Ruthless Compassion: Wrathful Deities in Early Indo-Tibetan Esoteric Buddhist Art* (London: Serindia, 1999), pp. 162–71.
5. Ibid., fig. 153; Roger Goepper and Jarslav Poncar, *Alchi, Ladakh's Hidden Buddhist Sanctuary: The Sumtsek* (London: Serindia, 1996), pp. 151–52; Sawa Ryuken et al., *Kobo Daishi and the Art of Esoteric Buddhism* (Tokyo: Tokyo National Museum, 1983), cat. nos. 120, 121, 135, 140, 148.
6. Li Lin-ts'an, *A Study of the Nan-chao and Ta-li Kingdoms in the Light of Art Materials Found in Various Museums* (Taibei: National Palace Museum, 1982), p. 117, fig. 120.

Cat. no. 48

Note *(Cont. from p. 211)*

1. Janet Baker, *Seeking Immortality: Chinese Tomb Sculpture from the Schloss Collection* (Santa Ana: Bowers Museum of Cultural Art, 1996), p. 53.

Cat. no. 50

(Cont. from p. 215) general.[2] The offering cake just to the left of Yama Dharmaraja (cat. key 50.19) is painted in considerable detail and faithfulness to the specific forms mandated for Gelugpa Vajrabhairava rituals. It "symbolizes the buddha-mind of Vajrabhairava."[3] However, teachings and images of Vajrabhairava are still part of the Sakya and Kagyu lineages as well. Pre-Gelugpa images, and most contemporary Sakya and Kagyu lineage versions of Vajrabhairava, show a different configuration for the nine heads. Instead of a 7-1-1 stack, the older ones have a 3-3-3 stack, as in catalog numbers 46 and 47.[4]

Directly above the central couple is a group of seven teachers (cat. key 50.2–8) forming a spiritual lineage of the Gelugpa. This is something of an idealized set, not a *sampradaya* (the chain of teachers through whom came the meditation practice of the main figures), as in other paintings in the exhibtion (cat. nos. 42, 43, 46, 51, 56). The group consists of Vajradhara (cat. key 50.2), the Mahasiddhas Tilopa and Naropa (cat. key 50.3–4), Atisha (972/82–1052), founder of the Kadampa lineage (cat. key 50.6), Tsongkapa (1357–1419), founder of the Gelugpa tradition (cat. key 50.7), a second image of Tsonkapa in the guise of a Mahasiddha as envisioned by Khedrup Geleg Pal Zangpo (1385–1438, cat. key 50.5), and finally one of the Dalai Lamas (cat. key 50.8). He holds the stem of a lotus and a long-life vase in his left hand, suggesting that he might have been alive when the work was painted. Without inscriptions or more specific attributes it is not possible to identify which Dalai Lama it is, but perhaps the seventh Kalzang Gyatso (1708–57), or the eighth Jampal Gyatso (1758–1804), are more likely than the ninth through twelfth, whose lives were short, or the sixth, whose reign was also cut short.

The protectors surrounding Vajrabhairava and his consort are arranged roughly into two groups consisting of wisdom in the upper half and worldly deities in the lower. This closely parallels the exhibition's categories of Enlightened and Dangerous Protectors, with Wrathful Buddhas at the center of the painting. Among the Enlightened Protectors are five different forms of Mahakala (cat. key 50.9–13), and both Palden Lhamo and Magzor Gyalmo (cat. key 50.15–16). The Chitipati (Smashana Adipati) are unusual in at least three respects. First, although in a Gelugpa painting, both carry the skull-topped staff instead of a stalk of grain (see cat. no. 12). Second, no conch or cowrie is visible; perhaps they were thought of as underneath the corpse they jointly stand on. Finally, their pose is one of nearly frontal embrace, instead of standing side-by-side.

The first pair of Dangerous Protectors includes the epic warrior, King Gesar, with his riding crop and spear (cat. key 50.18). Animal messengers fly out of his nimbus, a trait found on many images of

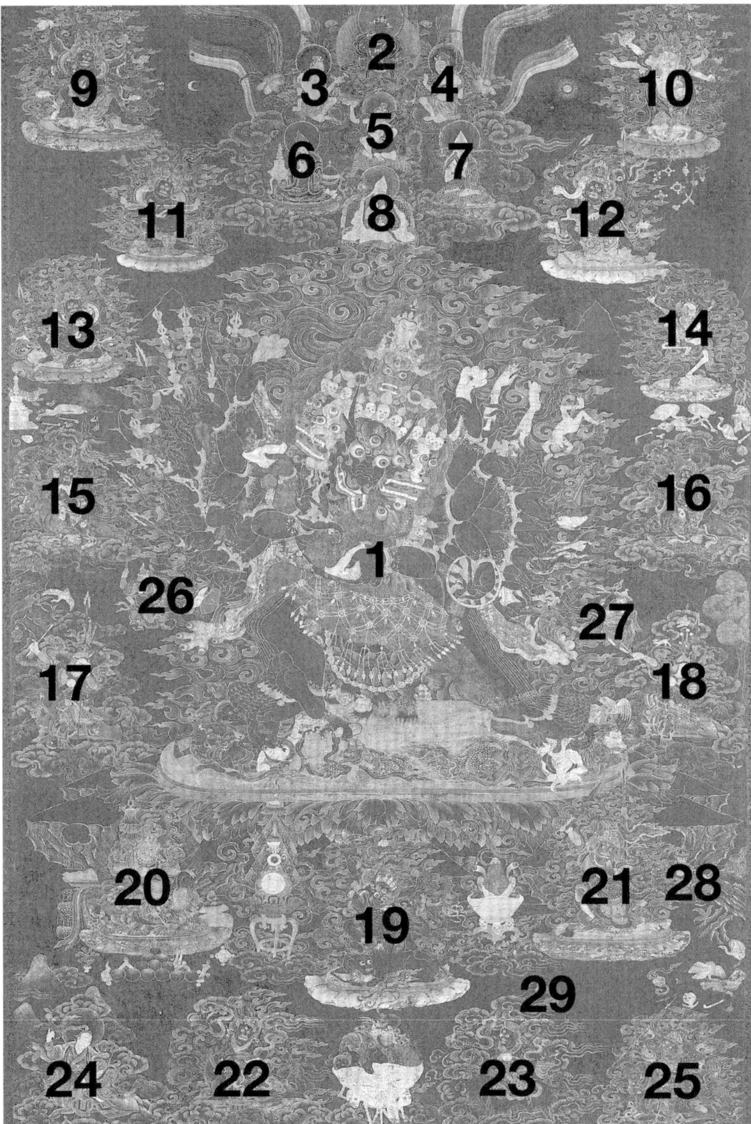

Gesar.[5] The mounted warrior who forms the pendant to Gesar is unidentified (cat. key 50.17). Perhaps a clue to his identity is the *terma* casket placed in a cave just above him.

In the top right corner, a rain of jewels and other precious objects falls from the two elephants being trampled by Shadbhuja Sita Mahakala (cat. key 50.10). On the diagonal opposite side of the painting, in the mid-lower left, one finds Vaishravana on a lion beside a stack of bolts of silk and tublike vase of jewels (cat. key 50.20). Since he is both a *dharma* protector and a wealth deity, these two scenes reflect the undertone of benefaction implied within the main purpose of protection at the essence of this work.

There are no inscriptions on this work and it appears to be untouched in terms of in-painting or restoration.

Notes

1. Robert Thurman, "Worlds of Transformation," in Marylin M. Rhie and Robert A. F. Thurman, *Worlds of Transformation: Tibetan Art of Wisdom and Compassion* (New York: Tibet House, 1999), p. 38.
2. Gyurme Dorje, "A Rare Series of Tibetan Banners," in *Pearls of the Orient: Asian*

Cat. key 50

1. Vajrabhairava and Vajravetali 2. Vajradhara 3. Tilopa 4. Naropa 5. Tsonkapa in the form of a Mahasiddha 6. Atisha 7. Tsonkapa 8. Dalai Lama, perhaps the seventh, Kalsang Gyatso (1708–57), or eighth, Jampal Gyatso (1758–1804) 9. Shadbhuja Mahakala 10. Shadbhuja Sita Mahakala 11. Panjarnata Mahakala 12. Chaturmukha Mahakala 13. Chaturbhuja Mahakala 14. Smashana Adipati (Chitipati) 15. Shri Devi Palden Lamo 16. Shri Devi Magzor Gyalmo 17. Unidentified 18. King Gesar 19. Yama Dharmaraja (outer), with consort Chamunda 20. Vaishravana on Lion 21. Begtse Chen 22. Shanglon Mahakala 23. Damchen Garwai Nagpo 24. Yudronma or chief of the Tenma Chunyi (the twelve indigenous goddesses of Tibet) 25. Tsiu Marpo

Treasures from the Wellcome Library, ed. Nigel Allan (London: Serindia, 2003), p. 165.

3. Dorje, "Rare Series," p. 165. Rituals for offerings to Vajrabhairava are translated in *Meditation on Vajrabhairava*, ed. Sharpa Tulku with Richard Guard, 2nd edition (Dharamsala: Library of Tibetan Works and Archives, 2000).
4. See, for example, Sakya-style images on the Himalayan Art Website items 198, 295, 388, 73516, 83722, 90326. Item 73511 is a relatively recent Sakya painting with the Gelugpa-style stack of heads (late 19th–20th century). This is probably the error of an artist more accustomed to Gelugpa patrons.
5. For comparable images of Gesar, see Himalayan Art Website items 79418, 87625, 90705, 90715; and Do Khyentse Hungkar Dorje et al., *Tangkas in Golog: The Tangka Album of Lung-ngon Monastery* (Beijing: Encyclopedia of China Publishing, 2001), p. 211.

Cat. no. 51

(Cont. from p. 218) penetrating sound of the horse's neigh, can definitely be traced back to India, and in one sense, he was a personification of this power.[5] In Tibetan contexts, Hayagriva is continues to be understood as the "embodiment of the speech of the Buddhas."[6]

The overall composition and particular details of this painting bear a number of archaic elements that suggest a date of the late thirteenth or early fourteenth century. The central couple dominates the space, and is large in scale compared to all the other figures who are in two different scales depending on placement. There is a system of registers and columns of deities which are rigidly set off from each other, though without the structural borders on twelfth- and early-

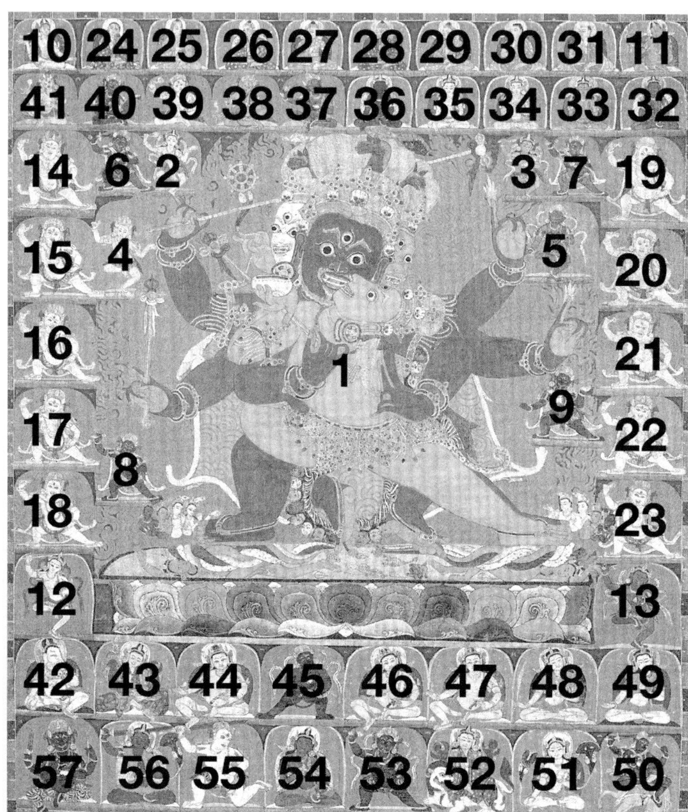

Cat. key 51

1. Hayagriva (Tamdrin Dregpa Kundrol) and Krodhishvari **2–9.** Retinue figures of the mandala; the Tibetan names are found on *tsagli* cards of this mandala; see Himalayan Art Website thematic set 888. **10.** Pashini, female gate-keeper of South, yellow **11.** Sphota, female gate-keeper of West, red **12.** Ankushi, female gate-keeper of East, white **13.** Ghanta, female gate-keeper of North, Green **14–23.** The first is Hayagriva with single horse's head, protector of the West. The other protectors are not distinguished from each other so they can't be identified individually but their Tibetan names are found on *tsagli* cards of this mandala; see Himalayan Art Website thematic set 888. **24.** The terton, Drugu Yangwang (?) **25–31.** Nyingma lineage of this *terma*. **32.** Amoghasiddhi Tathagata **33.** Amitabha Tathagata **34.** Vairochana Tathagata **35.** Ratnasambhava Tathagata **36.** Akshobhya Tathagata **37–41.** Semi-wrathful representatives of the Karma, Padma, Buddha, Vajra and Ratna families. They may represent the consorts of the Tathagatas. **42.** Ganapati **43.** Vaishravana **44.** Yellow Jambhala **45.** Black Jambhala **46.** Yellow Jambhala 2 **47.** Yellow Jambhala 3 **48.** Yellow Vasudhara **49.** White Sitapatatra (without parasol; restorer's error?) **50.** Shri Devi, Palden Lhamo **51.** White Tara **52.** Vaishravana on Lion **53.** Krodha Vajrapani **54.** Vajravidarana **55.** White Achala **56.** Black Manjushri **57.** Four-armed Mahakala

thirteenth-century compositions. There is no attempt at creating a shared setting or landscape to connect the registers. The distribution of teachers at the top, retinue figures related to the main couple on the sides, and the protectors, benefactors and wealth deities in the lower registers, also has counterparts in early paintings. Another early feature is the triangular gold finials behind the back-rest bolsters against which many of the deities sit. Finally, the triangular gold crests on the tiaras of many of the figures, and the gold-outlined brick-like border of alternating colors are common features in paintings dated from the eleventh through the fourteenth century.[7]

The arrangement of the deities around the central couple of Hayagriva and Krodhishvari creates groupings that imply a mandala.[8] There are eight retinue figures, of which four are peaceful female goddesses (cat. key 51.2–5) and four blue male wrathful protectors (cat. key 51.6–9), four inner gate-keepers (cat. key 51.10–13), and ten outer wrathful protectors of the eight directions, zenith and nadir (cat. key 51.14–23). This is a mandala of twenty-three deities, or twenty-four counting Hayagriva's consort Krodhishvari, one that is included in the Rinchen Terdzo Chenmo (Great Jewel Treasury), and credited to Drugu Yangwang of the late eleventh to mid twelfth century. He is probably the first of the six layman on the left side of the top register (cat. key 51.24). After Drugu Yangwang, the next five wear distinctive hats associated with the Nyingma lineage (cat. key 51.25–29). At the end of the line on the right, two monks sit in a respectful manner (cat. key 51.30–31).

In the second register, the five deities on the right are the five Tathagatas (cat. key 51.32–36). On the left side of the same row are five bodhisattva-like deities, who may be female (cat. key 51.37–41). Each holds a skull bowl in their left hand, but a different object in the right; four of them resemble the four offering goddesses (cat. key 51.2–5), who also have skull bowls, but in a slightly more wrathful mode. Since they are connected to the five Tathagatas by color and, with one exception, order, perhaps they are intended to represent the consorts of the Tathagatas. However, since there has been considerable repainting on the surface, the precise iconographic details cannot be relied upon uncritically.

The bottom two registers depict deities not part of the "implied mandala." Several of them are wealth deities, but others are protectors, benefactors and wealth deities. For their identification, please refer to the numbered chart and key below.

Notes

1. The name of the *terma* is *Hayagriva Liberating All Hindrances* (Tibetan: *dpal rta mgrin dreg pa kun sgrol*), revealed by Gru-gu Yang-dbang and later reinforced by 'Jam-dbyang Mkhyen-brtse'i-dbang-po. It is found in the *Rin chen gter mdzod chen mo*, vol. 40, pp. 237–474, reproduction of the Stod-lun Msthur-phu redaction in Bhutan, 1976–80; bibliographic details can be found at TBRC Resource Code W20578. On Drugu Yangwang, see "Masters of the Nyingma Lineage," *Crystal Mirror* 11 (1995), p. 123. Besides the usual OM–AH–HUM consecration *mantras* on the back, written in red, there is a longer inscription, only partly legible, consisting of mantras relating to various deities important in the Nyingma lineage, including Garuda, Vajrakila, Yamantaka/Yamari, Vajrapani, and Mahakala
2. For a description of the Rinchen Terzo and the intentions of the editor, see E. Gene Smith, *Among Tibetan Texts: History & Literature of the Himalayan Plateau* (Boston: Wisdom Publications, 2001), p. 262. A summary of its contents is found in Jamgon Kongtrul Lodro Thaye, *The Autobiography of Jamgön Kongtrul: A Gem of Many Colors*, Richard Barron, trans. (Ithaca: Snow Lion Publications, 2003), pp. 521–26.
3. Martin Boord, *A Bolt of Lightning from the Blue: The vast commentary on Vajrakila that clearly defines the essential points* (Berlin: Khordong, 2002), pp. 128, 188
4. The white and red *garudas* are clear, though it appears that the restorer was not completely sure about the blue one and blurred the details. They are actually part of the retinue, and in extant *tsagli* sets, are depicted separately, as are all the other forms in the implied mandala. For their names, see Himalayan Art Website thematic set 888.
5. For an introduction to Hayagriva in Indian texts and images, see Rob Linrothe, *Ruthless Compassion: Wrathful Deities in Early Indo-Tibetan Esoteric Buddhist Art* (London: Serindia, 1999), pp. 82–141.
6. Tulku Thondup, *Masters of Meditation and Miracles: Lives of the Great Buddhist Masters of India and Tibet* (Boston: Shambhala, 1999), p. 101. See also Dudjom Rinpoche, Jikdrel Yeshe Dorje, *The Nyingma School of Tibetan Buddhism, Its Fundamentals and History* (Boston: Wisdom Publications, 1991), p. 479.
7. For older paintings that share one or more features with this painting, see Steven M. Kossak and Jane Casey Singer, *Sacred Visions: Early Paintings from Central Tibet* (New York: Metropolitan Museum of Art, 1998), cat. nos. 31 and 40, both dated to the 14th century. Superficially, the Vajrakila Vajrakumara in a private collection, also an early Nyingma painting, has a number of comparable features, including

the way the side figures interrupt the edges of the nimbus of the main figure and his retinue; Pratapaditya Pal, *Himalayas: An Aesthetic Adventure* (Chicago: The Art Institute of Chicago, 2003), cat. no. 137. However, both the Hayagriva painting, and to a much greater extent, the Vajrakila painting, have been restored, making it dangerous to make detailed comparisons. See also Himalayan Art Website item nos. 65036, 65125, 73812, and 89979.

8. Christian Luczanits has identified the iconography of a number of paintings of Tathagatas that collectively present the iconography of Vajradhatu mandalas, though each painting does not appear in the symmetrical arrangement of a mandala. Christian Luczanits, "On the Iconography of Thangkas dedicated to the five Tathagatas," in *Aspects of Tibetan Art*, edited by E. F. Lo Bue (Leiden: Brill, in press; Proceedings of the Ninth Seminar of the International Association for Tibean Studies, Oxford, 2003). This type of painting can be termed an "implied mandala."

Cat. no. 52

(Cont. from p. 221) both Western Tibet and Eastern India. Several elements militate against a Western Tibetan provenance. First, the base rests on angled legs that terminate in feet. There is a prominent hanging triangle in the middle of the lowest horizontal bar, above which is a pair of addorsed lions with exaggeratedly curved backs. Between them is a medallion with an incised design that resembles the trefoil mark between the horns of the *garuda* at the apex. Above the lions, on a thin vertical surface, is an incised and die-punched design of alternating triangles. The lotus base on which Vajrapani stands has a single row of down-turned lotus petals in a distinctive form: rather puffy, with an outline incised on the borders, and a tip that turns sharply up. Finally, the nimbus is worth taking note of for its shape—long and narrow, curved at the top with the *garuda* finial. The nimbus also has a double-band structure, the inner band with a different pattern but exactly following the shape of the outer border with its pierced flaming pattern.

None of these features can be found in Kashmiri or Western Tibetan metalwork except as rare exceptions, and even then, never with more than one of these features. On the other hand, many of these elements are present in examples of Eastern Indian metalwork (especially from Kurkihar) between the ninth and eleventh centuries.[3] Western Tibetan metalwork examples almost always have a flat base, and combine a head nimbus with a body nimbus, not one continuous shape. The nimbus is usually rounder than in Eastern India, and very rarely has a parallel double band structure.

Eastern Indian and Western Tibetan metalwork are frequently inlaid with silver and copper. This work has neither. Its inscription on the back appears to have been added later, in a modified *nagari* script, rather crudely written and undeciphered. One of the problems with accepting an Eastern Indian provenance is the shape of the eyes. One would expect the curved, wave-shaped eyes, certainly in a Buddha or bodhisattva. The slightly bulging, hooded eyes actually resemble Kashmiri-derived almond-shaped eyes. However, the rather softly articulated torso and body parts bring it closer to Eastern India than to the more brittle structure of Kashmiri-derived torsos, with strongly articulated upper chest, tapering rib cage and abdomen. Given the correspondence of minor features to works from Eastern India, this seems slightly more likely. Perhaps the anomalies can be explained by its relative roughness. Nevertheless, the work exudes a power and the conviction of a designer who, with the prominence of the snakes and the *garuda*, had Vajrapani's *naga*-subduing quality in mind.

Notes

1. Compare the winged *garudas* biting down on snakes between the legs of two 14th-century Vajrapani sculptures in Ulrich von Schroeder, *Buddhist Sculptures in Tibet*, vol. 2, *Tibet & China* (Hong Kong: Visual Dharma Publication, 2001), pls. 326B–C. Discussion of the *garuda* and its archetypal rivalry with *nagas* as found in Sanskrit texts is found in Kurakichi Shiratori, "The Mu-nan-chu of Ta'-ch'in and the Cintamani of India," *Memoirs of the Research Department of the Toyo Kunko* 11 (1939): 2–54.
2. Ulrich von Schroeder, *Indo-Tibetan Bronzes* (Hong Kong: Visual Dharma Publications, 1981), pl. 33A.
3. Ulrich von Schroeder, *Buddhist Sculptures in Tibet*, vol. 1, *India and Nepal* (Hong Kong: Visual Dharma Publication, 2001), pls. 69a–c, 70–75, 82C, 86C.

Cat. no. 53

(Cont. from p. 222) few old patches visible on the back. However, there has been considerable repainting on the front, particularly on the main figure. Although still conveying the main qualities of an old painting, the present painting surface cannot be accepted uncritically.

Notes

1. Other paintings in this style include a Vajrapani in the Rubin Museum of Art, unfortunately extensively repainted; a Mahakala painting in the Navin Kumar collection; a painting in the Essen collection; and a painting in a private collection. See Himalayan Art website item 65088; Pratapaditya Pal, *Tibet: Tradition and Change* (Albuquerque [NM] Museum, 1997), pp. 104–5, 110–11; M. Rhie's essay in this volume, fig. 2.4; Gerd-Wolfgang Essen and Tsering Tashi Thingo, *Die Götter des Himalaya: Buddhistische Kunst Tibets* (Munich: Prestel-Verlag, 1989), cat. no. 99; Amy Heller, "On the Development of the Iconography of Acala and Vighnantaka in Tibet," in *Embodying Wisdom: Art, Text and Interpretation in the History of Esoteric Buddhism*, ed. Rob Linrothe and Hernik H. Sorensen (Copenhagen: Seminar for Buddhist Studies, 2001), fig. 4.
2. This attribute is not well understood and particularly liable to misinterpretation. A Vajrapani painting in the Kumbum at Gyantse is captioned in Chinese and in English, "The Blue Vajrapani with Iron Pipes in Hand" (Chinese: *lanse tieguan jingang shou*); Xiong Wenbing et al., *The Kumbum of Gyantse Palcho Monastery in Tibet* (Chengdu: Tibet People's Publishing House & Sichuan Nationalities Publishing House, 2001), p. 123.
3. For the development of these deities in Indian art and Vajrapani's role, see Rob Linrothe, *Ruthless Compassion: Wrathful Deities in Early Indo-Tibetan Esoteric Buddhist Art* (London: Serindia, 1999).
4. The offerings are understood to be water for drinking, water for washing, flowers, incense, scented water, food, music, and in a separate dish, the light of a lamp. A similar composition, with seven offering tripods, is found in an early painting in the Metropolitan Museum of Art, New York; see Steven M. Kossak and Jane Casey Singer, *Sacred Visions: Early Paintings from Central Tibet* (New York: Metropolitan Museum of Art, 1998), cat. no. 1, where the painting is dated to the 11th century. They are also found in a Western Tibetan painting in the Los Angeles County Museum of Art; see Pratapaditya Pal, *Art of Tibet* (Los Angeles County Museum of Art, 1983), cat. no. P3.
5. A close counterpart to this type of hat is on a *tsagli* in the Virtue Collection; see Pratapaditya Pal and Julia Meech-Pekarik, *Buddhist Book Illuminations* (Hong Kong: Ravi Kumar Publishers, 1988), pl. 41b. Broad-brimmed hats of a related, though not identical style are found in the top register of a cloth painting reproduced in Kossak and Singer,

Cat. no. 54

(Cont. from p. 225) Buddha. Both appear prominently in very similar form, larger-than-life-size, carved in the late thirteenth century among the cliffs at Feilaifeng in Hangzhou, sponsored by the Mongol Yuan government.[3] Here they are painted in an early style that relates to thirteenth-century painting. Compare the Vajrapani of catalog number 51 (detail and cat. key 51.53), as well the styles of catalog numbers 37 and 53.[4] There are tiny mica flecks in some of the pigments, giving the illustrations a shimmering quality.

The themes of the first three illustrated folios of this manuscript give insight into the pantheon and relative status of wrathful deities in about the thirteenth century. One might expect a Wrathful Buddha such as Vajrapani to have a significantly higher position than a wealth deity such as Vaishravana. Although he is placed on the proper right, and therefore the more prestigious position in relation to Vaishravana, the difference is minimal. In fact, our three-fold classification of Wrathful Buddha, Enlightened Protector, and Dangerous Protector is situated within the parameters of an interpretation based on the fully developed Himalayan Buddhist system, not on a historical evolution that began in India. In other words, it is based more on revelation than on history; it is synchronic, not diachronic. A more historical approach would acknowledge that the earliest representations of wrathful Vajrapani were as personifications of the *vajra* (an *ayudhapurusha*) who were attendants to the peaceful bodhisattva Vajrapani in Indian sculpture of the sixth and seventh centuries. Wrathful Vajrapani and the other early wrathful deities such as Hayagriva and Yamantaka were tertiary, as they are literally here, though they gradually increase in importance to become the primary paradigm at the core of Esoteric Buddhism or Vajrayana.[5] This early image in the reconstructed context still retains a kind of embedded memory of an earlier phase.

Notes

1. See Valrae Reynolds et al., *Catalogue of the Newark Museum Tibetan Collection*, vol. 3, *Sculpture and Painting* (Newark Museum, 1986), pp. 125–29; and Pratapaditya Pal and Julia Meech-Pekarik, *Buddhist Book Illuminations* (Hong Kong: Ravi Kumar Publishers, 1988), pp. 138–42.
2. According to E. Gene Smith, the varied number of lines on the second, third, and fifth folios is standard, though the presence of illumination on the verso, not the recto is somewhat unusual (personal communication, April 2004). The second folio is P1994.21.10; third folio is P1995.1.5; see Himalayan Art Website item 700123.
3. Himalayan Art Website items 73235 and 73243. These are niches 32 and 75; see Rob Linrothe, "The Commissioner's Commissions: Late Thirteenth Century Tibetan and Chinese Buddhist Art In Hangzhou Under the Mongols," in Xie

Jisheng et al., *Jiangnan Zangchuanfojiao Yishu: Hangzhou Feilaifeng Shike Zaoxiang* (Hangzhou: Zhejiang Guji Chubanshe, 2004).

4. For manuscript illuminations on a Prajnaparamita text, offering some comparisons in scale of the writing and painting style, see the Newark manuscript radio-carbon dated to the end of the 12th century; Reynolds et al., *Newark Museum Tibetan Collection*, vol. 3, pp. 139–41; and Nathalie Bazin et al., *Rituels tibétains: Visions secrètes du Ve Dalai Lama* (Paris: Musée national des Arts asiatiques-Guimet, 2002), cat. no. 39.
5. Rob Linrothe, *Ruthless Compassion: Wrathful Deities in Early Indo Tibetan Esoteric Buddhist Art* (London: Serindia, 1999), pp. 3–61; Ronald M. Davidson, *Indian Esoteric Buddhism: a social history of the Tantric movement* (New York: Columbia University Press, 2002).

Cat. no. 55

(Cont. from p. 226)

The combination of Tibetan writing in relief against a flat background below figures in an elaborate floral design is unusual. Each half, upper and lower, resembles a Tibetan book cover in its proportions, but together, the shape precludes that function. The thickness of the piece of wood is also greater than most book covers, and instead of beveled edges as is customary on top covers, there is a raised frame around the carved area. The back and sides are planed smooth, but not finished. Two holes were drilled into the top of the work at a diagonal so they emerge on the center back. The panel must have been fixed to some larger composition with other such panels. Stylistically and functionally, this panel relates to a number of wooden panels of Newari workmanship that clearly belong to the same set.[2] Most of the known examples depict peaceful deities, usually one to a panel, not three as here, and they are slightly more elongated in their rectilinear proportions. Nor do they have writing on them, suggesting this work belonged to a different set.

Newari artists have been carving architectural wooden panels for the Tibetans at least since the eighth century. Wooden narrative panels survive in the Jokhang temple of Lhasa, for example, one of the oldest and still the most revered of Tibetan Buddhist temples.[3] Accomplished wooden sculpture is much more common in Nepal than in Tibet, particularly for various architectural elements including brackets, window screens and complex icons.

Notes

1. Inscription: *Om ni lam bha ra dha ra bajra pan ni hum hum phat; Om Nilambara dhara Vajrapani HUM HUM PHAT.* In Tibetan, Vajrapani Nilambaradhara is Pal Chagna Dorje Go Ngonchen (*dpal phag na rdo rje gos sngon can*). The *Drub Tab Kuntu* (TBRC item W21253, vol. 3, pp. 213–57, vol. 11, pp. 476–78) gives three lineages for this form of Vajrapani. The first two belong to the Avadhuti tradition and the third to the Drozang tradition. The first lineage begins: Acharya Avadhutipa Tradition: Vajra Dakini, Suvarna Avadhutipa, Atisha, Geshe Rolpa Garge, Geshe Dze Gyepub, Sakyapa Chenpo, Sonam Tsemo, Dragpa Gyaltsen, Sakya Pandita, Chogyal Pagpa, etc. The second lineage begins with Vajrapani and then follows the Kadam Lha Shi lineage of Atisha. The third lineage begins: Vajradhara, Vajrapani, Chodze Chokyi Dorje, Pal Kuntu Zangpo, Acharya Drozang Nyingpo, Kache Rinchen Dorje, Brahmin Jnana, Jowo Jita Deva, Zangskar Lotsawa Pagpa Sherab (11th century), Yorpa Joton, Chal Sonam Rinchen, Jipu Padma Tashi, Tagpa Jozang, Lotsawa Jampai Pal, Lhachen Sonam Wangchug, Sonam Senge, Yartse Rinchen Senge, Buton Rinchen Drub (1290–1364), etc.
2. See Himalayan Art Website items 65118 and 65191.
3. Construction of the Jokhang began in the 7th century. Ulrich von Schroeder, *Buddhist Sculptures in Tibet*, vol. 1, *India and Nepal* (Hong Kong, Visual Dharma, 2001), pp. 406–31.

Cat. no. 56

(Cont. from p. 229) massive figure of Vajrapani at the center, his white-edged facial features clearly defined in an oval face. This sense of overpowering command is intensified by the projection of his left foot over the edge of a lotus pedestal.

The top of the painting shows thirteen figures, each in their own arched enclosure. Only Vajradhara at the center, and Vajrapani on his right look outward. The rest turn inward toward the central figure. They include Indian pandits, Tibetan monks, and laymen. Ten Tibetan monks are shown in the rigidly set off side registers, above six wrathful protectors. The upper register and the monks on the sides no doubt illustrate one of the lineages for Nilambara Vajrapani, the one that includes the great Zangskar translator, Pagpa Sherap, here in the white layman's robe, third from the right.[3] Although this lineage and the Nilambara Vajrapani practice enters Tibet among Kadampa Buddhists, it is later transmitted into Sakya. Evidence that this painting is Sakya is found in the lower register, which features customary deities used for curing disease (or acting as a prophylactic against them), for protection, and wealth.[4] The donor or patron depicted in the lower left corner is seated in an elaborately curtained chamber in front of an altar on which sits a sculpture of Vajradhara. On the same shelf are a tray mandala, *stupa*-reliquary, and water flask. Beneath are other offerings.

A number of features of this painting relate to the murals in the Kumbum of Gyantse in a Newari-based style, datable to the second quarter of the fifteenth century.[5] A date of the early fifteenth century seems appropriate. Until and unless the unread, effaced inscriptions at the bottom can be recovered, giving historical information, or the later members of the lineage can identified, the dating must rely on formal elements of style alone.[6]

Notes

1. Monier Monier-Williams, *A Sanskrit-English Dictionary* (1899; reprint, Oxford: Clarendon Press, 2000), p. 566.
2. The names of the *nagas* are: Vasuki, Hulunta, Padma, Mahapadma, Karkota, Kulika, Takshaka, and Shankhapala. They are the kings of the various *naga* races and represent the subjugation of various obstacles and the accomplishment of skillful activities.
3. Vajradhara, Vajrapani, Chodze Chokyi Dorje, Pal Kuntu Zangpo, Acharya Drozang Nyingpo, Kache Rinchen Dorje, Brahmin Jnana, Jowo Jita Deva, Zangskar Lotsawa Pagpa Sherab (11th century), Yorpa Joton, Chal Sonam Rinchen, Jipu Padma Tashi, Tagpa Jozang, Lotsawa Jampai Pal, Lhachen Sonam Wangchug, Sonam Senge, Yartse Rinchen Senge, Buton Rinchen Drub (1290–1364), etc.
4. Starting from the left, after the donor or patron, the deities in the lower register are: White Tara, Green Tara, Manjushri, four-armed Avalokiteshvara, Parnashavari, White Achala, Bhurkumkuta, Vaishravana on a lion, Panjarnata Mahakala, Shri Devi Palden Lhamo, Legden Mahakala. Shri Devi Palden Lhamo, the second from the right, is in the Sakya form: four hands, with sword and skull bowl in the right, and spear and trident in the left. Marpa's (Kagyu) Shri Devi holds a purba and trident in the left hands. She also has her legs shackled together.
5. These include the shape of the lotus and jewelry, treatment of the face, hair, snakes, and scarves (including the one that loops around his head), the jeweled arches over the smaller figures, the relative independence of the flame-shaped edges of the main nimbus, and the scrolling, garment patterns etc. Compare Franco Ricca and Erberto Lo Bue, *The Great Stupa of Gyantse: A Complete Tibetan Pantheon of the Fifteenth Century* (London: Serindia, 1993), pls. 17–20, 38–48, 51–54; Xiong Wenbing et al., *The Kumbum of Gyantse Palcho Monastery in Tibet* (Chengdu: Tibet People's Publishing House & Sichuan Nationalities Publishing House, 2001), pls. 110–15, 190.
6. Marylin Rhie and Robert Thurman came to a similar conclusion regarding the dating, placing it between the 14th-century murals at Shalu and the Gyantse Kumbum murals; see Marylin M. Rhie and Robert A. F. Thurman, *Wisdom and Compassion: The Sacred Art of Tibet, Expanded Edition* (New York: Tibet House, 1996), p. 445.

Cat. no. 57

(Cont. from p. 230)

beneath the prone figure on whom she tramples (see detail). It is surprisingly detailed for its size and corresponds well to a fifteenth-century Karma Kagyu *tangka* painting of a five-deity Vajravarahi mandala in the RMA (see detail below).[3] As in the painting, the tips of the two crossed triangles on the base have *svastika* signs, surrounded by borders of skulls and *vajras.*[4] On the eastern and western inner lotus petals are a *vajra* and *padma* representing two of the four *yoginis* surrounding her. The feet and head of the prone figure obscure the southern and northern symbols of the other two *yoginis*, a jewel and a sword.

This work has a few archaistic elements, particularly the triangular plaques in the crown, which have led to a date of the thirteenth century in the past.[5] However, in the authors' opinion, the elongated proportions, beaded swags on the crown, tight swoop of the scarf-ends that tie the crown above the ears, and the complex structure of the petals of the lotus base relate better to fifteenth-century sculpture.[6] It is an impressive work of three-dimensional sculpture, dynamic and powerful.

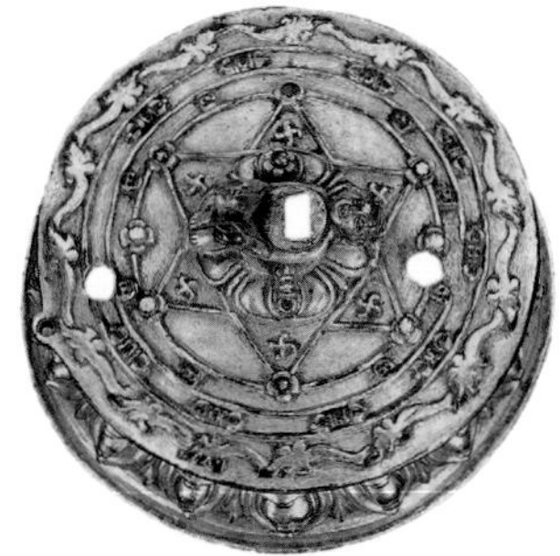

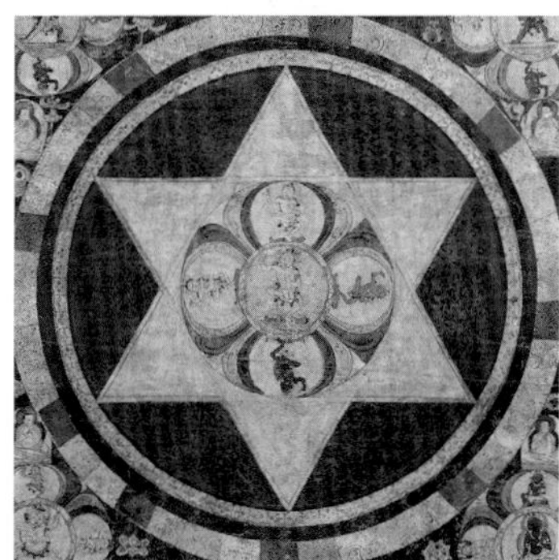

Top: Cat. no. 57, detail

Bottom: Vajravarahi mandala, detail
Tibet, 15th c.
Mineral pigments on cloth
Overall size 19½ x 14½ in. (49.5 x 36.8cm)
F1997.7 (HA94)

Notes

1. John Huntington and Dina Bangdel, *The Circle of Bliss: Buddhist Meditational Art* (Columbus: Columbus Museum of Art, 2003), p. 238.
2. Tibetan: *dor je pag mo*; English: the Vajra Sow. This form of Vajravarahi arises from the Chakrasamvara cycle of *tantras* belonging to the wisdom (mother) class of *Anuttarayoga Tantra* among Sarma practioners. It is practiced predominantly in the Kagyu and Sakya Schools. Along with numerous variations in appearance such as Vajrayogini and the Fierce Black One, Vajravarahi remains one of the most popular and special tutelary deity practices. Among Karma Kagyupa, she is the principal Wrathful Buddha and tutelary deity of the Six Yogas of Naropa. The lineage of her teaching among them begins: Vajradhara, Tilopa, Naropa, Marpa (1012–97), Milarepa (1040–1123), Dagpo Sonam Rinchen, Lord Dusum Kyenpa (1110–93), Rechen, Pom Dragpa, Karma Pakshi (1206–83), etc.
3. Himalayan Art Website item 94.
4. Vajravarahi stands on a double *dharmodaya* (variant, *dharmakara*), the Sanskrit word for the Tibetan word *chos 'byung*. An English translation is "reality source." It refers to the physical shape of a tetrahedron, or four-sided object, with the point directed downward. The top plane, or side, is empty, giving the appearance of a three sided upside down pyramid. The three sides represent the three types of emptiness found in Mahayana Buddhism, wishless, signless, and emptiness itself. In all *tantric sadhanas* the deity arises out of emptiness, and this emptiness can be represented by a *dharmodaya*.
5. Denise Patry Leidy and Robert A. F. Thurman, *Mandala: The Architecture of Enlightenment* (New York: Asia Society Galleries, 1997), cat. no. 17.
6. Unlike jewelry of the 13th to 14th century, which merges into the body, her jewelry stands off the surface. Compare the 13th/14th-century Vajravarahi in Ulrich von Schroeder, *Buddhist Sculptures in Tibet*, vol. 2, *Tibet & China* (Hong Kong: Visual Dharma Publication, 2001), pl. 289B and pls. 267B–D (16th-century examples). The breasts and jewelry resemble the more elaborate 15th-century Vajraharai in the Potala; see ibid., pl. 266D. Probably the closest comparison, particularly in the proportions, scarf loops at the ears, and elaborate turquoise-encrusted jewelry, is with the Vajradhara in the Newark Museum, also dated to the 15th century; see Valrae Reynolds, *From the Sacred Realm: Treasures of Tibetan Art from the Newark Museum* (Munich: Prestel, 1999), pl. 141. Another comparison is with the 15th-century peaceful Green Tara; see Bowers Museum of Cultural Art, *Tibet Treasures from the Roof of the World* (Santa Ana, Cal.: Bowers Museum, 2003), cat. no. 82.

Cat. no. 58

(Cont. from p. 231)

three round red eyes. The right hand holds a curved knife upraised and the left a skull bowl of blood [held] to the heart. In the bend of the left elbow, as the nature of method, appears a *katvanga* staff. Wearing an elephant hide as an upper garment and a tiger skin as a lower garment; adorned with snakes and bones. Dark yellow hair bristles upward, the remainder falling loose. With a crown of five dry human skulls, a necklace of fifty fresh [heads]. The left leg is extended in a half dance posture pressing on the heart of a human corpse. [She appears] youthful and dwelling in the middle of a blazing mass of fire.[5]

The emulation of earlier style is not an isolated phenomenon, or confined to painting. (This issue is also raised in the entry for catalog number 40 in relation to a Nepalese painting.) It has been noticed before in relation to sixteenth-century painting in a Kagyu Taglung context.[6] A number of possible explanations have been offered, including the need to add to a preexisting set of images, extending a series of lineage portraits, for instance. It may also reflect the antiquarian interests of knowledgeable patrons, as seems to be the case with Choying Dorje, the Tenth Karmapa (1604–74).[7] In other cases, it is a matter of copying images—or replicas of images—which are believed to be particularly sacred, as is the case for the Arya Avalokiteshvara (Pagpa Chenrezig) image in Tibet.[8] There may be other reasons as well.[9] Until much more is known about the context of the creators, which ones are relevant here is not yet possible to say.

Notes

1. Nathalie Bazin et al., *Rituels tibétains: Visions secrètes du Ve Dalai Lama* (Paris: Musée national des Arts asiatiques-Guimet, 2002), cat. nos. 22, 27, 29. Like others in the group, the McCormick *tsagli* has an inscription on the back in the *umed* script confined to the outlines of a *chorten*.
2. The Pema Lingpa painting is in the Asian Art Museum of San Francisco, the Chong Moon Lee Center for Asian Art and Culture, Avery Brundage Collection, 1992.344, "Padmasambhava as Guru Drakpoche," 20¾ x 11⅛ inches; published by the Museum in a 2002 calendar titled "Buddhist Painting," on the August month. The Chokyi Gocha painting is illustrated in Heather Stoddard et al., *Portraits of the Masters: Bronze Sculptures of the Tibetan Buddhist Lineages*, ed. Donald Dinwiddie (Serindia: Chicago, 2003), p. 55, fig. 38.
3. Troma Nagmo; Sanskrit: Krishna Krodhini; English: the Fierce Black One.
4. Translation by Jeff Watt, April 1998.
5. From a visualization by Terdag Lingpa Gyurme Dorje (1646–1714) and Minling Lochen Dharmashri (1654–1718), *sgrub thabs 'dod 'jo 'bum bzang* (TBRC item W18), trans. Jeff Watt, April 1998.

Although in this case, because of the other closely related images, this came out of a Nyingma *terma* tradition, another practice lineage belongs to the Zhije School of Padampa Sanggye in the 11th century, but has now been adopted by all the Sarma Schools of Tibetan Buddhism to a greater or lesser extent. The early lineage began as follows: Vajradhara, Jnana Dakini, Virupa, Brahmin Aryadeva, Padampa Sanggye, etc.

6. Amy Heller, *Tibetan Art* (Milan: Jaca Book, 1999), p. 196, caption to pls. 103–4.
7. Ulrich von Schroeder, *Buddhist Sculptures in Tibet*, vol. 2, *Tibet & China* (Hong Kong: Visual Dharma Publication, 2001), pp. 796–819.
8. Ibid, pp. 820–25.
9. See the discussion of this issue in Stoddard et al., *Portraits of the Masters*, pp. 56–57.

Cat. no. 59

(Cont. from p. 236) include various demons and spirits, and found near the top of the painting are the animals of the four directions: white yak, dragon, tiger, and *garuda*, the king of birds.

At the top center is a peaceful deity hardly differentiated from the six surrounding human teachers. At the bottom are protectors of the Bön religion. Red in color and riding a red horse is the protector Tsen. Dark blue and riding a black horse is Sipai Gyalmo, Queen of the World, with three faces and six hands. Other protectors with animal heads stand at the sides.[6]

Notes

1. Tibetan: *dkar nag dmar gsum.*
2. Samten G. Karmay, ed. and trans., *The Treasury of Good Sayings, A Tibetan History of Bon* (Delhi: Motilal Banarsidass, 2001), p. 45, n. 2.
3. Tibetan: *dbal rong.*
4. The liturgical texts describe Tonpa Shenrab as sitting in the upward swirling hair of Tagla Membar.
5. Four Tibetan name inscriptions on the front of the painting identify two retinue deities and two clusters of figures: *rbad pa'i ma mo sde bzhi/ thugs las sprul pa'i ma mo sde lnga/ khrag gdong/ bcud dril.*
6. For a description of Tagla Membar from an almost identical painting with the same composition, see Per Kvaerne, *The Bon Religion of Tibet, the Iconography of a Living Tradition* (London: Serindia, 1995), pp. 124–25.

Cat. no. 60

(Cont. from p. 240) by the mouth on the belly), prominent round cheeks, enlarged eyebrows, and the beard encircling the jaw and chin.

Kneeling on the ledge at Vishnu's feet are a *naga raja* (snake-king) on the left, Privithi, the personification of the earth, in the center, and Lakshmi, Vishnu's consort on the right. A short inscription was carved into the wet clay on the front lower edge, now damaged beyond legibility.

Note

1. Mary Slusser, *Nepal Mandala* (Princeton, N.J.: Princeton University Press, 1982), pp. 240–41.

Cat. no. 61

(Cont. from p. 243) Brahmanical pantheon."[1] Other examples of syncretism are the Chakrasamvara- and Hevajra-like couple in the upper corners (see detail).[2] The Ganesha in the upper left is more familiar in Hindu contexts, as the stepson of Shiva, but he too plays an important role in Buddhist Vajrayana. A final noteworthy example of the late syncretic attitude is the structure of the eight charnel grounds (*smashana*) separated by rivers, four on each side. Along with Shiva-*lingams* in a *yoni*-base, to be expected in a painting depicting Shiva, there are *stupas* which, though mandated by Buddhist texts as included in each of the charnel grounds (see cat. no. 10), suggest that the same charnel grounds were used by both Hindus and Buddhists.

Notes

1. John Huntington and Dina Bangdel, *The Circle of Bliss: Buddhist Meditational Art* (Columbus: Columbus Museum of Art, 2003), p. 194. Other relevant comparisons are the Vishvarupa Mahasamvara of cat. no. 77 in the same source, and Mahottama Heruka of cat. nos. 139–41.
2. The Chakrasamvara-like figure has eighteen arms, instead of twelve, while the Hevajra-like figure has sixteen hands holding *kapala*, like Hevajra, but has eleven heads instead of eight. Compare cat. nos. 42, 44, 45. Both Pal and Slusser mention closely related paintings of ca. 1800–50. Pal writes of the "strong influences of Buddhist imagery," while Slusser states it is "imitative of Buddhist imagery;" see Pratapaditya Pal, *The Arts of Nepal, Part II: Painting* (Leiden: E. J. Brill, 1978), p. 91; Mary Shepherd Slusser, *Nepal Mandala: A Cultural Study of the Kathmandu Valley* (1982; reprint, Kathmandu: Mandala Book Point, 1998), caption to pl. 512.

Cat. no. 62

(Cont. from p. 244) artists were able to pack a great deal of narrative into a single image.

Note

1. See Rob Linrothe, *Ruthless Compassion: Wrathful Deities in Early Indo-Tibetan Esoteric Buddhist Art* (London: Serindia, 1999), pp. 201–3, 212 n. 14.

Cat. no. 63

Notes *(Cont. from p. 245)*

1. V. P. Dwivedi, "An Unusual Devi Image from Kannauj," *Oriental Art* 17, no. 1 (1971): 60–62.
2. Jane Casey et al., *Divine Presence: Art of Indian and the Himalayas* (Barcelona: Casa Asia, 2003), cat. no. 19.

Cat. no. 64

(Cont. from p. 248) Ground (cat. nos. 10–12), Chamunda is depicted as a skeletal figure, with a fierce, compelling beauty. A scholar has recently probed the nature of this mix of fascination and revulsion:

> Whereas ideal physical beauty is often approached in human beings, the image of Camunda comes from the depths of our imagination and thus is more than human, having no limitations; hence her numinous power and our fascination for that which it truly awesome.[4]

Chamunda is a quintessential example of the paradox of the "demonic divine" as expressed in Hindu art.

Notes

1. For such sketchbooks, see M. L. B. Blom, *Depicted Deities: painter's model books in Nepal* (Groningen: E. Forsten, 1989).
2. Pratapaditya Pal, *Hindu Religion and Iconology According to the* Tantrasara (Los Angeles: Vichitra, 1981), p. 67.
3. The various Puranas in which Chamunda features, under one name or another, are comprehensively gathered and reviewed by Thomas E. Donaldson, *Tantra and Sakta Art of Orissa* (New Delhi: D.K. Printworld, 2002), pp. 302–12 (the rest of the chapter contains invaluable information on the iconography of all the Matrikas). The importance of Chamunda in the Kathmandu Valley is also described in Mary Shepherd Slusser, *Nepal Mandala: A Cultural Study of the Kathmandu Valley* (1982; reprint, Kathmandu: Mandala Book Point, 1998), pp. 329–33.
4. Donaldson, *Tantra and Sakta Art*, p. 440.

Cat. no. 65

(Cont. from p. 252) couple, yet also connected to them by sharing an atmosphere of sorts. Only one monk looks directly at the viewer: in the second register, far right. This is probably the teacher of the donor. The side figures include two pairs of solitary wrathful figures—probably inner retinue figures in this implied mandala, though Black Jambhala's presence on the right is puzzling—and five pairs of wrathful protectors embracing consorts, quite close to the main couple. These are no doubt the ten outer protectors (see cat. nos. 18, 51). At the bottom are four peaceful offering goddesses, and four wrathful gate guardians.

There are a number of similarities between this painting and two in a private European collection identified as "RRE."[3] In all three paintings the fine gold lines penetrate the entire background, including the ruled off areas of the top and bottom. Tiny licks of gold paint indicating flames, as at the edges of the nimbi of the wrathful side figures of the Rubin Vajrapani and Vajrayogini and Vajrapani on either side of Vajradhara at the top, is used selectively in the other paintings. They are seen on the larger wrathful retinue figure at the bottom center of the RRE Vajrabhairava, and on the ten wrathful protectors at the bottom of the RRE Guhyasamaja. Since the latter two paintings have been dated late fourteenth to early fifteenth century, a similar date for the Rubin Vajrapani would appear warranted.

However, a few features are hard to reconcile with this date. It is difficult, for instance, to find such active, animated scarves at that time. To be sure, there are active scarves that seem to move of their own accord found in murals at the Gyantse Kumbum, but they do not approach the complexity and scaled diminishment of each fold as the scarves tumble downward in a pyramid shape.[4] In structure, they look much more like garment folds found on seventeenth-century and later paintings and metalwork (cat. nos. 12, 26).[5] Another oddity is the treatment of the upper part of the background. Although there is a scrolling pattern at the bottom, the upper part has gold lines drawn on the dark blue-green background, depicting clouds scudding across the sky. This is unprecedented for an early painting, but recalls the treatment of the sky in *nag-tang* such as in catalog numbers 17 and 31. Later painting regularly distinguishes the top and the bottom of the background, and creates a continuous landscape setting, with sky above, ground and water below, and mountains in between. Early paintings make no such attempt. As already mentioned, the scrolling design can be seen on the RRE Vajrabhairava, but handled differently. It penetrates the upper and lower registers, but not the side columns, as it does in the Rubin painting, and it is uniform throughout, not changing into clouds near the top. A further anomaly is the shape of the oblate nimbus, which is quite bulbous in the middle, and then tapers as it meets the lotus pedestal. Early nimbi are flatter on the sides, as in catalog number 56.

One way to resolve these contradictions is to suggest that the Rubin Vajrapani is a latter painting done in an earlier style, as is the case with other paintings in the exhibition, for example, catalog number 58. However, comparison of the front and back of this painting raises other issues which suggest an alternative explanation. There is no question that the painting has had a great deal of in-painting. The back, which has no inscriptions (nor are there any on the front), is battered and water stained, as would be expected in a fifteenth-century painting. No stains or discolorations are visible on the front, however. A few areas of bare fabric have been left unrestored, noticeable most easily at the top center, around and in Vajradhara, giving some sense of what the rest of the painting may once have looked like. Based on this evidence, it now seems most likely that the painting has been heavily restored, that it was indeed an early fifteenth-century painting done in a style worked out in the fourteenth, but that in the process of restoration—probably in the twentieth century—later elements were added anachronistically to fill in areas that were nearly bare. This explains the disparity between back and front, and between fourteenth- and fifteenth-century formal qualities with eighteenth-century elements. In spite of the considerable restoration, it still conveys a strong sense of the original intentions of its patron and artist. And it still holds its weight in the comparison of wrathful and peaceful forms of the same deity.

Notes

1. Drugpa Kagyu *sadhana* text, *rjes su gnang ba nyi shu rtsa gnyis kyi chog chings lo rgyu bcas rgas tshangs spros 'bring du bkod pa tshogs gsung reg zig bzhugs so*, second deity description, of Utsarya Vajrapani. This is a Drugpa Kagyu collection of twenty-two initiations and accompanying sadhana practices together with lists of lineage teachers.
2. bSod nams rgya mtsho, *The Ngor Mandalas of Tibet*, 2 vols., revised by Musashi Tachikawa et al. (Tokyo: Centre for East Asian Cultural Studies, 1989/91), mandala no. 49. "Implied mandala" refers to a work that is not arranged as a symmetrical graph as in catalog numbers 35, 42–44, 46, but does include the deities who would be found in such a plan. There are several Rechungpa Vajrapani lineages; none of the ones checked so far fits the group around Vajradhara exactly.
3. The collection designated as RRE has a Vajrabhairava and and Guhyasamaja; both are published in Amy Heller, *Tibetan Art* (Milan: Jaca Book, 1999), pls. 80 and 97. The Guhyasamaja is also published in John C. Huntington and Dina Bangdel, *The Circle of Bliss: Buddhist Meditational Art* (Columbus: Columbus Museum of Art, 2003), cat. no. 135. Heller dates the Vajrabhairava to the "late fourteenth to early fifteenth century," and the Guhyuasamaja to the 16th century. This dating is based on radiocarbon dating providing a range between the 15th to 17th century, and apparently Heller decided on a dating in the middle of that range. A 15th-century date is not excluded by the radiocarbon evidence, and Huntington and Bangdel prefer a late-14th-century date based on stylistic judgements, but settle on the early 15th century, which seems reasonable.
4. Franco Ricca and Erberto Lo Bue, *The Great Stupa of Gyantse: A Complete Tibetan Pantheon of the Fifteenth Century* (London: Serindia, 1993), pls. 38, 40–42, 53, 66. Similar ones are found on 13th-century paintings, but as the fluttering head scarves against the plain head-nimbi of Tathagatas; see Steven M. Kossak and Jane Casey Singer, *Sacred Visions: Early Paintings from Central Tibet* (New York: Metropolitan Museum of Art, 1998), cat. nos. 4, 23a–c.
5. They are very close to those on the 18th-century Simhamukha, Himalayan Art Website item 65261.

Cat. no. 66

Notes *(Cont. from p. 253)*

1. David Jackson, "Some Karma Kagyupa Paintings in the Rubin Collections," in Marylin M. Rhie and Robert A. F. Thurman, *Worlds of Transformation: Tibetan Art of Wisdom and Compassion* (New York: Tibet House, 1999), pp. 102–14. See also idem, "Si tu Pan chen and the Thangka Treasures of Palpung: The Great Eighteenth Century Lama Connoisseur and His Revival of Buddhist Painting in Eastern Tibet," mss. June 2003 (in press), pp. 73–79.
2. Rob Linrothe, *Ruthless Compassion: Wrathful Deities in Early Indo-Tibetan Esoteric Buddhist Art* (London: Serindia, 1999), figs. 10, 13, 15, 30, 32. See also John Huntington and Dina Bangdel, *The Circle of Bliss: Buddhist Meditational Art* (Columbus: Columbus Museum of Art, 2003), cat. nos. 51–52, and pp. 197–99.
3. Jackson, "Some Karma Kagyupa Paintings," pp. 90–92. Jackson also has a chapter on Situ Panchen in idem, *A History of Tibetan Painting* (Vienna: Osterreichischen Akademie der Wissenschaften, 1996), pp. 259–87.

Exhibition Checklist | Demonic Divine: Himalayan Art and Beyond

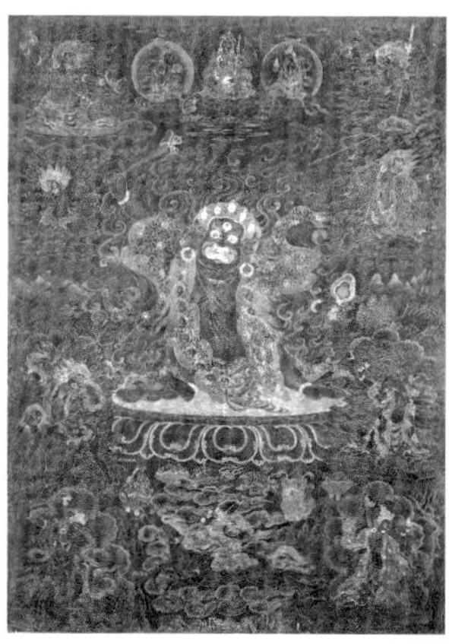

Cat. no. 1
Durtro Lhamo
Protectress of Discovered Texts

Tibet, 18th c.
Mineral pigments on cloth
29½ x 20½ in. (74.9 x 52.1 cm)
Collection of Shelley and Donald Rubin
(HA 1053)

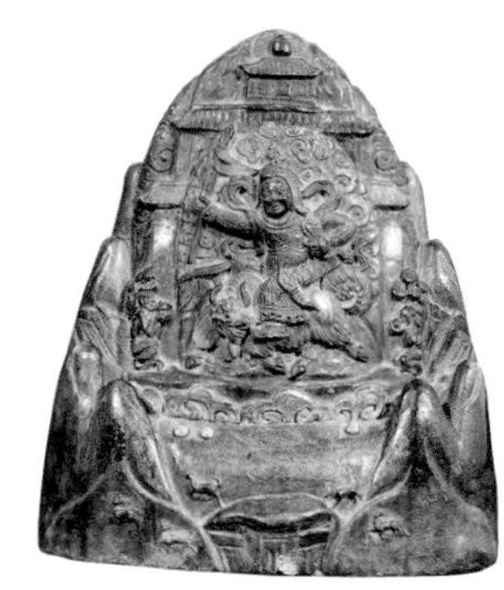

Cat. no. 4
Kula Khari
Protector of Lodrak

Tibet, 19th c.
Painted terracotta
9¾ x 8¼ x 4¾ in.
(24.8 x 21 x 12.1 cm)
Acc. no. C2002.7.3 (HA 65079)

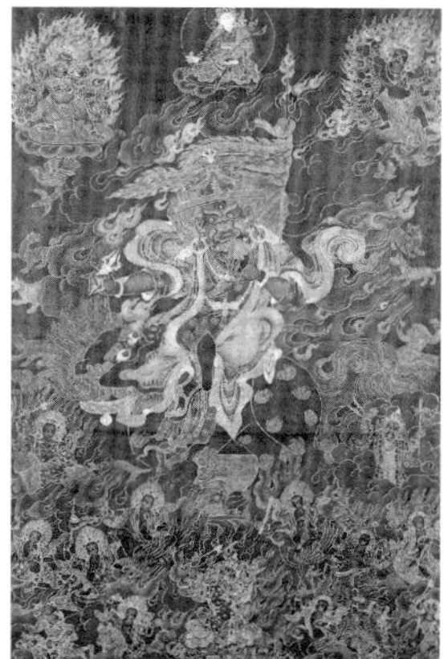

Cat. no. 2
Dorje Legpa
Protector of Discovered Texts

Tibet, 19th c.
Mineral pigments on cloth
17¾ x 11¾ in. (45.1 x 29.8 cm)
Collection of Shelley and Donald Rubin
(HA 93)

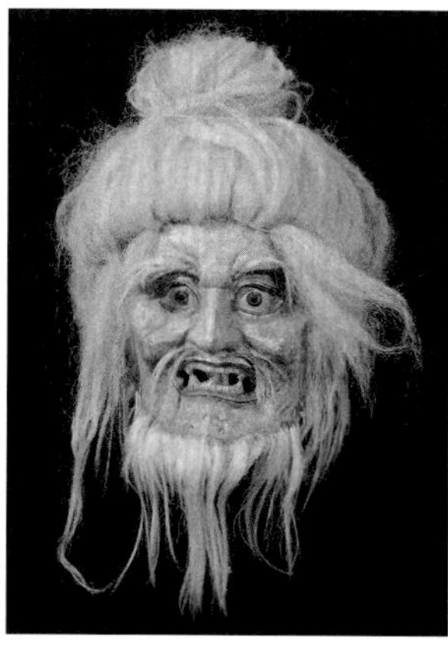

Cat. no. 5
Mask for Ritual Dance

Mongolia, Tibet, or China,
19th–20th c.
Papier-mâché with yak or horse hair
17¾ x 13½ x 11 in. (45.1 x 34.3 x 27.9 cm)
Acc. no. C2003.8.1 (HA 65190)

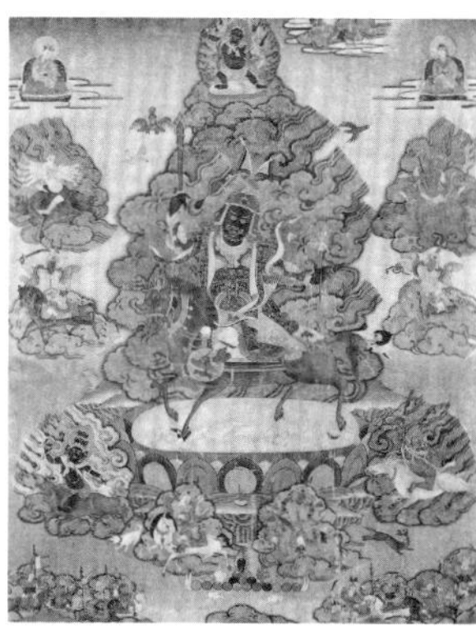

Cat. no. 3
Draglha Gonpo
Protector of Serta and Lhagang monastery

Eastern Tibet, second half of the 19th c.
Mineral pigments on cloth
20¼ x 15½ in. (51.4 x 39.34 cm)
Collection of Shelley and Donald Rubin
(HA 862)

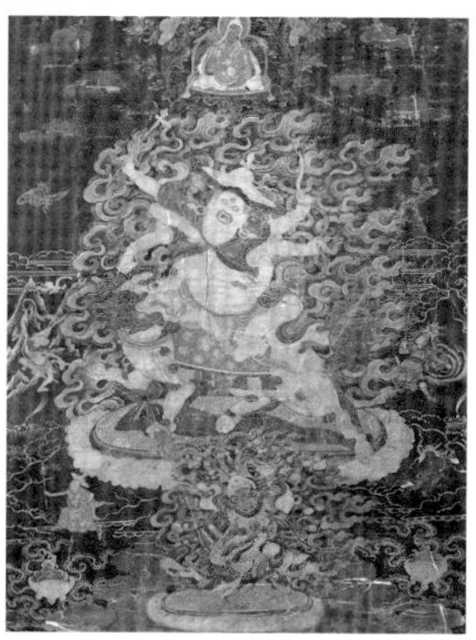

Cat. no. 6
Pehar Gyalpo
Chief Protector of the State

Tibet, late 17th or 18th c.
Mineral pigments on cloth
13¼ x 9¾ in. (33.7 x 24.8 cm)
Acc. no. F1997.35.3 (HA 551)

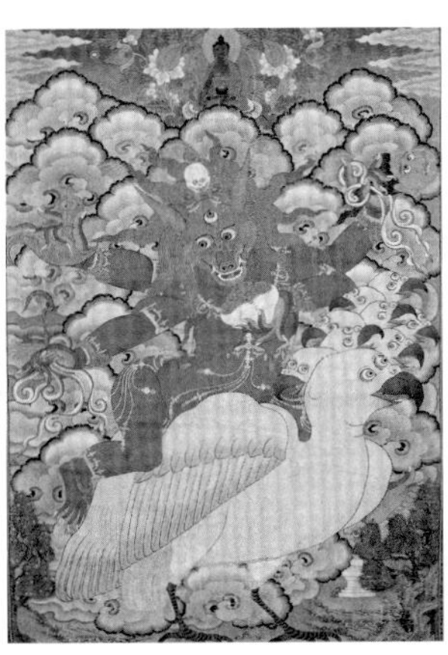

Cat. no. 7
Kandroi Tsomo Chechang Mar
Red Wolf-headed Mistress of Dakinis

Tibet, 19th c.
Mineral pigments on cloth
34¼ x 23½ in. (86.4 x 59.7 cm)
Collection of Shelley and Donald Rubin
(HA 192)

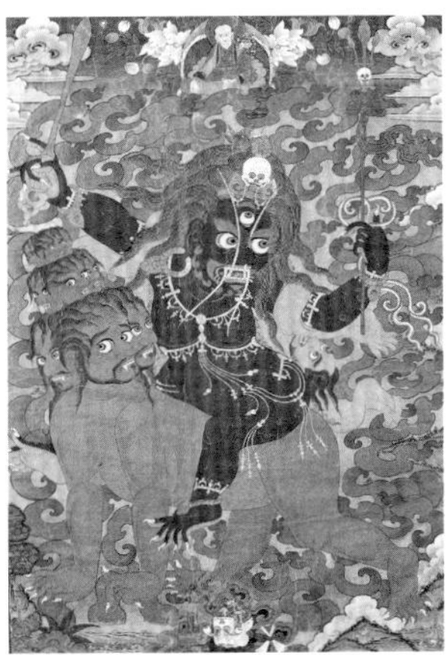

Cat. no. 8
Sinpoi Tsomo Jigje Mar
Red Zombie-riding Protectress

Tibet, 19th c.
Mineral pigments on cloth
33 x 23¾ in. (83.8 x 60.3 cm)
Collection of Shelley and Donald Rubin
(HA 193)

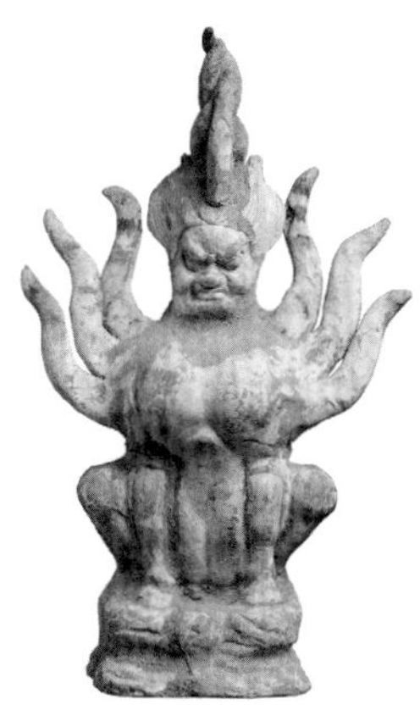

Cat. no. 9
Tomb Guardian

China, late 7th c.
Red clay with white slip
and pigment traces
H. 14¾ in. (37.5 cm)
Schloss Collection, New York

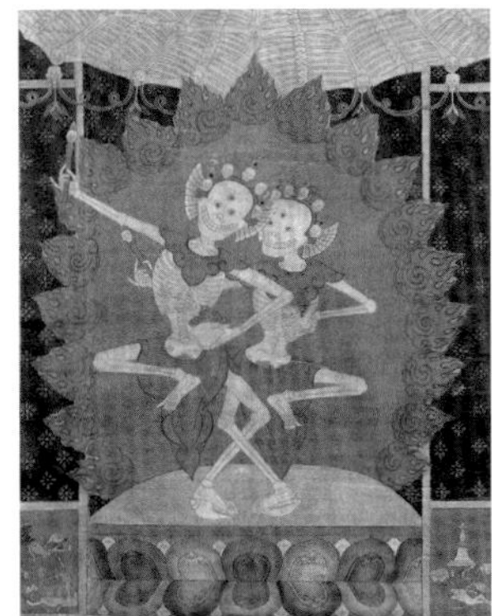

Cat. no. 10
Smashana Adipati
Lords of the Charnel Ground

Tibet, 15th c.
Mineral pigments on cloth
18 x 14½ in. (45.7 x 36.8 cm)
Acc. no. F1996.16.5 (HA 462)

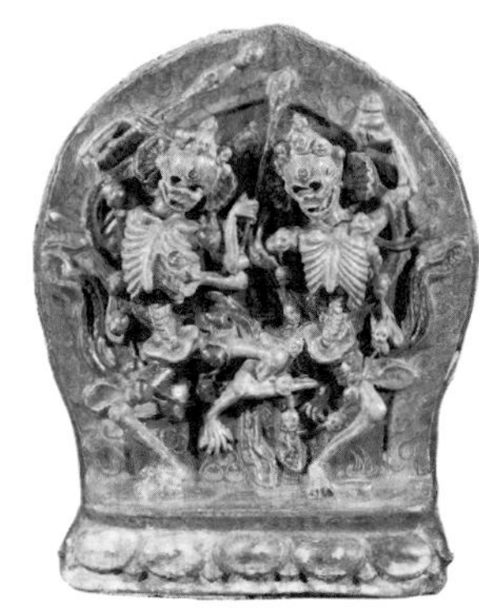

Cat. no. 11
Smashana Adipati
Lords of the Charnel Ground

Tibet, 18th c.
Painted terracotta
6¼x 5¼ x 1¼ in.
(15.9 x 13.3 x 3.2 cm)
Acc. no. C2002.36.1 (HA 65149)

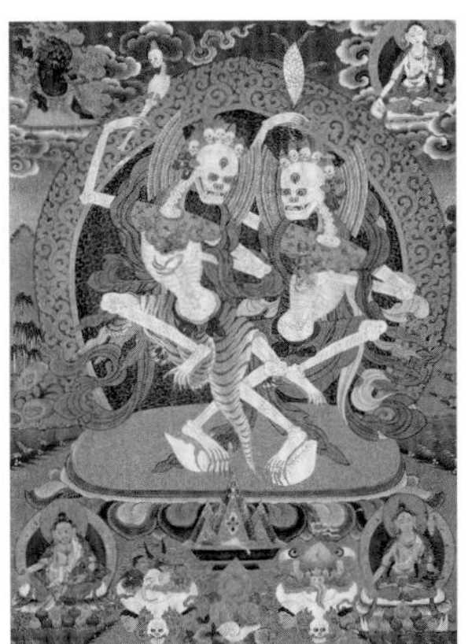

Cat. no. 12
Smashana Adipati
Lords of the Charnel Ground

Tibet, 19th c.
Mineral pigments on cloth
23¼ x 17 in. (59 x 43.2 cm)
Collection of Shelley and
Donald Rubin
(HA 302)

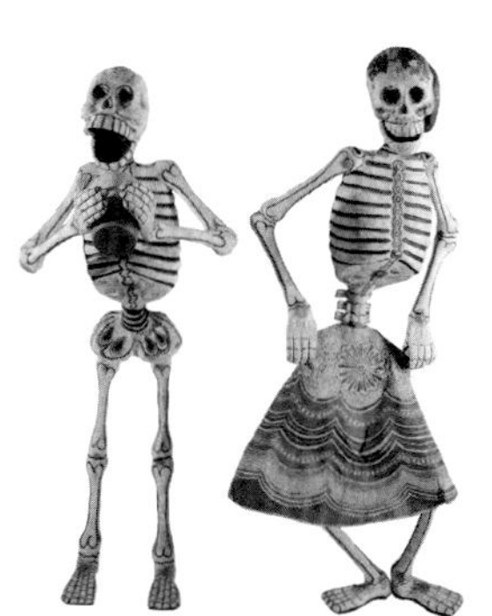

Cat. no. 13
Pareja de Esqueletos
(Skeleton Couple)

Pedro Linares (1907–1992), Mexico
Painted papier-mâché
Male figure: 69 x 27 x 32 in.
(175.3 x 68.6 x 81.3 cm)
Female figure: 73 x 30 x 15 in.
(185.4 x 76.2 x 38.1 cm)
El Museo del Barrio, New York
Gift of Margery Nathanson
Acc. nos. F96.26.20 and F96.26.21

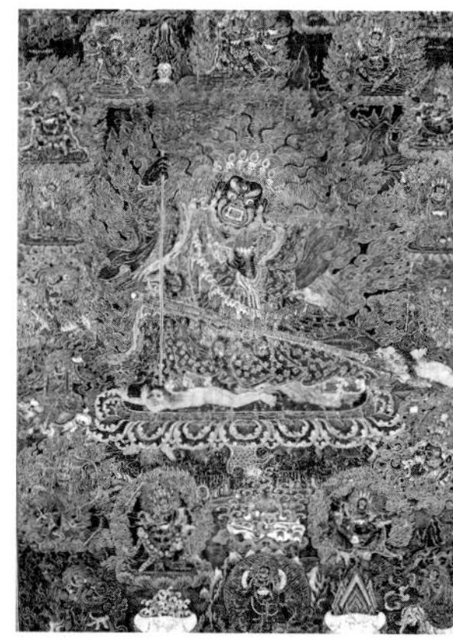

Cat. no. 16
Mahakala
Maning (Eunuch)

Tibet or Bhutan, 19th c.
Mineral pigments on cloth
33 x 21¼ in. (83.8 x 54 cm)
Acc. no. F1997.30.4 (HA 387)

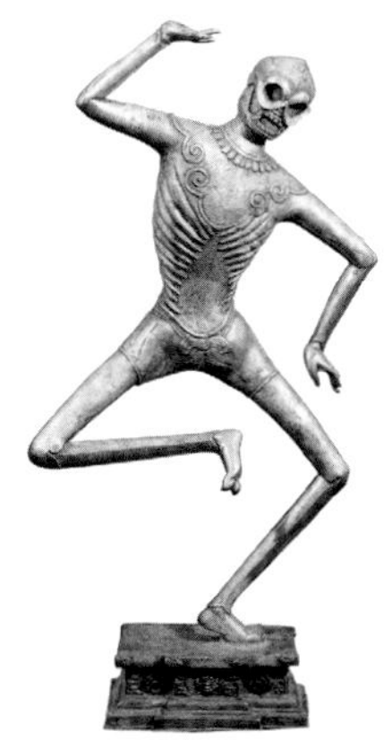

Cat. no. 14
One of a Pair of Long Trumpet-horn Stands

Himalayan culture, ca. 17th c.
Metalwork
29 x 13½ x 7 in. (73.7 x 34.3 x 17.8 cm)
Collection of Navin Kumar, New York

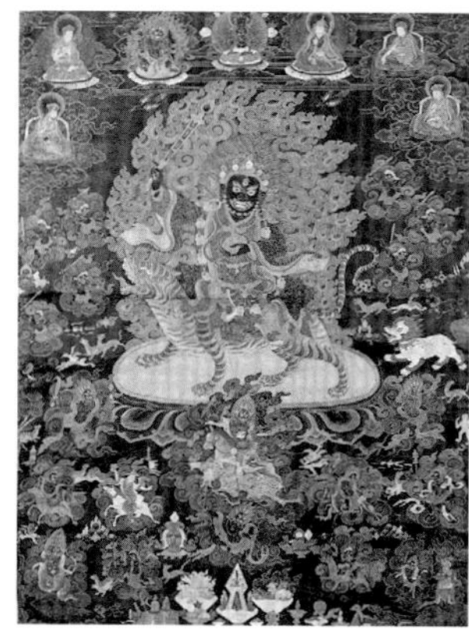

Cat. no. 17
Mahakala
Vyaghra Vahana (Tiger-rider)

Tibet, late 18th–early 19th c.
Mineral pigments on cloth
26¼ x 19½ in. (66.7 x 49.5 cm)
Acc. no. C2002.38.2 (HA 65192)

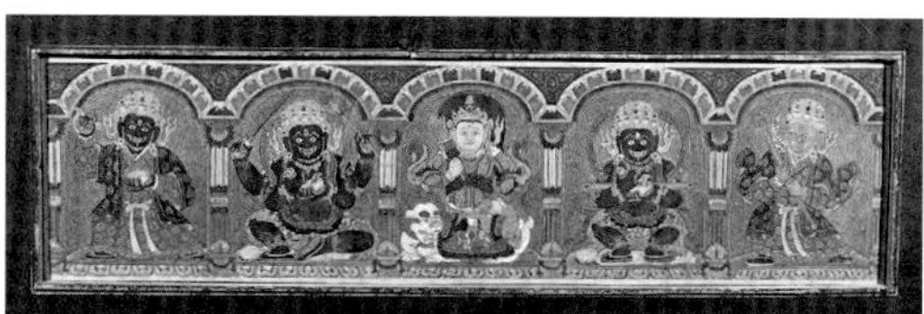

Cat. no. 15
Illuminated Manuscript Page with Four Forms of Mahakala and Vaishravana, King of the Northern Direction

China, 15th c.
Mineral pigments on paper
9½ x 27½ in. (24.1 x 69.9 cm)
Acc. no. F1998.19.2 (HA 700048)

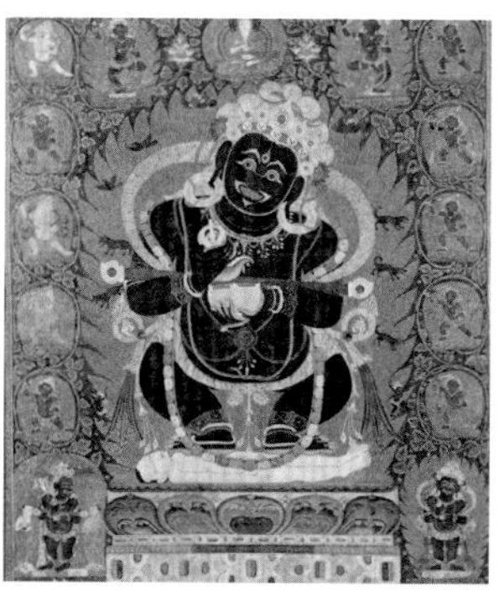

Cat. no. 18
Mahakala
Panjarnata (Lord of the Pavilion)

Tibet, late 15th c.
Mineral pigments on cloth
37⅜ x 31½ in. (94.9 x 80 cm)
Collection of Navin Kumar, New York

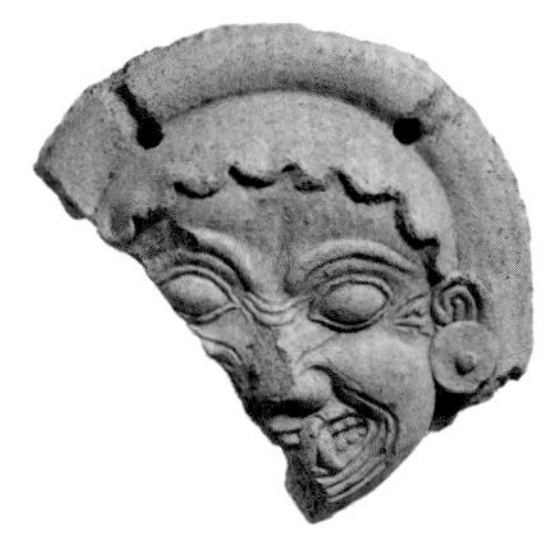

Cat. no. 19
Fragmentary Antefix-Gorgonion

Etruscan or South Italian,
6th–5th c. BCE
Terracotta
H. 8¼ in. (21 cm)
The Metropolitan Museum of Art,
Gift of Mr. and Mrs. Jonathan P. Rosen,
1991
Acc. no. 1991.171.44

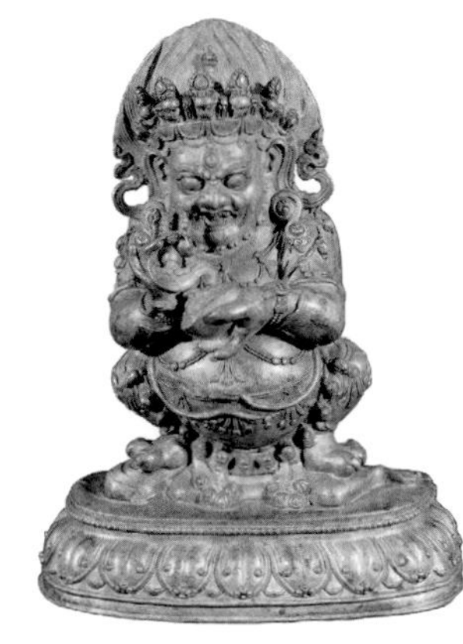

Cat. no. 22
Mahakala
Panjarnata
(Lord of the Pavilion)

Nepal or Tibet, 18th c.
Metalwork
11 x 10 x 4½ in.
(27.9 x 25.4 x 11.4 cm)
Acc. no. C2001.7.1 (HA 65018)

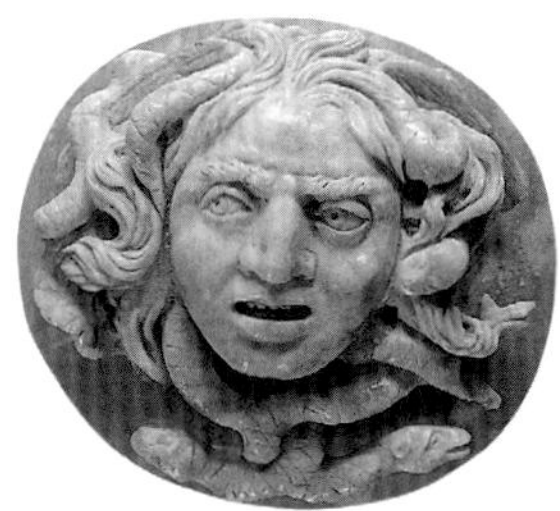

Cat. no. 20
Cameo of Medusa with Serpents

Western Europe, Post-Classical (after 4th c. CE)
Grey stone, carnelian with sardonyx back
2 x 1⅞ in. (5.1 x 4.8 cm)
University of Pennsylvania Museum of Archaeology and Anthropology
Acc. no. 29-128-2183

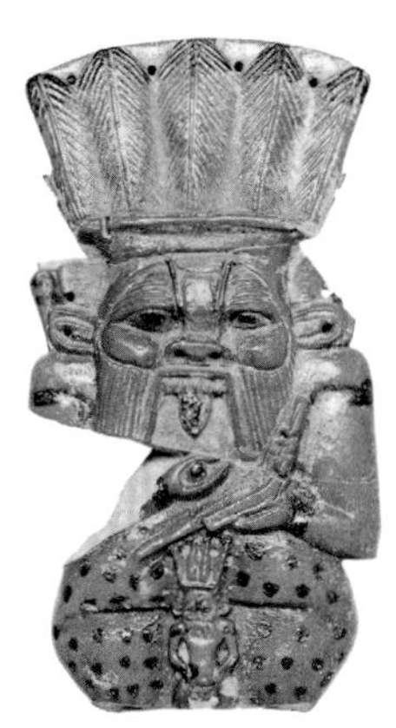

Cat. no. 23
Bes-image

Egyptian, 22nd–25th dynasty
(ca. 945–656 BCE)
Faience with turquoise glaze
6⅞ x 3⅝ x ⅞ in.
(17.5 x 9.2 x 2.3 cm)
Brooklyn Museum of Art,
Charles Edwin Wilbour Fund
Acc. no. 37.309E

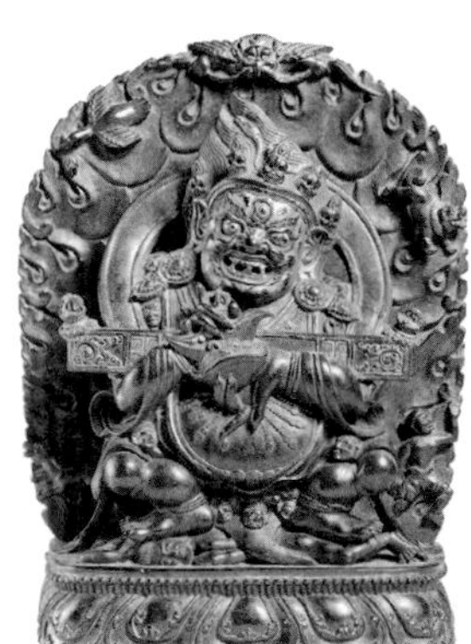

Cat. no. 21
Mahakala, Panjarnata
(Lord of the Pavilion)

Tibet, 15th c.
Stone
10¼ x 6¾ x 3½ (26 x 17.1 x 8.9 cm)
Acc. no. C2002.10.2 (HA 65085)

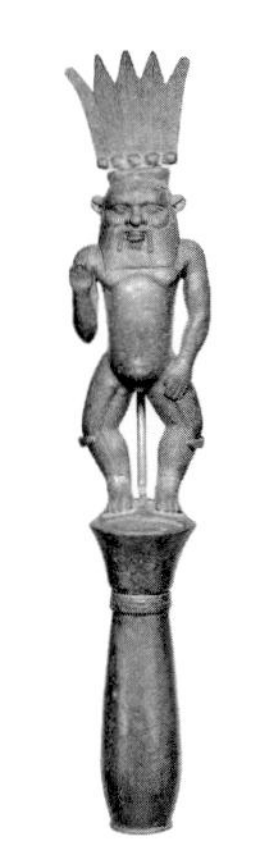

Cat. no. 24
Finial with Bes-image

Egyptian, 22nd–25th dynasty
(ca. 945–656 BCE)
Bronze
16 x 2⅞ in. (40.6 x 7.3 cm)
Brooklyn Museum of Art,
Charles Edwin Wilbour Fund
Acc. no. 46.127

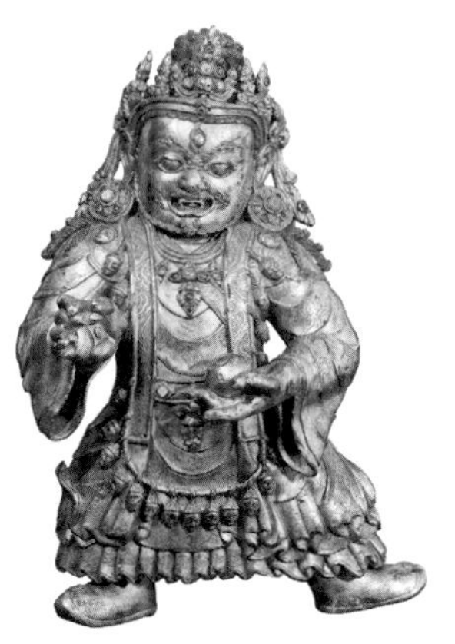

Cat. no. 25
Mahakala
Legden (Excellent One)

Tibet, ca. 15th c.
Metalwork with inlaid stones
13½ x 9 x 5¾ in. (34.3 x 22.9 x 14.6 cm)
Acc. no. C2003.10.3 (HA 65208)

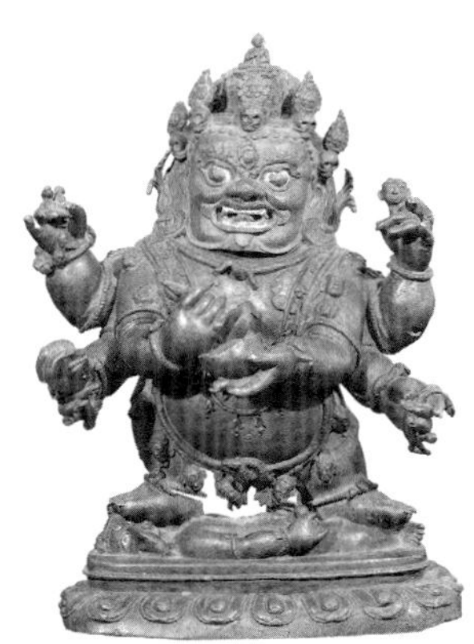

Cat. no. 28
Mahakala
Shadbhuja (Six Hands)

Tibet, 14th c.
Metalwork
12⅜ x 8⅜ x 5¼ in.
(31.4 x 21.3 x 13.3 cm)
Collection of Shelley and Donald Rubin
(HA 700065)

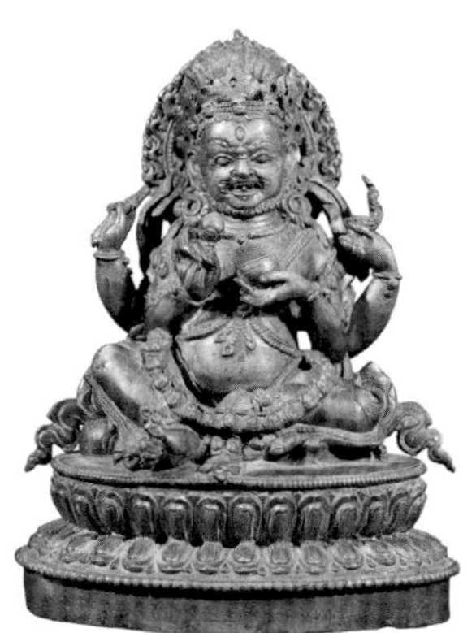

Cat. no. 26
Mahakala,
Chaturbhuja (Four Hands)

Tibet, 17th c.
Metalwork
8½ x 6 x 4 in.
(21.6 x 15.2 x 10.2 cm)
Collection of Navin Kumar, New York
(HA 90059)

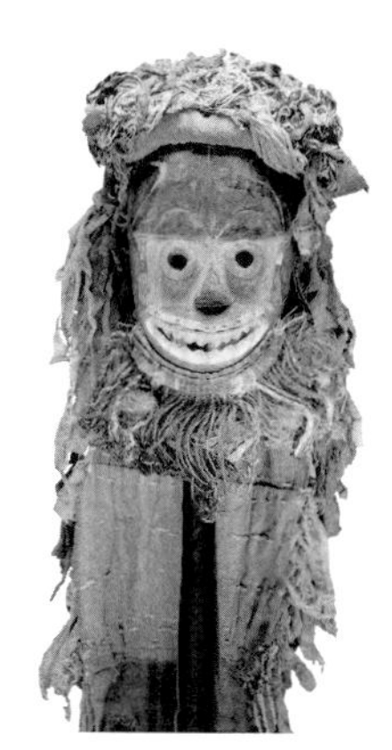

Cat. no. 29
Mask

Liberia, Africa (Krau, Guere culture),
20th c.
Mixed media (including wood, brass, beads, grass fibers, imported cotton cloth, raffia, cotton thread, and mud pigment)
24 x 15 x 117 in. (61 x 38.1 x 297.2 cm)
American Museum of Natural History,
New York
Acc. no. 90.2/9327

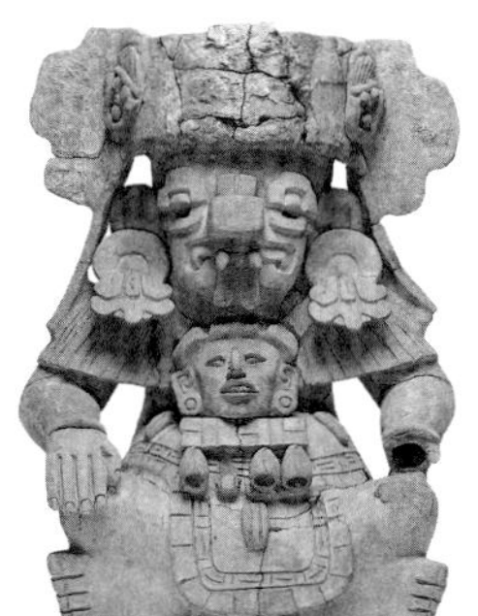

Cat. no. 27
Funeral Urn

Mexico, Oaxaca, Xoxocotlan, (Zapotec culture), ca. Monté Alban III (250–500 CE)
Clay
23⅝ x 19¾ x 13¾ in.
(60 x 50.2 x 34.9 cm)
American Museum of Natural History,
New York
Acc. no. 1898-30

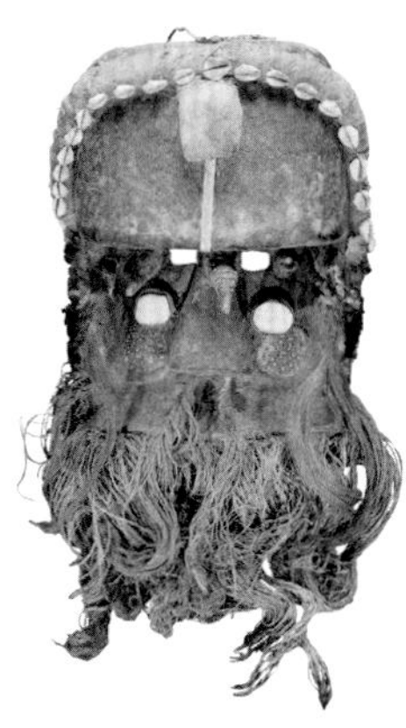

Cat. no. 30
Mask

Liberia, Africa (Krau, Guere culture),
20th c.
Mixed media (including wood, plant fiber, cowrie shells, aluminum metal, antelope horn, iguana skin, bushcat fur, horse hair, porcelain shards, and mud pigment)
30 x 24 x 12 in. (76.2 x 61 x 30.5 cm)
American Museum of Natural History,
New York
Acc. no. 90.2/9330

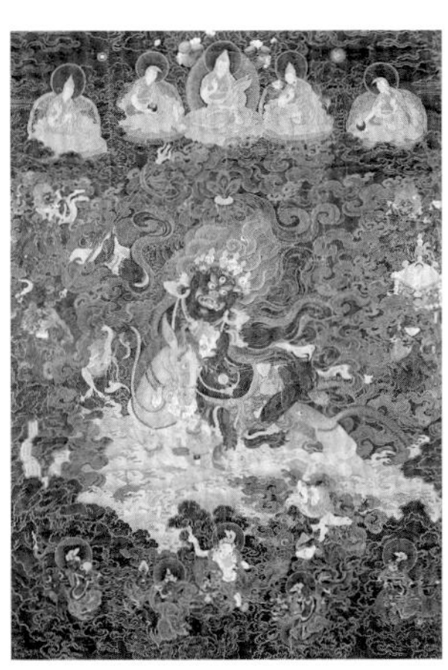

Cat. no. 31
Shri Devi, Magzor Gyalmo
Queen who Has the Power
to Turn Back Armies

Central Tibet, mid-18th c.
Mineral pigments on cloth
33¼ x 22¾ in. (84.5 x 57.8 cm)
Collection of Shelley and Donald Rubin
(HA 105)

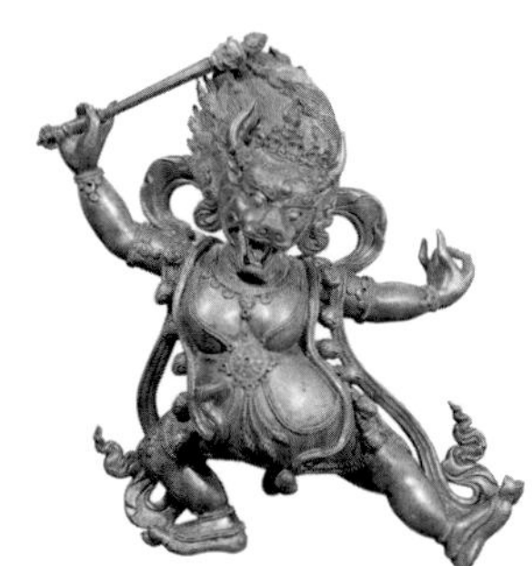

Cat. no. 34
Yama Dharmaraja with
Buffalo Head
Destroyer of the King of Hell

Tibet, 17th–18th c.
Metalwork, inset coral
and turquoise
10½ x 8 x 3 in.
(26.7 x 20.3 x 7.6 cm)
Collection of Shelley and Donald
Rubin (HA 700009)

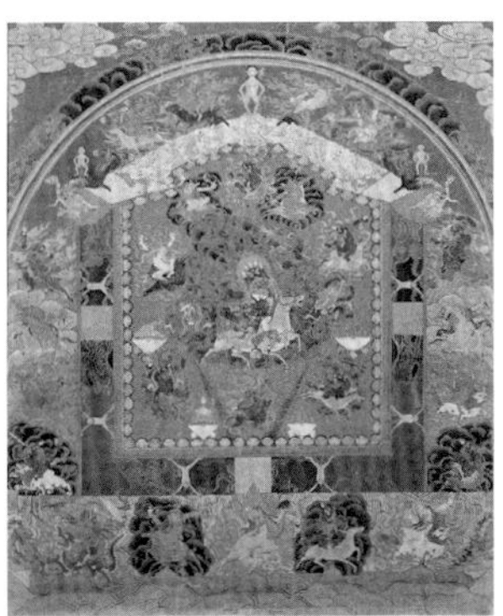

Cat. no. 32
Shri Devi, Magzor Gyalmo
Queen who Has the Power
to Turn Back Armies

Tibet, 19th c.
Mineral pigments on cloth
25 x 20⅜ in. (63.5 x 51.8 cm)
Collection of Shelley and Donald Rubin
(HA 140)

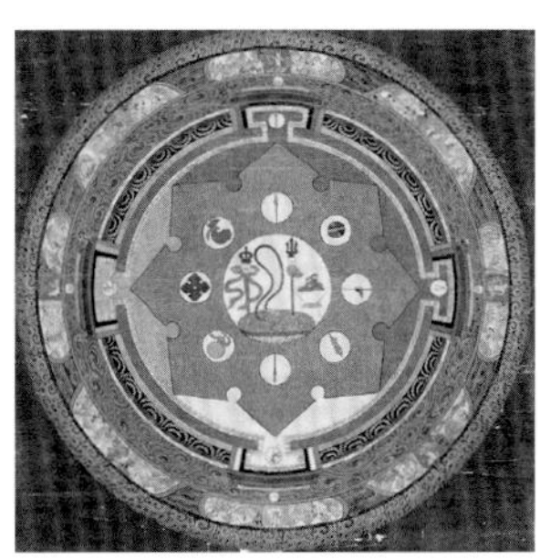

Cat. no. 35
Symbol Mandala of Yama
Dharmaraja and Chamunda

Tibet, 18th c.
Mineral pigments on cloth
12 x 12 in. (30.5 x 30.5 cm)
Acc. no. F1996.11.1 (HA 436)

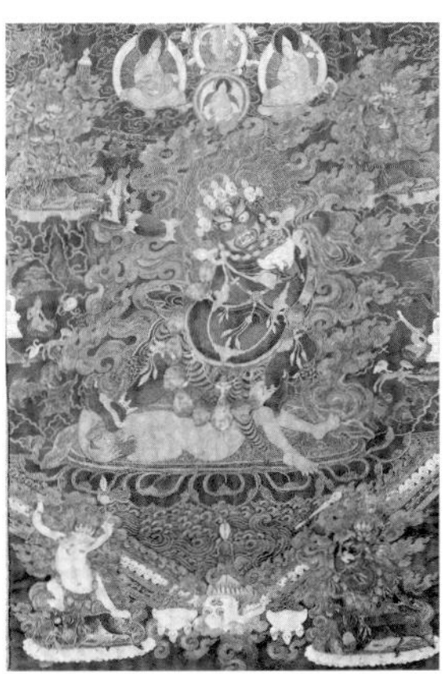

Cat. no. 33
Yama Dharmaraja with
Demon Head
Destroyer of the King of Hell

Central Tibet, second half of the 18th c.
Mineral pigments on cloth
16¾ x 11 in. (42.5 x 27.9 cm)
Collection of Shelley and Donald Rubin
(HA 159)

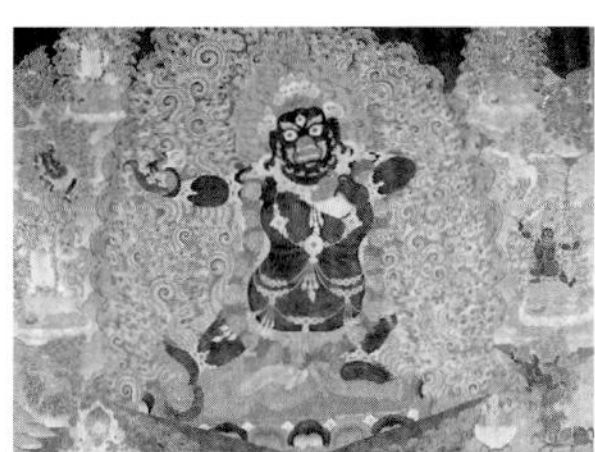

Cat. no. 36
Yama Dharmaraja with
Demon Head
Destroyer of the King of Hell

Tibet, 18th–19th c.
Mineral pigments on cloth
73¾ x 96½ in.
(185.4 x 245.1 cm)
Collection of Navin Kumar,
New York

Note: Catalog numbers 37–41 were shown at the Asia Society, New York, in a special exhibition, *Wrathful Deities in Buddhist Art: An Installation to Celebrate the Opening of the Rubin Museum of Art*, March 23–August 22, 2004.

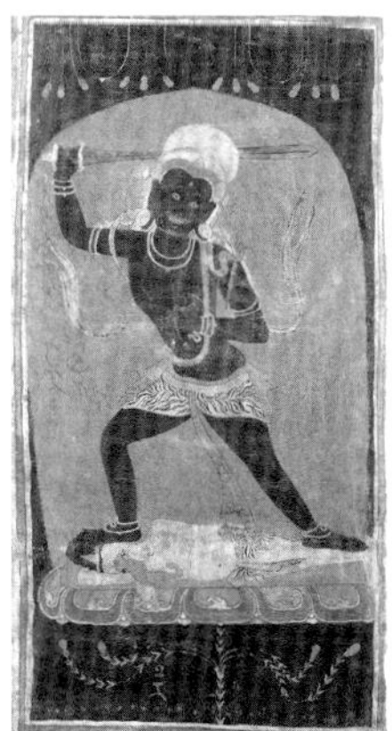

Cat. no. 37
Achala
(The Immovable One)

Tibet or Eastern India, 11th–12th c.
Mineral pigments on cloth
6¾ x 14 in. (17.1 x 35.6 cm)
Collection of Shelley and Donald Rubin
(HA 594)
Also exhibited at Asia Society

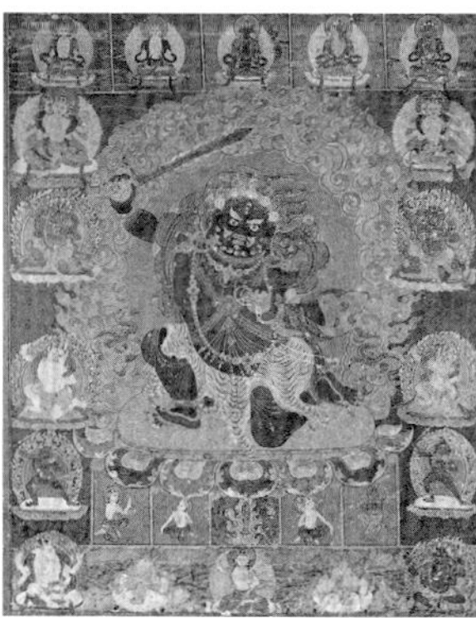

Cat. no. 40
Achala
(The Immovable One)

Nepal, dated 1871
Mineral pigments on cloth
17¼ x 14 in. (43.8 x 35.6 cm)
Collection of Shelley and Donald Rubin
(HA 100045)
Exhibited at Asia Society only

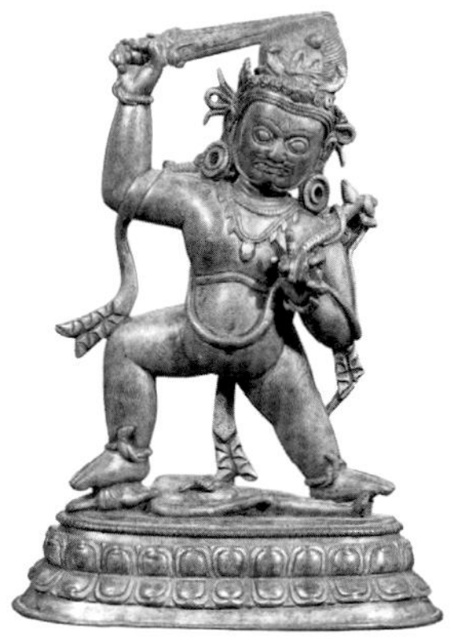

Cat. no. 38
Achala
(The Immovable One)

Tibet, 13th c.
Metalwork, inlaid turquoise
9 x 6¼ x 2½ in. (22.9 x 15.9 x 6.4 cm)
Acc. no. F1998.19.1 (HA 700047)
Exhibited at Asia Society only

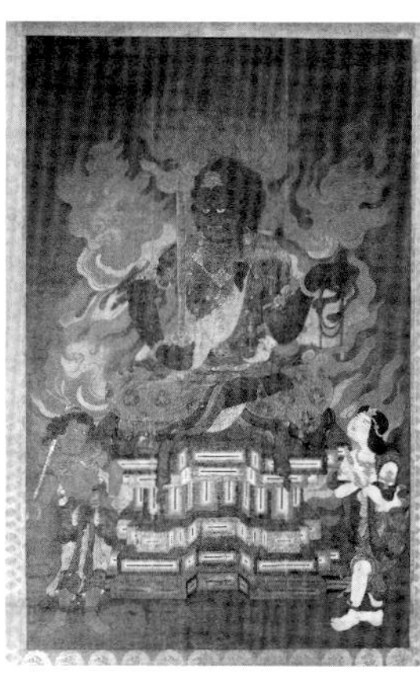

Cat. no. 41
Fudo Myo-o (Achala Vidyaraja) with Two Attendants

Japan, Kamakura period, early 14th c.
Hanging scroll; ink, color, and gold on silk
72 x 45 in. (182.9 x 114.3 cm)
Asia Society, New York
Mr. and Mrs. John D. Rockefeller 3rd Collection
Acc. no. 1979.209
Exhibited at Asia Society only

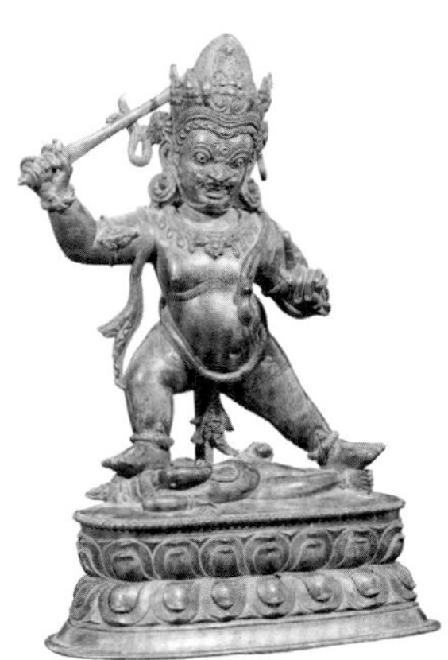

Cat. no. 39
Achala
(The Immovable One)

Tibet, ca. 13th–14th c.
Metalwork
13¼ x 9½ x 4¼ in.
(33.7 x 24.1 x 10.8 cm)
Acc. no. F1997.50.1 (HA 700044)
Exhibited at Asia Society only

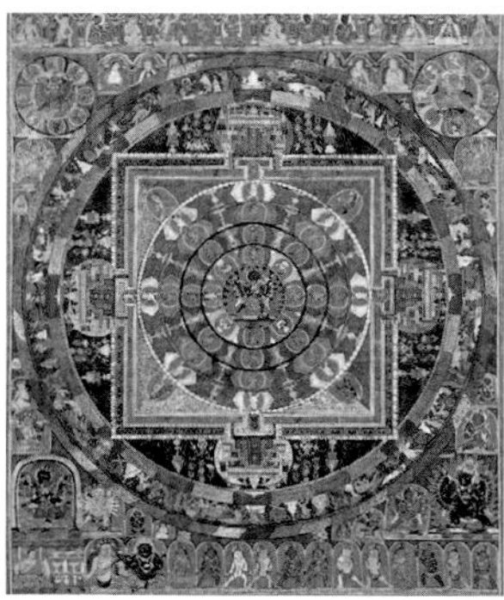

Cat. no. 42
Chakrasamvara with Twelve Hands and Vajrayogini Mandala

Tibet, late 15th–16th c.
Mineral pigments on cloth
26½ x 22 in. (67.3 x 55.9 cm)
Collection of Shelley and Donald Rubin
(HA 97)

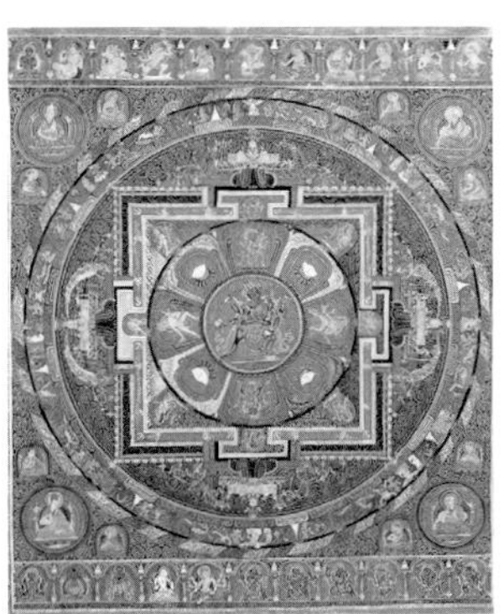

Cat. no. 43
Chakrasamvara with Six Hands and Vajrayogini Mandala

Tibet, ca. 1500
Mineral pigments on cloth
21½ x 17½ in. (54.6 x 44.5 cm)
Acc. no. C2001.9.1 (HA 65020)

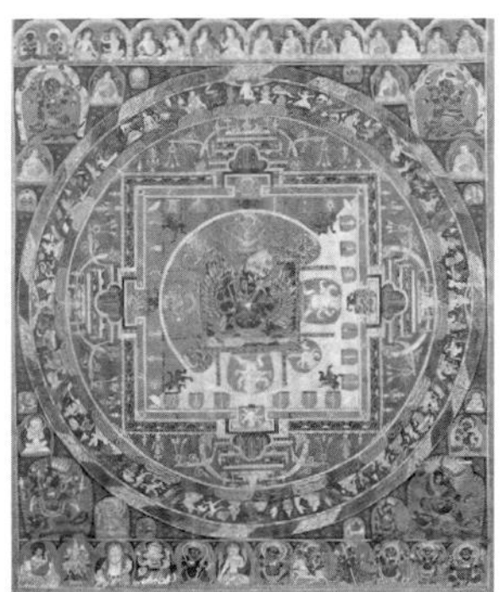

Cat. no. 46
Vajrabhairava Mandala

Tibet, late 15th–16th c.
Mineral pigments on cloth
29½ x 24½ in. (74.9 x 62.2 cm)
Collection of Navin Kumar, New York (HA 900095)

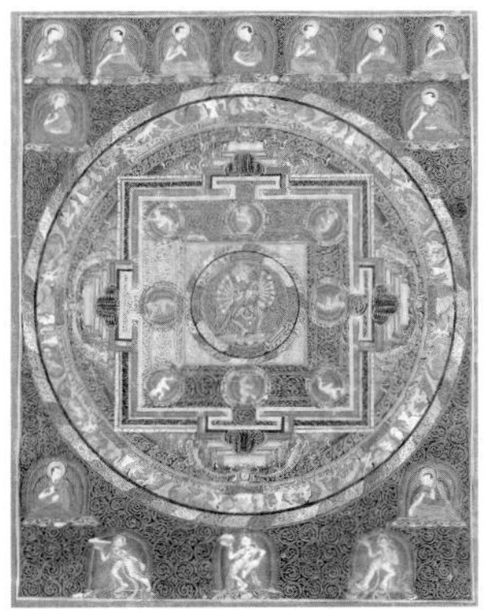

Cat. no. 44
Hevajra with Nairatmya Mandala

Tibet, ca. late 16th c.
Mineral pigments on cloth
14½ x 11½ in. (36.8 x 29.2 cm)
Collection of Shelley and Donald Rubin (HA 964)

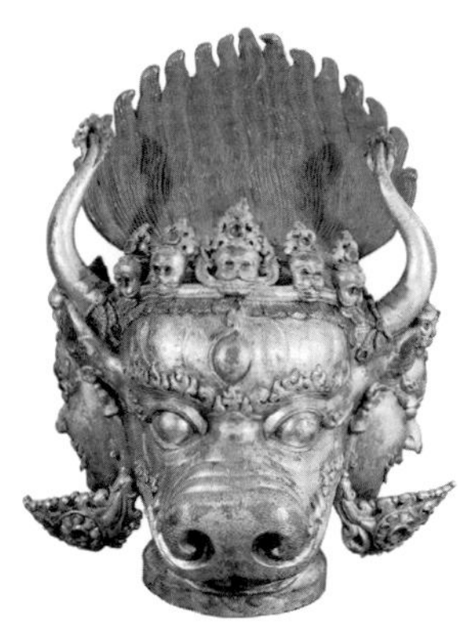

Cat. no. 47
Vajrabhairava, Fragment

Tibet, 15th–16th c.
Metalwork with inlaid stones
8¼ x 6¼ x 4¾ in.
(21x 15.9 x 12.1 cm)
Acc. no. C2002.40.1 (HA 65160)

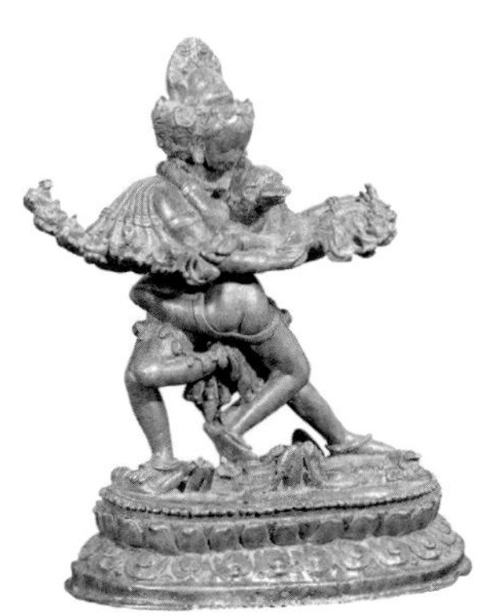

Cat. no. 45
Hevajra with Nairatmya

Nepal, 14th c.
Copper
7¾ x 6½ x 3 in. (19.7 x 16.5 x 7.6 cm)
Collection of Shelley and Donald Rubin (HA 700066)

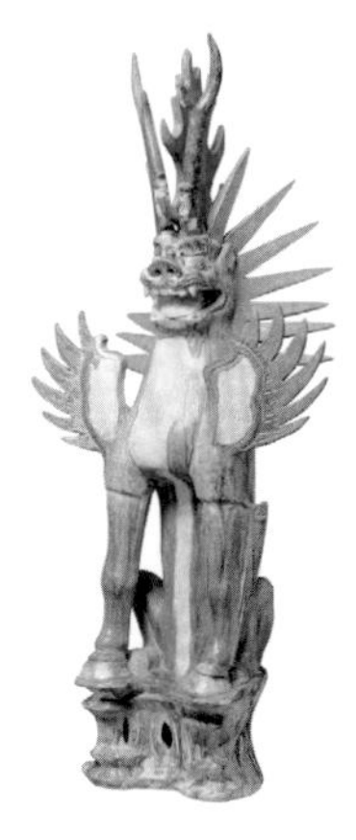

Cat. no. 48
Tomb Guardian

China, early 8th c.
White pottery with *sancai* glaze and pigment traces
H. 37½ in. (95.3 cm)
Schloss Collection, New York

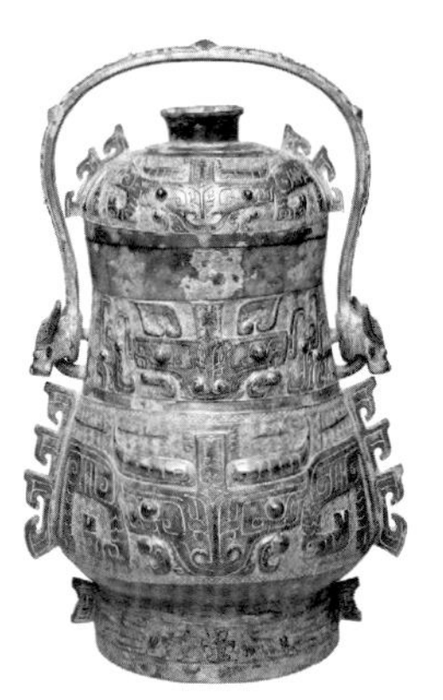

Cat. no. 49
Wine Vessel: *You*

North China: Western Zhou period, ca. late 11th c. BCE
Bronze
H. 14⅞ (37.8 cm), including handle; W. 8¾ (22.23 cm), across flanges
Asia Society, New York
Mr. and Mrs. John D. Rockefeller 3rd Collection
Acc. no. 1979.100 a,b

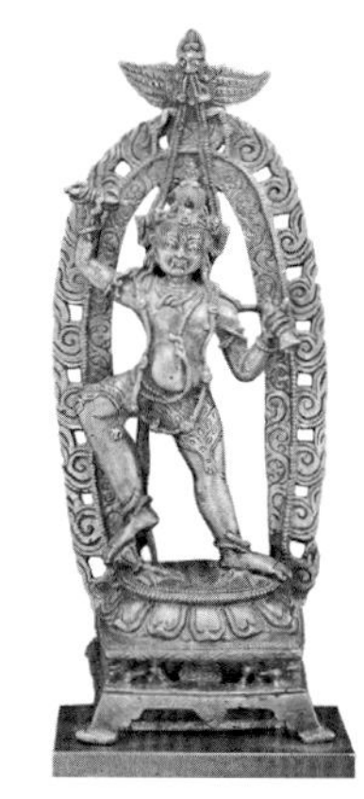

Cat. no. 52
Vajrapani Trampling Snakes

Eastern India or Western Tibet (?), ca. 10th–11th c.
Metalwork
10½ x 4 in. (26.7 x 10.2 cm)
Collection of Michael and Beata McCormick, New York

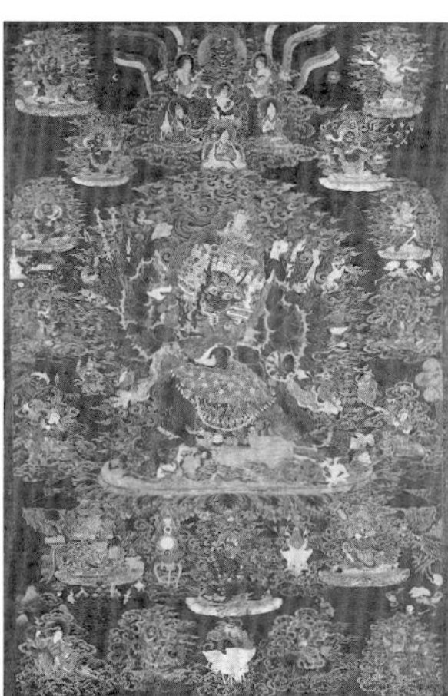

Cat. no. 50
Vajrabhairava with Vajravetali

Tibet, 18th c.
Mineral pigments on cloth
26 x 17 in. (66 x 43.2 cm)
Acc. no. C2002.21.2 (HA 65113)

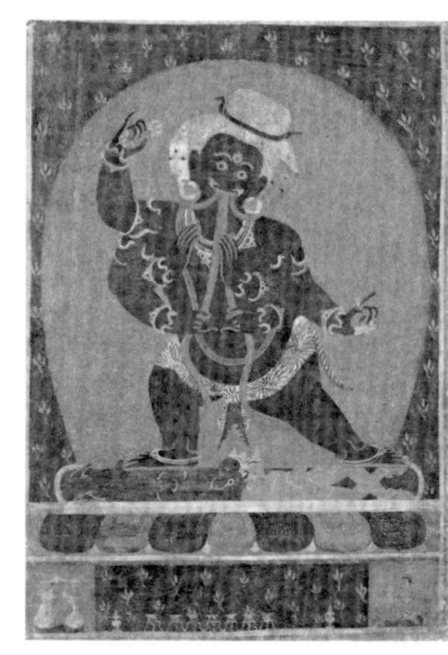

Cat. no. 53
Mahachakra Vajrapani, Great Wheel Vajra Holder

Tibet, ca. 12th c.
Mineral pigments on cloth
27 x 19¾ x 6¾ in.
(68.58 x 50.2 x 17.1 cm)
Acc. no. C2002.25.1 (HA 65128)

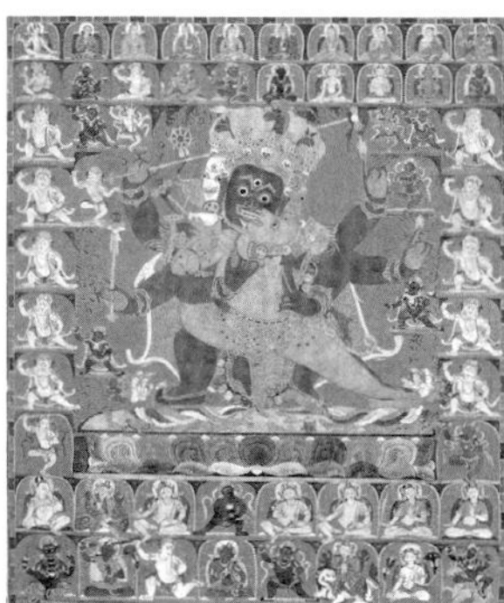

Cat. no. 51
Hayagriva with Six Hands and Consort

Tibet, ca. 1300
Mineral pigments on cloth
26 x 21¼ in. (66 x 54 cm)
Collection of Navin Kumar, New York

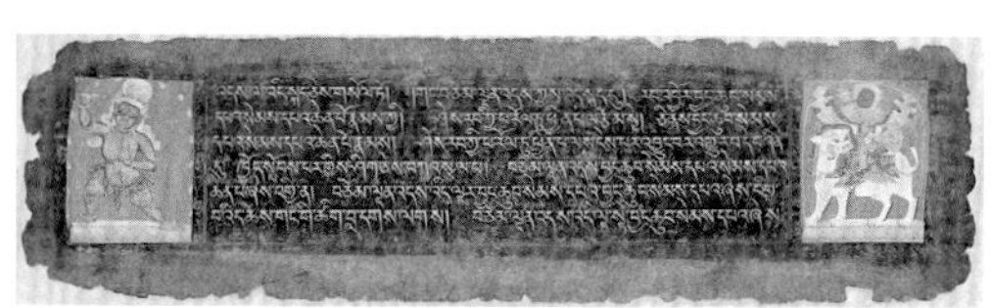

Cat. no. 54
Illuminated manuscript page of a philosophical Prajnaparamita text
Vajrapani, Vajra Holder (left)
Vaishravana, King of the Northern Direction (right)

Tibet, ca. late 13th c.
Pigments, gold, silver, and ink on paper
8 x 28 in. (20.3 x 17.1 cm)
Collection of Shelley and Donald Rubin (HA 700115)

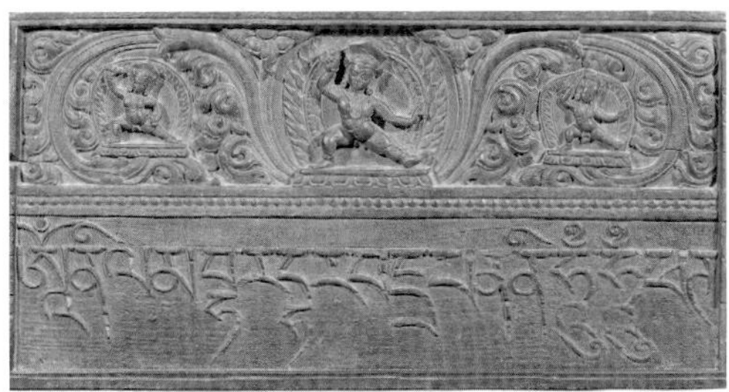

Cat. no. 55
Vajrapani Nilambaradhara, Vajra Holder

Tibet, 14th c.
Wood
9 x 17¾ x 1½ in. (22.9 x 45.1 x 3.8 cm)
Collection of Shelley and Donald Rubin (HA 700005)

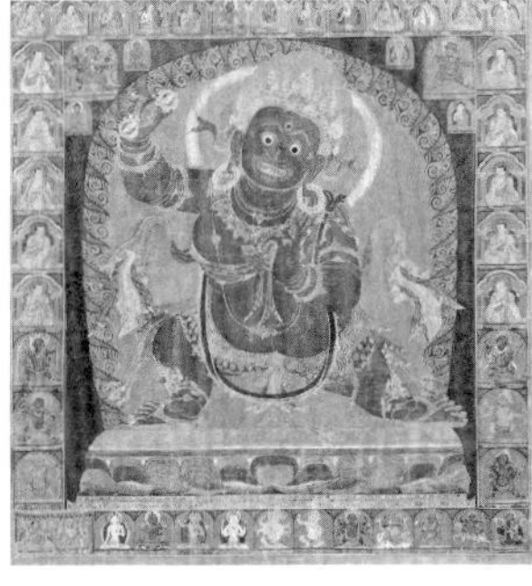

Cat. no. 56
Vajrapani, Lord of Secrets

Tibet, early 15th c.
Mineral pigments on cloth
36 x 32 in. (91.4 x 81.3 cm)
Collection of Michael and Beata McCormick, New York (HA 90135)

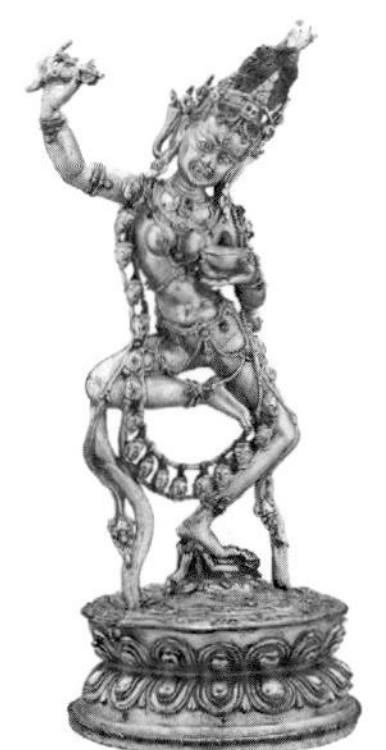

Cat. no. 57
Vajravarahi

Tibet, 15th c.
Gilt metal
9½ x 3½ in. (24.1 x 8.9 cm)
Collection of Michael and Beata McCormick, New York (HA 90164)

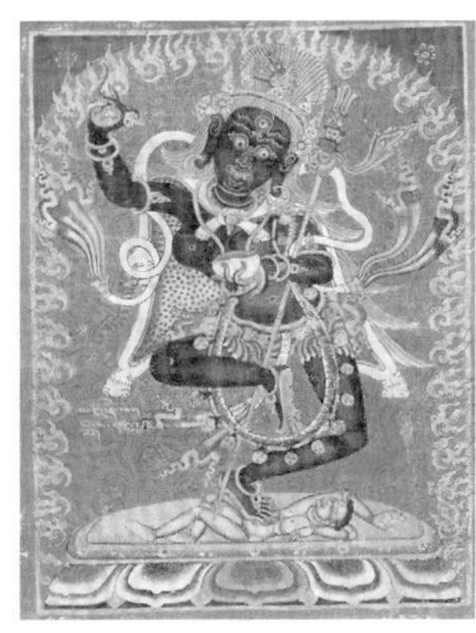

Cat. no. 58
Vajravarahi, Krodha Kali (Fierce Black One)

Tibet, second half of the 16th c.
Mineral pigments on cloth
5 x 4¼ in. (12.7 x 10.8 cm)
Collection of Michael and Beata McCormick, New York

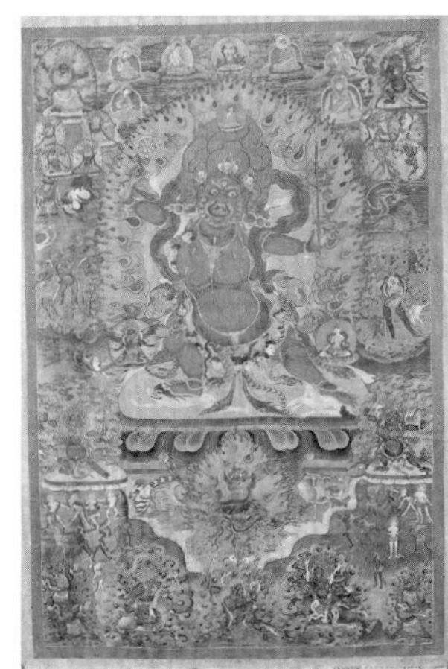

Cat. no. 59
Tagla Membar (Flaming Tiger-God)

Tibet, 19th c.
Mineral pigments on cloth
39 x 25¾ in. (99.1 x 65.4 cm)
Collection of Shelley and Donald Rubin (HA 200041)

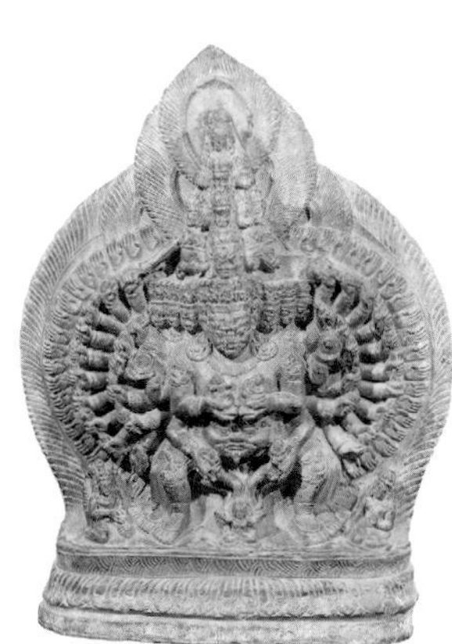

Cat. no. 60
Vishnu Vishvarupa Universal Form

Nepal, 17th–18th c.
Clay
20 x 14½ x 4 in.
(50.8 x 36.8 x 10.2 cm)
Acc. no. C2003.12.3 (HA 65214)

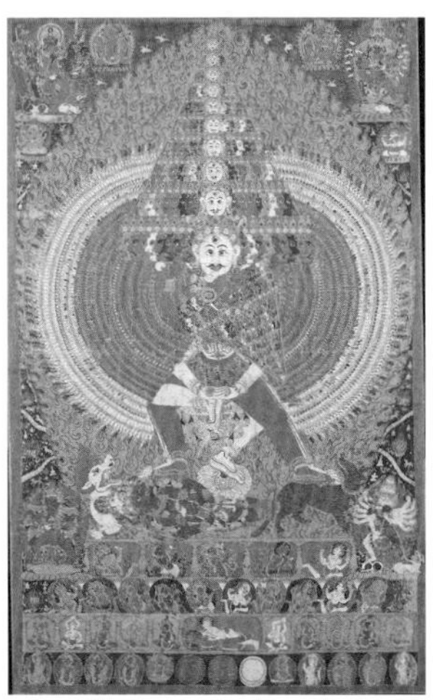

Cat. no. 61
Shiva Vishvarupa
Universal Form with Consort

Nepal, mid-19th c.
Mineral pigments on cloth
63 x 38 in. (160 x 96.5 cm)
Acc. no. C2003.20.2 (HA 65250)

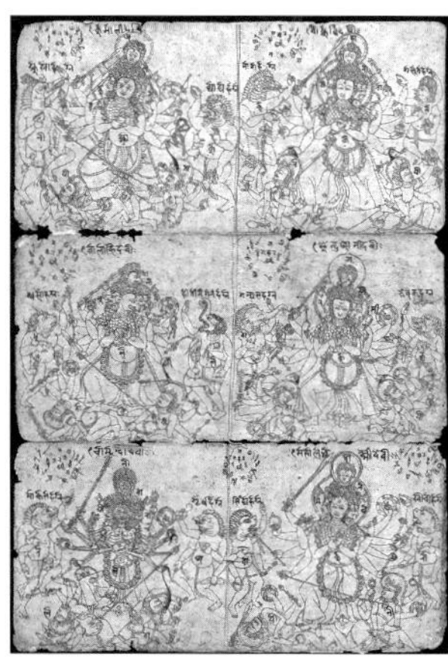

Cat. no. 64
Page from an artist's manual

Nepal, 18th–19th c.
Ink on paper
16¾ x 11½ in. (42.5 x 29.2 cm)
Acc. no. C2003.10.1 (HA 65238)

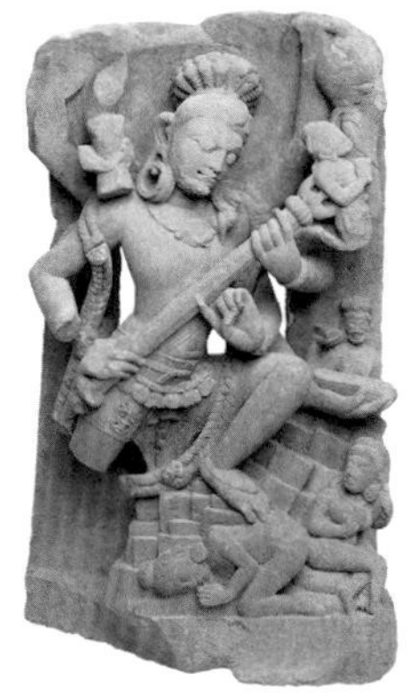

Cat. no. 62
Shiva Andhakashuramurti

Rajasthan, India, late 8th c.
Red sandstone
27¼ x 16⅜ x 11¼ in.
(69.2 x 41.6 x 28.6 cm)
Brooklyn Museum of Art
Gift of the Ernest Erikson Foundation, Inc.
Acc. no. 86.227.145

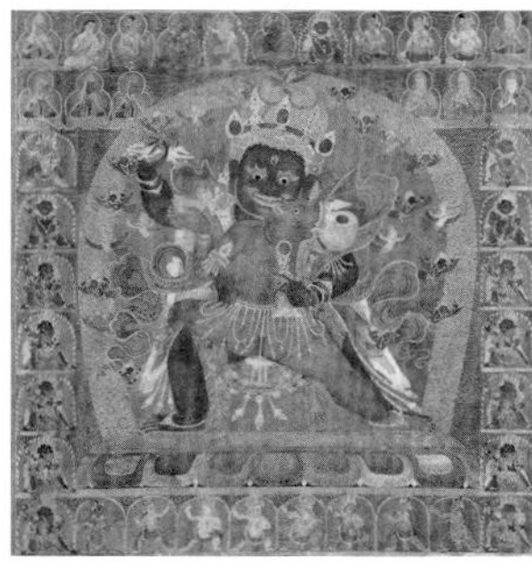

Cat. no. 65
Vajrapani, Lord of Secrets

Tibet, early 15th c.
Mineral pigments on cloth
17¼ x 16¼ in. (43.8 x 41.3 cm)
Collection of Shelley and Donald Rubin
(HA 11)

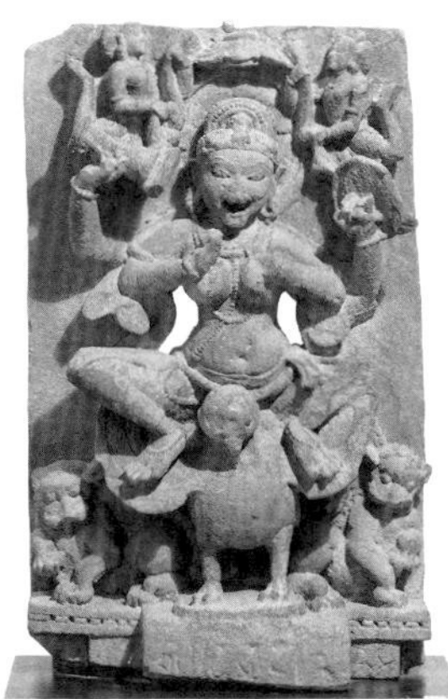

Cat. no. 63
Devi

India, 10th c.
Stone
H. 19¼ in. (48.9 cm)
Collection of Michael Cohn, New York

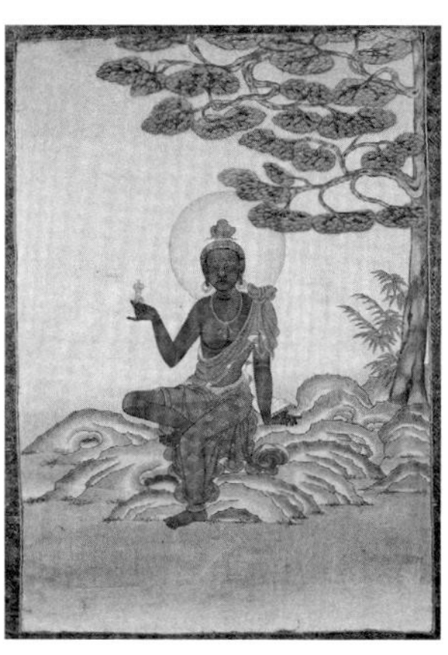

Cat. no. 66
Vajrapani, Lord of Secrets

Eastern Tibet, 19th c.
Mineral pigments on cloth
31¾ x 20½ in. (80.6 x 52.1 cm)
Acc. no. F1997.40.5 (HA 586)

Glossary

This glossary includes terms and non-personal proper names. For persons or the names of individual deities, see the index. (See also the Glossary on the Himalayan Art Website, from which many of these definitions were adapted.)

Amdo
A region of Northeastern Tibet as ethnographically (not politically) defined; now incorporated into the Chinese provinces of Qinghai, Gansu and Sichuan.

amrita
Nectar, ambrosia; an elixir of longevity.

amulet
(Tibetan: *tog chag*). Small metal objects thought to be created in the ground by lightning striking the earth; thus *tog chag* means "lightning metal." Some objects are recognizable and others are in abstract shapes. Old garment clasps, book buckles, bits and pieces of horse bridles, are all gathered together under this one term.

appliqué
A type of textile in which pieces of cloth (often silk) in different colors are cut into pieces and sewn together to make a composition; a *tangka* made in this way is called an appliqué *tangka*.

attribute
A symbolic object associated with a particular subject based on well-known examples and textual iconography; deities are recognized by attributes they hold, such as a *vajra*, sword, or book.

black-ground painting
(Tibetan: *nag-tang*). A type of painting with gold outlines on a black background, colors sometimes added to a varying, but usually limited, degree.

blockprint
A woodcut image in a relief technique where (usually) the outlines are carved into the surface, allowing ink to pool in the grooves and marking the page when it is printed. The same techinique was used for printing books.

bodhisattva
(Tibetan: *jang chub sem pa*). Idealized beings in the appearance of youthful heavenly gods, generally male and richly attired in silks and jewels. They represent the principal students of the Buddha according to the Mahayana Sutras of Northern Buddhism.

Bön religion
The indigenous religion of Tibet and the Himalayan regions; according to adherents, it was founded by Tonpa Shenrab of Tazik, Central Asia, eight thousand years ago.

brocade
Textiles usually of Indian or Chinese silk, often with elaborate design, used to frame the borders of cloth paintings.

chorten
See *stupa*.

dakini
Female spirits, witches, *yoginis*, and deities; both human and divine, they are often teachers within Tantric Buddhism.

Dharma
The teachings of the Buddha, though originally it meant "law," or the ethical path of religion in general.

dharmachakra
Literally "wheel of dharma," it usually refers to a gesure in teaching, in which both hands are brought together in front of the heart, the index finger and thumb touching.

dhoti
The wraparound cloth skirt worn by Bodhisattva and other male and female deities.

donor
An individual, family, or group of people responsible for commissioning an artwork. It is common in Nepalese and Tibetan paintings to find the donors of the painting depicted at the bottom right or left of a painting.

Esoteric Buddhism
Also known as Tantrayana (the path of the *tantras*) and Vajrayana (the path of the *vajra*). A late form of Buddhism growing within the Mahayana school in India, incorporating the techniques of visualization and practice.

garuda
Both a mythical creature and a deity, half man and half bird, found in the Hindu, Bön, and Buddhist religions.

Gelug
A Tibetan monastic lineage also known as the Ganden School, and New Kadampa. It was founded by Tsongkapa in the early fifteenth century. It was very active in promoting the monastic system and creating very large monasteries that housed thousands of monks.

ground
The primary layer of paint or sizing applied to the canvas or cotton cloth of a painting, often fusing with the cloth and becoming the substratum.

iconometry
The geometric rules, drawing guides, and measurements used in the creation of correctly proportioned figures in Himalayan art.

illuminated manuscript
A book with pages on which miniature paintings (often figures or narrative scenes) are made as decorations.

initiation cards
See *tsagli*.

Kadam
A Buddhist lineage in Tibet founded by the Indian master Atisha (972/82–1054) and his lay Tibetan disciple Dromton. The Gelug tradition considers itself a revival of Kadam.

Kagyu
A Buddhist tradition tracing its teachings back to Indian Mahasiddhas Tilopa and Naropa and the Tibetan masters Marpa and Milarepa.

Kham
A region of Eastern Tibet as ethnographically (not politically) defined; now incorporated into the Chinese provinces of Sichuan, Yunnan, Qinghai and the Tibetan Autonomous Region (TAR).

lama
Tibetan translation for the Sanskrit term *guru*, meaning a religious teacher or preceptor in South Asia. Often mistakenly used as if synonymous with *monk*. In Vajrayana Buddhism, the term is specifically used for a *Tantric* teacher. The titles of *acharya* or *kalyanamitra* are used for *Sutrayana*, or ordinary, religious teachers.

lantsa
Ornamental Sanskrit script, also called *ranjana*.

lineage
A tradition or school, within Himalayan Buddhism, sharing an emphasis on certain teachings, and tracing back through a particular line of teachers. Among the major lineages, or sets of lineages, are the Nyingma, Sakya, Kagyu, and Gelug.

long-life vase.
A vase containing amrita, an elixir of longevity.

Mahasidha
The great Hindu and Buddhist Tantric practitioners of medieval India. Also known as "adept" and *sidha*. Most were male yogis, but they also include kings, monks and female *yoginis*.

Mahayana (Great Vehicle)
The Buddhism of Northern India, the Himalayas, China and East Asia, generally featuring philosophy based on the *Prajnaparamita* (Perfection of Wisdom) texts and featuring an expanded role for lay people and Bodhisattvas.

makara
A mythical sea creature having a snout like an elephant and the body like an alligator.

mala
Prayer beads on a string; a Christian equivalent is a rosary.

mandala
A symmetrical diagram, highly technical and precise, representing the entire universe; the container and contained, animate and inanimate. Mandalas are painted on cloth, on the ceilings of temples, as murals, fashioned from metal, wood, stone or textiles, constructed of colored threads, and also from colored sand.

mantra
A letter (or combination of letters) representing a sound which is considered an essence and associated with a deity. Originally written in Sanskrit, but also transliterated using Tibetan script.

mudra
Generally used to refer to a hand gesture with predetermined significance and associations. Literally, it means a "seal" and has other technical meanings in Esoteric Buddhism.

naga
A mythical serpentine creature appearing as human or snake, or both together, either with a human torso above and coiled snakes tail below, or as a human with snake hoods above and behind the head. They are treasure-gatherers who inhabit watery regions.

Newar
A ethnic and social group inhabiting Nepal since early historical times. Usually refers to a hereditary group particularly adept at painting and sculpture; they played important roles in the early periods of art in Tibet, and continued to be commissioned by Tibetan donors.

nimbus, nimbi
The circle of light surrounding the head or body of a spiritual figure; thus "head nimbus," and "body nimbus."

Nyingma
The oldest of the four main schools (Nyingma, Sakya, Kagyu, and Gelug), established with the founding of Samye Chokor Ling monastery in the eighth century by Padmasambhava and Shantirakshita. Nyingma means "old," or "ancient," and differs from the other three schools in a number of ways. The three later schools are collectively called the Sarma schools, meaning "new." A significant characteristic of the Nyingma is that it has no central authority. All of the other schools have a clear authority and hierarchy.

Offerings
A particular subject of Buddhist painting or sculpture, representing items of clothing, weapons, or food, and meant as offerings for various deities. Often offerings are found at or towards the bottom of a painting, though there are also paintings largely consist of offerings.

padma
A lotus flower, conventionally used as an attribute, or as a pedestal or dais for a deity.

Pata
An Indian painting on cloth.

Prajnaparamita Sutra.
A philosophical text in various forms and lengths, known as the "Perfection of Wisdom," and personified by a female deity holding a text. As a text, it is also an attribute held by the Bodhisattva Manjushri.

Purana
Indian Sanskrit texts, which are often the source for the study and iconographic descriptions of Hindu gods and deities. They tend to feature epic stories.

Purba
A peg, shaped like a three-sided dagger, a ritual object represented three-dimensionally in metal, wood, or crystal; for pegging down disturbances and obstacles arising in the practice of Tantric Buddhism.

Raksha/Rakshasi
Dangerous male and female spirits and daemons of classical Indian literature. Their fearsome appearance became the model for wrathful Buddhist deities such as Mahakala, characterized by round bulbous red eyes, gaping slathering mouths with large bared canine teeth, flaming hair, large bellied and thick limbed.

ranjana
See *lantsa*.

repoussé
Sculpture or decoration hammered into relief from the reverse side of a metal.

Sakya
One of the four mains traditions of Tibetan Buddhism. Khon Konchog Gyalpo founded the Sakya School in 1073 with the construction of the first temple at a place called *sa kya* (white earth), Tsang, Tibet. The following teachers are generally credited with the founding and shaping of the Sakya School of Tibetan Buddhism: Sachen Kunga Nyingpo (1092–1158), Sonam Tsemo (1142–82), Dragpa Gyaltsen (1147–1216), Sakya Pandita (1182–1251), and Chogyal Pagpa (1235–80).

Sarma
The "new schools" (Sakya, Kagyu, and Gelug), in contrast to the Ancient school (Nyingma).

siddha
See Mahasiddha.

stupa (Tibetan: chorten)
(Tibetan: chorten). Originally a funerary mound, adapted into Buddhism as a dome-like reliquary structure with a base and finial, made of brick, stone, metal, or clay, etc. Also a ritual object symbolically representing the mind of complete enlightenment.

sutra
Indian Buddhist texts, often written in Pali or Sanskrit language, the iconographic source for images of Shakyamuni Buddha, the bodhisattvas and Arhats.

tangka
A Himalayan painting executed on cloth or paper. Usually mounted in cloth brocade.

tantra
Meaning "continuum," a genre of Hindu and Buddhist religious literature featuring teachings associated with Tantric Hinduism and Esoteric Buddhism.

Tantrayana, Tantric Buddhism
See Esoteric Buddhism.

tarjani
A gesture conveying admonition or threat; the index finger is raised, the others curled into the palm, sometimes while simultaneously holding a lasso. It is generally made by wrathful deities such as Achala.

Tathagata
(Tibetan: *de shin sheg pa.* English: Thus Gone One). A general term of respect for all Buddhas, having gone, passed beyond cyclic existence.

terma
A "revealed treasure text," either discovered in a hiding place deposited at the time of Padmasambhava (eighth century), placed into the mind stream, or through visionary experience.

terton
A "treasure revealer," one who has discovered a *terma.*

torma
(Sanskrit: *bali*). A dough sculpture, cone-shaped and sometimes elaborately decorated and colored, used as stylized food offerings in Bön and Buddhist rituals and initiations. Sometimes referred to as an offering cake.

tsagli
Small paintings, generally the size of playing cards, created in sets and used in Buddhist and Bön rituals and initiations, featuring illustrations of deities, animals, objects, attributes, and abstract images such as *yantras.*

vajra
(Tibetan: *rdo rje.* English: the best stone). Sometimes translated as "thunderbolt" and "diamond scepter," this originally Sanskrit word has several meanings: 1) Originally a weapon made from the bones of a *rishi*; 2) the scepter of the Hindu god Indra; 3) a name and symbol representing Esoteric or Tantric Buddhism and Vajrayana. As a Buddhist scepter it is a small object made of metal and having five or nine prongs at each end that bend inward to form a rounded enclosure. As a ritual object it is usually accompanied by a bell (Sanskrit: *ghanta*).

Vajrayana
See Esoteric Buddhism.

Yaksha, Yakshi
Male and female nature spirits of India, of classical Indian literature and folk beliefs. Absorbed into and transformed variously in Hinduism and Buddhism.

Yantra
Technical paintings, drawings, and blockprints of diagrams showing auspicious conjunctions or the ritual control of demons, sometimes used as talismans.

yidam
Meditation or "tutelary" deity. In this exhibition and catalog, Wrathful Buddhas are *yidam,* though not all *yidam* are wrathful.

Photography Credits

R. Linrothe essay: Fig. 1.36
Photo © 2003 British Museum, London

R. Linrothe essay: Figs. 1.34, 1.39–47
Photos, Rob Linrothe

M. Rhie essay: Fig. 2.1
Photo after *Xueyu cangzhen* (Treasures from Snow Mountains) (Shanghai: Shanghai shushua chubansha, 2001), no. 18.

M. Rhie essay: Fig. 2.3
Image after photo by Jaroslav Poncar in Roger Goepper, *Alchi* (Boston: Shambhala Limited Editions, 1996), p. 30.

M. Rhie essay: Fig. 2.5
Photo © 2004 Museum Associates / LACMA

M. Rhie essay: Fig. 2.8
Photo, Young Rhie

M. Rhie essay: Fig. 2.9
Photo after U. von Schroeder. 2001
Buddhist Sculptures in Tibet, Vol. Two, p. 892, pl. 206A.

M. Rhie essay: Fig. 2.12
Photo after *Precious Deposits: Historical Relics of Tibet, China* (Beijing: Morning Glory Publishers, 2000), 3: no. 43.

M. Rhie essay: Fig. 2.15
Photo after Marylin M. Rhie and Robert A.F. Thurman, *Cibei zihui (Wisdom and Compassion)* (Tapei: The China Times, 1998): no. 90.

M. Rhie essay: Fig. 2.16
Photo © 2003 Museum of Fine Arts, Boston

M. Rhie essay: Fig. 2.17
Photo © 1994 Philadelphia Museum of Art

M. Rhie essay: Fig. 2.24
photo after *Sajiasi (Sakya Monastery)* (Beijing: Wenwu chubanshe, 1985), pl. 36.

Cat. no. 13
Photo, Bruce Schwarz, El Museo del Barrio, NY

Cat. no. 19
© 2003 The Metropolitan Museum of Art, NY

Cat. no. 20
© 2003 University of Pennsylvania Museum of Archaeology and Anthropology

Cat. nos. 23, 24, 62
Photos, Brooklyn Museum of Art, NY

Cat. nos. 27, 29, 30
Photos, 2003 Craig Chesek and Jackie Beckett, American Museum of Natural History, NY

Cat. nos. 41, 49
Photos, Lynton Gardiner, Asia Society, NY

Cat. nos. 52, 58
Photos © 2003 by Dennis Cowley, NY

Cat. no. 57
Photo © 1997 by John Bigelow Taylor, NY

Index

Entries in Bold refer to names of exhibits. An *f* after page number indicates an illustration